TURNING
PAPER
TO
GOLD

Other books by Joseph Raymond LeFontaine:

INTERNATIONAL BOOK COLLECTORS DIRECTORY
A HANDBOOK FOR BOOK LOVERS
POPULAR AUTHORS AND THEIR BOOKS
THE PAPER MINER'S MANUAL

TURNING PAPER TO GOLD

Joseph Raymond LeFontaine

BETTERWAY PUBLICATIONS, INC.
WHITE HALL, VIRGINIA

Published by Betterway Publications, Inc.
Box 219
Crozet, VA 22932

Cover design by Deborah Chappell
Typography by TechType

The publisher and the author assume no liability, implied or otherwise, in the use of the information presented in this book. Users should be aware that book values differ widely throughout North America and Europe, and are subject to the laws of supply and demand. Always keep in mind that the value of any merchandise is that which a willing buyer will pay a willing seller.

Library of Congress Cataloging-in-Publication Data

LeFontaine, Joseph Raymond
        Turning paper to gold: how to make money with old books, magazines, comics, sheet music, and other printed paper collectibles.
/ Joseph Raymond LeFontaine.
        p. cm.
    Includes index.
    ISBN 0-932620-97-3 (pbk.) : $17.95
    1. Books--Prices. 2. Printed ephemera--Prices. 3. Book collecting. 4. Printed ephemera--Collectors and collecting.
I. Title
Z1000.L45 1988
332-63--dc19   88-2838
                                                         CIP

This book is for my grandchildren

SHERYL and SHELLY
MATTHEW
JENNIFER, ANDREW, and DANIEL
TAMAR and NATHAN

THIS BOOK IS WRITTEN FOR.....

.....the hundreds of thousands of persons throughout the world, and particularly those in North America, who are fascinated by old books and other forms of printed paper collectibles.

Even though the primary focus is on making money NOW with these plentiful collectibles, very nearly everything in the book is equally applicable to the collector or the unabashed investor. For if you are a collector, already active or would-be, it doesn't really matter if your goal is to leave your collection or accumulation to an institution or your heirs, or to serve as your retirement fund, you still want to buy wisely with the hope that what you have acquired will appreciate in value in the future.

FOREWORD

The title of this book is TURNING PAPER TO GOLD. Of course, no one can really do that, but what I will tell you now can be the next best thing.

If you want to learn of any easy and fun way to make some extra money — keep reading. How much can you make? That's really impossible to say. It depends on how much time, effort, and money you want to invest. First, in learning, and then in doing.

For some of you, the financial aspect won't enter it to it at all. If you simply want to collect for pleasure you'll be able to follow an intelligent path. You will be able to buy wisely and properly care for your nuggets.

The nuggets — your raw material — are all around you wherever you live. Unrecognized by almost everyone (except you, after you finish reading this book). They can be found at flea markets; tag, garage and yard sales; country and city auctions; in attics barns, and basements; trunks, drawers and closets; in rummage and junk stores; in old warehouses, sheds, and storerooms; and in a large variety of other places which you will learn to recognize when you encounter them.

Once you absorb the knowledge I provide you in this book you will constantly find things that would never have caught your attention before. And every time that happens it will be an opportunity to put MONEY in your pocket.

The nicest part of it all is that you can be doing something which will give you a great deal of pleasure with a very small outlay of hard cash, and with a very high potential return in prestige and admiration from your friends, relatives, and acquaintances...and at the same time you might also be making some big, extra dollars.

Do you know of any undertaking which you could attempt, either part or full time, which could provide you with a list of over 18,000 items every single week throughout the year of things which people are so anxious to buy that they are advertising for them? I DO!

These are some of the nuggets I mentioned. They are everywhere — it does not matter where you live — you can unearth some.

I recently checked an issue of just one of the trade publications for this field and here is what I found. There were the advertisements of approximately 660 booksellers, book search services, and libraries, listing over 18,000 book titles they were searching for. That's close to a million titles in the course of a single year!

If the average selling price for each of these titles were as little as $10 (and that is very conservative) this represents a market potential of nearly $10 million. Wherever you may live, you are going to be able to find some of these titles and sell them at a nice profit — right from your home.

What is really interesting about what I have just told you is that none of these advertisers are collectors, or retail buyers (with libraries being an exception) — they are all dealers of one type or another — store front, scout, search service, picker, etc., who must mark up each title they buy before they resell it to a collector or library, and sometimes to another dealer. So, if the $10 million I mentioned above represents what is essentially wholesale buying, then we are really looking at a possible $20 million retail market — just for *used books*. As I said, that is very conservative — many out-of-print books sell for far more then $10 — sometimes for hundreds of dollars.

I AM GOING TO TELL YOU HOW TO GET YOUR SHARE OF THIS MARKET

What qualifies me to do that? I think it will be self-evident from the contents of this book. I am certain you will agree with me by the time you finish your first reading. I hope you will be as excited as I am. By way of background, I will tell you that I have been in this business for over 30 years, as the proprietor of antiquarian bookstores, as a book scout and picker, as a list and catalog compiler, and as a private collector.

Everything you read in this book is based on something which I have done myself, and represents knowledge which I have acquired the hard way and usually at considerable expense.

I am also the author of *The International Book Collectors Directory* which can be found in the reference section of many libraries throughout North America and 43 other countries. You will also find additional background in my listing in *Who's Who in the West*, and in *Contemporary Authors, Volume 106*.

When I started in this business there were no books or guides such as this to show me where the pitfalls were. As a result, YOU have the opportunity to benefit from my experiences. Everything I tell you how to do is based on the very real experience of *learning what not to do*.

Another thing. Even if you have no intention of trying to make a living or additional income from TURNING PAPER TO GOLD, almost everything in this book is equally applicable to you as a collector or investor. You still need this information in order to collect or invest wisely.

You can benefit from my experience. Everything I explain to you is based on the very real experience of what NOT to do.

It is not difficult.

It is a lot of fun.

It is dignified.

It is REWARDING.

One secret you will not discover here is how to get rich quickly. I cannot pass that secret along because I have yet to discover it.

So, read on and discover how to "TURN PAPER TO GOLD."

CONTENTS

1.
PUTTING MONEY IN YOUR POCKET— FAST

There is a huge and ever growing market in North America for used in-print as well as out-of-print books and other types of printed material. Much of this material was ephemeral (lasting a very short time) in nature when it was originally published.

As a result, most of this material is difficult to find for new needs or as a replacement for worn out, lost, or stolen materials. Hence, it is much sought after by scholars, librarians, and collectors. Even though you will be primarily concerned with printed *paper* materials, there are other forms of interest. For example, much printed material occurs on metals such as beer cans (there are thousands of collectors), advertising signs, tin containers for food such as candy, cigars, tobacco tins and tags, and many similar items — the list is almost endless.

The major emphasis throughout this book will be on old (usually but not always), used, out-of-print books simply because they are the most plentiful and most in demand. Bear in mind, however, that much of this information, even though primarily oriented to books is equally applicable to all other forms of printed material such as newspapers, magazines, prints, posters, broadsides, and the things mentioned above, and many other things you will learn about later in the book.

My point is — all of these things can be found right near your home — no matter where you live. I mentioned above, difficult to find, but I want to qualify that. It's only difficult for those who do not know what to look for and how to recognize it when they find it.

A TRUE STORY

Here's a little story for you. It is absolutely true. Not long ago a business firm in New York City threw out some stored merchandise. Its employees were told they could take anything they could use. One alert person spotted an old beat-up book, and on a hunch decided to show it to an auctioneer he would be seeing later that day. His hunch paid off.

The book turned out to be a rare 16th Century book, EUPHEUS, OR THE ANATOMY OF WIT, by John Lyly.

That old beat-up book was subsequently sold at auction for $8500. This provided quite a handsome profit for that alert, and lucky, person even after subtracting the auctioneer's commission. On a lesser scale, these occurrences happen almost daily for those with knowledge — and I'm going to show you how it can happen to you.

SOME FACTS TO CONSIDER!

Each year the major auction houses, in the United States alone, sell several million dollars worth of scarce and rare books, prints, autographic material, photographs, historical documents and other forms of printed collectibles. A very high percentage of auction sales are to dealers, so that figure, to a large extent, represents the wholesale market. The ultimate retail value would be much higher since dealers in turn sell to collectors, libraries, and other institutions — and often just to each other.

Every year the 38,000-plus libraries in North America spend many millions of dollars just to REPLACE books which are lost due to wear or theft. Most of these books are out-of-print and can only be replaced by searching for them and buying them in the out-of-print market.

This is done by using the services of booksellers, booksearch services, and scouts (or pickers). I will explain just how that works further on in the book and tell you how to get your share of that business.

In addition, thousands of libraries maintain Special Subject and Author Collections. They purchase millions of dollars of scarce and rare books and other types of printed material to augment their collections.

No one really knows how many used-book stores, as well as the specialized persons that deal in scarce and rare books, there really are in the United States. Possibly over 8,000. Hundreds of them advertise regularly for books which their clients are looking for. Even the ones who do not advertise will always have a file or "Wants List" of titles they need. Library "Wants Lists" often contain hundreds of titles.

The total number of collectors, which includes libraries, of books and all the other types of printed collectibles, is beyond estimating. Certainly it is in the millions. That is, if we define as a collector someone who has a continuing interest in accumulating the works of particular authors, or those on a particular subject, or the illustrations of a particular artist/illustrator, or any of the other items you will find listed in Chapter 7. Most of them rely on the offerings they receive by mail — from people like you and me — who may be hundreds or thousands of miles away. Nevertheless, we may have items they need for their collections.

TURNING PAPER TO GOLD ... find what is needed ... buy low and sell high ... where to prospect for your nuggets ... how to reach the people who want them. Keep reading!

Are there really enough nuggets out there to make it worth your while to learn what is in this book either as a business or hobby? Absolutely!

Perhaps as many as a third of a billion books have been printed since Johann Gutenberg produced the first printed book in 1455 — over 530 years ago. Books, not titles. At first, a few hundred copies of a title was all that could be managed. Now, it is not uncommon for a book to sell several million copies and go through several printings within a short time after first publication.

Every year, over 50 thousand new titles are published in the United States alone. The majority of these will probably never again be worth the original retail price. BUT, a significant and important percentage of them may become the high priced collectible books of tomorrow. This has been true since 1455.

The most popular, and often the most valuable, printed collectibles of today relate to; sports, medicine and science, 'classic' authors, Americana (the term for early or scarce material about American history and the development of our country), private press books, first editions of important authors, color plate, photography, early science fiction, mystery/detective, and so forth. More about this later. Also you can refer to the lists of collectible authors you will find in the Appendices.

Not too many years ago a prominent New York rare book dealer stated, "Most rich people collect not for enjoyment but for investment ... The greatest men and women in the history of the world have been book collectors; the Ptolemies including Cleopatra, the Medici, the list is endless."

Another equally prominent antiquarian book authority said, "Once upon a time one could still collect the very earliest imprints on this continent such as the Bay Psalm book of 1640. No more. But many of the greatest collections of Americana are, nevertheless, *still to be built* and many of the great subjects are still up for grabs. Various aspects of black history or the history of women, and the many great and small social movements of the 18th, 19th, and 20th centuries."

"In America, the great movements — college education, Prohibition, public hospitals — grew up from below, from the grass roots, and were not, as in England, merely bestowed from above. The pamphlets, broadsides, newspapers and books of these 'people's movements' are not yet systematically being collected. The collectors who do so in the future will not only be important contributors to American history, but will also have a hell of a good time all the while."

RECYCLING INFORMATION, KNOWLEDGE, AND PLEASURE

You can be part of this tremendously fulfilling experience. You will have a part in RECYCLING INFORMATION, KNOWLEDGE, AND PLEASURE. All you need do is; first, scan this book, second, read it thoroughly, third, carry it with you when you go prospecting.

You can experience the thrill of discovering

books or other printed collectibles of value; the fine first edition, the tattered but rare treatise that only a few other people have been able to unearth. With diligence and knowledge you will be able to assemble a collection or inventory that will give you a sense of personal satisfaction, and perhaps have historical significance. You will also discover that as your collection or inventory expands and you uncover the harder to find nuggets, the value of your holdings will increase remarkably.

You will be dealing with interesting and enjoyable material — things which are also fascinating to look upon, hold, research, catalog, and SELL. This is material which will give you a great sense of self-satisfaction which can come from discovery. Followed by the gratification that results from selling something for many times what you paid for it.

HAVE FUN WHILE YOU MAKE MONEY

Going to swap meets, flea markets, and garage or yard sales can be lot's of fun. Especially when you have a purpose — to make a discovery that will put dollars in your pocket or purse and a big smile on your face. That's also why this can be a part-time venture and still be lucrative. Most swap meets and so forth are held on weekends.

It can also be fun to shop the classified advertisements in specialized antiques magazines and newspapers. Probably the advertiser won't have your specialized knowledge and the material is just something to get rid of at any price obtainable.

There will be no greater thrill for you than the one which you will experience when you send someone a quotation for a book which they have advertised for, you discovered, and they send you a CHECK.

You will get another thrill when you receive your first reply to an inexpensive advertisement which you can run, offering to buy old books, magazines, valentines, posters, or any other collectible item I am going to tell you about.

I remember the first time I ran such an ad. It was in an upstate New York weekly newspaper. Here is what the ad said, as I recall after 30-odd years. "Wanted to buy. Old books, advertising, magazines. Write and describe, give phone, to __."

I received several replies, mostly from rural addresses offering all kinds of things; old trade catalogs, books, advertising brochures and signs, newspapers, you name it. Of course, I called all of them to get more specific information. Some were duds, of course, everyone has a different idea of what is old.

One reply in particular, is still vivid in my mind after all these years. It was from an elderly lady who simply said she had a trunk full of old books in the attic and would I like to come and look at them. You bet I would. I thought that even if the books were no good, the trunk might be valuable.

What a find! That trunk was full of old children's books from the period 1850 to 1880. Many were in poor condition, which is normal for children's books, but some were very good and very salable. At that time I was pretty much a neophyte to the business but thought I was being very astute to offer her $10 for the lot (including the trunk), which she accepted.

Eventually I sold those books for a total of several hundred dollars, one at a time. A few years later I had learned enough to realize that I could have gotten many times that sum had I known what I was doing. I had been lucky. But it taught me a lesson. I'll pass that knowledge along to you so that you won't make the same mistake.

I might also add that had I known what I was doing I would certainly have offered that lady a great deal more money. I took advantage of her but only because of my ignorance. I'll have more to say about this later, but, always pay fair prices when you are dealing with people you know do not have any knowledge of your business unless they are dealers themselves.

SWAP MEETS AND FLEA MARKETS

I can also recall going to a swap meet about a year later and finding a small book which cost me 25 cents. It was an early American edition of Robinson Crusoe, published in 1794. By the way, that is not the correct title of the first edition. It is THE LIFE AND MOST SURPRISING ADVENTURES OF ROBINSON CRUSOE OF YORK, MARINER ... by Daniel Defoe.

I remembered seeing an advertisement in *The Antique Trader* placed by a gentlemen in New England who collected children's books. I simply put the book in an ordinary #10 business envelope (it was that small) along with a note asking him if he could use the book. I had no idea what it was worth and didn't know how to find out. If he wanted the book, would he just send me a check? Thank goodness, I was dealing with an honest man. By return mail I received a check for $125.

That made me smile — I thought I had discovered a new type of gold mine.

That's when I had the inspiration for the title to this book. Best of all, I had not taken advantage of anyone, however unwittingly. The buyer set the price.

I could tell you hundreds of stories like this, from my own experience, and from that of other dealers throughout the country. But I won't. I would rather you experience your own stories in future.

By now you should be excited and certainly curious about what comes next. So, keep reading. First, scan the Table of Contents so you know what is here. Then read the book carefully. Carry it with you whenever you go prospecting.

MISTAKES ARE CHEAP

Don't be afraid to make some mistakes. It really won't hurt if you follow my advice.

The knowledge you need to get started is all right here. It's really not that extensive. Some trade terms must be learned. A knowledge of how to use readily available reference material is needed. Add a little study to that and you may just stumble across those nuggets in your own backyard.

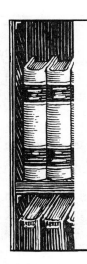
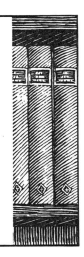

2.
RECOGNIZE THE WHEAT—DISCARD THE CHAFF

Any book, manuscript or other item of printed material which is of importance is also potentially valuable. The actual value will depend on how many copies are available and how many prospective buyers there are. Four things determine value:

- **IMPORTANCE**
- **SUPPLY**
- **DEMAND**
- **CONDITION**

WHAT IS VALUABLE?

The kinds of books and other printed materials which have potential value include the whole range of historical and nostalgic subjects — from a paper bound guide for emigrants of the Gold Rush periods, to the poems of Edna St. Vincent Millay printed on Japan Vellum, to early Victorian valentines.

Of great interest in the American market today are two dominant categories: Americana; and the first editions of important books, or books by important authors. However, there are dozens of lesser categories which offer great profit making potential for the astute and knowledgeable searcher or "scout." That's how I will refer to you from now on.

You will be "scouting" out all those nuggets waiting for you. In the antiques business such people are referred to as "pickers." They make a good living by going around to farmhouses, or whatever, throughout the country offering to buy anything old (almost) that people are willing to part

with. When they have a truckload they drive to the nearest antique shop and resell their finds — usually at a fat profit. You will not have to do that. I will tell you of much easier ways to do your paper mining.

TAKING OUT THE MYSTERY

What is Americana? Webster's New Collegiate Dictionary defines it as "Materials concerning or characteristic of America, its civilization, or its culture."

It is the history of the American scene which includes all of the Americas — North, Central and South. Anything and everything that deals with the history, exploration and development of the New World. Often, the term Americana is used in the narrow sense to mean only that which pertains to the United States.

It is true that a large proportion of collectors of Americana are really only interested in things which pertain to the United States, to the exclusion of Canada, Mexico, and the other Central and South American countries. However, that is gradually changing and you should be interested in all forms of Americana in its broadest sense.

Books or other printed material published prior to World War II in any of the following fields are typical Americana and are of potential value: State, local, county and city history; adventure, travel and exploration; Indians and Indian captivities; almanacs; Indian laws and treaties; territorial laws; overland narratives; travel atlases and view books; Utah and the Mormons; the old Northwest; the Middle West; the Far West; state laws and Constitutions; the Confederacy; railroads and canals; Davy Crockett; Daniel Boone; Mike Fink; Andrew Jackson; the Black Hills gold rush; Colorado and the mines.

The California gold rush; the Kansas gold rush; Oklahoma and oil; Texas oil and cattle; the Great Plains and the Rockies; sporting and hunting; the Northwest coast; the fur trade; the Dakotas; Arizona; California; Oregon; Indian fighting on the Western frontier; the Civil War; the Revolutionary War; outlaws and badmen; government documents; Alabama; Georgia; Louisiana; Mississippi. The list is virtually endless but this should give you a pretty good idea.

You will not learn of all of the nuggets of Americana in this book so keep this in mind: most in demand are first-hand contemporary (written during the same period of time) narratives concerning these phases of American history. Voyages and explorations of the Sixteenth and Seventeenth centuries — the personal narratives of English, French and Spanish adventurers; the pioneer movement across the Alleghenies in the 18th century; the wars against the Indians and the French, especially narratives of captivity among the Indians; the Revolution and the Civil War — from both sides; the westward expansion across the plains and Rockies to California; journals of explorers, trappers, traders; 'Forty-Niners'; overland emigration and Indian fighting.

These are the most readily salable items of printed Americana, whether books, pamphlets, posters, broadsides, or what have you. Since everything except some books was largely ephemeral in nature, they are as a consequence scarce or rare and of special interest.

Nearly as important in interest, and highly salable, are books, pamphlets, posters, etc., relating to the early history of American economics, science, medicine, transportation, marine activity (especially whaling), and so forth. Items about early American sports, and children's books, also fetch tidy sums.

No matter what the type of material you are considering — Americana, first editions, movie posters — remember that condition is of great importance. Only great rarities are salable when they are in poor condition or incomplete. Even the loss of a single page or plate (illustration) can cause a tremendous decrease in value. Items must be clean, untorn, and free of water staining or "foxing." (See chapter 10 for the definition of that term)

Always bear in mind — AGE does *not* necessarily determine value. Massachusetts was old when Montana was young. The assumption that age increases value is based partly on another assumption — that old things are harder to come by. Very often, this is simply not true. It is a mistake that most antique dealers are prone to make when dealing with printed material.

For example, many more books have been printed in the past than most people realize. During the second half of the 15th century an estimated 40,000 different books (called incunabula) were printed. From then until now the presses have never been still. It is not at all difficult to purchase 17th and 18th century books for less than $50. Remember what I said about importance?

What about old books that you, or someone you know, owns? Chances are that most of them are worthless. Or perhaps one of them could be worth a small fortune. Several years ago a New England woman found a copy of TAMERLANE by Edgar Allan Poe. It was the rare 1827 first edition, in wraps (an early paperback). Not too long ago a copy of this book was sold at auction for $123,000. There is no telling what another copy might bring today. But if you find one you will probably be able to retire on the proceeds.

Literally, thousands on thousands of valuable books and other items of paper Americana or nostalgia are still lying hidden throughout the country in boxes, trunks, drawers, attics, basements, barns, and countless other forgotten hiding places. They are worth hundreds, sometimes thousands, of dollars depending on importance, scarcity, demand, and condition.

Again I will remind you that age does not necessarily determine value. Many modern books, for example, have considerable value to collectors. Much sought after first editions are often rare and valuable. Only two copies of TWILIGHT by Robert Frost, his first book of poems, are known to exist. If you happen to find a third copy you will whistle all the way to the bank.

Many important scientific books are modern. A notable one is A METHOD OF REACHING EXTREME ALTITUDES by Robert Goddard. Published in 1919, it describes principles used over 50 years later to land men on the moon. Copies of this book sold for $550-750 in the 1970's. Einstein's first piece on the theory of relativity, published in a scientific journal, will sell for at least $650.

Sporting books, old and modern, can command very high prices. The oldest American sporting book is SPORTSMAN'S COMPANION, OR AN ESSAY ON SHOOTING, by Charles Bell, published in 1738 in New York. Several modern day famous authors have also contributed collectible books on hunting and fishing. Zane Grey, Ernest Hemingway, Erle Stanley Gardner of Perry Mason fame, to name a few.

Sporting books need not be written by famous authors, or be very old, to be collectible. Some fishing books have become classics because of their contents. One is MODERN DRY-FLY CODE by Vincent Marinaro which was published at $6.95 in 1951. Today, you can sell a copy for at least $75.

Many of the most desirable sporting books were published in limited editions between 1927 and 1941 by the Derrydale Press of New York city. Some of these books bring very high prices. An example is ATLANTIC SALMON FISHING by Charles Phair. This book was published in 1937, in a deluxe limited edition of 200 copies, at an original price of $250. Today, a copy will bring at least $4500.

Even the regular edition, limited to 950 copies and issued at $25 will bring over $200. All the Derrydale Press books are wanted by collectors and specialty dealers, and bring high prices.

Between 1943 and 1955 the firm of Alfred A. Knopf published the Borzoi Books For Sportsmen series. These, too, bring good prices. An example being HUNTING IN THE ROCKIES by Jack O'Conner, first published in 1947. A fine first edition copy in dust jacket should bring at least $250.

There have been significant changes in the out-of-print and rare book market in the past 20-30 years. Major auction sales of a great number of literary and Americana collections have taken place both in the United States and abroad. These sales have tended to elevate prices to new highs, not only for individual titles, but for all related books in the various fields.

To the average layman, the field of old books and related printed paper materials is pretty much a mystery. This mystique is perpetuated by a small group of self styled rare (antiquarian) book dealers. The dealers themselves are not rare, though many of them certainly qualify as antiquarian — it's the books that are being referred to. They are mostly concentrated in New York, Los Angeles, San Francisco, and to a lesser extent, Chicago.

Many of the things which you will learn in this book represent know-how that this small circle of elitist dealers would prefer you did not have. Why? The less you know about book values, the more likely it will be that you will accept unfairly low prices for your nuggets from them. The other side of the coin, is that this still remains one of the few fields of endeavor which offers a high possibility for making substantial profits, either from the investment standpoint, or as a dealer, which is not yet overly populated with opportunists. This is because so many of the so-called trade secrets have remained just that — trade secrets. Until this book, that is. I'm telling many of them to you now.

SOME THINGS TO LOOK FOR

Here is a partial list of the kinds of printed paper and other materials which can be sold in the huge collectibles market. These are the nuggets you will be scouting for, and perhaps selling, with the knowledge you will have when you finish this book.

ADVERTISING	LITHOGRAPHS
ALMANACS	LOBBY CARDS
ART	MAGAZINES
ATLASES	MANUSCRIPTS
AUTOGRAPHS	MAPS
BADGES	MEDALS
BANNERS	MENUS
BILLS	NEWSPAPERS
BOOKS	PAMPHLETS
BROADSIDES	PAPER DOLLS
BROCHURES	PASSPORTS
CALENDARS	PHOTOGRAPHS
COUNTER CARDS	PINBACK BUTTONS
CATALOGS	PLAYING CARDS
CERTIFICATES	POSTCARDS
CHARTS	POSTERS
CHECKS	PREMIUMS
CIGAR BANDS	PRESS BOOKS
CIRCULARS	PRINTS
COMIC STRIPS	PROGRAMS
CONTAINERS	PROSPECTUSES
CURRENCY	PUNCHBOARDS
DIARIES	SCRAPBOOKS
DIRECTORIES	SCRIPTS
DISPLAYS	SHEET MUSIC
DOCUMENTS	SHIP'S LOGS
FANS	STAMPS
GAMES	TICKETS
HANDBILLS	TIMETABLES
INVITATIONS	TRADE CARDS
INVOICES	VALENTINES
LABELS	WALLPAPER
LEAFLETS	

This list is by no means complete, but it will give you some idea of how big the market really is.

SOME POPULAR MYTHS TO IGNORE

There are a great many myths floating around in this business. One of the most obtrusive is the belief that all old Bibles have some value. A small percentage do. Here are some others to keep in mind.

MYTH: All McGuffey's Readers, and similar old school books are worth something. Not so — most are worthless except as curiosities. There are thousands of reproductions floating around.

MYTH: Sets of encyclopedias can be sold if only one or two volumes are missing. Wrong — they are almost impossible to sell even when complete. *Never* buy them, no matter how cheap, do not even accept them as a gift. They just take up lots of space, and time. And they are *heavy*.

MYTH: Books about disasters, such as the Johnstown flood, the Mount Pelée eruption, the San Francisco earthquake, the Chicago fire, etc., are valuable. Wrong again — because most books such as this were run-of-the-mill, cheap, overnight printings with lurid covers, and are plentiful. Do not bother with this type of book unless it is in very fine condition and you can buy it for a dollar or less. You will see a lot of these in antique shops, usually overpriced.

MYTH: One-hundred or more years old Gift books (Annuals with ornamental bindings, good engravings, and contributions by noted writers) are scarce and bring good prices. Wrong — most of the writings were reprints, often used without the author's permission. There is an exception, however. THE GIFT, Philadelphia, 1836, which contained the first appearance of a celebrated Edgar Allan Poe story.

MYTH: A book is unique and valuable because some of the pages were bound in up-side-down. Wrong — it must be valuable for other reasons first.

MYTH: Odd volumes from sets may have value because "somebody must need it to complete their set." Wrong — do you know who that somebody is? Unless they are very early works of importance, and you already know who to sell it to, do not buy odd volumes. Always check the title page of any book you buy to make sure it is not part of a set. And remember, there is a difference between a 'series' and a 'set.'

MYTH: Any old copy of BEN HUR or MUTINY ON THE BOUNTY is of value because they made a movie of these stories. Wrong — except for those books which are illustrated with scenes from the movie or the play. There is a limited market for illustrated versions of classics which have been made into movies among movie memorabilia collectors.

3.
THE MEASURE OF VALUE

I'll repeat that throughout this book I am going to primarily be discussing books. However, please bear in mind that almost everything is equally applicable to all other forms of printed materials such as magazines, pamphlets, posters, broadsides, prints, or any other form of ephemeral printing.

What kind of books are valuable? How to determine the value? What is a first edition and how do you determine that status? How do you describe an old book? Who are some of the authors whose first editions are valuable? What can be sold? Who to sell it to? How much to pay? How much to sell for? How to go about selling?

I will answer all these questions for you and best of all, I will tell you what *not* to buy. You will not have to make all the costly and discouraging mistakes I made in the beginning.

I want to emphasize something. Once you have bought whatever it is that you feel is a valuable nugget — make sure you know *exactly what it is* that you have before you offer it for resale to anyone. *Do not* rush off to the nearest bookseller with a bunch of junk. You may end up with a very red face. And you do not want to sell an item which may be worth several hundred dollars for just a fraction of its value because you did not take the time for a bit of simple research.

BECOMING INFORMED

One of the simplest, and by far the most productive, methods of keeping informed about which books are in demand and being sought after, is by regularly reading *AB Bookmans Weekly*. This weekly publication is a treasure house of information for buying, selling, or collecting books

and other printed material. It is probably the most important tool at your disposal after this book and THE INTERNATIONAL BOOK COLLECTORS DIRECTORY. I will be more specific on the best way to use AB in a later chapter.

AB Bookmans Weekly is published 48 times a year. The subscription price includes a free copy of *AB Bookmans* YEARBOOK which will also become an indispensable tool for you. You can obtain subscription information by writing: AB Bookmans Weekly, P.O. Box AB, Clifton, NJ 07015, USA. You might also check your local library to see if they have a copy which you can inspect.

BOOKS TO AVOID

Don't buy these types of books until you have some experience in this field. It will not be long. Even then, they are poor risks unless you become a specialist dealer.

Sermons and religious books in general; gift books or the more modern version, coffee-table books; dictionaries and encyclopedias; medical and legal books; cookbooks; gardening; text books of all types unless printed before 1830; most almanacs; anthologies; the Readers Digest Condensed Book volumes; any "Book Club" editions; and most magazines, especially news, sport, western, romance, true confessions. There are some exceptions which I will mention later.

There is virtually no market for reprints of novels or poetry, no matter who the author is, or sets of books by the classic authors such as Charles Dickens, Hawthorne, et al. Some of the reprint publishers to be wary of are A.L. Burt, Hurst, Henneberry, Grosset & Dunlap, Tower, Triangle,

Blakiston, Altemus, Readers Digest, and many others.

There are certain older authors whose books are quite commonly seen in antiques shops and which as a general rule ought to be avoided. Not because they aren't worth reading or collecting, many are, but because they are common and were widely reprinted and few people today find them of interest or collect them. The first editions of many of these authors can be quite valuable but they are scarce and reprints are plentiful. When you know more about recognizing first editions you will be able to buy (or price) such books with assurance.

Some of these authors are Zane Grey, Rex Beach, Max Brand, Ralph Connor, Marie Corelli, James Oliver Curwood, Erle Stanley Gardner, Ernest Haycox, G.A. Henty, Grace Livingston Hill, Peter B. Kyne, L.M. Montgomery, Baroness Orczy, Ellery Queen, Charles Alden Seltzer, Luke Short, Stewart Edward White, Harold Bell Wright, and many others. This will give you some idea though.

You will learn to recognize many of them by scanning the copyright page of any book you are thinking of buying. One trick you will soon adopt is to just scan the spines of a box or shelf of books and simply not bother to even pick up any with the names I have mentioned above.

You must also keep in mind that paperbacks can also be valuable, both old and modern. Paperbacks have been around for a long time and in the old book trade they are often referred to as books with 'wraps.' Which simply means stiff paper cover. Wraps on older books were not usually illustrated the way modern paperbacks are. Two of our most famous American books were paperbacks.

One is TAMERLANE AND OTHER POEMS By a Bostonian (Edgar Allan Poe), Boston, 1827. The other is THE PROSE ROMANCES OF EDGAR ALLAN POE, Uniform Serial Edition...No.1, containing THE MURDERS IN THE RUE MORGUE and THE MAN THAT WAS USED UP, Philadelphia, 1843.

A copy of this book, with facsimile wraps, sold in 1974 for $20,000. There is no telling how much a complete copy would bring at auction should another ever be discovered — perhaps more than a quarter-of-a-million dollars. This is also a good example of the price difference which can result when a book has defects (the original covers missing in this case).

Some well known contemporary authors who have had many paperback first editions are Ray Bradbury, John D. MacDonald, Jack Kerouac, Tom Robbins, and many, many other science fiction and mystery writers.

So, remember these important points:

- **OLD IS RELATIVE**
- **MODERN CAN BE VALUABLE**
- **SUBJECT IS OF IMPORTANCE**
- **AUTHORS AND ILLUSTRATORS NAMES MUST BE REMEMBERED**
- **FIRST EDITIONS MUST BE RECOGNIZED AND IDENTIFIED**

AGE VERSUS VALUE!

So it's old! Is it valuable? What does valuable really mean? Valuable is subjective and means different things to different people. It often depends on whether you are a buyer or seller. But for the purpose of this book, we will assume that an item is valuable if it has a retail value of at least $10 and you can make a 200% profit if you sell it, or is worth at least twice the purchase price if you are investing. This doesn't mean that you will not be able to buy many things which you will sell for less than $10, but when you do you will usually make several hundred percent profit. I will explain that later.

Now, to illustrate the point about prices for "old" versus "recent" books, here are some comparative prices taken from auction records, and dealer catalogs, in the past few years.

OLDER BOOKS

Date	Publication	Author & Title	Price
1664	Bible	NOVUM TESTAMENTUM SYRIACUM...	$135
1679	—	ADVICE...NOBILITY...QUALIFICATIONS ...OF KNIGHTS, ETC.	$32
1680	Burg	TRUE NARRATIVE...DUKE OF BUCKINGHAM	$40
1729	Ames	AN ASTRONOMICAL DIARY, OR, AN ALMANACK	$45
1746	Centlivre	THE BUSIE BODY, A COMEDY	$30
1769	Anon.	ACCOUNT OF THE BARBARITY OF THE RUSSIANS, ETC.	$50
1779	Abercrombie	THE BRITISH FRUIT-GARDENER	$80
1792	—	AN ALMANACK & REGISTER FOR THE ISLAND OF JAMAICA	$145
1797	Rowson	AMERICAN SPECTATOR, OR MATRIMONIAL PRECEPTOR	$45
1829	—	AN...AMERICAN PRIMER...FOR LITTLE CHILDREN	$30
1832	—	AN ADDRESS...FEMALES...BY AN ENGLISHWOMAN	$48
1837	Allen	MR. ALLEN'S REPORT...ON SLAVERY, ETC.	$25
1842	Addison	HISTORY OF THE KNIGHTS	$40
1845	Barker	FRANCISCO, OR THE PIRATE OF THE PACIFIC	$45
1846	Simms	THE AMERICAN SPY	$100
1850	Marvel	THE REVERIES OF A BACHELOR	$75
1854	Avery	MRS. PARTINGTONS CARPET BAG OF FUN	$38
1858	Beebe	THE HISTORY OF PERU	$65
1858	Holmes	THE AUTOCRAT OF THE BREAKFAST TABLE	$60
1858	Longfellow	THE COURTSHIP OF MILES STANDISH	$85
1863	Addey	LIFE AND MILITARY CAREER...JACKSON, ETC.	$50
1865	May	LITTLE PRUDY	$75
1865	Bowman	SHERMAN AND HIS CAMPAIGN	$25
1871	Adams	CHAPTERS OF ERIE AND OTHER ESSAYS	$35
1871	Alcott	LITTLE MEN	$125
1871	Miller	SONGS OF THE SIERRAS	$75
1876	Cornell	HISTORY OF PENNSYLVANIA, ETC.	$27
1879	Holmes	JOHN LOTHROP MOTLEY: A MEMOIR	$50
1881	Alger	FROM CANAL BOY TO PRESIDENT	$40
1891	Allen	FLUTE AND VIOLIN...KENTUCKY TALES	$25
1896	Field	THE LOVE AFFAIRS OF A BIBLIOMANIAC	$45
1904	Abbey	THE POEMS	$25

AND SOME MORE RECENT BOOKS

Date	Publication	Author & Title	Price
1915	Maugham	OF HUMAN BONDAGE	$850
1916	Anderson	WINDY MC PHERSON'S SON	$1000
1919	Grey	GREAT GAME FISHING AT CATALINA	$650
1923	Hemingway	THREE STORIES AND TEN POEMS	$4000+
1924	Hemingway	IN OUR TIME	$3000
1924	Faulkner	THE MARBLE FAUN	$4800
1924	Hemingway	IN OUR TIME	$3500+
1926	Hemingway	THE SUN ALSO RISES	$2000+
1926	Milne	WINNIE-THE-POOH	$350
1927	Faulkner	MOSQUITOES	$1000
1927	Hemingway	MEN WITHOUT WOMEN	$650
1928	Ackley	CROSSING THE PLAINS...EARLY DAYS IN CALIF.	$150
1929	Faulkner	THE SOUND AND THE FURY	$1225
1929	Hemingway	A FAREWELL TO ARMS	$600
1932	Faulkner	SALMAGUNDI	$850
1933	Hemingway	WINNER TAKES NOTHING	$250
1935	Algren	SOMEBODY IN BOOTS	$400
1935	Hind	INTRO. TO THE HISTORY OF THE WOODCUT...2 vol.	$150
1945	Eder	HISTORY OF PHOTOGRAPHY	$125
1946	Agee	LET US NOW PRAISE FAMOUS MEN	$300
1947	Hunter	PAPERMAKING, 2nd Edition	$75
1949	Adams	MY CAMERA IN YOSEMITE VALLEY	$500
1958	Hunter	MY LIFE WITH PAPER	$125
1972	Adams	WATERSHIP DOWN	$250

As you can see, old books are not necessarily valuable, and valuable books are not necessarily old.

Where do prices come from? There are many sources for book prices such as you see above. But there is no single source which can give you the current values for all old and/or out-of-print books. That would be impossible for there have been millions of titles published since the invention of movable type.

If there were such a source it would consist of hundreds of volumes — you would need a small library just to store such a set.

Even then, the best you would have would be a rough idea only of the value of any particular title. Why? Because the price shown might be old, one obtained at auction and essentially a wholesale price, or may have been taken from a booksellers catalog and there would be no way of knowing if the dealer ever really obtained that price — the book may still be sitting on the shelf. Furthermore, the price shown might be for a copy in fine condition and yours is only good, or vice versa.

If it were an auction price it might not be typical because a rivalry between bidders may have forced the price abnormally high. Or perhaps bad weather may have kept bidders away and the item went for a song. Or lots of other reasons. But, do not despair, there is an answer as you will see.

We will continue this discussion on the relationship of value to age. Many old books were written by authors who never achieved any fame, or by authors who are long forgotten — deservedly. If these books were trash when they were written then they are still trash. That's also true for modern books. On the other hand, modern books by good authors, especially those printed in small editions, may be many times more valuable then older works published in very large editions. Books written by important authors before they became famous are quite likely to have been printed in small quantities and became scarce very quickly — and thus valuable.

One such example is William Faulkner's THE MARBLE FAUN which you may have noticed in the list you just read. This book of poems was first published in 1924. Take another look at the price!

I will repeat — old is relative. If you know the date that printing was first introduced into a locality it will help you to determine just what 'old' really means. The date 1796 can be important if it appears on the title page of a book printed in Detroit; it may not be too important for a book printed in Boston.

IMPORTANT DATES FOR YOU TO KNOW

Here is the order in which printing first appeared in some of the various states:

Massachusetts — 1639
Virginia — 1682
Pennsylvania and Maryland — 1685
New York — 1693
Connecticut — 1709
Rhode Island — 1727
South Carolina — 1731
North Carolina — 1749
New Jersey — 1754 (possibly earlier)
New Hampshire — 1756
Delaware — 1761
Georgia — 1762
Louisiana — 1764
Vermont — 1780
Florida — 1783
Maine — 1785
Kentucky — 1787
Tennessee — 1791
Ohio — 1793
Michigan — 1796
Mississippi — 1797-98
California — 1833
New Mexico — 1834
Wyoming — 1867

These dates are important for you to keep in mind because they will help you to appreciate the relativity of old, and perhaps keep you from embarrassing yourself if you offer someone a book printed in Philadelphia in 1826 just because it is 159 years old. It certainly doesn't qualify as an early imprint. However, a book printed in San Francisco in 1850 would certainly be a very early imprint even though it's 24 years younger than the Philadelphia book.

Such a book would have value aside from its subject matter or author. Remember, however, that other than the earliest imprints of a locality, age is still secondary to subject matter and the author's importance.

BIBLES

There are only four American Bibles you should be aware of when you are scouting until you become experienced.

The first is the Bible which the Reverend John Eliot translated into Indian language. It was printed at Cambridge, Massachusetts, in 1661 and 1663. It's important because it was the first Bible printed in the United States and contains the Gospel in the Natick Indian language. It is also an early Cambridge imprint and a complete copy is rare. It represented a tremendous literary feat because the Natick Indians had no written language until Reverend Eliot created one for them, and then taught them to read it. The correct title of the book is MAMUSSE WUNNEET UPANA-TAMWE UP-BIBLUM GOD, Cambridge, 1663. A second edition printed in Cambridge in 1685 is also rare and valuable. If you should discover one while you're scouting you will be able to take a very long vacation. Several years ago a copy was sold at auction for $43,000.

The second Bible printed in the United States was German. It was printed in Germantown, Pennsylvania, in 1743, by Christopher Saur (Sauer or Sower). It, too, is rare and valuable.

The third important Bible was the first one printed in English in this country. It was published by Robert Aitken, in Philadelphia, in 1781-82. The date itself is important because before the American Revolution, the right to print Bibles in English was licensed by the British Crown and no one in America had been given the privilege. So we had to wait until after the Revolution to print a Bible in English.

The fourth Bible of importance was the first Catholic Bible to be printed in America. It was published by Carey, Stewart and Company of Philadelphia, in 1790. Keep looking for these Bibles — avoid all the rest in the beginning.

ABOUT NEWSPAPERS

Almost without exception, newspapers are of little value except to a specialist dealer. Particularly those of the 19th Century (1800-1899). This is true for single copies or bound "runs" unless you are buying them to fill an order from a library or collector. Even a complete Civil War run might be hard to sell despite the historical interest. An exception would be a run of Confederate newspapers, especially those which were printed on wallpaper due to the paper shortage in the South during the war years.

If you do buy any newspaper make sure that it is genuine. You must be especially careful of any copy of the *Vicksburg Daily Citizen* of July 4, 1863.

Another no-no would be a complete run of newspapers for the years of the War of 1812. Even if genuine there would be no great value. Also be on guard for Lincoln and Washington facsimiles. One is the *New York Herald* of April 15, 1865, announcing the death of Lincoln. Even genuine copies are of no great value.

Many other early newspapers have also been reproduced. One of the best known being the January 4, 1800, issue of the *Ulster County Gazette*. Over 60 different facsimiles have been published over the years — only two genuine copies have been recorded.

Other 18th Century newspapers which have been reproduced in facsimile are *The Boston Gazette* of March 12, 1770, announcing the Boston Massacre; the first issue of the *Boston Newsletter* of 1704; the *New-England Courant* of 1723, the first paper published by Benjamin Franklin; a *Massachusetts-Spy* of 1775; a *Pennsylvania Packet* of 1776, containing the Declaration of Independence; and a *Maryland Journal* of 1783, with news of the Peace Treaty. There are exceptions to all this, but until you gain some experience you will do best by avoiding all newspapers.

AUTHORS AND THEIR FIRST BOOKS

Now we will get back to books of importance. I have already told you about important subject matter to be on the lookout for. Appendix 2 contains a list of over 2,400 collectible authors and their first published book, with place and date of publication. I have also noted pseudonyms where applicable. This list is of importance to you for two reasons. First, because the authors are collectible; second because usually an author's first book is the keystone book for any collection and often the scarcest and most valuable.

Use this list along with the authors and illustrators listed in the other Appendices. You need not try to memorize the lists. However, if you read them over several times you will find that you have a surprising ability for recall later on.

Carry this book with you when you are searching for nuggets.

FIRST EDITIONS

When booksellers, librarians, and collectors talk about books by important authors they are almost always referring to the first editions of the authors' books. SO — what is a first edition?

In the bibliographic sense, a first edition is the first appearance in print of a work in book form. To realize the importance of the first edition you must think of a book as a collectible object such as a work of art. The first edition is an original to book collectors, and always preferred to a later printing, just as a collector of paintings prefers an original to a copy.

This is especially true for the first editions of any significant works in any field of human endeavor — medicine, the arts, sciences, agriculture, history, discovery, and of course, for authors who become famous.

The term "first edition" deserves some explanation because it has assumed different meanings as printing technology and economic factors changed throughout the years. Prior to 1800, page forms for a book were generally broken up immediately after running off the first printed version of a book.

After 1800, however, it became practical to leave the type 'standing' intact after the first printing run. Then, if a second printing were required the printer could simply put the forms back on the press and run off a second 'impression.' Technically, both runs could be considered impressions of the first edition since the type was not changed. Nevertheless, both print runs cannot be considered 'firsts.'

One run came before the other, perhaps years before, and only the first impression copies from the first printing run are the truly valuable ones — the "First" edition. This is what is meant when the term is used in a catalog or any other writing relating to book collecting or bibliography.

The problem, of course, is how to tell a first edition from a later one! And there is no really simple answer. A general guide is that a book is probably a first edition if the date on the title page agrees with the copyright date, which is usually on the verso (back side) of the title page. But that is not always true. Some books are published without a dated title page and often without even the publisher's name or the place of publication. In those cases, it will be necessary for you to do some research. This book is a good starting point.

The best way to start is to learn more about 'firsts', 'issues', and 'points' by studying those invaluable tools called bibliographies. These are usually available at your local library. A bibliography will give the printing history of the works of one author, or of the works on one subject. As an example of this kind of help, you already have information at hand on over 5,000 books.

You also have the names and pseudonyms (pen name) of hundreds of additional authors and illustrators. There are standard bibliographies available for almost any subject, author of importance, or other area of bibliography which you might encounter. Appendix 8 provides many useful references.

They are not infallible but they are an indispensable aid. A bibliography will also tell you other things which a complete copy of a book must include to identify its edition — for example, the number of illustrations, or the color of the binding.

Sometimes identifying a first edition can be very difficult. For instance, identifying identically dated books which have variant issues. These variations occur in some books, and bibliographers must separate the first edition into the various issues, or states, and refer to the distinguishing features as 'points.'

Here is one example: THE SONG OF HIAWATHA by Henry Wadsworth Longfellow was published in Boston in 1855. However, not every copy dated 1855 is a true first edition. The valuable 'first issue' of the first edition contains advertisements that are dated November, 1855. This is the first point that distinguishes the edition, first issue, and its consequently higher price.

Other points used in determining first issue, or state, can be a missing letter in a word, a piece of broken type flawing a printed letter, differences in binding cloth, color, or type, insertion of an 'errata' (correction) slip, differences in end papers, presence or absence of maps, and so forth. Here are some more examples of points which help determine first issue.

Pearl Buck's novel of China, THE GOOD EARTH, was published in 1931. In the first few copies, "flees" was misprinted for "fleas" in line 17 on page 100. This misprint was noticed and corrected during the printing run. Now, booksellers and catalogers who list the first issue refer to it in their catalogs as "First edition, first issue," and subsequently corrected copies are "first edition, second issue." The first, uncorrected copy is the more valuable. So, bear in mind, collectors and booksellers place the emphasis on the earliest issue — always. If you are either buying or selling a copy of this book you would certainly want to verify this 'point.'

An example of a point which is not a misprint is found in the first edition of Ernest Hemingway's A FAREWELL TO ARMS, which has two issues. The first edition, first issue, does not have the usual printed notice stating "None of the characters in this book is a living person." This notice was added to the book in the second printing (issue) to prevent some of Hemingway's friends from complaining, with good cause, as they were the characters in the novel.

Another famous point is in the dedication of General Lew Wallace's Biblical novel BEN HUR. The first issue has a dedication page reading "To the Wife of my Youth." Mrs. Wallace, who was very much alive, thought this might lead people to think that she was no longer around.

So, she insisted that later editions should read "To the Wife of my Youth Who Still Abides With Me."

Who are some of the authors whose works are valuable in first editions? All of those listed in the various appendices of this book.

Are all books marked first editions valuable? Certainly not. If the author, or what he or she has to say, is not of importance, than nothing is going to make the book valuable to anyone. The majority of the thousands of books which will be published this year will probably be marked first edition — but very few will ever again be worth the original publisher's retail price — and perhaps aren't at the outset.

THE IMPORTANCE OF CONDITION IN DETERMINING VALUE

The value of any item — book, magazine, or any piece of ephemera, is drastically affected by condition. Nothing will reduce the value of any printed item as severely as poor condition.

You may not think it matters if an illustration from a book is missing or torn, or two or three pages have coffee or water stains, or the covers are loose — but IT DOES. Any defect reduces the value. When you offer an item for sale and do not describe the condition completely you will get it back from a buyer — fast. You must be complete-

ly honest and describe what, if anything, is wrong. If you have priced it accordingly you will have no problems.

Would you buy a cracked or chipped piece of porcelain? If you did, you would not pay more than a fraction of the price for one in good condition. Would you buy a postage stamp for your collection if a corner had been torn off? Or if it was defaced by a heavy cancellation?

You might feel that your book with a loose binding, or missing end papers, can be repaired. So can the cracked or chipped porcelain. But neither may be worth the cost of repair unless of great rarity and value. Even if the repair were successful it still would not approach the value of an undamaged item.

There are exceptions to bad condition. Use common sense. Do not try to offset the poor condition with crutches such as "I was told that this once belonged to Marilyn Monroe," or, "This book came on one of the first ships to round the 'Horn' on the way to California," or, "See that name there, George Hoover. well, maybe he was related to President Hoover." Even if you could prove such things — SO WHAT!

There are several things which should be kept in mind relative to copies of hardcover books which are not new. It is the distinction between "used," "secondhand," "rare," and "antiquarian." All of which often appear as part of a bookseller's business name or are appended to indicate the type of merchandise sold. They are often used as synonyms, but in fact there are true distinctions in my mind.

Let's start with a "secondhand" copy of a book. A secondhand book can also be "used" but not necessarily. And, of course, it may have had many previous owners, not just two. Possibly it has never actually been read. The one thing that all secondhand books have in common is that they have had one or more previous owners. However, a secondhand book may show evidence of shelf wear, the extent of which may indicate its age, and which is not related to wear due to handling from being read. There may be other defects present which are not related to being used such as foxing, wormholes or page discoloration or print-through.

Now, let's consider a "used" copy of a book. It is a copy which has been read and shows it. Condition of a used copy can vary from poor to fine.

There may be barely perceptible evidence of its having been read, or there could be evidence of considerable abuse such as underlining, creased corners, stains, fingermarks, notes, tears, etc. All affect condition and value. The book could be 200 years old, or may have been published last month.

Secondhand or used books can be in- or out-of-print and a bookseller may have both to offer. If a hardcover book is still available from the original publisher than it is still in-print. It may also be in-print in a hardcover reprint edition by another publisher, or by a book club. The paperback edition of any book which was originally published in a hardcover edition is, of course, also a reprint.

Secondhand or used copies of a hardcover book which is still in-print bring quite a bit less than new copies. This may range from 50% of the original cover price if the book is in "like new" condition, downward to as little as 10% if it is badly shelfworn or reader abused. And perhaps nothing. And the economics of the book business are that a bookseller would not pay more than 50% of the price he could expect to sell it for — even less if it is in plentiful supply or other copies are presently in stock.

One thing a lot of us tend to forget is that collectible titles which were published many years ago, and were perhaps out of print for a long time, may be back in print. Perhaps they have never been out-of-print. Many books by the classic or better known writers are kept in print. Books by Mark Twain, L. Frank Baum, Ernest Hemingway, F. Scott Fitzgerald, and most of the better known children's writers are good examples. You may not see them on the shelf at your local B. Dalton or Waldenbooks store, but nevertheless, they can be ordered from a publisher for you. So, unless you are a collector concerned with first editions only, new copies of many classic titles are available.

If you are concerned with selling a copy of such a title, you must remember that if you have an old reprint you are competing with a newer reprint and that affects the price you can expect. This is why it is important to do your homework when you wish to value or sell a book. Most libraries will allow you to check the current edition of *Books In Print* and this should be one of the very first things you should do if you are concerned with the possible value of a book. Certainly, if you

wish to be a serious bookseller, the latest or at least a fairly recent edition of *Books In Print* is a must.

This will also explain why, if you have ever quoted a price for a book which you own to a bookseller who has advertised for the book, your price might have been too high. The bookseller's customer may have only been interested in "any" copy of the title. If the book is still in print, then the bookseller's customer certainly expects to pay much less for a used or secondhand copy then for a new copy. On the other hand, if the customer is a collector or library looking for a first edition, a much higher price can be expected.

The point is, quoting a first edition price to a bookseller wanting a used copy of an in-print book can be very frustrating. The problem is aggravated by booksellers who do not provide that distinction in their advertising. In fairness, it may be because their customer did not tell them. It may also be because they did not do their homework either. Perhaps if they had, they could have told the customer the book was available new through their local new book store.

I'll take a few paragraphs right here to discuss the difference between **RARE** and **SCARCE** in referring to old books. Both terms have been frequently abused by booksellers. Usually, but not always, through ignorance. One definition of **rare** which I have heard for many years was "a title which would be offered for sale no less often than once every 20 years or more."

In the strictest sense both terms can be used synonymously but the definition which I much prefer is the usage given in my American Heritage Dictionary. It is: **Rare** and **scarce** both describe what is in infrequent or short supply. But **Rare** usually implies unusual quality and value enhanced by permanent infrequency. **Scarce** emphasizes mere infrequency, with the implication that it is temporary."

That's all well and good. The problem is knowing if the particular catalog or description you are reading uses it this way. If the bookseller using the term is a very knowledgeable one, with many years of experience, than the use of either term will probably be accurate and the balance of the description, as well as the title itself, will clarify this.

However, either term can be badly misused by less experienced dealers or collectors. The most frequent offense, in my experience, has been the use in describing books which the seller has never heard of (either by title or author) and thus an immediate assumption is made that it is either **scarce** or **rare**. The distinction being made without regard to fact. In truth, the title may be in plentiful supply in other parts of the country, and indeed, often in other parts of the same city. However, its use provides an ostensible justification for an unrealistic price. I have even seen **scarce** used in reference to titles which are still in-print, or available as remainders at less than the original publisher's price.

A further complication can occur even with more experienced booksellers or collectors who do have access to the several book price guides which are available. This is when the failure to find a title listed in the guides leads to the assumption that the title must be either **scarce** or **rare**. But this is not necessarily so. Example: the title can't be found in American Book Prices Current even after examining a run of many years. The reason may be that copies simply don't have sufficient value to be included, as well as being too common to have been ever offered at auction.

I should also mention that even if a title is **scarce/rare**, that does not automatically equate with valuable. Even for a title which exists in only two known copies, a third copy may have little value if no one wants that third copy. There were literally thousands of religious titles printed in the 17th and 18th century which fall into that category.

Always do your homework before buying or trying to sell a title which you suspect, or hope, is **scarce/rare**.

CONDITION

Here are some specific things which are fatal to the value of any printed collectible. Always remember them when you are buying, and if you should have a flawed item to sell, bear that in mind when you set the price.

BINDINGS (COVERS): Cloth — the most usual form of binding. Missing; loose; dirty; water stained; partially chewed by mice, roaches, or the dog; marked by rims of liquid containers; damage of any kind; excessive wear; fading of color, pictorial design or lettering; fraying.

Leather — Same as for cloth. In addition, leather is more susceptible to scuffing and peeling.

Paper — Usually referred to as "Wraps" or "Wrappers." Tears are bad and even worse if they have been repaired with transparent tape. Excessive rust marking from staples does not help either. Be especially watchful for missing pages.

Other — There are other types of bindings you may encounter, such as silk, linen, vellum, buckram. deerskin, denim, silver and other metals. Any fault will lower the value just as for cloth, leather or paper.

END PAPERS (FLY LEAVES): These are the blank pages at the front and the back of a book. If they are missing the book is not complete. Sometimes they were removed because they had been scribbled on, or the former owner did not want a name seen when the book was passed on. Nevertheless, their absence reduces value. Do not ever remove them no matter what the condition.

Writing on end papers can reduce the value *unless* it is the author's or someone else of importance or fame — providing you can prove it. Even if in poor condition, and perhaps not even a first edition, MOBY DICK would be valuable if the writing — in INK — said "From the author, Herman Melville, to the Captain of the whaling ship North Star." However, if it said instead, "From Joe Doakes to his good friend Pete Smith, Christmas, 1910," it would mean less than nothing.

A somewhat soiled cookbook inscribed "From P.T. Barnum to the idol of his heart — Jenny Lind," would certainly raise the price (Barnum brought the 'Swedish Nightingale' to America). However, "From the Ladies Garden Club to Maggie Jones" would be meaningless.

Pen or pencil notes on the margins of pages (annotating) are generally detrimental unless you could somehow prove that the comments written in a LIFE OF WASHINGTON were in Abraham Lincoln's own hand. Then you would have a very large nugget no matter the condition.

TITLE PAGE, TABLE OF CONTENTS, LIST OF ILLUSTRATIONS (front matter): Always check to see if these pages have been marked with library stamps or any other useless and detrimental writing or marks.

Be sure to check — by actual count (collating) — that all of the illustrations (plates) are still present and have not been crayoned or otherwise defaced. This is one of the easiest errors to make. Do not be lazy. A customer who makes the unhappy discovery that an illustration is missing has a right to be very unhappy indeed. He will surely return the book to you along with some pointed comments because you did not check properly. It is not excusable

THE TEXT: Check for missing or loose pages, foxing (see the Glossary), underlining, scribbling, and annotating.

ADVERTISEMENTS: Check for missing, or damaged, advertising pages if you know or suspect that they should be there. These are often an important point for determining edition or issue status. If missing, the book is imperfect.

BOOKPLATES: Decorative bookplates do not normally decrease the value. An important 'association' bookplate — that of an important or famous person — can often enhance the value considerably. However, if there is evidence that a bookplate has been removed, leaving an ugly scar, the value will be reduced. It's acceptable to place a new and attractive bookplate over the scar.

ERRATA SLIPS: Sometimes typographical errors were discovered before the book left the publisher's premises. The publisher may have printed a slip correcting these errors and 'tipped' it into the book (glued it in), usually at the front of the book. Sometimes it was just loosely inserted. In any event, it must be reported to a prospective buyer if you, or the buyer, is aware that its presence is required. If it has been lost it could seriously affect the value.

SOME EXCEPTIONS TO GOOD CONDITION: As is often the case after you have been given the rules, you learn when they can be broken. For example, a scarce color plate (illustrated) book can be in terrible condition BUT if any of the plates are still in good condition they will have some value.

Just one plate from the original elephant folio edition of Audubon's BIRDS OF AMERICA can be worth thousands of dollars. These plates are the size of a small kitchen table so you will not have any trouble recognizing one when you encounter it.

Warning — Do not be fooled by reprints of Audubon's, or other early and modern reprints of valuable bird, flower, animal, costume, and other plates. Many of the better plates have been reproduced in this century and sometimes sell for only a few dollars each.

Especially notorious in this regard are the reprints of Currier and Ives lithographs which have been reproduced as calendars for many years

by the Traveler's Insurance Company. Do not ever buy an old print unless you can inspect the back of it first, as well as all the margins.

Sometimes you might think you can make more money by removing the plates from a book that is in poor condition, then you could by restoring it. That is really a no-no. I ask you, please, do not give in to that temptation. In the long run it will not be worth the damage to your reputation as a conscientious scout or dealer. It's considered to be quite reprehensible.

In the specialized fields of art and science, extremely scarce books can be valuable even if the title page, or several text pages are missing. Why? Because such books are needed in university and other scholarly libraries. These libraries can complete a defective book by obtaining a facsimile of the missing pages from other institutions. The restored copy will not have the same monetary value as a complete original but it will still be useful to scholars.

On the other hand, it is very difficult to find an exception for literary first editions unless they are rare, like the Poe book I mentioned earlier. For the collector, there is no substitute for a complete first edition in fine condition.

Another exception occurs in the case of bindings. Books and pamphlets that were originally issued in wraps of some kind are often found in rebound condition, with the original 'wraps' bound in. This was done to preserve the original covers and may not effect the value too drastically.

LOST, STRAYED, OR STOLEN

You may have, or seen for sale, books which have in them library ownership stamps or other evidence of ownership. What should you do about them? If the book is marked 'discard' or 'surplus' or 'duplicate - unwanted' you need do nothing because libraries have the right to dispose of surplus.

The book with library identification and no notice such as above is the puzzle. It may have been stolen, or perhaps it was overdue and the borrower just gave it away or left it in some book shop's outdoor bargain bin.

In any event, you should not consider the book yours until you have found out if the library wants it back. This can be a Herculean task. If the library is in your home town a quick telephone call or personal visit can settle the matter quickly. But suppose you live in Texas and the book bears the markings of a library in a Vermont town! What then?

You can write to Vermont and ask about it. Or you can simply mail the book back.

But you paid good money for it! So did the taxpayers who bought the book for the library in the first place. Consider it a good public relations gesture. If it is a really scarce or valuable book the library will often compensate you for returning it.

The loss of books from libraries costs taxpayers in the United States millions of dollars each year. One big city public library, with guards at all doors, is known to have 'lost' three huge Webster's Dictionaries within twelve months. A major cause of thefts results from books which are borrowed in order to remove the illustrations, especially if the artist is important and collected, such as Maxfield Parrish, Frederic Remington, and others.

Most of the books which appear in salvage and thrift stores with library markings are not worth more than a dime or quarter... but it will cost the library which owns them several dollars (and perhaps hundreds) each to replace them.

This is without including the cost of the paperwork involved. If they can not afford to replace them, then the public is deprived of access to that book. Many salvage shops and thrift stores now screen the books which they receive and make an attempt to return them.

In some cities, booksellers set aside any library books which they might acquire when purchasing a quantity of books from someone. If notified, the library will arrange to pick them up. Some libraries have asked dealers not to leave library books in a home, but to take them along with others and see that they find their way back to the library. This would be a nice practice for you to follow — but don't do so at the risk of a punch in the nose!

When a bookseller's catalog uses the words 'ex-lib' or 'ex-libris' (Latin for 'out of the library') it means that the book has library markings. You can be fairly sure that in such cases the book is a legitimate library discard. Reputable booksellers will not offer a doubtful book.

4.
IMPORTANT AUTHORS AND ILLUSTRATORS

Now that you know of some of the things which create value, and those which will decrease it, you should start to become familiar with the names to watch for. You need to do this so that you will have memory recall whenever you have an opportunity to look over a box or shelf of books or other printed paper. Or when you read a bookseller's catalog, attend a rummage sale, country auction, flea market, or swap meet. Bear in mind that for non-fiction material you are concerned with subject matter and the actual author is not always of primary importance. For novels, poetry, and other literary writings it is the author and edition that are important.

Presented in the various appendices are comprehensive, but by no means complete, lists of authors, and illustrators, of all types of works: novels, biographies, essays, poetry, science fiction, mystery and detective, histories, narratives — they cover the entire gamut of writing.

In many cases you will find books with the author and illustrators combined. For example; TOM SAWYER by Mark Twain and illustrated by Norman Rockwell. This particular book would be collectible for the illustrator only since Rockwell was not yet born when TOM SAWYER was first published.

APPENDIX 1 — AUTHORS: THEIR TRUE NAMES AND PSEUDONYMS (PEN NAMES)

Appendix 1 provides the TRUE NAMES OF AUTHORS AND THEIR PSEUDONYMS. This appendix contains over 4000 names of authors who use one or more pen names and those pen names. The use of pseudonyms has been so prevalent for many years. Indeed, many authors seldom or never published a book using their true name, for various reasons.

A good example is Frederick Schiller Faust, best known as Max Brand. Of his over 200 published books, only three books of verse were published with his true name of Faust. The rest were published using at least 13 different pseudonyms and he used over 50 names in his magazine writings.

In selecting the authors to be included, I have chosen both living and deceased authors if they are generally considered collectible or of enduring reader interest. I have also selected a nearly equal number from the genres of most interest, i.e., mystery, science fiction/fantasy, children's, western, romance/gothic, and mainstream novels.

This is a compilation which is not available in any other single reference and is both a useful reference and an informative source of literary trivia.

Any collector, librarian, or bookseller wishing to know if a known author's name is the true name, as well as other pen names which that particular author may have used or still uses, should refer to Appendix 1 at the outset.

This appendix does not provide names of authors who did not use any pseudonyms. As a general rule, if you do not find a currently popular author's name in Appendix 1 it probably means that the name is of a new author who will perhaps be included in the next edition of this book.

When a name is not located in Appendix 1, you should always check Appendix 2. Appendix 2 provides information on the first books of important and collectible authors who may or may not have already been listed in Appendix 1. If an author and first book is listed in Appendix 2 you can safely assume that other books by the same author are also of importance. You may also find books by that author listed in one of the Value Guide Appendices 4 and 5.

APPENDIX 2 — 2,400 FIRST BOOKS BY COLLECTIBLE AUTHORS

The importance of this list for anyone hoping to assemble complete author collections should be obvious. Many authors published their first book using a pseudonym, or anonymously, and this information is also provided.

It makes no particular difference if your interest is only in first editions, or if any edition will do when trying to assemble a complete author collection. This list will provide the correct title of an author's first book(s).

This list provides the names of hundreds of authors who do not appear on any other list in this book, particularly if the author did not use any pseudonym(s). You can safely assume that any author appearing in this list can be considered collectible.

As a general rule, an author's first book is the most difficult to find. Not necessarily the most expensive, however. There are many reasons for this. First of all, publishers are usually reluctant to take a chance on a large printing for the first book of a new author, thus first books are often small printings. Often as few as six copies for copyright purposes.

You will also discover from a study of the listings, that first books are likely to be books of verse or non-fiction books. Many authors who have achieved great prominence in a certain genre, such as mysteries, or as mainstream authors, may have written their first book as a juvenile, a school text, many forms of non-fiction, or perhaps, a scientific tome. Sometimes even as a paper for a doctorate.

Often they are privately printed editions — a euphemism for self-published in many instances. A very high percentage of them, particularly in the science fiction, adventure, and mystery fields were originally published as paperbacks. You can recognize these by names such as Ace, Bantam, Avon, Paperback Library, etc.

As a result of these factors, the first book often becomes the key book in assembling an author collection. When a first edition is required it often becomes a near impossibility to locate one and the price can become truly astronomical.

If I were a beginning collector or scout interested in assembling a collection most likely to increase in value — to use that word that most antiquarian book sellers hate — INVESTMENT — I think I would go for a collection of first books by authors in a particular genre such as mystery or children's books, or as a general collection of either fiction or non-fiction.

In using this Appendix, please note that when an author published more than one book in his first year of publication I have noted them all without trying to indicate precedence. This would be beyond the scope of this book and I suggest that in those cases where you are interested in that particular author you consult available bibliographies.

APPENDIX 3 — ILLUSTRATORS TO LOOK FOR

Appendix 3 lists artists who are primarily known as book or magazine illustrators. You should be on the look out for anything which they have illustrated. Often, these will be later editions of the "classics."

Many, of course, became best known for their magazine illustrations, such as Norman Rockwell and his work for *The Saturday Evening Post*, though he also did much work for many other magazines. Frederic Remington achieved considerable fame for his illustrations for *Harper's Weekly*, as did Winslow Homer, Howard Pyle, and Maurice Zogbaum.

In any event, a good working recall of these names will allow you to scan magazines with a purpose — to look for 'name' illustrators. They are very marketable.

5.
THE IMPORTANCE OF PSEUDONYMS

A knowledge of the pseudonyms, or pen names, used by many authors is of considerable importance to you. Some very important authors used as many as 50 or more names. The champion is probably Frederick Schiller Faust whose best known pen name is Max Brand. We know of over 50 names which he used and there seems little doubt that there are others yet to be discovered. A close runner up to Faust is probably John Creasey. As with many authors, not all pseudonyms were used for book writings. Quite often many of the pseudonyms were used in writing for the pulp magazines.

WHY YOU NEED TO KNOW THEM

An author collection, whether being made by a library or a private collector, must necessarily include the books written under any pseudonyms. In most cases, the pseudonymous books are more difficult to find because far fewer scouts will have the necessary knowledge to recognize them. In fact, sometimes the collectors themselves will be unaware of their existence. This is where you can really shine and harvest many nuggets.

Appendix 1 includes thousands of pseudonyms as well as the the real names of many collectible authors. The list is alphabetical and will either give you the real name of the author or will provide you with additional names the author has used. You will find other books on the subject listed in Appendix 8.

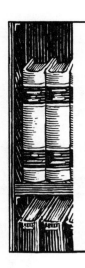
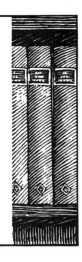

6.
MAGAZINES CAN
BE VALUABLE

Magazines are a very broad field, and save for the exceptions which I will discuss, one in which you should be cautious about involving yourself until you become quite experienced. Above all, don't get excited by the person who comes to you with the dramatic announcement that they have a complete run of *Life* magazine, right from issue number one. Even if you receive them as a gift they will be more trouble than they are worth. Where would you store several thousand issues while you try to sell them one or a few at a time? Only a very small percentage of Life issues have any value at all — and that is only to movie buffs who collect Marilyn Monroe and James Dean covers, etc.

This is also true for the other magazines which are no longer being published such as *Collier's*, *Liberty*, *Look*, and so on. Some of these are worth buying because of the cover illustrators such as Norman Rockwell, Maxfield Parrish, and others. But you must first learn which artists are collected AND who wants to buy them. Even so, don't pay more than $1 each until you really know what you are doing.

The *National Geographic* is another magazine for you to stay away from except for issues published between 1898 and 1920. Those early issues are valuable and your best bet with them is to quote them to a specialist. You will find their advertisements in *AB Bookman's Weekly*, *The Antique Trader*, and *Collector's News*. Don't start buying them with the idea that you can assemble a complete collection. It's nearly impossible to locate the issues from the first few years it was published. To my knowledge there are only two complete collections extant.

You can learn more about the magazine field from some of the references mentioned in Appendix 8.

WHICH ARE VALUABLE AND WHY

Having said what you read above, I'll tell you about magazines which you can sell very profitably if you follow the guidelines I am now going to give you. I will also list some of these magazines. Refer to this list whenever you are out scouting and spot any magazines which you suspect may be "possible's."

In almost every case, you will only buy these magazines if they contain articles or stories by one of the authors, or illustrations by one of the artists, listed in any of the Appendices. So — this means you must scan the table of contents of any magazine you contemplate buying for a recognizable author's or illustrator's name.

Here are a few examples of what I mean. *Harper's Weekly* and *Harper's Monthly* will often have illustrations by Frederic Remington and Winslow Homer. Be on the lookout for these issues and be sure and check to make sure the illustrations are still there. It is common to run across these magazines and discover too late, that someone has previously removed the illustration. Be particularly cautious when you find these magazines in antique shops. The *Saturday Evening Post* published over 400 covers by Norman Rockwell, many of which bring $100 or more from collectors. Winslow Homer illustrations can bring several hundred dollars each.

You will find short stories and articles by many famous writers in some of the magazines such as *The American Mercury* (William Faulkner). *Ken* magazine (the forerunner to *Esquire*) and

Esquire published authors such as Ernest Hemingway, John Dos Passos, and many others. *Playboy* magazine is also collectible for its author content as well as its centerfolds. Always check copies of *Playboy* to make certain that the centerfold is still present.

Many authors who later achieved considerable fame using their own names wrote for the pulp magazines using a variety of pseudonyms as well. Almost all of the pulp magazines are now collectible, and some such as *Black Mask* can bring several hundred dollars each from libraries and private collectors trying to assemble complete collections.

The pulps were published from the late teens until the early 50s. They generally sold for a nickel or a dime, and in addition to the important authors who got their start in them, they also featured lurid covers by collectible artists.

You can learn more about all of these kinds of magazines by sending for the specialist dealer's catalogs which are advertised in many of the trade magazines I have listed in Chapter 8, and the catalogs of booksellers (see Chapter 7).

Here is a partial list of magazines to be on the alert for:

American Mercury, The Art Interchange, Atlantic, The Bachelor of Arts, The Bookman, Boy's Life (with Rockwell covers), *Century, Colliers, Esquire, Evergreen, Godey's, Graham's, Harper's Weekly, Harper's Monthly, Illustrated American, International, Judge, Ken, Liberty, Life* (not the picture magazine), *Lippincott's, McClure's, Overland, Peterson's, Police Gazette* (early), *Punch, Recreation, Saturday Evening Post* (for illustrators), *Scribner's, St. Nicholas, Sunday World, To Date, Vogue,* and most pre-1950 movie magazines.

Pulp magazines have a very good collectors market, primarily libraries assembling collections of all in certain genres, or early works by authors who were prolific writers for these magazines, often using a variety of pseudonyms and writing in a wide variety of genres.

Some of the better known magazines are *Air Wonder Stories, Amazing Detective Tales, Amazing Stories, A. Merritt Fantasy Magazine, Astonishing Stories, Argosy, All-Story, Adventure, All Detective, Avenger, Astounding Stories, The Blue Book, Bill Barnes Air Adventures, Black Mask* (the most sought after pulp of them all), *Breezy Stories, Comet Stories, Cosmic Stories, Clues Detective Stories.*

Dime Mystery Detective, Dare-Devil Aces, Doc Savage, Doctor Death, Detective Story, Dusty Ayres...Battle Aces, Detective Fiction Weekly, Dime Mystery, EErie Stories, Famous Fantastic Mysteries, Fantastic Adventure, Fantasy Book, Future Fiction, Fight Stories, Ghost Stories, G-8 and His Battle Aces, Green Lama, Horror Stories, Jungle Stories, Magic Carpet, Mammoth Adventure, Mystery Stories, Mysterious Wu-Fang, Nick Carter, Navy Stories, Nickel Western, New York Stories, Oriental Stories, Over the Top, Operator #5.

Planet Stories, Popular Magazine, Pirate Stories, Phantom Detective, The Parisienne, Parisian Life, Pep Stories, Railroad Stories, RAF Aces, Racketeer Stories, Star Adventures, Science Fiction Magazine, Science Wonder Stories, Scientific Detective Monthly, Sinister Stories, Spicy Mystery, Startling Mystery, Startling Stories, Strange Stories, Strange Tales, Sea Stories, Sport Story Magazine, Sky Birds, Spy Novels, Saucy Stories, Spicy Adventure, Spicy Detective, Spicy Western.

Spicy Mystery, The Shadow, Secret Agent "X", The Spider, Tales of Magic and Mystery, Ten Detective Aces, Terror Tales, The Thrill Book, Thrilling Mystery, Thrilling Wonder Stories, Terence X. O'Learys War Birds, Uncanny Stories, Uncanny Tales, Unknown, Weird Tales, Wonder Stories, The Wizard, War Birds, War Stories, Wings, Wild West Weekly, Western Story, The West, Western Round-Up, Western Tales, Zero.

7.
PRINTED COLLECTIBLES EVERYWHERE

Yes, they really are. Wherever you may go in your search for books, you will also find an amazing variety of other printed collectibles. Most of these will be on paper, but you will also find them in the form of lithography on tin, glass, cardboard, leather, Celluloid, plastic, and cloth.

Some of these items will bring unbelievably high prices from specialty dealers and collectors throughout North America. You have to be astute enough to recognize them when you see them, buy them at the right price, and know how to sell them for what they are worth. Sounds simple doesn't it. Well, it is simple.

In this and later chapters I'll tell you how to accomplish this. First, though, let's concentrate on how to recognize them. Take another look at the list in Chapter 2 of the things which can be sold. Now we will consider it in more detail.

ADVERTISING

Generally speaking, I am referring to early (pre-1930) advertising items such as display cards, counter cards, store signs, posters, brochures, trade cards, boxes and containers of all types. The subject matter can be just about anything. Tobacco, food, patent medicines, clothing, farm equipment, drinks such as soda, beer, wine and whiskey, automobiles, trucks, motorcycles, carriages and wagons, harness, travels by ship, train or plane, games, and just about anything else you can possibly imagine. Trade catalogs for general merchandise firms and specialized products bring good prices. To a lesser extent there is a market for items up through the early 50s.

ART

I am really referring to old prints rather than original art in the traditional mediums. You will find these in books, magazines, and as individual pieces which will normally have been framed.

Often the frames themselves have considerable value. A study of the illustrators listed in Appendix 3 is important. Since this is a major specialty all by itself, I would suggest that you also study some of the references I have included in Appendix 8. You should also send for as many catalogs as you can from the specialty dealers whose advertisements you will see if you subscribe to any of the publications I mention or which are listed in Chapter 7.

ATLASES AND MAPS

There is a good market for early atlases and maps which are in GOOD condition. Early means prior to about 1870 for North America. Maps which show geographic boundaries, and place names, which no longer exist are of considerable interest. Also maps showing routes of the pioneer explorers, early railroads, early aviation routes, military campaigns, population centers, canals, pre-dam sites, etc. Important and early hand colored maps bring very high prices. Some of the important publishers of atlases are Colson, Mitchell, and the United States and Canadian governments.

AUTOGRAPHS AND HISTORICAL DOCUMENTS

This is a very large specialized field and generally you will sell anything you discover in this field to a specialty dealer. Here again, you will find them advertising in the publications I mention.

The field includes more than simple signatures, which of course aren't printed at all. Often autographic material is both printed and holographic (hand written). If the item is by a person of interest or importance, it is collectible and valuable. This includes letters, deeds, diaries, notes, checks, photographs which were signed or inscribed by the subject, book manuscripts, sheet music compositions, autographed and presentation copies of books, and so forth. In some cases the person need not have been famous. For example, a ships log of a whaling voyage can be very valuable even though the Captain himself may have never become famous. The same would be true of a soldier's diary written during the Civil War which describes a famous or important battle from a first hand participants viewpoint. Often, notoriety can be more valuable than laudable fame. A John Dillinger item may be more valuable than J. Edgar Hoover's.

Another example; John F. Kennedy's autograph is worth about $150 — but the signature of his assassin, Lee Harvey Oswald, can bring as much as $350. One reason, of course, is that there are far fewer Oswald signatures in existence. Dillinger letters are worth about $55. A signed photograph of Al Capone could bring as much as $400, and a holographic letter perhaps $1,000. A Jesse James letter might bring between $5,000 and $10,000, and a letter from Billy the Kid, over $10,000. A letter written by John Wilkes Booth, who assassinated Lincoln, is worth double that of most Lincoln letters. A letter by Robert F. Kennedy may bring $75-100 but one by Sirhan Sirhan could will bring over $350.

BADGES AND PIN-BACK BUTTONS

The most valuable badges are those of law enforcement officers, especially those of the early West; sheriffs, marshals, rangers, and their deputies. Others of value include fire fighters, detective agencies, Indian agents, military personnel of all types, fraternal lodges, etc. You must be careful here, because there are a great many fake law enforcement badges to be found at swap meets, flea markets, and as an inevitable result, in antique shops.

Pin-backs are far more common. Just to clarify, a pin-back button is one with a pin device on the back for attaching it to clothing and you are likely to see them everywhere. They have been, and still are, issued for just about everything; political figures, comic characters, convention commemoratives, fairs and expositions, and so forth. Here again,

some of the more valuable ones have been issued as replicas and you must be very careful when you buy these. However, if you inspect them closely you can usually determine if they really are original.

This may be a good time for me to mention that you should always carry a small loupe (pocket magnifier) with you. A 10x power is good, 15x or 20x even better. You will find uses for it constantly when you're out scouting for nuggets.

BANNERS AND BROADSIDES

These are found in all sorts of material, but usually banners will be of cloth — broadsides will be of paper or cardboard. They usually announce events or make some sort of announcement. For example, announcing the eminent arrival of a circus or carnival; ship, train, or stage coach arrivals and departures; wanted person announcements; rewards; significant news events of community interest, and more. Here, as in all items we talk about, condition is important.

CATALOGS

This is a major area of interest. Manufacturer's catalogs are usually more valuable than those of wholesalers or retailers such as Sears. Many of the early Sears catalogs have been reproduced in facsimile by the thousands so you must be careful if you consider buying one.

The kind of catalogs that bring high prices are from manufacturers of steam engines, windmills, guns, musical instruments, toys, farm machinery, cars, horse drawn vehicles, airplanes, motorcycles, bicycles, jewelry, watches, clocks, housewares, pottery and porcelain, silverware, clothing, patent medicines, writing instruments, furniture, etc. Also included in this category are service and repair manuals, spare parts lists, and so forth.

One of the biggest reasons this is such a good market is that antique dealers, writers, and collectors are able to identify and date many items by locating them in these catalogs.

CERTIFICATES, CHECKS, INVOICES, BUSINESS FORMS

All of these forms of ephemeral printed material are of interest if they are old and have engraved illustrations on them. The more ornate the better. If they relate to an obsolete type of business such as carriage making or buggy whips, so much the better. Naturally, they must be in good condition.

LABELS

Of collector interest are cigar box labels, cigar bands, whiskey and beer labels, patent medicines, early food and drink, and anything else of an unusual nature. At present I advise you to avoid fruit crate labels as the market seems to be flooded with them — some of which I suspect are not very old.

COMIC STRIPS

This is a good market. Be on the lookout for the early comic characters, especially the Sunday newspaper issues, which were usually in color. The more consecutive issues you can find, the better.

Of special interest are *Buck Rogers, Flash Gordon,* early *Prince Valiant, Alley Oop, Popeye, Katzenjammer Kids, Life With Father, Gasoline Alley, Betty Boop, The Yellow Kid, Buster Brown,* early *Dick Tracy, Mickey Mouse, Moon Mullins, Winnie Winkle* — in fact, just about anything before 1940. Condition is important.

GAMES

All sorts of early parlor games are collectible. They are very difficult to find in good condition, in the original box, and complete since they were ephemeral in nature. Of special interest are the paper doll sets and paper doll cutout books that are still intact. Early coloring books (which haven't been colored yet) are also good, especially if the subject is a movie star or comic character.

MOVIE AND ENTERTAINMENT

This is a field of great interest to thousands of collectors and dealers. The range of collectible materials is wide; programs, press books, film scripts, magazines, lobby cards, posters, still photographs, autographic items, home film projector versions of cartoons, serials, and movies, and now, of course, video tape recordings.

Of special interest and value are any of the materials which relate to the silent film era and its stars. Also the stars themselves who have attained a special mystique such as Humphrey Bogart, James Dean, Valentino, Garbo, Mae West, Chaplin, Harold Lloyd, Fatty Arbuckle, Abbott & Costello, the Marx Brothers, the Ritz Brothers, Errol Flynn, Clark Gable, John Wayne, Marilyn Monroe, etc.

PLAYING CARDS

There are many collectors of playing cards and organizations of collectors. Of interest are unusual designs and those having association interest. An example, those issued by railroads, especially those no longer in existence. The same is true for steamships and steamship lines, airlines, hotels, gambling casinos, social clubs and organizations, and political groups and parties.

Some collectors are only interested in themes such as flowers, animals and birds, buildings, famous persons, scenics, and what have you. Complete decks are the most valuable but even a single card can be valuable if it is old, unusual, and rare. Hand-painted cards dating back to medieval times can be worth thousands of dollars.

POSTCARDS

This is another very large collecting field with literally thousands of collectors and hundreds of specialist dealers. You will find several references for further study listed in Appendix 8. You can also write the postcard collector clubs for additional information. By all means, send for dealer catalogs and lists so you can get a feel for the pricing structure and the specialized way postcards are marketed.

Some of the more important postcard names you must be aware of are Winsch, Clapsaddle, Tuck, Brundage, O'Neill, Wain, Thiele, and De-Longpre. Themes, or subjects, which you should be on the lookout for are views, greetings, war, aviation, ships, cars, comic characters, flags, costume, railroad, birds, fishes, animals, military, rodeo, amusement parks, fire-fighting, mining, Indians, sports of all types, deformities, erotica, covered bridges, old hotels and public buildings, resorts, cowboys, hold-to-light type cards, and any unusual depiction.

There is very little market for standard tourist type view cards no matter what part of the world they are from with the exception of pre-Castro Cuba and old Japan.

TRADE CARDS, ADVERTISING

These were colorful cards of various sizes given out by business firms for just about any product or service imaginable. They usually carried a brief advertising message on one side and the advertisers name superimposed on the image on the other.

The range of picture subjects would be similar to those for postcards. Often the lithography was outstanding and the work of many collectible illustrators was represented.

CARDS — TOBACCO, GUM, CANDY, CEREAL, FOOD, BEVERAGE

These are best exemplified by the bubble gum cards which are still collected today and are big business. Most popular are the baseball and football cards, some of which bring prices in the hundreds of dollars.

Also popular with older collectors are the cigarette cards which were issued as subject series such as war, costume and uniforms, animals, birds, planes, trains, flags, comic characters, ships, freaks, and so forth. Complete series of these cards bring substantial prices.

SPORT'S COLLECTIBLES

In addition to the cards mentioned above, there is also a huge variety of other printed sports collectibles which are much in demand. Some of them are; books, programs, pins, yearbooks, photos, prints, advertisements, souvenir programs, almanacs, posters, yearbooks, handbills, caps, t-shirts, jackets, and autographed items of all kinds.

SHEET MUSIC

There are a great many collectors in this field and several specialist dealers. Of special interest are sheet music with stage and screen stars on the covers of songs related to the pictures or stage productions in which the star appeared.

Also of interest are the music or songs of thematic interest such as our American wars, and ethnic groups, as well as Negroes and the South. Many famous illustrators also provided covers for sheet music so be on the lookout for these.

VALENTINES

Victorian valentines are the primary object of interest here. They were often quite elaborate,

having several layers which progressively folded outward as the valentine was opened to form a 3-dimensional effect. I have seen some with as many as seven levels when fully opened and they are often truly beautiful They are difficult to find in good condition and some will bring prices in the hundreds of dollars.

POSTERS

This is a large and lucrative field. Some posters sell for thousands of dollars. Artist and subject matter are of great importance here and many very famous artists also did poster work at some stage in their careers. Some who did are Toulouse-Lautrec, Joan Miro, Salvadore Dali, Alexander Calder, Will Bradley, Norman Rockwell, Frank Brangwyn, Howard Chandler Christy, J.C. Leyendecker, Ben Shahan, Alphonse Mucha, and many other famous names.

The range of subjects is vast; movie themes and stars, circus and carnival, the various wars, military recruiting, advertising, travel, autos, bicycles, ships, stage plays, books and magazine promotions, sound recordings, video's, concerts, and other special events.

The best way to familiarize yourself with this field is by obtaining dealer catalogs and studying them, reading the various price guides available, and visiting the shop of a poster specialist if at all possible.

To summarize this chapter, just about anything that is printed and more than 30 years old is collectible and thus of value. Somewhere there is a collector, and probably a specialist dealer, who needs your nugget.

Never forget condition — I can't emphasize that too much. If an item is in poor condition don't bother with it no matter how old it is or how cheap. If it is being offered for only a few dollars that's probably all it is worth and it will cost you far more to sell it than you paid for it — if you are ever able to. There is no point in your trying to be in this business for nickels and dimes. And you do not want to acquire a reputation for dealing in poor quality merchandise.

8.
WORKING TOOLS AND
REFERENCE MATERIALS

I hope that you realize by now that an indispensable working tool is this book you're reading. There are others which are going to be useful too. Some of them are more important than others and, of course, they serve different purposes. You'll also be happy to know that none are very expensive.

To start making money using this book (in addition to the nuggets you'll soon be mining) you need a comfortable and well lighted place to sit and read, a table or desk, and some writing material. It will also be helpful to have some form of transportation, but you can still get started even if you are handicapped in some way.

You do not need a lot of money in order to get started — but you do need to invest your time. Time for study, writing a few letters or postcards, visiting your local library, and going prospecting. Best of all, you can look forward to enjoying yourself. Even if you never make any money you will have a nice return in the pleasant experiences which will occur and some fascinating knowledge which you will accumulate.

INSTANT KNOW-HOW

There are two very important additional tools available to you. I strongly urge you to invest in both as soon as you make the decision to use the knowledge I'm giving you. If you don't feel you can afford them right at the beginning, perhaps you will be able to find one or both at your local library. Both of these tools are book oriented, and books are the printed collectible that I suggest you concentrate on in the beginning. First, because they are easiest to sell, and secondly, because they are the most plentiful.

The number one tool is *AB Bookmans Week-*

ly which I have already mentioned. It is important because every single issue carries the advertisements of hundreds of book dealers who are looking for thousands upon thousands of book titles that they have customers for. Private collectors are not permitted to advertise for "Books Wanted" in *Bookmans Weekly*, though they are permitted to advertise "Books For Sale."

Every issue also contains news of the out-of-print book field, announcements of coming events of interest, book reviews, and a large section of books for sale. Of greatest importance to you are those thousands of books that someone wants to buy.

At the outset, by carefully reading all those advertisements, you will develop a very strong sense or feeling, for what kinds of books are wanted, by which authors, which subjects, and specialty categories. Certain titles will also stick with you for recall when you are out prospecting. Occasionally these advertisements even list the price the advertiser is willing to pay. So even though you haven't yet acquired any books to sell you will develop a sense of what is wanted in the market.

You may not be able to recall who was advertising for any particular title (but you may surprise yourself), however you will recall that someone did and know that you have a green light for a possible purchase. Why possible? Because you must still follow the rules as regards issue and condition.

Occasionally you will notice several dealers advertising for the same book. That isn't necessarily because a lot of people are looking for it at the same time — it's more likely that a collector has written to several search services at the same time and asked them all to look for that book. It would indicate however, that it is a title that may be difficult to find thus the multiple activity on the part of the collector.

Later on, after you have accumulated a stock (inventory), you will be scanning these ads for the items you already have on hand. When you find one, or several, you will be on your way to making sales — and profits.

Your next most important tool will be the various price guides which are available to you at your local library unless you are in a very rural area. There are four primary sources of prices of used and out-of-print books.

A HANDBOOK FOR BOOKLOVERS by Joseph Raymond LeFontaine. This is my own book and contains many thousands of collectible books and their values. Published by Prometheus Books, 700 East Amherst St., Buffalo, NY 14215, it will be available in the summer of 1988. Reservations are suggested.

THE BOOK COLLECTORS HANDBOOK OF BOOK VALUES by Van Allen Bradley. A new edition has been published approximately every three years since its inception. However, Bradley died a few years ago and it is questionable if new editions will be published. Try to obtain the last edition in the out-of-print market if you can.

AMERICAN BOOK PRICES CURRENT. This is an annual compilation of book prices received at auctions throughout North America and Great Britain. Published since 1895, the prices are essentially wholesale prices since most auction purchases are by dealers who in turn resell to their clients at retail.

BOOKMANS PRICE INDEX. Published annually this series lists prices taken from dealers' catalogs. Of some value as a guide only, since there is no way of knowing if any particular price was ever obtained by the dealer offering the book. Lists books in varying conditions as well as later printings. Large libraries will have copies of some, if not all of the above, in their reference section.

Last, but probably the most important for you, are current dealers' catalogs. You obtain these by requesting them. They are usually free. They are a great source of current pricing information for thousands upon thousands of books as well as other printed collectibles. By reading these

catalogs you will become amazingly knowledgeable about this field in a very short time. Not only will you learn what is being sold and for how much, but you will find them to be a great source of bibliographical information AND your working guide on how to write your own catalog when the time comes.

How do you find out who is offering catalogs? First, by reading, and then writing to the booksellers I have listed in Appendix 7. Next, by reading any or all of the following periodicals. Some will be available at the library. Others you will have to subscribe to. Usually you can purchase a sample issue of any of these for a token amount. A postcard to any of them will get you subscription information and the cost of a sample issue.

Collectors News. P.O. Box 156, Grundy Center, IA 50638. Published monthly. Approximately the same as *The Antique Trader* but with much more editorial material, i.e., authoritative articles. Also contains my monthly column ALL ABOUT BOOKS ... AND THEIR AUTHORS.

The Antique Trader. P.O. Box 1050, Dubuque, IA 52001. Published weekly, approximately 172 pages per issue, tabloid size. Contains "Wanted" and "For Sale" classified ads of hundreds of collectors and dealers. Almost every conceivable type of collectible can be found in each issue with good emphasis on books, magazines, and other paper collectibles. Also authoritative and interesting articles, announcements of flea markets, antique shows, and auctions.

The West Coast Peddler. P. O. Box 5134, Whittier, CA 90607. Monthly. Distributed throughout the Western states. A good scouting guide. Contains my monthly column BIBLIOPHILE: COLLECTING BOOKS FOR FUN AND PROFIT.

American Book Collector. 274 Madison Avenue, New York, NY 10016. Six times per year. Articles, news, and reviews for the book collector. A major source of available book dealers' catalogs.

As you become involved in this field you will also learn of other useful periodicals, many of which are regionally oriented and may be of specific help to you. The periodicals I have mentioned above will be of the greatest value to you immediately. You will learn of others as time goes by.

On a more prosaic level you will also need a supply of 3 x 5 inch blank file cards, and some postage prepaid postal cards from the post office will be useful.

I'll explain the use of the file cards in a later chapter. Obtain them in a few different colors if you can. It will simplify things when you begin cataloging your nuggets. The postal cards will be used for requesting catalogs and for quoting your nuggets to prospective buyers.

A typewriter is helpful but not absolutely necessary unless you are unable to hand print legibly. You might also want to buy a file card box and a set of blank index divider cards. Later on when your sales income justifies it you might also want to have some inexpensive stationery and business cards printed, or have a rubber stamp made with your name or a business name of your choosing.

9.
THE WAY TO THE HIDDEN TREASURE

No matter where you live, be it a large city or a small village, East, West, North, or South, there are nuggets all around you. Now I'll tell you all the places and ways to do your prospecting. You can do it right at home if you wish or if you are handicapped, or out in the field as the inclination and available time permit.

By now, I hope you have a pretty good idea of what to look for. Once you know where to look you will be on your way to making as much or as little extra money as you wish. Or to being a very wise collector, if that's your goal. Spend as much time as you wish — a few evenings a week, or a few hours on the weekend — or all day, every day. Work at your own pace and choose your own hours. Midnight or mid-afternoon, whatever pleases you.

FLEA MARKETS AND SWAP MEETS

They are really one and the same thing for your purposes and are excellent places for you to do your prospecting. There are hundreds of them occurring all over the country, in almost every community, all year around. They are held indoors and outdoors, at operating as well as abandoned drive-in theaters, race tracks, sports stadiums, convention halls, motels, farm yards, fields, and parking lots.

They range in size from less than 20 sellers to those like the Rose Bowl Swap Meet in Pasadena, California. A typical Sunday will have several hundred sellers and an attendance of over 20,000 shoppers. Sellers run the gamut from those who come on a one-time basis to clean out the garage accumulation to major antique dealers and booksellers who operate regular store front shops.

These meets are usually held on weekends, though in some parts of the country there is being one held every single day of the week, all the year around. They are usually announced in your local newspapers or over the local radio stations.

Here are some tips to help you become a wise and successful prospector. Get there as early as possible — before they open for business — which may be before dawn.

Don't worry about arriving before the meet is actually open to the public. Most of the time you'll be able to get in as you will be taken to be a seller. A very large business is often done among the sellers themselves before the meet opens. In fact, some sellers really participate in order to get first crack at the merchandise the other sellers have brought. They hope to cream off all the real goodies before YOU get there. So, beat them to the punch — be there first.

Don't hesitate to bargain with sellers. If you see something you want and think perhaps it is too high priced, ask the seller if they will accept the price that you think is right. That's the name of the game. If they won't accept your offer early in the day, they might if they still have the item later in the day, especially if they have not had a good day.

On the other hand, if it is a bargain at the price asked, don't be foolish. Pay the price and be happy. Your time is valuable and while you are trying to save a few pennies you might be missing out on another bargain at the next stall.

If the sun is expected to be out that day be sure to dress lightly and wear something on your head. Wear your most comfortable shoes — you may walk a lot of miles and be on your feet for hours.

Always bring some folded shopping bags with you, the kind with handles. Sellers are often thoughtless about providing bags or boxes. It's even a good idea to put some empty cartons in the car. You never know what sort of bonanza you might run across. It would be a shame to miss out on some real finds because you have no way to cart them home. I remember one time coming across a seller who had hundreds of collectible books priced at fifty cents each. But I was only able to buy 40 or 50 of them because I had not come prepared. There wasn't a book that I couldn't have resold for at $10 and some would have brought several times that. Don't let that ever happen to you.

Always look through every box of books or paper that you spot no matter how trashy it might appear at first glance. The nugget is often at the very bottom and the reason it's still there is because everyone else was lazy. Be especially alert for boxes that are under tables. Very often, they have been overlooked by your rival scouts.

Even if you don't spot anything of interest at a stall or space, make it your business to ask "Do you have any books or paper materials?" The seller may not have brought them with him, and might possibly have an entire truckload at home or still in the trunk of the car.

The seller may reply that there are none at present but often turns down opportunities to buy them. If that happens be sure to leave your name and address along with a request that you be notified the next time it happens. Offer to pay a finder's fee for such tips. Say, 5% of whatever you spend. And then keep your word. There might be many more such opportunities from the same source.

It's also a good idea to have a little flyer or business card with your name and address, and some information on what you are interested in buying. Leave one with every seller who might possibly be a future source.

GARAGE, YARD, TAG, ATTIC, MOVING SALES

These are among the best prospecting sources over the long term. You learn of them by reading the classified ads in local papers in the merchandise for sale sections. Also, keep your eyes open for signs posted on light and telephone poles as you drive around your community. It's even more important to be an early bird here than it is with swap meets.

If a telephone is provided, call as soon as possible and ask if they have any books or printed material for sale. If they don't, you've saved yourself a fruitless trip.

If they do, a few questions as to what, can do the same thing. If all they have is a bunch of schoolbooks that shouldn't interest you. But if it sounds as if they have some goodies, then ask if you can come right over — before the sale even starts. Most of the time you will be invited. If not, at least you know that you should be there early on the day of the actual sale.

If you find several sales occurring on each day of the weekend that you would like to attend, plan your itinerary beforehand so you can save time and needless running from one end of town to another. Also, remember what I said about carrying shopping bags and cartons with you.

Here's another thing to remember that applies to any of your buying activities. If you plan on paying for your purchases by check, carry some strong identification with you. Better yet, is to plan on paying in cash (currency). You will be surprised at how many sellers will not accept checks from anyone, especially those who have come to a swap meet from out of town. It may be because they need money too badly to wait for checks to clear. Perhaps they may not even have a bank account in which to deposit checks And it is not unusual to be offered a better price if you can pay with cash.

Here's another important thing. Many sellers are not prepared to provide a receipt. Carry one of those blank receipt books which you can get at any stationery store. When necessary you can fill one out right on the spot for the seller to sign and you'll have a record of your purchase. If you don't feel it necessary to do this, at least carry a small notebook with you and record the details of every purchase immediately. Example: $3.25 — 7 books; $16 — poster. Don't wait until you get home. If you have had an active day you will invariably forget what was spent and for what.

THRIFT SHOPS OPERATED BY SOCIAL SERVICE AGENCIES/PRIVATE ORGANIZATIONS

These shops, and sometimes one-time sales, are sponsored by the Salvation Army, Goodwill, Veterans Organizations, church and youth groups, etc. They can be an excellent source of nuggets but there are a few things to be careful of. Make it your business to visit them on a regular basis. Try to make friends with the person(s) responsible for pricing books and other paper items. Very often that person may already have an arrangement with a book scout or dealer to pick over the merchandise before it is placed on the floor for sale. Perhaps you can replace that scout or bookseller.

If, after visiting a store several times without finding anything of value despite a large stock you can just bet that someone in the store has a private arrangement going. Drop the store from your list if you can't make your own arrangement.

Even though you will occasionally find some nuggets at this type of store, for the most part you will run into the more common items such as book club editions, and lots of ex-library material, which you should not be tempted to buy unless it's for personal use, not resale.

One very bad habit these stores have is either marking the prices in crayon or ink on the endpapers, or using stick-on price tags on the dust jackets. All are very difficult to remove without damage and unless the item is a real gem don't bother with them. If the store people are friendly and you don't suspect some sort of arrangement as I mentioned above, you might ask them to mark all prices in books, at least, with a soft pencil.

Needless to say, this is something you should always do if you should find a need to place prices in your own books. Never, never use a pen.

ANTIQUE SHOPS, SECOND-HAND SHOPS, JUNK SHOPS

On occasion you can find a nugget in these shops. However, you will probably discover that many antique shops overprice books because they tend to treat them as if they were similar to furniture, porcelain, and other objects whose age is visually obvious. That is, the older a book is the more valuable it must be. This is, of course, simply not true as I have all ready discussed. They also tend to justify shabby condition as having some virtue in demonstrating value related to age. So, even when you find a likely book it will probably be overpriced. These stores are also where you are quite likely to find facsimile editions of various printed items being offered. The McGuffey's readers and Sears catalogs, for example, or any of the old newspapers I mentioned earlier.

Here, too, is where you will find the facsimile Currier and Ives print mounted in an old appearing frame and often priced as if it were an original being offered as a bargain. In all fairness to the stores, it is ignorance which is probably in operation here, not any deliberate attempt to defraud. The net effect on you, if you buy any of these items will be the same, however. You will have paid for legitimate merchandise and received a sham which you cannot recover from unless you in turn perpetuate the deceit.

Do your homework, don't be afraid to ask questions — and don't buy unless the seller will allow you a reasonable time to authenticate the purchase and return it if it is not what it was represented to be.

Any honest dealer will be happy to accommodate you on this request for they have nothing to knowingly conceal. If they have made a mistake they will appreciate having it pointed out to them in order to protect their reputation.

Many of these shops can also be fine sources of your nuggets. Since they often acquire the kind of things you are interested in along with those which are their primary interests, they will often price these items too low because time and their available reference materials don't permit them to research them properly. Quite often these items end up tucked away in drawers, hidden behind other merchandise, or left to accumulate in boxes left in odd corners. Look in all these places. Open the drawers of all cabinets which are offered for sale. They are the favorite dumping place for many dealers, who then forget about them. Always ask what the dealer has in the back room — this question often turns up a virtual mother lode of material which the owner just hasn't wanted to bother with or has had no room to display.

USED-BOOK STORES

These can be one of your very best prospecting sources. That may sound a bit odd but it's true. Many of these stores are operated by people without the slightest real interest in books except as merchandise, just as groceries, hardware, or shoes are. You will know far more about the value of used books, old or recent, after you finish this book than they will. Unless they buy this book too.

In any event, their merchandise will generally be priced on the basis of a simple markup on whatever was paid — usually not very much. Hardcover books for 50 cents to a dollar are the norm, with no particular attempt to peg the price to any intrinsic merit of the book or author. Sometimes big thick books are marked higher than small thin ones — pricing by size. That is very much to your advantage if this seems to be the practice.

Look their merchandise over very carefully. If you think you are going to find quite a few good items, go to the proprietor and ask if he will give you a discount or special price if you make a large purchase. Very often you'll be offered more than you could have hoped for.

Sometimes this type of store will have a place behind the cash register area where the "rare" books are kept. You can usually spot this soon after you enter the store. Scan the backstrips of these books quickly for recognizable titles, authors and publishers. Remember the list of reprint publishers in Chapter 2? Now is when that list will be helpful. You may spot several names of reprint publishers in the so-called "rare" book section. If this store owner thinks that an Altemus edition of Jack London's CALL OF THE WILD is a first edition, you may discover some mighty fine nuggets in that store. Reason! The fine first editions are also likely to go unrecognized for what they are.

What about the used-book store where it is obvious the proprietor is very knowledgeable about books? You can still find many great bargains. In my experience, this is the very best source of nuggets for many reasons. Why? One reason is because no dealer who has, for example, 20,000 books on his shelves can possibly re-price each book every year as their value increases due to inflation, increasing scarcity, changes in collectors' interests, etc.

You may discover books on the shelf which were originally priced 5 or 10 years ago and are now considerably underpriced. Perhaps a book is marked $4. You know that this book, in the condition it is in, now sells for at least $20. You buy it and you have a nice potential profit in hand. Another reason a book may be underpriced is because the dealer specializes in a specific type of book, perhaps Americana, and is not particularly interested in mystery novels and does not keep up with that field. Again, this means an opportunity for you. A third reason is that the market for cer-

tain types of books in your community may be quite poor and so the dealer has to keep his prices down. People buy those types of books from him for reading, not collecting. You, however, have a market wherever the postal service delivers and can sell that book that has been sitting on his shelf for years.

Perhaps at this point I should discuss in a bit more depth the distinction between a used-book store and an antiquarian bookseller. It won't be hard for you to tell them apart in the field.

The antiquarian bookseller will usually have a much more presentable shop. Neater and better organized. You won't have to scan too many shelves to recognize the kind of stock he has. If most of the titles make your heart skip a beat, check a few prices. They will usually be marked in the upper right hand corner of the front free endpaper — in pencil. Often the price will have a code beneath it. That's the sure tip-off that the proprietor is a knowledgeable book person. The code represents the price paid for the book. I'll tell you more about using a code yourself later.

PERIODICALS, ADVERTISEMENTS

The periodicals I mentioned in Chapter 8 are good hunting grounds which you can prospect without ever leaving home. All these publications, and many others like them, as well as your local news and shopping papers, carry classified advertising for book sellers, antique shops, and scouts like yourself who have books and all sorts of printed materials for sale.

You will find lots of great bargains. You will also find ads for common items with ridiculously high prices. And now you will discover that one of the reasons this book is so valuable to you is that I have taught you the difference. These periodicals also offer catalogs which you can send for. Then, you can shop the catalogs.

When you do see a bargain advertised you must act fast. There may be other people out there who have become just as knowledgeable as you — perhaps they also bought this book. But if you act fast you might get the item before they even read the ad. If it's a really good higher priced item, it may be worth making a phone call, long distance if necessary. If the item hasn't been sold ask that it be held until they receive your check. Then mail the check immediately.

Naturally, you will have asked enough questions to make sure the item is what you want. For example, if it is a book having known "points" you can ascertain them. And you can determine or verify condition.

If you can't telephone because no number was available, then write immediately and enclose payment. Be sure to state exactly what you are ordering. If there are points then spell them out in your letter and state that the money should be returned if the book does not meet your criteria. Or is not in the condition you specify. Be sure and mention the name of the publication you saw the ad in, and the date. Many dealers advertise in several publications each month.

Always enclose a stamped self-addressed envelope (SASE) with your order. If the item is already sold the dealer will use it to return your check. Otherwise your check may just be torn up and your order ignored. Sad to say, many dealers do just that when they receive several orders for the same item, all with checks, and feel it to be too expensive and time consuming to return them.

I consider the practice utterly reprehensible and anyone who does this should not be allowed to advertise further in the periodical in question.

Many of these dealers state in their ads that they will do just that, as if warning you provides justification for such a shabby business practice.

Here's a happy thought now. Early in my book selling career I badly underpriced a book which I had advertised. Even so, it was priced for a healthy profit. I received over 40 checks in the mail within a week. Wouldn't it have been nice to have had 40 copies of that book? Anyway, I was happy to mail all those checks back. I now had 40 new names for my mailing list to use in future. And if I had known then what I know now — I could have filled some of those additional orders. You will know how if this happy situation ever occurs for you. Oh yes! About underpricing the book. It will happen. Don't lose any sleep when it does as long as you aren't actually out-of-pocket.

You will make up for that time and time again with books you buy for nickels and dimes and sell for many, many dollars.

To summarize, read the periodicals you subscribe to (or that the library does) as soon as they arrive. Act promptly on the finds. Send for as many dealer catalogs as you see offered. Aside from their shopping possibilities they are the nucleus of your pricing reference library.

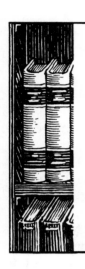
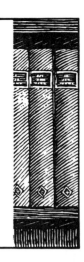

10.
THE CARE AND FEEDING
OF YOUR NUGGETS

Inasmuch as you will not be operating a store — in fact, probably you will be using the kitchen table for your office — it is important that you develop a simple system for keeping track of your inventory and storing it so that it will not be necessary to ever handle anything more than a few times until you sell an item.

The first time will be immediately after buying, and the second time will be after you have sold it and are ready to ship it.

The simplest system that I know of is one I used for many years, until I was able to computerize my inventory. For now I'll assume that you don't have a computer and perhaps never will. At least not for the purposes we are discussing. My system involves the 3 x 5 inch file cards I recommended you buy in an earlier chapter. If you haven't done so yet now is the time. You will make a card for each and every item you purchase. The card will contain all the information you will ever need in future. Once the card is completed you can store the book, or whatever, until it's time to ship it to someone.

About storing! Shelves are fine but not necessary. If you keep books on open shelves they are subject to fading and soiling from dust and other nasty things in the air. But you can see them and admire them. Just make sure they stand upright — as little leaning as possible as that will eventually distort the whole book.

The best is to store them in sturdy cartons which can be closed tightly with the books standing upright as if they were on a shelf. An alterna-

tive is to place them in the carton with the spine up. Do not lay them flat and on top of each other. It won't hurt to place each book in a plastic bag to prevent them rubbing against each other. Number each carton in a prominent place so you can locate the carton quickly when you need to retrieve a book.

Store all other paper items such as magazines, small prints, valentines, handbills, etc. flat. Posters and larger prints can be rolled but not too tightly and do not put a rubber band in contact with the original. Place a sheet of writing paper under the point which the rubber band will contact, or else use transparent tape instead of a rubber band on the protective sheet.

Other types of smaller flat material such as photographs, autographic items, or anything else which might be fragile should be stored in standard file folders and filed upright after being properly labeled. Be cautious about using plastic material to protect thinner paper material. When sealed tight it cannot breathe and any retained moisture can result in mildewing.

Keep all stored material in a clean, well ventilated, and dry place. Remember to fill out your file card FIRST. Don't try to rely on memory after you've put them away.

Before I get into an explanation on how to fill out your file cards I suggest you familiarize yourself with the following glossary of terms and the explanation of the Roman Numeral System which follows. You will encounter this fairly often in older books and it's important to be able to date them.

BOOK TERMS AND ABBREVIATIONS:

Advance copy—A copy of the first edition of a book, usually one of the first off the presses, so likely to be first issue. Released by the publisher prior to the scheduled publication date for review purposes. They may be specially bound, left unbound, or bound in wrappers.

Advts.—The pages of advertisements bound into many books.

Americana—Any book, map, broadside, document, pamphlet, print or other printed material dealing historically with the American scene. This includes Canada, the United States, and Mexico — all of North America.

Anonymous (Anon.)—A book which does not provide the name of the author.

Association copy—Any book, or other item, which bears an identifiable relationship to the author or some other famous person by the inclusion of a signature, photograph, letter laid in, etc.

Auction prices—Prices realized for books sold at auction. In the U.S. the major book auctions are held in New York, Chicago, Los Angeles, and San Francisco. As a rule, you should consider auction prices as wholesale values since they are largely attended by book sellers.

Author's copy—A book which has been the authors personal copy and is so inscribed and signed, or has his bookplate. This adds a premium to the normal value.

Autographed copy—Any book signed by the author. Also see Inscribed copy.

Backstrip—The common term for the spine of a book. What you see when the book is standing between two other books on a shelf. Sometimes the backstrip is of a different material than the rest of the binding. Example: boards with cloth backstrip; cloth with leather backstrip.

Bibliography—(Biblio.) An alphabetically arranged list of books about a special subject or author. Usually providing considerable detailed information.

Bibliophile—A lover of books. What I hope you will become if you aren't one already.

Bibliopole—A hater of books. Please, don't be one.

Binding (Bndg)—The cover of a book. May be any of a wide variety of materials.

Blind stamping—Any impression of lettering or ornament in the surface of a binding, without the addition of coloring or gilding.

Bookplate—A printed, and usually ornamental label pasted on an endpaper or flyleaf to indicate ownership. Does not normally detract from a book's value and may enhance it if it is that of a famous person and signed. Most bookplates carry the words "ex libris" which means "from the library of ..."

Buckram—A type of coarse linen or cotton used for bindings, especially by libraries.

Calf (calfbound)—A binding of leather made from calf skin.

Case—See binding.

Cloth (Clo. or Cl.)—The material used for binding most modern hard cover books.

Collate—To check a book page by page to see that every page is present. This is very important for illustrated books in order to assure that all the plates or illustrations are present.

Colophon—A final notice, usually at the back of a book, which gives the name of the printer or publisher and sometimes, in the case of a limited edition, the number of copies printed and details as to paper and type used. Often important as a "point." In modern books this information is often found on the copyright page. Sometimes an ornamental device is a part of the colophon.

Color Plate (Clr. Pl.)—Colored illustrations in a book. May be hand or mechanically colored. See Plates.

Compiler (Comp.)—One who compiles a book, bringing its contents together from various sources, such as an anthology, almanac, or directory.

Condition—The physical state of a book or any printed item relative to its original state when it was first published. This is one of the most important factors affecting value aside from rarity, and one of the most troublesome.

Contemporary binding—A binding which dates from the same time period in which the book was published. Not necessarily the original binding. At one time books were sold unbound and the purchaser would then have the book bound in a style of his own choosing — perhaps so that all the books in his library would be in uniform bindings.

Copyright page—The page carrying the copyright notice(s). Normally the back, or verso, of the title page. Often provides much information in addition to the copyright date, sometimes including the true name of a pseudonymous author.

Covers bound in—When a book is rebound because the original covers are damaged and beyond repair the original covers may be bound into the new binding as evidence of the book's authenticity. This is quite common for books which were originally issued in wrappers and have been rebound in cloth or leather.

CWO—Check with order.

Dampstained—Staining or discoloration caused by excessive moisture.

Desiderata—A list of books or other collectibles wanted by a collector, library, or dealer. More commonly known as a Wants List.

Dust jacket (DJ)—Printed or pictorial paper cover used to protect the binding of a book. Normally issued with the book by the publisher. Printed dust jackets date from about 1832. Plain jackets were used much earlier. If a book was issued with a printed dust jacket it is considered incomplete if it is missing. Some dealers refer to jackets as dust wrappers (DW).

Ed.—Abbreviation for editor or edition.

Edition—The total quantity of books printed for a publisher at one time. See First edition.

End papers—The pages, which may be blank or printed, pasted to the inside covers of a book. A second set may also be present which are not pasted down. These are known as free end papers or fly leaves.

Errata slip—A printed slip containing corrections to printing errors in the book discovered after the printing was completed. The slip may be pasted (tipped) in or inserted loosely. Sometimes it is an important point in determining the first issue of a first edition and if missing will adversely affect value.

Ex-lib (Ex-library)—A book bearing library stamps or markings, a card pocket, etc. If the book has been legitimately disposed of by the library it will be marked "discard" on an end paper or the title page. Legitimate discards bring much lower prices than normal books no matter what the condition. Illegitimate discards should be completely avoided.

Facsimile—An exact photograph or photocopy of a page, book, or catalog.

First edition (1st ed.)—The first time an "edition" of a book is printed. The first edition may have several "issues" since the press can be stopped during the printing run to make a correction to a plate. At that point all copies run with the error become the "first issue," and copies run after the correction is made become the "second issue." This can occur several times, creating several issues of the first edition. Further, each issue can be divided into states for other changes such as changing the type or color of the binding. Studying the descriptions in price guides, catalogs, and bibliographies will provide you with many examples of edition, issue, and state, and the importance of "points" in their determination. You will find many examples in the value guides I have provided in Appendixes 4 and 5.

Folding map; folding plate (Fldg.)—A map or illustration printed on a sheet larger than the book and folded to protect it. They are usually bound in, but sometimes a pocket will be provided as part of the book's cover. Missing maps or folding maps will lower a book's value considerably.

Foxed, foxing—Reddish brown spotting (freckling) caused by iron oxide particles in the paper which have literally rusted. It may mar text and plates. Foxing should always be noted when describing condition, particularly if it affects either text or pictorial image.

Frayed—see Rubbed.

Half title—The book title appearing on an otherwise blank page preceding the title page. Sometimes called the "bastard title."

Hinge—The point in a binding where the covers join the backstrip. The terms "hinge cracking" or "hinges weak" indicate that the cover is beginning to separate from the body of the book. This condition should always be noted. Do not try to repair this condition yourself.

In-print—A book which is still available from a publisher. Not necessarily the original publisher.

Label—This has two meanings. First, a cover or backstrip label is a printed paper, cloth or leather slip with the title and authors name which is pasted on an otherwise blank surface. Label (pasted in) usually means a library or some other notice pasted to an endpaper.

Laid-in—Any material such as a letter, errata slip, photograph, newspaper review, etc., which is loosely inserted in a book. Also see Tipped in.

Large paper copy—A book printed on paper larger than the regular trade edition and providing much wider margins. Normally on better grade paper and nearly always as a limited edition signed by the author and sometimes the illustrator.

Limited edition—Any edition consisting of a specific number of copies and having characteristics which distinguish it from the trade edition or other editions. Generally a limited edition is numbered indicating which copy it is from the total number of copies issued. It may also be signed by the author and/or illustrator.

Mint—A book in the same condition as when first issued by the publisher. Some booksellers use the term "as new."

n.d. (no date)—A notation indicating that a book shows no date of publication on the title or copyright page. If the date of publication is known from other sources or there is only a copyright date, that date will be placed within parenthesis. Example: Boston, n.d. (1866); or, Boston, (1866).

n.p. (no place)—A notation indicating that a book shows no place of publication. If the place of publication is known from other sources it will be shown in parenthesis. Example: n.p. (Boston), n.d.(1866); or, (Boston, 1866).

Original cloth (Orig. cl.)—The original publisher's cloth binding.

Offsetting—A term used to describe the effect when pictures or type have reproduced themselves on an adjacent page. Probably occurs when the ink is not completely dry when a book is assembled.

Out-of-print (O.P.)—A book no longer available from any publisher. When a desirable book is out-of-print its price begins to rise in the after market. However, the mere fact that a book is out-of-print will not increase its value if none existed in the first place.

Paperbound—See paperback; Wrappers.

Parts (Pts.)—Some books were originally published (issued) in consecutive parts, or serialized in a magazine, in advance of regular book publication, with paper covers. Often they were bound together after all parts were issued. A complete set of the original parts of such books is often the most desirable form as many collectors feel that this is the true first edition. Inasmuch as such sets are fragile and difficult to save they can command very high prices. Many first works by Charles Dickens and Conan Doyle were first issued in parts.

Pictorial cloth (Pict. cl.)—A cloth binding with a printed or blind stamped pictorial design.

Picture label—A large picture label pasted on the front cover of a book to provide a cover illustration.

Pirated edition—An unauthorized reprint of a book, poem, print, item of music, etc.

Plates (Plts)—Another word for pictures, sometimes on a different paper than the text. Also can refer to the type from which a book is printed.

POB—Post office box.

Point—An identifying characteristic which helps to determine the edition, issue, or state of a book. There are numerous variations that can occur such as typographical errors, broken typefaces, misspellings, changes of binding, deletions or additions, errata slips, etc.

pp.—Abbreviation for pages, as 263pp.

Ppd—Postpaid.

Presentation copy—A book inscribed by an author to a particular person.

Pseudonym—(pen name) The assumed or pen name of an author. For example, Mark Twain is the pseudonym of Samuel Langhorne Clemens. You will find pseudonyms of collectible authors in Appendix 1.

Rare—A book, or other paper collectible which is extremely scarce. Usually all known copies

Rare—A book, or other paper collectible which is extremely scarce. Usually all known copies are kept track of. Rarity in itself does not command a high price — demand and condition must also be present.

Rebacked—Replacement of the original backstrip with a new one.

Rebound—Replacing the original binding. Also called recasing.

Recto—The right hand page of a book.

Rubbed—A binding which shows evidence of wear and fraying. Another word for scuffed.

SASE—Self-addressed stamped envelope.

Scarce—An item which may be hard to find but is not necessarily rare. An out-of-print book will become scarce if there is much demand for it.

Scout—You. One who locates scarce and rare books and other paper collectibles, buys them if the price is right, and sells them to dealers, libraries, and sometimes, to collectors.

Scuffed—See Rubbed.

Sewed—A method of binding thin books or pamphlets with wrappers by stitching them together with thread.

Shaken—A book having loose pages, or signatures, or with the entire body of the book loose within its cover.

Signature—A section of a book consisting of 8, 12, 16, or 32 pages which were originally folded from a single printed sheet.

Slip case—A cardboard, pasteboard, or leather protective case made to fit, and protect, a book.

Spine—See Backstrip

Started—Denotes a signature which has become loose when a book is not otherwise shaken, viz, signature started.

Text—The main content of a book as distinguished from the forematter, index, etc.

Tipped in—This means that extra plates, errata slips, or other material has been lightly glued into the book at an appropriate place.

Title page (T.P.)—The key page at the front of the book which usually contains the title, author's name, date and place of publication, publisher's name, and other information needed to properly describe a book.

Uncut—Refers to the edges of pages in a book which were not trimmed to be even with each other. See Unopened.

Unopened—Refers to the untrimmed foredges of a book which are still joined, just as they came from the printer. It indicates that the book has not been read, and can increase the book's value if it is otherwise still in good condition. This is very seldom found in modern books. See Uncut.— I once discovered an unopened book, published in the early 1920s, on the circulating shelf of a large public library. No one, in over 50 years had wanted to read that book!

Verso—The left hand page of a book. The copyright page is usually a verso page. See Recto.

Want List—See Desiderata

Water stained/damaged—Stains or discoloration caused by water. Difficult to remedy because it usually shrinks or warps pages and bindings. Very seldom can you ever sell a water damaged book.

Woodcut—A picture reproduced by carving a block of wood and inking it.

Wrappers (Wraps.)—Paper, stiff paper, or pliable material used as a book or pamphlet cover. Our modern paperback. Older books were quite commonly bound in wrappers and tend to become rare because of their inherent fragility.

BOOK SIZES

Book sizes are often a puzzle to the average book person. If you have a lot of modern books they are all probably the size known as octavo, or 8vo. If your books are odd size measure them by inches and be guided by the following table to find the proper size description.

32mo— 4-5 inches tall.

16mo— Roughly 5-6 inches tall.

12mo— Approximately 6-7 inches tall. The usual modern paperback size.

8vo— The size of the ordinary hardbound novel. Roughly 8 inches tall.

4to— Approximately 10 inches tall. The size of the usual coffee table book.

Folio— 12 or more inches tall.

Elephant folio— A very large book, about the size of a sheet of your newspaper.

ROMAN NUMERALS

Roman numerals for dating books was quite common until late in the 19th Century. When you acquire such a book it is a good idea for you to translate the date to Arabic numbering as a convenience both to yourself and to anyone you might quote the book to.

You can write the Arabic number beneath the Roman number on the title page — lightly — in pencil. Both versions should be noted on your catalog card, thus: MDXXX (1530); or, MDCCCLXV (1865).

Here is the code — most large dictionaries have conversion tables which you can also use.

M is 1,000, D is 500, C is 100, L is 50, X is 10, V is 5, I is 1.

Example: MDXXX is the year 1,530. MDL is 1550.

M	=	1,000
D	=	500
XXX	=	30
		1,530

M	=	1,000
D	=	500
L	=	50
		1,550

Example: MDCCCLXIV is the year 1864.

M	=	1,000
D	=	500
CCC	=	300
L	=	50
X	=	10
IV	=	4
		1,864

The year 1900 is MCM

The year 2000 is MM

The year 2100 will be MMC

If a smaller value letter is placed before a larger value one, you subtract:

CM	=	900
CD	=	400
XL	=	40
IX	=	9
IV	=	4

If a smaller value letter follows a larger value one, you add:

MC	=	1,100
DC	=	600
LX	=	60
XI	=	11
VI	=	6

CATALOGING YOUR NUGGETS

Now that you understand the language I'll show you how to complete your 3 x 5 inch file cards for each item. Once you understand how to do this you will be able to prepare individual quotes, or lists and catalogs without ever having to handle your inventory again until it's time to ship it to a buyer.

Here is how a typical catalog card will look for a novel.

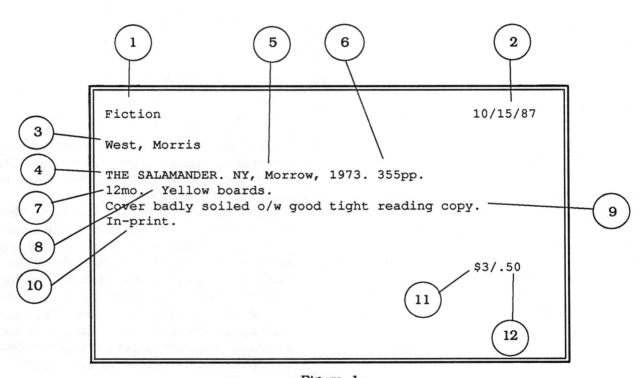

Figure 1

As you can see, there are a lot of little circled numbers. That's your road map, and here is what those numbers mean.

1. Content - a novel.
2. The date you acquired the book.
3. The author's name - Morris West.
4. The title - THE SALAMANDER.
5. The place of publication, publisher, and date of publication: NY, Morrow, 1973.
6. The total number of numbered pages in the book - 355pp.
7. The size of the book - 12mo.
8. The cover material and color - Yellow boards.
9. The condition of the book - Cover badly soiled o/w (otherwise) good, tight, reading copy.
10. Edition status - The book is still in-print. This means that even if the book were in "as new" condition the most you could charge for it at retail would be half of the original cover price.
11. The price you have decided to sell it for.
12. The price you paid for the book.

```
Publishing                                    10/15/87

Bailey Jr., Herbert S.
THE ART AND SCIENCE OF BOOK PUBLISHING
NY, Harper & Row, (1970). 1st edition
Appendices, bibliography, index.
216pp. 12mo. Yellow/orange cloth
Fine in DJ.  OP.

$4.50/.50
```

Figure 2

Here is another example but of a non-fiction book. You'll note that more information is required.

Since this is non-fiction the subject is shown in the upper left hand corner. Non-fiction books are filed by subject first, and then alphabetically by author. All fiction is filed alphabetically by author even if you sub-divide by genre, i.e., mystery, science fiction, etc.

The card also notes that the book has appendices, a bibliography, and an index. DJ means dust jacket. OP means the book is out-of-print, so you can disregard the original published price in determining your own selling price.

You can use this system to catalog anything — a movie poster, magazine, autographed photograph, railroad timetable, it doesn't matter. Just be sure to describe the item completely.

Now, let's take a look at the title page of an actual book to see how you found the information for your catalog card.

Figures 3A and 3B are the title page and the back of that title page from a popular 19th Century reference book. Once again, follow the numbers.

1. This is the complete title of the book and as you can see it is a lengthy title. Only a portion of this was shown on the cover of the book. Always determine the correct title by the title page rather than relying on the cover title.

2. This is the author's name. It may be a true name or a pen name. If you discover that it is a pen name then you should note the true name within parenthesis.

3. A statement that the book is illustrated. This is your tip-off to check (collate) to make sure all the illustrations are present. If there is a list of illustrations following the Table of Contents you can use it as a guide for locating each illustration and inspecting it to make sure it hasn't been torn or defaced. Even one missing or damaged illustration affects the value of a book. Needless to say, if all are missing, the book has no value unless it is an extreme rarity.

4. The place where the book was published. If more than one place is listed, then the first one should be noted in any description of the book.

5. The publisher's name.

6. The date the book was published. Sometimes found here, and occasionally on the verso (copyright) page.

7. The copyright date and the name of the copyright holder. Since this repeats the information shown on the title page we do not need to enclose it in parenthesis.

8. The printer's name and address. Not normally of any importance but occasionally useful in determining issue.

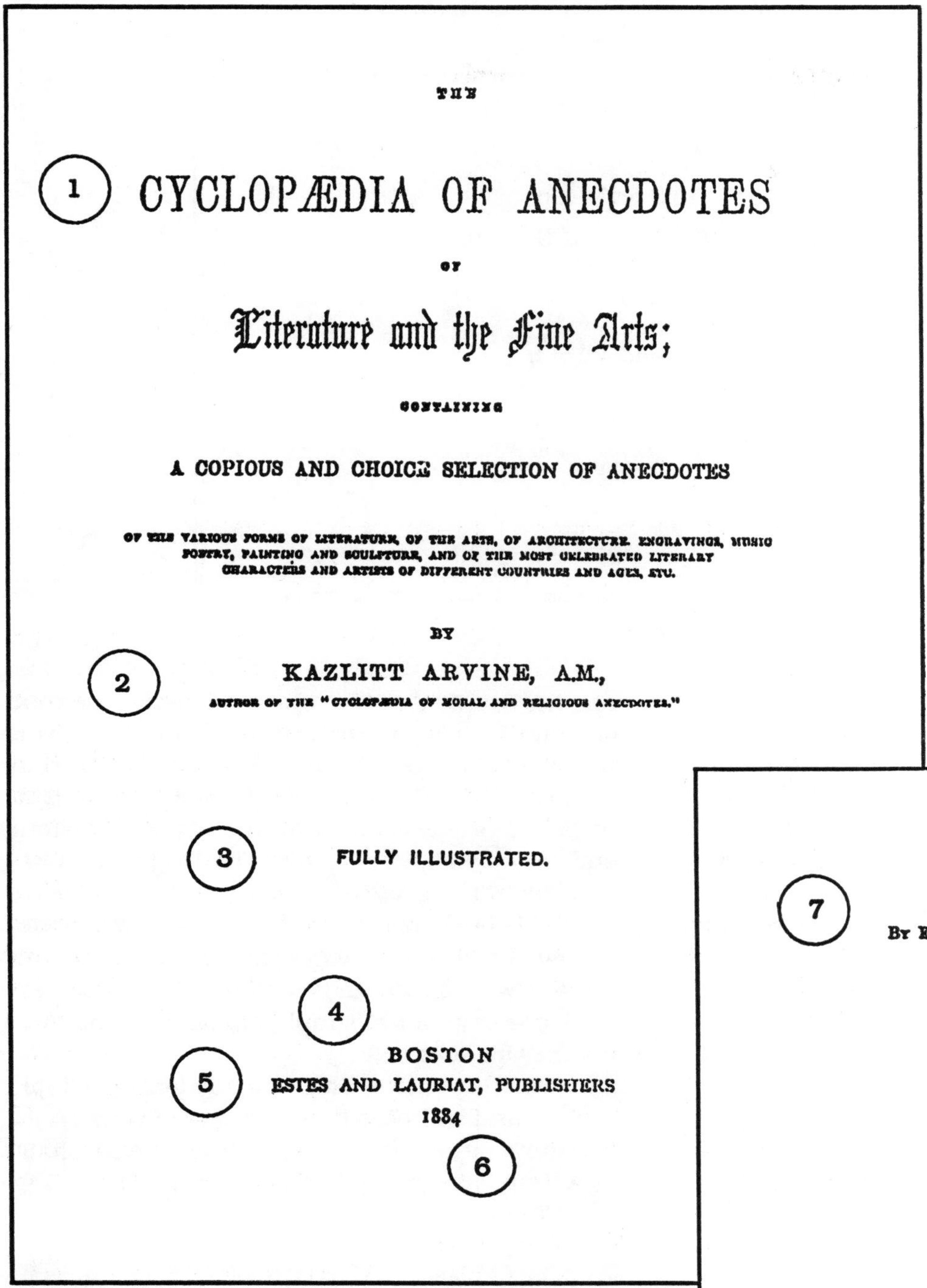

THE

① CYCLOPÆDIA OF ANECDOTES

OF

Literature and the Fine Arts;

CONTAINING

A COPIOUS AND CHOICE SELECTION OF ANECDOTES

OF THE VARIOUS FORMS OF LITERATURE, OF THE ARTS, OF ARCHITECTURE, ENGRAVINGS, MUSIC
POETRY, PAINTING AND SCULPTURE, AND OF THE MOST CELEBRATED LITERARY
CHARACTERS AND ARTISTS OF DIFFERENT COUNTRIES AND AGES, ETC.

BY

② **KAZLITT ARVINE, A.M.,**

AUTHOR OF THE "CYCLOPÆDIA OF MORAL AND RELIGIOUS ANECDOTES."

③ FULLY ILLUSTRATED.

④

BOSTON

⑤ ESTES AND LAURIAT, PUBLISHERS
1884

⑥

Figure 3A

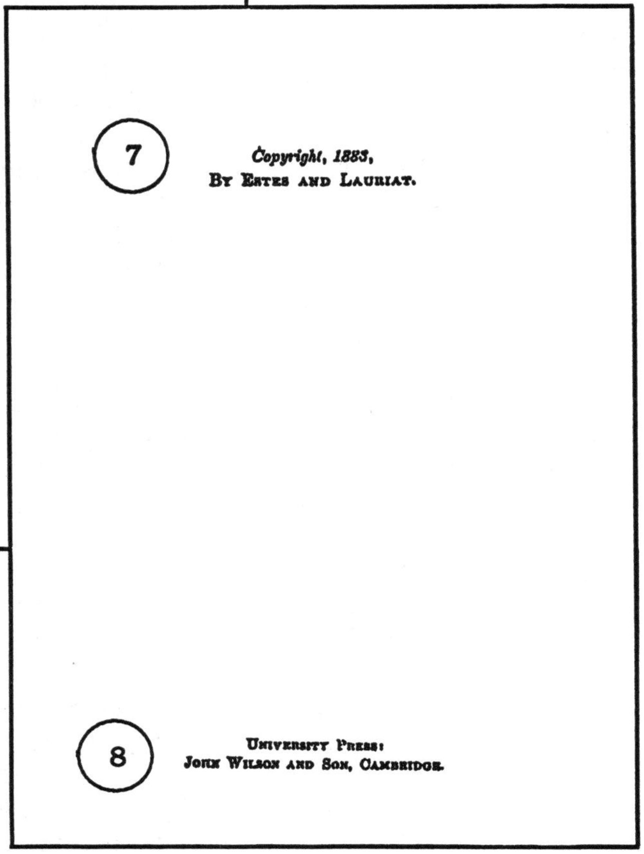

⑦ *Copyright, 1883,*
BY ESTES AND LAURIAT.

⑧ UNIVERSITY PRESS:
JOHN WILSON AND SON, CAMBRIDGE.

Figure 3B

```
Reference                                      10/21/87

Kazlitt, Arvine
THE CYCLOPAEDIA OF ANECDOTES OF LITERATURE AND THE FINE
ARTS, ETC.
Boston, Estes and Lauriat, 1984.
Illustrated. 696pp. plus index.
Small 4to. Decorative embossed cloth.
Near Fine.

$20/1
```

Figure 4

If you prepare a catalog card for this book, here is how it should look.

You could copy this description verbatim to prepare an entry for a list or catalog (with the exception of the price you paid for the book).

Your catalog cards can be filed in standard card file boxes, or even in an old shoe box. You can use blank dividers to enter your subject headings or alpha sequence.

You will need at least two sets for books. One, alphabetical, for all literary writings; novels, poetry, whatever, because you file these by author's last name.

The other set you will categorize by subjects. In the beginning your categories can be quite broad. For instance, Western Americana, Ships and the Sea, Travel, Exploration. Later on, as your accumulate more stock or begin to specialize, you may want to break the broad categories down in greater detail. For example, Western Americana might be broken down into the various Western states, or by activity such as rustling, cattle raising, gold mining, etc.

This is where the use of various colored cards is also helpful. For example, one color for all literary writing, another for non-fiction. Or perhaps one color for biography, another for history, another for science.

Be imaginative. This is really quite a simple system and will permit you to review your entire inventory sitting at your desk or in an easy chair, or a lawn chair in the back yard or patio.

11.
A BARGAINERS GUIDE

HOW MUCH SHOULD I PAY?

A simple question with a fairly complex answer. Certainly no more than you have to — never so much that you cannot make a profit.

Here are some guidelines that will help to minimize any mistakes you will make while you are learning. Later on, as you absorb more and more of the information that is available to you, you will develop your own sense of value and a higher level of confidence in your own judgment

Don't buy anything that you don't think you can resell for less than $5 — it won't repay you for the time and effort. This applies to single items or lots. For example a "lot" of postcards. You buy 12 for 5 cents each — you must resell them as a "lot" for at least $5. So, don't buy that dozen cards unless you fairly certain they will be worth at least $5.

With the exception of the types of books I have already mentioned to you, you are safe in buying most books if you pay less than $1 each for them. This holds true for almost any other single item except for postcards. This is because you will work on the basis of averaging.

If, in the course of a week or month, you buy 200 books, it would be perfectly all right to pay several dollars for some of them so long as a substantial proportion of the remainder of them are bought for less than $1 each. Your goal is an average price for the 200 books. Here's how that might work out.

You buy 14 books for $3 each, 24 for $1.50 each, and 162 for 50 cents apiece. You have bought a total of 200 books (or any items) for a total of $159. That makes an average price per item of 80 cents ($159 divided by 200 = .0795).

Now let's take a look at how you might profit

from this example after you have sold all those items.

You sell the first fourteen $3 items for $15 each; the twenty-four $1.50 items for $8 each; and the one-hundred and sixty-two items for the minimum of $5 each.

Here is the total return:

14	x $15	=	$210
24	x 8	=	192
162 x	5	=	810
The total		=	$1212

That is an average selling price of $6.06 for each item ($1212 divided by 200). Your average cost was 80 cents. Your gross profit per item = $5.26.

Looking at it another way, you invested $159 and received a return of $1212. That is a gross profit of $1053 on a $159 investment.

The point of this is to show you that by averaging you can afford to pay more for some books, that is operate on a smaller profit margin, because the averaging will protect you until you become more experienced. Of even greater importance is the fact that even had a large proportion of those books been worthless the averaging would still have protected you. Your gross profit would have been considerably reduced, but nearly all of them would have to have been worthless for you to actually lose money.

Suppose, however, you had really goofed when you bought those 200 books and over half of them were totally worthless and you had to give or throw them away. Where would you stand? You sell the balance of the 100 books for the average of $6.06 each. Your return is now $606 for your investment of $159. You have still made nearly 400% profit. That's not too hard to take, is it?

So, don't ever hesitate to buy good, clean books — as many as you can afford as long as the price is less than $1 each. You will have many opportunities to do just that in future.

After you become more familiar with prices by studying Appendices 4 and 5, your recall ability will start to operate for you when you are out scouting. As a general rule, if you have some feeling for the price you will be able to sell an item for, even if you have no specific buyer in mind, you can pay at least 25 percent of that price without too much concern that you will get hurt. If you think you can sell the item for $25 you can pay at least $6.25 - $8.

If it will sell for $100, don't hesitate to pay at least $25 and go up to $50 if you think you can sell it quickly.

When you do have a waiting buyer, from a Want List for example, you can pay as much as much as 50 percent of the selling price because of the quick turnover. You can also pay higher prices when you know the item in question is in demand because you have seen multiple advertisements for it.

What I have said so far applies to single items. Suppose you have been offered a box, or several, of books at a garage sale or in response to an ad you have run! What then? First, don't single out individual items and make individual offers. Make one offer for the entire lot even though there may be many books which you know are just plain junk. Why? Because people can be very greedy and as soon as you single out something you'll have planted the idea that the item is choice. The seller will then decide to have someone else make an offer on it.

At that point you are faced with the need to explain why you don't make offers on single items or you will have opened the door to having to make an offer on each and every item in those boxes. After you have considerable experience you'll be able to sort such accumulations into two piles — those you will make a single offer for, and those you are not interested in. But at that point, you will have the necessary knowledge to comfortably explain the why of your choices without embarrassing yourself.

Instead, here's what you should do. Go through the entire lot carefully and mentally separate the salable items from the dreck. Count up the number of good items and multiply that quantity by the average price you have decided you can pay for each item. That total sum is your offer for the entire lot. After you get the lot back home you can discard the unwanted items and catalog the ones you will keep.

Here's an example. After inspecting the lot you have been offered and making a quick mental count you know you are considering 50 books, but only 20 of them are really salable. You decide that you're willing to pay $1.50 each for those 20, or a total of $30. You offer the seller $30 for the entire lot. To the seller, that will sound like a nice round number and your offer will probably be accepted.

If you separate out those 20 books and offer $1.50 each you will have a problem on your hands. $1.50 isn't a nice round number. Your seller will then recall that the book cost $15 and want to know why you won't pay $10 for it. And perhaps may have decided that it should bring more than was originally paid. After all, it was written by Herman Schlumpf and he has a new best seller out.

Even worse would be offering the seller say, $10 for one of the books and $1 each for the others. First, the seller will want to know why the others aren't also worth more. Second, the seller may conclude that if it's worth $10 it may well be worth more and another dealer had better be called in. Why should you be trusted?

Either way there's a good chance your offer will be refused. It's just human nature to over-value most of our possessions when offered the chance to sell them. It doesn't matter that the day before this same person was all but ready to throw the books in the trash or donate them to the Salvation Army.

This is a good time to say — don't you be greedy. Pay fair prices when it is up to you to make an offer. Don't take advantage of the sellers need for money if you are aware of one, or ignorance. In the long run the reputation for being fair will benefit you. That kind of word spreads far more rapidly then you might think, especially in small communities. Don't offer $2 for a $100 book just because you think you can get away with it.

First of all, the seller may be testing you and be well aware that the particular book is worth much more than your offer. Even if that's not the case, you might find yourself in an embarrassing situation. If the $2 offer is refused and you want the book badly, how can you explain a new offer of $20 or $30. Your credibility will certainly suffer at the very least. And if that seller later calls in someone else who offers $30 immediately, what will he think of you? Either you don't know what you are doing (the kindest thought) or you are a crook (the probable thought).

Offer the fair price in the beginning. After all, even if you pay $30 you still stand to make $70. Is that so bad?

When you are asked to make an offer take the time to think about it, offer the top price you know you can pay and stick with it.

Incidentally, when you are first shown the books that are for sale, you should always start out by asking how much the seller wants for them. Most of the time you won't be able to get an answer other than "What will you offer," "I don't know," or something similar. But if you are quoted a figure that sounds reasonable, reply that you'll have to look them over first. Proceed as before, and after you have made your mental computation, either say you accept the figure quoted or counter with the one you have in mind.

This is the only time you should accept a number which is much lower than your own mental sum. The seller has set the price — it is all right for you to accept. Nice little old ladies being excepted. The unwritten law of "let the buyer beware" works both ways.

Let's go back a moment now to that lot of books. You've bought them. Twenty of them are good. What do you do with the rest of them? First, you look them over more carefully when you get them all home. You may have missed a few good items because you were in a hurry. But if even after looking them over again, they are still junk the rule of averaging has protected you and you can throw them away. But not in the trash. Donate them to someone for whatever tax deduction you can obtain. Get a receipt from whoever you donate them to. It does not have to have a value on it — just a notation of how many books or whatever were donated and the organizations name. Even if you bought the lot at a church rummage sale you can donate the unwanted books to another church.

12.
PAYDAY

There is an old maxim "The value of something is what it will bring." Nothing could be truer in this business. If you know what the right price should be for an book you are well on your way to making a sale and the profit you deserve for your efforts.

The right price is not necessarily what a price guide tells you was received at an auction, or what a dealer has listed it for in a fancy catalog. However, the auction price is the better indicator because it does represent an actual sale. Furthermore it is more likely to be a wholesale price and provides a basis for determining the correct retail value. The dealer's price reflects an opinion of what the retail price ought to be, or it may be wishful thinking. You have no way of knowing if the book was actually ever sold for that price. UNLESS it is a catalog from one of the very knowledgeable and experienced book sellers. There are many of them but it will be some time before you will know which ones they are.

In the beginning it will be far better for you to operate on the premise of using prices which will make your items attractive to other booksellers. That is, your prices will be essentially wholesale prices. This will also make it easier to sell to libraries and collectors since you will be offering them a bargain. You will still be able to make a nice profit and turn over your nuggets much faster. In turn, the cash flow will help you to build your inventory faster without additional out-of-pocket investment.

In the process of finding your nuggets, particularly with books, you must remember these distinctions. Old books — pre-1900 for this discussion — are termed "antiquarian;" books newer than that can be termed either "out-of-print" or "in-print."

HOW MUCH IS IT WORTH? ♦
SOME RULES

RULE 1:

In-print books should be priced at about 40% of the original publishers price. This is usually marked on the flap of the dust jacket. Even so, they must be in very good to fine condition. It follows, of course, that you should not pay more than 10 percent of the cover price in the first place. If the book's cover price was $16.95 your selling price should be $7-8, and you should not have paid more than $1.75 for it and preferably less.

RULE 2:

If the book is out-of-print, or antiquarian, and you can find a price reference in any of the guides, or perhaps in Appendix 4 or 5 of this book, than price your book at 80% of the price you find. You must also assume that the price reference is for a copy in very good or better condition. If your copy is less than that adjust the price downward. Perhaps only 50% of the reference price if your book's condition is only good. Here is where the Value Guide, Appendix 10, will come in handy.

If you cannot find a price reference for the specific title you have, then you must try to find prices for other books by the same author written about the same period in time, or books on the same subject, and use that as your guide. You can't however, use a comparison between an author's first book and a much more recent one.

When all else fails, use your own judgment

and price the book so that it will return you a fair profit. The few times that you will seriously underprice an item will not hurt you in the long run and you may never know it anyway.

WHO WANTS IT IF I DON'T?

If you are really convinced that the book is of considerable value, then you can offer it to the closest rare book seller and ask for an offer. Don't bother doing this unless you feel it has a value over $25 — it won't be worth the trouble. Try quoting it to specialist dealer(s) and adjust your price downward if need be. A dealer will offer you 30 to 50% of the retail value if he has an immediate customer for the book. If he doesn't but wants to buy it for stock the offer might be for 20-30%. This is fair considering the nature of the market, and a bookseller's overhead and the nature of inventory turnover, which differs from most other retail businesses.

Here is something you should not do. It is done fairly often by neophyte book scouts and sellers who are either lazy or ignorant. What I am referring to is the practice of placing a classified advertisement in one of the antique periodicals for books and asking for "make offer."

This type of advertising is the label of an amateur, and knowledgeable dealers and collectors will usually ignore such ads because they will assume (rightly) that the advertiser isn't really interested in selling the items at that point — only fishing for correct pricing. No one wants to waste time either educating you or participating on an amateur form of an auction. Another reason is that you won't be trusted to describe a book correctly, particularly as to condition, if you are considered an amateur.

There are several distinct markets you can sell to and there is a different approach to determine the selling price for each one. Top prices come from private individuals or collectors. Next come the libraries who buy for their research departments or for the circulating shelves.

Last, but actually your number one market are the book sellers and search services. They are the easiest to sell to after you know how to approach them, but you must always remember that they buy in order to resell.

13.
SELLING, INVENTORY, AND
QUOTE CARDS

Let's take a more detailed look at each of the markets and the way in which you can reach them.

SELLING

Your best and largest source of customers is *AB Bookmans Weekly* which I told you about in an earlier chapter. This periodical will provide you with the names of hundreds of book sellers, search services, and institutional libraries who are actively looking for, and buying, thousands of books by mail. In addition to who, AB also tells you what — thousands of book titles and author names, or subjects they need material about. In the course of reading AB for just a few weeks, you will develop a feel for book scouting that will amaze you.

You will, rather unconsciously, absorb a high percentage of this information and this will trigger a recall at the appropriate times. You can expect your life to change once you finish this book. Why? Because you will never again go anywhere where you will not be looking around you, for, and at, books. You will be unable to pass a book, or group of books, without a pause to scan the titles.

You respond to this huge potential market by quoting to these specific advertisers those items which you have and that they want to buy. You can also compile all these names to create your own mailing list of prospects for books and other items which you will acquire. And you'll prepare your own lists or catalogs.

Another source of prospective customers and their wants are the various weekly and monthly periodicals which serve the antiques and collectibles field such as *Collectors News*. Immediately, I have supplied you with the names of over 250 North American book search services whose primary business is locating books for private and institutional collectors, and other persons and businesses who need specific books for research and reference purposes.

These search services are very important for you. If you decide at some point in the future to become more heavily involved in this book business, becoming a search service yourself will probably be the most logical way for you to enter.

Search services undertake to locate books, and other items, which are needed and not available to their customers from their local sources. They are used quite heavily by libraries needing to replace books which have either worn out or have been stolen, and to build their own specialty collections. Nearly all of the larger public libraries maintain special collections of subjects which they have interests in, especially local and regional history and the works of authors native to the region.

A search service is essentially a simple business and is one way to enter this business without the need to accumulate an inventory of any sort. You only buy an item **AFTER you have sold it and been paid for it** (except for libraries). To illustrate how one operates I'll give you a hypothetical transaction involving yourself.

You stop and visit with the local librarian and in the course of the conversation you ask if there are any books which they need. In reply, you are handed a short list of regional history books which they need to expand their collection. There are seven entries on the list. Each gives the author's name and the complete title of the book as well as date and place of original publication and publisher's name.

You only need ask two questions at this point,

and only if you are dealing directly with someone. The first question is, "Must these be first editions?", the other question is "Will you accept copies if they need to be rebound?" No matter what the answers are, you can proceed.

The very first thing you do, if you have any out-of-print book stores near you is to check and see if they have any of these books. You might get a surprise. It happens. Librarians are often too busy to shop locally, even by telephone — book sellers are often too busy or lack the imagination to look in their own backyard. You can do your checking by telephone in all likelihood.

Let's say, however, that you do locate one of the books in this way. What do you do? First, you identify yourself as a book scout and say you have a search requirement for that particular title. Ask for a title page description to verify that it is indeed the book you want, ask for YOUR price, and ask for a good description of the condition. Also ask if they will hold the book for you for two weeks while you contact your customer. The book seller does NOT have to know who your customer is.

Now you add your own markup to the price the book seller quoted you. This can be anywhere from 50% to 100% depending on the actual cost. The more expensive the book, the smaller the markup can be. This can also vary as a function of the type of book. If you happen to be searching for a good used copy of a book which is still in-print, obviously you must follow the guidelines I have already given you as to pricing. But if you do some checking and discover that the proper value of the book in question is $65, that is the price you should use.

If the price the book seller quoted you is around that, then you must look elsewhere for a copy. If the price quoted you is, say, $45, then you could proceed knowing you can make a quick $20. If the price is considerably less than that you must decide if you want to quote the $65 price or something less to show the librarian how reasonable you are.

Bear in mind that librarians are often quite knowledgeable and may know precisely how much a copy of that book should cost in the condition you have found. If you have no guidance on what the price should be, then simply add whatever markup you feel is appropriate, including the cost of shipping the book, to the price quoted you. If,

in this example, the price quoted you was $40, I would suggest marking it up 50% which would make it $60 and add $2 more for shipping. You quote $62 postpaid to the library. I'll show how how to prepare a quote very soon.

If the library accepts your offer they will send you a purchase order. It may be a quite formal document or it may be a simple letter telling you fine, ship the book and your invoice. You have made a sale. Now you can buy the book. If this same transaction had occurred with a collector, you would have asked for payment in advance with the order. You will have been paid BEFORE you have to buy the book.

Essentially, that is the way any search service operates. If you understand that it will make it easier to sell to them. Any price you quote to a search service has to have a markup added to it before that information reaches the service's client.

Your customer is the search service and you must satisfy your customer. The search service's customer in turn must be satisfied and the service must rely on the accuracy of your description of the book because they will simply repeat it to their customer.

If you have not been accurate the service will be very unhappy should they buy the book from you. First, they will have to start over again, second, they will have to notify their customer as to what happened and perhaps lose the customer, and third, go to the expense of returning the book to you and asking for a refund because they paid you in advance. Some search services will not pay you in advance until they have some experience in dealing with you. You may be honest but may not have enough experience to properly describe a book, especially its condition, which is often a subjective judgment

Search services obtain their clients in many different ways. Some advertise in the classified sections of large national magazines. Some solicit Wants Lists from libraries on a regional and often national basis. Many advertise their services in special interest magazines, such as *Writers Digest, American History Illustrated, The Armchair Detective,* or what have you. At some point in the future you will be able to do the same thing.

Some search services make it a policy to never buy for inventory and maintain no stock whatsoever unless it is by unfortunate accident (such as having a book returned because it was not described properly and being unable to obtain satisfaction from the original seller). Other search services are adjuncts of larger book seller operations who will undertake to locate books for their customers whether they are private collectors or institutions.

Getting back to how you can work with search services. Many of them publish periodic and often quite lengthy lists of the books and other items they are searching for. A postcard request to be placed on their mailing list will bring these lists to you. You then screen them for books which you might have or have seen somewhere recently and quote them. You also carry these lists with you when you are out scouting. You are now looking for all those books.

You can also write public and institutional libraries, starting with those closest to you, and ask for their Wants List if they have a current one. Write all the colleges and universities within your state to start with. Expand to other states when you are ready. A legible but simple letter offering your services as a scout should do the trick. Address it to the Acquisitions Librarian.

Now, back to AB again. Each issue of AB is essentially an accumulation of Wants Lists from book sellers all over the country, and occasionally from other countries. Libraries are also allowed to advertise in AB and occasionally do. For the most part though, the libraries prefer to work through a search service or community book seller. This is because the search service can perform the time consuming screening of the quotes which will be received. It is not uncommon for a search service to receive dozens of quotes for an in-print title or a plentiful best seller which has gone out-of-print.

For the most part, all the books that you will find being advertised for in AB represent a customer that a bookseller has. Occasionally book sellers will advertise for all books in a particular category, or by a particular author, for their stock. In responding to any AB advertisement, or Wants List, always remember that your price has to be marked up and still remain fair and reasonable. You cannot sell at retail to another bookseller. You can do so to a library or a private collector. Private collectors are not allowed to advertise in the Books Wanted section of AB, which forces them to turn to the book seller or search service.

How can you reach the collector market? There are several ways. Collectors can, and do, advertise in the other periodicals such as *Collectors News*. They will send you their Wants Lists if you drop them a postcard asking for it. *The American Book Collector* can be particularly helpful in this respect, however their readers are generally quite sophisticated as collectors and you will not be able to sell the more common books to them.

You can also develop your own collector mailing list by advertising in these publications yourself. Placing such an advertisement can be quite productive and need not be expensive. It should read something like this:

Active Scout seeks Wants Lists of books and printed collectibles. No obligation. (Your name and address).

Once you begin to accumulate Wants Lists, including those which you might make yourself from your study of various issues of AB, always carry them when you go scouting. A 3-ring binder is ideal for the purpose. Of course, you should also be carrying this book with you.

INVENTORY AND QUOTE CARDS

Selling to AB advertisers or to anyone who has supplied you with a Wants List is quite simple in execution. You send a quotation. Your prospect sends you an order, usually accompanied by a check. You ship the book. If you are functioning as a search service you must first buy the book yourself. In the beginning however, we will assume you are quoting a nugget you have already bought and have in your inventory.

Now is when you put your inventory cards to work. No need to handle the book itself at this point unless you forgot something when you made up the inventory card.

Card quotes are the primary method for quoting single items. You can use postage prepaid postal cards which can be purchased at the post office, or you can use ordinary 3 x 5 file cards. Since postal cards are already stamped you need to be careful in filling them out. The 3 x 5 cards either require a stamp, or must be placed in an envelope. Either will accomplish your purpose.

I do not recommend that you put several quotes on a single sheet of paper. It makes it quite difficult for your prospect to evaluate your quote alongside others which will be received. When the quotes are received they are segregated by author or title and held for a short period of time in order for all anticipated quotes to arrive from various parts of the country — and often from overseas. If you have placed two or more quotes on a single sheet, the only way the segregating can be done is by cutting your quote sheet apart. That is awkward and time consuming. Unless you are offering something quite scarce, or unusually cheap, your entire quote sheet may be discarded.

So, a single quote card or slip for each item you intend to quote. If you have several for one address, they all can go into a single envelope.

Please refer back to the catalog card illustrated in chapter 10 for THE ART AND SCIENCE OF BOOK PUBLISHING by Herbert S. Bailey, Jr.

Let us suppose you have been reading through an issue of AB and Sam Jones Books is advertising for a copy of the Bailey book, or for "Books on publishing, any."

The ad line reads, Bailey — Art & Science of Publishing. Your recall is working just fine and you know you have the Bailey book. You go to your file and remove the catalog card for the Bailey book. If this is the only book you are going to quote to Tom Jones Books, you address a postal card to him. On the reverse side you complete a card like this example, using the information on your catalog card.

Now, let's review this example card and see just what information you have provided either from your catalog card or from what you will adopt as your standard terms. Follow the numbers which are circled.

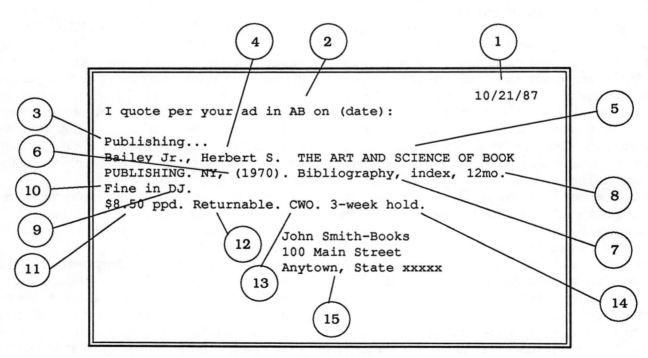

Figure 5

1. The date you prepare this card. It is important because it is related to item 14.
2. You are quoting his advertisement in AB *Bookmans Weekly* on (give the cover date).
3. If you were responding to an ad line just for Books on Publishing you would complete this.
4. The author's name in full as it appears on the title page.
5. The book's title just as it appears on the title page.
6. Place and date of publication from the title page.
7. State that the book has a bibliography and an index.
8. The size of the book.
9. It has a dust jacket.
10. The condition is Fine. This includes the dust jacket. If the dust jacket is in a different condition than the book itself, you must note the condition of each.
11. Your price for the book including shipping.
12. If the book is not satisfactory for any reason it can be returned for a refund. You won't be able to sell any book without this statement.
13. CWO means "Check with order." *Always* with private collectors, sometimes with search services, never with libraries. Nevertheless, state this as part of your terms (except libraries) and let the buyer take exception if desired.
14. You will hold the book for three weeks after the date shown at the top of the card. After that you are free to offer the book to someone else.
15. Your name and address — legibly. Though this may seem obvious, it is not unusual to receive quote cards that don't have one. Particularly if you use a rubber stamp. It so easy to forget. Don't rely on it being on one of a group of cards either. The cards will be separated. It is a bit difficult for your prospect to order if he doesn't know who you are.

You can follow this format to quote any book, or any other item of printed material. Later on, if you find that you are doing a lot of quoting you can have this card pre-printed following the format in Figure 6.

```
                                           (Date)

I quote per your (ad, Want List) in _____
_____ on (date):

Author: _____
Title:  _____
Place:  _____ Date: _____ Size: _____
Cond:   _____
Remarks: _____
         _____

Price: _____ Terms: Ppd, CWO, returnable.
_____ weeks hold.
                      John Smith, Books
                      100 Main Street
                      Anytown, State xxxxx
```

Figure 6

There is one more thing you should get in the habit of doing. On your catalog card make a brief entry noting when, to whom, and how much, you quoted. Very simple; 7/24 Jones $3.50. When the order comes from Jones you can verify the price is correct. You may have reduced it from the price noted on your inventory card because Jones is a dealer.

Now, set this catalog card aside for the next 3 weeks. If you haven't received an order by then, you can return it to your file until you are ready to use it again.

When it happens that you have quoted a book several times without selling it, as your entry record will show, it is time to consider reducing the price on the next quote. For whatever reason, your price is obviously too high.

Now, here is something you must recognize when you are quoting books. It isn't unusual for an advertiser to receive dozens of quotes for some common titles, particularly if it is a book that is still in-print. After you gain some experience, you will know which books these are and probably won't bother quoting them anymore.

But until then, don't be disappointed when you don't get an order by return mail for every quote you send out.

After your prospect receives all the cards he can reasonably expect, which will take several days after the advertisement runs, or you are responding to a Wants List, the quotes will be reviewed and compared against the specific requirement the client has provided. Quotes which do not meet that requirement are then discarded. For example, as to condition. If the customer specified a fine copy and you quoted very good and someone else quoted fine, you've lost the sale. Now your prospect will compare the prices for all the fine copy quotes and choose the lowest. You shouldn't have quoted in the first place if your copy wasn't "fine."

Next, your prospect must add the markup to the chosen quote and contact the customer to advise that the desired copy has been located and the price is $_. Sometimes this is done by telephone, but usually by mail. So, more time has to elapse for a letter to go out and a reply to be received. Further, the customer may have to pay in advance and your prospect may wait until the check clears before he places his own order to you.

Only then, can you expect to receive an order. That is why your quote has to be good for 3 weeks. Quite often that isn't long enough.

Quoting becomes a numbers game. When you have enough inventory to maintain a reasonable volume of quotes outstanding at all times, you will be able to anticipate that a certain percentage of them will turn into sales. This in turn will depend on how active you are prospecting and how many nuggets you turn up.

For various reasons, you should bear these rules of thumb in mind at all times.

It is easier to sell higher priced books than low priced ones. They are usually scarcer and in most cases have established a price track record. I would rather sell one $100 book than ten $10 books and I always keep this in mind when prospecting.

Always buy the finest condition available. Don't buy anything but **fine** for lower priced and common titles, especially if they are still in-print.

Don't buy books without dust jackets unless you know for a fact that they are difficult to acquire any other way.

14.
LISTS AND CATALOGS

After you have accumulated an inventory of books or other printed collectibles you can begin to offer lists of the items you have for sale. These lists can consist of mixed items or be confined to a single type such as books, magazines, posters, or whatever else you might have in quantity.

Your list or lists are then mailed to a selected list of dealers, collectors, libraries, or all three. All the sources I've previously mentioned can provide you the names. This is also another use for Appendices 6 and 7. Booksellers who offer catalogs of books are also prime prospects for your lists. That's how they obtain many of the items which they, in turn, offer in their catalogs.

You can also advertise the availability of your list in any of the collector's periodicals. You can offer it free with a self-addressed and stamped envelope (SASE), or for a loose stamp, or for a nominal charge such as $1. However, don't charge for the list unless it has unusual items and your advertisement states this.

Lists are easy to prepare. Type them on 8 1/2 x 11 inch white paper and then reproduce the pages by having them offset printed at a "quick print" shop, or by having them photocopied. Type with care and with a fresh ribbon because the printed copies will be no better than your original.

Next, staple the pages together, fold them, and insert into an addressed #10 business envelope, and mail.

Be prepared to wait at least a week for your first reply. Perhaps longer. Most of your prospects probably receive many catalogs and lists and yours will have to wait its turn before being read.

A catalog is nothing more than a longer and more elaborate list. It will contain several pages and be folded to resemble a small booklet. A common size is 5 1/2 inches wide by 8 1/2 inches tall. This is the size which results when you fold an 8 1/2 x 11 inch sheet at the center. You can type your original copy across the 5 1/2 inch width for each page and the printer will set the pages side by side when he prepares the offset plates. Printed on both sides of an 8 1/2 x 11 sheet the result is four pages per sheet.

The starting point for either a catalog or list is your catalog cards. Choose the items you want to include and organize them alphabetically by author, or in groups by subject matter or type of collectible item, i.e., books, magazines, or other paper ephemera.

On the first page, at the top, place your name and address. If you have a business letterhead it will do just fine but it isn't really necessary. Then the date — month and year only — and an identification. The simplest is to number them as you issue them, starting with number 1. Or you can use a code number which would include the date and general content. For example, if your first list will be general Americana titles, and it will be issued in July of 1988, the code number could be List 788-1AM (July, 1988, List 1, Americana).

Now, here's an example of what your list or catalog page might look like. Use this as a guide for preparing your own lists.

John Smith Books
100 Main Street
Anytown, State xxxxx

LIST NO.1
GENERAL BOOKS

July, 1988
Terms: CWO, returnable, postpaid

1. Alsberg, Henry (Editor). THE AMERICAN GUIDE. NY, (1949). 1348pp. 8vo. Near fine. $12
2. Bacon, James. HOLLYWOOD IS A FOUR LETTER TOWN. Chicago, 1976. 324pp. 8vo. Wraps. Advance uncorrected proof copy dated May 28, 1976. Near fine. $20
3. Carlova, John. MISTRESS OF THE SEAS (Anne Bonney). NY, (1964). frontis 12mo. Fine. $5
4. cummings, e.e. 73 POEMS. NY, (1963). 73pp. 8vo. Boards. Near fine in fair DJ. $14
5. Jackson, W. Turrentine (editor). TWENTY YEARS ON THE PACIFIC SLOPE. New Haven, 1965. Frontis, biblio., index. 224pp. 12mo. Yellow boards. Fine. $12.50

and continue with as many items and pages as you wish

OTHER WAYS TO SELL

If you live in a large community you can simply bring your nuggets to local booksellers or specialist dealers. Than either accept or reject the offers for the items they are interested in.

If you are able to accumulate a sufficient number of really good titles — perhaps 50 or more with values in excess of $50 each — you can offer them at auction through any of the well-known auction galleries. Most are located in New York City. Write one or more of them and describe what you have or make a list. Don't send anything unless they tell you to. You may get more than you expected for them this way. A disadvantage for this method is that you may have to wait several months before the books are placed on sale, and perhaps several more weeks before you are paid.

15.
GOOD BUSINESS PRACTICES

Even though you will find this business to be enjoyable you must still remember that it IS a business and you must conduct it like one if you want it to be profitable. Large or small, this is essentially a mail order business and there are some rules to be observed.

Your address or geographic location has no bearing on your eventual success. Starting at home will have no effect on your prospects. Indeed, it's essential. You can avoid such costs as office space, furniture, electricity, telephone, and so forth.

CHOOSING A NAME FOR YOUR BUSINESS

Many beginners think that the average person is more inclined to order products from a company instead of an individual and are overly concerned with using an impressive business name. There is no basis in fact for this belief. In fact, just the contrary in the out-of-print books field. Your buyers are only interested in what you have to offer — not your name. You will discover this is true when you read the names of advertisers in the publications I've told you about.

So, there is no reason not to use your own name for the business UNLESS it's a long name, one difficult to pronounce, or because you don't want anyone else to know what you're doing.

If you decide to use a fictitious name, choose one that is indicative of the type of business. Try to avoid one which is already being used or can be confused with similar names. Check several issues of AB Bookmans Weekly to give yourself some idea of the more common names and variations thereof. And don't use a "cute" name that includes the word "Shoppe." Another term to avoid is

"Enterprises," it shrieks of amateurism. If your name is George Jones or Betty Smith, just go ahead and style yourself as George Jones-Books, or Betty Smith-Bookseller.

YOUR BUSINESS LETTERHEAD

As soon as practical you should obtain some business stationery. At first, all you need are some letterheads and #10 business envelopes. They should include your name, address, and a telephone number, and indicate what your business is if your business name doesn't. The printing needn't be elaborate, but a distinctive design does help to promote customer recognition. If you can't afford a small quantity of printed stationery, a well made rubber stamp will do to get started. I have included a short list of business stationery suppliers at the end of this chapter. Write for their catalogs — they can give you some good design ideas as well as being an inexpensive source.

CONDUCTING YOUR BUSINESS EFFICIENTLY

It's essential that you handle your day-to-day operations efficiently even if you only operate on a part-time basis. You need to operate economically and with a minimum of lost time. And you must keep accurate records that will let you see the profit from individual transactions and the current financial state of the business. You must also keep your records up to date at all times. Most stationery stores sell simplified book keeping systems which are simple to use and satisfy all IRS requirements. I recommend that you obtain such a system as soon as possible and get started on the right foot by keeping track of all your expenses right from the start.

HANDLING CORRESPONDENCE. All your business correspondence should be typed, not handwritten, on your business letterhead (even if it is just a rubber stamp). And nobody will ever know whether you typed with two fingers or can do 90 words a minute. You want to create a good impression and very often hand written letters simply won't be read even if you won many prizes for penmanship in school.

Naturally, you want to keep correspondence as simple as possible. You can respond to routine catalog or information requests using neatly typed Postal Cards. Try to avoid conditions which will lead to lengthy correspondence. For example, by filling orders promptly you can avoid having to reply to inquiries and complaints about orders. Don't get involved in continuing correspondence with customers by arguing about requests for returns — give the customer the benefit of the doubt. If it becomes a habit, take that name off your mailing list.

Keep copies of all your non-routine correspondence and file them alphabetically in the appropriate category so you can find them quickly when needed.

PROCESS ORDERS PROMPTLY. I can't overemphasize this. Delay in filling orders results in inquiries and COMPLAINTS and often, a demand for a refund. Promptly notify a customer if an item has been sold and return the check. Don't just write "Sorry, sold" on the order and mail it back. Take the time to at least write a brief note to say thanks for the order and asking them if they would like you to search for another copy of the item. And to ask for their Want List. You'll make friends and create a lot of good will by doing this.

Always try to ship orders the same day you receive them. Don't delay shipping an order while you wait for a check to clear unless a large sum is involved. The bad checks you might get, if any, will be few and far between, and probably not worth the trouble that results from delayed orders. If you cannot ship immediately, acknowledge receiving the order and advise when you will ship. This will forestall inquiries and complaints and show your customer that you're paying attention. In addition, you don't want to run afoul of Postal Regulations.

PROCESSING YOUR ORDERS. When you are ready to start your selling activities you will need to open a bank account in the name which you have decided to use, especially if it is fictitious. Deposit all checks received as soon as possible.

If the order is from an institutional buyer such as a library you won't receive payment with the order no matter what the terms were in your list or catalog. You should not even quote CWO to such customers. You will either have to invoice them when the item is shipped, or complete voucher forms which they will send you with the order. So, ship promptly, and invoice or complete voucher forms immediately. You will be paid AFTER the buyer receives the item and inspects it. This may take several weeks but be patient — you will be paid eventually.

Some of the larger antiquarian booksellers may also refuse to pay in advance until they have some experience doing business with you. This is understandable because they have all been hurt at one time or another by neophyte scouts and dealers who have misdescribed items through ignorance. By and large, they are all honest and you need not fear that if you ship the item you won't be paid.

Occasionally you may encounter a dealer who is slow in paying. If this happens more than once, just remove the name from your mailing list. Collectors should always be expected to pay in advance until you have done business with them several times or unless you know who they are beforehand. They all expect this and will not be offended.

The actual shipping of an item requires care on your part. It does no good to sell an item described as "as new, or mint" and ship it so poorly that it arrives damaged. First of all, your customer may not believe it was damaged in transit and decide you misdescribed it deliberately. Even if that is not the case, you'll have a disappointed customer who may be wary of ever doing business with such a careless person again.

Books are easy to ship. Whether one or several, wrap each book in a double thickness of newspaper. It won't hurt to put each one in a plastic "baggie" first — it makes them look nicer when the package is opened and provides some additional protection from scuffing. The outer wrapping should be good THICK brown wrapping paper. Seal all seams with paper or reinforced plastic tape. Don't use thin transparent tape. You can also buy "Jiffy" type padded bags at the stationery store and some Post Offices and they work just fine. Address the package to your customer, be sure to include your return address, and print in the lower left hand corner "Special Fourth Class Rate — Book(s)," and take it to the Post Office.

Other types of printed items can be mailed in reinforced envelopes. Posters should be mailed in heavy-wall cardboard tubes which are usually sold in stationery stores. Don't ever fold a poster to ship it even it it shows evidence of having been folded in the past.

INQUIRIES AND COMPLAINTS. When you receive a letter of inquiry from a customer, answer it promptly and provide all the information you have available. Your records, if you kept them properly, will show when the order was filled and shipped. If you haven't filled the order, do so immediately if you can and inform the customer it has been sent, with an apology for the delay.

INSURANCE. It's a good idea to insure all shipments over a certain value. I suggest $50. If a shipment is lost or damaged, file a claim immediately and refund the customer's money.

If you do a good job packing your items you won't have many damage claims and a lost shipment is really quite unusual. I've never had one lost in over 25 years.

RETURNS. If a customer returns an item and requests a refund give it promptly AFTER you receive it and can verify that it is the same one you sent and has not been damaged. Don't argue over the matter no matter what the reason given. It isn't worth the hassle you may involve yourself in.

CUSTOMER RECORDS. It is to your advantage to keep good customer records. The records should include details of all orders received from each customer and all correspondence between you and the customer.

Your customer record should include a card with the customer's name and address and detailed notes for each purchase including date, description of the item(s), and prices. An example card is shown in Figure 7.

The cards should be separated by merchandise category, such as books, magazines, posters, autographs, or whatever other categories are appropriate. If a customer purchases more than one type of item, make one master card to show all the items and file it under one major category, or alphabetically. Then make additional cards to place in the other category files which refer you to the location of the master card.

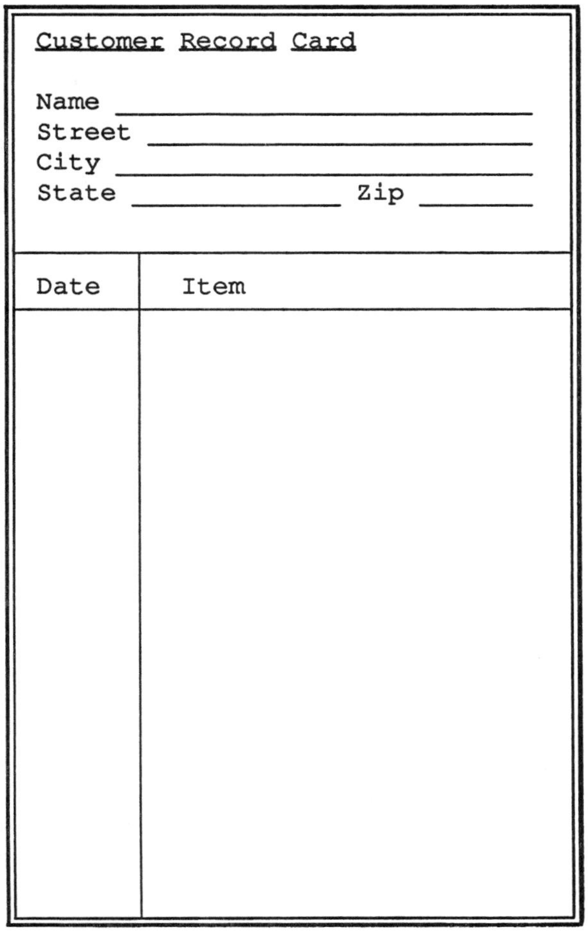

Figure 7

SUPPLIES. For your convenience, I've provided this list of sources for stationery and printing. Write for their catalogs. Compare prices before ordering.

Amity Hallmark Ltd., POB 929, Flushing, NY 11354

Walter Drake Co., Drake Building, Colorado Springs, CO 80949

The Drawing Board, POB 505, Dallas, TX 75221

Harlo Printing Co., 16721 Hamilton, Detroit, MI 48203

Postal Instant Press (PIP) — This is a franchise chain with shops located in hundreds of communities throughout the country. See your "Yellow Pages" directory.

Speedy Offset Printers, 23902 Aurora, Bedford, OH 44146

Stationery House Inc., POB 1393, Hagerstown, MD 21740

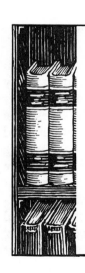
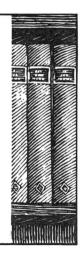

16.
LAWS AND TAXATION

Even if you are only a part-time dealer or scout there are some laws you must pay attention to, and you can't avoid taxes. I'll discuss some of them briefly and I would suggest that if you have any questions you talk to an attorney or an accountant.

REGISTRATION, LICENSES, AND PERMITS

If you decide to conduct your business as a proprietor using your own name there are probably no legal requirements as to registration. However, if you intend to use a fictitious name you must comply with applicable registration requirements for your community or state.

In some places, assumed names, known as DBAs (Doing business as) must be registered at the County or City Clerk's office, and some states may require that the name be registered with the Secretary of State. Make it your business to find out which regulations will apply to you and comply with them. You can get this information from your accountant, lawyer, the County Clerk, or the nearest office of the Small Business Administration.

No license or permit is required from the federal government in order to conduct a business by mail. Some communities require you to obtain a business or occupational license. There may also be regulations governing retail and wholesale selling which might apply to your activities. Many may have zoning laws which divide the community into industrial, commercial, and residential areas. If so, businesses are only permitted to operate in the designated zone. Normally there is no problem for a person conducting a mail order business from a residence.

SALES TAX LAWS

If your community, or state, has a Sales Tax, you must learn how to comply with it. You will have to obtain a Resale Certificate Number. This is obtained by applying to the Franchise Tax Bureau or its equivalent in your state. Briefly, it permits you to purchase goods for resale without having to a pay a sales tax to the seller. You do this by giving the seller your Resale Number. You will also be required to collect the sales tax on your own retail sales to customers within your state. You do not have to collect the tax from out-of-state customers, or from buyers who intend to resell the item(s) and furnish you with a Resale Number. You must obtain this so your books can reflect both taxable and non-taxable sales.

Periodically you must remit all the taxes you have collected. You collect these taxes as an agent for the taxing authority. It is not your money, so be conscientious about this and avoid getting yourself into trouble.

FEDERAL, STATE, AND LOCAL TAXES

Make it your business to learn about the tax obligations you will be subject to. Your record keeping system should enable you to accurately determine your tax liabilities. Pay your taxes promptly and in full. Some of these obligations are:

Federal Taxes. These include corporate and personal income taxes, self-employment tax, and perhaps excise tax. If you employ help you will need to obtain a Federal Identification Number and withhold income taxes and Social Security payments from your employees' wages, and remit these to the federal government. If you are self employed you must also pay Social Security. You can obtain more information on all this by asking the nearest IRS office for a copy of "Tax Guide For Small Business."

State Taxes. These vary from state to state. The Small Business Administration can be helpful to you in determining which may apply to you.

POSTAL LAWS AND REGULATIONS

You will be doing most of your selling by mail so you must be aware of the various Postal Regulations which may effect you. They prohibit use of the mail for operating fraudulent schemes, or for any purpose contrary to the public interest. This is why you must be accurate when you describe any item which you offer for sale. You must fill or-

ders promptly and make refunds promptly. If you cannot fill an order within 30 days you must notify your customer and offer a refund if waiting longer is not acceptable. So, conduct your business the way you would want to be treated yourself. And keep good records.

There are other Postal Regulations which are also of importance to you. They concern classification of mail, limitations as to size and weight, postal rates, insurance, certification of mail, special delivery, special handling, C.O.D., reply permits, and various other services available to you. Ask at your Post Office for the various publications which they have available.

17.
GETTING STARTED—
NOW

Well — you've read the book. Now you have to STUDY it. When you do that you will be on your way to finding many nuggets and *Turning Paper To Gold*.

I've told you what to look for, how much to pay, how to sell and for how much. And you know how to keep your records.

The next step is up to you. Carry this book with you when you go prospecting. You'll have your first nugget in your hands soon.

As the old saying goes, "The Proof is in the Pudding." Can you think of a better way to find out for yourself that everything I've said will really work for you?

GOOD LUCK

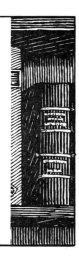

18.
TRIVIA—
BUT NOT TOO TRIVIAL

TRIVIA — BUT NOT TRIVIAL

Over the years I have received hundreds of questions about books and authors. I answer many of them in my monthly column's, ALL ABOUT BOOKS...AND THEIR AUTHORS, and BIBLIOPHILE: COLLECTING BOOKS FOR FUN AND PROFIT. I'll share some of the answers here.

Q.I recently bought a copy of HUCKLEBERRY FINN by Mark Twain, published by Grosset & Dunlap. It was copyrighted in 1884. Is this a first edition? How much is it worth?

A.No. It is an inexpensive reprint and worth only a few dollars if it is in good condition. It was quite common for reprint publishers to reproduce the original copyright page in their editions. It would be nice to think that this was done innocently!

The book was first published in 1884 in London and the correct title is ADVENTURES OF HUCKLEBERRY FINN by Samuel Langhorne Clemens. The first American edition was published in 1885, and showed Mark Twain (Clemens' pen name) as the author. There are many bibliographic points related to identifying a true first American edition. Among them are; "was" for "saw" in line 23 on page 57, and with page 283 on a stub.

A first American edition in good condition would be worth $1500-2500. It is also interesting to note that THE ADVENTURES OF TOM SAWYER was published in England and Canada before being published in this country even though all three editions were published in 1876.

Q.I recently saw a book whose title is THE BOOK OF HAMBURGS, etc., by L. Frank Baum. Is this

the same Baum who write the WIZARD OF OZ?

A.Yes, it is. It was his first book, published in 1886, and is about a breed of chickens (not sandwiches) and how to raise them. He wrote 81 books during his career, the most famous being THE WONDERFUL WIZARD OF OZ. He used several pen names; Hugh Fitzgerald, Edith Van Dyne, Laura Bancroft, Floyd Akers, Schuyler Stanton, and John Estes Cooke.

The first edition, first issue, of THE WONDERFUL WIZARD OF OZ can be identified by the title page date of 1900 and must have an 11-line colophon (not 13) on the back end paper.

There are also several binding states. Copies in good condition will bring $2500-3500. An extremely fine copy sold for $5400 in 1980 which was a record price. If you can send me more information from the title and copyright pages of your book I may be able to give you some idea of its value. Don't forget to describe the condition carefully.

Q.I have been collecting John D. MacDonald books for years. Can you tell me how many books he has written? What was his first book? How many TRAVIS MCGEE books are there?

A.So have I. His first book was a paperback, THE BRASS CUPCAKE, published in 1950. He has published over 70 books. So far, there are over 20 McGee titles. Interestingly, most of his first 60 books were paperback first editions. His first best selling hardcover title was CONDOMINIUM, published in 1977. He also wrote using the pen names of Peter Reed, John Wade Farrell, and Scott O'Hara.

Q.Were the Charlie Chan movies made from

books? If so, who wrote them?

A. The Charlie Chan mystery novels were all written by Earl Derr Biggers. Various screen writers adapted them to the movies, as well as writing original scripts based on the character. Biggers wrote six Chan books in all plus six other titles and several stage plays.

Q. I have a first edition of GONE WITH THE WIND by Margaret Mitchell published in June, 1936. How much is it worth?

A. I'm sorry, but you don't have a first edition. One of the questions I receive most often is about "GONE WITH THE WIND."

Here is how to tell if the copy you have is a true first edition. The book was published simultaneously in New York and London, by Macmillan, in 1936. The binding was gray cloth.

A true first edition must have "Published May, 1936" on the copyright page and no notice of any other printings.

There are also two issues of the dust jacket for the first edition. The first issue dust jacket lists "Gone with the Wind" in the second column of the Macmillan book list on the back panel. The second issue dust jacket lists the book at the top of the list in the first column.

The book, in a first issue dust jacket and in very good or better condition, would have a retail value between $650 and $900. In a second issue jacket, $450-600. Without a jacket, $175-250. Typographical errors are NOT an indication of a first edition.

Margaret (Munnerlyn) Mitchell was born in Atlanta, Georgia, in 1900 and died August 16, 1949. Gone with the Wind was her only book. She was awarded a Pulitzer Prize in 1937.

Q. How important is the condition of a collectible book? Is there a standard way to describe condition such as there is with stamps and coins? How does the condition affect the value?

A. It's very important and book collectors try to own the very best copy that they can afford. Value is directly related to importance, scarcity and condition. Very seldom will they accept a book simply because you might think it can be easily repaired. And they almost never are willing to accept an ex-library copy, particularly novels. No matter what the condition always mention if there is a dust jacket present and its condition.

Here are some terms used to describe condition and what they mean.

Mint or As New — just what it says. The book and its dust jacket should be just they way it first came from the publisher. No names or other marks of any kind and no evidence of having been read.

Fine — Almost as above except for slight evidence of having been read or of normal shelf wear commensurate with the books age. A neat owners name or a bookplate is acceptable, but always mention it if one is present.

Very Good — Some evidence of wear, minor tears in the dust jacket (don't ever repair them with cellophane type tape), neat former owner's names. The book must be sound and tight, with a minimum of dog-eared pages, and only light exterior soil.

Good — The average condition of most used books. Some soiling of the covers, name's, minor page abuse, sound and reasonably tight, all pages and illustrations present.

Fair — Covers badly soiled and/or loose, perhaps some loose pages or even missing pages. Describe all such defects carefully. Such a book must have some importance to be salable in this condition.

Poor — don't bother unless you know it is a great rarity and who might want it.

No matter what the general condition of a book is it must have its title page present.

Always, always, collate a book before you buy it. This means to make sure the title page and all other pages are present, and if it is illustrated check a make sure ALL the illustrations are also present. There is usually a list of illustrations following the table of contents which you can follow. This is a common fault with illustrated books bought at flea markets and service organization outlets such as The Salvation Army.

Be especially careful with books illustrated by the better known and collected artists such as Maxfield Parrish, Norman Rockwell, Jessie Wilcox Smith, Harrison Fisher, Arthur Rackham, Frederic Remington, and Winslow Homer (especially in Harper's Weekly).

In general you should view condition just as you

would any other antique. A loose cover on a book is in the same category as a crack in a plate or teacup, or a chip on the rim of a cut glass bowl. However, books also have some unique aspects as regards condition, particularly in regards to evidence of aging.

One of these is a condition called "foxing," something you have perhaps heard of or seen without knowing what it is called. The paper will seem to have rust spots, sometimes lightly scattered, but often very heavily present and badly obscuring the text or an illustration. And that's just what it is — rust. Iron in the paper which has been affected by dampness over the years. Too much is bad in older books — any at all is bad in more modern books.

Q. I have several Tarzan books by Edgar Rice Burroughs. How can I tell if they are first editions and how much they are worth?

A. During Burroughs' lifetime there were only six publishers of his books. The McClurg publishing firm of Chicago published most of them. Other publishers were Macauley of New York, Vollard of Joliet, Illinois, Metropolitan of New York, Burroughs of Tarzana, California, and Whitman of Racine, Wisconsin.

If your books were published before 1950 by any other publisher then they are reprints and have far less value than the first editions. The Grosset & Dunlap reprints are the most common and many of them do have some value. I cannot help you with placing a value on your books unless you let me know the titles, publishers, illustrators name, and condition, which is very important. First editions are hard to find in good or better condition, and scarce with dust jackets. A dust jacket in good condition can easily triple the normal value of a title.

The first Tarzan book was TARZAN OF THE APES, published in 1914 by McClurg. There were 24 Tarzan books in all published during Burroughs' lifetime. He also wrote many science fiction books.

Q. When was the book 1984 by George Orwell first published? Is a first edition valuable?

A. The correct title is NINETEEN EIGHTY-FOUR by Eric Arthur Blair. It was first published in London in 1949, in a green cloth binding. With dust jacket and in good condition it would be worth at least $500. The first American edition was published as 1984, later in 1949 in New York, in a gray cloth binding, using Blair's pseudonym of George Orwell.

In good condition and red (first issue) dust jacket it is worth at least $250. Blair was British and died in 1950 at the age of 47.

Q. I saw a copy of THE MARBLE FAUN by William Faulkner at our Salvation Army store. The price is $15. Is that a good buy? I know he was an important author but it's poetry and I see a lot of other poetry books there for 50 cents and a dollar.

A. Run, don't walk, back to that store and pray that it is still there. THE MARBLE FAUN was Faulkner's first book and there were only about 500 copies issued. If the book has mottled green boards and printed paper labels, and published in Boston, copyrighted 1924, it is a first edition and worth $7500 or more. Please let me know if you get it!

Q. I have been collecting paperbacks by Dashiell Hammett for some time now but I think I would like to collect the first editions of some of his books. I would especially like to find a copy of THE MALTESE FALCON. What do I look for?

A. The Maltese Falcon was first published in 1930, in New York, in a gray cloth binding. With dust jacket and in good condition it will probably cost you at least $2500. Without a jacket, perhaps as much as $750.

Q. My grandmother passed away and left me many books. One of them is MOBY-DICK; or, THE WHALE by Herman Melville. The date on the first page is 1851. The publisher was from New York city. How much is it worth?

A. It is probably the first American edition. If the publishers name is blind stamped into the cover and there are six blank pages at the front and the back then it is. In fine condition it might be worth as much as $10,000.

The book was first published in London in 1851, in three volumes. The title was simply THE WHALE. It was bound in bright-blue and cream colored cloth with pale yellow end papers. In fine condition it would probably bring at least $20,000.

Q. One of my favorite western movies has always been DESTRY RIDES AGAIN. Did Max Brand write this? Did he write many other western's. Did he use any pen names?

A. Yes, he wrote the book the movie was made from. It was one of over 200 books which he wrote. Max Brand is a pen name for Frederick Schiller Faust, who also wrote under many other names. Among them are Frank Austin, George Owen Baxter, Walter C. Butler, George Challis, Peter Dawson, Martin Dexter, Evan Evans, John Frederick, Frederick Frost, David Manning, Peter Henry Morland, Huge Owen, and Nicholas Silver.

Perhaps it will surprise you to know that he also wrote the Dr. Kildare books which became the basis for many popular movies and a television series. Faust also wrote over 300 hundred western stories, primarily for the pulp magazines, between 1918 and 1938, several screen plays, and 3 books of verse. He died on May 12, 1944, at age 52.

Q. The television series MURDER SHE WROTE has become my favorite. Can you tell me something about Agatha Christie? Does she write all the scripts?

A. My favorite also. No, she doesn't write the scripts. She died in January 12, 1976 at age 86. She was a prolific writer of mysteries with 109 books to her credit. She also wrote several novels using the pen name of Mary Westmacott, and sixteen stage plays.

Several of her books have been made into movies. Probably the best known is MURDER ON THE ORIENT EXPRESS which was first published in London, in 1934. Another is TEN LITTLE INDIANS, published as a paperback in New York in 1965. However it was originally published in England as TEN LITTLE NIGGERS in 1939; then published in the U.S. as AND THEN THERE WERE NONE in 1940.

She received the Mystery Writers of America Grand Master Award in 1954, and the New York Drama Critics Circle Award in 1955. Also a C.B.E. (Commander, Order of the British Empire) in 1956, and a D.B.E. (Dame Commander, Order of the British Empire) in 1971.

Q. I would like to collect the Perry Mason books by Earl Gardiner. Will this be difficult? Did he write other books?

A. Yes, unless you look for the books by Erle Stan-ley Gardner, who also wrote using the pen names of A.A. Fair, Carleton Kendrake, Charles M. Green, Charles Kenny, Charles J. Kenny, Robert Park, and Les Tilray, .

In addition to the Perry Mason books, his novels also featured the continuing characters of Terry Clane, Sheriff Bill Eldon, Doug Selby, Gramps Wiggins, Bertha Cool, and Donald Lam. Some of the most collectible of his books are those he wrote about Baja California.

There are 82 Perry Mason books in all, of the 148 books Gardner wrote. He died March 11, 1970 at age 71. The last Perry Mason book was published posthumously in 1973.

Q. Who created the radio and book character The Shadow?

A. Walter B. Gibson created the character "The Shadow" at the request of a pulp magazine publisher, Street & Smith.

The first Shadow story appeared in 1931 under Gibson's pseudonym of Maxwell Grant. He has written nearly 300 Shadow novels, many of which have never been published in book form.

Gibson has also written over 60 other books, mostly about magic and cards. He was a stage magician and a confidant of Houdini, Thurston, and Dunninger.

Q. What is a polyglot Bible?

A. A polyglot Bible is one with several different lan-guage versions within the same book. One of the most valuable editions is the "MITHRIDATES" of Adelung, which contains the Lord's Prayer in more than 400 languages.

Q. Who was the first author to use a typewriter?

A. Mark Twain (Samuel Langhorne Clemens) was the first author to prepare typewritten book manuscripts. He wrote both THE ADVEN-TURES OF TOM SAWYER, and LIFE ON THE MISSISSIPPI, in 1875, using a Remington typewriter.

Q. How many Nero Wolfe novels are there? What is the title of the first one?

A. There are 46 Nero Wolfe novels by Rex (Tod-hunter) Stout. The first one was FER-DE-LANCE, published in 1934. The last one, A FAMILY AFFAIR was published in 1975. Stout wrote over 60 novels all together. He died October 27, 1975, at age 89.

Q.I have heard that Barbara Cartland has written over 300 books. Does that make her the champion writer?

A.No, not by a long shot. Isaac Asimov has also passed that number as have several other authors. My candidate is Enid Blyton, a British author. Most of her books were children's books. She wrote 561 books between 1924 and 1969, plus many plays.

Not too far behind her is Ursula Bloom. She wrote over 500 books between 1903 and 1979. Most of them were romance and Gothic novels. Her first books were TIGER, and WINIFRED, both published in 1903 when she was 7 years old. She wrote under her own name as well as the pen names of Sheila Burns, Mary Essex, Rachel Harvey, Deborah Mann, Lozania Prole, and Sara Sloane. She passed away October 29, 1984.

Q.Was Louisa May Alcott (LITTLE MEN, LITTLE WOMEN) a women's rights advocate?

A.Yes. They called themselves suffragettes in those days. To quote her, "I believe that it is as much a right and duty for women to do something with their lives as for men and we are not going to be satisfied with such frivolous parts as you have given us."

Q.Were there libraries as we know them in ancient times?

A. The Alexandrian Library was the largest library of the ancient world, founded by Ptolemy Soter, in Alexandria, near the beginning of the Third Century B.C. It supposedly contained 700,000 manuscripts.

Q.How many copies of the Bible have been printed?

A.Enough to have leveled a great many forests. Between 1816 and 1975, approximately 2.46 billion copies of the Bible were printed.

Q.Has the Bible ever been censored?

A.Yes it has. In 1833, Noah Webster published a censored version of the Bible. It deleted all words for sex, or elimination.

Q.Is the TV program Believe It Or Not based on a book?

A.It was a newspaper column. Robert Ripley started his Believe It Or Not column in December, 1918. It was originally called Chumps and Champs. He was a sports cartoonist for the New York Globe.

Q.I recently saw a news item about Henry James and one of his books. What was it about?

A.It was probably about his book THE AMBASSADORS which was first published, correctly, in England. By 1958 it had been reprinted five times in America — and four of these printings reversed the order of chapters 28 and 29.

Q.I know that Oscar Wilde spent some time in prison. Did he write any of his books while there?

A.He wrote DE PROFUNDIS, APOLOGIA, and BALLAD OF READING GOAL, while in prison, in 1895-97.

Q.When did the bestseller lists first start appearing?

A.The first American bestseller list appeared in the February, 1895, issue of *The Bookman*. It listed 16 books. Three authors had two books each on the list. The books were:

TRILBY by George du Maurier
PETER IBBETSON by George du Maurier
THE PRISONER of Zenda by Anthony Hope
THE DOLLY DIALOGUES by Anthony Hope
THE MANXMAN by Hall Caine
SLUM STORIES OF LONDON by H.W. Nevinson
BESIDE THE BONNIE BRIAR BUSH by Ian Maclaren
THE GOOD SHIP MOHOCK by W. Clark Russell
THE RALSTONS by F. Marion Crawford
THE AMERICAN COMMONWEALTH by James Bryce
BARABBAS by Marie Corelli
THE ADVENTURES OF SHERLOCK HOLMES by A. Conan Doyle
COFFEE AND REPARTEE by John Kendrick Bangs
THE GREEN CARNATION by Henry Drummond
THE ASCENT OF MAN by Henry Drummond
SOCIAL EVOLUTION by Benjamin Kidd

...and how many of those did you recognize?

Q. How long have book clubs been around?

A. The first book club was the Book-Of-The-Month Club, founded in New York City in 1926. The first selection offered members was THE LOVING HUNTSMAN by Sylvia Townsend Warner. It was distributed to 4,750 members.

Q. When did the first printing press arrive in America?

A. The first printing press in America was imported from England by the Reverend Jess Glover in 1638.

Q. When was the first book printed in America?

A. The first privately printed book in America was John Eliot's COMMUNION OF CHURCHES; or, the Devine Management of Gospel Churches by the Ordinance of Councils, Constituted in Order According to the Scriptures. It was printed in 1665 by Marmaduke Johnson in Cambridge, Massachusetts, and contained 40 pages.

Q. What was the first completely American book?

A. The first all American book; paper, ink, type, etc., was IMPENETRABLE SECRET, published in 1775, in Philadelphia.

Q. What is the name of the first newspaper published in America?

A. The first newspaper published in America was PUBLIC OCCURRENCES, in 1690. Next came THE BOSTON NEWS LETTER, in 1704.

Q. Who wrote LITTLE BLACK SAMBO?

A. Helen Bannerman wrote THE STORY OF LITTLE BLACK SAMBO. It was published in England in 1899 by Grant Richards, and in the US in 1900 by Stokes. She was born in Scotland in 1863, lived for 30 years in India, and died in 1946. The book is now considered racist and used copies bring good prices.

Q. When was the first used-book store established in this country?

A. The first antiquarian book store was established in Boston in 1830 by Samuel Gardner Drake.

Q. When did book dust jackets first come into use?

A. The first book dust jacket was designed by John Keep for THE KEEPSAKE; a Gift for the Holidays, in 1833, in New York City.

Q. Who wrote "One of the lessons of history is that nothing is often a good thing to do and always a clever thing to say"?

A. Will Durant.

Q. Who was the first book reviewer?

A. Sarah Margaret Fuller. She was hired by Horace Greeley for the New York Tribune in December, 1844. She was paid a salary plus room and board with the Greeley's.

Q. Who was the first sports writer?

A. The first sports writer was Henry William Herbert around 1834. He is perhaps better known as Frank Forester.

Q. When was the first "advice" column written?

A. Dorothy Dix wrote the first advice column for the *New Orleans Picayune* in 1896.

Q. When was the first book for the blind published?

A. The first book for the blind was the GOSPEL OF ST. MARK, published in 1833 by the Pennsylvania Institute for the Instruction of the Blind.

Q. Do writers have bigger brains than average?

A. I doubt it. Sometimes I think it takes a small brain to be one considering the energy expended in proportion to the return. In any event, you decide. Here are some comparisons. ...Walt Whitmans brain weighed 44.85 ounces — George Gordon, Lord Byron's, weighed 82.25 ounces. The average mans brain weighs 49 ounces; womans 44 ounces — BUT bear in mind that the average man is larger than the average woman.

Q. I'm a redhead. Are there any famous redheaded writers?

A. You bet. Emily Dickinson, Sinclair Lewis, William Shakespeare, George Bernard Shaw, and Mark Twain were all redheads.

Q. Who wrote "You cannot fly like an eagle with the wings of a wren"?

A. William Henry Hudson.

Q.Does old age slow up a writer?

A.Old age slows up everyone that I know. However, George Bernard Shaw wrote FARFETCHED FABLES at the age of 93 and he was not exceptional.

Q.When was the book PILGRIM'S PROGRESS written?

A.In 1678, by John Bunyan, while he was in prison.

Q.I have heard that the novelist Gore Vidal as gay. Is that true?

A.He has admitted to it. As are many other writers...and butchers...and bakers...and candlestick makers. Here are two that may surprise you, though! Hans Christian Andersen and Horatio Alger.

Q.What is the Voynich manuscript?

A.The Voynich Manuscript is a 204 page volume, with multi-colored drawings, written in an unknown language. It was purchased in 1912 from a Jesuit college in Italy by the bookseller, Wilfred Voynich. It has been at Yale University since 1969.

Q.Who was the first female writer?

A.Aphra Ben (1640-1689) was the first professional female writer in English. She wrote 19 plays and 11 prose works after being a secret agent in Holland. She is buried at Westminster Abbey.

Q.I recently discovered two books my grandmother had tucked away in the attic. Neither one has an authors name so I would like to know who wrote them and if they have any value.

The first one is THE AMERICAN SHOOTER'S MANUAL. By a Gentleman of Philadelphia County. It was published in Philadelphia and it has a date of 1827. I think the cover is leather.

The other is HOBOMOK, A TALE OF EARLY TIMES. The title page says Boston, 1824. The cover seems to be paper over a stiff board of some sort. Both books are in very good condition. What can you tell me?

A.Something to make you smile. THE AMERICAN SHOOTER'S MANUAL is attributed to Dr. Jesse Y. Kester. If your copy has a frontispiece (a picture opposite the title page), 2 plates (illustrations), and an errata slip (giving corrections), than you have a first edition. The value? At least $2500.00 if sold to a library or collector.

HOBOMOK, A TALE OF EARLY TIMES, was written by Lydia Maria Child. You have a first edition of her first book. In bookish terminology the covers are called "boards." In good condition the book should bring at least $300.00 at retail.

Q.I watch and enjoy the television series Spencer. I see the name Robert Parker in the screen credits. Who is he and what does he have to do with the series?

A.Spencer is the Boston based detective character created by Robert Brown Parker, one of our finest private-eye tradition writers. He was born in Massachusetts in 1932, and received a Ph.D from Boston University in 1971.

During his career he has been an advertising copy writer, editor, lecturer, instructor, and professor at Northeastern University in Boston. He was the recipient of the Mystery Writers of America Edgar Allan Poe award in 1976.

The TV series is based on the Spencer character and Parker acts as consultant for the series. The first Spencer book was THE GODWULF MANUSCRIPT, published in 1973.

Q.I know THE STAR SPANGLED BANNER was written by Francis Scott Key. What else can you tell me about it?

A.Tell us if this helps? The original title of THE STAR SPANGLED BANNER was THE DEFENSE OF FORT HENRY. It was set to music by Ferdinand Durang, who patterned it after an old air titled Adams and Liberty.

It might also interest you to know that the song America was written by Samuel F. Smith, and set to the tune of GOD SAVE THE KING.

Q.Can you tell me anything about the "Blue Laws" and if they were actually printed?

A.Yes, I can, and they were. The Blue Laws originated in the "Dominion of New Haven" in Connecticut. They were called this because they were printed on blue paper. Some were very strange indeed. For example:

No food or lodging shall be offered to a heretic.

No one shall cross a river on the Sabbath but authorized clergymen.

No one shall kiss his or her children on the Sabbath or feasting days.

No one shall eat mince pies, dance, play cards, or play any instrument of music except the drum, trumpet or jewsharp.

No gospel minister shall join people in marriage. The magistrate may join them as he may do it with less scandal to Christ's church. (Can anyone explain that one?)

Q. Where does the phrase "I wandered lonely as a cloud" come from?

A. From DAFFODILS by William Wordsworth.

Q. When I was a child one of my favorite books was THE YEARLING by Marjorie Kinnan Rawlings. Did she write any other children's books?

A. Yes, she did. THE SECRET RIVER was posthumously published in 1955, two years after her death at age 57. She wrote 10 books in all and won the Pulitzer prize in 1939. All of her books would be enjoyable reading for young people as well as adults.

Q. I have seen books by Nick Carter which date back to the turn of the century. I've also seen paperbacks by this author on the book store racks. Is this the same author? Are the paperbacks reprints of the old books? If they are not reprints how old IS Nick Carter?

A. Nick Carter is what is known as a "house" name. There have been at least five "Nick Carter's" over the years. The first one was J. Russell Coryell. The others, not necessarily in this order have been Frederic Merrill Van Rensselaer Dey (1865-1922), Michael Angelo Avallone, Jr. (1924-), Willis Todhunter Ballard (1903-), and Dennis Lynds (1924-). Possibly there will be others in the future.

Most of the current paperbacks are not reprints of the old books. Since the start there have been hundreds of Nick Carter novels published as books and in pulp magazines.

Q. Can you tell me something about the TV character Zorro? I believe it was a Western series made back in the 50's.

A. Zorro, which means the fox, was created by the writer Johnston McCulley. The first appearance was in a serial published in *All Story Weekly* in 1919. In 1920 the first movie was made, The Mark of Zorro, starring Douglas Fairbanks. This was published as the first Zorro book in 1924.

The Zorro character became one of the most popular of all time, selling several million copies in America alone, and was featured in at least 24 movies and 82 television segments during 1957-59. The books have been translated into several languages. McCulley also wrote over 50 other western and mystery books, and several hundred short stories for the pulp magazines, several screenplays, and the television plays.

Q. I would like to know the value of the following book which is in very good condition but has no dust jacket...

SLAVE SONGS OF THE GEORGIA SEA ISLANDS by Lydia Parrish (wife of Maxfield Parrish, I understand). It is signed by her. The book was published in 1942 by Creative Age Press. It is a first edition and so stated. It is full of photographs of blacks but the photos on pages 80 and 81 are upside down as is the photo opposite page 64.

A. Your book is definitely a good find of a scarce title. There is no particular value added because of the inverted photos, or for the autograph, as the author signed many copies. I would suggest that a fair retail value for your copy would be $100-125.

Q. Please tell me if the following book is a first edition and/or if it has any value in its condition.

OF HUMAN BONDAGE by W. Somerset Maugham. Garden City, Doubleday, Doran, copyright, 1915. No dust jacket. Red cover well worn. Thanks!

A. I really can't tell you too much about the edition you have without more information. However, I suspect that it is a book club edition or a later printing by the original publisher.

The first edition must have the Doran imprint (device) on the title or copyright page, a misprint in line four of page 257, and be bound in green cloth. With a dust jacket, and in very good or better condition, the retail value would be at least $750. Hope this helps.

Now I would like to share some of the wisdom

of a remarkable writer with you — Samuel Langhorne Clemens, better known as MARK TWAIN. Here are some of his sayings.

"Noise proves nothing. Often a hen who has merely layed an egg cackles as if she had laid an asteroid."

"Fewer things are harder to put up with than the annoyance of a good example."

"The man who does not read good books has no advantage over the man who can't read them."

"Fame is a vapour, popularity an accident; the only earthly certainty is oblivion."

"Ethical man — a Christian holding four aces."

"There are those who would misteach us that to stick in a rut is consistency — and a virtue, and that to climb out of the rut is inconsistency — and a vice."

"Courage is resistance to fear, mastery of fear, not absence of fear."

"The reports of my death are greatly exaggerated."

"The human race is a race of cowards; and I am not only marching in that procession but carrying a banner."

"Let us be thankful for the fools. But for them the rest of us could not succeed."

"We may not pay Satan reverence, for that would be indiscreet, but we can at least respect his talents."

"It is better to deserve honours and not have them than to have them and not deserve them."

"It takes your enemy and your friend, working together to hurt you to the heart; the one to slander you and the other to get the news to you."

"It isn't so astonishing, the number of things that I can remember, as the number of things I can remember that weren't so."

"Richard Wagner, a musician who writes music which is better than it sounds."

"Pessimism is only the name that men of weak nerves give to wisdom."

"What a good thing Adam had — when he said he had a good thing, he knew nobody had said it before."

"Good breeding consists in concealing how much we think of ourselves and how little we think of the other person."

"I can live for two months on a good compliment."

"We are chameleons, and our partialities and prejudices change places with an easy and blessed facility."

"Get your facts first, and then you can distort 'em as much as you please."

"There are several good protections against temptation, but the surest is cowardice."

"If you tell the truth you don't have to remember anything."

"Few of us can stand prosperity. Another man's, I mean."

"The difference between the right word and the almost right word is the difference between lightning and the lightning bug."

"In Paris they simply stared when I spoke to them in French; I never did succeed in making those idiots understand their own language."

"I conceive that the right way to write a story for boys is to write so that it will not only interest boys but strongly interest any man who has ever been a boy. That immensely enlarges the audience."

"When I was a boy of fourteen, my father was so ignorant I could hardly stand to have the old man around. But when I got to be twenty-one, I was astonished at how much the old man had learned in seven years."

Q. What does it mean when a book is referred to as incunabula?

A. This is a word from the Latin meaning "in the cradle." It is applied to any book printed between 1450 and January 1, 1501. Actually it is the plural form of incunabulum. During that brief fifty year period more than 60,000 books were printed. There is a good market for even poor and incomplete specimens.

Most incunabula were printed in black letter or "Gothic" type. This was a heavy, broad type used when movable type was first introduced in Germany. A theory is that there was probably a deliberate attempt to fool the public into thinking that such printed books were really manuscripts. So the type was designed to resemble German script with wide and nearly unreadable characters.

Q. Why do some book catalogs refer to a "leaf" missing and others to a "page?" What's the difference?

A. Confusing isn't it? When a book is printed, the printer starts with a "sheet" of paper. This is folded, after printing several pages of the book on it, to make "leaves." Each side of the "leaf" thus has a page printed on it. So, strictly speaking, a single page cannot be missing since it would be impossible for only one side of a leaf to be missing. If a leaf is missing, than two pages are missing, even if one is blank. The best way to describe a missing page(s) is to state pages and missing.

Q. How small must a book be to qualify as a miniature book? Are they very valuable?

A. There is no real universal agreement on this among collectors or dealers but as a general rule three inches in height is the guideline. As with regular size books, value depends on content, condition, and scarcity.

Q. What is the difference between parchment and vellum?

A. Though both terms are generally used synonymously, there is an actual difference. Vellum is the name for parchment made from the skins of goats or calves. Very fine vellum is made from the skins of unborn animals.

Parchment is the name for leather used for writing, printing, or bookbinding made from the skins of various animals. For example, Calfskin parchment, sheep parchment, goatskin parchment, pigskin, etc.

Q. What does it mean when a book is described as having three-quarter leather binding?

A. The spine and tips of the corners are covered in leather. The rest of cover is cloth or boards. A half-binding has only the spine covered in leather.

MORE TRIVIA that's not so trivial...

There are over 2 billion books in the more than 100,000 libraries in the United States.

The longest overdue book on record was borrowed from the University of Cincinnati library in 1823 and returned 145 years later, in 1968. No fine had to be paid even though it was calculated to be $22,646.

The most prolific borrower seems to have been a New York City attorney, Joseph Feldman, who had accumulated over 15,000 overdue books from the New York Public Library. They were discovered in 1973, by fireman who were doing what they do best.

The U.S. Government Printing Office is the largest publisher in the world. It publishes over 6,000 new titles each year and mails out over 150 million items annually. The largest non-government publisher in the United States is Sears, Roebuck. Well over 5 billion copies of their catalog have been distributed since 1896. 175,000 tons of paper and one million gallons of ink are used each year to produce their catalogs.

Author John Creasey, who died in 1973, wrote 564 books using 13 pen names. He received 743 rejection slips before one of his mystery novels was accepted for publication. Other authors who persisted after numerous rejections: James Joyce received 22 for DUBLINERS; Pearl Buck — a dozen before THE GOOD EARTH was accepted.

A probable worlds record for a slow-selling book was a translation from Coptic to Latin of the New Testament by David Wilkins. It was published in 1716. 500 copies were sold in the next 191 years when it finally went out-of-print.

There are around 200 book clubs in the United States. They sell over 250 million of the over 1.6 billion books sold each year in the U.S.

Fiction pre-empted truth in Jules Verne's TWENTY THOUSAND LEAGUES UNDER THE SEA. His description of a periscope was so accurate that when it was actually invented a few years later, the inventor was refused an original patent.

The American Heritage Word Frequency Book list the twelve most commonly written words as: the, of, and, a, to, in, is, you, that, it, he, and for — in that order.

APPENDICES

Appendix 1

AUTHORS — THEIR TRUE NAMES AND PSEUDONYMS

Just what is a pseudonym? Do many authors use them? Why? Those are all reasonable questions — here are some of the answers.

The American Heritage Dictionary defines a pseudonym as; "A fictitious name assumed by an author; pen name." A great many authors use them. Some authors have used more than 50 pen names.

Why? Many reasons. One of the most common is because many authors can write more books than their regular publisher is willing to publish. So, for contractual reasons, they will go to other publishers and use a pen name. Another reason is that an author may not wish to have a particular type of book asociated with his true name. For example, a well-known poet might write a Gothic romance to keep bread on the table but would not want it known. So, the poet will use a pen name.

An author may also adopt a pen name because the true name may be difficult to pronounce or the publisher wants a name with more sales "sizzle." Very often a pen name is used to conceal the sex of the author. As you read through the following list you will find many examples of that. Men writing romance novels using a feminine pen name; women writing western novels using a macho male pen name.

In the following list keep this in mind to avoid confusion:

True names are printed entirely in upper case, followed by the "PN" for pen names(s), and the pen name or names are capitalized and in lower case, as well as right reading, i.e., first name first:

ABBOTT, JACOB ..... PN: Rollo

Pseudonyms (pen names) are printed in lower case, capitalized, last name first, followed by "TN:" and the author's true name in all upper case, last name first. Example:

Acre, Stephen ..... TN: GRUBER, FRANK

A

A, Dr. — TN: ASIMOV, ISAAC
A.A. — TN: ARMSTRONG, ANTHONY
A Bachelor of Arts — TN: BENTLEY, PHYLISS
A.E. — TN: RUSSELL, GEORGE WILLIAM
AARONS, EDWARD SIDNEY — PN: Paul Ayres, Edward Ronns
Abbey, Kieran — TN: REILLY, HELEN
Abbot, Sara — TN: ZOLOTOW, CHARLOTTE
Abbott, Alice — TN: BORLAND, KATHRYN
Abbott, Alice — TN: SPEICHER, HELEN ROSS
Abbott, Anthony — TN: OURSLER, CHARLES FULTON
ABRAHAMS, DORIS CAROLINE — PN: Caryl Brahms, Oliver Linden
ACLAND, ALICE — PN: Anne Marreco
Adair, Cecil — TN: EVERITT-GREEN, EVELYN
Adams, Bart — TN: BINGLEY, DAVID ERNEST
Adams, Chuck — TN: TUBB, EDWIN CHARLES
ADAMS, CLEVE FRANKLIN — PN: Franklin Charles, John Spain
ADAMS, CLIFTON — PN: Jonathan Grant, Matt Kinkaid, Clay Randall
ADAMS, HARRIET STRATEMEYER — PN: Victor W. Appleton II, Frank W. Dixon, Franklin W. Dixon, Laura Lee Hope, Carolyn Keene

ADAMS, JOHN — PN: Novanglus
Adams, Justin — TN: CAMERON, LOU
Adams, Perseus — TN: ADAMS, PETER ROBERT CHARLES
ADAMS, PETER ROBERT CHARLES — PN: Perseus Adams
ADAMS, WILLIAM TAYLOR — PN: Oliver Optic
ADDISON, JOSEPH — PN: Clio
Adelberg, Doris — TN: ORGEL, DORIS
Adeler, Max — TN: CLARK, CHARLES HEBER
Adler, Irene — TN: STORR, CATHERINE
Adrian, Frances — TN: POLLAND, MADELEINE ANGELA
Aesop — TN: LONIGAN, GEORGE THOMAS (NOT THE FAIRY TALES)
Affluent, Anthony — TN: FRANKLIN, BENJAMIN
Agar, Brian — TN: BALLARD, WILLIS TODHUNTER
Agate — TN: REID, WHITELAW
AGATE, JAMES — PN: Prentis, Richard
Aghill, Gordon — TN: GARRETT, RANDALL PHILLIP
AIKEN, CONRAD — PN: Samuel Jeake
Ainsbury, Ray — TN: VERRILL, ALPHEUS HYATT
AINSWORTH, MARY D. SALTER — PN: Mary D. Salter
Ainsworth, Harriet — TN: CADELL, VIOLET ELIZABETH
Ainsworth, Patricia — TN: BIGG, PATRICIA NINA
Aird, Catherine — TN: MC INTOSH, KINN HAMILTON
Airlie, Catherine — TN: MAC LEOD, JEAN S.
Akers, Alan Burt — TN: BULMER, HENRY KENNETH
Akers, Floyd — TN: BAUM, LYMAN FRANK
Alan, Sandy — TN: ULLMAN, ALLAN
Alardyce, Paula — TN: TORDAY, URSULA
ALBANESI, Madame EFFIE ADELAIDE MARIA — PN: Effie Rowlands
ALBERT, MARVIN H. — PN: Nick Quarry, Anthony Rome
Albrand, Martha — TN: FREYBE, HEIDI HUBERTA
Alcibiade — TN: PRAZ, MARIO
ALCOTT, LOUISA MAY — PN: A.M. Barnard
Aldanov, Mark — TN: LANDAU, MARK A.
ALDEN, ISABELLA M. — PN: Pansy
Alden, Sue — TN: FRANCIS, DOROTHY BRENNER
Alding, Peter — TN: JEFFRIES, RODERIC
Aldon, Adair — TN: MEIGS, CORNELIA LYNDE
Aleichem, Sholom — TN: RABINOVITCH, SOLOMON
Alexander, Joan — TN: CARNWORTH, Lady
ALEXANDER, ROBERT WILLIAM — PN: Joan Butler
Aliki — TN: BRANDENBERG, ALIKI
Allan, Dennis — TN: DENNISTON, ELINORE
Allan, Luke — TN: AMY, WILLIAM LACEY

ALLAN, MABEL ESTHER　　PN: Jean Estoril, Priscilla Hagon, Anne Pilgrim
Allbeury, Ted　　TN: ALLBEURY, THEODORE EDWARD LE BOUTHILLIER
ALLBEURY, THEODORE EDWARD
　LE BOUTHILLIER　　PN: Ted Allbeury, Richard Butler
Allen, Betsy　　TN: CAVANNA, BETTY
ALLEN, CHARLES GRANT
　BLAIRFINDIE　　PN: Cecil Power, Olive Pratt Rayner, Martin Leach
　　　Warborough
ALLEN, DON B.　　PN: T.D. Allen, Terry D. Allen
Allen, Grace　　TN: HOGARTH, GRACE
ALLEN, HENRY WILSON　　PN: Clay Fisher, Will Henry
Allen, John　　TN: PERRY, RITCHIE JOHN ALLEN
ALLEN, JOHN E.　　PN: Paul M. Danforth, Bisonius
ALLEN, KENNETH S.　　PN: Avis Murton Carter, Alastair Scott
Allen, T.D.　　TN: ALLEN, DON B.
Allen, Terry D.　　TN: ALLEN, DON B.
Allen, Woody　　TN: KONIGSBERG, ALLEN STEWART
Allen's Wife, Josiah　　TN: HOLLEY, MARIETTA
Allerton, Mary　　TN: GOVAN, CHRISTINE NOBLE
ALLIBONE, S.A.　　PN: Bibliophile
Allison, Clay　　TN: KEEVIL, HENRY JOHN
Allison, Sam　　TN: LOOMIS, NOEL MILLER
Allyson, Kym　　TN: KIMBRO, JOHN M.
ALSOP, MARY O'HARA　　PN: Mary O'Hara, Mary Sture-Vasa
ALVAREZ-DEL RAY, RAMON
　FELIPE SAN JUAN MARIO
　SILVIO ENRICO　　PN: Edson McCann, Lester Del Rey, Philip St. John, Erik
　　　Van Lhin, Kenneth Wright
Alvord, Burt　　TN: KEEVIL, HENRY JOHN
Amberley, Richard　　TN: BOURQUIN, PAUL HENRY JAMES
AMBLER, ERIC　　PN: Eliot Reed
Ambrose, Alice　　TN: LAZEROWITZ, ALICE AMBROSE
Ames, Clinton　　TN: GRAHAM, ROGER PHILLIPS
Ames, Jennifer　　TN: GREIG-SMITH, JENNIFER
Ames, Leslie　　TN: RIGONI, ORLANDO
AMES, SARAH RACHEL GAINHAM　　PN: Sarah Gainham
Amherst, Wes　　TN: SHAVER, RICHARD SHARPE
AMIS, KINGSLEY WILLIAM　　PN: Robert Markham
AMY, WILLIAM LACEY　　PN: Lacey Amy, Luke Allan
Anderson, Ella　　TN: MAC LEOD, ELLEN JANE
Anderson, Sonia　　TN: DANIEL, WILLIAM ROLAND
ANDREWS, LUCILLA MATHEW　　PN: Diana Gordon, Joanna Marcus
Andrews, V.C.　　TN: MARY AUSTIN
Andrezel, Pierre　　TN: BLIXEN, KAREN
ANGREMY, JEAN-PIERRE　　PN: Raymond Marlot, Pierre-Jean Remy
Angus, Ian　　TN: MACKAY, JAMES ALEXANDER
Anne Of Swansea　　TN: CURTIS, JULIA ANN KEMBLE
ANSLE, DOROTHY PHOEBE　　PN: Laura Conway, Hebe Elsna, Vicky Lancaster, Lyndon
　　　Snow
Anstey, F.　　TN: GUTHRIE, THOMAS ANSTEY
Anthony, C.L.　　TN: SMITH, DODIE
Anthony, Evelyn　　TN: WARD-THOMAS, EVELYN BRIDGET PATRICIA
Anthony, Peter　　TN: SHAFFER, ANTHONY JOSHUA and SHAFFER, PETER
　　　LEVIN
Anthony, Piers　　TN: JACOB, PIERS ANTHONY DILLINGHAM
Antoninus　　TN: EVERSON, WILLIAM
Anvil, Christopher　　TN: CROSBY, HARRY C.
Appleton, Victor W., II　　TN: ADAMS, HARRIET STRATEMEYER
Appleseed, Johnny　　TN: CHAPMAN, JOHN
April, Steve　　TN: ZINBERG, LEONARD S.
Archer, A.A.　　TN: JOSCELYN, ARCHIE LYNN
Archer, Frank　　TN: O'CONNOR, RICHARD
Archer, Ron　　TN: WHITE, TED THEODORE EDWIN
ARD, WILLIAM THOMAS　　PN: Ben Kerr, Mike Moran, Jonas Ward, Thomas Wills
Arden, J.E.M.　　TN: CONQUEST, GEORGE ROBERT ACWORTH
Arden, William　　TN: LYNDS, DENNIS

Arion	TN: CHESTERTON, G.K. (GILBERT KEITH)
Arlen, Leslie	TN: NICOLE, CHRISTOPHER ROBIN
Arlen, Michael	TN: KOUYOUMDJIAN, DIKRAN
ARMSTRONG, ANTHONY	PN: A.A.
ARMSTRONG, CHARLOTTE	PN: Jo Valentine
ARMSTRONG, DOUGLAS ALBERT	PN: Albert Douglas
Armstrong, Geoffrey	TN: FEARN, JOHN RUSSELL
Armstrong, Raymond	TN: LEE, NORMAN
ARMSTRONG, RICHARD	PN: Cam Renton
Arnett, Caroline	TN: TAYLOR, LOIS DWIGHT
Arnette, Robert	TN: GRAHAM, ROGER PHILLIPS
Arnold, Joseph H.	TN: HAYES, JOSEPH ARNOLD
AROUET, FRANCOIS MARIE	PN: Voltaire
Arp, Bill	TN: SMITH, CHARLES H.
Arrow, William	TN: ROTSLER, WILLIAM
Arthur, Frank	TN: EBERT, ARTHUR FRANK
Arthur, Peter	TN: PORGES, ARTHUR
Aruba, Hervé	TN: LE FONTAINE, JOSEPH RAYMOND HERVÉ
Ash, Fenton	TN: ATKINS, FRANK
Ash, Pauline	TN: WALKER, EMILY KATHLEEN
Ashdown, Clifford	TN: FREEMAN, RICHARD AUSTIN and PITCAIRN, J.J.
Ashe, Douglas	TN: BARDIN, JOHN FRANKLIN
Ashe, Gordon	TN: CREASEY, JOHN
Ashe, Mary Anne	TN: BRAND, MARY CHRISTIANNA MILNE
Ashford, Jeffrey	TN: JEFFRIES, RODERIC
Ashley, Elizabeth	TN: SALMON, ANNIE ELIZABETH
Ashley, Ellen	TN: SEIFERT, ELIZABETH
Ashley, Fred	TN: ATKINS, FRANK
Ashley, Gladys	TN: EWENS, GWENDOLINE WILSON
Ashton, Ann	TN: KIMBRO, JOHN M.
Ashton, Sharon	TN: VAN SLYKE, HELEN LENORE
ASHTON, WINIFRED	PN: Clemence Dane
ASIMOV, ISAAC	PN: Dr. A., Paul French
Askham, Francis	TN: GREENWOOD, JULIA EILEEN COURTNEY
Asquith, Nan	TN: PATTINSON, NANCY EVELYN
Assiac	TN: FRAENKEL, HEINRICH
Astley, Juliet	TN: LOFTS, NORAH
Aston, James	TN: WHITE, TERENCE HANBURY
ATHANAS, WILLIAM VERNE	PN: Ike Boone, Bill Colson, Bill Gordon, Anson Slaughter
Atheling, William, Jr.	TN: BLISH, JAMES BENJAMIN
ATHERTON, GERTRUDE FRANKLIN	PN: Frank Lin
ATKEY, PHILIP	PN: Pat Merriman, Barry Perowne
Atkinson, Mary	TN: HARDWICK, MOLLIE
Atlee, Philip	TN: PHILLIPS, JAMES ATLEE
Atterley, Joseph	TN: TUCKER, GEORGE
Atthill, Robin	TN: ATTHILL, ROBERT ANTHONY
ATKINS, FRANK	PN: Fenton Ash, Fred Ashley, Frank Aubrey
ATKINSON, NANCY	PN: Nancy Benko
ATTHILL, ROBERT ANTHONY	PN: Robin Atthill
Aubrey, Frank	TN: ATKINS, FRANK
AUBREY-FLETCHER, HENRY LANCELOT	PN: Henry Wade
AUCHINCLOSS, LOUIS	PN: Andrew Lee
AUDEMARS, PIERRE	PN: Peter Hodemart
August, John	TN: DE VOTO, BERNARD
Aumbry, Alan	TN: BAYLEY, BARRINGTON JOHN
Austin, Brett	TN: FLOREN, LEE
Austin, Frank	TN: FAUST, FREDERICK SCHILLER
AUSTIN, MARY	PN: Gordon Stairs, V.C. Andrews
Austwick, John	TN: LEE, AUSTIN
AVALLONE, MICHAEL ANGELO, JR.	PN: James Blaine, Nick Carter, Troy Conway, Priscilla Dalton, Mark Dane, Jean-Anne De Pre, Dora Highland, Steve Michaels, Dorothea Nile, Ed Noon, Edwina Noone, Vance Stanton, Sidney Stuart, Max Walker
AVERILL, ESTHER HOLDEN	PN: John Domino
Avery, A.A.	TN: MONTGOMERY, RUTHERFORD GEORGE

Avery, Al   TN: MONTGOMERY, RUTHERFORD GEORGE
Avery, Lynn   TN: TAYLOR, LOIS DWIGHT
Avery, Richard   TN: COOPER, EDMUND
AWDRY, RICHARD CHARLES   PN: Richard Charles
Axton, David   TN: KOONTZ, DEAN RAY
Aydy, Catherine   TN: TENNANT, EMMA CHRISTINA
Ayre, Thornton   TN: FEARN, JOHN RUSSELL
Ayres, Paul   TN: AARONS, EDWARD SIDNEY

B

Baba, Ali   TN: MACKAY, ALBERIGH
BABA, MEHER   PN: Merwan S. Irani
Babbitt, Robert   TN: BANGS, ROBERT B.
Bagby, George   TN: STEIN, AARON MARC
Bahl, Franklin   TN: GRAHAM, ROGER PHILLIPS
Baker, Asa   TN: DRESSER, DAVIS
Baker, Betty Doreen   TN: RENIER, ELIZABETH
BAKER, C.   PN: Circuit Breaker
BAKER, RAY STANNARD   PN: David Grayson
Balaam   TN: LAMB, GEOFFREY FREDERICK
Baldwin, Gordo   TN: GORDON CORTIS BALDWIN
BALDWIN, GORDON CORTIS   PN: Gordo Baldwin, Lew Gordon
BALL, ARMINE   PN: Armine Von Temski
BALL, DORIS BELL   PN: Josephine Bell
Ball, Zachary   TN: JANAS, FRANKIE-LEE
Ballantine, Bill   TN: BALLANTINE, WILLIAM OLIVER
BALLANTINE, WILLIAM OLIVER   PN: Bill Ballantine
BALLANTYNE, ROBERT MICHAEL   PN: Comus
Ballard, K.G.   TN: ROTH, HOLLY
Ballard, P.D.   TN: BALLARD, WILLIS TODHUNTER
Ballard, W.T.   TN: BALLARD, WILLIS TODHUNTER
Ballard, Willis T.   TN: BALLARD, WILLIS TODHUNTER
BALLARD, WILLIS TODHÚNTER   PN: Brian Agar, P.D. Ballard, W.T. Ballard, Willis T. Ballard,
                                             Parker Bonner, Sam Bowie, Nick Carter, Hunter
                                             D'Allard, Harrison Hunt, John Hunter, Neil Mac Neil,
                                             Clint Reno, John Shepherd, Clay Turner
Ballinger, Bill S.   TN: BALLINGER, WILLIAM SANBORN
BALLINGER, WILLIAM SANBORN   PN: Bill S. Ballinger, Frederic Freyer, B.X. Sanborn
BALOGH, PENELOPE   PN: Petronella Fox
Baltimore, J.   TN: CATHERALL, ARTHUR
Bancroft, Laura   TN: BAUM, LYMAN FRANK
Bandoff, Hope   TN: GUTHRIE, THOMAS ANSTEY
BANGS, ROBERT B.   PN: Robert Babbitt
Bannatyne, Jack   TN: GASTON, WILLIAM JAMES
Banner, Angela   TN: MADDISON, ANGELA MARY
BANNER, CHARLA ANN LEIBENGUTH   PN: Charla Ann Leibenguth
BANNISTER, PATRICIA V.   PN: Patricia Veryan
Bannon, Peter   TN: DURST, PAUL
Banton, Coy   TN: NORWOOD, VICTOR GEORGE CHARLES
Baraka, Imamu Amiri   TN: JONES, LE ROI
Barbette, Jay   TN: SPICER, BART and BETTY COE SPICER
Barclay, Ann   TN: GREIG-SMITH, JENNIFER
Barclay, Bill   TN: MOORCOCK, MICHAEL
BARCLAY, FLORENCE LOUISA   PN: Brandon Roy
Barclay, Marguerite   TN: JERVIS, MARGUERITE FLORENCE
Barcynska, Countess Helene   TN: JERVIS, MARGUERITE FLORENCE
BARDIN, JOHN FRANKLIN   PN: Douglas Ashe, Gregory Tree
Baretton, Grandall   TN: GARRETT, RANDALL
BARHAM, RICHARD   PN: Thomas Ingoldsby
BARKER, DUDLEY   PN: Lionel Black, Anthony Matthews, Tom Dudley-Gordon
BARKER, E.M.   PN: Nell Jordan
Barker, S. Omar   TN: BARKER, SQUIRE OMAR
BARKER, SQUIRE OMAR   PN: S. Omar Barker, Jose Canusi, Dan Scott, Phil Squires
Barlay, Bennett   TN: CROSSEN, KENDELL FOSTER
Barnard, A.M.   TN: ALCOTT, LOUISA MAY

BARNARD, MARJORIE FAITH   PN: M. Barnard Eldershaw
Barne, Kitty   TN: BARNE, MARION CATHERINE
BARNE, MARION CATHERINE   PN: Kitty Barne
BARNES, ARTHUR KELVIN   PN: Dave Barnes, Kelvin Kent
Barnes, Dave   TN: BARNES, ARTHUR KELVIN
BARNES, DJUNA   PN: Lydia Steptoe
BARNSLEY, ALAN GABRIEL   PN: Gabriel Fielding
Barretton, Grandall   TN: GARRETT, RANDALL PHILLIP
BARRIE, SUSAN   PN: Anita Charles, Pamela Kent
Barrington, E.   TN: BECK, LILY ADAMS
Barrow, Pamela   TN: HOWARTH, PAMELA
Barry, Jocelyn   TN: BOWDEN, JEAN
Barry, Mike   TN: MALZBERG, BARRY NORMAN
Bartholomew, Jean   TN: BEATTY, PATRICIA
BARTLETT, ANNA   PN: Amy Lothrop
BARTLETT, VERNON   PN: Peter Oldfield
BARTON, EUSTACE ROBERT   PN: Robert Eustace, Eustace Robert Rawlins
Barton, Jon   TN: JOHN B. HARVEY
BASS, CLARA MAY   PN: Claire May Overy
Bass, T.J.   TN: BASSLER, THOMAS J.
Basserman, Lujo   TN: SCHREIBER, HERMANN O.L.
BASSETT, RONALD LESLIE   PN: William Clive
BASSLER, THOMAS J.   PN: T.J. Bass
BATES, H.E.   PN: Flying Officer X
Bates, Harry   TN: BATES III, HIRAM GILMORE
BATES, HIRAM GILMORE, JR.   PN: Harry Bates, Anthony Gilmore, A.R. Holmes, H.G. Winter
BATTYE, GLADYS STARKEY   PN: Margaret Lynn
BAUM, LYMAN FRANK   PN: Floyd Akers, Laura Bancroft, John Estes Cooke, Hugh
                                   Fitzgerald, Suzanne Metcalf, Schuyler Stanton, Edith
                                   Van Dyne

Bax, Roger   TN: WINTERTON, PAUL
Baxter, George Owen   TN: FAUST, FREDERICK SCHILLER
BAXTER, JOHN   PN: Martin Loran
Baxter, Sanee V.   TN: NORWOOD, VICTOR GEORGE CHARLES
Baxter, Valerie   TN: MAYNELL, LAURENCE WALTER
BAYBARS, TANER   PN: Timothy Bayliss
Bayer, Sylvia   TN: GLASSCO, JOHN
BAYER, WILLIAM   PN: Leonie St. John
BAYLEY, BARRINGTON JOHN   PN: Alan Aumbry, P.F. Woods
Bayliss, Timothy   TN: BAYBARS, TANER
BB   TN: WATKINS-PITCHFORD, DENYS JAMES
Bean, Norman   TN: BURROUGHS, EDGAR RICE
BEARD, FRANCIS THOMAS   PN: Frank Beard
Beard, Frank   TN: BEARD, THOMAS FRANCIS
BEATTY, PATRICIA   PN: Jean Bartholomew
BEATY, BETTY   PN: Karen Campbell, Catherine Ross
BEATY, DAVID   PN: Paul Stanton
BEAUCHAMP, KATHLEEN   PN: Katherine Mansfield
Beauclerk, Helen De Vere   TN: BELLINGHAM, HELEN MARY DOROTHEA
BECHKO, PEGGY ANNE   PN: Bill Haller
BECK, LILY ADAMS   PN: E. Barrington, Louis Moredby
BECKWITH, BURNHAM PUTNAM   PN: John Putnam
Beeding, Francis   TN: PALMER, JOHN LESLIE and SAUNDERS, HILARY
                                   ADAM ST. GEORGE

Bedford, John   TN: HASTINGS, PHYLISS DORA
BELANEY, ARCHIBALD STANSFIELD PN: Grey Owl (Washaquonasin)
Bell, Acton   TN: BRONTE, ANNE
Bell, Carolyn   TN: RIGONI, ORLANDO
Bell, Currer   TN: BRONTE, CHARLOTTE
Bell, Ellis   TN: BRONTE, EMILY
BELL, ERIC TEMPLE   PN: John Taine
Bell, Georgianna   TN: RUNDLE, ANNE
Bell, Janet   TN: CLYMER, ELEANOR
Bell, Josephine   TN: BALL, DORIS BELL
Bellairs, George   TN: BLUNDELL, HAROLD
BELLEM, ROBERT LESLIE   PN: Franklin Charles, John A. Saxon

BELLINGHAM, HELEN MARY DOROTHEA — PN: Helen De Vere Beauclerk
BELLOC, HILAIRE — PN: H.B.
Belvedere, Lee — TN: GRAYLAND, VALERIE MERLE
Ben Shimon Halevi, Zev — TN: KENTON, WARREN
Benko, Nancy — TN: ATKINSON, NANCY
BENNETT, ARNOLD — PN: Jacob Tonson Gwendolyn
Bennett, Elizabeth Deare — TN: MERWIN, SAMUEL KIMBALL, JR.
BENNETT, GEOFFREY — PN: Sea-Lion
BENNETT, GERTRUDE BARROWS — PN: Francis Stevens
Bennett, H.O. — TN: HARDISON, OSBORNE B.
BENNETTS, PAMELA — PN: Margaret James
Benson, Daniel — TN: COOPER, COLIN SYMONS
Benson, Edwin — TN: SHAVER, RICHARD SHARPE
Benteen, John — TN: HAAS, BENJAMIN LEOPOLD
BENTLEY, EDMUND CLERIHEW — PN: E. Clerihew
BENTLEY, PHYLISS — PN: A Bachelor Of Arts
BENTON, PEGGIE — PN: Shifty Burke
Benyon, John — TN: HARRIS, JOHN WYNDHAM PARKES LUCAS BENYON
BERGER, EVELYN MILLER — PN: Evelyn Berger Brown
Berkeley, Anthony — TN: COX, ANTHONY BERKELEY
BERMAN, ED — PN: Otto Premier Check, Professor R.L. Dogg, Super Santa
Bernard, Robert — TN: MARTIN, ROBERT BERNARD
BERRY, BRYAN — PN: Rolf Garner
Berrington, John — TN: BROWNJOHN, ALAN
Betteridge, Anne — TN: POTTER, MARGARET EDITH
Betteridge, Don — TN: NEWMAN, BERNARD
Bettina — TN: BRENTANO, ELIZABETH
BEVAN, ANEURIN — PN: Celticus
Bexar, Phil — TN: BORG, PHILIP ANTHONY JOHN
Bey, Isabella — TN: BOSTICCO, MARY
BEYLE, MARIE HENRI — PN: Stendahl
Beynon, John — TN: HARRIS, JOHN WYNDHAM PARKES LUCAS BEYNON
Bibolet, R.H. — TN: KELLY, TIM
Bibliophile — TN: ALLIBONE, S.A.
Bickerstaff, Isaac — TN: STEELE & SWIFT and WEST, BENJAMIN
BICKHAM, JACK MILES — PN: Jeff Clinton, John Miles
BIDWELL, MARJORY ELIZABETH SARAH — PN: Elizabeth Ford, Mary Ann Gibbs
BIERCE, AMBROSE — PN: Dod Grile
BIGG, PATRICIA NINA — PN: Patricia Ainsworth
Biglow, Hosea — TN: LOWELL, JAMES RUSSELL
Billings, Josh — TN: SHAW, HENRY W.
Binder, Eando — TN: BINDER, EARL ANDREW and BINDER, OTTO OSCAR
BINDER, EARL ANDREW — PN: Eando Binder
BINDER, OTTO OSCAR — PN: Eando Binder, John Coleridge
BINGLEY, DAVID ERNEST — PN: Bart Adams, Adam Bridger, Abe Canuck, Dave Carver, Henry Carver, Larry Chatham, Henry Chesham, Will Coltman, Ed Coniston, Luke Dorman, George Fallon, David Horsley, Bat Jefford, Syd Kingston, Eric Lynch, James Martell, Colin North, Ben Plummer, Caleb Prescott, Mark Remington, John Roberts, Steve Romney, Frank Silvester, Henry Starr, Link Tucker, Christopher Wigan, Roger Yorke
Binkley, Anne — TN: RAND, ANN
BIRD, DENNIS LESLIE — PN: John Noel
Birkley, Dolan — TN: HITCHENS, JULIA CLARA CATHERINE DOLORES BIRK OLSEN
BIRNEY, HERMAN HOFFMAN — PN: David Kent
BIRO, BALINT STEPHEN — PN: Val Biro
Biro, Val — TN: BIRO, BALINT STEPHEN
BISHOP, CLAIRE HUCHET — PN: Claire Huchet
BISHOP, MORCHARD — PN: Oliver Stoner
Bisonius — TN: ALLEN, JOHN E.
Bixby, Ray Z. — TN: TRALINS, S. ROBERT
Black, Gavin — TN: WYND, OSWALD MORRIS
Black, Ishi — TN: GIBSON, WALTER B.

Black, Lionel	TN: BARKER, DUDLEY
Black, Mansell	TN: TREVOR, ELLESTON
Black, Veronica	TN: PETERS, MAUREEN
Blacker, Hereth	TN: CHALKE, H.D.
BLACKETT, VERONICA HEATH	PN: Veronica Heath
Blackstock, Charity	TN: TORDAY, URSULA
Blackstock, Lee	TN: TORDAY, URSULA
Blade, Alexander	TN: GARRETT, RANDALL PHILLIP
Blaine, James	TN: AVALLONE, MICHAEL ANGELO, JR.
BLAIR, ERIC ARTHUR	PN: George Orwell
BLAIR, KATHRYN	PN: Rosalind Brett, Celine Conway
BLAIR, WALTER	PN: Mortimer Post
Blaisdell, Anne	TN: LININGTON, BARBARA ELIZABETH
Blake, Alfred	TN: HARRIS, LARRY MARK
Blake, Andrew	TN: HARRIS, LARRY MARK
Blake, Jennifer	TN: MAXWELL, PATRICIA ANNE
Blake, Justin	TN: BOWEN, JOHN and BULLMORE, JEREMY
Blake, Ken	TN: BULMER, HENRY KENNETH
Blake, Nicholas	TN: DAY LEWIS, CECIL
Blake, Patrick	TN: EGLETON, CLIVE
Bland, Alexander	TN: GOSLING, NIGEL
Bland, E.	TN: NESBIT, EDITH
Bland, Fabian	TN: NESBIT, EDITH
Bland, Jennifer	TN: BOWDEN, JEAN
Blayn, Hugo	TN: FEARN, JOHN RUSSELL
Blayre, Christopher	TN: HERON-ALLEN, EDWARD
Bleeck, Oliver	TN: THOMAS, ROSS
Blight, Rose	TN: GREER, GERMAINE
BLINDER, ELLIOT	PN: Asa Elliot
BLISH, JAMES BENJAMIN	PN: William Atheling, Jr.
BLIXEN, Baroness KAREN	PN: Isak Dinesen, Pierre Andrezel
BLOCH, BARBARA	PN: Phoebe Edwards
BLOCH, ROBERT	PN: Collier Young
BLOCK, LAWRENCE	PN: Chip Harrison, Paul Kavanagh
BLOOD, MARIE	PN: Paige McKenzie
Blood, Matthew	TN: DRESSER, DAVIS
Blood, Matthew	TN: JOHNSON, RYERSON
BLOOM, URSULA HARVEY	PN: Sheila Burns, Mary Essex, Rachel Harvey, Deborah Mann, Lozania Prole, Sara Sloane
BLOOMFIELD, ANTHONY JOHN WESTGATE	PN: John Westgate
BLUNDELL, HAROLD	PN: George Bellairs
Blunt, Don	TN: BOOTH, EDWIN
Bluting, Edward	TN: GOREY, EDWARD
Bly, Nellie	TN: SEAMAN, ELIZABETH C.
Blyth, John	TN: HIBBS, JOHN
BLYTON, ENID MARY	PN: Mary Pollock
Boardman, Charles	TN: GRIFFITHS, CHARLES
BODINGTON, NANCY HERMIONE	PN: Shelley Smith
BODKIN, M. M'DONNELL	PN: Crom A Boo
Bold, Ralph	TN: GRIFFITHS, CHARLES
Bolitho, William	TN: RYALL, W.B.
Bond, Evelyn	TN: HERSHMAN, MORRIS
Bonehill, Capt. Ralph	TN: STRATEMEYER, EDWARD
Bonett, Emery	TN: CARTER, FELICITY WINIFRED and COULSON, JOHN HUBERT ARTHUR
Bonett, John & Emery	TN: CARTER, FELICITY WINIFRED and COULSON, JOHN HUBERT ARTHUR
BONFILS, Mrs. CHARLES	PN: Annie Laurie
BONHAM, BARBARA	PN: Sara North
BONNER, GERALDINE	PN: Hard Pan
Bonner, Parker	TN: BALLARD, WILLIS TODHUNTER
Bonner, Sherwood	TN: MAC DOWELL, KATHERINE
Bonney, Bill	TN: KEEVIL, HENRY JOHN
BONSALL, CROSBY NEWELL	PN: Crosby Newell
Bookman, Charlotte	TN: ZOLOTOW, CHARLOTTE

Boone, Ike   TN: ATHANAS, WILLIAM VERNE
BOOTH, EDWIN   PN: Don Blunt, Jack Hazard
Booth, Geoffrey   TN: TANN, JENNIFER
Booth, Irwin   TN: HOCH, EDWARD DENTINGER
BOOTH, ROSEMARY   PN: Frances Murray
BORG, PHILIP ANTHONY
   JOHN   PN: Phil Bexar, John Q. Pickard
Borland, Hal   TN: BORLAND, HAROLD GLEN
BORLAND, HAROLD GLEN   PN: Hal Borland, Ward West
BORLAND, KATHRYN   PN: Alice Abbot, Jane Land, Jane And Ross Land
BORNEMAN, ERNEST   PN: Cameron McCabe
BOSTICCO, MARY   PN: Isabelle Bey
Boston, Charles K.   TN: GRUBER, FRANK
BOSWORTH, ALLAN RUCKER   PN: Alamo Boyd
Boucher, Anthony   TN: WHITE, WILLIAM ANTHONY PARKER
BOUMA, JOHANAS L.   PN: Steve Shannon
BOUNDS, SYDNEY JAMES   PN: Wes Saunders
Bourne, Lesley   TN: MARSHALL, EVELYN
Bourne, Peter   TN: JEFFRIES, GRAHAM MONTAGUE
BOURQUIN, PAUL HENRY JAMES   PN: Richard Amberley
BOWDEN, JEAN   PN: Belinda Dell, Jocelyn Barry, Avon Curry, Jennifer Bland
Bowden, Jim   TN: SPENCE, WILLIAM JOHN DUNCAN
BOWEN, JOHN   PN: Justin Blake
Bowen, Marjorie   TN: CAMPBELL, GABRIELLE MARGARET VERE
BOWEN-JUDD, SARA   PN: Sara Woods
Bower, Barbara   TN: TODD, BARBARA EUPHAN
Bower, B.M.   TN: SINCLAIR-COWAN, BETHA MUZZY
Bowie, Jim   TN: NORWOOD, VICTOR GEORGE CHARLES
Bowie, Sam   TN: BALLARD, WILLIS TODHUNTER
Bowood, Richard   TN: DANIELL, ALBERT SCOTT
Box, Edgar   TN: VIDAL, EUGENE LUTHER GORE
Boyd, Alamo   TN: BOSWORTH, ALLAN RUCKER
Boyd, Frank   TN: KANE, FRANK
Boyd, John   TN: UPCHURCH, BOYD BRADFIELD
Boyd, Nancy   TN: MILLAY, EDNA ST. VINCENT
Boyer, Robert   TN: LAKE, KENNETH ROBERT
Boz   TN: DICKENS, CHARLES
BRACKMAN, ARNOLD C.   PN: Capt. Moss Bunker
Bradbury, E.P.   TN: MOORCOCK, MICHAEL
BRADBURY, RAY   PN: Leonard Spaulding
Bradfield, Nancy   TN: SAYER, NANCY MARGETTS
BRADLEY, IAN   PN: Duplex
BRADLEY, MARION ZIMMER   PN: Lee Chapman, John Dexter, Miriam Gardner, Valerie
                                                           Graves, Morgan Ives
Bradwell, James   TN: KENT, ARTHUR
Brady, William S.   TN: HARVEY, JOHN B.
BRAEME, CHARLOTTE M.   PN: Bertha Clay
Brahms, Caryl   TN: ABRAHAMS, DORIS CAROLINE
Brahams, Caryl   TN: SIMON, S.J.
Bramah, Ernest   TN: SMITH, ERNEST BRAMAH
BRAMESCO, NORTON J.   PN: Daedalus, Bram Norton
Bramwell, Charlotte   TN: KIMBRO, JOHN M.
Branch, Stephen   TN: ZWEIG, STEFAN
Brand, Clay   TN: NORWOOD, VICTOR GEORGE CHARLES
BRAND, MARY CHRISTIANNA
   MILNE   PN: Mary Ann Ashe, Annabel Jones, Mary Roland, China
                                                           Thompson
Brand, Max   TN: FAUST, FREDERICK SCHILLER
Brand, Victor   TN: NORWOOD, VICTOR GEORGE CHARLES
BRANDENBERG, ALIKI   PN: Aliki
Brandon, Joe   TN: DAVIS, ROBERT PRUNIER
Brandon, Sheila   TN: RAYNER, CLAIRE BERENICE
Brandt, Tom   TN: DEWEY, THOMAS BLANCHARD
BRAWNER, H.   PN: Geoffrey Coffin
Brennan, Christopher   TN: KININMONTH, CHRISTOPHER

BRENNAN, JOHN NEEDHAM HUGGARD	PN: John Welcome
BRENT, MADELINE	PN: a pseudonym
BRENT, PETER LUDWIG	PN: Ludovic Peters
BRENTANO, ELIZABETH	PN: Bettina
BRETNOR, REGINALD	PN: Grendel Briarton
Brett, Michael	TN: TRIPP, MILES BARTON
Brett, Rosalind	TN: BLAIR, KATHRYN
Brett, Simon Anthony Lee	TN: BREUER, MILES JOHN
BREUER, MILES JOHN	PN: Simon Anthony Lee Brett
Brewster, Benjamin	TN: FOLSOM, FRANKLIN BREWSTER
Briarton, Grendel	TN: BRETNOR, REGINALD
Bridge, Ann	TN: O'MALLEY, Lady MARY DOLLING
Bridger, Adam	TN: BINGLEY, DAVID ERNEST
BRIDGES, ROBERT	PN: Droch
BRIGHT, ROBERT	PN: Michael Douglas
Brisco, P.A.	TN: MATTHEWS, PATRICIA ANNE
Brisco, Patty	TN: MATTHEWS, PATRICIA ANNE
Britain, Dan	TN: PENDLETON, DONALD EUGENE
Brock, Lynn	TN: MC ALLISTER, ALISTER
Brock, Rose	TN: HANSEN, JOSEPH
Brock, Stuart	TN: TRIMBLE, LOUIS PRESTON
Brogan, James	TN: HODDER-WILLIAMS, JOHN CHRISTOPHER GLAZEBROOK
Bronson, Lynn	TN: LAMPMAN, EVELYN SIBLEY
BRONSTEIN, LEO DAVIDOVITCH	PN: Trotsky, Leon
BRONTE, ANNE	PN: Acton Bell
BRONTE, CHARLOTTE	PN: Currer Bell
BRONTE, EMILY	PN: Ellis Bell
Bronte, Louisa	TN: ROBERTS, JANET LOUISE
Brooker, Clark	TN: FOWLER, KENNETH ABRAMS
BROOKS, EDWY SEARLES	PN: Robert W. Comrade, Berkeley Gray, Victor Gunn, Carlton Ross
BROSSARD, CHANDLER	PN: Daniel Harper
Brother Antoninus	TN: EVERSON, WILLIAM
Brother Graham	TN: JEFFREY, GRAHAM
BROWN, BILL	PN: Rosalie Brown
Brown, Carter	TN: YATES, ALAN GEOFFREY
Brown, Douglas	TN: GIBSON, WALTER B.
Brown, Evelyn Berger	TN: BERGER, EVELYN MILLER
BROWN, MARGARET WISE	PN: Tomothy Hay, Golden Macdonald, Juniper Sage
BROWN, MORNA DORIS	PN: Elizabeth Ferrars, E.X. Ferrars
Brown, Peter Carter	TN: YATES, ALAN GEOFFREY
Brown, Rosalie	TN: BROWN, BILL & ROSALIE MOORE
BROWN, ROSALIE MOORE	PN: Rosalie Moore, Rosalie Brown
BROWN, ZENITH	PN: Brenda Conrad, Leslie Ford, David Frome
Browne, Barum	TN: DENNIS, GEOFFREY
Browne, Barum	TN: SAUNDERS, HILARY ADAM ST. GEORGE
BROWNE, CHARLES FARRAR	PN: Artemus Ward
Browning, Craig	TN: GRAHAM, ROGER PHILLIPS
Browning, Sterry	TN: GRIBBLE, LEONARD REGINALD
BROWNJOHN, ALAN	PN: John Berrington
BROXHOLME, JOHN	PN: Duncan Kyle, James Meldrum
Bruce, David	TN: PATCHETT, MARY ELWYN OSBORNE
Bruce, Leo	TN: CROFT-COOKE, RUPERT
Bruin, John	TN: BRUTUS, DENNIS
BRULLER, JEAN	PN: Vercors
BRUNDAGE, JOHN HERBERT	PN: John Herbert
BRUNNER, JOHN KILIAN HOUSTON	PN: Gill Hunt, John Loxmith, Keith Woodcott
Bruton, Connors	TN: EDWARD ROHEN
BRUTUS, DENNIS	PN: John Bruin
Bryan, Michael	TN: MOORE, BRIAN
BRYANS, ROBERT HARBISON	PN: Robin Bryans, Robert Harbison, Donald Cameron
Bryans, Robin	TN: BRYANS, ROBERT HARBISON
BRYANT, EDWARD WINSLOW	PN: Lawrence Talbot

Bryant, Peter — TN: GEORGE, PETER BRYAN
BRYNING, FRANCIS BERTRAM — PN: Frank Bryning, F. Cornish
Bryning, Frank — TN: BRYNING, FRANCIS BERTRAM
BUCHANAN, EILEEN MARIE
  DUELL — PN: Marie Buchanan, Rhona Petrie
Buchanan, Marie — TN: BUCHANAN, EILEEN MARIE DUELL
Buchanan, William — TN: BUCK, WILIAM RAY
BUCK, PEARL S. — PN: John Sedges
BUCK, WILLIAM RAY — PN: William Buchanan
Buckingham, Nancy — TN: SAWYER, JOHN and NANCY
Bude, John — TN: ELMORE, ERNEST CARPENTER
BUDRYS, ALGIRDAS JONAS — PN: Algis Budrys, Frank Mason
Budrys, Algis — TN: BUDRYS, ALGIRDAS JONAS
Buffalo Bill — TN: CODY, WILLIAM S.
Bullen Bear — TN: DONNELLY, AUSTIN S.
BULLMORE, JEREMY — PN: Justin Blake
BULLOCK, MICHAEL — PN: Michael Hale
Bull-us — TN: PAULDING, JAMES KIRK
BULMER, HENRY KENNETH — PN: Alan Burt Akers, Ken Blake, Ernest Corley, Arthur Frazier, Adam Hardy, Kenneth Johns, Philip Kent, Bruno Krauss, Neil Langholm, Karl Maras, Manning Norvil, Charles R. Pike, Andrew Quiller, Richard Silver, Tully Zetford
BULMER-THOMAS, IVOR — PN: Ivor Thomas
BULWER-LYTTON, EDWARD — PN: Owen Meredith
Bunker, Capt. Moss — TN: BRACKMAN, ARNOLD C.
Bunny — TN: SHULTZE, CARL E.
Buntline, Ned — TN: JUDSON, EDWARD
Bupp, Walter — TN: GARRETT, RANDALL PHILLIP
Burchell, Mary — TN: COOK, IDA
Burford, Eleanor — TN: HIBBERT, ELEANOR ALICE
BURGE, MILWARD RODON
  KENNEDY — PN: John Burke, Jonathan Burke, Owen Burke, Evelyn Elder, Harriet Esmond, John Frederick, Jonathan George, Joanna Jones, Milward Kennedy, Robert Milward Kennedy, Sara Morris, Martin Sands
Burgess, Anthony — TN: WILSON, JOHN ANTHONY BURGESS
Burgess, Trevor — TN: TREVOR, ELLESTON
Burgoyne, Elizabeth — TN: PICKLES, MABLE ELIZABETH
Burke, John — TN: BURGE, MILWARD RODON KENNEDY
Burke, John — TN: O'CONNER, RICHARD
BURKE, JOHN FREDERICK — PN: Joanna Jones
Burke, Jonathan — TN: BURGE, MILWARD RODON KENNEDY
Burke, Noel — TN: HITCHENS, JULIA CLARA CATHERINE DOLORES BIRK OLSEN
Burke, Owen — TN: BURGE, MILWARD RODON KENNEDY
Burke, Ralph — TN: GARRETT, RANDALL PHILLIP
Burke, Shifty — TN: BENTON, PEGGIE
Burnett, W.R. — TN: BURNETT, WILLIAM RILEY
BURNETT, WILLIAM RILEY — PN: W.R. Burnett, John Monahan, James Updyke
Burns, Rex — TN: SCHLER, RAOUL STEPHEN
Burns, Sheila — TN: BLOOM, URSULA HARVEY
Burns, Tex — TN: LA MOORE, LOUIS DEARBORN
BURROUGHS, EDGAR RICE — PN: Norman Bean, John Tyler McCulloch
BURROUGHS, WILLIAM SEWARD — PN: William Lee
BURROWES, MICHAEL ANTHONY
  BERNARD — PN: Mike Burrowes
Burrowes, Mike — TN: BURROWES, MICHAEL ANTHONY BERNARD
BURTON, ELIZABETH — PN: Susan Kerby
Burton, Miles — TN: STREET, CECIL JOHN CHARLES
Burton, Thomas — TN: LONGSTREET, STEPHEN
BUSH, CHARLIE CHRISTMAS — PN: Christopher Bush, Michael Home
Bush, Christopher — TN: BUSH, CHARLIE CHRISTMAS
Busybody, The — TN: FRANKLIN, BENJAMIN
BUTLER, GWENDOLINE — PN: Jennie Melville
Butler, Joan — TN: ALEXANDER, ROBERT WILLIAM

Butler, Nathan   TN: SOHL, JERRY GERALD ALLAN
Butler, Patrick   TN: DUNBOYNE, LORD
Butler, Richard   TN: ALLBEURY, TED THEODORE EDWARD LE
                                            BOUTHILLIER
BUTLER, SAMUEL   PN: Cellarius
Butler, Walter C.   TN: FAUST, FREDERICK SCHILLER
Butters, Dorothy Gilman   TN: GILMAN, DOROTHY
BUTTERWORTH, MICHAEL   PN: Sarah Kemp, Carola Salisbury
BUXTON, ANNE   PN: Anne Maybury, Katherine Troy
BYRNE, JOHN KEYES   PN: Hugh Leonard

C

Cade, Robin   TN: NICOLE, CHRISTOPHER ROBIN
CADELL, VIOLET ELIZABETH   PN: Harriett Ainsworth
CAESAR, R.D.   PN: Dudley James
Caillou, Alan   TN: LYLE-SMITH, ALAN
Cain, Paul   TN: RURIC, PETER
Caine, Hall   TN: CAINE, THOMAS HENRY HALL
CAINE, THOMAS HENRY HALL   PN: Hall Caine
Calder, Jason   TN: DUNMORE, JOHN
CALDWELL, JANE MIRIAM
  TAYLOR HOLLAND   PN: Max Reiner
Caliban   TN: PHILLIPS, HUBERT
Callahan, William   TN: GALLUN, RAYMOND ZINKE
Callas, Theo   TN: MC CARTHY, SHAUN LLOYD
Callender, Julian   TN: LEE, AUSTIN
Calvert, Mary   TN: DANBY, MARY
Calvin, Henry   TN: HANLEY, CLIFFORD
Cameron, Donald   TN: BRYANS, ROBERT HARBISON
Cameron, D.Y.   TN: COOK, DOROTHY MARE
Cameron, Ian   TN: PAYNE, DONALD GORDON
Cameron, Julie   TN: CAMERON, LOU
CAMERON, LOU   PN: Justin Adams, Julie Cameron
Campbell, Bridget   TN: SANCTUARY, BRENDA
Campbell, Cliff   TN: HECKELMANN, CHARLES NEWMAN
Campbell, Francis Stuart   TN: KUEHNELT-LEDDIHN, ERIK
CAMPBELL, GABRIELLE
  MARGARET VERE   PN: Marjorie Bowen, Robert Paye, George Preedy, Joseph
                                            Shearing, John Winch
CAMPBELL, GORDON   PN: Tom Dudley-Gordon
Campbell, Judith   TN: PARES, MARION STAPLYTON
Campbell, Karen   TN: BEATY, BETTY
CAMPBELL, WALTER STANLEY   PN: Stanley Vestal
Campbell, Wilfred   TN: CAMPBELL, WILLIAM
CAMPBELL, WILLIAM E.   PN: William March, Wilfred Campbell
CANADY, JOHN EDWIN   PN: Matthew Head
Canaway, Bill   TN: CANAWAY, W.H.
CANAWAY, W.H.   PN: Bill Canaway, William Hamilton, Hermes
Candy, Edward   TN: NEVILLE, BARBARA ALISON
Cannan, Joanna Maxwell   TN: PULLEIN-THOMPSON, JOANNA MAXWELL
CANNING, VICTOR   PN: Alan Gould
Cannon, Curt   TN: HUNTER, EVAN
Canuck, Abe   TN: BINGLEY, DAVID ERNEST
Canusi, Jose   TN: BARKER, SQUIRE OMAR
Cape, Judith   TN: PAGE, P.K.
CAPON, HARRY PAUL   PN: Noel Kenton
Carbury, A.B.   TN: CARR, ALBERT ZOTALKOFF
Carder, Leigh   TN: CUNNINGHAM, EUGENE
CAREW-SLATER, HAROLD JAMES   PN: James Carey
Carey, James   TN: CAREW-SLATER, HAROLD JAMES
Carfax, Caterine   TN: FAIRBURN, ELENOR
Carleon, D.M.   TN: SKINNER, JUNE O'GRADY
Carlisle, D.M.   TN: COOK, DOROTHY MARE
Carmichael, Harry   TN: OGNALL, LEOPOLD HORACE
Carnac, Carol   TN: RIVETT, EDITH CAROLINE

Carnac, Levin	TN: GRIFFITH-JONES, GEORGE CHETWYND
CARNWORTH, Lady	PN: Joan Alexander
Carol, Bill J.	TN: KNOTT, WILLIAM C.
Carpenter, Duffy	TN: HURLEY, JOHN J.
Carr, A.H.Z.	TN: CARR, ALBERT ZOTALKOFF
CARR, ALBERT ZOTALKOFF	PN: A.B. Carbury, A.H.Z. Carr
Carr, Catharine	TN: WADE, ROSALIND
Carr, Glyn	TN: STYLES, FRANK SHOWELL
CARR, JOHN DICKSON	PN: Carr Dickson, Carter Dickson, Roger Fairbairn
CARR, MARGARET	PN: Martin Carroll, Carole Kerr
Carr, Philippa	TN: HIBBERT, ELEANOR ALICE
Carr, Roberta	TN: ROBERTS, IRENE
CARR, TERRY GENE	PN: Norman Edwards
Carrick, Edward	TN: CRAIG, EDWARD ANTHONY
Carroll, Lewis	TN: DODGSON, CHARLES LUTWIDGE
Carroll, Martin	TN: CARR, MARGARET
Carson, S.M.	TN: GORSLINE, MARIE
Carstairs, Kathleen	TN: PENDOWER, JACQUES
Carter, Ashley	TN: WHITTINGTON, HARRY
Carter, Avis Murton	TN: ALLEN, KENNETH S.
Carter, Bruce	TN: HOUGH, RICHARD ALEXANDER
Carter, Elizabeth Eliot	TN: HOLLAND, CECELIA ANASTASIA
CARTER, FELICITY WINIFRED	PN: Emery Bonett, John & Emery Bonett
Carter, Nicholas	TN: DEY, FREDERIC MERRILL VAN RENSSELAER
Carter, Nick	TN: AVALLONE, MICHAEL ANGELO JR.
Carter, Nick	TN: BALLARD, WILLIS TODHUNTER
Carter, Nick	TN: CORYELL, J. RUSSELL
Carter, Nick	TN: DEY, FREDERIC MERRILL VAN RENSSELAER
Carter, Nick	TN: LYNDS, DENNIS
Carter-Brown, Peter	TN: YATES, ALAN GEOFFREY
CARTLAND, BARBARA HAMILTON	PN: Barbara McCorquodale
CARTMILL, CLEVE	PN: Michael Corbin
Carver, Dave	TN: BINGLEY, DAVID ERNEST
Carver, Henry	TN: BINGLEY, DAVID ERNEST
Cary, Jud	TN: TUBBS, EDWIN CHARLES
Caskoden, Edw.	TN: MAJOR, CHARLES
Cass, Zoe	TN: LOW, LOIS DOROTHEA
Cassandra	TN: CONNOR, WILLIAM
Cassels, Johgn	TN: DUNCAN, WILLIAM MURDOCH
Cassius	TN: FOOT, MICHAEL
Castlemon, H.C.	TN: FOSDICK, CHARLES AUSTIN
Castlemon, Harry	TN: FOSDICK, CHARLES AUSTIN
CATHER, WILLA	PN: Willa Sibert
CATHERALL, ARTHUR	PN: J. Baltimore, A.R. Channel, Dan Corby, Peter Hallard, Trevor Maine, Linda Peters, Margaret Ruthin
Catlow, Joanna	TN: LOWRY, JOAN
Caudwell, Christopher	TN: SPRIGG, CHRISTOPHER ST. JOHN
Cauldwell, Frank	TN: KING, FRANCIS
CAVANNA, BETTY	PN: Betsy Allen, Elizabeth Headley
Cave, Emma	TN: LASSALLE, CAROLINE
CEBULASH, MEL	PN: Glen Harlan, Jared Jansen
Cecil, Henry	TN: KELLER, DAVID HENRY
Cecil, Henry	TN: LEON, HENRY CECIL
Cellarius	TN: BUTLER, SAMUEL
Celticus	TN: BEVAN, ANEURIN
Chaber, M.E.	TN: CROSSEN, KENDELL FOSTER
Chace, Isobel	TN: HUNTER, ELIZABETH MARY TERESA
Chaffin, James B.	TN: LUTZ, GILES ALFRED
CHALKE, H.D.	PN: Hereth Blacker
Challice, Kenneth	TN: HUTCHIN, KENNETH CHARLES
Challis, George	TN: FAUST, FREDERICK SCHILLER
CHANCE, JOHN NEWTON	PN: J. Drummond, John Lymington, David C. Newton
Chance, Stephen	TN: TURNER, PHILIP WILLIAM
Chandler, Frank	TN: HARKNETT, TERRY WILLIAMS
Chandos, Fay	TN: SWATRIDGE, IRENE MAUDE
Chaney, Jill	TN: LEEMING, JILL

Channel, A.R.	TN: CATHERALL, ARTHUR
CHAPMAN, JOHN	PN: Johnny Appleseed
Chapman, Lee	TN: BRADLEY, MARION ZIMMER
Chapman, Walter	TN: SILVERBERG, ROBERT
CHARBONNEAU, LOUIS HENRY	PN: Carter Travis Young
Charles, Anita	TN: BARRIE, SUSAN
Charles, Franklin	TN: ADAMS, CLEVE FRANKLIN
Charles, Franklin	TN: BELLEM, ROBERT LESLIE
Charles, Henry	TN: HARRIS, MARION ROSE
Charles, Nicholas	TN: KUSKIN, KARLA
Charles, Richard	TN: AWDRY, RICHARD CHARLES
Charles, Theresa	TN: SWATRIDGE, IRENE MAUDE and SWATRIDGE, CHARLES
Charteris, Leslie	TN: YIN, LESLIE CHARLES BOWYER
Chartham, Robert	TN: SETH, RONALD
Chase, Adam	TN: FAIRMAN, PAUL W
Chase, Adam	TN: LESSER, MILTON
Chase, Jamed Hadley	TN: RAYMOND, RENE BRABAZON
Chatham, Larry	TN: BINGLEY, DAVID ERNEST
Check, Otto Premier	TN: BERMAN, ED
Chelton, John	TN: DURST, PAUL
CHERRY, CAROLYN JANICE	PN: C.J. Cherryh
Cherryh, C.J.	TN: CHERRY, CAROLYN JANICE
Chesham, Henry	TN: BINGLEY, DAVID ERNEST
Chesney, Weatherby	TN: HYNE, CHARLES JOHN CUTCLIFFE WRIGHT
Chesterton, Denise	TN: ROBINS, DENISE NAOMI
CHESTERTON, GILBERT KEITH	PN: Arion, G.K.C.
CHIPPERFIELD, JOSEPH EUGENE	PN: John Eland Craig
CHITTY, SIR THOMAS WILLES	PN: Thomas Hinde
Cholmondeley, Alice	TN: RUSSELL, COUNTESS MARY ANNETTE VON ARNIM
Christian, Jill	TN: DILCOCL, NOREEN
Christian, John	TN: DIXON, ROGER
Christie, Agatha	TN: MALLOWAN, DAME AGATHA MARY CLARISSA
Christopher, John	TN: YOUD, CHRISTOPHER SAMUEL
Churchill, Elizabeth,	TN: HOUGH, RICHARD ALEXANDER
Circuit Breaker	TN: BAKER, C.
Clare, Elizabeth	TN: COOK, DOROTHY MARE
CLARK, ALFRED ALEXANDER GORDON	PN: Cyril Hare
CLARK, CHARLES HEBER	PN: Max Adeler
Clark, Curt	TN: WESTLAKE, DONALD EDWIN
Clare, Ellen	TN: SINCLAIR, OLGA ELLEN
Clare, Helen	TN: CLARKE, PAULINE
CLARK, MAVIS THORPE	PN: Mavis Latham
Clark, Merle	TN: GESSNER, LYNNE
CLARK, PATRICIA DENISE	PN: Claire Lorrimer, Patricia Robins
CLARKE, BRENDA	PN: Brenda Honeyman
CLARKE, DAVID WALDO	PN: Dave Waldo
CLARKE, PAULINE	PN: Helen Clare
Clarkson, Helen	TN: MC CLOY, HELEN WORRELL CLARKSON
Clarkson, J.F.	TN: TUBB, EDWIN CHARLES
Clavers, Mary	TN: KIRKLAND, CAROLINE
Clay, Alison	TN: KEEVIL, HENRY JOHN
Clay, Bertha	TN: BRAEME, CHARLOTTE M.
Claypool, Jane	TN: MINER, JANE CLAYPOOL
CLAYTON, RICHARD HENRY MICHAEL	PN: William Haggard
CLEMENS, SAMUEL LANGHORNE	PN: Mark Twain
Clement, Hal	TN: STUBBS, HARRY CLEMENT
Cleri, Mario	TN: PUZO, MARIO
Clerihew, E.	TN: BENTLEY, EDMOND CLERIHEW
Clerk, N.W.	TN: LEWIS, CLIVE STAPLES
Cleve, John	TN: OFFUTT, ANDREW JEFFERSON V
Cleveland, John	TN: MC ELFRESH, ELIZABETH ADELINE
Clevinger, Paul	TN: NORWOOD, VICTOR GEORGE CHARLES
Clifford, Francis	TN: THOMPSON, ARTHUR LEONARD BELL

Clifford, Martin	TN: HAMILTON, CHARLES HAROLD ST. JOHN
Clinton, Jeff	TN: BICKHAM, JACK M
Clio	TN: ADDISON, JOSEPH
Clive, Dennis	TN: FEARN, JOHN RUSSELL
Clive, William	TN: BASSETT, RONALD LESLIE
CLUTTERBUCK, RICHARD	PN: Richard Jocelyn
CLYMER, ELEANOR	PN: Janet Bell, Elizabeth Kinsey
Coates, Sheila	TN: HOLLAND, SHEILA
Cobalt, Martin	TN: MAYNE, WILLIAM
COBBETT, WILLIAM	PN: Peter Porcupine
Coburn, L.J.	TN: HARVEY, JOHN B.
Cochran, Jeff	TN: DURST, PAUL
Cody, Al	TN: JOSCELYN, ARCHIE LYNN
Cody, John	TN: REPP, EDWARD EARL
Cody, Walt	TN: NORWOOD, VICTOR GEORGE CHARLES
CODY, WILLIAM S.	PN: Buffalo Bill
Coe, Tucker	TN: WESTLAKE, DONALD EDWIN
Coffey, Brian	TN: KOONTZ, DEAN RAY
Coffin, Geoffrey	TN: BRAWNER, H.
Coffin, Geoffrey	TN: MASON, FRANCIS VAN WYCK
Coffin, Peter	TN: LATIMER, JONATHAN WYATT
COFFMAN, VIRGINIA EDITH	PN: Victor Cross, Jeanne Duval, Virginia C. Du Vaul, Anne Stanfield
Cofyn, Cornelius	TN: LODER, JOHN DE VERE
Cofyn, Cornelius	TN: SAUNDERS, HILARY ADAM ST. GEORGE
Coghlan, Peggie	PN: STIRLING, JESSICA
COHEN, SIR FRANCIS	PN: Sir Francis Palgrave
Cole, Jackson	TN: HECKELMANN, CHARLES NEWMAN
Coleridge, John	TN: BINDER, OTTO OSCAR
COLES, CYRIL HENRY	PN: Manning Coles, Francis Gaite
Coles, Manning	TN: COLES, CYRIL HENRY and MANNING, ADELAIDE FRANCES OKE
Collier, Jane	TN: COLLIER, ZENA
Collier, Margaret	TN: TAYLOR, MARGARET STEWART
COLLIER, PRICE	PN: Percy Collins
COLLIER, ZENA	PN: Jane Collier
Collins, Hunt	TN: HUNTER, EVAN
Collins, Michael	TN: LYNDS, DENNIS
COLLINS, MICHAEL DALE	PN: Copeland
Collins, Percy	TN: COLLIER, PRICE
Collinson, Peter	TN: HAMMETT, SAMUEL DASHIELL
Collodi, Carlo	TN: LORENZINI, CARLO
COLLOMS, BRENDA	PN: Brenda Cross, Brenda Hughes
Colson, Bill	TN: ATHANAS, WILLIAM VERNE
Colt, Zandra	TN: STEVENSON, FLORENCE
Colter, Shayne	TN: NORWOOD, VICTOR GEORGE CHARLES
Coltman, Will	TN: BINGLEY, DAVID ERNEST
Colton, James	TN: HANSEN, JOSEPH
Colvin, James	TN: MOORCOCK, MICHAEL
COMPTON, DAVID GUY	PN: Guy Compton, Frances Lynch
Compton, Guy	TN: COMPTON, DAVID GUY
Comrade, Robert W.	TN: BROOKS, EDWY SEARLES
Comus	TN: BALLANTYNE, ROBERT MICHAEL
CONARAIN, ALICE NINA	PN: Elizabeth Hoy
Condray, Bruno	TN: HUMPHRYS, LESLIE GEORGE
Coniston, Ed	TN: BINGLEY, DAVID ERNEST
CONLY, ROBERT LESLIE	PN: Robert O'Brien
Connington, J.J.	TN: STEWART, ALFRED WALTER
Connolly, Paul	TN: WICKER, TOM
Connor, Ralph	TN: GORDON, CHARLES WILLIAM
CONNOR, WILLIAM	PN: Cassandra
Connors, Bruton	TN: ROHEN, EDWARD
CONQUEST, GEORGE ROBERT ACWORTH	PN: J.E.M. Arden
Conquest, Martin	TN: HAMILTON, CHARLES HAROLD ST. JOHN
Conquest, Owen	TN: HAMILTON, CHARLES HAROLD ST. JOHN

Conrad, Brenda — TN: BROWN, ZENITH
Conrad, Gregg — TN: GRAHAM, ROGER PHILLIPS
Conrad, Joseph — TN: KORZENIOWSKI, FEODOR J.K.
Conscience, A Good — TN: FRANKLIN, BENJAMIN
Constant, Stephen — TN: DANEFF, STEPHEN CONSTANTINE
Conway, Celine — TN: BLAIR, KATHRYN
Conway, E. Carolyn — TN: KERMOND, EVELYN CAROLYN CONWAY
Conway, Laura — TN: ANSLE, DOROTHY PHOEBE
Conway, Troy — TN: AVALLONE, MICHAEL ANGELO, JR.
COOK, DOROTHY MARE — PN: Elizabeth Clare, D.M. Carlisle, D.Y. Cameron
Cook, Howard — TN: HASKIN, DOROTHY C.
COOK, IDA — PN: Mary Burchell
COOK, JOHN LENNOX — PN: Lennox Cook
Cook, Lennox — TN: COOK, JOHN LENNOX
COOK, WILLIAM EVERETT — PN: Wade Everett, James Keene, Frank Peace
Coole, W.W. — TN: KULSKI, W.W.
Cook, Lyn — TN: WADELL, EVELYN MARGARET
Cooke, Arthur — TN: LOWNDES, ROBERT AUGUSTINE WARD
Cooke, John Estes — TN: BAUM, LYMAN FRANK
Cooke, Margaret — TN: CREASEY, JOHN
Cooke, M.E. — TN: CREASEY, JOHN
COOKE III, PHILIP ST. GEORGE — PN: Peter Hertzog
COOKSON, CATHERINE ANN — PN: Catherine Marchant
Coole, W.W. — TN: KULSKI, W.W.
Coolidge, Susan — TN: WOOLSEY, SARAH CHAUNCY
Coombs, Murdo — TN: DAVIS, FREDERICK CLYDE
COOPER, COLIN SYMONS — PN: Daniel Benson
COOPER, EDMUND — PN: Richard Avery
Cooper, Henry St. John — TN: CREASEY, JOHN
Cooper, Jeff — TN: FOX, GARDNER FRANCIS
Cooper, Jefferson — TN: FOX, GARDNER FRANCIS
Cooper, William — TN: HOFF, HARRY SUMMERFIELD
Copeland — TN: COLLINS, MICHAEL DALE
COPPEL, ALFRED — PN: Sol Galaxan, Robert Cham Gilman, Derfla Leppoc, A.C. Marin

COPPER, BASIL — PN: Lee Falk
Corbett, Chan — TN: SCHACHNER, NATHAN
Corbin, Michael — TN: CARTMILL, CLEVE
Corby, Dan — TN: CATHERALL, ARTHUR
Cordell, Alexander — TN: GRABER, GEORGE ALEXANDER
Corelli, Marie — TN: MACKAY, MARY
Corley, Ernest — TN: BULMER, HENRY KENNETH
Cornish, F. — TN: BRYNING, FRANK FRANCIS BERTRAM
CORNWELL, DAVID JOHN MOORE — PN: John Le Carre
Corren, Grace — TN: HOSKINS, ROBERT
Correy, Lee — TN: STINE, GEORGE HARRY
Corrigan, Mark — TN: LEE, NORMAN
Corteen, Wes — TN: NORWOOD, VICTOR GEORGE CHARLES
Corvo, Baron Frederick — TN: ROLFE, FREDERICK
Cory, Desmond — TN: MC CARTHY, SHAUN LLOYD
CORYELL, J. RUSSELL — PN: Nick Carter
Costello, P.F. — TN: GRAHAM, ROGER PHILLIPS
Cotton, John — TN: FEARN, JOHN RUSSELL

COTTON, JOSE MARIO GARRY ORDONEZ EDMONDSON Y — PN: G.C. Edmondson, Kelly P. Gast
COULSON, JOHN HUBERT ARTHUR — PN: Emery Bonett, John & Emery Bonett
COULSON, JUANITA — PN: John J. Wells
COULSON, ROBERT STRATTON — PN: Thomas Stratton
COULTER, STEPHEN — PN: James Mayo
COUNSELMAN, MARY ELIZABETH — PN: Charles Dubois
COUSINS, MARGARET — PN: Avery Johns
COWEN, FRANCES — PN: Eleanor Hyde
Cowper, Richard — TN: MURRY, COLIN MIDDLETON
COX, ANTHONY BERKELEY — PN: Anthony Berkeley, Francis Iles
COX, WILLIAM ROBERT — PN: Mike Frederic, Joel Reeve, Roger G. Spellman, Jonas Ward

Craddock, Charles Egbert — TN: MURFREE, MARY NOAILLES
Craig, Alisa — TN: MAC LEOD, CHARLOTTE MATILDA
Craig, Brian — TN: STABLEFORD, BRIAN MICHAEL
CRAIG, EDWARD ANTHONY — PN: Edward Carrick
Craig, John Eland — TN: CHIPPERFIELD, JOSEPH EUGENE
Craig, Jonathan — TN: POSNER, RICHARD
Craig, M.S. — TN: CRAIG, MARY FRANCIS
CRAIG, MARY FRANCIS — PN: M.S. Craig, Alexis Hill, Mary Francis Shura
CRANE, STEPHEN — PN: Johnston Smith
Crawford, Robert — TN: RAE, HUGH CRAWFORD
Crayon, Geoffrey — TN: IRVING, WASHINGTON
Crayon, Porte — TN: STROTHER, DAVID
CREASEY, JOHN — PN: Gordon Ashe, M.E. Cooke, Margaret Cooke, Henry St. John Cooper, Norman Deane, Elise Fecamps, Robert Caine Frazer, Patrick Gill, Michael Halliday, Charles Hogarth, Brian Hope, Colin Hughes, Kyle Hunt, Peter Manton, J.J. Marric, James Marsden, Richard Martin, Rodney Mattheson, Anthony Morton, Ken Ranger, William K. Reilly, Tex Reilly, Jimmy Wilde, Jeremy York

Crecy, Jeanne — TN: WILLIAMS, JEANNE
Creighton, Don — TN: DRURY, MAXINE COLE
Crespigny, Charles De — TN: WILLIAMSON, ALICE MURIEL
Crespigny, Charles De — TN: WILLIAMSON, CHARLES NORRIS
CRICHTON, DOUGLAS — PN: Michael Douglas
CRICHTON, JOHN MICHAEL — PN: Michael Douglas, Jeffery Hudson, John Lange
CRISP, ANTHONY THOMAS — PN: Tony Crisp
Crisp, Tony — TN: CRISP, ANTHONY THOMAS
Crispin, Edmund — TN: MONTGOMERY, ROBERT BRUCE
CROFT-COOKE, RUPERT — PN: Leo Bruce
Crom A Boo — TN: M'DONNELL, BODKIN M.
Crompton, Richmal — TN: LAMBURN, RICHMAL CROMPTON
Cromwell, Elsie — TN: LEE, ELSIE
CROOK, COMPTON NEWBY — PN: Stephen Tall
CROSBY, HARRY C. — PN: Christopher Anvil
Cross, Amanda — TN: HEILBRUN, CAROLYN GOLD
Cross, Brenda — TN: COLLOMS, BRENDA
Cross, James — TN: PARRY, HUGH JONES
CROSS, JOHN KEIR — PN: Stephen Macfarlane, Susan Morley
Cross, Polton — TN: FEARN, JOHN RUSSELL
Cross, Victor — TN: COFFMAN, VIRGINIA EDITH
CROSSEN, KENDELL FOSTER — PN: Bennett Barlay, M.E. Chaber, Richard Foster, Christopher Monig, Clay Richards

CROWE, Lady BETTINA — PN: Peter Lum
Crowe, John — TN: LYNDS, DENNIS
Crowfield, Christopher — TN: STOWE, HARRIET BEECHER
Crowther, Brian — TN: GRIERSON, EDWARD DOBBYN
Crumarums — TN: CRUMB, R.
CRUMB, R. — PN: Crumarums, R. Cum
Cullingford, Guy — TN: TAYLOR, CONSTANCE LINDSAY
Culver, Kathryn — TN: DRESSER, DAVIS
Culver, Timothy J. — TN: WESTLAKE, DONALD EDWIN
Cum, R. — TN: CRUMB, R.
CUMBERLAND, MARTEN — PN: Kevin O'Hara
Cunningham, Cathy — TN: CUNNINGHAM, CHET
CUNNINGHAM, CHET — PN: Cathy Cunningham
CUNNINGHAM, EUGENE — PN: Leigh Carder
Cunningham, E.V. — TN: FAST, HOWARD MELVIN
Curry, Avon — TN: BOWDEN, JEAN
Curtin, Philip — TN: LOWNDES, MARIE ADELAIDE BELLOC
CURTIS, JULIA ANN KEMBLE — PN: Anne Of Swansea, Julia Hatton
Curtis, Peter — TN: LOFTS, NORAH
CURTIS, RICHARD — PN: Ray Lilly
CURTIS, SHARON — PN: Laura London
CURTIS, THOMAS DALE — PN: Laura London
Curtis, Tom — TN: PENDOWER, JACQUES
Curtis, Wade — TN: POURNELLE, JERRY EUGENE

Curtis, Will	TN: NUNN, WILLIAM CURTIS
Curzon, Lucia	TN: STEVENSON, FLORENCE
Cyclops	TN: LEONARD, JOHN

D

DACE, LETITIA	PN: Tish Dace
Dace, Tish	TN: DACE, LETITIA
Daedalus	TN: BRAMESCO, NORTON J.
Daemer, Will	TN: MILLER, BILL
D'Allard, Hunter	TN: BALLARD, WILLIS TODHUNTER
Dallas, John	TN: DUNCAN, WILLIAM MURDOCH
Dalton, Priscilla	TN: AVALLONE, MICHAEL ANGELO JR.
Daly, Maureen	TN: MC GIVERN, MAUREEN DALY
DANBY, MARY	PN: Mary Calvert
Dancer, J.B.	TN: HARVEY, JOHN B.
Dane, Clemence	TN: ASHTON, WINIFRED
Dane, Mark	TN: AVALLONE, MICHAEL ANGELO JR.
Dane, Mary	TN: MORLAND, NIGEL
DANEFF, STEPHEN CONSTANTINE	PN: Stephen Constant
Danforth, Paul M.	TN: ALLEN, JOHN E.
Dangerfield, Clint	TN: NORWOOD, VICTOR GEORGE CHARLES
DANIEL, GLYN EDMUND	PN: Dilwyn Rees
DANIEL, WILLIAM ROLAND	PN: Sonia Anderson
DANIELL, ALBERT SCOTT	PN: Richard Bowood, David Scott Daniell, John Lewesdon
Daniell, David Scott	TN: DANIELL, ALBERT SCOTT
DANIELS, DOROTHY	PN: Danielle Dorsett, Angela Gray, Cynthia Kavanaugh, Helaine Ross, Suzanne Somers, Geraldine Thayer, Helen Gray Weston
Daniels, Max	TN: GELLIS, ROBERTA LEAH
Daniels, Norman	TN: LEE, ELSIE
DANNAY, FREDERIC	PN: Daniel Nathan, Ellery Queen, Barnaby Ross
Danton, Rebecca	TN: ROBERTS, JANET LOUISE
Darby, Catherine	TN: PETERS, MAUREEN
Darby, J.N.	TN: GOVAN, CHRISTINE NOBLE
D'Arcy, Pamela	TN: ROBY, MARY LINN
Dare, Evelyn	TN: EVERETT-GREEN, EVELYN
Dark, Johnny	TN: NORWOOD, VICTOR GEORGE CHARLES
Darrich, Sybah	TN: DI PRIMA, DIANE
Davey, Jocelyn	TN: RAPHAEL, CHAIM
Davie-Martin, Hugh	TN: MC CUTCHEON, HUGH
DAVIES, JOAN H.	PN: Joan Drake
DAVIES, JOHN EVAN WESTON	PN: Berkley Mather
DAVIES, LESLIE PURNELL	PN: Leslie Vardre
DAVIES, PAUL	PN: P.C.W. Davies
Davies, P.C.W.	TN: DAVIES, PAUL
Daviot, Gordon	TN: MACKINTOSH, ELIZABETH
Davis, Don	TN: DRESSER, DAVIS
DAVIS, FREDERICK CLYDE	PN: Murdo Coombs, Stephen Ransome, Curtis Steele
DAVIS, JULIA	PN: F. Draco
DAVIS, NORBERT	PN: Harrison Hunt
Davis, Robert Hart	TN: WHITTINGTON, HARRY
DAVIS, ROBERT PRUNIER	PN: Joe Brandon
Dawlish, Peter	TN: KERR, JAMES LENNOX
Dawson, Elizabeth	TN: GEACH, CHRISTINE
Dawson, Peter	TN: FAUST, FREDERICK SCHILLER
DAY LEWIS, CECIL	PN: Nicholas Blake
De Forbes	TN: FORBES, DELORIS FLORINE STANTON
De Kiriline, Louise	TN: LAWRENCE, LOUISE DE KIRILINE
De La Guard, Theodore	TN: WARD, NATHANIEL
DE LA MARE, WALTER	PN: Walter Ramal
DE LA PASTURE, EDMEE ELIZABETH MONICA	PN: E.M. Delafield
De La Torre, Lillian	TN: MC CUE, LILLIAN BUENO
De Lima, Sigrid	TN: GREENE, SIGRID
De Pre, Jean-Anne	TN: AVALLONE JR., MICHAEL ANGELO

DE REGNIERS, BEATRICE SCHENK	PN: Tamara Kitt
De Saint-Luc, Jean	TN: GALSSCO, JOHN
DE SCHANSCHIEFF, JULIET DYMOKE	PN: Juliet Dymoke
De Vere, Jane	TN: WATSON, JULIA
DE VOTO, BERNARD AUGUSTINE	PN: John August, Cady Lewes
De Weese, Gene	TN: DE WEESE, THOMAS EUGENE
De Weese, Jean	TN: DE WEESE, THOMAS EUGENE
DE WEESE-WEHEN, JOY	PN: Jennifer Wade
DE WEESE, THOMAS EUGENE	PN: Gene De Weese, Jean De Weese, Thomas Stratton
Deane, Norman	TN: CREASEY, JOHN
Debrett, Hal	TN: DRESSER, DAVIS
Debrett, Hal	TN: ROLLINS, KATHLEEN
Decolta, Ramon	TN: WHITFIELD, RAOUL
Deer, M.J.	TN: SMITH, GEORGE HENRY
Deighton, Len	TN: DEIGHTON, LEONARD CYRIL
DEIGHTON, LEONARD CYRIL	PN: Len Deighton
Deitrich, Robert	TN: HUNT, HOWARD
Dekker, Carl	TN: LYNDS, DENNIS
Del Martia, Astron	TN: FEARN, JOHN RUSSELL
Del Rey, Lester	TN: ALVAREZ-DEL REY, RAMON FELIPE SAN JUAN MARIO SILVIO ENRICO
Del Rey, Lester	TN: FAIRMAN, PAUL W.
Delafield, E.M.	TN: DE LA PASTURE, EDMEE ELIZABETH MONICA
Delaney, Denis	TN: GREEN, PETER
DELANEY, MARY MURRAY	PN: Mary D. Lane
Dell, Belinda	TN: BOWDEN, JEAN
Delving, Michael	TN: WILLIAMS, JAY
Demaris, Ovid	TN: DESMARAIS, OVIDE E.
Demijohn, Thom	TN: DISCH, THOMAS MICHAEL and SLADEK, JOHN THOMAS
Deming, Kirk	TN: DRAGO, HARRY SINCLAIR
DEMING, RICHARD	PN: Max Franklin, Emily Moor, Nick Morino
Denholm, Mark	TN: FEARN, JOHN RUSSELL
DENISON, DULCIE WINIFRED CATHERINE	PN: Dulcie Gray
DENNIS, GEOFFREY	PN: Barum Browne
DENNISTON, ELINORE	PN: Dennis Allan, Rae Foley
DENT, LESTER	PN: Kenneth Robeson, Tim Ryan
Dentinger, Stephen	TN: HOCH, EDWARD DENTINGER
DERBY, GEORGE HORATIO	PN: Squibob
DERLETH, AUGUST WILLIAM	PN: Stephen Grendon, Tally Mason
DESMARAIS, OVIDE E.	PN: Ovid Demaris
Destry, Vince	TN: NORWOOD, VICTOR GEORGE CHARLES
Deveraux, Jude	TN: WHITE, JUDE GILLIAM
DEVINE, DAVID MC DONALD	PN: Dominic Devine
Devine, Dominic	TN: DEVINE, DAVID MCDONALD
Devon, Sarah	TN: WALKER, EMILY KATHLEEN
DEWEY, THOMAS BLANCHARD	PN: Tom Brandt, Cord Wainer
Dexter, John	TN: BRADLEY, MARION ZIMMER
Dexter, Martin	TN: FAUST, FREDERICK SCHILLER
Dexter, Peter	TN: SHAVER, RICHARD SHARPE
DEY, FREDERIC MERRILL VAN RENSSELAER	PN: Nicholas Carter, Nick Carter, Marmaduke Dey, Frederic Ormond, Varick Vanardy
Dey, Marmaduke	TN: DEY, FREDERIC MERRILL VAN RENSSELAER
Di Bassetto, Corns	TN: SHAW, GEORGE BERNARD
Di Guisa, Giano	TN: PRAZ, MARIO
DI PRIMA, DIANE	PN: Sybah Darrich
DICK, PHILIP K.	PN: Richard Phillips
DICK-LAUDER, SIR GEORGE	PN: George Lauder
DICKENS, CHARLES	PN: Boz
DICKINSON, JOHN	PN: A Pennsylvania Farmer
Dickinson, Margaret	TN: MUGGESON, MARGARET ELIZABETH
Dickson,Carr	TN: CARR, JOHN DICKSON

Dickson, Carter — TN: CARR, JOHN DICKSON
DILCOCL, NOREEN — PN: Jill Christian
Dimont, Penelope — TN: MORTIMER, PENELOPE
Dinesen, Isak — TN: BLIXEN, Baroness KAREN
DISCH, THOMAS MICHAEL — PN: Thom Demijohn, Leonie Hargrave, Cassandra Knye
Dix, Dorothy — TN: GILMER, ELIZABETH M.
Dixon, Frank W. — TN: ADAMS, HARRIET STRATEMEYER
Dixon, Franklin — TN: ADAMS, HARRIET STRATEMEYER
Dixon, Paige — TN: CORCORAN, BARBARA
DIXON, ROGER — PN: John Christian, Lewis Charles
Docherty, James L. — TN: RAYMOND, RENE BRABAZON
DODGE, MARY ABAGAIL — PN: Gail Hamilton
DODGSON, CHARLES LUTWIDGE — PN: Lewis Carroll
Dogg, Professor R.L. — TN: BERMAN, ED
Dogood, Mrs. Silence — TN: FRANKLIN, BENJAMIN
Dollar, Jimmy — TN: SHAGINYAN, MARIETTA SERGEYEVNA
Dominic, R.B. — TN: HENNISART, MARTHA
Dominic, R.B. — TN: LATIS, MARY J.
Dominic, Sister Mary — TN: PARKER, MARION DOMINICA HOPE
Domino, John — TN: AVERILL, ESTHER HOLDEN
Donalds, Gordon — TN: SHIRREFFS, GORDON DONALD
Donavan, John — TN: MORLAND, NIGEL
DONNELLY, AUSTIN S. — PN: Bullen Bear
Donovan, Dick — TN: MUDDOCK, JOYCE EMMERSON PRESTON
DONOVAN, JOHN — PN: Hugh Hennessey
Dooley, Martin — TN: DUNNE, PETER FINLEY
DOOLITTLE, HILDA — PN: H.D.
Dorman, Luke — TN: BINGLEY, DAVID ERNEST
Dorset, Richard — TN: SHAVER, RICHARD SHARPE
Dorsett, Danielle — TN: DANIELS, DOROTHY
Douglas, Albert — TN: ARMSTRONG, DOUGLAS ALBERT
Douglas, Arthur — TN: MORETON, DOUGLAS ARTHUR
Douglas, Barbara — TN: OVSTEDAL, BARBARA
Douglas, Michael — TN: BRIGHT, ROBERT
Douglas, Michael — TN: CRICHTON, JOHN MICHAEL and CRICHTON, DOUGLAS
DOUGLAS, NORMAN — PN: Narmyx
Douglas, R.M. — TN: MASON, DOUGLAS RANKINE
Douglas, Thorne — TN: HAAS, BENJAMIN LEOPOLD
Dowdy, Mrs. Regera — TN: GOREY, EDWARD
Dower, Penn — TN: PENDOWER, JACQUES
Dowley, D.M. — TN: MARRISON, LESLIE WILLIAM
Downes, Quentin — TN: HARRISON, MICHAEL
DOYLE, CHARLES — PN: Mike Doyle
Doyle, Mike — TN: DOYLE, CHARLES
DRACKETT, PHIL — PN: Paul King
Draco, F. — TN: DAVIS, JULIA
DRAGO, HARRY SINCLAIR — PN: Stewart Cross, Kirk Deming, Will Ermine, Bliss Lomax, J. Wesley Putnam, Grant Sinclair

Dragonet — TN: SIMS, GEORGE R.
Drake, Joan — TN: DAVIES, JOAN H.
Draper, Hastings — TN: JEFFRIES, RODERIC
DRESSER, DAVIS — PN: Asa Baker, Matthew Blood, Kathryn Culver, Don Davis, Hal Debrett, Brett Halliday, Anthony Scott, Anderson Wayne

Drew, Nicholas — TN: HARLING, ROBERT
Drinkrow, John — TN: HARDWICK, MOLLIE
Droch — TN: BRIDGES, ROBERT
Drummond, Charles — TN: GILES, KENNETH
Drummond, Ivor — TN: LONGRIGG, ROGER ERSKINE
Drummond, J. — TN: CHANCE, NEWTON
Drummond, V.H. — TN: SWETENHAM, MRS. ANTHONY
Drummond, Violet Hilda — TN: SWETENHAM, MRS. ANTHONY
DRURY, MAXINE COLE — PN: Don Creighton
Dryden, Lennox — TN: STEEN, MARGUERITE
Duvaul, Virginia C. — TN: COFFMAN, VIRGINIA EDITH
Dubois, Charles — TN: COUNSELMAN, MARY ELIZABETH

Dubois, M.   TN: KENT, ARTHUR
DUCHACEK, IVO   PN: Ivo Duka
Dudley, Helen   TN: HOPE-SIMPSON, JACYNTH
Dudley, Nancy   TN: TAYLOR, LOIS DWIGHT
Dudley-Gordon, Tom   TN: BARKER, DUDLEY
Dudley-Gordon, Tom   TN: CAMPBELL, GORDON
Dudley-Gordon, Tom   TN: GUTHRIE, TOM
Dudley-Smith, T.   TN: TREVOR, ELLESTON
DUFAULT, JOSEPH ERNEST
   NEPHTALI   PN: Will James
Duka, Ivo   TN: DUCHACEK, IVO D.
DUKE, MADELAINE   PN: Alex Duncan
Duke, Will   TN: GAULT, WILLIAM CAMPBELL
Dumas, Claudine   TN: MALZBERG, BARRY NORMAN
DUNBOYNE, Lord   PN: Patrick Butler
Duncan, Alex   TN: DUKE, MADELAINE
DUNCAN, ROBERT LIPSCOMB   PN: James Hall Roberts
DUNCAN, Mr.& Mrs. ROBERT   PN: W.R. Duncan
Duncan, W.R.   TN: DUNCAN, Mr. & Mrs. ROBERT L.
DUNCAN, WILLIAM MURDOCH   PN: John Cassells, John Dallas, Neill Graham, Martin
                                                  Locke, Peter Malloch, Lovat Marshall

DUNKERLEY, ELSIE JEANNETTE   PN: Elsie Oxenham
DUNLOP, AGNES M.R.   PN: Elisabeth Kyle, Jan Ralston
DUNMORE, JOHN   PN: Jason Calder
DUNNE, PETER FINLEY   PN: Martin Dooley
DUNNETT, DOROTHY   PN: Dorothy Halliday
Dunsany, Lord   TN: PLUNKETT, EDWARD JOHN MORETON DRAX
DUPIN, ARMANDINE AURORE   PN: George Sand
Duplex   TN: BRADLEY, IAN
Duplex   TN: HALLOWS, N.F.
Dupont, Paul   TN: FREWIN, LESLIE
Durham, Anne   TN: WALKER, EMILY KATHLEEN
Durham, David   TN: VICKERS, ROY C.
Durrant, Sheila   TN: GROVES, SHEILA
Durrant, Theo   TN: WHITE, WILLIAM ANTHONY PARKER
DURRELL, LAWRENCE GEORGE   PN: Charles Norden
DURST, PAUL   PN: Peter Bannon, John Chelton, Jeff Cochran, John Shane
Dustin, Charles   TN: GIESY, JOHN ULRICH
Duval, Jeanne   TN: COFFMAN, VIRGINIA EDITH
Duvaul, Virginia C.   TN: COFFMAN, VIRGINIA EDITH
Dwight, Allan   TN: TAYLOR, LOIS DWIGHT
Dwyer, K.R.   TN: KOONTZ, DEAN RAY
Dykes, Jack   TN: OWEN, JACK
Dymoke, Juliet   TN: DE SCHANSCHIEFF, JULIET DYMOKE

E

E.V.L.   TN: LUCAS, E.V.
E.W.H.   TN: HORNUNG, ERNEST WILLIAM
Eaglesfield, Francis   TN: GUIRDHAM, ARTHUR
Earle, William   TN: JOHNS, WILLIAM EARLE
Earp, Virgil   TN: KEEVIL, HENRY JOHN
EAST, FRED   PN: Roy Manning, Tom West
East, Michael   TN: WEST, MORRIS
Eastway, Edward   TN: THOMAS, EDWARD
Easton, Edward   TN: MALERICH, EDWARD P.
EBEL, SUZANNE   PN: Suzanne Goodwin, Cecily Shelbourne
EBERT, ARTHUR FRANK   PN: Frank Arthur
EDEN, DOROTHY   PN: Mary Paradise
Edgar, Josephine   TN: MUSSI, MARY
EDGINTON, HELEN MARION   PN: May Edginton
Edginton, May   TN: EDGINTON, HELEN MARION
Edmonds, Charles   TN: CARRINGTON, CHARLES EDMUND
Edmondson, G.C.   TN: COTTON, JOSE MARIO GARRY ORDONEZ
                                                  EDMONDSON Y

EDSON, JOHN THOMAS   PN: Rod Denver, Chuck Nolan

EDWARDS, LEO   PN: Edward Edson Lee
Edwards, Norman   TN: CARR, TERRY GENE
Edwards, Norman   TN: WHITE, THEODORE EDWIN
Edwards, Phoebe   TN: BLOCH, BARBARA
Edwards, Samuel   TN: GERSON, NOEL
Egan, Leslie   TN: LININGTON, BARBARA ELIZABETH
Egbert, H.M.   TN: EMANUEL, VICTOR ROUSSEAU
EGLETON, CLIVE   PN: Patrick Blake, John Tarrant
Eisner, Simon   TN: KORNBLUTH, CYRIL M.
El Dnomyar, Evreh Eniatnof   TN: LE FONTAINE, JOSEPH RAYMOND HERVÉ
Elbertus, Fra   TN: HUBBARD, ELBERT
Elder, Art   TN: MONTGOMERY, RUTHERFORD GEORGE
Elder, Evelyn   TN: BURGE, MILWARD RODON KENNEDY
ELDERSHAW, FLORA SYDNEY
  PATRICIA   PN: M. Barnard Eldershaw
Eldershaw, M. Barnard   TN: BARNARD, MARJORIE FAITH
Eldershaw, M. Barnard   TN: ELDERSHAW, FLORA SYDNEY PATRICIA
Elgin, Mary   TN: STEWART, DOROTHY MARY
Elia   TN: LAMB, CHARLES
Eliot, Anne   TN: TAYLOR, LOIS DWIGHT
Eliot, George   TN: EVANS, MARIAN (MARY ANN CROSS?)
Elizabeth   TN: RUSSELL, Countess MARY ANNETTE VON ARNIM
     BEAUCHAMP
Ellanby, Boyd   TN: BOYD, WILLIAM C.
ELLERBECK, ROSEMARY ANNE
  L'ESTRANGE   PN: Anna L'Estrange, Nicola Thorne, Katherine Yorke
ELLES, DORA AMY   PN: Patricia Wentworth
Elliot, Asa   TN: BLINDER, ELLIOT
Ellis, Louise   TN: WALKER, EMILY KATHLEEN
Ellis, Olivia   TN: FRANCIS, ANNE
ELLISON, VIRGINIA TIER   PN: Virginia Tier Howard
ELMORE, ERNEST CARPENTER   PN: John Bude
Elphinstone, Francis   TN: POWELL-SMITH, VINCENT
Elsna, Hebe   TN: ANSLE, DOROTHY PHOEBE
Elson, R.N.   TN: NELSON, RAY RADELL FARADAY
EMANUEL, VICTOR ROUSSEAU   PN: H.M. Egbert, Victor Rousseau
Embey, Philip   TN: PHILIPP, ELLIO ELIAS
Emsley, Clare   TN: PLUMMER, CLARE EMSLEY
English, Richard   TN: SHAVER, RICHARD SHARPE
Engren, Edith   TN: MC CAIG, ROBERT JESSE
Erickson, Walter   TN: FAST, HOWARD MELVIN
Ermine, Will   TN: DRAGO, HARRY SINCLAIR
ERNST, PAUL   PN: Kenneth Robeson
ERNST, PAUL FREDERICK   PN: Paul Frederick Stern
Erskine, Margaret   TN: WILLIAMS, MARGARET WETHERBY
Erskine, Rosalind   TN: LONGRIGG, ROGER ERSKINE
Esmond, Harriet   TN: BURKE, JOHN FREDERICK
Esohg, Lama   TN: GHOSE, AMAL
Essex, Mary   TN: BLOOM, URSULA HARVEY
Esteven, John   TN: SHELLABARGER, SAMUEL
Estoril, Jean   TN: ALLAN, MABEL ESTHER
ESTRIDGE, ROBIN   PN: Philip Loraine
Eton, Robert   TN: MEYNELL, LAURENCE WALTER
ETCHISON, BIRDIE L.   PN: Leigh Hunter
Euphan   TN: TODD, BARBARA EUPHAN
Eustace, Robert   TN: BARTON, EUSTACE ROBERT
Evan, Paul   TN: LEHMAN, PAUL EVAN
Evans, Evan   TN: FAUST, FREDERICK SCHILLER
Evans, Evan   TN: STOKER, ALAN
Evans, Frances   TN: CARTER, FRANCES MONET
EVANS, JULIA   PN: Polly Hobson
Evans, Tabor   TN: KNOTT, WILLIAM C.
EVELYN, JOHN MICHAEL   PN: Michael Underwood
Everett, Wade   TN: LUTZ, GILES ALFRED
Everett, Wade   TN: COOK, WILLIAM EVERETT
EVERETT-GREEN, EVELYN   PN: Cecil Adair, Evelyn Dare, H.F.E.

Ewing, Frederick R.	TN: WALDO, EDWARD HAMILTON
Excellent, Matilda	TN: FARSON, DANIEL NEGLEY
Eyre, Annette	TN: WORBOYS, ANNETTE ISOBEL

F

F.O.O.	TN: STREET, CECIL JOHN CHARLES
Fabrizius, Peter	TN: FABRY, JOSEPH B.
Fair, A.A.	TN: GARDNER, ERLE STANLEY
Fairbairn, Roger	TN: CARR, JOHN DICKSON
Faire, Zabrina	TN: STEVENSON, FLORENCE
FAIRFIELD, CICILY ISABEL	PN: Rebecca West
Fairfield, John	TN: LIVINGSTONE, HARRISON EDWARD
FAIRMAN, PAUL W.	PN: Adam Chase, Ivor Jorgensen, Lester Del Rey
Falk, Lee	TN: COPPER, BASIL
Falkirk, Richard	TN: LAMBERT, DEREK
Fallon, Martin	TN: PATTERSON, HENRY
Falstaff, Jake	TN: FETZER, HERMAN
Family Doctor, A	TN: HUTCHIN, KENNETH CHARLES
FANTONI, BARRY	PN: Sylvie Krin
Farely, Alison	TN: POLAND, DOROTHY
Fargo, Doone	TN: NORWOOD, VICTOR GEORGE CHARLES
FARIGOULE, LOUIS	PN: Jules Romains
Farley, Ralph Milne	TN: HOAR, ROGER SHERMAN
FARMER, PHILIP JOSE	PN: Kilgore Trout
Farndale, James	TN: FARNDALE, W.A.J.
Farquharson, Martha	TN: FINLEY, MARTHA F.
Farr, John	TN: WEBB, JACK
Farrell, Ben	TN: CEBULASH, MEL
Farrell, David	TN: SMITH, FREDERICK E.
Farrell, John Wade	TN: MacDONALD, JOHN DANN
Farrow, James S.	TN: TUBB, EDWIN CHARLES
FARSON, DANIEL NEGLEY	PN: Matilda Excellent
Farson, Negley	TN: FARSON, DANIEL NEGLEY
FAST, HOWARD MELVIN	PN: E.V. Cunningham, Walter Ericson
Faulis, Hugh	TN: MUNRO, NEIL
FAUST, FREDERICK SCHILLER	PN: Frank Austin, George Owen Baxter, Max Brand, Walter C. Butler, George Challis, Peter Dawson, Martin Dexter, Evan Evans, John Frederick, Frederick Frost, David Manning, Peter Henry Morland, Hugh Owen, Nicholas Silver
FEARN, JOHN RUSSELL	PN: Geoffrey Armstrong, Thornton Ayre, Hugo Blayn, Dennis Clive, John Cotton, Polton Cross, Astron Del Martia, Mark Denholm, Volsted Gridban, Timothy Hayes, Conrad G. Holt, Frank Jones, Paul Lorraine, Dom Passante, Laurence F. Rose, Doorn Sclanders, Joan Seager, Bryan Shaw, John Slate, Vargo Statten, K. Thomas, Earl Titan, Arthur Waterhouse, John Wernheim, Ephriam Winiki
Fecamps, Elise	TN: CREASEY, JOHN
Fecher, Constance	TN: HEAVEN, CONSTANCE
Feikema, Feike	TN: MANFRED, FREDERICK FEIKEMA
FEILDING, DOROTHY	PN: A. Fielding, A.E. Fielding
FEINBERG, BEA	PN: Cynthia Freeman
FELLIG, ARTHUR	PN: Weegee
Fellowes, Anne	TN: MANTLE, WINIFRED LANGFORD
FELTON, RONALD OLIVER	PN: Ronald Welsh
Fenner, Carol	TN: WILLIAMS, CAROL
Fenner, James R.	TN: TUBB, EDWIN CHARLES
Fenton, Mark	TN: NORWOOD, VICTOR GEORGE CHARLES
Fenwick, Elizabeth	TN: WAY, ELIZABETH FENWICK
Fenwick, E.P.	TN: WAY, ELIZABETH FENWICK
Ferguson, Evelyn	TN: NEVIN, EVELYN C.
Ferguson, Helen	TN: WOODS, HELEN
Fern, Fanny	TN: WILLIS, SARA PAYSON (SARA P. PARTON?)
Fernandez, Happy Craven	TN: FERNANDEZ, GLADYS CRAVEN

Ferrars, Elizabeth	TN: BROWN, MORNA DORIS
Ferrars, E.X.	TN: BROWN, MORNA DORIS
Ferrat, Jacques Jean	TN: MERWIN, SAMUEL KIMBALL, JR.
FETZER, HERMAN	PN: Jake Falstaff
Fiacc, Padraic	TN: O'CONNOR, PATRICK JOSEPH
FICHTER, GEORGE S.	PN: George Kensinger
Field, Gans T.	TN: WELLMAN, MANLEY WADE
Field, Peter	TN: MINES, SAMUEL
Field, Peter	TN: REPP, EDWARD EARL
Fielding, A.	TN: FIELDING, DOROTHY
Fielding, A.E.	TN: FIELDING, DOROTHY
Fielding, Hubert	TN: SCHONFIELD, HUGH JOSEPH
Fielding, Xan	TN: FIELDING, A.W.
Finch, Matthew	TN: FINK, MERTON
Finch, Merton	TN: FINK, MERTON
Finlay, William	TN: MACKAY, JAMES ALEXANDER
Finn, Mickey	TN: JARROLD, ERNEST
Finnegan, Robert	TN: RYAN, PAUL WILLIAM
Finney, Jack	TN: FINNEY, WALTER BRADEN
FINNEY, WALTER BRADEN	PN: Jack Finney
FINNIN, MARY	PN: John Hogarth
FISCHER, BRUNO	PN: Russell Gray
FISH, ROBERT L.	PN: A.C. Lamprey, Robert L. Pike, Lawrence Roberts
Fisher, A.E.	TN: FISHER, EDWARD
FISHER, STEPHEN GOULD	PN: Steve Fisher, Stephen Gould, Grant Lane
Fisher, Steve	TN: FISHER, STEPHEN GOULD
Fisher, Wade	TN: NORWOOD, VICTOR GEORGE CHARLES
Fiske, Sharon	TN: HILL, PAMELA
Fitt, Mary	TN: FREEMAN, KATHLEEN
Fitzalan, Roger	TN: TREVOR, ELLESTON
Fitz-Boodle, George	TN: THACKERY, WILLIAM MAKEPEACE
Fitzgerald, Barbara	TN: NEWMAN, MONA ALICE JEAN
Fitzgerald, Hugh	TN: BAUM, LYMAN FRANK
Fitzgerald, Julia	TN: WATSON, JULIA
Fitznoodle	TN: VALLENTINE, B.B.
Flannery, Sean	TN: HAGBERG, DAVID J.
Fleming, Caroline	TN: MATHER, ANNE
Fleming, Oliver	TN: MacDONALD, PHILIP
Fletcher, George U.	TN: PRATT, MURRAY FLETCHER
FLOREN, LEE	PN: Claudia Hall, Matthew Whitman Harding, Felix Lee Horton, Jason Stuart, Grace Lang, Marguerite Nelson, Lew Smith, Maria Sandra Sterling, Lee Thomas, Len Turner, Will Watson, Dave Wilson
Flying Officer "X"	TN: BATES, H.E.
Flynn, Jackson	TN: SHIRREFFS, GORDON DONALD
Foda, Aun	TN: FOXE, ARTHUR NORMAN
Foley, Rae	TN: DENNISTON, ELINORE
FOLSOM, FRANKLIN BREWSTER	PN: Lyman Hopkins
Forbes, Daniel	TN: KENYON, MICHAEL
Forbes, D.E.	TN: FORBES, DELORIS FLORINE STANTON
FORBES, DELORIS FLORINE STANTON	PN: De Forbes, D.E. Forbes, Forbes Rydell, Tobias Wells
Ford, David	TN: HARKNETT, TERRY WILLIAMS
Ford, Elbur	TN: HIBBERT, ELEANOR ALICE
Ford, Elizabeth	TN: BIDWELL, MARJORY ELIZABETH SARAH
Ford, Ford Maddox	TN: HUEFFER, FORD MADOX
Ford, Elizabeth	TN: BIDWELL, MARJORY ELIZABETH SARAH
Ford, Hilary	TN: YOUD, CHRISTOPHER SAMUEL
Ford, Kirk	TN: SPENCE, WILLIAM JOHN DUNCAN
Ford, Leslie	TN: BROWN, ZENITH
Ford, Norrey	TN: DILCOCK, NOREEN
Forrest, Norman	TN: MORLAND, NIGEL
Forman, Ginny	TN: ZACHERY, HUGH
Forrest, Felix C.	TN: LINEBARGER, PAUL MYRON ANTHONY
Forrest, Norman	TN: MORLAND, NIGEL
Forrester, Frank	TN: HERBERT, HENRY WILLIAM

Forrester, Mary — TN: HUMPHRIES, ELSIE MARY
FOSDICK, CHARLES AUSTIN — PN: H.C. Castlemon, Harry Castlemon
Fosse, Alfred — TN: JELLY, GEORGE OLIVER
Foster, George — TN: HASWELL, CHETWYND JOHN DRAKE
Foster, Iris — TN: POSNER, RICHARD
Foster, Richard — TN: CROSSEN, KENDALL FOSTER
Foster, Simon — TN: GLEN, DUNCAN
Foulds, E.V. — TN: FOULDS, ELFRIDA VIPONT
FOULDS, ELFRIDA VIPONT — PN: E.V. Foulds, Charles Vipont, Elfrida Vipont
Fowler, Sydney — TN: WRIGHT, SYDNEY FOWLER
Fox, Anthony — TN: FULLERTON, ALEXANDER
FOX, GARDNER FRANCIS — PN: Jeff Cooper, Jefferson Cooper, Jeffrey Gardner, James Kendricks, Simon Majoro, Kevin Matthews, Bart Somers

FOX, NORMAN ARNOLD — PN: Mark Sabin
Fox, Petronella — TN: BALOGH, PENELOPE
Foxx, Jack — TN: PRONZINI, BILL
Fra Elbertus — TN: HUBBARD, ELBERT
France, Anatole — TN: THIBAULT, JACQUES ANATOLE FRANCOIS
Francis, C.D.E. — TN: HOWARTH, PATRICK
FRANKEN, ROSE DOROTHY — PN: Margaret Grant, Franken Meloney
FRANKLIN, BENJAMIN — PN: Father Abraham, Anthony Affluent, The Busybody, A Good Conscience, Mrs. Silence Dogood, Philomath, Echo Proteus Esquire, Richard Saunders

Franklin, Max — TN: DEMING, RICHARD
Fraser, Jane — TN: PILCHER, ROSAMUNDE
FRAZEE, CHARLES STEVE — PN: Dean Jennings
Frazer, Andrew — TN: LESSER, MILTON
Frazer, Robert Caine — TN: CREASEY, JOHN
Frazier, Arthur — TN: BULMER, HENRY KENNETH
Frederic, Mike — TN: COX, WILLIAM ROBERT
Frederick, John — TN: FAUST, FREDERICK SCHILLER
Fredricks, Dr. Frank — TN: FRANCK, FREDERICK
FREEDGOOD, MORTON — PN: John Godey, Stanley Morton
Freeman, Cynthia — TN: FEINBERG, BEA
FREEMAN, KATHLEEN — PN: Mary Fitt, Stuart Mary Wick
FREEMAN, RICHARD AUSTIN — PN: Clifford Ashdown
Freeman, Thomas — TN: FEHRENBACH, T.R.
FREEMANTLE, BRIAN HARRY — PN: John Maxwell
French, Ashley — TN: ROBINS, DENISE NAOMI
French, Paul — TN: ASIMOV, ISAAC
FREWER, GLYN — PN: Mervyn Lewis
FREWIN, LESLIE — PN: Paul Dupont
FREYBE, HEIDI HUBERTA — PN: Martha Albrand, Katrin Holland, Christine Lambert
Freyer, Fredric — TN: BALLINGER, WILLIAM SANBORN
Frick, C.H. — TN: IRWIN, CONSTANCE
Friedman, Elias — TN: FRIEDMAN, JACOB HORACE
Friedman, John — TN: FRIEDMAN, JACOB HORACE
Frome, David — TN: BROWN, ZENITH
Frost, Frederick, — TN: FAUST, FREDERICK SCHILLER
Froy, Herald — TN: DEGHY, GUY
Froy, Herald — TN: WATERHOUSE, KEITH
FRY, CHRISTOPHER — PN: Christopher Harris
Furey, Michael — TN: WARD, ARTHUR HENRY SARSFIELD
FYFE, HORACE BROWNE — PN: Andrew Mac Duff

G

G.K.C. — TN: CHESTERTON, GILBERT KEITH
Gade, Henry — TN: PALMER, RAYMOND A.
Gage, Wilson — TN: STEELE, MARY QUINTARD
Gainham, Sarah — TN: AMES, SARAH RACHEL
Gaite, Francis — TN: COLES, CYRIL HENRY
Gaite, Francis — TN: MANNING, ADELAIDE FRANCIS OKE
Galaxan, Sol — TN: COPPEL, ALFRED
GALLUN, RAYMOND ZINKE — PN: William Callahan
GALSWORTHY, JOHN — PN: John Sinjohn

Galway, Robert Conington — TN: MC CUTCHAN, DONALD PHILIP
GANDLEY, KENNETH ROYCE — PN: Oliver Jacks, Kenneth Royce
Gant, Richard — TN: FREEMANTLE, BRIAN
Gard, Janice — TN: REEVES, JOYCE
Gard, Joyce — TN: REEVES, JOYCE
Garden, Bruce — TN: MACKAY, JAMES ALEXANDER
GARDNER, ERLE STANLEY — PN: A.A. Fair, Charles M. Green, Carleton Kendrake, Charles J. Kenny, Robert Park, Les Tillray

Gardner, Jeffrey — TN: FOX, GARDNER FRANCIS
Gardner, Miriam — TN: BRADLEY, MARION ZIMMER
GARFIELD, BRIAN FRANCIS WYNNE — PN: Bennett Garland, Alex Hawk, John Ives, Drew Mallory, Frank O'Brian, Jonas Ward, Brian Wynne, Frank Wynne

Garland, Bennett — TN: GARFIELD, BRIAN FRANCIS WYNNE
Garner, Rolf — TN: BERRY, BRYAN
Garnett, Mary Clew — TN: HAINS, T. JENKINS
Garnett, Roger — TN: MORLAND, NIGEL
Garrett, Gordon — TN: GARRETT, RANDALL PHILLIP
GARRETT, RANDALL PHILLIP — PN: Gordon Aghaill, Grandall Barretton, Alexander Blade, Alfred Blake, Andrew Blake, Walter Bupp, Ralph Burke, Gordon Garrett, David Gordon, Richard Greer, Laurence M. Janifer, Larry Mark Harris, Ivar Jorgensen, Darrel T. Langart, Clyde T. Mitchell, Mark Phillips, Robert Randall, Leonard G. Spencer, S.M. Tenneshaw, Gerald Vance, Barbara Wilson

Garrison, Frederick — TN: SINCLAIR, UPTON
Garth, Will — TN: KUTTNER, HENRY
Garve, Andrew — TN: WINTERTON, PAUL
GARVICE, CHARLES — PN: Charles Gibson, Caroline Hart
Gascoigne, Marguerite — TN: LAZARUS, MARGUERITE
Gast, Kelly P. — TN: COTTON, JOSE MARIO GARRY ORDONEZ EDMONDSON Y

Gaston, Bill — TN: GASTON, WILLIAM JAMES
GAULDEN, RAY — PN: Wesley Ray
GAULT, WILLIAM CAMPBELL — PN: Will Duke
Gay, Amelia — TN: HOGARTH, GRACE
Gayle, Emma — TN: FAIRBURN, ELEANOR
GEACH, CHRISTINE — PN: Elizabeth Dawson, Anne Lowing
Gearing-Thomas, G. — TN: NORWOOD, VICTOR GEORGE CHARLES
GEISEL, THEODOR SEUSS — PN: Theo Le Sieg, Seuss, Dr. Seuss
GELLIS, ROBERTA LEAH — PN: Max Daniels, Priscilla Hamilton, Leah Jacobs
George, Eliot — TN: FREEMAN, GILLIAN
George, Eugene — TN: CHEVALIER, PAUL EUGENE GEORGE
George, Jonathan — TN: BURKE, JOHN FREDRICK
GEORGE, PETER BRYAN — PN: Peter Bryant, Bryan Peters
GERMANO, PETER B. — PN: Jack Bertin, Barry Cord, Jim Kane
GERSON, NOEL — PN: Samuel Edwards
Gibb, Lee — TN: DEGHY, GUY
Gibb, Lee — TN: WATERHOUSE, KEITH
Gibbons, Margaret — TN: MAC GILL, Mrs. PATRICK MARGARET
Gibbs, Henry — TN: RUMBOLD-GIBBS, HENRY ST. JOHN CLAIR
Gibbs, Mary Ann — TN: BIDWELL, MARJORY ELIZABETH SARAH
Gibson, Charles — TN: GARVICE, CHARLES
Gibson, Josephine — TN: JOSLIN, SESLYE
Gibson, Josephine — TN: HINE, AL
Gibson, Josephine — TN: JOSLIN, SESYLE
GIBSON, WALTER B. — PN: Ishi Black, Douglas Brown, Maxwell Grant, Maborushi Kineji

GIESY, JOHN ULRICH — PN: Charles Dustin
GIGGAL, KENNETH — PN: Angus Ross
Gilbert, Anna — TN: MARGUERITE LAZARUS
Gilbert, Anthony — TN: MALLESON, LUCY BEATRICE
Gilbert, Manu — TN: WEST, JOYCE
Gilbert, Miriam — TN: PRESBERG, MIRIAM
Gilbert, Nan — TN: GILBERTSON, MILDRED
Gilbert, Sister Mary — TN: DE FREES, MADELINE

GILES, KENNETH — PN: Charles Drummond, Edmund McGirr
GILKYSON, BERNICE KENYON — PN: Bernice Kenyon
Gill, Patrick — TN: CREASEY, JOHN
Gillen, Lucy — TN: STRATTON, REBECCA
Gillette, Bob — TN: SHAW, BYNUM G.
Gilman, George C. — TN: HARKNETT, TERRY WILLIAMS
Gilman, Robert Cham — TN: COPPEL, ALFRED
GILMER, ELIZABETH M. — PN: Dorothy Dix
Gilmore, Anthony — TN: BATES, HARRY HIRAM GILMORE, III
GILMORE, JAMES R. — PN: Edmuns Kirke
Giovanni, Nicki — TN: GIOVANNI, YOLANDE C.
GIOVANNI, YOLANDE C. — PN: Nicki Giovanni
GIPIUS, ZINAIDA — PN: Zinaida Hippius
Gissing, George — TN: GLOUSTON, J. STORER
Glamis, Walter — TN: SCHACHNER, NATHAN
Glaser, Comstock — TN: GLASER, KURT
GLASKIN, G.M. — PN: Neville Jackson
GLASSCO, JOHN — PN: Jean De Saint-Luc
GLASSCOCK, ANNE — PN: Michael Bonner
GLIDDEN, FREDERICK DILLEY — PN: Luke Short
GLIDDEN, JONATHAN H. — PN: Peter Dawson
GLUT, DON F. — PN: Johnny Jason, Mick Rogers
Goaman, Muriel — TN: COX, EDITH MURIEL
Godey, John — TN: FREEGOOD, MORTON
GODFREY, LIONEL — PN: Elliott Kennedy
Godfrey, William — TN: YOUD, CHRISTOPHER SAMUEL
Goforth, Ellen — TN: FRANCIS, DOROTHY BRENNER
GOLDMAN, WILLIAM — PN: Harry Longbaugh
GOLDSTEIN, ARTHUR DAVID — PN: Albert Ross
Goldstone, A. — TN: GOLDSTONE, LAWRENCE ARTHUR
GOLDSTONE, LAWRENCE ARTHUR — PN: A. Goldstone, Lawrence Treat
GOODEN, ARTHUR HARRY — PN: Brett Rider
GOODRICH, SAMUEL B.F. — PN: Peter Parley
Goodwin, Suzanne — TN: EBEL, SUZANNE
GORDON, CHARLES WILLIAM — PN: Ralph Connor
Gordon, David — TN: GARRETT, RANDALL PHILLIP
Gordon, Diana — TN: ANDREWS, LUCILLA MATHEW
Gordon, Donald — TN: PAYNE, DONALD GORDON
Gordon, Fritz — TN: JARVIS, FREDERICK G.H.
GORDON, GORDON — PN: The Gordons
Gordon, Jane — TN: LEE, ELSIE
Gordon, Katharine — TN: PEARSON, KATHARINE
GORDON, MILDRED — PN: The Gordons
Gordon, Ray — TN: WAINWRIGHT, GORDON RAY
Gordon, Rex — TN: HOUGH, STANLEY BENNETT
GORDON, RICHARD — PN: Stuart Gordon, Alex R. Stuart
Gordon, Stewart — TN: SHIRREFFS, GORDON DONALD
Gordon, Stuart — TN: GORDON, RICHARD
Gordons, The — TN: GORDON, MILDRED
Gordons, The — TN: GORDON, GORDON
GOREY, EDWARD — PN: Edward Bluting, Mrs. Regera Dowdy, Redway Grode, O. Mude, Ogdred Weary, Dreary Wodge
Gorham, Michael — TN: FOLSOM, FRANKLIN BREWSTER
Gorky (Gorki?), Maxim — TN: PESHKOV, ALEXEL MAXIMOVITCH
Gorman, Ginny — TN: ZACHARY, HUGH
Gorsline, S.M. — TN: GORSLINE, MARIE
Goryan, Sirak — TN: SAROYAN, WILLIAM
Gottesman, S.D. — TN: LOWNDES, ROBERT AUGUSTINE WARD
Gottschalk, Laura Riding — TN: JACKSON, Mrs. SCHUYLER B.
GOULART, RONALD JOSEPH — PN: Josephine Kains, Julian Kearney, Howard Lee, Kenneth Robeson, Frank S. Shawn, Con Steffanson
Gould, Alan — TN: CANNING, VICTOR
Gould, Stephen — TN: FISHER, STEPHEN GOULD
GOVAN, CHRISTINE NOBLE — PN: J.N. Darby
GOYDER, MARGOT — PN: Margot Neville
Graaf, Peter — TN: YOUD, CHRISTOPHER SAMUEL

GRABER, GEORGE ALEXANDER	PN: Cordell Alexander
Graduate Of Oxford, A	TN: RUSKIN, JOHN
Grady, Tex	TN: WEBB, JACK
Graeme, Bruce	TN: JEFFRIES, GRAHAM MONTAGUE
Graeme, David	TN: JEFFRIES, GRAHAM MONTAGUE
Graeme, Roderic	TN: JEFFRIES, RODERIC
Graham, Charles S.	TN: TUBBS, EDWIN CHARLES
Graham, Ennis	TN: MOLESWORTH, MARY LOUISA
Graham, James	TN: PATTERSON, HENRY
Graham, Neill	TN: DUNCAN, WILLIAM MURDOCH
Graham, Robert	TN: HALDEMAN, JOE WILLIAM
GRAHAM, ROGER PHILLIPS	PN: Clinton Ames, Robert Arnette, Franklin Bahl, Alexander Blade, Craig Browning, Gregg Conrad, P.F. Costello, Inez Mc Gowan, Rog Phillips, Melva Rogers, Chester Ruppert, William Carter Sawtelle: A.R. Steber, Gerald Vance, Peter Worth
Graham, Tom	TN: LEWIS, HARRY SINCLAIR
Granados, Paul	TN: KENT, ARTHUR
Grandower, Elissa	TN: WAUGH, HILLARY BALDWIN
Grange, Peter	TN: NICOLE, CHRISTOPHER ROBIN
Granite, Tony	TN: POLITELLA, DARIO
Grant, Ambrose	TN: RAYMOND, RENE BRABAZON
Grant, Anthony	TN: PARES, MARION STAPYLTON
Grant, Landon	TN: GRIBBLE, LEONARD REGINALD
Grant, Margaret	TN: FRANKEN, ROSE DOROTHY
Grant, Maxwell	TN: GIBSON, WALTER B.
Grant, Maxwell	TN: LYNDS, DENNIS
Grantland, Keith	TN: NUTT, CHARLES
GRAVES, ROBERT RANKE	PN: Barbara Rich
Graves, Valerie	TN: BRADLEY, MARION ZIMMER
Gray, Angela	TN: DANIELS, DOROTHY
Gray, Berkeley	TN: BROOKS, EDWY SEARLES
Gray, Dorothy Kate	TN: HAYNES, DOROTHY K.
Gray, Dulcie	TN: DENISON, DULCIE WINIFRED CATHERINE
Gray, Elizabeth Janet	TN: VINING, ELIZABETH GRAY
Gray, Ellington	TN: JACOB, NAOMI ELLINGTON
Gray, Harriet	TN: ROBINS, DENISE NAOMI
Gray, Jane	TN: EVANS, CONSTANCE MAY
GRAY, PEARL ZANE	PN: Zane Grey
Gray, Russell	TN: FISHER, BRUNO
Grayson, David	TN: BAKER, RAY STANNARD
Great Merlini, The	TN: RAWSON, CLAYTON
Greaves, Richard	TN: MC CUTCHEON, GEORGE BARR
Green, Charles M.	TN: GARDNER, ERLE STANLEY
GREEN, PETER	PN: Denis Delaney
GREENE, SIGRID	PN: Sigrid De Lima
GREENWOOD, EDWARD ALISTER	PN: Ted Greenwood
Greenwood, Grace	TN: LIPPINCOTT, SARA JANE
Greenwood, Ted	TN: GREENWOOD, EDWARD ALISTER
Greer, Francesca	TN: JANAS, FRANKIE-LEE
GREER, GERMAINE	PN: Rose Blight
Greer, Richard	TN: GARRETT, RANDALL PHILLIP
Gregory, John	TN: HOSKINS, ROBERT
Gregory, Stephen	TN: PENDLETON, DONALD EUGENE
Grieg, Charles	TN: CRUICKSHANK, CHARLES GREIG
Greig, Maysie	TN: GREIG-SMITH, JENNIFER
GREIG-SMITH, JENNIFER	PN: Jennifer Ames, Ann Barclay, Maysie Greig, Mary Douglas Warre, Mary Douglas Warren
Grendon, Stephen	TN: DERLETH, AUGUST WILLIAM
Grenville, Pelham	TN: WODEHOUSE, PELHAM GRENVILLE
Grex, Leo	TN: GRIBBLE, LEONARD REGINALD
Grey, Belinda	TN: PETERS, MAUREEN
Grey, Brenda	TN: MACKINLAY, LEILA ANTIONETTE STERLING
Grey, Carol	TN: LOWNDES, ROBERT AUGUSTINE WARD
Grey, Charles	TN: TUBB, EDWIN CHARLES
Grey, Georgina	TN: ROBY, MARY LYNN

Grey, Louis   TN: GRIBBLE, LEONARD REGINALD
Grey Owl   TN: BELANEY, ARCHIBALD STANSFELD
GRIBBLE, LEONARD REGINALD   PN: Sterry Browning, Landon Grant, Leo Grex, Louis Grey,
                                                      Dexter Muir
Gridban, Volsted   TN: FEARN, JOHN RUSSELL
Gridban, Volsted   TN: TUBB, EDWIN CHARLES
GRIERSON, EDWARD DOBBYN   PN: Brian Crowther, John P. Stevenson
Grieve, C.M.   TN: MAC DIARMID, HUGH
Griff, Alan   TN: SUDDABY, DONALD
Griffin, Andrew   TN: HECKELMANN, CHARLES NEWMAN
Griffin, David   TN: MAUGHAM, ROBERT CECIL ROMER
Griffin, Jonathan   TN: GRIFFIN, ROBERT JOHN THURLOW
Griffith, George   TN: GRIFFITH-JONES, GEORGE CHETWYND
GRIFFITH-JONES, GEORGE
   CHETWYND   PN: Levin Carnac, George Griffith, Lara, Stanton March
Grile, Dod   TN: BIERCE, AMBROSE
GRIMM, CHERRY BARBARA   PN: Cherry Wilder
Grinnell, David   TN: WOLLHEIM, DONALD ALLEN
Grode, Redway   TN: GOREY, EDWARD ST. JOHN
Groener, Carl   TN: LOWNDES, ROBERT AUGUSTINE WARD
Groves, Georgina   TN: SYMONS, DOROTHY GERALDINE
GROVES, SHEILA   PN: Sheila Durrant
GRUBER, FRANK   PN: Stephen Acre, Charles K. Boston, John K. Vedder
Gunn, Victor   TN: BROOKS, EDWY SEARLES
GUTHRIE, THOMAS ANSTEY   PN: F. Anstey, Hope Bandoff, William Monarch Jones
GUTHRIE, TOM   PN: Tom Dudley-Gordon
Gwendolyn, Jacob Tonson   TN: BENNETT, ARNOLD
GWINN, CHRISTINE MARGARET   PN: Christine Kelway

H

H.B.   TN: BELLOC, HILAIRE
H.D.   TN: DOOLITTLE, HILDA
H.F.E.   TN: EVERETT-GREEN, EVELYN
H.H.   TN: JACKSON, HELEN HUNT
HAAS, BENJAMIN LEOPOLD   PN: John Benteen, Thorne Douglas, Richard Meade
HAAVIKKO, PAAVO JUHANI   PN: Anders Lieksman
Haddon, Christopher   TN: PALMER, JOHN LESLIE
Hagar, Judith   TN: POLLEY, JUDITH ANNE
HAGBERG, DAVID J.   PN: Sean Flannery, David James
Haggard, Paul   TN: LONGSTREET, STEPHEN
Haggard, William   TN: CLAYTON, RICHARD HENRY MICHAEL
Hagon, Proscilla   TN: ALLAN, MABEL ESTHER
HALDEMAN, JOE WILLIAM   PN: Robert Graham
Hale, Michael   TN: BULLOCK, MICHAEL
Haliburton, Hugh   TN: ROBERTSON, JAMES LOGIE
HALIBURTON, THOMAS   PN: Sam Slick
Hall, Adam   TN: TREVOR, ELLESTON
Hall, Aylmer   TN: HALL, NORAH E.L.
Hall, Claudia   TN: FLOREN, LEE
Hall, Evan   TN: HALLERAN, EUGENE EDWARDS
Hall, Holworthy   TN: PORTER, HAROLD EVERETT
Hall, John Ryder   TN: ROTSLER, WILLIAM
HALL, NORAH E.L.   PN: Aylmer Hall
Hall, O.M.   TN: HALL, OAKLEY MAXWELL
HALL, OAKLEY MAXWELL   PN: O.M. Hall, Jason Manor
Hallard, Peter   TN: CATHERALL, ARTHUR
Haller, Bill   TN: BECHKO, PEGGY ANNE
HALLERAN, EUGENE EDWARDS   PN: Evan Hall
Halliday, Brett   TN: DRESSER, DAVIS
Halliday, Dorothy   TN: DUNNETT, DOROTHY
Halliday, Michael   TN: CREASEY, JOHN
HALLOWS, N.F.   PN: Duplex
Halls, Geraldine   TN: JAY, GERALDINE MARY
Hamill, Ethel   TN: WEBB, JEAN FRANCIS
HAMILTON, ALEXANDER   PN: Publius

HAMILTON, CHARLES HAROLD
    ST. JOHN   PN: Martin Clifford, Owen Conquest, Frank Richards, Hilda
                                          Richards
Hamilton, Clive   TN: LEWIS, CLIVE STAPLES
HAMILTON, EDMOND   PN: Brett Sterling
Hamilton, Gail   TN: DODGE, MARY ABAGAIL
Hamilton, Hervey   TN: ROBINS, DENISE NAOMI
Hamilton, Julia   TN: WATSON, JULIA
Hamilton, Priscilla   TN: GELLIS, ROBERTA LEAH
Hamilton, Wade   TN: FLOREN, LEE
Hamilton, William   TN: CANAWAY, W.H.
HAMMETT, SAMUEL DASHIELL   PN: Peter Collinson
Hammond, Jane   TN: POLAND, DOROTHY
Hammond, Ralph   TN: INNES, RALPH HAMMOND
Hampton, Mark   TN: NORWOOD, VICTOR GEORGE CHARLES
HANLEY, CLIFFORD   PN: Henry Calvin
Hannon, Ezra   TN: HUNTER, EVAN
HANSEN, JOSEPH   PN: Rose Brock, James Colton
HANSHEW, THOMAS W.   PN: Charlotte Mary Kinsley
HARBAGE, ALFRED BENNETT   PN: Thomas Kyd
Harbison, Robert   TN: BRYANS, ROBERT HARBISON
Hard Pan   TN: BONNER, GERALDINE
Harding, George   TN: RAUBENHEIMER, GEORGE HARDING
HARDING, LEE JOHN   PN: Harold G. Nye
Harding, Matthew Whitman TN: FLOREN, LEE
Harding, Todd   TN: REYNOLDS, DALLAS MC CORD
Harding, Wes   TN: KEEVIL, HENRY JOHN
HARDWICK, MOLLIE   PN: Mary Atkinson, John Drinkrow
HARDISON, OSBORNE B.   PN: H.O. Bennett
Hardy, Adam   TN: BULMER, HENRY KENNETH
Hardy, Laura   TN: HOLLAND, SHEILA
Hare, Cyril   TN: CLARK, ALFRED ALEXANDER GORDON
Hargrave, Leonie   TN: DISCH, THOMAS MICHAEL
HARKNETT, TERRY WILLIAMS   PN: Frank Chandler, David Ford, George G. Gilman, Jane
                                      Harman, Joseph Hedges, William M. James, Charles R.
                                      Pike, William Pine, James Russell, Thomas H. Stone,
                                      William Terry
Harlan, Glen   TN: CEBULASH, MEL
Harland, Marion   TN: TERHUNE, MARY VIRGINIA
Harle, Elizabeth   TN: ROBERTS, IRENE
Harley, John   TN: MARSH, JOHN
HARLING, ROBERT   PN: Nicholas Drew
Harman, Jane   TN: HARKNETT, TERRY WILLIAMS
Harper, Daniel   TN: BROSSARD, CHANDLER
Harriford, Daphne   TN: HARRIS, MARION ROSE
Harris, Christopher   TN: FRY, CHRISTOPHER
Harris, J.B.   TN: HARRIS, JOHN WYNDHAM PARKES LUCAS BEYNON
HARRIS, JOHN   PN: Mark Hebden, Max Hennessy
HARRIS, JOHN WYNDHAM
    PARKES LUCAS BEYNON   PN: John Beynon, J.B. Harris, Johnson Harris, John
                                      Wyndham
Harris, Johnson   TN: HARRIS, JOHN WYNDHAM PARKES LUCAS BEYNON
Harris, Larry Mark   TN: GARRETT, RANDALL PHILLIP
HARRIS, MARION ROSE   PN: Henry Charles, Daphne Harriford
Harrison, Bruce   TN: PANGBORN, EDGAR
Harrison, Chip   TN: BLOCK, LAWRENCE
HARRISON, GILBERT   PN: Sedulous
HARRISON, MICHAEL   PN: Quentin Downes
Harrison, Whit   TN: WHITTINGTON, HARRY
Harsch, Hilya   TN: JELLY, GEORGE OLIVER
Hart, Caroline   TN: GARVICE, CHARLES
Hart, Jon   TN: HARVEY, JOHN B.
Harte, Marjorie   TN: MC EVOY, MARJORIE
HARTLEY, ELLEN R.   PN: Ellen Raphael Knauff
Harvester, Simon   TN: RUMBOLD-GIBBS, HENRY ST. JOHN CLAIR
Harvey, Caroline   TN: POTTER, JOANNA

HARVEY, JOHN B.

Harvey, Rachel
HASKIN, DOROTHY C.
Hastings, Graham
HASTINGS, PHYLISS DORA
Haswell, Jock
HASWELL, CHETWYND JOHN
    DRAKE
Hatton, Julia
Havil, Anthony
Hawk, Alex
Hawk, Alex
HAWKINS, SIR ANTHONY HOPE
HAWTHORNE, JULIAN
Hay, Timothy
HAYES, JOSEPH ARNOLD
Hayes, Timothy
Haygood, G. Arnold
Hayward, Richard
Hayward, Richard
Hazard, Jack
Head, Matthew
Headley, Elizabeth
Healey, Ben
HEALEY, BENJAMIN JAMES
Heard, Gerald
HEARD, HENRY FITZGERALD
Heath, Sandra
Heath, Sharon
Heath, Veronica
HEAVEN, CONSTANCE
Hebden, Mark
Heberden, M.V.
HEBERDEN, MARY VIOLET
HECKELMANN, CHARLES NEWMAN

Hedges, Joseph
Hegan, Alice Caldwell
Hegesippus
HEILBRUN, CAROLYN GOLD
HEINLEIN, ROBERT

Held, Peter
Henderson-Howat, Gerald
Hennessey, Hugh
Hennessy, Max
HENNISSART, MARTHA
Henry, O.
Henry, Will
HENSON, JAMES MAURY
Henson, Jim
Henty, G.A.
HENTY, GEORGE ALFRED
Herald, Kathleen
Herbert, Henry K.
Herbert, John
Hermes
HERON-ALLEN, EDWARD
HERSHMAN, MORRIS
HERTZOG, EMILE
Hertzog, Peter
Hervé, Joseph
Hervey, Raymond

PN: Jon Barton, William S. Brady, L.J. Coburn, J.B. Dancer,
    Jon Hart, William M. James, James Mann, John J. Mc
    Laglen, Thom Ryder, J.D. Sandon, Jonathan White
TN: BLOOM, URSULA HARVEY
PN: Howard Clark
TN: JEFFRIES, RODERIC
PN: John Bedford, Julia Mayfield
TN: HASWELL, CHETWYND JOHN DRAKE

PN: Jock Haswell
TN: CURTIS, JULIA ANN KEMBLE
TN: PHILIPP, ELLIOT ELIAS
TN: GARFIELD, BRIAN FRANCIS WYNNE
TN: KELTON, ELMER
PN: Anthony Hope
PN: Judith Hollinshead
TN: BROWN, MARGARET WISE
PN: Joseph H. Arnold
TN: FEARN, JOHN RUSSELL
TN: SLAUGHTER, FRANK GILL
TN: KENDRICK, BAYNARD H.
TN: KENDRICK, BAYNARD HARDWICK
TN: BOOTH, EDWIN
TN: CANADAY, JOHN EDWIN
TN: CAVANNA, BETTY
TN: HEALEY, BENJAMIN JAMES
PN: Ben Healey, J.G. Jeffreys, Jeremy Sturrock
TN: HEARD, HENRY FITZGERALD
PN: Gerald Heard
TN: WILSON, SANDRA
TN: RITCHIE, CLAIRE
TN: BLACKETT, VERONICA HEATH
PN: Constance Fecher, Christina Merlin
TN: HARRIS, JOHN
TN: HEBERDEN, MARY VIOLET
PN: M.V. Heberden, Charles L. Leonard
PN: Cliff Campbell, Jackson Cole, Andrew Griffin, Charles
    Lawton, Charles Mann, Chuck Mann, Mat Rand, James
    Rourke, Charles Smith, Reeve Walker
TN: HARKNETT, TERRY WILLIAMS
TN: RICE, ALICE CALDWELL
TN: SCHONFIELD, HUGH JOSEPH
PN: Amanda Cross
PN: Anson Mac Donald, Lyle Monroe, John Riverside, Caleb
    Saunders
TN: VANCE, JOHN HOLBROOK
TN: HOWAT, GERALD
TN: DONOVAN, JOHN
TN: HARRIS, JOHN
PN: R.B. Dominic, Emma Lathen
TN: PORTER, WILLIAM SIDNEY OR SYDNEY
TN: ALLEN, HENRY WILSON
PN: Jim Henson
TN: HENSON, JAMES MAURY
TN: HENTY, GEORGE ALFRED
PN: G.A. Henty
TN: PEYTON, KATHLEEN W.
TN: KNIBBS, HENRY HERBERT
TN: BRUNDAGE, JOHN HERBERT
TN: CANAWAY, W.H.
PN: Christopher Blayre, Nora Helen Wardell
PN: Evelyn Bond
PN: Andre Maurois
TN: COOKE III, PHILIP ST. GEORGE
TN: LE FONTAINE, JOSEPH RAYMOND HERVÉ
TN: LE FONTAINE, JOSEPH RAYMOND HERVÉ

HEUMAN, WILLIAM   PN: George Kramer
Hext, Harrington   TN: PHILLPOTTS, EDEN
Heyer, Georgette   TN: Mrs. GEORGE RONALD ROUGIER
ROUGIER, Mrs. GEORGE RONALD   PN: Georgette Heyer, Stella Martin
HIBBERT, ELEANOR ALICE   PN: Eleanor Burford, Philippa Carr, Elbur Ford, Victoria
                                        Holt, Kathleen Kellow, Jean Plaidy, Ellalice Tate
HIBBS, JOHN   PN: John Blyth
Hicks, Eleanor   TN: COERR, ELEANOR BEATRICE
Higgins, Jack   TN: PATTERSON, HENRY
Highland, Dora   TN: AVALONNE, MICHAEL ANGELO JR.
HIGHSMITH, PATRICIA   PN: Claire Morgan
HILDICK, E.W.   PN: Wallace Hildick
Hildick, Wallace   TN: HILDICK, E.W.
Hill, Alexis   TN: CRAIG, MARY FRANCIS
HILL, CHRISTOPHER   PN: K.E. Holme
Hill, H. Haverstock   TN: WALSH, JAMES MORGAN
Hill, James   TN: JAMESON, MARGARET STROM
Hill, Grace Livingston   TN: HILL-LUTZ, GRACE LIVINGSTON
HILL, PAMELA   PN: Sharon Fiske
HILL, REGINALD   PN: Dick Morland, Patrick Ruell, Charles Underhill
HILL-LUTZ, GRACE LIVINGSTON   PN: Grace Livingston, Grace Livingston Hill, Marcia
                                        Macdonald
HILTON, JAMES   PN: Glen Trevor
HINCKLEY, HELEN   PN: Helen Jones
Hinde, Thomas   TN: CHITTY, SIR THOMAS WILLES
HINE, AL   PN: Josephine Gibson, G.B. Kirtland
Hippius, Zinaida   TN: GIPIUS, ZINAIDA
HITCHINS, JULIA CLARA
    CATHERINE DELORES BIRK
    OLSEN   PN: Dolan Birkley, Noel Burke, D.B. Olsen
HOAR, ROGER SHERMAN   PN: Ralph Milne Farley
Hobart, Robert   TN: LEE, NORMAN
Hobart, Robertson   TN: LEE, NORMAN
Hobson, Polly   TN: EVANS, JULIA
HOCH, EDWARD DENTINGER   PN: Irwin Booth, Stephen Dentinger, Pat McMahon, R.L.
                                        Stevens, Mr. X
Hockaby, Stephen   TN: MITCHELL, GLADYS MAUDE WINIFRED
HOCKING, MONA NAOMI ANNE
    MESSER   PN: Mona Messer
HODDER-WILLIAMS, JOHN
    CHRISTOPHER GLAZEBROOK   PN: James Brogan
Hodemart, Peter   TN: AUDEMARS, PIERRE
HODGES, DORIS M.   PN: Charlotte Hunt
Hofer, Peter   TN: KORTNER, PETER
HOFF, HARRY SUMMERFIELD   PN: William Cooper
HOFFMAN, LEE   PN: Georgia York
HOGAN, ROBERT RAY   PN: Clay Ringold
Hogarth, Charles   TN: CREASEY, JOHN
HOGARTH, GRACE   PN: Grace Allen, Amelia Gay
Hogarth, John   TN: FINNIN, MARY
Hogarth, Jr.   TN: KENT, ROCKWELL
Holbrook, John   TN: VANCE, JOHN HOLBROOK
Holden, Matthew   TN: PARKINSON, ROGER
HOLDING, JAMES   PN: Ellery Queen, Jr.
HOLLAND, CECELIA ANASTASIA   PN: Elizabeth Eliot Carter
HOLLAND, ISABELLE   PN: Francesca Hunt
HOLLAND, JOSIAH   PN: Timothy Titcomb
Holland, Katrin   TN: FREYBE, HEIDI HUBERTA
Holland, Kel   TN: WHITTINGTON, HARRY
HOLLAND, SHEILA   PN: Sheila Coates, Laura Hardy, Charlotte Lamb, Sheila
                                        Lancaster
HOLLEY, MARIETTA   PN: Josiah Allen'S Wife
Hollinshead, Judith   TN: HAWTHORNE, JULIAN
Hollis, H.H.   TN: RHAMEY, BEN
Holm, Saxe   TN: JACKSON, HELEN HUNT
HOLMAN, CLARENCE HUGH   PN: Clarence Hunt

Holme, K.E. — TN: HILL, CHRISTOPHER
Holmes, A.R. — TN: BATES, HARRY HIRAM GILMORE, III
Holmes, Gordon — TN: SHIEL, MATTHEW PHIPPS
Holmes, H.H. — TN: WHITE, WILLIAM ANTHONY PARKER
Holmes, John — TN: SOUSTER, RAYMOND
Holt, Conrad G. — TN: FEARN, JOHN RUSSELL
Holt, Tex — TN: JOSCELYN, ARCHIE LYNN
Holt, Victoria — TN: HIBBERT, ELEANOR ALICE
Holton, Leonard — TN: WIBBERLEY, LEONARD PATRICK O'CONNER
Home, Michael — TN: BUSH, CHARLIE CHRISTMAS
Homes, Geoffrey — TN: MAINWARING, DANIEL
Honeyman, Brenda — TN: CLARKE, BRENDA
Hope, Anthony — TN: HAWKINS, SIR ANTHONY HOPE
Hope, Brian — TN: CREASEY, JOHN
Hope, Laura Lee — TN: ADAMS, HARRIETT STRATEMEYER
Hope, Margaret — TN: KNIGHT, ALANNA
Hope, Marion — TN: PARKER, MARION DOMINICA HOPE
Hope, Alice L. — TN: LIGHTNER, ALICE MARTHA
HOPE-SIMPSON, JACYNTH — PN: Helen Dudley
Hopf, Alice L. — TN: LIGHTNER, ALICE MARTHA
Hopkins, Lightnin' — TN: HOPKINS, SAM
Hopkins, Lyman — TN: FOLSOM, FRANKLIN BREWSTER
HOPKINS, SAM — PN: Lightnin' Hopkins
HOPKINSON, SIR HENRY THOMAS — PN: Tom Hopkinson
Hopkinson, Tom — TN: HOPKINSON, SIR HENRY THOMAS
Hopley, George — TN: HOPLEY-WOOLRICH, CORNELL GEORGE
HOPLEY-WOOLRICH, CORNELL
   GEORGE — PN: George Hopley, William Irish, Cornell Woolrich
HOPSON, WILLIAM L. — PN: John Sims
HORNE, GEOFFREY — PN: Gil North
HORNUNG, ERNEST WILLIAM — PN: E.W.H.
Horsley, David — TN: BINGLEY, DAVID ERNEST
Horton, Felix Lee — TN: FLOREN, LEE
HOSKEN, CLIFFORD JAMES
   WHEELER — PN: Richard Keverne
HOSKINS, ROBERT — PN: Grace Corren, John Gregory, Susan Jennifer, Michael
   Kerr
Houdini, Harry — TN: WEISS, EHRICH
HOUGH, RICHARD ALEXANDER — PN: Bruce Carter, Elizabeth Churchill, Pat Strong
HOUGH, STANLEY BENNETT — PN: Rex Gordon, Bennett Stanley
Houston, R.B. — TN: RAE, HUGH CRAWFORD
Howard, Captain — TN: SENARENS, LUIS PHILIP
Howard, Hartley — TN: OGNALL, LEOPOLD HORACE
Howard, Jean — TN: MAC GIBBON, JEAN
Howard, Linden — TN: MANLEY-TUCKER, AUDRIE
Howard, Mary — TN: MUSSI, MARY
HOWARD, ROBERT B. — PN: Patrick Irvin
Howard, Virginia Tier — TN: ELLISON, VIRGINIA HOWELL
HOWARTH, PAMELA — PN: Pamela Barrow
HOWAT, GERALD — PN: Gerald Henderson-Howat
Howes, Jane — TN: SHIRAS, WILMAR HOUSE
Hoy, Elizabeth — TN: CONARAIN, ALICE NINA
Hubbard, Cal — TN: HUBBARD, ELBERT
HUBBARD, ELBERT — PN: Cal Hubbard, Fra Elbertus
HUBBARD, GEORGE BARRON — PN: Amos Moore
Hubbard, L. Ron — TN: HUBBARD, LAFAYETTE RON
HUBBARD, LAFAYETTE RON — PN: L. Ron Hubbard, Rene La Fayatte, Kurt Von Rachen
Huchet, Claire — TN: BISHOP, CLAIRE HUCHET
Hudson, Jan — TN: SMITH, GEORGE HENRY
Hudson, Jeffery — TN: CRICHTON, JOHN MICHAEL
HUEFFER, FORD MADOX — PN: Ford Madox Ford
Hughes, Brenda — TN: COLLOMS, BRENDA
Hughes, Colin — TN: CREASEY, JOHN
Hughes, Elizabeth — TN: ZACHARY, HUGH
Hughes, Matilda — TN: MAC LEOD, CHARLOTTE MATILDA
HUGHES, WALTER LLEWELLYN — PN: Hugh Walters

Hughes, Zach	TN: ZACHARY, HUGH
Hull, Opal I.	TN: LEHNUS, OPAL HULL
Hull, Richard	TN: SAMPSON, RICHARD HENRY
Humprhys, Geoffrey	TN: HUMPRHYS, LESLIE GEORGE
HUMPRHYS, LESLIE GEORGE	PN: Bruno Condray, Geoffrey Humprhys
Hunt, Charlotte	TN: HODGES, DORIS M.
Hunt, Clarence	TN: HOLMAN, CLARENCE HUGH
HUNT, E. HOWARD	PN: David St. John
Hunt, Francesca	TN: HOLLAND, ISABELLE
Hunt, Gill	TN: BRUNNER, JOHN KILIAN HOUSTON
Hunt, Gill	TN: TUBB, EDWIN CHARLES
Hunt, Harrison	TN: BALLARD, WILLIS TODHUNTER
Hunt, Harrison	TN: DAVIS, NORBERT
HUNT, HOWARD	PN: Robert Deitrich
Hunt, Kyle	TN: CREASEY, JOHN
Hunter	TN: LUTZ, GILES ALFRED
HUNTER, ELIZABETH MARY Teresa	TN: CHACE, ISOBEL
HUNTER, EVAN	PN: Curt Cannon, Hunt Collins, Ezra Hannon, Richard Marsten, Ed McBain
Hunter, Hall	TN: MARSHALL, EDISON TESLA
Hunter, John	TN: BALLARD, WILLIS TODHUNTER
Hunter, Leigh	TN: ETCHISON, BIRDIE L.
HURLEY, JOHN J.	PN: Duffy Carpenter, S.S. Rafferty
Huston, Fran	TN: MILLER, R.S.
HUTCHIN, KENNETH CHARLES	PN: Kenneth Challice
HUTTEN, Baroness BETSY RIDDLE VON	TN: RIDDLE, BETSEY
Hyde, Eleanor	TN: COWEN, FRANCES
HYNDMAN, JANE LEE	PN: Lee Wyndham
HYNE, CHARLES JOHN CUTCLIFFE WRIGHT	PN: Weatherby Chesney

I

Iams, Jack	TN: IAMS, SAMUEL H., JR
IAMS, SAMUEL H., JR.	PN: Jack Iams
Iles, Francis	TN: COX, ANTHONY BERKELEY
Incogniteau, Jean-Louis	TN: KEROUAC, JEAN LOUIS LEBRID
Informa, Tion	TN: LE FONTAINE, JOSEPH RAYMOND HERVE'
Ingham, Daniel	TN: LAMBOT, ISOBEL MARY
Inglis, Susan	TN: MACKIE, DORIS
Ingoldsby, Thomas	TN: BARHAM, RICHARD
Innes, Hammond	TN: INNES, RALPH KAMMOND
Innes, Jean	TN: SAUNDERS, JEAN
Innes, Michael	TN: STEWART, JOHN INNES MACKINTOSH
INNES, RALPH HAMMOND	PN: Ralph Hammond, Hammond Innes
Inspector F.	TN: RUSSELL, WILLIAM
Irani, Merwan S.	TN: BABA, MEHER
Ireland, Doreen	TN: LORD, DOUGLAS
Irish, William	TN: HOPLEY-WOOLRICH, CORNELL GEORGE
Ironquill	TN: WARE, EUGENE E. FITCH
Irvin, Patrick	TN: HOWARD, ROBERT E.
IRVING, JOHN TREAT	PN: John Quod
IRVING, WASHINGTON	PN: Geoffrey Crayon, Diedrich Knickerbocker, Jonathan Oldstyle
Irwin, G.H.	TN: PALMER, RAYMOND A.
Irwin, G.H.	TN: SHAVER, RICHARD SHARPE
Ives, Morgan	TN: BRADLEY, MARION ZIMMER

J

Jacks, Oliver	TN: GANDLEY, KENNETH ROYCE
Jackson, E.F.	TN: TUBB, EDWIN CHARLES
Jackson, Everatt	TN: MUGGESON, MARGARET ELIZABETH
JACKSON, HELEN HUNT	PN: H.H., Saxe Holm

Jackson, Neville	TN: GLASKIN, G.M.
Jackson, Sara	TN: THOMAS, SARA
JACKSON, Mrs. SCHUYLER B.	PN: Laura Riding
JACOB, NAOMI ELLINGTON	PN: Ellington Gray
Jaffa, George	TN: WALLACE-CLARKE, GEORGE
Jeake, Samuel	TN: AIKEN, CONRAD
JACOB, PIERS ANTHONY DILLINGHAM	PN: Piers Anthony
Jacobs, Leah	TN: GELLIS, ROBERTA LEAH
Jacobs, T.C.H.	TN: PENDOWER, JACQUES
Jaffa, George	TN: WALLACE-CLARKE, GEORGE
JAKES, JOHN WILLIAM	PN: Alan Payne, Jay Scotland
James, David	TN: HAGBERG, DAVID J.
James, Dudley	TN: MAYNE, WILLIAM
James, Dudley	TN: CAESAR, R.D.
James, Dynely	TN: MAYNE, WILLIAM
James, Margaret	TN: BENNETTS, PAMELA
James, Matthew	TN: LUCEY, JAMES D.
James, P.D.	TN: JAMES, PHYLISS DOROTHY
JAMES, PHYLISS DOROTHY	PN: P.D. James
James, Will	TN: DUFAULT, JOSEPH ERNEST NEPHTALI
James, William M.	TN: HARKNETT, TERRY WILLIAMS
James, William M.	TN: HARVEY, JOHN B.
Jameson, Eric	TN: TRIMMER, ERIC J.
JAMESON, MARGARET STROM	PN: James Hill, William Lamb
JANAS, FRANKIE-LEE	PN: Zachary Ball
Janet, Lillian	TN: RESSLER, LILLIAN
Janet, Lillian	TN: O'DANIEL, JANET
Janifer, Laurence M.	TN: GARRETT, RANDALL PHILLIP
Jansen, Hank	TN: NORWOOD, VICTOR GEORGE CHARLES
Jansen, Jared	TN: CEBULASH, MEL
Japrisot, Sebastian	TN: ROSSI, JEAN BAPTISTE
JARRETT, CORA	PN: Faraday Keene
Jason, Jerry	TN: SMITH, GEORGE HENRY
Jason, Johnny	TN: GLUT, DON F.
Jason, Stuart	TN: FLOREN, LEE
Jason, Veronica	TN: JOHNSTON, VELDA
Jawien, Andrzej	TN: POPE JOHN PAUL II
Jay, Charlotte	TN: JAY, GERALDINE MARY
JAY, GERALDINE MARY	PN: Geraldine Halls, Charlotte Jay
Jay, Marion	TN: SPALDING, RUTH
Jefford, Bat	TN: BINGLEY, DAVID ERNEST
JEFFRIES, GRAHAM MONTAGUE	PN: Peter Bourne, Bruce Graeme, David Graeme
JEFFRIES, RODERIC	PN: Peter Alding, Jeffrey Ashford, Hastings Draper, Roderic Graeme, Graham Hastings
JEFFREY, GRAHAM	PN: Brother Graham
Jeffrey, William	TN: PRONZINI, BILL
Jeffreys, J.G.	TN: HEALEY, BENJAMIN JAMES
Jeffs, Rae	TN: SEBLEY, FRANCES RAE
JELLY, GEORGE OLIVER	PN: Hilya Harsch
JENKINS, WILLIAM FITZGERALD	PN: Murray Leinster,
JENKS, GEORGE C.	PN: W.B. Lawson
Jennifer, Susan	TN: HOSKINS, ROBERT
Jennings, Dean	TN: FRAZEE, CHARLES STEVE
Jerome, Joseph	TN: SEWELL, BROCARD
JERVIS, MARGUERITE FLORENCE	PN: Marguerite Barclay, Countess Helene Barcynska, Oliver Sandys
Jocelyn, Richard	TN: CLUTTERBUCK, RICHARD
John, Nancy	TN: SAWYER, JOHN
John, Nancy	TN: SAWYER, NANCY
JOHN PAUL II, POPE	PN: Jawien Andrzej, Karol Wojtyla
Johns, Avery	TN: COUSINS, MARGARET
Johns, Foster	TN: SELDES, GILBERT
Johns, Geoffrey	TN: WARNER, GEOFFREY JOHN
Johns, Kenneth	TN: BULMER, HENRY KENNETH
JOHNS, WILLIAM EARL	PN: William Earle
Johnson, A.E.	TN: JOHNSON, ANNABELL JONES

Keith, J. Kilmeny	TN: MALLESON, LUCY BEATRICE
Kell, Joseph	TN: WILSON, JOHN ANTHONY BURGESS
KELLAR, JOHN W.	PN: Cholly Knickerbocker
KELLER, DAVID HENRY	PN: Henry Cecil
Kellow, Kathleen	TN: HIBBERT, ELEANOR ALICE
KELLY, TIM	PN: R.H. Bibelot
KELTON, ELMER	PN: Alex Hawk, Lee Mc Elroy
Kelway, Christine	TN: GWINN, CHRISTINE MARGARET
Kemp, Sarah	TN: BUTTERWORTH, MICHAEL
Kendall, Lace	TN: STOUTENBERG, ADRIEN
Kendrake, Carleton	TN: GARDNER, ERLE STANLEY
KENDRICK, BAYNARD HARDWICK	PN: Richard Hayward
Kendricks, James	TN: FOX, GARDNER FRANCIS
Kennedy, Elliott	TN: FOX, GARDNER F.
Kennedy, Elliott	TN: GODFREY, LIONEL
KENNEDY, JOSEPH CHARLES	PN: X.J. Kennedy
Kennedy, Milward	TN: BURGE, MILWARD RODON KENNEDY
Kennedy, Robert Milward	TN: BURGE, MILWARD RODON KENNEDY
Kennedy, X.J.	TN: KENNEDY, JOSEPH CHARLES
Kenneggy, Richard	TN: NETTELL, RICHARD
Kenny, Charles J.	TN: GARDNER, ERLE STANLEY
Kenny, Kathryn	TN: KRULL, KATHLEEN
Kenny, Kevin	TN: KRULL, KATHLEEN
Kensinger, George	TN: FICHTER, GEORGE S.
Kent, Arthur	TN: BRADWELL, JAMES
KENT, ARTHUR	PN: M. Dubois, Alexander Karol
Kent, Alexander	TN: REEMAN, DOUGLAS
Kent, David	TN: BIRNEY, HERMAN HOFFMAN
Kent, Fortune	TN: TOOMBS, JOHN
Kent, Helen	TN: POLLEY, JUDITH ANNE
Kent, Kelvin	TN: BARNES, ARTHUR KELVIN
Kent, Mallory	TN: LOWNDES, ROBERT AUGUSTINE WARD
Kent, Pamela	TN: BARRIE, SUSAN
Kent, Philip	TN: BULMER, HENRY KENNETH
KENT, ROCKWELL	PN: Hogarth, Jr.
Kenton, Maxwell	TN: SOUTHERN, TERRY
Kenton, Noel	TN: CAPON, HARRY PAUL
KENTON, WARREN	PN: Zev Ben Shimon Halevi
Kenyon, Bernice	TN: GILKYSON, BERNICE KENYON
KENYON, MICHAEL	PN: Daniel Forbes
Keppel, Charlotte	TN: TORDAY, URSULA
Kerby, Susan	TN: BURTON, ELIZABETH
Kern, Gregory	TN: TUBB, EDWIN CHARLES
Kerouac, Jack	TN: KEROUAC, JEAN LOUIS LEBRID
KEROUAC, JEAN LOUIS LEBRID	PN: Jean-Louis Incogniteau, Jack Kerouac
Kerr, Ben	TN: ARD, WILLIAM THOMAS
Kerr, Carole	TN: CARR, MARGARET
KERR, JAMES LENNOX	PN: Peter Dawlish
Kerr, M.E.	TN: MEAKER, MARIJANE
Kerr, Michael	TN: HOSKINS, ROBERT
Kershaw, Peter	TN: LUCIE-SMITH, EDWARD
KETCHUM, PHILIP L.	PN: Miriam Leslie, Mack Saunders
Kevern, Barbara	TN: SHEPHERD, DONALD LEE
Keverne, Richard	TN: HOSKEN, CLIFFORD JAMES WHEELER
Kiefer, Middleton	TN: KIEFER, WARREN AND MIDDLETON, HARRY
KIEFER, WARREN	PN: Middleton Kiefer
Kimbro, Jean	TN: KIMBRO, JOHN M.
KIMBRO, JOHN M.	PN: Kym Allyson, Ann Ashton, Charlotte Bramwell, Jean Kimbro, Katheryn Kimbrough
Kimbrough, Katheryn	TN: KIMBRO, JOHN M.
Kineji, Maborushi	TN: GIBSON, WALTER B.
King, Arthur	TN: LAKE, KENNETH ROBERT
KING, FRANCIS	PN: Frank Cauldwell
King, Norman A.	TN: TRALINS, S. ROBERT
King, Paul	TN: DRACKETT, PHIL
King, Vincent	TN: VINSON, REX THOMAS

KINGLSEY, CHARLES	PN: Parson Lot
Kingsley, Charlotte Mary	TN: HANSHEW, THOMAS W.
Kingston, Syd	TN: BINGLEY, DAVID ERNEST
KININMONTH, CHRISTOPHER	PN: Christopher Brennan
Kinkaid, Matt	TN: ADAMS, CLIFTON
Kinsey, Elizabeth	TN: CLYMER, ELEANOR
Kinsley, Charlotte Mary	TN: HANSHEW, THOMAS W.
Kirk, Michael	TN: KNOX, WILLIAM
Kirke, Edmuns	TN: GILMORE, JAMES R.
KIRKLAND, CAROLINE	PN: Mary Clavers
Kirtland, G.B.	TN: HINE, AL
Kirtland, G.B.	TN: JOSLIN, SESYLE
Kitt, Tamara	TN: DE REGNIERS, BEATRICE SCHENK
KLASS, PHILIP	PN: William Tenn
Knauff, Ellen Raphael	TN: HARTLEY, ELLEN R.
KNIBBS, HENRY HERBERT	PN: Henry K. Herbert
Knickerbocker, Cholly	TN: KELLAR, JOHN W.
Knickerbocker, Diedrich	TN: IRVING, WASHINGTON
KNIGHT, ALANNA	PN: Margaret Hope
Knight, David	TN: PRATHER, RICHARD SCOTT
KNIGHT, FRANCIS EDGAR	PN: Frank Knight, Cedric Salter
Knight, Frank	TN: KNIGHT, FRANCIS EDGAR
Knight, Gareth	TN: WILBY, BASIL LEE
Knight-Patterson, W.M.	TN: KULSKI, W.W.
Knott, Bill	TN: KNOTT, WILLIAM S.
Knott, Will C.	TN: KNOTT, WILLIAM S.
KNOTT, WILLIAM C.	PN: Bill J. Carol
KNOTT, WILLIAM S.	PN: Bill Knott, Will C. Knott
KNOWLES, MABEL WINIFRED	PN: Lester Lurgan, May Wynne
Knox, Bill	TN: KNOX, WILLIAM
Knox, Calvin M.	TN: SILVERBERG, ROBERT
KNOX, WILLIAM	PN: Michael Kirk, Bill Knox, Robert Mac Leod, Noah Webster
Knye, Cassandra	TN: DISCH, THOMAS MICHAEL and SLADEK, JOHN THOMAS
KOESTLER, ARTHUR	PN: Vigil
KONIGSBERG, ALLEN STEWART	PN: Woody Allen
KONIGSBERG, HANS	PN: Hans Koning
Koning, Hans	TN: KONIGSBERG, HANS
KOONTZ, DEAN RAY	PN: David Axton, Brian Coffey, K.R. Dwyer
KORNBLUTH, CYRIL M.	PN: Simon Eisner, Cyril M. Judd, Jordan Park
KORTNER, PETER	PN: Peter Hofer
KORZENIOWSKI, TEODOR J.K.	PN: Joseph Conrad
KOS, ERIH	PN: Erich Kosch
Kosch, Erich	TN: KOS, ERIH
KOSINSKI, JERZY	PN: Joseph Novak
KOUYOUMDJIAN, DIKRAN	PN: Michael Arlen
Kramer, George	TN: HEUMAN, WILLIAM
Krauss, Bruno	TN: BULMER, HENRY KENNETH
Krin, Sylvie	TN: FANTONI, BARRY
Kruger, Paul	TN: SEBENTHAL, ROBERTA ELIZABETH
KRULL, KATHLEEN	PN: Kathryn Kenny, Kevin Kenny
KUEHNELT-LEDDIHN, ERIK	PN: Francis Stuart Campbell
KULSKI, W.W.	PN: W.W. Coole, W.M. Knight-Patterson
KURLAND, MICHAEL JOSEPH	PN: Jennifer Plum
KURNITZ, HARRY	PN: Marco Page
KUSKIN, KARLA	PN: Nicholas Charles
KUTTNER, HENRY	PN: Will Garth, Lewis Padgett
Kyd, Thomas	TN: HARBAGE, ALFRED BENNETT
Kyle, Duncan	TN: BROXHOLME, JOHN
Kyle, Elizabeth	TN: DUNLOP, AGNES M.R.
Kyle, Sefton	TN: VICKERS, ROY C.

L

La Fontaine, Raymond	TN: LE FONTAINE, JOSEPH RAYMOND HERVÉ
La Fayette, Rene	TN: HUBBARD, LAFAYETTE RON

LA MOORE, LOUIS DEARBORN	PN: Tex Burns, Louis L'Amour, Jim Mayo
Lacey, Amy	TN: AMY, WILLIAM LACEY
Lacy, Ed	TN: ZINBERG, LEONARD S.
Ladd, Veronica	TN: MINER, JANE CLAYPOOL
LAKE, KENNETH ROBERT	PN: Arthur King, Ken Roberts, Xeno
Laker, Rosalind	TN: OVSTEDAL, BARBARA
LAMB, CHARLES	PN: Elia
Lamb, Charlotte	TN: HOLLAND, SHEILA
LAMB, GEOFFREY FREDERICK	PN: Balaam
Lamb, William	TN: JAMESON, MARGARET STROM
Lambert, Christine	TN: FREYBE, HEIDI HUBERTA
LAMBOT, ISOBEL MARY	PN: Daniel Ingham
LAMBURN, RICHMAL CROMPTON	PN: Richmal Crompton
Lamont, Marianne	TN: RUNDLE, ANNE
L'Amour, Louis	TN: LA MOORE, LOUIS DEARBORN
LAMPMAN, EVELYN SIBLEY	PN: Lynn Bronson
Lamprey, A.C.	TN: FISH, ROBERT L.
Lancaster, Sheila	TN: HOLLAND, SHEILA
Lancaster, Vicky	TN: ANSLE, DOROTHY PHOEBE
Lance, Leslie	TN: SWATRIDGE, IRENE MAUDE
Land, Jane	TN: BORLAND, KATHRYN
Land, Jane	TN: SPEICHER, HELEN ROSS
Land, Jane & Ross	TN: BORLAND, KATHRYN
Land, Jane & Ross	TN: SPEICHER, HELEN ROSS
LANDAU, MARK A.	PN: Mark Aldanov
Lane, Grant	TN: FISHER, STEVE STEPHEN GOULD
Lane, Mary D.	TN: DELANEY, MARY MURRAY
Lanf, Frances	TN: MANTLE, WINIFRED LANGFORD
LANG, ANDREW	PN: A Huge Longway
Lang, Grace	TN: FLOREN, LEE
Lang, King	TN: TUBB, EDWIN CHARLES
Langart, Darrel T.	TN: GARRETT, RANDALL PHILLIP
Lange, John	TN: CRICHTON, JOHN MICHAEL
LANGE, JOHN FREDERICK JR.	PN: John Norman
Langford, Jane	TN: MANTLE, WINIFRED LANGFORD
Langholm, Neil	TN: BULMER, HENRY KENNETH
Langstaff, Launcelot	TN: PAULDING, JAMES KIRK
'Lantern'	TN: MARQUIS, DON
Lantry, Mike	TN: TUBB, EDWIN CHARLES
Lara	TN: GRIFFITH-JONES, GEORGE CHETWYND
LARDNER, RING	PN: Jack Keefe, Old Wilmer
LASSALLE, CAROLINE	PN: Emma Cave
LATHAM, JEAN LEE	PN: Julian Lee
Latham, Mavis	TN: CLARK, MAVIS THORPE
Latham, Philip	TN: RICHARDSON, ROBERT SHIRLEY
Lathen, Emma	TN: HENNISART, MARTHA and LATIS, MARY J.
LATIMER, JONATHAN WYATT	PN: Peter Coffin
LATIS, MARY J.	PN: R.B. Dominic, Emma Lathen
Lattin,Anne	TN: TAYLOR, LOIS DWIGHT
Lauder, George	TN: DICK-LAUDER, SIR GEORGE
LAUNAY, ANDRE	PN: Droo Launay
Launay, Droo	TN: LAUNAY, ANDRE
Laurie, Annie	TN: BONFILS, Mrs. CHARLES
Laurin, Anne	TN: MC LAURIN, ANNE
Lavond, Paul Dennis	TN: LOWNDES, ROBERT AUGUSTINE WARD
Lawless, Anthony	TN: MACDONALD, PHILIP
Lawrence, Lesley	TN: LEWIS, LESLEY
LAWRENCE, LOUISE DE KIRILINE	PN: Louise De Kiriline
Lawrence, P.	TN: TUBB, EDWIN CHARLES
Lawson, Chet	TN: TUBB, EDWIN CHARLES
Lawson, Michael	TN: RYDER, M.L.
Lawson, Dr. Philip	TN: TRIMMER, ERIC J.
Lawson, W.B.	TN: JENKS, GEORGE C.
Lawton, Charles	TN: HECKELMANN, CHARLES NEWMAN
LAZARUS, MARGUERITE	PN: Marguerite Gascoigne, Anna Gilbert

LAZEROWITZ, ALICE AMBROSE — PN: Alice Ambrose
Le Cagat, Benat — TN: WHITAKER, RODNEY
Le Carre, John — TN: CORNWELL, DAVID JOHN MOORE
LE FONTAINE, JOSEPH RAYMOND HERVÉ — PN: Hervé Aruba, Dan Cingfox, El Dnomyar Evreh Eniatnof, Sebastain Largo Gregory, Joseph Hervé, Raymond Hervey, Tion Informa, Raymond LaFontaine, Ray LeFontaine, Charlotte Raymond, Joseph Raymond
Lefontaine, Ray — TN: LE FONTAINE, JOSEPH RAYMOND HERVÉ
Lefontaine, Raymond — TN: LE FONTAINE, JOSEPH RAYMOND HERVÉ
Le Jeune, Anthony — TN: THOMPSON, EDWARD ANTHONY
Lemon, Lynn — TN: WERT, LYNETTE L.
Le Sieg, Theo — TN: GEISEL, THEODOR SEUSS
Lea, Ed — TN: RICHELSON, GERALDINE
Lear, Peter — TN: LOVESEY, PETER
Leavor, Ruth — TN: TOMALIN, RUTH
Lee, Andrew — TN: AUCHINCLOSS, LOUIS
LEE, AUSTIN — PN: John Austwick, Julian Callender
Lee, Edward Edson — TN: EDWARDS, LEO
LEE, ELSIE — PN: Elsie Cromwell, Norman Daniels, Jane Gordon, Lee Sheridan
Lee, Howard — TN: GOULART, RONALD JOSEPH
Lee, Julian — TN: LATHAM, JEAN LEE
LEE, MANFRED BENNINGTON — PN: Ellery Queen, Ellery Queen Jr., Barnaby Ross
Lee, Matt — TN: MERWIN, SAMUEL KIMBALL, JR.
LEE, NORMAN — PN: Raymond Armstrong, Mark Corrigan, Robertson Hobart
LEE, WAYNE CYRIL — PN: Lee Sheldon
Lee, William — TN: BURROUGHS, WILLIAM SEWARD
LEEMING, JILL — PN: Jill Chaney
LEHMAN, PAUL EVAN — PN: Paul Evan
LEHNUS, OPAL HULL — PN: Opla I. Hull
Leibenguth, Charla Ann — TN: BANNER, CHARLA ANN LEIBENGUTH
Leigh, Roberta — TN: LINDSAY, RACHAEL
Leinster, Murray — TN: JENKINS, WILLIAM FITZGERALD
LEISK, DAVID JOHNSON — PN: Crockett Johnson
Lenin — TN: ULYANOV, VLADIMIR ILYICH
LEON, HENRY CECIL — PN: Henry Cecil
Leonard, Charles L. — TN: HEBERDEN, MARY VILET
Leonard, Hugh — TN: BYRNE, JOHN KEYES
LEONARD, JOHN — PN: Cyclops
Leppoc, Derfla — TN: COPPEL, ALFRED
Leslie, Miriam — TN: PHILIP L. KETCHUM
Leslie, O.H. — TN: SLESAR, HENRY
LESSER, MILTON — PN: Adam Chase, Andrew Frazer, Stephen Marlowe, Jason Ridgeway, C.H. Thames
Lester, Jane — TN: WALKER, EMILY KATHLEEN
L'Estrange, Anna — TN: ELLERBECK, ROSEMARY ANNE L'ESTRANGE
Lewes, Cady — TN: DE VOTO, BERNARD AUGUSTINE
Lewesdon, John — TN: DANIELL, ALBERT SCOTT
LEWIS, ALFRED HENRY — PN: Quin
Lewis, C.D. — TN: LEWIS, CECIL DAY
LEWIS, CECIL DAY — PN: C.D. Lewis, Nicholas Blake
Lewis, Charles — TN: DIXON, ROGER
Lewis, C.S. — TN: LEWIS, CLIVE STAPLES
LEWIS, CLIVE STAPLES — PN: N.W. Clerk, Clive Hamilton, C.S. Lewis
LEWIS, D.B. WYNDHAM — PN: Timothy Shy
LEWIS, HARRY SINCLAIR — PN: Tom Graham
LEWSI, J.R. — PN: Roy Lewis
LEWIS, LESLIE — PN: Lesley Lawrence
Lewis, Mervyn — TN: FREWER, GLYN
Lewis, Roy — TN: LEWIS, J.R.
Lewis, Voltaire — TN: RITCHIE, EDWIN
LEXAU, JOAN M. — PN: Joan L. Nodset
LEY, ROBERT ARTHUR — PN: Martin Luther, Arthur Sellings
Leyton, Sophie — TN: WALSH, SHEILA
Lieksman, Anders — TN: HAAVIKKO, PAAVO JUHANI

LIGHTNER, ALICE MARTHA	PN: Alice L. Hopf
Lilly, Ray	TN: CURTIS, RICHARD
Lin, Frank	TN: ATHERTON, GERTRUDE
Lincoln, Geoffrey	TN: MORTIMER, JOHN
Lindars, Barnabas	TN: LINDARS, FREDERICK C.
LINDARS, FREDERICK C.	PN: Barnabas Lindars
Linden, Oliver	TN: ABRAHAMS, DORIS CAROLINE
LINDSAY, RACHEL	PN: Roberta Leigh, Janey Scott
LINEBARGER, PAUL MYRON ANTHONY	PN: Felix C. Forrest, Carmichael Smith, Cordwainer Smith
LININGTON, BARBARA ELIZABETH	PN: Anne Blaisdell, Lesley Egan, Egan O'Neill, Dell Shannon
LIPKIND, WILLIAM	PN: Will
LITTLE, CONSTANCE	PN: Conyth Little
Little, Conyth	TN: LITTLE, CONSTANCE
Little, Conyth	TN: LITTLE, GWENYTH
Little, Francis	TN: MACAULEY, FRANCES C.
LITTLE, GWENYTH	PN: Conyth Little
Livingston, Grace	TN: HILL, GRACE LIVINGSTON
LOCKE, DAVID	PN: Petroleum V. Nasby
Locke, Martin	TN: DUNCAN, WILLIAM MURDOCK
LOCKRIDGE, FRANCES & RICHARD	PN: The Lockridge'S
Lockridge'S, The	TN: LOCKRIDGE, FRANCES & RICHARD
LODER, JOHN DE VERE	PN: Cornelius Cofyn
LOFTS, NORAH	PN: Juliet Astley, Peter Curtis
Logan, Jake	TN: RIFKIN, SHEPARD
Lohrman, Paul	TN: SHAVER, RICHARD SHARPE
Lomax, Bliss	TN: DRAGO, HARRY SINCLAIR
London, Jack	TN: LONDON, JOHN GRIFFITH
LONDON, JOHN GRIFFITH	PN: Jack London
London, Laura	TN: CURTIS, SHARON
London, Laura	TN: CURTIS, THOMAS DALE
LONG, FRANK BELKNAP	PN: Lyda Belknap Long
Long, Lyda Belknap	TN: LONG, FRANK BELKNAP
Long, William Stuart	TN: STUART, VIVIAN
Longbaugh, Harry	TN: GOLDMAN, WILLIAM
Longdon, George	TN: RAYER, FRANCIS GEORGE
LONGRIGG, ROGER ERSKIN	PN: Ivor Drummond, Roselind Erskin
LONGSTREET, STEPHEN	PN: Thomad Burton, Paul Haggard, David Ormsbee, Henri Weiner
Longway, A. Huge	TN: LANG, ANDREW
LONIGAN, GEORGE THOMAS	PN: Aesop
LOOMIS, NOEL MILLER	PN: Sam Allison, Benj. Miller, Frank Miller, Silas Water
Lorac, E.C.R.	TN: RIVETT, EDITH CAROLINE
Loraine, Philip	TN: ESTRIDGE, ROBIN
Loran, Martin	TN: BAXTER, JOHN
LORD, DOUGLAS	PN: Doreen Ireland
Lord, Jeffrey	TN: NELSON, RAY RADELL FARADAY
Lord, Nancy	TN: TITUS, EVE
LORENZINI, CARLO	PN: Carlo Collodi
LORING, EMILIE	PN: Josephine Story
Loring, Peter	TN: SHELLABARGER, SAMUEL
Loris	TN: VON HOFMANNSTHAL, HUGO
Lorraine, Paul	TN: FEARN, JOHN RUSSELL
Lorrimer, Claire	TN: CLARK, PATRICIA DENISE
Lothrop, Amy	TN: BARTLETT, ANNA
LOTHROP, HARRIET	PN: Margaret Sidney
Loti, Pierre	TN: VIAUD, L.M. JULIEN
Lourie, Helen	TN: STORR, CATHERINE
Lovell, Marc	TN: MC SHANE, MARK
LOVESEY, PETER	PN: Peter Lear
Low, Dorothy Mackie	TN: LOW, LOIS DOROTHEA
LOW, LOIS DOROTHEA	PN: Zoe Cass, Dorothy Mackie Low, Lois Paxton
LOWELL, JAMES RUSSELL	PN: Hosea Biglow
Lowing, Anne	TN: GEACH, CHRISTINE

LOWNDES, MARIE ADELAIDE
  BELLOC   PN: Philip Curtin
LOWNDES, ROBERT AUGUSTINE
  WARD   PN: Arthur Cooke, S.D. Gottesman, Carol Grey, Carl
                                      Groener, Mallory Kent, Paul Dennis Lavond, John
                                      Macdougal, Wilfred Owen Morley, Richard Morrison,
                                      Robert Morrison, Michael Sherman, Peter Michael
                                      Sherman, Lawrence Woods
LOWRY, JOAN   PN: Joanna Catlow
Loxmith, John   TN: BRUNNER, JOHN
LUCAS, E.V.   PN: E.V.L., V.V.V.
Lucas, Victoria   TN: PLATH, SYLVIA
LUCEY, JAMES D.   PN: Matthew James
LUCIE-SMITH, EDWARD   PN: Peter Kershaw
Ludlow, Geoffrey   TN: MEYNELL, LAURENCE WALTER
LUDLUM, ROBERT   PN: Jonathan Ryder, Michael Shepherd
Luellen, Valentina   TN: POLLEY, JUDITH ANNE
Lum, Peter   TN: CROWE, Lady BETTINA
Lurgan, Lester   TN: KNOWLES, MABEL WINIFRED
Luther, Martin   TN: LEY, ROBERT ARTHUR
LUTYENS, MARY   PN: Esther Wyndham
LUTZ, GILES ALFRED   PN: James B. Chaffin, Wade Everett, Alex Hawk, Hunter
Lyall, David   TN: SWAN, ANNIE S.
LYLE-SMYTHE, ALAN   PN: Alan Caillou
Lymington, John   TN: CHANCE, JOHN NEWTON
Lynch, Eric   TN: BINGLEY, DAVID ERNEST
Lynch, Frances   TN: COMPTON, DAVID GUY
LYNDS, DENNIS   PN: William Arden, Nick Carter, Michael Collins, John
                                      Crowe, Carl Dekker, Maxwell Grant, Mark Sadler

Lynn, Margaret   TN: BATTYE, GLADYS STARKEY
LYNNE, JAMES BROOM   PN: James Quartermain
Lynton, Ann   TN: RAYNER, CLAIRE BERENICE
Lyons, Delphine C.   TN: SMITH, EVELYN E.

M

Maborushi, Kineji   TN: GIBSON, WALTER B.
Mac Creigh, James   TN: POHL, FREDERIK
MAC DIARMID, HUGH   PN: C.M. Grieve
Mac Donald, Anson   TN: HEINLEIN, ROBERT
Mac Donald, Golden   TN: BROWN, MARGARET WISE
Mac Donald, John   TN: MILLAR, KENNETH
MAC DONALD, JOHN DANN   PN: John Wade Farrell, Scott O'Hara, Peter Reed
Mac Donald, John Ross   TN: MILLAR, KENNETH
Mac Donald, Marcia   TN: HILL-LUTZ, GRACE LIVINGSTON
Mac DONALD, PHILIP   PN: Oliver Fleming, Anthony Lawless, Martin Porlock
Mac Donald, Ross   TN: MILLAR KENNETH
Mac Donall, Robertson   TN: MAIR, GEORGE BROWN
Mac Dougal, John   TN: LOWNDES, ROBERT AUGUSTINE WARD
MAC DOWELL, KATHERINE   PN: Sherwood Bonner
Mac Duff, Andrew   TN: FYFE, HORACE BROWNE
Mac Farlane, Stephen   TN: CROSS, JOHN KEIR
MAC GIBBON, JEAN   PN: Jean Howard
MAC GILL, Mrs. PATRICK
  MARGARET   PN: Margaret Gibbons
MAC GREGOR, JAMES MURDOCH   PN: J.T. Mc Intosh, H.J. Murdoch
Mac Intyre, Elisabeth   TN: ELDERSHAW, ELISABETH
Mac Laren, Ian   TN: WATSON, JOHN MAC LAREN
MAC LEAN, ALISTAIR STUART   PN: Ian Stuart
Mac Lean, Art   TN: SHIRREFFS, GORDON DONALD
Mac Lean, Arthur   TN: TUBB, EDWIN CHARLES
MAC LEOD, CHARLOTTE MATILDA   PN: Alisa Craig, Matilda Hughes
MAC LEOD, ELLEN JANE   PN: Ella Anderson
Mac Leod, Fiona   TN: SHARP, WILLIAM
MAC LEOD, JEAN S.   PN: Catherine Airlie
Mac Leod, Robert   TN: KNOX, (BILL) WILLIAM

Mac Neil, Duncan
Mac Neil, Neil
MAC PHERSON, A.D.L.
Mac Thomas, Ruaraidh
MC ALLISTER, ALISTER
Mc Bain, Ed
Mc Cabe, Cameron
MC CAIG, ROBERT JESSE
Mc Call, Anthony
Mc Call, Vincent
Mc Cann, Edson

Mc Cann, Edson
MC CARTHY, SHAUN LLOYD
MC CLARY, THOMAS CALVERT
MC CLOY, HELEN WORRELL
   CLARKSON
MC COMAS, JESSE FRANCIS
MC CONNELL, JAMES DOUGLAS
   RUTHERFORD
Mc Cord, Whip
Mc Corquodale, Barbara
Mc Crorey, Sanders
MC CUE, LILLIAN
Mc Culloch, John Tyler
MC CUTCHAN, DONALD PHILIP
MC CUTCHEON, GEORGE BARR
MC CUTCHEON, HUGH
MC ELFRESH, ELIZABETH
   ADELINE
Mc Elroy, Lee
MC EVOY, MARJORIE
MC GAUGHY, DUDLEY DEAN
Mc Girr, Edmund
MC GIVERN, MAUREEN DALY
MC GIVERN, WILLIAM PETER
Mc Gowan, Inez
Mc Grath, Morgan
MC ILWAIN, DAVID

MC INTOSH, KINN HAMILTON
Mc Intosh, J.T.
Mc Kenna, Evelyn
Mc Kenzie, Paige
MC LEAN, ALISTAIR
Mc Laglen, John J.
MC LAURIN, ANNE
Mc Llowery, Frank
Mc Mahon, Pat
MC NEILE, HERMAN CYRIL
Mc Quill, Thirsty
Mc Roberts, Agnessan
MC SHANE, MARK
MACAULEY, FRANCES C.
MACHEN, ARTHUR
MACKAY, ALBERIGH
MACKAY, JAMES ALEXANDER
MACKAY, MARY
MACKIE, DORIS
MACKINLAY, LEILA
   ANTOINETTE STERLING
MACKINTOSH, ELIZABETH
Macumber, Mari
MADDISON, ANGELA MARY
Maddock, Stephen

TN: MC CUTCHAN, DONALD PHILIP
TN: BALLARD, WILLIS TODHUNTER
PN: Sara Seale
TN: THOMSON, DEREK S.
PN: Lynn Brock, Anthony Wharton
TN: HUNTER, EVAN
TN: BORNEMAN, ERNEST
PN: Edith Engren
TN: KANE, HENRY
TN: MORLAND, NIGEL
TN: ALVAREZ-DEL REY, RAMON FELIPE SAN JUAN MARIO
   SILVIO ENRICO
TN: POHL, FREDERIK
PN: Theo Callas, Desmond Cory
PN: Calvin Peregoy

PN: Helen Clarkson
PN: Webb Marlowe

PN: Douglas Rutherford
TN: NORWOOD, VICTOR GEORGE CHARLES
TN: CARTLAND, BARBARA HAMILTON
TN: COUNSELMAN, MARY ELIZABETH
PN: De La Torre, Lillian
TN: BURROUGHS, EDGAR RICE
PN: Robert Conington Galway, Duncan Macneil, T.I.G. Wigg
PN: Richard Greaves
PN: Hugh Davie-Martin

PN: John Cleveland, Jane Scott, Elizabeth Wesley
TN: KELTON, ELMER
PN: Marjorie Harte
PN: Dudley Dean, Dean Owen, Brian Wynne
TN: GILES, KENNETH
PN: Maureen Daly
PN: Bill Peters
TN: GRAHAM, ROGER PHILLIPS
TN: RAE, HUGH C.
PN: Will Daemer, Whit Masterson, Wade Miller, Dale Wilmer,
   Bob Wade, Robert Wade, Charles Eric Maine, Richard
   Rayner, Robert Wade
PN: Catherine Aird
TN: MAC GREGOR, JAMES MURDOCH
TN: JOSCELYN, ARCHIE LYNN
TN: BLOOD, MARIE
PN: Ian Stuart
TN: HARVEY, JOHN B.
PN: Anne Laurin
TN: KEEVIL, HENRY JOHN
TN: HOCH, EDWARD DENTINGER
PN: Sapper
TN: WALLACE, BRUCE
TN: MEEK, PAULINE PALMER
PN: Marc Lovell
PN: Francis Little
PN: Leolinus Siluriensis
PN: Ali Baba
PN: Ian Angus
PN: Marie Corelli
PN: Susan Inglis

PN: Brenda Grey
PN: Gordon Daviot, Josephine Tey
TN: SANDOZ, MARI
PN: Angela Banner
TN: WALSH, JAMES MORGAN

Maddox, Carl	TN: TUBB, EDWIN CHARLES
Maine, Charles Eric	TN: MC ILWAIN, DAVID
Maine, Trevor	TN: CATHERALL, ARTHUR
MAINWARING, DANIEL	PN: Geoffrey Homes
MAJOR, CHARLES	PN: Edw. Caskoden
Majors, Simon	TN: FOX, GARDNER FRANCIS
MALLESON, LUCY BEATRICE	PN: Anthony Gilbert, J. Kilmeny Keith, Anne Meredith
Malloch, Peter	TN: DUNCAN, WILLIAM MURDOCH
Mallory, Drew	TN: GARFIELD, BRIAN FRANCIS WYNNE
Mallowan, Agatha Christie	TN: MALLOWAN, Dame AGATHA MARY CLARISSA
MALLOWAN, Dame AGATHA MARY CLARISSA	PN: Agatha Christie, Agatha Christie Mallowan, Mary Westmacott
MALZBERG, BARRY NORMAN	PN: Mike Barry, Claudine Dumas, Mel Johnson, Lee W. Mason, Francine De Natale, K.M. O'Donnell, Gerrold Watkins
MANFRED, FREDERICK FEIKEMA	PN: Feike Feikema
MANLEY-TUCKER, AUDRIE	PN: Linden Howard
Mann, Abel	TN: CREASEY, JOHN
Mann, Charles	TN: HECKELMANN, CHARLES NEWMAN
Mann, Chuck	TN: HECKELMANN, CHARLES NEWMAN
Mann, Deborah	TN: BLOOM, URSULA
MANN, EDWARD BEVERLY	PN: Peter Field, Zachary Strong
Mann, James	TN: HARVEY, JOHN B.
MANN, THOMAS	PN: Paul Thomas
Manners, Alexandra	TN: RUNDLE, ANNE
MANNING, ADELAIDE FRANCES OKE	PN: Manning Coles, Francis Gaite
Manning, David	TN: FAUST, FREDERICK SCHILLER
Manning, Marsha	TN: GRIMSTEAD, HETTIE
MANNING, ROSEMARY	PN: Mary Voyle
Manning-Sanders, Ruth	TN: SANDERS, RUTH
Manor, Jason	TN: HALL, OAKLEY MAXWELL
Mansfield, Katherine	TN: BEAUCHAMP, KATHLEEN
MANTLE, WINIFRED LANGFORD	PN: Frances Lanf, Jane Langford
Manton, Peter	TN: CREASEY, JOHN
Maras, Karl	TN: BULMER, HENRY KENNETH
March, William	TN: CAMPBELL, WILLIAM E.
Marchant, Catherine	TN: COOKSON, CATHERINE ANN
Marcus, Joanna	TN: ANDREWS, LUCILLE MATTHEW
Marin, A.C.	TN: COPPEL, ALFRED
Markham, Robert	TN: AMIS, KINGSLEY WILLIAM
Marlot, Raymond	TN: ANGREMY, JEAN-PIERRE
Marlowe, Hugh	TN: PATTERSON, HENRY
Marlowe, Stephen	TN: LESSER, MILTON
Marlowe, Webb	TN: MC COMAS, JESSE FRANCIS
MARQUIS, DON	PN: Lantern, Sundial
Marreco, Anne	TN: ACLAND, ALICE
Marric, J.J.	TN: CREASEY, JOHN
MARRISON, LESLIE WILLIAM	PN: D.M. Dowley
Marsden, James	TN: CREASEY, JOHN
Marsh, Jean	TN: MARSHALL, EVELYN
MARSH, JOHN	PN: Grace Richmond
MARSHALL, EDISON TESLA	PN: Hall Hunter
MARSHALL, EVELYN	PN: Lesley Bourne, Jean Marsh
Marshall, Joanne	TN: RUNDLE, ANNE
Marshall, Lovat	TN: DUNCAN, WILLIAM MURDOCH
Marshall, Raymond	TN: RAYMOND, RENE BRABAZON
Marsten, Richard	TN: HUNTER, EVAN
Martell, James	TN: BINGLEY, DAVID ERNEST
Martin, Ellis	TN: RYAN, MARAH ELLIS
MARTIN, PATRICIA MILES	PN: Miska Miles
MARTIN, RHONA	PN: Rhona M. Neighbour
Martin, Richard	TN: CREASEY, JOHN
MARTIN, ROBERT BERNARD	PN: Robert Bernard
Martin, Ruth	TN: RAYNER, CLAIRE BERENICE
Martin, Stella	TN: ROUGIER, Mrs. GEORGE RONALD

Marvel, Ik   TN: MITCHELL, DONALD G.
MASON, DOUGLAS RANKINE   PN: R.M. Douglas, John Rankine
MASON, FRANCIS VAN WYCK   PN: Geoffrey Coffin, Frank W. Mason, Ward Weaver
Mason, Frank   TN: BUDRYS, ALGIRDAS JONAS
Mason, Frank W.   TN: MASON, FRANCIS VAN WYCK
Mason, Lee W.   TN: MALZBERG, BARRY NORMAN
Mason, Tally   TN: DERLETH, AUGUST WILLIAM
Masterson, Whit   TN: MILLER, BILL
Masterson, Whit   TN: WADE, ROBERT
MATHER, ANNE   PN: Caroline Fleming
Mather, Berkely   TN: DAVIES, JOHN EVAN WESTON
Matheson, Rodney   TN: CREASEY, JOHN
Matthews, Anthony   TN: BARKER, DUDLEY
Matthews, Kevin   TN: FOX, GARDNER FRANCIS
MATTHEWS, PATRICIA ANNE   PN: P.A. Brisco, Patty Brisco, Laura Wylie
MAUGHAM, ROBERT CECIL ROMER   PN: David Griffith, Robin Maugham
Maugham, Robin   TN: MAUGHAM, ROBERT CECIL ROMER
Maurois, Andre   TN: HERZOG, EMILE
Maxwell, John   TN: FREEMANTLE, BRIAN HARRY
MAXWELL, PATRICIA ANNE   PN: Jennifer Blake
Maxwell, Vicky   TN: WORBOYS, ANNETTE ISOBEL
May, Sophie   TN: CLARKE, REBECCA SOPHIA
MAY, WINIFRED JEAN   PN: Wynne May
May, Wynne   TN: MAY, WINIFRED JEAN
Maybury, Anne   TN: BUXTON, ANNE
Mayfield, Julia   TN: HASTINGS, PHYLISS DORA
MAYNE, WILLIAM   PN: Martin Cobalt, James Dynely
MAYNELL, LAURENCE WALTER   PN: Valerie Baxter
Mayo, James   TN: COULTER, STEPHEN
Mayson, Marina   TN: ROGERS, ROSEMARY
MEADE, ELIZABETH THOMASINA   PN: L.T. Meade
Meade, L.T.   TN: MEADE, ELIZABETH THOMASINA
Meade, Richard   TN: HAAS, BENJAMIN LEOPOLD
MEAKER, MARIJANE   PN: M.E. Kerr
MEARS, LEONARD F.   PN: Marshall Grover, Marshall Mc Coy, Johnny Nelson
MEEK, STERNER ST. PAUL   PN: Sterner St. Paul
MEIGS, CORNELIA LYNDE   PN: Adair Aldon
Meldrum, James   TN: BROXHOLME, JOHN
Melikow, Loris   TN: VON HOFMANNSTHAL, HUGO
Melmoth, Sebastian   TN: WILDE, OSCAR FINGAL
Meloney, Franken   TN: FRANKEN, ROSE DOROTHY
Melville, Anne   TN: POTTER, MARGARET EDITH
MELVILLE, HERMAN   PN: Salvatore R. Tarnmoor
Melville, Jennie   TN: BUTLER, GWENDOLINE
Mentor   TN: LAKE, KENNETH ROBERT
MERCER, CECIL WILLIAM   PN: Dornford Yates
Meredith, Anne   TN: MALLESON, LUCY BEATRICE
Meredith, Owen   TN: BULWER-LYTTON, EDWARD
Merezhkovsky, Zinaida   TN: GIPPIUS, ZINAIDA
Merlin, Christina   TN: HEAVEN, CONSTANCE
Merlin, David   TN: MOREAU, DAVID MERLIN
Merlini, The Great   TN: RAWSON, CLAYTON
MERRIL, JOSEPHINE JUDITH   PN: Cyril Judd
Merrill, P.J.   TN: ROTH, HOLLY
Merriman, Pat   TN: ATKEY, PHILIP
MERTZ, BARBARA LOUISE GROSS   PN: Barbara Michaels, Elizabeth Peters
MERWIN, SAMUEL KIMBALL, JR.   PN: Elizabeth Deare Bennett, Jacques Jean Ferrat, Matt Lee,
                                                                        Carter Sprague
Messer, Mona   TN: HOCKING, MONA NAOMI ANNE MESSER
Metcalf, Suzanne   TN: BAUM, LYMAN FRANK
MEYNELL, LAURENCE WALTER   PN: Valerie Baxter, Robert Eton, Geoffrey Ludlow, A.
                                                                        Stephen Tring
Michaels, Barbara   TN: MERTZ, BARBARA LOUISE GROSS
Michaels, Dale   TN: RIFKIN, SHEPPARD
Michaels, Kristin   TN: WILLIAMS, DOROTHY JEANNE
Michaels, Steve   TN: AVALONNE, MICHAEL ANGELO, JR.

MIDDLETON, HARRY   PN: Middleton Kiefer
Miles, John   TN: BICKHAM, JACK M.
Miles, Keith   TN: TRALINS, S. ROBERT
Miles, Miska   TN: MARTIN, PATRICIA MILES
Militant   TN: SANDBURG, CARL A.
MILLAR, KENNETH   PN: John Macdonald, John Ross Macdonald, Ross
                                       Macdonald
MILLARD, JOSEPH JOHN   PN: Joe Millard
MILLAY, EDNA ST. VINCENT   PN: Nancy Boyd
Miller, Benj.   TN: LOOMIS, NOEL MILLER
MILLER, BILL   PN: Will Daemer, Whit Masterson, Wade Miller, Dale Wilmer
MILLER, CINCINNATUS HEINE   PN: Joaquin Miller
Miller, Frank   TN: LOOMIS, NOEL MILLER
Miller, Joaquin   TN: MILLER, CINCINNATUS HEINE
Miller, Jon   TN: MILLER, JOHN GORDON
Miller, Olive Thorne   TN: MILLER, HARRIETT MANN
MILLER, R.S.   PN: Fran Huston
Miller, Wade   TN: MILLER, BILL
Miller, Wade   TN: WADE, ROBERT
Milne, A.A.   TN: MILNE, ALAN ALEXANDER
Mitchell, Clyde T.   TN: GARRETT, RANDOLPH PHILLIP
MINER, JANE CLAYPOOL   PN: Jane Claypool, Veronica Ladd
MITCHELL, DONALD   PN: Ik Marvel
MITCHELL, GLADYS MAUDE WINIFRED   PN: Stephen Hockaby, Malcolm Torrie
Mitchell, Scott   TN: GODFREY, LIONEL
Moamrath, M.M.   TN: PUMILIA, (JOE) JOSEPH F.
MODELL, MERRIAM   PN: Evelyn Piper
MOLESWORTH, MARY LOUISA   PN: Ennis Graham
Moliere   TN: POQUELIN, JEAN BAPTISTE
Molin, Charles   TN: MAYNE, WILLIAM
Monahan, John   TN: BURNETT, WILLIAM RILEY
Monig, Christopher   TN: CROSSEN, KENDELL FOSTER
Monro, Gavin   TN: MONRO-HIGGS, GERTRUDE
Monroe, Lyle   TN: HEINLEIN, ROBERT
MONTGOMERY, ROBERT BRUCE   PN: Edmund Crispin
MONTGOMERY, RUTHERFORD
    GEORGE   PN: A.A. Avery, Al Avery, Art Elder, Everitt Proctor
Moor, Emily   TN: DEMING, RICHARD
MOORCOCK, MICHAEL   PN: Bill Barclay, E.P. Bradbury, James Colvin
Moore, Amos   TN: HUBBARD, GEORGE BARRON
MOORE, BRIAN   PN: Michael Bryan
MOORE, C.L.   PN: Lewis Padgett
Moore, Austin   TN: MUIR, AUGUSTUS
Moore, Rosalie   TN: BROWN, ROSALIE MOORE
Moran, J-L   TN: WHITAKER, RODNEY
Moran, Mike   TN: ARD, WILLIAM THOMAS
More, Caroline   TN: CONE, MOLLY
Moresby, Louis   TN: BECK, LILY ADAMS
MORETON, DOUGLAS ARTHUR   PN: Arthur Douglas
Moreton, John   TN: COHEN, MORTON
Morgan, Claire   TN: HIGHSMITH, PATRICIA
Morgan, Marjorie   TN: CHIBNALL, MARJORIE MC CALLUM
Morice, Anne   TN: SHAW, FELICITY
Morich, Stanton   TN: GRIFFITH-JONES, GEORGE CHETWYND
Morino, Nick   TN: DEMING, RICHARD
Morland, Dick   TN: HILL, REGINALD
MORLAND, NIGEL   PN: Mary Dane, John Donavan, Norman Forrest, Roger
                                       Garnett, Vincent McCall, Neal Shepherd
Morland, Peter Henry   TN: FAUST, FREDERICK SCHILLER
Morley, Susan   TN: CROSS, JOHN KEIR
Morley, Wilfred Owen   TN: LOWNDES, ROBERT AUGUSTINE WARD
Morren, Theophil   TN: VON HOFMANNSTHAL, HUGO
Morris, John   TN: CARGILL, MORRIS
Morris, John   TN: HEARNE, JOHN
Morris, Julian   TN: WEST, MORRIS
Morris, Sara   TN: BURKE, JOHN FREDERICK

Morris, Sara	TN: BURGE, MILWARD RODON KENNEDY
MORRISSEY, JOSEPH LAWRENCE	PN: Henry Richards, Richard Saxon
Morrison, Richard	TN: LOWNDES, ROBERT AUGUSTINE WARD
Morrison, Robert	TN: LOWNDES, ROBERT AUGUSTINE WARD
Morrison, Roberta	TN: WEBB, JEAN FRANCIS
Morse, Carol	TN: HALL, MARJORY
Mortimer, Charles	TN: CHAPMAN-MORTIMER, WILLIAM CHARLES
Mortimer, Chapman	TN: CHAPMAN-MORTIMER, WILLIAM CHARLES
MORTIMER, JOHN	PN: Geoffrey Lincoln
MORTIMER, PENELOPE	PN: Penelope Dimont
Morton, Anthony	TN: CREASEY, JOHN
MORTON, SARA WENTWORTH	PN: Philenia
Morton, Stanley	TN: FREEDGOOD, MARTIN
Moss, Nancy	TN: MOSS, ROBERT
Moss, Roberta	TN: MOSS, ROBERT
Mossman, Burt	TN: KEEVIL, HENRY JOHN
Mossop, Irene	TN: SWATRIDGE, IRENE MAUD
Motley, Mary	TN: DE RENEVILLE, MARY MARGARET MOTLEY
Mountfield, David	TN: GRANT, NEIL
Muddock, J.E.	TN: MUDDOCK, JOYCE EMMERSON PRESTON
MUDDOCK, JOYCE EMMERSON PRESTON	PN: Dick Donovan, J.E. Muddock
Mude, O.	TN: GOREY, EDWARD ST. JOHN
MUGGESON, MARGARET ELIZABETH	PN: Margaret Dickinson, Everatt Jackson
Muir, Dexter	TN: GRIBBLE, LEONARD
Mun	TN: MUNRO, LEAF
Mundy, Max	TN: SCHOFIELD, SYLVIA ANNE
Munro, H.H.	TN: MUNRO, HECTOR HUGO
MUNRO, HECTOR HUGO	PN: H.H. Munro, Saki
Munro, Mary	TN: HOWE, DORIS
Munro, Ronald Eadie	TN: GLEN, DUNCAN
Murdoch, H.J.	TN: MC GREGOR, JAMES MURDOCH
MURFREE, MARY NOAILLES	PN: Charles Egbert Craddock
MURPHY, LAWRENCE AGUSTUS	PN: Steven C. Lawrence, C.L. Murphy
Murray, Beatrice	TN: POSNER, RICHARD
Murray, Frances	TN: BOOTH, ROSEMARY
Murray, Jill	TN: WALKER, EMILY KATHLEEN
MURRY, COLIN MIDDLETON	PN: Richard Cowper
Mussey, Virginia T.H.	TN: ELLISON, VIRGINIA HOWELL
MUSSI, MARY	PN: Josephine Edgar, Mary Howard
Myers, Harriet Kathryn	TN: WHITTINGTON, HARRY

N

Napier, Mark	TN: LAFFIN, JOHN
Napier, Mary	TN: WRIGHT, PATRICIA
'Narmyx'	TN: DOUGLAS, NORMAN
Nasby, Petroleum V.	TN: LOCKE, DAVID
Nasier, Alcofribas	TN: RABELAIS, FRANCOIS
Nash, Newlyn	TN: HOWE, DORIS
Nash, Newlyn	TN: HOWE, MURIEL
Natale, Francine De	TN: MALZBERG, BARRY NORMAN
Nathan, Daniel	TN: DANNAY, FREDERIC
Naylor, Eliot	TN: FRANKAU, PAMELA
Neal, Hilary	TN: NORTON, OLIVE MARION
Neighbour, Rhona M.	TN: MARTIN, RHONA
Neilson, Marguerite	TN: TOMPKINS, JULIA
Nelson, Marguerite	TN: FLOREN, LEE
Nelson, R.N.	TN: NELSON, RADELL FARADAY
NELSON, RADELL FARADAY	PN: R.N. Nelson, Ray Nelson, Jeffrey Lord
Nelson, Ray	TN: NELSON, RADELL FARADAY
NESBIT, EDITH	PN: E. Bland, Fabian Bland
Nesbit, Troy	TN: FOLSOM, FRANKLIN BREWSTER
NETTELL, RICHARD	PN: Richard Kenneggy
NEVILLE, BARBARA ALISON	PN: Edward Candy

Neville, Margot	TN: GOYDER, MARGOT
Neville, Margot	TN: JOSKE, ANNE NEVILLE GOYDER
Newell, Crosby	TN: BONSALL, CROSBY
Newman, Barbara	TN: NEWMAN, MONA ALICE JEAN
NEWMAN, BERNARD	PN: Don Betteridge
Newman, Margaret	TN: POTTER, MARGARET
Newton, David C.	TN: CHANCE, JOHN NEWTON
NEWTON, DWIGHT BENNETT	PN: Dwight Bennett, Clement Hardin, Ford Logan, Hank Mitchum, Dan Temple
Nicholas, F.R.E.	TN: FREELING, NICHOLAS
Nichols, Peter	TN: YOUD, CHRISTOPHER SAMUEL
Nicholson, C.R.	TN: NICOLE, CHRISTOPHER ROBIN
Nicholson, Christina	TN: NICOLE, CHRISTOPHER ROBIN
Nicholson, Jane	TN: STEEN, MARGUERITE
NICHOLSON, MARGARET BETA	PN: Margaret Yorke
Nicholson, Robin	TN: NICOLE, CHRISTOPHER ROBIN
NICKSON, ARTHUR THOMAS	PN: Arthur Hodson, Roy Peters, John Saunders, Matt Winstan
NICOLE, CHRISTOPHER ROBIN	PN: Leslie Arlen, Robin Cade, Peter Grange, Mark Logan, Christina Nicholson, C.R. Nicholson, Robin Nicholson, Alison York, Andrew York
Nile, Dorothea	TN: AVALLONE, MICHAEL ANGELO, JR.
Noble, Charles	TN: PAWLEY, MARTIN
Nodset, Joan L.	TN: LEXAU, JOAN M.
Noel, John	TN: BIRD, DENNIS LESLIE
NOLAN, FREDERICK	PN: Frederick H. Christian
Noon, Ed	TN: AVALLONE, MICHAEL ANGELO, JR.
Noone, Edwina	TN: AVALLONE, MICHAEL ANGELO, JR.
Norden, Charles	TN: DURRELL, LAWRENCE
Norden, Helen Brown	TN: LAWRENSON, HELEN
Norman, James	TN: SCHMIDT, JAMES NORMAN
Norman, John	TN: LANGE, JOHN
North, Andrew	TN: NORTON, ALICE MARY
North, Colin	TN: BINGLEY, DAVID ERNEST
North, Gil	TN: HORNE, GEOFFREY
North, Howard	TN: TREVOR, ELLESTON
North, Sara	TN: BONHAM, BARBARA
NORTON, ALICE MARY	PN: Andrew North, Andre Norton, Allen Weston
Norton, Andre	TN: NORTON, ALICE MARY
Norton, Bess	TN: NORTON, OLIVE MARION
Norton, Bram	TN: BRAMESCO, NORTON J.
NORTON, OLIVE MARION	PN: Hilary Neal, Bess Norton, Kate Norway
Norvil, Manning	TN: BULMER, HENRY KENNETH
Norway, Kate	TN: NORTON, OLIVE MARION
NORWAY, NEVIL SHUTE	PN: Nevil Shute
NORWOOD, VICTOR GEORGE CHARLES	PN: Jim Bowie, Coy Banton, Sane V. Baxter, Clay Brand, Victor Brand, Shayne Colter, Walt Cody, Paul Clevinger, Johnny Dark, Vince Destry, Wes Corteen, Doone Fargo, Clint Dangerfield, Mark Fenton, Wade Fisher, G. Gearing-Thomas, Mark Hampton, Hank Jansen, Nat Karta
Novak, Joseph	TN: KOSINSKI, JERZY
Novanglus	TN: ADAMS, JOHN
NOWLAN, PHILIP FRANCIS	PN: Frank Phillips
Norman, John	TN: LANGE, JOHN FREDERICK, JR.
NUNN, WILLIAM CURTIS	PN: Will Curtis
NUTT, CHARLES	PN: Charles Beaumont, Keith Grantland
Nye, Harold G.	TN: HARDING, LEE JOHN
NYE, NELSON CORAL	PN: Clem Colt, Drake C. Denver

O

O'Brian, Frank	TN: GARFIELD, BRIAN FRANCIS WYNNE
O'Brien, Clancy	TN: SMITH, GEORGE HENRY
O'Brien, Robert C.	TN: CONLY, ROBERT LESLIE

O'Brien, Saliee — TN: FRANKIE-LEE, JANAS
O'Connor, Patrick — TN: WIBBERLEY, LEONARD PATRICK O'CONNOR
O'CONNOR, RICHARD — PN: Frank Archer, John Burke, Patrick Wayland
O'DANIEL, JANET — PN: Lillian Janet
O'Donnell, K.M. — TN: MALZBERG, BARRY NORMAN
O'Dowd, Cornelius — TN: LEVER, CHARLES
O'Gorman, Ned — TN: O'GORMAN, EDWARD CHARLES
O'Grady, Rohan — TN: SKINNER, JUNE O'GRADY
O'Hara, Kevin — TN: CUMBERLAND, MARTEN
O'Hara, Mary — TN: ALSOP, MARY O'HARA
O'Hara, Scott — TN: MAC DONALD, JOHN DANN
O. Henry — TN: PORTER, WILLIAM SYDNEY
O'Laoghaire, Liam — TN: O'LEARY, LIAM
O'Leary — TN: KUEHNELT-LEDDIHN, ERIK
O'MALLEY, Lady MARY DOLLING — PN: Ann Bridge
O'Nair, Mairi — TN: EVANS, CONSTANCE MAY
O'Neill, Egan — TN: LININGTON, BARBARA ELIZABETH
O'Neill, Rose Cecil — TN: WILSON, Mrs. HARRY LEON
O'ROURKE, FRANK — PN: Kevin Connor, Frank O'Malley, Patrick O'Malley
O'Shea, Sean — TN: TRALINS, S. ROBERT
O'Toole, Rex — TN: TRALINS, S. ROBERT
OFFUTT, ANDREW JEFFERSON V. — PN: John Cleve
Ogilvy, Gavin — TN: BARRIE, J.M.
OGNALL, LEOPOLD HORACE — PN: Harry Carmichael, Hartley Howard
Old Sleuth — TN: HALSEY, HARLAN P.
Old Wilmer — TN: LARDNER, RING
Oldfield, Peter — TN: BARTLETT, VERNON
Oldstyle, Jonathan — TN: IRVING, WASHINGTON
Oliver, Mark — TN: TYLER-WHITTLE, MICHAEL
OLSEN, ALFRED JOHN, JR. — PN: Bob Olsen
Olsen, Bob — TN: OLSEN, ALFRED JOHN, JR.
Olsen, D.B. — TN: HITCHENS, JULIA CLARA CATHERINE DELORES BIRK OLSEN

OLSEN, THEODORE VICTOR — PN: Joshua Stark, Christopher Storm, Cass Willoughby
Oneal, Zibby — TN: ONEAL, ELIZABETH
OPPENHEIM, EDWARD PHILLIPS — PN: Anthony Partridge
Optic, Oliver — TN: ADAMS, WILLIAM TAYLOR
Orczy, Baroness — TN: ORCZY, EMMA MAGDALENA ROSALIA MARIA JOSEFA BARBARA

ORCZY, EMMA MAGDALENA ROSALIA MARIA JOSEFA BARBARA — PN: Baroness Orczy
ORGEL, DORIS — PN: Doris Adelberg
ORLEY, JOHN — PN: Allen Tate
Ormond, Frederic — TN: DEY, FREDERIC MERRILL VAN RENSSELAER
Ormsbee, David — TN: LONGSTREET, STEPHEN
Orwell, George — TN: BLAIR, ERIC ARTHUR
Osborne, David — TN: SILVERBERG, ROBERT
Oswalt, Sabine — TN: MAC CORMACK, SABINE G.
Otis, James — TN: KALER, JAMES OTIS
Ouida — TN: DE LA RAMEE, LOUISE
OURSLER, CHARLES FULTON — PN: Anthony Abbot
OVERHOLSER, WAYNE D. — PN: John S. Daniels, Lee Leighton, Mark Morgan, Wayne Roberts, Dan J. Stevens, Joseph Wayne

Overy, Claire May — TN: BASS, CLARA MAY
OVSTEDAL, BARBARA — PN: Barbara Douglas, Rosalind Laker, Barbara Paul
Owen, Caroline Dale — TN: SNEDEKER, CAROLINE DALE
Owen, Edmund — TN: TELLER, NEVILLE
Owen, Hugh — TN: FAUST, FREDERICK SCHILLER
OWEN, JACK — PN: Jack Dykes
Oxenham, Elsie — TN: DUNKERLEY, ELSIE JEANETTE

P

Padgett, Lewis — TN: KUTTNER, HENRY and MOORE, CATHERINE LUCILLE
Page, Emma — TN: TIRBUTT, HONORIA

Page, Marco	TN: KURNITZ, HARRY
Palgrave, Sir Francis	TN: COHEN, SIR FRANCIS
Palinurus	TN: CONNELLY, CYRIL
PALMER, CHARLES STUART	PN: Jay Stewart
PALMER, JOHN LESLIE	PN: Francis Beeding, David Pilgrim
PALMER, RAYMOND A.	PN: Henry Gade, G.H. Irwin, Frank Patton, J.W. Pelkie, Wallace Quitman, A.R. Steber, Morris J. Steel
PANGBORN, EDGAR	PN: Bruce Harrison
Pansy	TN: ALDEN, ISABELLA MACDONALD
Paradise, Mary	TN: EDEN, DOROTHY
PARGETER, EDITH MARY	PN: Ellis Peters
PARISH, MARGARET CECILE	PN: Peggy Parish
Parish, Peggy	TN: PARISH, MARGARET CECILE
Park, Jordan	TN: KORNBLUTH, CYRIL M.
Park, Jordan	TN: POHL, FREDERIK
Park, Robert	TN: GARDNER, ERLE STANLEY
Parker, Leslie	TN: THIRKELL, ANGELA
Parley, Peter	TN: GOODRICH, SAMUEL G.
Parson Lot	TN: KINGSLEY, CHARLES
Partington, Mrs.	TN: SHILLABER, BENJAMIN P.
Partridge, Anthony	TN: OPPENHEIM, EDWARD PHILLIPS
Passante, Dom	TN: FEARN, JOHN RUSSELL
PATCHETT, MARY ELWYN OSBORNE	PN: David Bruce
Pater, Elias	TN: FRIEDMAN, JACOB HORACE
Paterson, Harry	TN: PATTERSON, HENRY
Paterson, Judith	TN: JONES, JUDITH PATERSON
Paterson-Jones, Judith	TN: JONES, JUDITH PATERSON
PATON WALSH, GILLIAN	PN: Jill Paton Walsh
Patrick, Maxine	TN: MAXWELL, PATRICIA ANNE
Patrick, Q.	TN: WEBB, RICHARD WILSON
Patrick, Q.	TN: WHEELER, HUGH CALLINGHAM
PATTEN, LEWIS BYFORD	PN: Lewis Ford, Len Leighton, Joseph Wayne
PATTEN, WILLIAM G.	PN: Burt L. Standish
PATTERSON, HARRY	PN: Martin Fallon, James Graham, Jack Higgins
PATTERSON, HENRY	PN: Hugh Marlowe
PATTINSON, NANCY EVELYN	PN: Nan Asquith
Patton, Frank	TN: PALMER, RAYMOND A. and SHAVER, RICHARD SHARPE
Paul, Barbara	TN: OVSTEDAL, BARBARA
PAUL, ELLIOT HAROLD	PN: Brett Rutledge
Paul, John	TN: WEBB, CHARLES HENRY
PAULDING, JAMES KIRK	PN: Bull-Us, Launcelot Langstaff
Paxton, Lois	TN: LOW, LOIS DOROTHEA
Paye, Robert	TN: CAMPBELL, GABRIELLE MARGARET VERE
Payne, Alan	TN: JAKES, JOHN WILLIAM
Pearce, A.H.	TN: QUIBELL, AGATHA HUNT
PEDLER, CHRISTOPHER MAGNUS HOWARD	PN: Kit Pedler
Pedler, Kit	TN: PEDLER, CHRISTOPHER MAGNUS HOWARD
Peekner, Ray	TN: PUECHNER, RAY
Pelkie, J.W.	TN: PALMER, RAYMOND A.
Pell, Robert	TN: HAGBERG, DAVID J.
Pemberton, Thomas	TN: HOPKINSON, SIR HENRY THOMAS
Pembroke, Thomas	TN: HORTON, MILES
Pembroke, Thomas	TN: HOPKINSON, SIR HENRY THOMAS
Pena, Ramon Del Valley	TN: DEL VALLE-INCLAN, RAMON
PENDLETON, DONALD EUGENE	PN: Dan Britain, Stephen Gregory
Pendennis, Arthur	TN: THACKERAY, WILLIAM MAKEPEACE
Pender, Marilyn	TN: PENDOWER, JACQUES
PENDOWER, JACQUES	PN: Kathleen Carstairs, Tom Curtis, Penn Dower, T.C.H. Jacobs, Marilyn Pender, Anne Penn
Penmare, William	TN: NISOT, ELIZABETH
Penn, Anne	TN: PENDOWER, JACQUES
Pennsylvania Farmer	TN: DICKINSON, JOHN
Penoyre, Mary	TN: MORGAN, MERY PENOYRE

Pentecost, Hugh — TN: PHILIPS, JUDSON PENTECOST
Perch, Philemon — TN: JOHNSTON, RICHARD
Peregoy, Calvin — TN: MC CLARY, THOMAS CALVERT
Perkins, Virginia Chase — TN: CHASE, VIRGINIA
Perley — TN: POORE, BENJAMIN PERLEY
Perowne, Barry — TN: ATKEY, PHILIP
PERRY, RITCHIE JOHN ALLEN — PN: John Allen
Perseus, Peter — TN: THACKERAY, WILLIAM MAKEPEACE
Peters, Bill — TN: MC GIVERN, WILLIAM PETER
Peters, Bryan — TN: GEORGE, PETER BRYAN
Peters, Elizabeth — TN: MERTZ, BARBARA LOUISE GROSS
Peters, Ellis — TN: PARGETER, EDITH MARY
Peters, Geoffrey — TN: PALMER, MADELYN
Peters, Linda — TN: CATHERALL, ARTHUR
Peters, Ludovic — TN: BRENT, PETER LUDWIG
PETERS, MAUREEN — PN: Veronica Black, Catherine Darby, Belinda Grey, Levanah Lloyd, Judith Rothman, Sharon Whitby

Petrie, Rhona — TN: BUCHANAN, EILEEN MARIE DUELL
Peyton, K.M. — TN: PEYTON, KATHLEEN W.
PEYTON, KATHLEEN M. — PN: K. Peyton
Pfaal, Hans — TN: POE, EDGAR ALLAN
Pflaum, Susanna Whitney — TN: PFLAUM-CONNOR, SUSANNA
Philenia — TN: MORTON, SARA WENTWORTH
PHILIPS, JUDSON PENTECOST — PN: Hugh Pentecost
PHILLIFENT, JOHN THOMAS — PN: John Rackham
Phillips, Frank — TN: NOWLAN, PHILIP FRANCIS
PHILLIPS, JAMES ATLEE — PN: Philip Atlee
Phillips, Mark — TN: GARRETT, RANDALL PHILLIP and HARRIS, LARRY MARK

Phillips, Richard — TN: DICK, PHILIP K.
Phillips, Rog — TN: GRAHAM, ROGER PHILLIPS
PHILLPOTTS, EDEN — PN: Harrington Hext
Philomath — TN: FRANKLIN, BENJAMIN
Phiz — TN: BROWNE, H.K.
Pierce, Matthew — TN: LUCEY, JAMES D.
Pike, Charles R. — TN: BULMER, HENRY KENNETH
Pike, Robert L. — TN: FISH, ROBERT L.
PILCHER, ROSAMUNDE — PN: Jane Fraser
Pilgrim, Anne — TN: ALLAN, MABEL ESTHER
Pilgrim, David — TN: PALMER, JOHN LESLIE
Pilgrim, David — TN: SAUNDERS, HILARY ADAM ST. GEORGE
Pilgrom, Derral — TN: ZACHARY, HUGH
Pindar, Peter — TN: WOLCOTT, JOHN
Piper, Evelyn — TN: MODELL, MERRIAM
PITCAIRN, J.J. — PN: Clifford Ashdown
Plaidy, Jean — TN: HIBBERT, ELEANOR ALICE
Player, Robert — TN: JORDAN, ROBERT FURNEAUX
Pluche, Jeames De La — TN: THACKERAY, WILLIAM MAKEPEACE
PLUMMER, CLARE EMSLEY — PN: Clare Emsley
PLUNKETT, EDWARD JOHN MORETON DRAX — PN: Lord Dunsany
POCOCK, HENRY ROGER ASHWELL — PN: Robert Pocock
POE, EDGAR ALLAN — PN: Haus Pfaal
POHL, FREDERIK — PN: James Mac Creigh, Edson Mc Cann, Jordan Park
POLLAND, MADELEINE ANGELA — PN: Frances Adrian
Pollock, Mary — TN: BLYTON, ENID MARY
Ponder, Patricia — TN: MAXWELL, PATRICIA ANNE
PONSONBY, DORIS ALMON — PN: Doris Rybot, Sarah Tempest
POORE, BENJAMIN PERLEY — PN: Perley
POPE, ALEXANDER — PN: Martinus Scriblerus
POQUELIN, JEAN BAPTISTE — PN: Moliere
Porcupine, Peter — TN: COBBETT, WILLIAM
PORGES, ARTHUR — PN: Peter Arthur, Pat Rogers
Porlock, Martin — TN: MacDONALD, PHILIP
Portal, Ellis — TN: POWE, BRUCE
Porte Crayon — TN: STROTHER, DAVID H.
PORTER, ELEANOR HODGMAN — PN: Eleanor Stuart

Porter, Gene Stratton | TN: PORTER, GENEVA GRACE STRATTON
PORTER, GENEVA GRACE
   STRATTON | PN: Gene Stratton Porter
PORTER, WILLIAM SYDNEY
   OR SIDNEY | PN: O. Henry
Post, Mortimer | TN: BLAIR, WALTER
POSTL, KARL | PN: Charles Sealsfield
POTTER, JOANNA | PN: Caroline Harvey, Joanna Trollope
POTTER, MARGARET EDITH | PN: Anne Betteridge, Anne Melville, Margaret Newman
POUND, EZRA | PN: Alfred Venison
POURNELLE, JERRY EUGENE | PN: Wade Curtis
Powell, Richard Stillman | TN: BARBOUR, RALPH HENRY
Power, Cecil | TN: ALLEN, CHARLES GRANT BLAIRFINDIE
Powers, M.L. | TN: TUBB, EDWIN CHARLES
PRATHER, RICHARD SCOTT | PN: David Knight, Douglas Ring
PRATT, MURRAY FLETCHER | PN: George U. Fletcher
Pre, Jean-Anne, De | TN: AVALLONE, MICHAEL ANGELO JR.
Preedy, George | TN: CAMPBELL, GABRIELLE MARGARET VERE
Prentis, Richard | TN: AGATE, JAMES
Preston, Richard | TN: LINDSAY, JACK
Price, Evadne | TN: SMITH, HELEN ZENNA
Price, Jennifer | TN: HOOVER, HELEN
PRITCHARD, JOHN WALLACE | PN: Ian Wallace
Proctor, Everitt | TN: MONTGOMERY, RUTHERFORD GEORGE
Prole, Lozania | TN: BLOOM, URSULA HARVEY
PRONZINI, BILL | PN: Jack Foxx, William Jeffrey, Alex Saxon
Proteus Esquire, Echo | TN: FRANKLIN, BENJAMIN
Publius | TN: HAMILTON, ALEXANDER (with others)
Pumilla, Joe | TN: PUMILLA, JOSEPH F.
PUMILLA, JOSEPH F. | PN: M.M. Moamrath, Joe Pumilla
Pure, Simon | TN: SWINNERTON, FRANK
Putnam, John | TN: BECKWITH, BURNHAM PUTNAM
Putney, Gail J. | TN: FULLERTON, GAIL
PUZO, MARIO | PN: Mario Cleri
PYESHKOV, ALEXEI | PN: Maxim Gorky

Q

'Q' | TN: QUILLER-COUCH, SIR ARTHUR
Quarles | TN: POE, EDGAR ALLAN
Quartermain, James | TN: LYNNE, JAMES BROOM
Queen, Ellery | TN: DANNAY, FREDERIC and LEE, MANFRED BENNINGTON
Queen, Ellery | TN: VANCE, JOHN HOLBROOK
Queen, Ellery | TN: WALDO, EDWARD HAMILTON
Queen, Ellery, Jr. | TN: DANNAY, FREDERIC and LEE, MANFRED B.
Queen, Ellery, Jr. | TN: HOLDING, JAMES
Quentin, Patrick | TN: WEBB, RICHARD WILSON and WHEELER, HUGH CALLINGHAM
Quest, Erica | TN: SAWYER, JOHN and NANCY
Quiller, Andrew | TN: BULMER, HENRY KENNETH
QUILLER-COUCH, SIR ARTHUR | PN: Q
Quin, Dan | TN: LEWIS, ALFRED HENRY
Quin, Mike | TN: RYAN, PAUL WILLIAM
Quitman, Wallace | TN: PALMER, RAYMOND A.
Quod, John | TN: IRVING, JOHN TREAT

R

RABELAIS, FRANCOIS | PN: Alcofribas Nasier
RABINOVITCH, SOLOMON | PN: Sholom Aleichem
Rackham, John | TN: PHILLIFENT, JOHN THOMAS
Radcliffe, Janette | TN: ROBERTS, JANET LOUISE
Radford, E. & M.A. | TN: RADFORD, EDWIN ISAAC
Radford, E. & M.A. | TN: RADFORD, MONA AUGUSTA
RADFORD, EDWIN ISAAC | PN: E. & M.A. Radford
RADFORD, MONA AUGUSTA | PN: Radford, E. & M.A.

RAE, HUGH CRAWFORD — PN: Robert Crawford, R.B. Houston, Stuart Stern, Jessica Stirling

Rafferty, S.S. — TN: HURLEY, JOHN J.
Ralston, Jan — TN: DUNLOP, AGNES M.R
Ralston, Jan — TN: KYLE, ELISABETH
Ramal, Walter — TN: DE LA MARE, WALTER
Ramsey, Eric — TN: HAGBERG, DAVID J.
Ramsbottom. Dorothea Julia — TN: THACKERAY, WILLIAM MAKEPEACE
Rand, Brett — TN: NORWOOD, VICTOR GEORGE CHARLES
Rand. William — TN: ROSS, WILLIAM
Randall, Janet — TN: YOUNG, JANET RANDALL
Randall, Robert — TN: GARRETT, RANDALL PHILLIP and SILVERBERG, ROBERT

Randell, Beverley — TN: PRICE, BEVERLEY JOAN
RANDOLPH, GEORGIANA ANN — PN: Craig Rice, Daphne Sanders, Michael Venning
Randolph, Marion — TN: RODELL, MARIE FREID
Rangely, Olivia — TN: ZACHARY, HUGH
Ranger, Ken — TN: CREASEY, JOHN
Rankine, John — TN: MASON, DOUGLAS RANKINE
Ransome, Stephen, — TN: DAVIS, FREDERICK CLYDE
RAPHAEL, CHAIM — PN: Jocelyn Davey
RATHBONE, ST. GEORGE HENRY — PN: Harrison Adams, Hugh Allen, Oliver Lee Clifton, Duke Duncan, Aleck Forbes, Lieutenant Keene, Marline Manly, Mark Merrick, Warne Miller, M.D., Harry St. George, Col. J.M. Travers

Rattray, Simon — TN: TREVOR, ELLESTON
Rawlins, Eustace Robert — TN: BARTON, EUSTACE ROBERT
Raworth, Tom — TN: RAWORTH, THOMAS MOORE
RAWSON, CLAYTON — PN: The Great Merlini, Stuart Towne
Raycraft, Stan — TN: SHAVER, RICHARD SHARPE
RAYER, FRANCIS GEORGE — PN: George Longdon, Milward Scott, Roland Worchester
Raymond, Charlotte — TN: LE FONTAINE, JOSEPH RAYMOND HERVÉ
Raymond, Joseph — TN: LE FONTAINE, JOSEPH RAYMOND HERVÉ
Raymond, Mary — TN: HEATHCOTT, MARY
RAYMOND, RENE BRABAZON — PN: James Hadley Chase, James L. Docherty, Ambrose Grant, Raymond Marshall

RAYNER, CLAIRE BERENICE — PN: Sheila Brandon, Ann Lyton, Ruth Martin
Rayner, Olive Pratt — TN: ALLEN, CHARLES GRANT BLAIRFINDIE
Rayner, Richard — TN: MC ILWAIN, DAVID
Read, Jan — TN: READ, JOHN HILTON
Read, Miss — TN: SAINT, DORA JESSIE
Reade, Hamish — TN: GRAY, SIMON
Reault, Mary — TN: CHALLANS, MARY
Redmayne, Barbara — TN: HOWE, MURIEL
Reed, Eliot — TN: AMBLER, ERIC
Reed, Eliot — TN: RODDA, CHARLES
Reed, Kit — TN: REED, LILLIAN
REED, LILLIAN — PN: Kit Reed
Reed, Peter — TN: MACDONALD, JOHN DANN
REEMAN, DOUGLAS — PN: Alexander Kent
Rees, Dilwyn — TN: DANIEL, GLYN EDMUND
REESE, JOHN — PN: John Jo Carpenter, Cody Kennedy Jr.
REEVES, JOYCE — PN: Joyce Gard
Regan, Brad — TN: NORWOOD, VICTOR GEORGE CHARLES
Regester, Seeley — TN: VICTOR, METTA FULLER
REILLY, HELEN — PN: Kieran Abbey
Reilly, William K. — TN: CREASEY, JOHN
Reiner, Max — TN: CALDWELL, JANET MIRIAM TAYLOR HOLLAND
Reitchi, Jack — TN: REITCHI, JOHN GEORGE
REITCHI, JOHN GEORGE — PN: Jack Ritchie
REIZENSTEIN, ELMER — PN: Elmer Rice
Remy, Pierre-Jean — TN: ANGREMY, JEAN-PIERRE
Renier, Elizabeth — TN: BAKER, BETTY DOREEN
Renton, Cam — TN: ARMSTRONG, RICHARD
REPP, EDWARD EARL — PN: John Cody, Peter Field
Revere, M.P. — TN: WILLIAMSON, ALICE MURIEL

Revere, M.P.	TN: WILLIAMSON, CHARLES NORRIS
REYNOLDS, DALLAS MC CORD	PN: Todd Harding, Mack Reynolds, Maxine Reynolds
Reynolds, Mack	TN: REYNOLDS, DALLAS MC CORD
Reynolds, Maxine	TN: REYNOLDS, DALLAS MC CORD
RHAMEY, BEN	PN: Hollis, H.H.
Rhode, John	TN: STREET, CECIL JOHN CHARLES
Rice, Craig	TN: RANDOLPH, GEORGIANA ANN
Rice, Elmer	TN: REIZENSTEIN, ELMER
Rich, Barbara	TN: GRAVES, ROBERT RANKE
Rich, Barbara	TN: JACKSON, Mrs. SCHUYLER B.
Richards, Clay	TN: CROSSEN, KENDELL FOSTER
Richards, Frank	TN: HAMILTON, CHARLES HAROLD ST. JOHN
Richards, Henry	TN: MORRISSEY, JOSEPH LAWRENCE
Richards, Hilda	TN: HAMILTON, CHARLES HAROLD ST. JOHN
RICHARDSON, ROBERT SHIRLEY	PN: Philip Latham
Richmond, Grace	TN: MARSH, JOHN
RICHMOND, ROALDUS FREDERICK	PN: Roe Richmond
Rickard, Bob	TN: RICKARD, ROBERT J.M.
Ridgway, Jason	TN: LESSER, MILTON
Riding, Laura	TN: GOTTSCHALK, LAURA RIDING
Riding, Laura	TN: JACKSON, Mrs. SCHUYLER B.
RIEFE, ALAN	PN: Barbara Riefe
Riefe, Barbara	TN: RIEFE, ALAN
RIFKIN, SHEPARD	PN: Jake Logan
RIGSBY, VECHEL HOWARD	PN: Mark Howard, Vechel Howard
RILEY, JAMES WHITCOMB	PN: Benjamin F. Johnson
Riley, Tex	TN: CREASEY, JOHN
Ring, Douglas	TN: PRATHER, RICHARD SCOTT
Ripley, Jack	TN: WAINWRIGHT, JOHN
RITCHIE, CLAIRE	PN: Sharon Heath
Ritchie, Jack	TN: REITCHI, JOHN GEORGE
Riverside, John	TN: HEINLEIN, ROBERT
Rives, Amelie	TN: TROUBETSKOI, PRINCESS
RIVETT, EDITH CAROLINE	PN: Carol Carnac, E.C.R. Lorac
ROAN, TOM	PN: Adam Rebel
ROARK, GARLAND	PN: George Garland
Roberts, I.M.	TN: ROBERTS, IRENE
ROBERTS, IRENE	PN: Roberta Carr, Elizabeth Harle, I.M. Roberts, Ivor Roberts, Iris Rowland, Irene Shaw
Roberts, Ivor	TN: ROBERTS, IRENE
Roberts, James Hall	TN: DUNCAN, ROBERT LIPSCOMB
ROBERTS, JANET LOUISE	PN: Louisa Bronte, Rebecca Danton, Janette Radcliffe
Roberts, Ken	TN: LAKE, KENNETH ROBERT
Roberts, Lawrence	TN: FISH, ROBERT L.
Robertson, Elspeth	TN: ELLISON, JOAN AUDREY
ROBERTSON, FRANK CHESTER	PN: Robert Crane, Frank Chester Field
ROBERTSON, KEITH CARLTON	PN: Carlton Keith
Robeson, Kenneth	TN: DENT, LESTER
Robeson, Kenneth	TN: ERNST, PAUL
Robeson, Kenneth	TN: GOULART, RONALD JOSEPH
ROBINS, DENISE NAOMI	PN: Denise Chesterton, Ashley French, Harriet Gray, Hervey Hamilton, Julia Kane, Francesca Wright
Robins, Patricia	TN: CLARK, PATRICIA DENISE
ROBINSON, JOAN MARY GALE	PN: Joan Gale Thomas
Robson, Dirk	TN: ROBINSON, DEREK
ROBY, MARY LINN	PN: Pamela D'Arcy, Georgina Grey, Elizabeth Welles, Mary Wilson
Rochard, Henry	TN: CHARLIER, ROGER HENRI
ROCKLIN, ROSS LOUIS	PN: Ross Rocklynne
Rocklynne, Ross	TN: ROCKLIN, ROSS LOUIS
RODDA, CHARLES	PN: Eliot Reed
RODELL, MARIE FREID	PN: Marion Randolph
Rodger, Alec	TN: RODGER, THOMAS ALEXANDER
Roffman, Jan	TN: SUMMERTON, MARGARET
Rogers, Floyd	TN: SPENCE, WILLIAM JOHN DUNCAN
Rogers, Keith	TN: HARRIS, MARION ROSE

Rogers, Melva — TN: GRAHAM, ROGER PHILLIPS
Rogers, Mick — TN: GLUT, DON F.
Rogers, Pat — TN: PORGES, ARTHUR
ROGERS, ROSEMARY — PN: Marina Mayson
Rohmer, Sax — TN: WARD, ARTHUR HENRY SARSFIELD
Roland, Mary — TN: BRAND, MARY CHRISTIANNA MILNE
ROLFE, FREDERICK — PN: Baron Corvo
ROLLINS, KATHLEEN — PN: Hal Debrett
Rollo (Books) — TN: ABBOTT, JACOB
Rolls, Anthony — TN: VULLIAMY, COLWYN EDWARD
ROLVAAG, OLLE EDVART — PN: Paal Morck
Romains, Jules — TN: FARIGOULE, LOUIS
Ronns, Edward — TN: AARONS, EDWARD SIDNEY
ROOS, AUDREY — PN: Kelley Roos
Roos, Kelley — TN: ROOS, AUDREY and WILLIAM
ROOS, WILLIAM — PN: William Rand, Kelley Roos
Rose, Laurence F. — TN: FEARN, JOHN RUSSELL
Ross, Albert — TN: GOLDSTEIN, ARTHUR DAVID
Ross, Angus — TN: GIGGAL, KENNETH
Ross, Barnaby — TN: DANNAY, FREDERIC and LEE, MANFRED BENNINGTON
Ross, Carlton — TN: BROOKS, EDWY SEARLES
Ross, Catherine — TN: BEATY, BETTY
Ross, Clarissa — TN: ROSS, WILLIAM
Ross, Dana — TN: ROSS, WILLIAM
Ross, Helaine — TN: DANIELS, DOROTHY
Ross, Jonathan — TN: ROSSITER, JOHN
Ross, Laurence — TN: HYLAND, ANN
Ross, Leonard Q. — TN: ROSTEN, LEO
Ross, Marilyn — TN: ROSS, WILLIAM
Ross, Mary Adelaide Eden — TN: PHILLPOTTS, ADELAIDE
ROSS, W.E.D. — PN: Clarissa Ross, Marilyn Ross
ROSS, ZOLA HELEN — PN: Helen Arre, Bert Iles, Z.H. Ross
Rosse, Jan — TN: STRAKER, J.F.
ROSSITER, JOHN — PN: Jonathan Ross
Rostand, Robert — TN: HOPKINS, ROBERT SYDNEY
ROSTEN, LEO — PN: Leonard Q. Ross
ROTH, HOLLY — PN: K.G. Ballard, P.J. Merrill
Rothman, Judith — TN: PETERS, MAUREEN
ROTSLER, WILLIAM — PN: William Arrow, John Ryder Hall
ROUGIER, Mrs. GEORGE RONALD — PN: Georgette Heyer, Stella Martin
Rousseau, Victor — TN: EMANUEL, VICTOR ROUSSEAU
Rowan, Deirdre — TN: WILLIAMS, JEANNE
ROWLAND, DONALD SYDNEY — PN: Annette Adams, Jack Bassett, Hazel Baxter, Karla Benton, Helen Berry, Lewis Brant, Alison Bray, William Brayce, Fenton Brockley, Oliver Bronson, Chuck Buchanan, Rod Caley, Roger Carlton, Janita Cleve, Sharon Court, Vera Craig, Wesley Craille, John Delaney, John Dryden, Freda Fenton, Charles Field, Graham Garner, Burt Kroll, Helen Langley, Henry Lansing, Harvey Lant, Irene Lynn, Hank Madison, Chuck Mason, Stuart Mc Hugh, G.J. Morgan, Glebe Morgan, Edna Murray, Lorna Page, Olive Patterson, Alvin Porter, Alex Random, W.J. Rimmer, Donna Rix, Matt Rockwell, Charles RnSCoe, Minerva Rosetti, Norford Scott, Valerie Scott, Bart Segundo, Bart Shane, Frank Shaul, Clinton Spurr, Roland Starr, J.D. Stevens, Mark Suffling, Kay Talbot, Will Travers, Sarah Vine, Elaine Vinson, Rick Walters, Neil Webb
Rowland, Iris — TN: ROBERTS, IRENE
Rowlands, Effie — TN: ALBANASI, Madame EFFIE ADELAIDE MARIA
Roy, Brandon — TN: BARCLAY, FLORENCE LOUISA
Roy, Rob — TN: MAC GREGOR, JOHN
Royce, Kenneth — TN: GANDLEY, KENNETH ROYCE
RUBEL, JAMES LYON — PN: Timothy Hayes, Mason Mac Rae
Rudd, Margaret — TN: NEWLIN, MARGARET RUDD
Rudomin, Esther — TN: HAUTZIG, ESTHER

Ruell, Patrick	TN: HILL, REGINALD
RUMBOLD-GIBBS, HENRY ST. JOHN CLAIR	PN: Henry Gibbs, Simon Harvester
RUNDLE, ANNE	PN: Georgianna Bell, Marianne Lamont, Alexandra Manners, Joanne Marshall, Jeanne Summers
Ruppert, Chester	TN: GRAHAM, ROGER PHILLIPS
Rusholm, Peter	TN: POWELL, ERIC
RUSSELL, GEORGE WILLIAM	PN: A.E.
RUSSELL, Countess MARY ANNETTE VON ARNIM BAUCHAMP	PN: Elizabeth, Alice Cholmondeley
Russell, Shane	TN: NORWOOD, VICTOR GEORGE CHARLES
RUSSELL, WILLIAM	PN: Inspector F; Inspector Robert Warneford, Rn; Waters
Rusticus	TN: FOWLER, J.K.
Rutherford, Douglas	TN: MC CONNELL, JAMES DOUGLAS RUTHERFORD
Ruthin, Margaret	TN: CATHERALL, ARTHUR
Rutledge, Brett	TN: PAUL, ELIOT HAROLD
RYALL, W.B.	PN: William Bolitho
RYAN, PAUL WILLIAM	PN: Robert Finnegan, Mike Quin
Ryan, Tim	TN: DENT, LESTER
Rybot, Doris	TN: PONSONBY, DORIS ALMON
Rydell, Forbes	TN: FORBES, DOLORIS FLORINE STANTON
Rydell, Forbes	TN: RYDELL, HELEN
RYDELL, HELEN	PN: Forbes Rydell
Rydell, Wendell	TN: RYDELL, WENDY
Ryder, Jonathan	TN: LUDLUM, ROBERT
Rye, Anthony	TN: YOUD, CHRISTOPEHR SAMUEL

S

Sabre, Dirk	TN: LAFFIN, JOHN
Sadler, Mark	TN: LYNDS, DENNIS
Sage, Juniper	TN: BROWN, MARGARET WISE
St. John, David	TN: HUNT, E. HOWARD
St. John, Leonie	TN: BAYER, WILLIAM
St. John, Mabel	TN: COOPER, HENRY ST. JOHN
St. John, Nicole	TN: JOHNSTON, NORMA
St. John, Philip	TN: ALVAREZ-DEL RAY, RAMON FELIPE SAN JUAN MARI?
St. Paul, Sterner	TN: MEEK, STERNER ST. PAUL
Saki	TN: MUNRO, HECTOR HUGH
Salisbury, Carola	TN: BUTTERWORTH, MICHAEL
Salisbury, John	TN: CAUTE, DAVID
SALMON, ANNIE ELIZABETH	PN: Elizabeth Ashley
Salop, Lynne	TN: HAWES, LYNNE SALOP
Salter, Cedric	TN: KNIGHT, FRANK FRANCIS EDGAR
Salter, Mary D.	TN: AINSWORTH, MARY D. SALTER
SAMPSON, RICHARD HENRY	PN: Richard Hull
Sanborn, B.X.	TN: BALLINGER, WILLIAM SANBORN
Sand, George	TN: DUPIN, ARMANDINE AURORE
SANDBURG, CARL A.	PN: Militant
SANDERS, DOROTHY LUCIE	PN: Lucy Walker
Sanders, Daphne	TN: RANDOLPH, GEORGIANNA ANN
Sanders, Jeanne	TN: RUNDLE, ANNE
Sanders, Martin	TN: BURKE, JOHN FREDERIC
SANDOZ, MARI	PN: Mari Macumber
Sands, Martin	TN: BURKE, JOHN
Sandys, Oliver	TN: JERVIS, MARGUERITE FLOREN
Sapper	TN: MC NEILE, HERMAN CYRIL
Sarban	TN: WALL, JOHN W.
SAROYAN, WILLIAM	PN: Sirak Goryan
Saunders, Caleb	TN: HEINLEIN, ROBERT
SAUNDERS, HILARY ADAM ST. GEORGE	PN: Francis Beeding, David Pilgrim
Saunders, Richard	TN: FRANKLIN, BENJAMIN
Saunders, Wes	TN: BOUNDS, SYDNEY JAMES
Savage, David	TN: HOSSENT, HARRY

Savage, Richard	TN: ROE, IVAN
Savallo, Dona Teresa De	TN: WILLIAMSON, ALICE MURIEL
Savallo, Dona Teresa De	TN: WILLIAMSON, CHARLES NORRIS
Sawtelle, William Carter	TN: GRAHAM, ROGER PHILLIPS
SAWYER, JOHN and NANCY	PN: Nancy Buckingham, Nancy John, Erica Quest
Saxon, Alex	TN: PRONZINI, BILL
Saxon, John A.	TN: BELLEM, ROBERT LESLIE
Saxon, Richard	TN: MORRISSEY, JOSEPH LAWRENCE
Saxton, Judith	TN: TURNER, JUDITH
SAYERS, JAMES DENSON	PN: Denver Bardwell, Dan James
Scarrott, Michael	TN: FISHER, A. STANLEY T.
SCHACHNER, NATHAN	PN: Chan Corbett, Walter Glamis
SCHLER, RAOUL STEPHEN	PN: Rex Burns
SCHLEIN, MIRIAM	PN: Lavinia Stanhope
SCHMIDT, JAMES NORMAN	PN: James Norman
SCHOEPFLIN, HAROLD VINCENT	PN: Harl Vincent
Schofield, Jonathan	TN: STREIB, DAN
Schofield, Paul	TN: TUBB, EDWIN CHARLES
Sclanders, Doorn	TN: FEARN, JOHN RUSSELL
Scofield, Jonathan	TN: TOOMBS, JOHN
Scotland, Jay	TN: JAKES, JOHN WILLIAM
Scott, Alastair	TN: ALLEN, KENNETH S.
Scott, Anthony	TN: DRESSER, DAVIS
Scott, Dana	TN: ROBERTSON, CONSTANCE NOYES
Scott, Jane	TN: MC ELFRESH, ELIZABETH ADELINE
Scott, Janey	TN: LINDSAY, RACHEL
Scott, Milward	TN: RAYER, FRANCIS GEORGE
Scott, Warwick	TN: TREVOR, ELLESTON
Scriblerus, Martinus	TN: POPE, ALEXANDER
Scrum, R.	TN: CRUMB, R.
Seager, Joan	TN: FEARN, JOHN RUSSELL
Seale, Sara	TN: MAC PHERSON, A.D.L.
Sealsfield, Charles	TN: POSTL, KARL
Seare, Nicholas	TN: WHITAKER, RODNEY
Searls, Hank	TN: SEARLS, JR., HENRY HUNT
SEARLS JR., HENRY HUNT	PN: Hank Searls
Sebastian, Gregory Largo	TN: LE FONTAINE, JOSEPH RAYMOND HERVÉ
Sebastian, Lee	TN: SILVERBERG, ROBERT
Sedges, John	TN: BUCK, PEARL S.
Sedulous	TN: HARRISON, GILBERT
See, John Van	TN: VANCE, JOHN HOLBROOK
See-Lion	TN: BENNETT, GEOFFREY MARTIN
SEED, CECILE EUGENIE	PN: Jenny Seed
Seed, Jenny	TN: SEED, CECILE EUGENIE
SEIFERT, ELIZABETH	PN: Ellen Ashley
Selden, George	TN: THOMPSON, GEORGE SELDEN
SELDES, GILBERT	PN: Foster Johns
Sellings, Arthur	TN: LEY, ROBERT ARTHUR
SELTZER, CHARLES ALDEN	PN: Hiram Hopkins
SENARENS, LUIS PHILIP	PN: Captain Howard
Seuss	TN: GEISEL, THEODOR SEUSS
Seuss, Dr.	TN: GEISEL, THEODOR SEUSS
Severn, David	TN: UNWIN, DAVID STORR
Seymour, Alan	TN: WRIGHT, SYDNEY FOWLER
SHAFFER, ANTHONY JOSHUA	PN: Peter Antony
SHAFFER, PETER LEVIN	PN: Peter Anthony
Shane, Rhondo	TN: NORWOOD, VICTOR GEORGE CHARLES
Shane, Victor	TN: NORWOOD, VICTOR GEORGE CHARLES
Shannon, Dell	TN: LININGTON, BARBARA ELIZABETH
SHAPPIRO, HERBERT ARTHUR	PN: Burt Arthur, Herbert Arthur
SHARKEY, JOHN MICHAEL	PN: Mike Johnson, Jack Sharkey
Sharp, Luke	TN: BARR, ROBERT
SHARP, WILLIAM	PN: Fiona Mac Leod
SHAVER, RICHARD SHARPE	PN: Wes Amherst, Edwin Benson, Peter Dexter, Richard Dorset, Richard English, G.H. Irwin, Paul Lohrman, Frank Patton, Stan Raycraft

SHAW, BERNARD	PN: Corns Di Bassetto
Shaw, Brian	TN: TUBB, EDWIN CHARLES
Shaw, Bryan	TN: FEARN, JOHN RUSSELL
SHAW, FELICITY	PN: Anne Morice
Shawn, Frank S.	TN: GOULART, RONALD JOSEPH
SHAW, HENRY WHEELER	PN: Josh Billings
Shaw, Irene	TN: ROBERTS, IRENE
Shearing, Joseph	TN: CAMPBELL, GABRIELLE MARGARET VERE
Shelbourne, Cecily	TN: EBEL, SUZANNE
SHELDON, ALICE HASTINGS	PN: Raccoona Sheldon, James Tiptree, Jr.
Sheldon, Racoona	TN: SHELDON, ALICE HASTINGS
Sheldon, Lee	TN: LEE, WAYNE C.
Sheldon, Roy	TN: TUBB, EDWIN CHARLES
SHELLABARGER, SAMUEL	PN: John Estevan, Peter Loring
Shepard, Neal	TN: MORLAND, NIGEL
Shepherd, John	TN: BALLARD, WILLIS TODHUNTER
Shepherd, Michael	TN: LUDLUM, ROBERT
Sheridan, Lee	TN: LEE, ELSIE
SHEPHERD, DONALD LEE	PN: Barbara Kevern
Shepherd, Neal	TN: MORLAND, NIGEL
Sheraton, Neil	TN: SMITH, NORMAN EDWARD MACE
Sherman, Michael	TN: LOWNDES, ROBERT AUGUSTINE WARD
Sherman, Peter Michael	TN: LOWNDES, ROBERT AUGUSTINE WARD
SHIEL, MATTHEW PHIPPS	PN: Gordon Holmes
SHIRAS, WILMAR HOUSE	PN: Jane Howes
Shone, Patric	TN: HANLEY, JAMES
Shore, Norman	TN: SMITH, NORMAN EDWARD MACE
Shumsky, Zena	TN: COLLIER, ZENA
Shura, Mary Francis	TN: CRAIG, MARY FRANCIS
Shute, Nevil	TN: NORWAY, NEVIL SHUTE
Shy, Timothy	TN: LEWIS, D.B. WYNDHAM
Siady, Fred M.	TN: SAIDY, FAREED MILHEM
Sibert, Willa	TN: CATHER, WILLA
Sidney, Margaret	TN: LOTHROP, HARRIET MULFORD
Sihanouk, Norodom	TN: SIAHNOUK, SAMDECH NORODOM
Siller, Van	TN: VAN SILLER, HILDA
Siluriensis, Leolinus	TN: MACHEN, ARTHUR
Silver, Nicholas	TN: FAUST, FREDERICK SCHILLER
Silver, Richard	TN: BULMER, HENRY KENNETH
SILVERBERG, ROBERT	PN: Walter Chapman, Ivar Jorgensen, Calvin M. Knox, David Osborne, Robert Randall, Lee Sebastian, S.M. Tenneshaw
Simon, Robert	TN: MUSTO, BARRY
SIMON, S.J.	PN: Caryl Brahms
Simons, Jim	TN: SIMONS, JAMES MARCUS
Sinclair, Alisdair	TN: CLYNE, DOUGLAS
Sinclair, James	TN: STAPLES, REGINALD
SINCLAIR, OLGA ELLEN	PN: Ellen Clare
SINCLAIR, UPTON	PN: Frederick Garrison, Arthur Stirling
SINCLAIR-COWAN, BERTHA MUZZY	PN: B.M. Bower
Singer, Adam	TN: KARP, DAVID
Sinjohn, John	TN: GALSWORTHY, JOHN
SKINNER, JUNE O'GRADY	PN: A. Carleon, Rohan O'Grady
SLADEK JOHN THOMAS	PN: Thom Demijohn, Casandra Knye
Slate, John	TN: FEARN, JOHN RUSSELL
Slater, Cedric	TN: KNIGHT, FRANCIS EDGAR
SLAUGHTER, FRANK GILL	PN: G. Arnold Haygood, C.V. Terry
SLESAR, HENRY	PN: O.H. Leslie
Slick, Jonathan	TN: STEPHENS, ANN SOPHIA
Slick, Sam	TN: HALIBURTON, THOMAS C.
Sloane, Sara	TN: BLOOM, URSULA HARVEY
Small, Ernest	TN: LENT, BLAIR
Smith, Bryan	TN: KNOTT, WILLIAM C.
Smith, Caeser	TN: TREVOR, ELLESTON
Smith, Carmichael	TN: LINEBARGER, PAUL MYRON ANTHONY

Statten, Vargo	TN: FEARN, JOHN RUSSELL
Staunton, Schuyler	TN: BAUM, LYMAN FRANK
Steber, A.R.	TN: GRAHAM, ROGER PHILLIPS and PALMER, RAYMOND A.
STEEGMULLER, FRANCIS	PN: David Keith, Byron Steel
Steel, Byron	TN: STEEGMULLER, FRANCIS
Steel, Kurt	TN: KAGEY, RUDOLF
Steele, Curtis	TN: DAVIS, FREDERICK CLYDE
STEELE, HARWOOD ELMES ROBERT	PN: Howard Steele
STEELE, MARY QUINTARD	PN: Wilson Gage
Steele, Morris J.	TN: PALMER, RAYMOND A.
STEEN, MARGUERITE	PN: Lennox Dryden, Jane Nicholson
Steffanson, Con	TN: GOULART, RONALD JOSEPH
STEIN, AARON MARC	PN: George Bagby, Hampton Stone
Stein, Ben	TN: STEIN, BENJAMIN
Stendhal	TN: BEYLE, MARIE HENRI
STEPHENS, ANN SOPHIA	PN: Jonathan Slick
Steptoe, Lydia	TN: BARNES, DJUNA
Sterling, Brett	TN: HAMILTON, EDMOND
Sterling, Maria Sandra	TN: FLOREN, LEE
Stern, Paul Frederick	TN: ERNST, PAUL FREDERICK
Stern, Stuart	TN: RAE, HUGH CRAWFORD
Stevens, Blaine	TN: WHITTINGTON, HARRY
Stevens, Francis	TN: BENNETT, GERTRUDE BARROWS
Stevens, John	TN: TUBB, EDWIN CHARLES
Stevens, R.L.	TN: HOCH, EDWARD DENTINGER
Stevens, Robert Tyler	TN: STAPLES, REGINALD
STEVENSON, FLORENCE	PN: Zandra Colt, Lucia Curzon, Zabrina Faire
Stevenson, John P.	TN: GRIERSON, EDWARD DOBBYN
STEWART, ALFRED WALTER	PN: J.J. Connington
Stewart, David	TN: POLITELLA, DARIO
STEWART, DOROTHY MARY	PN: Mary Elgin
Stewart, Jay	TN: PALMER, CHARLES STUART
Stewart, Jean	TN: NEWMAN, MONA ALICE JEAN
STEWART, JOHN INNES MACKINTOSH	PN: Michael Innes
Stewart, Will	TN: WILLIAMSON, JOHN STEWART
STINE, GEORGE HARRY	PN: Lee Correy
Stine, Hank	TN: STINE, HENRY EUGENE
STINE, HENRY EUGENE	PN: Hank Stine
Stirling, Arthur	TN: SINCLAIR, UPTON
Stirling, Jessica	TN: COGHLAN, MARGARET M. PEGGIE
Stirling, Jessica	TN: RAE, HUGH CRAWFORD
Stockbridge, Dorothy	TN: TILLETT, DOROTHY STOCKBRIDGE
STOCKTON, FRANCIS RICHARD	PN: Stockton, Frank R.
Stockton, Frank R.	TN: STOCKTON, FRANCIS RICHARD
STOKER, ALAN	PN: Evan Evans
Stone, Hampton	TN: STEIN, AARON MARC
Stoner, Oliver	TN: BISHOP, MORCHARD
Stong, Pat	TN: HOUGH, RICHARD ALEXANDER
Storm, Christopher	TN: OLSEN, T.V.
STORR, CATHERINE	PN: Irene Adler, Helen Lourie
STOUTENBURG, ADRIEN	PN: Lace Kendall
Storm, Virginia	TN: SWATRIDGE, IRENE MAUD
Story, Josephine	TN: LORING, EMILIE
Strachey, Barbara	TN: HALPERN, BARBARA STRACHEY
Strange, John Stephen	TN: TILLETT, DOROTHY STOCKBRIDGE
Strange, Lord	TN: DRUMMOND, JOHN
Stranger, Joyce	TN: WILSON, JOYCE MURIEL
STRATEMEYER, EDWARD	PN: Arthur M. Winfield
STRATTON, REBECCA	PN: Lucy Gillen
Stratton, Thomas	TN: COULSON, ROBERT STRATTON
Stratton, Thomas	TN: DE WEESE, THOMAS EUGENE
Stravolgi, Bartolomeo	TN: TUCCI, NICCOLO
Street, C.J.C.	TN: STREET, CECIL JOHN CHARLES
STREET, CECIL JOHN CHARLES	PN: Miles Burton, John Rhode, C.J.C. Street

STREIB, DAN	PN: J. Faragut Jones
STRETE, CRAIG	PN: A Cherokee Indian Writer
Stretton, Hesba	TN: SMITH, SARAH HANNAH
Strong, Pat	TN: HOUGH, RICHARD ALEXANDER
Strong, Susan	TN: REES, JOAN
STROTHER, DAVID	PN: Porte Crayon
Strover, Dorothea	TN: TINNE, DOROTHEA
Stuart, Alex	TN: GORDON, RICHARD
Stuart, Alex R.	TN: GORDON, RICHARD
Stuart, Clay	TN: WHITTINGTON, HARRY
Stuart, Eleanor	TN: PORTER, ELEANOR HODGEMAN
Stuart, Ian	TN: MAC LEAN, ALISTAIR STUART
Stuart, Logan	TN: WILDING, PHILIP
Stuart, Sidney	TN: AVALLONE, MICHAEL ANGELO, JR.
STUART, VIVIAN	PN: William Stuart Long
STUBBS, HARRY CLEMENT	PN: Hal Clement
Stultifer, Morton	TN: CURTIS, RICHARD
Sture-Vasa, Mary	TN: ALSOP, MARY O'HARA
Sturgeon, Theodore	TN: WALDO, EDWARD HAMILTON
Sturrock, Jeremy	TN: HEALEY, BENJAMIN JAMES
Stuyvesant, Alice	TN: WILLIAMSON, ALICE MURIEL
Stuyvesant, Alice	TN: WILLIAMSON, CHARLES NORRIS
STYLES, FRANK SHOWELL	PN: Glyn Carr
Subond, Valerie	TN: GRAYLAND, VALERIE MERLE
SUDDABY, DONALD	PN: Alan Griff
Sue, Eugene	TN: SUE, MARIE JOSEPH
SUE, MARIE JOSEPH	PN: Eugene Sue
Sullivan, Sean Mei	TN: SOHL, JERRY GERALD ALLAN
Sullivan, Vernon	TN: VIAN, BORIS
Summers, Diana	TN: SMITH, GEORGE HENRY
Summers, Essie	TN: SUMMERS, ETHEL SNELSON
SUMMERS, ETHEL SNELSON	PN: Essie Summers
Summers,Jeanne	TN: RUNDLE, ANNE
Summers, Rowena	TN: SAUNDERS, JEAN
SUMMERTON, MARGARET	PN: Jan Roffman
Sundarananda	TN: NAKASHIMA, GEORGE KATSUTOSHI
'Sundial'	TN: MARQUIS, DON
Super Santa	TN: BERMAN, ED
Sutherland, Elizabeth	TN: MARSHALL, ELIZABETH SOUTHERLAND
Sutton, John	TN: TULLETT, DENIS
Sutton, Henry	TN: SLAVITT, DAVID
Sutton, I.M.	TN: COAD, FREDERICK ROY
SWAN, ANNIE S.	PN: David Lyall
SWATRIDGE, CHARLES	PN: Theresa Charles
SWATRIDGE, IRENE MAUDE	PN: Fay Chandos, Theresa Charles, Leslie Lance, Irene Mossop, Virginia Storm, Jan Tempest
SWINNERTON, FRANK	PN: Simon Pure
Sydney, Cynthia	TN: TRALINS, S. ROBERT
SYMONS, DOROTHY GERALDINE	PN: Georgina Groves
Syntax, Dr.	TN: COOMBE, WILLIAM

T

Taine, John	TN: BELL, ERIC TEMPLE
Talbot, Lawrence	TN: BRYANT JR, EDWARD WINSLOW
Tall, Stephen	TN: CROOK, COMPTON NEWBY
Tarnmoor, Salvatore R.	TN: MELVILLE, HERMAN
Tarrant, John	TN: EGLETON, CLEVE
Tate, Allen	TN: ORLEY, JOHN
Tate, Ellalice	TN: HIBBERT, ELEANOR ALICE
Taylor, H. Baldwin	TN: WAUGH, HILLARY BALDWIN
TAYLOR, CONSTANCE LINDSAY	PN: Guy Cullingford
TAYLOR, LOIS DWIGHT	PN: Caroline Arnett, Lynn Avery, Nancy Dudley, Allan Dwight, Anne Eliot, Anne Lattin
TAYLOR, PHOEBE ATWOOD	PN: Alice Tilton
Tempest, Jan	TN: SWATRIDGE, IRENE MAUD MOSSOP

Tempest, Sarah	TN: PONSONBY, DORIS ALMON
Tempest, Victor	TN: PHILIPP, ELLIOT ELIAS
Tenn, William	TN: KLASS, PHILIP
TENNANT, EMMA CHRISTINA	PN: Catherine Aydy
Tenneshaw, S.M.	TN: GARRETT, RANDALL PHILLIP and SILVERBERG, ROBERT
Terry, C.V.	TN: SLAUGHTER, FRANK GILL
Terson, Peter	TN: PATTERSON, PETER
Tertz, Abram	TN: SINTAVSKY, ANDREY
Tey, Josephine	TN: MACKINTOSH, ELIZABETH
THACKERAY, WILLIAM MAKEPEACE	PN: George Fitz-Boodle, Arthur Pendennis, Peter Perseus, Jeames De La Pluche, Dorothea Julia Ramsbottom, Ikey Solomons, Jr., Michael Angelo Titmarsh, Theophile Wagstaff, Lancelot Wagstaff, Charle Yellowplush
Thames, C.H.	TN: LESSER, MILTON
THAYER, EMMA REDINGTON	PN: Lee Thayer
Thayer, Geraldine	TN: DANIELS, DOROTHY
Thayer, Lee	TN: THAYER, EMMA REDINGTON
THIBAULT, JACQUES ANATOLE FRANCOIS	PN: Anatole France
THIMBLETHORPE, JUNE SYLVIA	PN: Sylvia Thorpe
THIRKELL, ANGELA	PN: Leslie Parker
Thomas, Joan Gale	TN: ROBINSON, JOAN MARY GALE
Thomas, Ivor	TN: BULMER-THOMAS, IVOR
Thomas, K.	TN: FEARN, JOHN RUSSELL
Thomas, Lee	TN: FLOREN, LEE
Thomas, Paul	TN: MANN, THOMAS
THOMAS, ROSS	PN: Oliver Bleek
THOMPSON, ARTHUR LEONARD BELL	PN: Francis Clifford
Thompson, China	TN: BRAND, MARY CHRISTIANNA MILNE
THOMPSON, EDWARD ANTHONY	PN: Anthony Lejeune
Thompson, Eileen	TN: PANOWSKI, EILEEN JANET THOMPSON
THOMPSON, GEORGE SELDEN	PN: George Selden
Thompson, Wolf	TN: SETON, ERNEST THOMPSON
Thomson, Edward	TN: TUBB, EDWIN CHARLES
Thomson, Joan	TN: CHARNOCK, JOAN PAGET
Thomson, Jonathan H.	TN: THOMSON, DAISY HICKS
Thorne, Nicola	TN: ELLERBECK, ROSEMARY ANNE L'ESTRANGE
Thorpe, Sylvia	TN: THIMBLETHORPE, JUNE SYLVIA
Thribb, E.J.	TN: FANTONI, BARRY
Tibber, Robert	TN: FRIEDMAN, ROSEMARY
Tibber, Rosemary	TN: FRIEDMAN, ROSEMARY
Tilbury, Quenna	TN: WALKER, EMILY KATHLEEN
TILLET, DOROTHY STOCKBRIDGE	PN: Dorothy Stockbridge, John Stephen Strange
Tillray, Les	TN: GARDNER, ERLE STANLEY
Tilton, Alice	TN: TAYLOR, PHOEBE ATWOOD
Tinker, Beamish	TN: JESSE, F. TENNYSON
TINNE DOROTHEA	PN: Dorothea Strover, E.D. Tinne
Tinne, E.D.	TN: TINNE, DOROTHEA
TIPPETTE, GILES	PN: Wilson Young
Tiptree Jr., James	TN: SHELDON, ALICE HASTINGS
TIRBUTT, HONORIA	PN: Emma Page
Titan, Earl	TN: FEARN, JOHN RUSSELL
Titcomb, Timothy	TN: HOLLAND, JOSIAH G.
Titmarsh, Michael Angelo	TN: THACKERAY, WILLIAM MAKEPEACE
TITUS, EVE	PN: Nancy Lord
TODD, BARBARA EUPHAN	PN: Barbara Bower, Euphan
Todd, Paul	TN: POSNER, RICHARD
TOMALIN, RUTH	PN: Ruth Leaver
Tomkinson, Constance	TN: WEEKS, Lady CONSTANCE AVARD
TOOMBS, JOHN	PN: Fortune Kent, Jonathan Scofield
TORDAY, URSULA	PN: Paula Allardyce, Charity Blackstock, Lee Blackstock, Charlotte Keppel
Torrie, Malcolm	TN: MITCHELL, GLADYS MAUDE WINIFRED

Towne, Stuart — TN: RAWSON, CLAYTON
Tracy, Leland — TN: TRALINS, S. ROBERT
Trailrider — TN: HYLAND, ANN
Trainor, Richard — TN: TRALINS, S. ROBERT
TRALINS, S. ROBERT — PN: Norman A. King, Keith Miles, Sean O'Shea, Rex O'Toole, Cynthia Sydney, Leland Tracy, Richard Trainor, Ruy Traube, Dorothy Verdon

TRANTER, NIGEL GODWIN — PN: Nye Tredgold
Traube, Ruy — TN: TRALINS, S. ROBERT
Traver, Robert — TN: VOELKER, JOHN DONALDSON
Travers, Kenneth — TN: HUTCHIN, KENNETH CHARLES
Travis, Gerry — TN: TRIMBLE, LOUIS PRESTON
Treat, Lawrence — TN: GOLDSTONE, LAWRENCE ARTHUR
Tredgold, Nye — TN: TRANTER, NIGEL GODWIN
Tree, Gregory — TN: BARDIN, JOHN FRANKLIN
Trehearne, Elizabeth — TN: ALBRITTON, CAROL
Trehearne, Elizabeth — TN: MAXWELL, PATRICIA ANNE
Tresilian, Liz — TN: GREEN, ELISABETH SARA
Tressidy, Jim — TN: NORWOOD, VICTOR GEORGE CHARLES
Trevanian — TN: WHITAKER, RODNEY
Treves, Kathleen — TN: WALKER, EMILY KATHLEEN
TREVOR, ELLESTON — PN: Mansell Black, Trevor Burgess, T. Dudley-Smith, Roger Fitzalan, Adam Hall, Howard North, Simon Rattray, Warwick Scott, Caesar Smith

Trevor, Glen — TN: HILTON, JAMES
Trevor, William — TN: COX, WILLIAM TREVOR
TRIMBLE, LOUIS PRESTON — PN: Stuart Brock, Gerry Travis
Tring, A. Stephen — TN: MEYNELL, LAURENCE WALTER
TRIPP, MILES BARTON — PN: Michael Brett
Trollope, Joanna — TN: POTTER, JOANNA
Trotsky, Leon — TN: BRONSTEIN, LEO DAVIDOVITCH
Trout, Kilgore — TN: FARMER, PHILIP JOSE
Troy, Katherine — TN: BUXTON, ANNE
Troy, Simon — TN: WARRINER, THURMAN
TUBB, EDWIN CHARLES — PN: Chuck Adams, Jud Cary, J.F. Clarkson, James S. Farrow, James R. Fenner, Charles S. Graham, Charles Grey, Volstad Gridban, Gill Hunt, E.F. Jackson, Gregory Kern, King Lang, Mike Lantry, P. Lawrence, Chet Lawson, Arthur Mac Lean, Carl Maddox, M.L. Powers, Paul Schofield, Brian Shaw, Roy Sheldon, John Stevens, Edward Thomson

TULLETT, DENIS — PN: John Sutton
Turner, Bill — TN: TURNER, W. PRICE
Turner, Len — TN: FLOREN, LEE
Turner, Mary — TN: LAMBOT, ISOBEL MARY
TURNER, PHILIP WILLIAM — PN: Stephen Chance
Twain, Mark — TN: CLEMENS, SAMUEL LANGHORNE
Twist, Ananias — TN: NUNN, WILLIAM CURTIS

U

ULYANOV, VLADIMIR ILYICH — PN: Lenin
Unada — TN: GLIEWE, UNADA G.
Uncle Gordon — TN: ROE, F. GORDON
Uncle Remus — TN: HARRIS, JOEL CHANDLER
Underhill, Charles — TN: HILL, REGINALD
Underwood, Michael — TN: EVELYN, JOHN MICHAEL
Underwood, Miles — TN: GLASSCO, JOHN
UNGERER, JEAN THOMAS — PN: Tomi Ungerer
Ungerer, Tomi — TN: UNGERER, JEAN THOMAS
UNWIN, DAVID STORR — PN: David Severn
UPCHURCH, BOYD BRADFIELD — PN: John Boyd
Updyke, James — TN: BURNETT, WILLIAM RILEY
Usco — TN: GERD, JACOB STERN
Usse, Peter — TN: YEUR, VICTOR OLIVER
UTTLEY, ALICE JANE — PN: Alison Uttley

Uttley, Alison   TN: UTTLEY, ALICE JANE

V

V.V.V.   TN: LUCAS, E.V.
Valentine, Alec   TN: ISAACS, ALAN
Valentine, Douglas   TN: WILLIAMS, GEORGE VALENTINE
Valentine, Jo   TN: ARMSTRONG, CHARLOTTE
Van Dine, S.S.   TN: WRIGHT, WILLARD HUNTINGTON
Van Dyne, Edith   TN: BAUM, LYMAN FRANK
Van Heller, Marcus   TN: ZACHARY, HUGH
Van Lhin, Erik   TN: ALVAREZ-DEL REY, RAMON FELIPE SAN JUAN MARIO SILVIO ENRICO

Van See, John   TN: VANCE, JOHN HOLBROOK
VAN SILLER, HILDA   PN: Van Siller
VAN SLYKE, HELEN LENORE   PN: Sharon Ashton
Van Someren, Liesje   TN: PUTLAND-VAN SOMEREN, ELIZABETH
VAN WYCK MASON, FRANK   PN: Geoffrey Coffin, Frank W. Mason, Ward Weaver
Vanardy, Varick   TN: DEY, FREDERIC MERRILL VAN RENSSELAER
Vance, Gerald   TN: GARRETT, RANDALL PHILLIP
Vance, Gerald   TN: GRAHAM, ROGER PHILLIPS
Vance, Jack   TN: VANCE, JOHN HOLBROOK
VANCE, JOHN HOLBROOK   PN: Peter Held, John Holbrook, Ellery Queen, Jack Vance, John Van See, Alan Wade

VANCE, WILLIAM E.   PN: George Cassidy
Vane, Bret   TN: KENT, ARTHUR
Vane, Michael   TN: HUMPHRIES, SYDNEY VERNON
Vardre, Leslie   TN: DAVIES, LESLIE PURNELL
Varley, John Philip   TN: MITCHELL, LANGDON E.
Vedder, John K.   TN: GRUBER, FRANK
Venables, Terry   TN: WILLIAMS, GORDON
VENABLES, TERRY   PN: P.B. Yuill
VERRILL, ALPHEUS HYATT   PN: Ray Ainsbury
Venison, Alfred   TN: POUND, EZRA
Venning, Michael   TN: RANDOLPH, GEORGIANNA ANN
Vercors   TN: BRULLER, JEAN
Verdon, Dorothy   TN: TRALINS, S. ROBERT
Verne, Jules   TN: OLCHEWITZ, M.
Verval, Alain   TN: GREENWOOD, THOMAS
Verval, Alain   TN: LANDE, LAWRENCE MONTAGNE
Veryan, Patricia   TN: BANNISTER, PATRICIA V.
Vestal, Stanley   TN: CAMPBELL, WALTER STANLEY
VIAN, BORIS   PN: Vernon Sullivan
Vicarion, Count Palmiro   TN: LOGUE, CHRISTOPHER
VICKERS, ROY C.   PN: David Durham, Sefton Kyle, John Spencer
Victor, Charles B.   TN: PUECHNER, RAY
VIDAL, EUGENE LUTHER GORE   PN: Edgar Box
Vigil   TN: KOESTLER, ARTHUR
Vigil, Lawrence   TN: FINNIN, MARY
Viliers, Guy   TN: GOULDING, PETER GEOFFREY
Vincent, Harl   TN: SCHOEPFLIN, HAROLD VINCENT
Vindicator   TN: HOPKINSON, Sir HENRY THOMAS
VINING, ELIZABETH GRAY   PN: Elizabeth Janet Gray
VINSON, REX THOMAS   PN: Vincent King
Vipont, Charles   TN: FOULDS, ELFRIDA VIPONT
Vipont, Elfrida   TN: FOULDS, ELFRIDA VIPONT
Vitezovic, T.   TN: KUEHNELT-LEDDIHN, ERIK
VOELKER, JOHN DONALDSON   PN: Robert Traver
Voltaire   TN: AROUET, FRANCOIS-MARIE
Von Rachen, Kurt   TN: HUBBARD, LA FAYETTE RON
Von Tempski, Armine   TN: BALL, ARMINE
Voyle, Mary   TN: MANNING, ROSEMARY
VULLIAMY, COLWYN EDWARD   PN: Anthony Rolls

W

WILDING, PHILIP   PN: Logan Stuart
Williams, Arnold   TN: MEADOWCROFT, ERNEST
Williams, J.R.   TN: WILLIAMS, DOROTHY JEANNE
Williams, J. Walker   TN: WODEHOUSE, PELHAM GRENVILLE
Wilder, Cherry   TN: GRIMM, CHERRY BARBARA
Wiley, John   TN: GRAHAM, ROGER PHILLIPS
Wiley, Margaret L.   TN: MARSHALL, MARGARET LENORE
Wilkins, Mary   TN: FREEMAN, MARY ELEANOR WILKINS
Will   TN: LIPKIND, WILLIAM
Williams, Arnold   TN: MEADOWCROFT, ERNEST
WILLIAMS, DOROTHY JEANNE   PN: Megan Castell, Jeanne Crecy, Jeanne Foster, Kristin
                                                         Michaels, Deirdre Rowen, J.R. Williams
WILLIAMS, GEORGE VALENTINE   PN: Douglas Valentine
WILLIAMS, GORDON   PN: P.B. Yuill
Williams, J.R.   TN: WILLIAMS, DOROTHY JEANNE
Williams, J. Walker   TN: WODEHOUSE, PELHAM GRENVILLE
WILLIAMS, JAY   PN: Michael Delving
WILLIAMS, MARGARET WETHERBY   PN: Margaret Erskine
WILLIAMSON, ALICE MURIEL   PN: Charles De Crespigny, M.P. Revere, Dona Teresa De
                                                         Savallo, Alice Stuyvesant, Mrs. Harcourt Williamson
WILLIAMSON, CHARLES NORRIS   PN: Charles De Crespigny, M.P. Revere, Dona Teresa De
                                                         Savallo, Alice Stuyvesant, Mrs. Harcourt Williamson
Williamson, Mrs. Harcourt   TN: WILLIAMSON, ALICE MURIEL & CHARLES NORRIS
Williamson, Jack   TN: WILLIAMSON, JOHN STEWART
WILLIAMSON, JOHN STEWART   PN: Will Stewart, Jack Williamson
WILLIS, EDWARD HENRY,
    Baron WILLIS OF
    CHISLEHURST   PN: Ted Willis
WILLIS, SARA P.   PN: Fanny Fern
Willis, Ted   TN: WILLIS, EDWARD HENRY
Willoughby, Cass   TN: OLSEN, T.V.
Willoughby, Hugh   TN: HARVEY, NIGEL
Willoughby, Lee Davis   TN: WEBB, JEAN FRANCIS
Wilmer, Dale   TN: MILLER, BILL
Wilmer, Dale   TN: WADE, ROBERT
Wilson, Barbara   TN: HARRIS, LARRY MARK
Wilson, Christine   TN: GEACH, CHRISTINE
Wilson, Dave   TN: FLOREN, LEE
Wilson, David   TN: MAC ARTHUR, DAVID WILSON
Wilson, Dick   TN: WILSON, RICHARD GARRATT
Wilson, Gwendoline   TN: EWENS, GWENDOLINE WILSON
WILSON, JOHN ANTHONY BURGESS   PN: Anthony Burgess, Joseph Kell
WILSON, JOYCE MURIEL   PN: Joyce Stranger
Wilson, Mary   TN: ROBY, MARY LINN
Winch, John   TN: CAMPBELL, GABRIELLE MARGARET VERE
Winchester, Kay   TN: WALKER, EMILY KATHLEEN
Windham, Basil   TN: WODEHOUSE, PELHAM GRENVILLE
Wine, Dick   TN: POSNER, RICHARD
Winfield, Arthur M.   TN: STRATEMEYER, EDWARD
Winiki, Ephriam   TN: FEARN, JOHN RUSSELL
Winslow, Kent   TN: WOODWORTH, FRED
Winter, H.G.   TN: BATES, HARRY HIRAM GILMORE III
WINTERTON, PAUL   PN: Roger Bax, Andrew Garve, Paul Somers
Wodehouse, P.G.   TN: WODEHOUSE, PELHAM GRENVILLE
WODEHOUSE, PELHAM GRENVILLE   PN: Pelham Grenville, C.P. West, J. Walker Williams, P.G.
                                                         Wodehouse, Basil Windham
Wodge, Dreary   TN: GOREY, EDWARD ST. JOHN
Wojtyla, Karol   TN: POPE JOHN PAUL II
WOLCOTT, JOHN   PN: Peter Pindar
WOLLHEIM, DONALD ALLEN   PN: David Grinnell
Wood, Catherine   TN: ETCHISON, BIRDIE L.
WOOD, EDGAR ALLARDYCE   PN: Kerry Wood
Wood, Kerry   TN: WOOD, EDGAR ALLARDYCE
Woodcott, Keith   TN: BRUNNER, JOHN KILIAN HOUSTON
Woodruff, Philip   TN: MASON, PHILIP
WOODS, HELEN   PN: Helen Ferguson, Anna Kavan

Woods, Lawrence	TN: LOWNDES, ROBERT AUGUSTINE WARD
Woods, P.F.	TN: BAYLEY, BARRINGTON JOHN
Woods, Sara	TN: BOWEN-JUDD, SARA
Woodward, Lilian	TN: MARSH, JOHN
WOODWORTH, FRED	PN: I.R. Ybarra
Woolrich, Cornell	TN: HOPLEY-WOOLRICH, CORNELL GEORGE
WOOLSEY, SARAH CHAUNCY	PN: Susan Coolidge
Worboys, Anne	TN: WORBOYS, ANNETTE ISOBEL
WORBOYS, ANNETTE ISOBEL	PN: Annete Eyre, Vicky Maxwell, Anne Worboys, Anne Eyre Worboys
Worcester, Roland	TN: RAYER, FRANCIS GEORGE
WORMSER, RICHARD EDWARD	PN: Ed Friend
Worth, Peter	TN: GRAHAM, ROGER PHILLIPS
Wright, Francesca	TN: ROBINS, DENISE NAOMI
Wright, Kenneth	TN: ALVAREZ-DEL REY, RAMON FELIPE SAN JUAN MARIO SILVIO ENRICO
Wright, Rowland	TN: WELLS, CAROLYN
Wright, S. Fowler	TN: WRIGHT, SYDNEY FOWLER
WRIGHT, SYDNEY FOWLER	PN: Sydney Fowler, Alan Seymour, S. Fowler Wright
WRIGHT, WILLARD HUNTINGTON	PN: Van Dine, S.S.
Wylie, Laura	TN: MATTHEWS, PATRICIA ANNE
WYND, OSWALD MORRIS	PN: Gavin Black
Wyndham, Esther	TN: LUTYENS, MARY
Wyndham, John	TN: HARRIS, JOHN WYNDHAM PARKES LUCAS BEYNON
Wyndham, Lee	TN: HYNDMAN, JANE LEE
Wynne, Brian	TN: GARFIELD, BRIAN FRANCIS WYNNE
Wynne, Frank	TN: GARFIELD, BRIAN FRANCIS WYNNE
Wynne, May	TN: KNOWLES, MABEL WINIFRED

X

X, Mr.	TN: HOCH, EDWARD DENTINGER
Xeno	TN: LAKE, KENNETH ROBERT

Y

Yaffe, Alan	TN: YORINKS, ARTHUR
Yarnall, Sophia	TN: JACOBS, SOPHIA YARNALL
YATES, ALAN GEOFFREY	PN: Carter Brown, Peter Carter Brown, Peter Carter-Brown
Yates, Dornford	TN: MERCER, CECIL WILLIAM
Ybarra, I.R.	TN: WOODWORTH, FRED
Yellowplush, Charle	TN: THACKERAY, WILLIAM MAKEPEACE
YEUR, VICTOR OLIVER	PN: Peter Usse
YIN, LESLIE CHARLES BOWYER	PN: Leslie Charteris
York, Alison	TN: NICOLE, CHRISTOPHER ROBIN
York, Andrew	TN: NICOLE, CHRISTOPHER ROBIN
York, Georgia	TN: HOFFMAN, LEE
York, Jeremy	TN: CREASEY, JOHN
Yorke, Katherine	TN: ELLERBECK, ROSEMARY ANNE L'ESTRANGE
Yorke, Margaret	TN: NICHOLSON, MARGARET BEDA
YOUD, CHRISTOPHER SAMUEL	PN: John Christopher, Hilary Ford, William Godfrey, Peter Graaf, Peter Nichols, Anthony Rye, C.S. Youd
Youd, C.S.	TN: YOUD, CHRISTOPHER SAMUEL
Young, Angela	TN: YARDLEY, ALICE
Young, Carter Travis	TN: CHARBONNEAU, LOUIS HENRY
Young, Collier	TN: BLOCH, ROBERT
YOUNG, GORDON RAY	PN: Hugh Richmond
Young, Jan	TN: YOUNG, JANET RANDALL
Young, Rose	TN: HARRIS, MARION ROSE
Young, Wilson	TN: TIPPETTE, GILES
Yuill, P.B.	TN: WILLIAMS, GORDON and VENABLES, TERRY
Yun, Leong Gor	TN: ELLISON, VIRGINIA HOWELL

Z

Zachary, Elizabeth	TN: ZACHARY, HUGH

ZACHARY, HUGH

Zetford, Tully
ZIEGLER, RICHARD
Ziliox, Marc
Ziller, Robert
Zinberg, Len
ZINBERG, LEONARD S.
ZOLOTOW, CHARLOTTE
Zonik, Eleanor Dorothy
ZWEIG, STEFAN

PN: Ginny Gorman, Elizabeth Hughes, Zach Hughes, Peter Kanto, Derral Pilgrom, Olivia Rangely, Marcus Van Heller, Elizabeth Zachary
TN: BULMER, HENRY KENNETH
PN: Robert Ziller
TN: FICHTER, GEORGE S.
TN: ZIEGLER, RICHARD
TN: ZINBERG, LEONARD S.
PN: Steve April, Ed Lacy, Len Zinberg
PN: Sara Abbot, Charlotte Bookman
TN: GLASER, ELEANOR DOROTHY
PN: Stephen Branch

Appendix 2
FIRST BOOKS BY COLLECTIBLE AUTHORS

The importance of this list for anyone hoping to assemble complete author collections should be obvious. Many authors published their first book using a pseudonym, or anonymously, and this information is also provided.

It makes no particular difference if you collect only first editions, or if any edition will do when trying to assemble a complete author collection. This list will provide the correct title of an author's first book(s).

This list provides the names of hundreds of authors who do not appear on any other list in this book, particularly if the author did not use any pseudonym(s). You can safely assume that any author appearing in this list can be considered collectible.

As a general rule, an author's first book is the most difficult to find. Not necessarily the most expensive, however. There are many reasons for this. First of all, publishers are usually reluctant to take a chance on a large printing for the first book of a new author, thus first books are often small printings. Often as few as six copies for copyright purposes.

You will also discover from a study of the listings, that first books are likely to be books of verse or non-fiction books. Many authors who have achieved great prominence in a certain genre, such as mysteries, or as mainstream authors, may have written their first book as a juvenile, a school text, many forms of non-fiction, or perhaps, a scientific tome. Sometimes even as a paper for a doctorate.

Often they are privately printed editions — a euphemism for self-published in many instances. A very high percentage of them, particularly in the science fiction, adventure, and mystery fields were originally published as paperbacks. You can recognize these by names such as Ace, Bantam, Avon, Paperback Library, etc.

As a result of these factors, the first book often becomes the key book in assembling an author collection. When a first edition is required it often becomes a near impossibility to locate one and the price can become truly astronomical.

If I were a beginning collector interested in assembling a collection most likely to increase in value — to use that word that most antiquarian book sellers hate — INVESTMENT — I think I would go for a collection of first books by authors, either in a particular genre such as mystery or children's books, or as a general collection of either fiction or non-fiction.

In using this list, please note that when an author published more than one book in his first year of publication I have noted them all without trying to indicate precedence. This would be beyond the scope of this book and I suggest that in those cases where you are interested in that particular author you consult available bibliographies.

A

A Cherokee Indian Writer — IF ALL ELSE FAILS, WE CAN WHIP THE HORSE'S EYES AND MAKE HIM CRY AND SLEEP, as Craig Strete. Amsterdam, 1976.

Aarons, Edward Sidney — DEATH IN A LIGHTHOUSE, as Edward Ronns. New York, Phoenix, 1938.

Abbey, Edward — JONATHAN TROY. New York, Dodd Mead, 1954.

Abbott, Alice (Pseudonym) — SOUTHERN YANKEES. Indianapolis, Bobbs Merrill, 1960.

Abrahams, Doris Caroline — THE MOON ON MY LEFT, as Caryl Brahms. London, 1930.

Acland, Alice — CAROLINE NORTON, 1948.

Adams, Andy — THE LOG OF A COWBOY. Boston, Houghton Mifflin, and London, Constable, 1903.

Adams, Cleve Franklin — AND SUDDEN DEATH. New York, Dutton, 1940.

Adams, Clifton — THE DESPERADO. New York, Fawcett, 1950; London, Fawcett, 1953.

Adams, Henry Brook — CHAPTERS OF ERIE, AND OTHER ESSAYS. 1871.

Adams, Leonie — THOSE NOT ELECT. New York, 1925.

Adams, Peter Robert Charles — THE LAND AT MY DOOR. 1965.

Adams, Richard — WATERSHIP DOWN. London & New York, 1972.

Ade, George — ARTIE 1896.

Adlard, Mark — INTERFACE. London, Sidgwick & Jackson, 1971; New York, Ace, 1977.

Agee, James — PERMIT ME VOYAGE. New Haven, 1934.

Ahlswede, Ann — DAY OF THE HUNTER. New York, Ballantine, 1960 HUNTING WOLF. New York, Ballantine, 1960.

Aiken, Conrad — EARTH TRIUMPHANT AND OTHER TALES IN VERSE. New York, 1914.

Aiken, Joan Delano — ALL YOU'VE EVER WANTED AND OTHER STORIES. London, Cape, 1953.

Ainsworth, Ruth Gallard — TALES ABOUT TONY. London, 1936.

Albanesi, Madame Effie Adelaide Maria — MARGERY DAW, published anonymously. London & New York, 1886.

Albee, Edward — THE ZOO STORY AND THE SANDBOX. New York, 1960, wraps — THE ZOO STORY. THE DEATH OF BESSIE SMITH, THE SANDBOX, New York,1960; London, 1962.

Albert, Marvin H. — LIE DOWN WITH LIONS. New York, Fawcett, 1955; London, Red Seal, 1957.

Alcott, Louisa May — FLOWER FABLES. Boston, Briggs, 1855.

Aldington, Richard — IMAGES 1910-1915. London, 1915.

Aldiss, Brian Wilson — THE BRIGHTFOUNT DIARIES. London, Faber, 1955.

Aldrich, Thomas Bailey — THE BELLS; A COLLECTION OF CHIMES. New York, Derby, 1855.

Alger, Jr., Horatio — BERTHA'S CHRISTMAS VISION: AN AUTUMN SHEAF. Boston, 1856.

Algren, Nelson — SOMEBODY IN BOOTS. New York, 1935.

Allbeury, Theodore Edward Le Bouthillier — A CHOICE OF ENEMIES, as Ted Allbeury. New York, St.

Martin's, 1972; London, Davies, 1973.

Allen, Charles Grant Blairfindie — PHYSIOLOGICAL AESTHETICS, as Grant Allen. London, King, 1877; New York, Appleton, 1878.

Allen, Henry Wilson — NO SURVIVORS, as Will Henry. New York, Random, 1950; London, Corgi, 1952.

Allen, James Lane — FLUTE AND VIOLIN. 1891.

Allen, Terry D. And Don B. — DOCTOR IN BUCKSKIN, as T.D. Allen. New York, Harper, 1951.

Allen, Jr., William Hervey — BALLADS OF THE BORDER. Privately printed, 1916.

Allen, Woody — DON'T DRINK THE WATER. New York, 1967.

Allingham, Margery Louise — BLACKKERCHIEF DICK: A TALE OF MERSEA ISLAND. London, Hodder & Stoughton, and New York, Doubleday, 1923.

Alsop. Mary O'Hara — LET US SAY GRACE, as Mary Sture-Vasa. Boston, Christopher, 1930.

Ambler, Eric — THE DARK FRONTIER. London, Hodder & Stoughton, 1936.

Anderson, Maxwell — WHITE DESERT (play).

Anderson, Sherwood — WINDY MC PHERSON'S SON. 1916.

Andrews, Lucilla Mathew — THE PRINT PETTICOAT. London, Harrap, 1954.

Arbor, Jane — THIS SECOND SPRING. London, Mills & Boon, 1948.

Arlen, Michael — THE LONDON VENTURE. London, Heinemann, and New York, Dodd Mead, 1920.

Armstrong, Charlotte — Lay On, MacDuff. New York, Coward McCann, 1942; London, Gifford, 1943.

Ashton, Elizabeth — THE PIED TULIP. London, Mills & Boon, 1969; Toronto, Harlequin, 1970.

Asimov, Isaac — PEBBLE IN THE SKY. New York, Doubleday, 1950; London, Corgi, 1958 — I, ROBOT. New York, Gnome, 1950; London, Grayson, 1952.

Asprin, Robert Lynn — THE COLD CASH WAR. New York, St. Martin's, and London, New English Library, 1977.

Athanas, William Verne — THE PROUD ONES, as Verne Athanas. New York, Simon & Schuster, 1952; London, Rich & Cowan, 1953.

Atherton, Gertrude Franklin — WHAT DREAMS MAY COME, as Frank Lin. Chicago, Belford Clarke, 1888; as Gertrude Atherton, London, Routledge, 1889.

Atkey, Philip — ARREST THESE MEN!, as Barry Perowne. London, Cassell, 1932.

Atkins, Frank — THE DEVIL-TREE OF EL DORADO, as Fenton Ash. London, Hutchinson, 1896; New York, New Amsterdam, 1897.

Atkins, John Alfred — THE DISTRIBUTION OF FISH, London, Fabian Society, 1941.

Aubrey-Fletcher, Henry Lancelot — THE VERDICT OF YOU ALL, as Henry Wade. London, Constable, 1926; New York, Payson & Clarke, 1927.

Austin, Mary — THE LAND OF LITTLE RAIN. Boston, Houghton Mifflin, 1903.

Ayres, Ruby Mildred — CASTLES IN SPAIN: THE CHRONICLES OF AN APRIL MONTH. London, Cassell, 1912.

B

Baker, Betty Doreen — THE GENEROUS VINE, as Elizabeth Renier. London, Hurst & Blackett, 1962; New York, Ace, 1972.

Baldwin, Faith — MAVIS OF GREEN HILL. Boston & London, 1921.

Baldwin, Gordon Cortis — TROUBLE RANGE. London, Hale, 1956; New York, Arcadia, 1959 — TRAIL NORTH. London, Hale, 1956; New York, Arcadia, 1957.

Baldwin, James — GO TELL IT ON THE MOUNTAIN. New York, 1953.

Baldwin, Joseph G. — THE FLUSH TIMES OF ALABAMA AND MISSISSIPPI. New York, 1853.

Ballantyne, Robert Michael — HUDSON'S BAY; OR, EVERY-DAY LIFE IN THE WILDS OF NORTH AMERICA, as R. M. Ballantyne. Edinburgh, Blackwood, 1848.

Ballard, James Graham — THE WIND FROM NOWHERE, as J.G. Ballard. New York, Berkley, 1962; London, Penguin, 1967 — THE VOICES OF TIME AND OTHER STORIES, as J.G. Ballard. New York, Berkley, 1962 — BILLENIUM AND OTHER STORIES, as J. G. Ballard. New York, Berkley, 1962.

Ballard, Willis Todhunter — SAY YES TO MURDER. New York, Putnam, 1942.

Bangs, John Kendrick — THE LORGNETTE, as J.K.B. New York, 1886.

Bannister, Patricia V. — THE LORD AND THE GYPSY, as Patricia Veryan. New York, Walker, 1978; as DEBT OF HONOUR. London, Souvenir Press, 1980.

Barclay, Florence Louisa — GUY MERVYN, as Brandon Roy. London, 1891, 3V.

Barker, Squire Omar — VIENTOS DE LAS SIERRAS, WINDS OF THE MOUNTAINS, as S. Omar Barker. Privately printed, 1922.

Barnes, Arthur Kelvin — INTERPLANETARY HUNTER. New York, Gnome, 1956.

Barrett, Neal, Jr. — KELWIN. New York, Lancer, 1970.

Barrie, Sir James Matthew — BETTER DEAD. London, 1888.

Barrie, Susan — MISTRESS OF BROWN FURROWS. London, 1952.

Barry, Jane — THE LONG MARCH. New York, Appleton Century Crofts, 1955.

Barth, John Simmons — THE FLOATING OPERA. New York, Appleton Century Crofts, 1956.

Barthelme, Donald — COME BACK, DR. CALIGARI. Boston, 1964.

Bassler, Thomas J. — HALF PAST HUMAN, as T.J. Bass. New York, Ballantine, 1971.

Bates, Hiram Gilmore, III — SPACE HAWK: THE GREATEST OF INTERPLANETARY ADVENTURES, as Anthony Gilmore, with D.W. Hall. New York, Greenberg, 1952.

Battye, Gladys Starkey — TO SEE A STRANGER, as Margaret Lynn. London, Hodder & Stoughton, 1961; New York, Doubleday, 1962.

Baum, Lyman Frank — THE BOOK OF HAMBURGS: A BRIEF TREATISE UPON THE MATING, REARING, AND MANAGEMENT OF THE DIFFERENT VARIETIES OF HAMBURGS (chickens), by L. Frank Baum. Hartford (CT), Stoddard, 1886.

Baxter, John — THE OFF-WORLDERS. New York, Ace,

1966; as THE GOD KILLERS. Sydney (AUS), Horwitz, 1968.

Bayley, Barrington John — STAR VIRUS. New York, Ace, 1970.

Beach, Rex Ellingwood — THE SPOILERS. New York, Harper, 1906; London, Hodder & Stoughton, 1912.

Beagle, Peter S. — A FINE AND PRIVATE PLACE. New York, 1960.

Bean, Myrtle Amelia — THE FANCHER TRAIN. New York, Doubleday, 1958; as THE VENGEANCE TRAIL. London, Hamish Hamilton, 1958.

Bear, Gregory Dale — HEGIRA, as Greg Bear. New York, Dell, 1979 — PSYCHLONE, as Greg Bear. New York, Ace, 1979.

Beaty, Betty — SOUTH TO THE SUN. London, 1956.

Beauclerk, Helen — THE GREEN LACQUER PAVILION. London & New York, 1926.

Bechdolt, Frederick Ritchie — 9009, with James Hopper. New York, McClure, 1908.

Bechko, Peggy Anne — NIGHT OF THE FLAMING GUNS. New York, Doubleday, 1974 — GUNMAN'S JUSTICE. New York, Doubleday, 1974.

Beck, Lily Adams — THE KEY OF DREAMS. New York, 1922; THE NINTH VIBRATION AND OTHER STORIES. New York, 1922.

Beecher, Harriet Elizabeth — PRIZE-TALE: A NEW ENGLAND SKETCH, as Harriet Beecher Stowe. Lowell, 1834.

Beecher, John — "AND I WILL BE HEARD". New York, 1940.

Behrman, S.N. — BEDSIDE MANNERS (play). 1924.

Bell, Eric Temple — THE CYCLOTOMIC QUINARY QUINTIC. New York, Columbia Univ., 1912.

Bellah, James Warner — SKETCH BOOK OF A CADET FROM GASCONY. New York, Knopf, 1923.

Bellamy, Edward — SIX TO ONE: A NANTUCKET IDYL. New York, Putnam, and London, Sampson Low, 1878.

Bellingham, Helen Mary Dorothea — THE GREEN LACQUER PAVILION. London & New York, 1926.

Belloc, Joseph Hilaire Pierre — VERSES AND SONNETS. London, 1896.

Bellow, Saul — DANGLING MAN. New York, 1944.

Benet, Stephen Vincent — FIVE MEN AND POMPEY. 1915.

Benet, William Rose — MERCHANTS FROM CATHAY AND OTHER POEMS. New York, 1913.

Benford, Gregory Albert — DEEPER THAN THE DARKNESS. New York, Ace, 1970; London, Gollancz, 1979.

Bennett, E.A. — A MAN FROM THE NORTH, as Arnold Bennett. London, 1898.

Bennett, Gertrude Barrows — THE HEADS OF CERBERUS, as Francis Stevens. Reading (PA), Polaris Press, 1952.

Bennetts, Pamela — THE BORGIA PRINCE. London, 1968.

Berckman, Evelyn Domenica — THE EVIL OF TIME. New York, Dodd Mead, 1954; London, Eyre & Spottswoode, 1955.

Beresford, Elisabeth — THE TELEVISION MYSTERY. London, 1957.

Beresford, John Davys — THE EARLY HISTORY OF JACOB STAHL. London, Sidgwick & Jackson, and Boston, Little Brown, 1911.

Berger, Thomas Louis — CRAZY IN BERLIN. New York, Scribner, 1958.

Bernstein, Aline — THREE BLUE SUITS. New York, 1933.

Berrigan, Daniel — TIME WITHOUT NUMBER. New York, 1957.

Berry, Bryan — AND THE STARS REMAIN. London, Panther, 1952 — BORN IN CAPTIVITY. London, Panther, 1952 — DREAD VISITOR. London, Panther, 1952.

Berry, Don — TRASK. New York, Viking, and London, Hutchinson, 1960.

Berryman, John — POEMS. Norfolk, 1942.

Bessie, Alvah C. — DWELL IN THE WILDERNESS. New York, 1935.

Best, Oswald Herbert — GARRAM THE HUNTER, as Herbert Best. New York, Doubleday, 1930; London, Lane, 1935.

Bester, Alfred — THE DEMOLISHED MAN. Chicago, Shasta, and London, Sidgwick & Jackson, 1953 — WHO HE? New York, Dial, 1953.

Betjeman, John — MOUNT ZION, OR IN TOUCH WITH THE INFINITE. London, 1931.

Bevan, Gloria — THE DISTANT TRAP. London, 1969.

Bickham, Jack Miles — GUNMAN'S GAMBLE. New York, Ace, 1958; London, Hale, 1959.

Bidwell, Marjory Elizabeth Sarah — FOG, as Elizabeth Ford. London, 1933.

Bierce, Ambrose — THE FIEND'S DELIGHT. 1872.

Bigg, Patricia Nina — THE FLICKERING CANDLE, as Patricia Ainsworth. London, 1968.

Biggers, Earl Derr — SEVEN KEYS TO BALDPATE. Indianapolis, Bobbs Merrill, 1913; London, Mills & Boon, 1914.

Biggle, Lloyd, Jr. — THE ANGRY ESPERS. New York, Ace, 1961; London, Hale, 1968.

Binder, Otto Oscar — THE NEW LIFE, as John Coleridge. New York, Columbia, 1940 — MARTIAN MARTYRS, as John Coleridge. New York, Columbia, 1940.

Bindloss, Harold Edward — IN THE NIGER COUNTRY. Edinburgh, Blackwood, 1898.

Bingham, John Michael Ward, Lord Clanmoris — MY NAME IS MICHAEL SIBLEY. London, Gollancz, and New York, Dodd Mead, 1952.

Bingley, David Ernest — MOSSYHORN TRAIL, as Christopher Wigan. London, Mills & Boon, 1957 — OPERATION PEDESTAL, as David Horsley. London, Brown Watson, 1957.

Bird, Robert Montgomery — CALAVAR; OR, THE KNIGHT OF THE CONQUEST. 1834.

Birney, Herman Hoffman — KING OF THE MESA, as Hoffman Birney. Philadelphia, Penn, 1927; London, Long, 1928.

Bischoff, David Frederick — THE SEEKER, with Christopher Lampton. Toronto, Laser, 1976.

Bishop, John Peale — POETRY: GREEN FRUIT. 1917.

Bishop, Michael — A FUNERAL FOR THE EYES OF FIRE. New York, Ballantine, 1975; London, Sphere, 1978.

Bixby, Jerome Lewis — THE DEVIL'S SCRAPBOOK. New York, Brandon, 1964 — SPACE BY THE TALE. New York, Ballantine, 1964.

Black, Laura — GLENDRACO. New York, London, 1977.

Blackburn, Paul — THE DISSOLVING FABRIC. Mallorca, 1955.

Blackmore, Jane — TOWARDS TOMORROW. London, 1941.

Blackmur, R.P. — T.S. ELIOT. Cambridge, 1928.

Blackwood, Algernon Henry — THE EMPTY HOUSE AND OTHER GHOST STORIES. London, Nash, 1906; New York, Vaughan, 1915.

Blair, Eric Arthur — DOWN AND OUT IN PARIS AND LONDON, as George Orwell. London, Gollancz, and New York, Harper, 1933.

Blair, Kathryn — GREEN LEAVES, as Rosalind Brett. Hanley (ENG), 1947 — PAGAN INTERLUDE, as Rosalind Brett. Hanley, 1947 — SECRET MARRIAGE, as Rosalind Brett, London, 1947.

Blake, Forrester Avery — RIDING THE MUSTANG TRAIL. New York, Scribner, 1935.

Blake, Stephanie — FLOWERS OF FIRE. Chicago, 1977.

Blish, James Benjamin — JACK OF EAGLES. New York, Greenberg, 1952; London, Nova, 1955.

Bloch, Robert — SEA-KISSED. London, Utopian, 1945 — THE OPENER OF THE WAY. Sauk City (WI), Arkham, 1945.

Bloom, Ursula Harvey — TIGER. Privately printed, 1903 — WINIFRED. Privately printed, 1903.

Blunden, Edmund — PASTORALS: A BOOK OF VERSES. London, 1916.

Bly, Robert — THE SILENCE IN THE SNOWY FIELDS. Middletown, 1962.

Bodenheim, Maxwell — MINNA AND MYSELF. New York, 1918.

Bodington, Nancy Hermione — BACKGROUND FOR MURDER, as Shelley Smith. London, Swan, 1942.

Bogan, Louise — BODY OF THIS DEATH: POEMS. New York, 1923.

Boland, Bertram John — WHITE AUGUST, as John Boland. London, Joseph, and New York, Arcadia, 1955.

Bond, Nelson Slade — MR. MERGENTHWIRKER'S LOBBLIES AND OTHER FANTASTIC TALES. New York, Coward McCann, 1946.

Bone, Jesse F. — OBSERVATIONS ON THE OVARIES OF INFERTILE AND REPORTEDLY INFERTILE DAIRY CATTLE, Corvallis, Oregon State College, 1954.

Bonham, Frank — LOST STAGE VALLEY. New York, Simon & Schuster, 1948; Kingswood (ENG), World's Work, 1950.

Booth, Edwin — SHOWDOWN AT WARBIRD. New York, Ace, 1957 — JINX RIDER. New York, Ace, 1957.

Booth, Rosemary — PONIES ON THE HEATHER, as Frances Murray. London, Collins, 1966.

Borg, Philip Antony John — SHERIFF OF CLINTON, as Jack Borg. London, Jenkins, 1954 — HELLBENT TRAIL, as Jack Borg. London, Jenkins, 1954.

Borland, Harold Glen — HEAPS OF GOLD, as Hal Borland. Privately printed, 1922.

Borland, Kathryn — SOUTHERN YANKEES, as Alice Abbott. Indianapolis, 1960.

Bosworth, Allan Rucker — WHEREVER THE GRASS GROWS. New York, Doubleday, 1941; London, Cassell, 1942 — STEEL TO THE SUNSET, as Alamo Boyd. New York, Arcadia, 1941.

Bouma, Johanas L. — DANGER TRAIL. New York, Popular Library, 1954.

Bounds, Sydney James — DIMENSION OF HORROR. London, Panther, 1953 — VENGEANCE VALLEY, as Wes Saunders. Leicester (ENG), Fiction House, 1953.

Bourdillon, Francis — AMONG THE FLOWERS, AND OTHER POEMS. London, 1878.

Bova, Benjamin William — THE STAR CONQUERORS, as Ben Bova. Philadelphia, Winston, 1959.

Bowen-Judd, Sara — BLOODY INSTRUCTIONS, as Sara Woods. London, Collins, and New York, Harper, 1962.

Bower, Bertha Muzzy — CHIP, OF THE FLYING U, as B.M. Bower. New York, Dillingham, 1906; London, Nelson, 1920.

Bowles, Jane — TWO SERIOUS LADIES. New York, 1943.

Bowles, Paul — TWO POEMS. New York, 1934, wraps.

Boyle, Kay — SHORT STORIES. Paris, 1929.

Brackett, Leigh Douglass — NO GOOD FROM A CORPSE. New York, Coward McCann, 1944.

Bradbury, Raymond Douglas — DARK CARNIVAL, as Ray Bradbury. Sauk City, Arkham, 1947; London, Hamish Hamilton, 1948.

Bradford, Richard Roark — RED SKY AT MORNING. Philadelphia, Lippincott, 1968; London, Hodder & Stoughton, 1969.

Bradley, Marion Zimmer — SONGS FROM RIVENDELL. Privately printed, 1959.

Bragg, William Frederick — STARR OF WYOMING, as W.F. Bragg. London, Wright & Brown, 1936.

Braine, John — ROOM AT THE TOP. London, 1957.

Braithwaite, William S. — LYRICS OF LIFE AND LOVE. Boston, 1904.

Braun, Matthew — MATTIE SILKS, as Matt Braun. New York, Popular Library, 1972; London, Coronet, 1974 — BLACK FOX, as Matt Braun. New York, Fawcett, 1972; London, Coronet, 1973.

Brennan, John Needham Huggard — RED COATS GALLOPING, as John Welcome. London, Constable, 1949.

Brent, Madeleine — TREGARON'S DAUGHTER. London & New York, 1971.

Brent, Peter Ludwig — CRY VENGEANCE, as Ludovic Peters. London and New York, Abelard Schuman, 1961.

Bretnor, Reginald — THROUGH SPACE AND TIME WITH FERDINAND FEGHOOT, as Grendel Briarton. Berkeley (CA), Paradox, 1962.

Breuer, Miles John — THE GIRL FROM MARS, with Jack Williamson. New York, Stellar, 1929.

Brinnin, John Malcolm — THE GARDEN IS POLITICAL. New York, 1942.

Britt, Katrina — A KISS IN A GONDOLA. London, 1968.

Broderick, Damien — A MAN RETURNED. Sydney (AUS), Horwitz, 1965.

Bromfield, Louis — THE GREEN BAY TREE. New York, 1924.

Bromige, Iris Amy Edna — THE TRACEYS. London, 1946.

Brooks, Gwendoline — A STREET IN BRONZEVILLE. New York, 1945.

Brooks, Van Wyck — VERSES BY TWO UNDERGRADUATES (with John Hall Wheelock). 1905.

Broster, Dorothy Kathleen — CHANTEMERLE with Gertrude Winifred Taylor. London & New York, 1911.

Brown, Charles Brockden — ALCUIN. 1798.

Brown, Dee Alexander — WAVE HIGH THE BANNER. Philadelphia, Macrae Smith, 1942.

Brown, Fredric — THE FABULOUS CLIPJOINT. New York, Dutton, 1947; London, Boardman, 1949.

Brown, James Cooke — LOGLAN, with L.F. Brown. Gainesville (FL), Loglan Institute, 5 vols., 1963-75.

Brown, Joseph Paul Summers — JIM KANE, as J.P.S. Brown. New York, Dial, 1970; as POCKET MONEY, as J.P.S. Brown. London, Sphere, 1972.

Browne, Charles Farrar — ARTEMUS WARD: HIS BOOK. 1862.

Brunner, John Kilian Houston — HORSES AT HOME. London, Spring, 1958.

Bryher, Winifred — THE LAMENT FOR ADONIS. London, 1918, wraps.

Bryant, Edward Winslow, Jr. — AMONG THE DEAD AND OTHER EVENTS LEADING UP TO THE APOCALYPSE. New York, Macmillan, 1973.

Bryant, William Cullen — THE EMBARGO; OR, SKETCHES OF THE TIMES: A SATIRE. 1808.

Buchan, John — SIR QUIXOTE OF THE MOORS. London & New York, 1895.

Buchanan, Eileen Marie Duell — DEATH IN DEAKINS WOOD, as Rhona Petrie. London, Gollancz, 1963; New York, Dodd Mead, 1964.

Budrys, Algirdas Jonas — FALSE NIGHT, as Algis Budrys. New York, Lion, 1954; London, Mayflower, 1963.

Buechner, Frederick — A LONG DAY'S DYING. New York, 1950.

Bullen, Frank T. — THE CRUISE OF THE "CACHALOT." London, 1898.

Bulmer, Henry Kenneth — SPACE TREASON, as Kenneth Bulmer, with A.V. Clarke. London, Panther, 1952 — CYBERNETIC CONTROLLER, as Kenneth Bulmer, with A.V. Clarke. London, Panther, 1952 — ENCOUNTER IN SPACE, as Kenneth Bulmer. London, Panther, 1952.

Bunner, H.C. — A WOMAN OF HONOR. Boston, 1883.

Bunting, Basil — REDIMICULUM MATELLARUM. Milan, 1930.

Burchardt, William Robert — THE WILDCATTERS, as Bill Burchardt. New York, Ace, 1963.

Burdette, Robert J. — THE RISE AND FALL OF THE MUSTACHE. Burlington, 1877.

Burdick, Eugene Leonard — THE NINTH WAVE. Boston, Houghton Mifflin, and London, Gollancz, 1956.

Burford, Lolah — VICE AVENGED: A MORAL TALE. New York & London, 1971.

Burge, Milward Rodon Kennedy — THE BLESTON MYSTERY, as Robert Millward Kennedy, with A. Gordon MacDonnell. London, Gollancz, 1928; New York, Doubleday, 1929.

Burgess, Frank Gelett — THE PURPLE COW! SF, 1895, 8 leaves.

Burghley, Rose — AND BE THY LOVE. London, 1958.

Burgin, George Brown — HIS LORDSHIP, AND OTHERS. London, 1893.

Burke, Kenneth — THE WHITE OXEN AND OTHER STORIES. New York, 1924.

Burnett, Frances Hodgson — THAT LASS O'LOWRIE'S. New York, 1877.

Burnett, William Riley — LITTLE CAESAR, as W.R. Burnett. New York, Dial, and London, Cape, 1929.

Burns, John Horne — THE GALLERY. New York, 1947.

Burns, Walter Noble — A YEAR WITH A WHALER. New York, Outing, 1913.

Burroughs, Edgar Rice — TARZAN OF THE APES. Chicago, McClurg, 1914; London, Methuen, 1917.

Burroughs, John — NOTES ON WALT WHITMAN AS POET AND PERSON. 1867.

Burroughs, William Seward—JUNKIE: CONFESSIONS OF AN UNREDEEMED DRUG ADDICT, as William Lee. New York, Ace, 1953; London, Digit, 1957.

Burt, Katharine — THE BRANDING IRON. Boston, Houghton Mifflin, and London, Constable, 1919.

Busch, Niven — TWENTY-ONE AMERICANS, BEING PROFILES OF SOME PEOPLE IN OUR TIME, TOGETHER WITH SILLY PICTURES OF THEM DRAWN BY DE MISKEY. New York, Doubleday, 1930.

Butler, Gwendoline — RECEIPT FOR MURDER. London, 1956.

Butler, Samuel — A FIRST YEAR IN CANTERBURY SETTLEMENT. London, 1863.

Butterworth, Michael — THE SOUNDLESS SCREAM. London, Long, and New York, Doubleday, 1967.

Butts, Mary — SPEED THE PLOW AND OTHER STORIES. London, 1923.

Buxton, Anne — THE BEST LOVE OF ALL, as Anne Maybury. London, Mills & Boon, 1932 — THE ENCHANTED KINGDOM, as Anne Maybury. London, Mills & Boon, 1932 — THE LOVE THAT IS STRONGER THAN LIFE, as Anne Maybury. London, Mills & Boon, 1932 — LOVE TRIUMPHANT, as Anne Maybury. London, Mills & Boon, 1932.

Bynner, Witter — AN ODE TO HARVARD AND OTHER POEMS. Boston, 1907.

C

Cabell, James Branch — THE EAGLE'S SHADOW. New York, 1904.

Cable, George Washington — OLD CREOLE DAYS. 1879.

Cable, James Branch — THE EAGLE'S SHADOW. 1904.

Cadell, Violet Elizabeth — MY DEAR AUNT FLORA. London, 1946.

Cain, James Mallahan — OUR GOVERNMENT. New York, 1930.

Caine, Thomas Henry Hall — RICHARD III AND MACBETH: A DRAMATIC STUDY, as Hall Caine. London, 1877.

Caird, Janet Hinshaw — ANGUS THE TARTAN PARTAN. London, 1961.

Caldwell, Erskine — THE BASTARD. New York, 1929.

Caldwell, Janet Miriam Taylor Holland — DYANSTY OF DEATH, as Taylor Caldwell. New York, 1938.

Calisher, Hortense — IN THE ABSENCE OF ANGELS. Boston, 1951.

Callaghan, Morley — STRANGE FUGITIVE. New York, 1928.

Cameron, Lou — ANGEL'S FLIGHT. New York, Fawcett, 1960; London, Muller, 1962.

Campbell, Gabrielle Margaret Vere — THE VIPER OF MILAN, as Marjorie Bowen. London, Alston Rivers, and New York, McClure Phillips, 1906.

Campbell, Roy — THE FLAMING TERRAPIN. London, 1924.

Capote, Truman — OTHER VOICES, OTHER ROOMS. New York, 1948.

Capps, Benjamin Franklin — HANGING AT COMANCHE WELLS. New York, Ballantine, 1962.

Carleton, William M. — FAX: A CAMPAIGN POEM. Chicago, 1868.

Carr, Robyn — CHELYNNE. Boston, 1980.

Carter, Forrest — THE REBEL OUTLAW, JOSEY WALES. Gantt (AL). Whipporwill, 1973; as GONE TO TEXAS, London, Weidenfeld & Nicolson, 1975.

Carter, Linwood Vrooman — THE WIZARD OF LEMURIA, as Lin Carter. New York, Ace, 1965.

Cartland, Barbara Hamilton — JIG-SAW. London, 1925.

Case, David — THE CELL: THREE TALES OF HORROR. New York, 1969.

Case, Robert Ormond — JUST BUCKAROOS. New York, Chelsea House, 1927.

Castaneda, Carlos — THE TEACHINGS OF DON JUAN/A YAQUI WAY OF KNOWLEDGE. Berkeley, 1968.

Cather, Willa Sibert — APRIL TWILIGHTS. Boston, Badger, 1903.

Cawein, Madison J. — BLOOMS OF THE BERRY. Louisville, 1887.

Chance, John Newton — MURDER IN OILS. London, Gollancz, 1935 — WHEELS IN THE FOREST. London, Gollancz, 1935.

Chandler, Raymond Thornton — THE BIG SLEEP. New York, 1939.

Channing, William Ellery — THE DUTIES OF CHILDREN. Boston, 1807.

Chapman, Hester Wolferstan — SHE SAW THEM GO BY. London & Boston, 1933.

Chappell, Mollie — LITTLE TOM SPARROW. Leeds, 1950.

Charbonneau, Louis Henry — NO PLACE ON EARTH. New York, Doubleday, 1958; London, Jenkins, 1966.

Chase, Borden — EAST RIVER. New York, Crowell, 1935.

Cheever, John — THE WAY SOME PEOPLE LIVE. New York, 1943.

Chesnutt, Charles W. — THE CONJURE WOMAN. Boston, 1899.

Chesterton, Gilbert Keith — GREYBEARDS AT PLAY: LITERATURE AND ART FOR OLD GENTLEMAN: RHYMES AND SKETCHES, as G.K. Chesterton. London, Brimley Johnson, 1900 — THE WILD KNIGHT AND OTHER POEMS, as G.K. Chesterton. London, Richards, 1900.

Chisholm, Arthur Murray — THE BOSS OF WIND RIVER, as A.M. Chisholm. New York, Doubleday, 1911.

Chivers, Thomas Holley — THE PATH OF SORROW. Franklin, 1832.

Christie, Agatha Mary Clarissa — THE MYSTERIOUS AFFAIR AT STYLES, as Agatha Christie. London, Lane, 1920; New York, Dodd Mead, 1927.

Clark, Charles Heber — OUT OF THE HURLY-BURLY, as Max Adeler. Philadelphia, 1874. Also the first book illustrated by A.B. Frost.

Clark, Patricia Denise — THE ADVENTURES OF THE THREE BABY BUNNIES, as Patricia Robins. London, Nicholson & Watson, 1934.

Clark, Walter Van Tilburg — CHRISTMAS COMES TO HJALSEN. Reno (NV), Reno Publishing House, 1930.

Clarke, Arthur Charles — INTERPLANETARY FLIGHT: AN INTRODUCTION TO ASTRONAUTICS. London, Temple Press, 1950; New York, Harper, 1951.

Clarke, David Waldo — MODERN ENGLISH WRITERS, as Dave Waldo. London, Longman, 1947.

Clavell, James — KING RAT. Boston, 1962.

Cleeve, Brian Talbot — THE FAR HILLS. London, 1952.

Clemens, Samuel Langhorne — THE CELEBRATED JUMPING FROG OF CALAVERAS COUNTY AND OTHER SKETCHES, by Mark Twain. New York, Webb, 1867.

Cleugh, Sophia — MATILDA, GOVERNESS OF THE ENGLISH. New York, 1924.

Cobb, Irvin S. — BACK HOME. New York, 1912.

Coburn, Walter J. — THE RINGTAILED RANNYHANS, as Walt Coburn. New York, Century, 1927.

Cockrell, Marian — YESTERDAY'S MADNESS. New York, 1943.

Cody, Stetson — CACTUS CLANCY RIDES. London, Allen, 1949.

Coffman, Virginia Edith — MOURA. New York, 1959.

Coghlan, Peggie — THE SPOILED EARTH, as Jessica Stirling, with Hugh C. Rae. London, Hodder & Stoughton, 1974; as STRATHMORE. New York, Delacorte, 1975.

Coldsmith, Donald C. — HORSIN' AROUND, as Don Coldsmith. San Antonio, Naylor, 1975.

Collin, Marion — ROMANTIC FICTION with Anne Britton. London, 1960.

Collins, Wilkie — MEMOIRS OF THE LIFE OF WILLIAM COLLINS, R.A. London, 1848, 2v.

Comfort, Will Levington — TROOPER TALES: A SERIES OF SKETCHES OF THE REAL AMERICAN PRIVATE SOLDIER. New York, Street & Smith, 1899.

Compton-Burnett, Ivy — DOLORES. Edinburgh, 1911.

Conarain, Alice Nina — LOVE IN APRON STRINGS, as Elizabeth Hoy. London, 1933.

Condon, Richard Thomas — THE OLDEST CONFESSION. New York, Appleton Century Crofts, 1958; as THE HAPPY THIEVES. New York, Bantam, 1962.

Conly, Robert Leslie — THE SILVER CROWN, as Robert C. O'Brien. New York, Atheneum, 1968; London, Gollancz, 1973.

Connolly, Cyril — THE ROCK POOL. Paris, 1936 .

Conroy, Jack — THE DISINHERITED. New York, 1933.

Constiner, Merle — HEARSE OF A DIFFERENT COLOR. New York, Phoenix, 1952.

Cook, Ida — WIFE TO CHRISTOPHER, as Mary Burchell. London, 1936.

Cook, William Everett — FRONTIER FEUD, as Will Cook. New York, Popular Library, 1954 — PRAIRIE GUNS, as Will Cook. New York, Popular Library, 1954.

Cook, William Wallace — HIS FRIEND THE ENEMY. New York, Dillingham, 1903.

Cookson, Catherine Ann — KATE HANNIGAN. London, 1950.

Coolidge, Dane — HIDDEN WATER. Chicago, McClurg, 1910.

Coolidge, Susan — THE NEW YEAR'S BARGAIN. Boston, Roberts, and London, Warne, 1872.

Cooper, Courtney Ryley — US KIDS: VERSES. Kansas City, Kellog Baxter, 1910.

Cooper, Henry St. John — BULL-DOGS AND BULL-DOG BREEDING. London, Jarrolds, 1905.

Cooper, James Fenimore — PRECAUTION: A NOVEL. 1820.

Cooper, Jilly — HOW TO STAY MARRIED. London, 1969.

Coover, Robert — THE ORIGIN OF THE BRUNISTS. New York, 1966.

Corle, Edwin — MOJAVE: A BOOK OF STORIES. New York, Liveright, 1934.

Cornwell, David John Moore — CALL FOR THE DEAD, as John Le Carre. London, Gollancz, 1961; New York, Walker, 1962.

Cort, Van — THE RANGERS OF BLOODY SILVER. New York, Phoenix, 1941; as BLOOD ON THE MOON. London, Hodder & Stoughton, 1941.

Costain, Thomas Bertram — FOR MY GREAT FOLLY. New York, 1942.

Coulson, Juanita — CRISIS ON CHEIRON. New York, Ace, 1967.

Courtney, Caroline — DUCHESS IN DISGUISE. New York & London, 1979 — A WAGER FOR LOVE. New York & London, 1979 — LOVE UNMASKED. New York & London, 1979 — GUARDIAN OF THE HEART. New York, 1979 — DANGEROUS EXPERIMENT. New York, 1979.

Coward, Noel — "I'LL LEAVE IT TO YOU." London, 1920.

Cowen, Frances — IN THE CLUTCH OF THE GREEN HAND . London, 1929.

Cox, William Robert — MAKE MY COFFIN STRONG. New York, Fawcett, 1954; London, Fawcett, 1955.

Coxe, Louis — THE SEA FARING AND OTHER POEMS. New York, 1947.

Cozzens, James Gould — CONFUSION. Boston, 1924.

Craig, Mary Francis — SIMPLE SPIGOTT. New York, 1960.

Crane, Hart — WHITE BUILDINGS: POEMS. 1926.

Crane, Stephen — MAGGIE: A GIRL OF THE STREETS. 1892.

Crews, Harry — THE GOSPEL SINGER. New York, 1968.

Cronin, A.J. — HATTER'S CASTLE. London, 1931.

Crook, Compton Newby — THE STARDUST VOYAGES, as Stephen Tall. New York, Berkley, 1975.

Crosby, Caresse — CROSSES OF GOLD: A BOOK OF VERSE. Paris, 1925.

Crosby, Harry C. — THE DAY THE MACHINES STOPPED, as Christopher Anvil. Derby (CT), Monarch, 1964.

Crothers, Samuel Mc Cord — MISS MUFFET'S CHRISTMAS PARTY. St. Paul, 1892.

Crowe, Cecily — MISS SPRING. New York, 1953.

Cullen, Countee — COLOR. New York, 1925.

Cullum, Ridgewell — THE DEVIL'S KEG. London, Chapman & Hall, 1903; as THE STORY OF THE FOSS RIVER RANCH. Boston, Page, 1903.

Cummings, E.E. — EIGHT HARVARD POETS. 1917.

Culp, John Hewett, Jr. — BORN OF THE SUN. New York, Sloane, 1959; London, Deutsch, 1963.

Cunningham, Chet — BUSHWHACKERS AT CIRCLE K. New York, Avalon, 1969.

Cunningham, Eugene — THE REGULATION GUY. New York, Cornhill, 1922; GYPSYING THROUGH CENTRAL AMERICA. New York, Dutton, and London, Unwin, 1922.

Curry, Peggy Simson — FIRE IN THE WATER. New York, McGraw Hill, 1951; London, Muller, 1952.

Curtis, Thomas Dale And Sharon — A HEART TOO PROUD, as Laura London. New York, Dell, 1978.

Curwood, James Oliver — THE COURAGE OF CAPTAIN PLUM. Indianapolis, Bobbs Merrill, 1908; London, Hodder & Stoughton, 1925 — THE WOLF HUNTERS: A TALE OF ADVENTURE IN THE WILDERNESS. Indianapolis, Bobbs Merrill, 1908; London, Cassell, 1917.

Cushman, Dan — MONTANA, HERE I BE! New York, Macmillan, 1950; London, Laurie, 1953.

D

Dahlberg, Edward — BOTTOM DOGS. London, 1929.

Dailey, Janet — NO QUARTER ASKED. London, Mills & Boon, 1974; Toronto, Harlequin, 1976 — SAVAGE LAND. London, Mills & Boon, 1974; Toronto, Harlequin, 1976.

Danbury, Iris — THE GENTLE INVADER. London, Mills & Boon, 1957.

Daniels, Dorothy — THE DARK RIDER, as Geraldine Thayer. New York, Avalon, 1961 — THE CADUCEUS TREE, as Suzanne Somers. New York, Avalon, 1961.

Dannay, Frederic — THE ROMAN HAT MYSTERY, as Ellery Queen, with Manfred B. Lee. New York, Stokes, and London, Gollancz, 1929.

Darcy, Clare — GEORGINA. New York, Walker, 1971.

Davenport, Marcia — MOZART. New York, Scribner, 1932.

Davidson, Donald — AN OUTLAND PIPER. Boston, 1924.

Davies, John Evan Weston — THE ACHILLES AFFAIR, as Berkely Mather. London, Collins, and New York, Scribner, 1959.

Davies, W.H. — THE SOUL'S DESTROYER, AND OTHER POEMS. London, 1905.

Davis, Dorothy Salisbury — THE JUDAS CAT. New York, Scribner, 1949.

Davis, Harold Lenoir — HONEY IN THE HORN, as H.L. Davis. New York, Harper, and London, Lovat Dickson & Thompson, 1935.

Davis, Rebecca — MARGARET HOWTH: A STORY OF TO-DAY. Boston, 1862.

Day, Robert S. — THE LAST CATTLE DRIVE. New York, Putnam, and London, Secker & Warburg, 1977.

Day-Lewis, Cecil — BEECHEN VIGIL & OTHER POEMS. London, 1925.

De Forest, John W. — HISTORY OF THE INDIANS OF CONNECTICUT. 1851.

De La Pasture, Edmee Elizabeth Monica — ZELLA SEES HERSELF, as E.M. Delafield. London, Heinemann, & New York, Knopf, 1917.

De La Roche, Mazo Louise — EXPLORERS OF THE DAWN. New York & London, 1922.

De Morgan, William — JOSEPH VANCE. London, 1906.

De Rosso, Henry Andrew — .44, as H.A. De Rosso. New York, Lion, 1953; London, Mills & Boon, 1957.

De Schanschieff, Juliet Dymoke — THE SONS OF THE TRIBUNE: AN ADVENTURE ON THE ROMAN WALL. London, 1956.

De Voto, Bernard Augustine — THE CROOKED MILE. New York, Minton Balch, 1924.

De Vries, Peter — BUT WHO WAKES THE BUGLER. Boston, 1940.

De Weese-Wehen, Joy — STAIRWAY TO A SECRET. New York, Dutton, 1953.

Decker, William — TO BE A MAN. Boston, Little Brown, 1967.

Deeping, George Warwick — UTHER AND IGRAINE. London, Richards, & New York, Outlook, 1903.

Deland, Margaret — THE OLD GARDEN AND OTHER VERSES. Boston, 1886.

Delderfield, Ronald Frederick — THESE CLICKS MADE HISTORY: THE STORIES OF STANLEY "GLORIOUS" DEVON, FLEET STREET PHOTOGRAPHER. Exmouth, ENG, 1946.

Dell, Ethel Mary — THE WAY OF AN EAGLE. New York, 1911.

Dell, Floyd — WOMEN AS WORLD BUILDERS. Chicago, 1913.

Delmar, Vina — BAD GIRL. New York, 1928.

Denver, Lee — GUN FEUD AT SUNROCK. London, Skeffington, 1951.

Deutsch, Babette — BANNERS. New York, 1919.

Dewlen, Al — THE NIGHT OF THE TIGER. New York, 1956.

Di Donato, Pietro — CHRIST IN CONCRETE. Chicago, 1937.

Dick, Philip Kindred — SOLAR LOTTERY. New York, Ace, 1955; as WORLD OF CHANCE. London, Rich & Cowan, 1956 — A HANDFUL OF DARKNESS. London, Rich & Cowan, 1955; Boston, Gregg Press, 1978.

Didion, Joan — RUN RIVER. New York, 1963.

Dingwell, Joyce — AUSTRALIAN HOSPITAL. London, 1955.

Diver, Katherine Helen Maud — THE ENGLISHWOMAN IN INDIA, as Maud Diver. Edinburgh Scot, 1909.

Dobson, Austin — VIGNETTES IN RHYME. London, 1873.

Doctorow, Edgar Laurence — WELCOME TO HARD TIMES, as E.L. Doctorow. New York, 1960.

Dodge, Mary Mapes — THE IRVINGTON STORIES, as M.E. Dodge. New York, O'Kane, 1865 — HANS BRINKER; OR, THE SILVER SKATES: A STORY OF LIFE IN HOLLAND. New York, O'Kane, 1865; as THE SILVER SKATES, London, Sampson Low, 1867.

Dodgson, Charles Lutwidge — THE FIFTH BOOK OF EUCLID TREATED ALGEBRAICALLY — as C.L. Dodgson. Oxford, Parker, 1858.

Donleavy, J.P. — THE GINGER MAN. Paris, 1955.

Doolittle, Hilda — SEA GARDEN: IMAGIST POEMS, as H.D. London, 1916 .

Dorn, Edward — WHAT I SEE IN THE MAXIMUS POEMS. Ventura, 1960.

Douglas, Lord Alfred — POEMES. Paris, 1896.

Dowler, James Ross — PARTNER'S CHOICE. New York, 1958.

Doyle, Arthur Conan — A STUDY IN SCARLET. London, Ward Lock, 1888; Philadelphia, Lippincott, 1890.

Drago, Harry Sinclair — WHOSO FINDETH A WIFE, as J. Wesley Putnam. New York, 1914.

Dreiser, Theodore — SISTER CARRIE. 1900.

Dresser, Davis — MARDI GRAS MADNESS, as Anthony Scott. New York, 1934.

Drinkwater, John — POEMS. Birmingham, 1903.

Du Maurier, Daphne — THE LOVING SPIRIT. London & New York, 1931.

Dufault, Joseph Ernest Nephtali — COWBOYS NORTH AND SOUTH, as Will James. New York, and London, Scribner, 1924.

Duffield, Anne — MISS MAYHEW AND MING YUN: A STORY OF EAST AND WEST. New York, 1928.

Dunbar, Paul Laurence — OAK AND IVY. Dayton, 1893.

Duncan, Robert Lipscomb — THE Q DOCUMENT, as James Hall Roberts. New York, Morrow, 1964; London, Cape, 1965.

Dunkerley, Elsie Jeanette — GOBLIN ISLAND, as Elsie Oxenham. London, Collins, 1907.

Dunlop, Agnes M.R. — THE BEGONIA BED, as Elisabeth Kyle. London, Constable, and Indianapolis, Bobbs Merrill, 1934.

Dunne, John Gregory — DELANO: THE STORY OF THE CALIFORNIA GRAPE STRIKE. New York, 1967.

Dunnett, Dorothy — THE GAME OF KINGS. New York, 1961.

Durham, Marilyn — THE MAN WHO LOVED CAT DANCING. New York & London, 1972.

Durrell, Lawrence George — QUAINT FRAGMENT: POEMS WRITTEN BETWEEN THE AGES OF SIXTEEN AND NINETEEN. London, Cecil Press, 1931.

Durst, Paul — DIE, DAMN YOU! New York, 1952.

Dwyer-Joyce, Alice Louise — PRICE OF INHERITANCE. London, 1963.

E

East, Fred — MEDDLING MAVERICK, as Tom West. New York, Dutton, 1944; London, Ward Lock, 1946.

Eastlake, William Derry — GO IN BEAUTY. New York, 1956.

Easton, Robert Olney — THE HAPPY MAN. New York, 1943.

Ebel, Suzanne — LOVE, THE MAGICIAN. London, 1956.

Eberhart, Mignon Good — THE PATIENT IN ROOM 18. New York, London, 1929.

Eberhart, Richard — A BRAVERY OF EARTH. London, 1930.

Eddison, E.R. — THE WORM OUROBOROS. London, 1922.

Eden, Dorothy — SINGING SHADOWS. London, 1940.

Edginton, Helen Marion — THE WEIGHT CARRIERS, as May Edginton. London, 1909.

Edmonds, Walter Dumaux — ROME HAUL. Boston, 1929.

Edson, John Thomas — TRAIL BOSS. London, 1961.

Edwards, Anne — A CHILD'S BIBLE. London, 1967.

Eggleston, Edward — MR. BLAKE'S WALKING-STICK: A CHRISTMAS STORY FOR BOYS AND GIRLS. 1870.

Ehrlich, John Gunther — REVENGE, as Jack Ehrlich. New York, 1958.

Eliot, T.S. — PRUFROCK AND OTHER OBSERVATIONS. London, 1917.

Elkin, Stanley — BOSWELL. New York, 1964.

Ellerbeck, Rosemary Anne L'Estrange — INCLINATION TO MURDER. London, 1965.

Elles, Dora Amy — A CHILD'S RHYME BOOK, as Patricia Wentworth. London, Melrose, 1910 — A MARRIAGE UNDER THE TERROR. London, Melrose, and New York, Putnam, 1910.

Ellison, Harlan Jay — RUMBLE. New York, Pyramid, 1958; THE DEADLY STREETS. New York, Ace, 1958; London, Digit, 1959.

Ellison, Ralph — INVISIBLE MAN. New York, 1952.

Elston, Allan Vaughan — COME OUT AND FIGHT! New York, 1941.

Emanuel, Victor Rousseau — DERWENT'S HORSE, as Victor Rousseau. London, Methuen, 1901.

Emerson, Ralph Waldo — LETTER — TO THE SECOND CHURCH AND SOCIETY. 1832.

Erdman, Loula Grace — SEPARATE STAR. New York, 1944.

Ernenwein, Leslie — GUNSMOKE GALOOT. New York, 1941.

Erskine-Lindop, Audrey Beatrice Noel — FORTUNE MY FOE. New York, 1947.

Ertz, Susan — MADAME CLAIRE. London & New York, 1923.

Estleman, Loren D. — THE OKLAHOMA PUNK. Canoga Park, 1976.

Estridge, Robin — THE FUTURE IS TOMORROW. London, Davies, 1947.

Evans, Max — SOUTHWEST WIND. San Antonio, 1958.

Evarts, Sr., Hal George — THE CROSS-PULL. New York, & London, 1920 .

Evarts, Hal George Jr. — ROLLING AHEAD. Paris, 1945.

Evelyn, John Michael — MURDER ON TRIAL, as Michael Underwood. London, Hammond, 1954; New York, Washburn, 1958.

Everett, Edward — A DEFENSE OF CHRISTIANITY. Boston, 1814.

Everson, Bill William — THESE ARE THE RAVENS. San Leandro, 1935.

Ewing, Juliana Horatia — MELCHIOR'S DREAM AND OTHER TALES. London, Bell & Daldy, 1862; Boston, Roberts, 1886.

Exley, Frederick — A FAN'S NOTES. New York, 1968.

F

Fante, John — WAIT UNTIL SPRING, BANDINI. New York, 1938.

Farnes, Eleanor — MERRY GOES THE TIME. London, 1935.

Farnol, John Jeffry — MY LADY CAPRICE. London & New York, 1907.

Farrell, Cliff — FOLLOW THE NEW GRASS. New York, 1945.

Farrell, James T. — YOUNG LONIGAN: A BOYHOOD IN CHICAGO. New York, 1932.

Fast, Howard Melvin — TWO VALLEYS. New York, Dial; London, Dickson, 1934.

Faulkner, William — THE MARBLE FAUN. Boston, 1924.

Faust, Frederick Schiller — THE UNTAMED, as Max Brand. New York, Putnam, 1919; London, Hodder & Stoughton, 1952.

Fearing, Kenneth Flexner — ANGEL ARMS. New York, 1929.

Feibleman, James K. — DEATH OF THE GOD IN MEXICO. New York, 1931.

Feinberg, Bea — A WORLD FULL OF STRANGERS, as Cynthia Freeman. New York, 1975.

Fellows, Catherine — LEONORA. London, 1972.

Felton, Ronald Oliver — THE BLACK CAR MYSTERY, as Ronald Welch. LONDON, Pitman, 1950.

Ferber, Edna — DAWN O'HARA: THE GIRL WHO LAUGHED. New York, 1911.

Fergusson, Harvey — CAPITOL HILL. New York, 1923.

Ferlinghetti, Lawrence — PICTURES OF THE GONE WORLD. San Francisco, 1955.

Ferrini, Vincent — NO SMOKE. Portland, 1941.

Field, Eugene — TRIBUNE PRIMER. Denver, 1881.

Field, Rachel Lyman — THE POINTED PEOPLE: VERSES AND SILHOUETTES . New Haven & London, 1924.

Finley, Glenna — DEATH STRIKES OUT. New York, 1957.

Finney, Charles G. — THE CIRCUS OF DOCTOR LAO. New York, 1935.

Firbank, Arthur Ronald — ODETTE D'ANTREVERNES. London, 1905.

Fisher, Vardi Alveroo — SONNETS: TO AN IMAGINARY MADONNA. New York, 1927.

Fitzgerald, F. Scott — THIS SIDE OF PARADISE. New York, 1920.

Fitzgerald, Robert — POEMS. New York, 1935.

Fitzgerlad, Valerie — ZEMINDAR. London, 1981.

Flanner, Janet — THE CUBICAL CITY. New York, 1926.

Fleming, Ian Lancaster — CASINO ROYALE. London, 1953.

Fletcher, John Gould — FIRE AND WINE. London, May, 1913.

Flynn, Robert Lopez — NORTH TO YESTERDAY. New York & London, 1967.

Flynn, Thomas Theodore — IT'S MURDER!, as T.T. Flynn. London, 1950.

Foreman, Leonard London — DON DESPERADO, as L.L. Foreman. New York, 1941.

Forester, C.S. — A PAWN AMONG KINGS. London, 1924.

Forster, Edward Morgan — WHERE ANGELS FEAR TO TREAD, as E.M. Forster. Edinburgh, Blackwood, 1905; New York, Knopf, 1920.

Foster, Walter Bertram — THE LOST GALLEON OF DOUBLOON ISLAND, as W. Bert Foster. Philadelphia, 1901.

Fowler, Kenneth Abrams — OUTCAST OF MURDER MESA. New York, 1954.

Fowles, John — THE COLLECTOR. London, 1963.

Fox, John, Jr. — A CUMBERLAND VENDETTA AND OTHER STORIES. New York, 1896.

Fox, Norman Arnold — GUN-HANDY. New York, 1941.

Frankau, Gilbert — ETON ECHOES: A VOLUME OF HUMOROUS VERSE. Eton (ENG), 1901.

Franken, Rose Dorothy — PATTERN. New York, 1925.

Frazee, Charles Steve — RANGE TROUBLE, as Dean Jennings. New York, Phoenix, 1951; — SHINING MOUNTAINS. NEW YORK, Rinehart, 1951; London, Muller, 1053.

Frederic, Harold — SETH'S BROTHER'S WIFE. New York, 1887.

Freeman, Mary E. Wilkins — DECORATIVE PLAQUES. 1883.

Freneau, Philip — A POEM ON THE RISING GLORY OF AMERICA. 1772.

Friedman, Bruce Jay — STERN. New York, 1962.

Friedman, I.K. — THE LUCKY NUMBER. Chicago, 1896.

Frost, Robert — A BOY'S WILL. 1913.

Fry, Christopher — THE BOY WITH A CART. London, 1939.

Fry, Roger — GIOVANNI BELLINI. London, 1899.

G

Gaddis, William — THE RECOGNITIONS. New York, 1955.

Gaines, Ernest — CATHERINE CARMIER — New York, 1964.

Gale, Zona — ROMANCE ISLAND. 1906.

Gallagher, Patricia — THE SONS AND THE DAUGHTERS. New York & London, 1961.

Gandley, Kenneth Royce — MY TURN TO DIE, as Kenneth Royce. London, Barker, 1958.

Gann, Walter — THE TRAIL BOSS. Boston, 1937.

Gardiner, Dorothy — THE TRANSATLANTIC GHOST. New York & London, 1933.

Gardner, John Edmund — THE RESURRECTION. New York, 1966.

Garfield, Brian Francis Wynne — RANGE JUSTICE. NEW YORK, 1960.

Garland. Hannibal Hamlin — UNDER THE WHEEL: A MODERN PLAY IN SIX SCENES. 1890.

Garvice, Charles — EVE AND OTHER VERSES. Privately printed, 1873.

Gaskin, Catherine — THIS OTHER EDEN. London, 1947.

Gass, William H. — OMENSETTER'S LUCK. New York, 1966.

Gaulden, Ray — THE ROUGH AND LONELY LAND. London, 1957.

Gavin, Catherine Irvine — LOUIS PHILIPPE, KING OF THE FRENCH. London, 1933.

Geisel, Theodor Seuss — AND TO THINK THAT I SAW IT ON MULBERRY STREET, as Dr. Seuss. New York, Vanguard, 1937; London, Country Life, 1939.

Gellis, Roberta Leah — KNIGHT'S HONOR. New York, 1964.

George, Henry — OUR LAND AND LAND POLICY, NATIONAL AND STATE. San Francisco, 1871.

Germano, Peter B. — TRAIL BOSS FROM TEXAS, as Barry Cord. New York, Phoenix, and London, Foulsham, 1948.

Giggal, Kenneth — THE MANCHESTER THING, as Angus Ross. London, Long, 1970.

Gilbert, W.S. — A NEW AND ORIGINAL EXTRAVAGANZA ENTITLED DULCAMARA; OR, THE LITTLE DUCK AND THE GREAT QUACK. London, 1866.

Gilder, Richard Watson — THE NEW DAY. New York, 1876.

Giles, Janice Holt — THE ENDURING HILLS. Philadelphia, 1950.

Giles, Kenneth — SOME BEASTS NO MORE. London, Gollancz, 1965; New York, Walker, 1968.

Gill, Brendan — DEATH IN APRIL AND OTHER POEMS. Windham, 1935.

Gipson, Frederick Benjamin — FABULOUS EMPIRE: COLONEL ZACK MILLER'S STORY, as Fred Gipson. Boston, 1946.

Gissing, George — WORKERS IN THE DAWN. London, 1880.

Glasgow, Ellen — THE DESCENDANT. 1897.

Glasscock, Anne — KENNEDY'S GOLD, as Michael Bonner. New York, Doubleday, 1960; London, Collins, 1961.

Glidden, Frederick Dilley — THE FEUD AT SINGLE SHOT, as Luke Short. New York, Farrar & Rinehart, and London, Collins, 1936.

Glidden, Jonathan H. — THE CRIMSON HORSESHOE, as Peter Dawson. New York, Dodd Mead, and London, Collins, 1941 — THE STAGLINE FEUD, as Peter Dawson. New York, Dodd Mead, 1941; London, Collins, 1942.

Gluyas, Constance — THE KING'S BRAT. Englewood Cliffs, 1972.

Glyn, Elinor — THE VISITS OF ELIZABETH. London, 1900.

Godden, Margaret Rumer — CHINESE PUZZLE. London, 1936.

Godwin, Gail — THE PERFECTIONISTS. New York, 1970.

Golding, William Gerald — POEMS. London, Macmillan, 1934; New York, Macmillan, 1935.

Goldstone, Lawrence Arthur — BRINGING SHERLOCK HOME, as Lawrence Treat. New York, Doubleday, 1930.

Gooden, Arthur Henry — CROSS KNIFE RANCH. London, 1933.

Goodman, Paul — TEN LYRIC POEMS. New York, 1934.

Gordon, Charles William — GWEN'S CANYON, as Ralph Connor. Toronto, Westminster, 1898 — BEYOND THE MARSHES, as Ralph Connor. Toronto, Westminster, 1898 — BLACK ROCK: A TALE OF THE SELKIRKS, as Ralph Connor. Toronto, Westminster; Chicago, Revell, and London, Hodder & Stoughton, 1898.

Gordon, Ethel Edison — WHERE DOES THE SUMMER GO? New York, 1967.

Goudge, Elizabeth De Beauchamp — THE FAIRIES' BABY AND OTHER STORIES. London, 1919.

Goyder, Margot & Anne Neville — MARIETTA IS STOLEN, as Margot Neville. London, Parsons, 1922.

Goyen, William — THE HOUSE OF BREATH. New York, 1950.

Graham, Roger Phillips — TIME TRAP, as Rog Phillips. Chicago, Century, 1949.

Grahame, Kenneth — PAGAN PAPERS. London, 1894.

Grau, Shirley Ann — THE BLACK PRINCE AND OTHER STORIES. New York, 1955.

Graves, John — GOODBYE TO A RIVER. New York, 1960.

Graves, Robert Ranke — OVER THE BRAZIER. London, Poetry Bookshop, 1916; New York, St. Martin's, 1975 — GOLIATH AND DAVID. London, Chiswick, 1916.

Gray, Pearl Zane — BETTY ZANE, as Zane Grey. New York, 1903.

Green, Henry — BLINDNESS. New York, 1926.

Greene, Graham — BABBLING APRIL: COLLECTED POEMS. Oxford, 1925.

Gregory, Horace — CHELSEA ROOMING HOUSE. New York, 1930.

Gregory, Jackson — UNDER HANDICAP. New York, 1914.

Grieg-Smith, Jennifer — PEGGY OF BEACON HILL, as Maysie Greig. Boston, 1924.

Greve, Felix Paul Berthold Friedrich — WANDERUNGEN, as Frederick Philip Grove. Privately printed, 1902 — HELENA UND DAMON, as Frederick Philip Grove. Privately Printed, 1902.

Grimm, Cherry Barbara — THE LUCK OF BRIN'S FIVE, as Cherry Wilder. New York, Atheneum, 1977; London, Angus & Robertson, 1979.

Grimstead, Hettie — PAINTED VIRGIN. London, 1931.

Grove, Frederick Herridge — FLAME OF THE OSAGE, as Fred Grove. New York, 1958.

Grove, Frederick Philip — WANDERUNGEN. Privately printed, 1902 — HELENA UND DAMON. Privately printed, 1902.

Gruber, Frank — PEACE MARSHALL. New York, 1939.

Grundy, Mabel Sarah Barnes — A THAMES CAMP. Bristol (ENG), 1902.

Guiney, Louise Imogen — SONGS AT THE START. Boston, 1884.

Gulick, Grover C. — COWBOY, FISHERMAN, HUNTER, as Bill Gulick, with Larry Mersfelder. Kansas City, 1942.

Guthrie, Jr., Alfred Bertram — MURDERS AT MOON DANCE, as A.B. Guthrie. New York, 1943.

Guthrie, Ramon — TROBAR CLUS. Northampton, 1923.

Guthrie, Thomas Anstey — VICE VERSA; OR, A LESSON TO FATHERS, as F. Anstey. London, Smith Elder, and New York, Appleton, 1882.

H

Haas, Benjamin Leopold — THE FORAGERS, as Ben Haas. New York, Simon & Schuster, 1962; London, Davies, 1963.

Haggard, Henry Rider — CETYWAYO AND HIS WHITE NEIGHBOURS; OR, REMARKS ON RECENT EVENTS IN ZULULAND, NATAL, AND THE TRANSVAAL. London, Trubner, 1882.

Haines, Pamela — TEA AT GUNTER'S. London, 1974.

Hale, Lucretia Peabody — THE STRUGGLE FOR LIFE. Boston, Walker Wise, 1861.

Haley, J. Evetts — THE XIT RANCH OF TEXAS. Chicago, 1929.

Hall, James — TRIAL AND DEFENSE OF FIRST LIEUTENANT JAMES HALL. 1820.

Hall, James Norman — KITCHENER'S MOB. Boston, 1916.

Hall, Oakley Maxwell — MURDER CITY, as O.M. Hall. New York, 1949.

Halleck, Fitz-Greene — POEMS, BY CROAKER & CO., AND CROAKER. 1819.

Halleran, Eugene Edward — NO RANGE IS FREE, as E.E. Halleran. Philadelphia, 1944.

Hamilton, Charles Harold St. John — SCHOOLBOY SERIES: THE SECRET OF THE SCHOOL, THE BLACK SHEEP OF SPARSHOTT, FIRST MAN IN, LOOKING AFTER LAMB, as Frank Richards. 4 vols. London, Merrett, 1946.

Hamilton, Donald Bengtsson — DATE WITH DARKNESS. New York, 1947.

Hammett, Samuel Dashiell — RED HARVEST. New York, 1929.

Hampson, Anne — ETERNAL SUMMER. London, 1969.

Harbage, Alfred Bennett — THOMAS KILLIGREW: CAVALIER DRAMATIST. Philadelphia, Univ. of Pennsylvania, and London, Oxford University, 1930.

Hardwick, Mollie — THE JOLLY TOPER, with Michael Hardwick. London, 1961

Hardy, William George — ABRAHAM, PRINCE OF UR. New York, 1935.

Harknett, Terry Williams — THE BENEVOLENT BLACKMAILER. London, Hale, 1962 — THE SCRATCH ON THE SURFACE. London, Hale, 1962.

Harris, Joel Chandler — UNCLE REMUS: HIS SONGS AND HIS SAYINGS: THE FOLKLORE OF THE OLD PLANTATION. New York, Appleton, 1881; as UNCLE REMUS AND HIS LEGENDS OF THE OLD PLANTATION. London, Bogue, 1881; as UNCLE REMUS; OR, MR. FOX, MR. RABBIT, AND MR. TERRAPIN, London, Routledge, 1881.

Harris, John Wyndham Parkes Lucas Beynon — THE SECRET PEOPLE, as John Beynon. London, Newnes, 1935; as J.B. Harris, New York, Lancer, 1964 — FOUL PLAY, as John Beynon. London, Newnes, 1935.

Harris, Larry Mark — PAGAN PASSIONA, with Randall Garrett. New York, Galaxy, 1959.

Harris, Marilyn — KING'S EX. New York & London, 1967.

Harris, Mark — TRUMPET TO THE WORLD. New Yoek, 1946.

Harris, Rosemary Jeanne — THE SUMMER-HOUSE. London, 1956.

Harrison, Edith Elizabeth Tatchell — COFFEE AT DOBREE'S. London, 1965.

Harte, Bret — CONDENSED NOVELS AND OTHER PAPERS. New York, 1867; THE LOST GALLEON AND OTHER TALES, 1867.

Harvey, John B. — AVENGING ANGEL, as Thom Ryder. London, 1975.

Hastings, Phyliss Dora — AS LONG AS YOU LIVE. London, 1951.

Hawkes, John — FIASCO HALL, as J.C.B. Hawkes, Jr. Cambridge, 1943.

Hawkins, Sir Anthony Hope — A MAN OF MARK, as Anthony Hope. London, 1890.

Hawthorne, Nathaniel — FANSHAWE: A TALE. 1828

Hay, John — JIM BLUDSO OF THE PRAIRIE BELL, AND LITTLE BREECHES. Boston, 1871.

Haycox, Ernest — FREE GRASS. New York, 1929.

Healey, Benjamin James — WAITING FOR A TIGER, as Ben Healey. London, Hale, and New York, 1965.

Hearn, Lafcadio — STRAY LEAVES FROM STRANGE LITERATURE. 1884.

Heaven, Constance — QUEEN'S DELIGHT, as Constance Fecher. London, 1966.

Hecht, Anthony — A SUMMONING OF STONES. New York, 1954.

Heckelmann, Charles Newman — JUNGLE MENACE. New York, 1937 — CLARKVILLE'S BATTERY; OR, BASEBALL VERSUS GANGSTERS, as Charles Lawton. New York, 1937.

Heinlein, Robert Anson — ROCKET SHIP GALILEO. New York, Scribner, 1947; London, New English Library, 1971.

Heller, Joseph — CATCH-22. New York, 1961.

Hemingway, Ernest — THREE STORIES AND TEN POEMS. Paris, 1923.

Hendryx, James Beardsley — THE PROMISE: A TALE OF THE GREAT NORTHWEST. New York, 1915.

Hennissart, Martha — BANKING ON DEATH, as Emma Lathen, with Mary J. Latis. New York, Macmillan, 1961; London, Gollancz, 1962.

Henty, George Alfred — A SEARCH FOR A SECRET, as G.A. Henty. London, Tinsley, 3 vols., 1867.

Herbst, Josephine — NOTHING IS SACRED. New York, 1928.

Hergseheimer, Joseph — THE LAY ANTHONY. New York, 1914.

Heron-Allen, Edward — DE FIDICULIS OPUSCULUM, as Christopher Blayre. Privately printed, 9 vols., 1882-1941.

Heuman, William — GUNS AT BROKEN BOW. New York, 1950; FIGHTING FIVE. New York, 1950.

Heyer, Georgette — THE BLACK MOTH. London & Boston, 1921.

Heyward, Du Bose — SKYLINES AND HORIZONS. New York, 1924.

Hibbert, Eleanor Alice — DAUGHTER OF ANNA, as Victoria Holt. London, 1941.

Hichens, Robert Smythe — THE COASTGUARD'S SECRET. London, 1886.

Hill, Grace Livingston — A CHAUTAUQUA IDYL. Boston, 1887.

Hill, Pamela — FLAMING JANET: A LADY OF GALLOWAY. London, 1954.

Hillyer, Robert — SONNETS AND OTHER LYRICS. Cambridge, 1917.

Hilton, James — CATHERINE HERSELF. London, Unwin, 1920.

Himes, Chester Bomar — IF HE HOLLERS LET HIM GO. New York, 1947.

Hintze, Naomi Agans — BURIED TREASURE WAITS FOR YOU. Indianapolis, 1962.

Hitchens, Julia Clara Catherine Dolores Birk Olsen — THE CLUE IN THE CLAY, as D.B. Olsen. New York, Phoenix, 1938.

Hobart, Donald Bayne — THE WHISTLING WADDY: A WESTERN STORY. New York, 1928; DOUBLE SHUFFLE. New York, 1928.

Hodge, Jane Aiken — MAULEVER HALL. London & New York, 1964.

Hoffman, Lee — GUNFIGHT AT LARAMIE. New York, Ace, 1966; London, Gold Lion, 1975 — THE LEGEND OF BLACKJACK SAM. New York, Ace, 1966.

Hogan, Robert Ray — EX-MARSHALL. New York, 1956.

Holland, Isabelle — CECILY . Philadelphia, 1967.

Holland, Sheila — LOVE IN A MIST. London, Hale, 1971.

Holmes, John Clellon — GO. New York, 1952.

Holmes, Oliver Wendell — THE HARBINGER: A MAY GIFT. 1833.

Hopley-Woolrich, Cornell George — COVER CHARGE, as Cornell Woolrich. New York, Boni & Liveright, 1926.

Hopson, William L. — GUN-THROWER. New York & London, 1940.

Horgan, Paul — LAMB OF GOD. Privately printed, 1927.

Horne, Geoffrey — WINTER. London, Hutchinson, 1957.

Horner, Lance — MANDINGO, with Kyle Onstott. Richmond, 1957

Hosken, Clifford James Wheeler — CARTERET'S CURE, as Richard Keverne. London, Constable, and Boston, Houghton Mifflin, 1926.

Hough, Emerson — THE SINGING MOUSE STORIES. New York, 1895.

Housman, Laurence — A FARM IN FAIRYLAND. London, 1894.

Houston, Tex — THE SHERIFF OF HAMMER COUNTY. London, 1956.

Hovey, Richard — POEMS. Washington, 1880.

Howard, Robert Ervin — A GENT FROM BEAR CREEK. London, 1937.

Howatch, Susan Elizabeth — THE DARK SHORE. New York, 1965.

Howe, Mark A. De Wolfe — RARI NANTES: BEING VERSES AND A SONG. Boston, 1893.

Howells, William Dean — POEMS OF TWO FRIENDS (with John Piatt); LIVES AND SPEECHES OF ABRAHAM LINCOLN AND HANNIBAL HAMLIN, both 1869.

Hubbard, George Barron — WITHOUT COMPROMISE, as George Hubbard, with Lilian Bennet-Thompson. New York, Century, 1922.

Hueffer, Ford H. Madox — THE BROWN OWL. London, 1892.

Huffaker, Clair — BADGE FOR A GUNFIGHTER. New York & London, 1957.

Hufford, Susan — MIDNIGHT SAILING. New York, 1975.

Hughes, Langston — THE WEARY BLUES. New York, 1926.

Hughes, Richard Arthur Warren — THE SISTERS' TRAGEDY. Oxford, 1922.

Hughes, Ted — THE HAWK IN THE RAIN. London, 1957.

Hughes, Walter Llewellyn — BLAST OFF AT WOOMERA, as Hugh Walters. London, Faber, 1957; as BLAST-OFF AT 0300. New York, Criterion, 1958.

Hull, Edith Maude — THE SHEIK, as E.M. Hull. London, 1919.

Humphrey, William — THE LAST HUSBAND AND OTHER STORIES. New York & London, 1953.

Huneker, James — MEZZOTINTS IN MODERN MUSIC. New York, 1899.

Hunt, Leigh — JUVENILIA; OR, A COLLECTION OF POEMS, as J.H.L. Hunt. London, 1801.

Hunter, Elizabeth Mary Teresa — THE AFRICAN MOUNTAIN, as Isobel Chace. London, 1960.

Hunter, Evan — THE BIG FIX. No place, Falcon, 1952 — FIND THE FEATHERED SERPENT. Philadelphia, Winston, 1952.

Hurley, John J. — FATAL FLOURISHES, as S.S. Rafferty. New York, Avon, 1979.

Hurst, Fannie — JUST AROUND THE CORNER: ROMANCE EN CASSEROLE. New York, 1914.

Huxley, Aldous Leonard — THE BURNING WHEEL. Oxford, Blackwell, 1916.

Hyndman, Jane Lee — SIZZLING PAN RANCH, as Lee Wyndham. New York, Crowell, 1951.

I

Iams, Samuel H., Jr. — NOWHERE WITH MUSIC. New York, Longman, 1938.

Iannuzzi, John Nicholas — WHAT'S HAPPENING? New York, Barnes, and London, Yoseloff, 1963.

Ingelow, Jean — A RHYMING CHRONICLE OF INCIDENTS AND FEELINGS, anonymously. London, Longman, 1850.

Innes, Ralph Hammond — THE DOPPELGANGER. London, Jenkins, 1937.

Irving, Washington — LETTERS OF JONATHAN OLDSTYLE, GENT. 1802-03.

Irwin, Margaret Emma Faith — HOW MANY MILES TO BABYLON? London, Constable, 1913.

Ish-Kishor, Sulamith — THE BIBLE STORY. New York, United Synagogue, 1921.

J

Jackman, Stuart Brooke — PORTRAIT IN TWO COLOURS. London, Faber, 1948; New York, Scribner, 1949.

Jackson, Jesse — CALL ME CHARLEY. New York, Harper, 1945.

Jackson, Shirley Hardie — THE ROAD THROUGH THE WALL. New York, Farrar Straus, 1948.

Jacob, Naomi Ellington — JACOB USSHER. London, Butterworth, 1925.

Jacob, Piers Anthony Dillingham — CHTHON, as Piers Anthony. New York, Ballantine, 1967; London, Macdonald, 1970.

Jakes, John William — THE TEXANS RIDE NORTH. Philadelphia, Winston, 1952.

James, Henry — A PASSIONATE PILGRIM AND OTHER TALES. 1875.

James, Phyliss, Dorothy — COVER HER FACE. London, Faber, 1962; New York, Scribner, 1966.

Jarrell, Randall — FIVE YOUNG AMERICAN POETS, with others. New York, New Directions, 1940.

Jarrett, Cora — PECCADILLOES, as Faraday Keene. New York, Day, 1929; London, Noel Douglas, 1930.

Jay, Geraldine Mary — THE KNIFE IS FEMININE, as Charlotte Jay. London, Collins, 1951.

Jeffers, Robinson — FLAGONS AND APPLES. 1912.

Jeffries, Roderic — BRANDY AHOY!, as Roderic Graeme. London, Hutchinson, 1951.

Jellicoe, Ann — SOME UNCONSCIOUS INFLUENCES IN THE THEATRE. London and New York, Cambridge Univ., 1967.

Jenkins, William Fitzgerald — SCALPS, as Murray Leinster. New York, Brewer & Warren, 1930; as WINGS OF CHANCE, London, Hamilton, 1935.

Jenks, George Charles — DOUBLE CURVE DAN, THE PITCHER DETECTIVE. New York, Beadle & Adams, 1883.

Jepson, Selwyn — THE QUALIFIED ADVENTURER. London, Hutchinson, and New York, Harcourt Brace, 1922.

Jervis, Marguerite Florence — THE ACTIVITIES OF LAVIE JUTT, as Marguerite Barclay, with Armiger Barclay. London, 1911.

Jesse, Fryniwyd Tennyson — THE MILKY WAY. London, Heinemann, 1913; New York, Doran, 1914.

Jessup, Richard — THE CUNNING AND THE HAUNTED. New York, Fawcett, 1957; London, Fawcett, 1958.

Jewett, Sarah Orne — DEEPHAVEN. 1877.

Jobson, Hamilton — THEREFORE I KILLED HIM. London, Long, 1968.

Johns, William Earl — THE CAMELS ARE COMING. London, Hamilton, 1932 — MOSSYFACE, as William Earl. London, Mellifont, 1932 — THE PICTORIAL FLYING COURSE, with Harry M. Schofield. London, Hamilton, 1932 — FIGHT PLANES AND ACES. London, Hamilton, 1932.

Johnson, Annabell Jones — AS A SPECKLED BIRD. New York, Crowell, 1956; London, Hodder & Stoughton, 1958.

Johnson, Barbara Ferry — LIONORS. New York, Avon, 1975; London, Sphere, 1977.

Johnson, Dorothy Marie — BEULAH BUNNY TELLS ALL. New York, Morrow, 1942; as MISS BUNNY INTERVENES, London, Chapman & Hall, 1948.

Johnson, Edgar Raymond — THE BIG ROCK CANDY, with Annabell Jones Johnson. New York, Crowell, 1957.

Johnson, Emil Richard — SILVER STREET. New York, Harper, 1968; as THE SILVER STREET KILLER, London, Hale, 1969.

Johnston, Mary — THE PRISONERS OF HOPE: A TALE OF COLONIAL VIRGINIA. Boston, Houghton Mifflin, 1898; as THE OLD DOMINION, London, Constable, 1899.

Johnston, Norma — THE WISHING STAR. New York, Funk & Wagnalls, 1963.

Johnston, Velda — ALONG A DARK PATH. New York, Dodd Mead, 1967; Aylesbury (ENG), Milton House, 1974.

Jones, Dennis Feltham — COLOSSUS. London, Hart Davis, 1966; New York, Putnam, 1967.

Jones, Diana Wynne — CHANGEOVER. London, Macmillan, 1970.

Jones, Douglas C. — THE TREATY OF MEDICINE LODGE: THE STORY OF THE GREAT TREATY COUNCIL AS TOLD BY EYEWITNESSES. Norman, Univ. of Oklahoma, 1966.

Jones, Langdon — THE EYE OF THE LENS. New York, Macmillan, 1972.

Jones, Nard — OREGON DETOUR. New York, Payson & Clarke, 1930.

Jones, Neil Ronald — THE PLANET OF THE DOUBLE SUN. New York, Ace, 1967 — THE SUNLESS WORLD. New York, Ace, 1967 — SPACE WAR. New York, Ace, 1967 — TWIN WORLDS. New York, Ace, 1967.

Jones, Raymond F. — RENAISSANCE. New York, Gnome, 1951 — THE ALIEN. New York, Galaxy, 1951 — THE TOYMAKER. Los Angeles, Fantasy, 1951.

Jordan, June — WHO LOOK AT ME! New York, Crowell, 1969.

Jordan, Robert Furneaux — THE CHARM OF THE TIMBER HOUSE. London, Nicholson & Watson, 1936.

Joscelyn, Archie Lynn — THE GOLDEN BOWL. Cleveland, World, 1931.

Joslin, Sesyle — WHAT DO YOU SAY, DEAR? New York, Scott, 1958; London, Faber, 1960.

Jowett, Margaret — CANDIDATE FOR FAME. London, Oxford Univ., 1955.

Judah, Aaron — TOMMY WITH THE HOLE IN HIS SHOE. London, Faber, 1957.

Juster, Norton — THE PHANTOM TOLLBOOTH. New York, Epstein & Carroll, 1961; London, Collins, 1962.

K

Kahl, Virginia C. — AWAY WENT WOLFGANG! New York, Scribner, 1954.

Kamm, Josephine Mary — ALL QUIET AT HOME. London, Longman, 1936.

Kane, Frank — ABOUT FACE. New York, Curl, 1947.

Kane, Henry — A HALO FOR NOBODY. New York, Simon & Schuster, 1947; London, Boardman, 1950.

Kantor, Mac Kinlay — DIVERSEY. New York, Coward McCann, 1928.

Kapp, Colin — TRANSFINITE MAN. New York, Berkely, 1964; as THE DARK MIND. London, Corgi, 1965.

Karp, David — THE VOICE OF THE FOUR FREEDOMS. Privately printed, 1942.

Kaye, Geraldine — TALES FOR MALAYAN CHILDREN. Singapore, Moore, 1956.

Keating, Henry Reymond Fitzgerald — DEATH AND THE VISITING FIREMEN. London, Gollancz, 1959; New York, Doubleday, 1973.

Keats, Ezra Jack — MY DOG IS LOST, with Pat Cherr. New York, Crowell, 1960.

Keeler, Harry Stephen — THE VOICE OF THE SEVEN SPARROWS. London, Hutchinson, 1924; New York, Dutton, 1928.

Keene, Day — THIS IS MURDER, MR. HERBERT, AND OTHER STORIES. New York, Avon, 1948.

Keeping, Charles William James — BLACK DOLLY. Leicester (ENG), Brockhampton, 1966; as MOLLY O' THE MOORS. Cleveland, World, 1966.

Keith, Harold Verne — BOYS' LIFE OF WILL ROGERS. New York, Crowell, 1937.

Kelland, Clarence Budington — QUIZZER NO. 20, BEING QUESTIONS AND ANSWERS ON INSURANCE. Detroit, Sprague, 1911.

Keller, David Henry — THE KELLERS OF HAMILTON TOWNSHIP: A STUDY IN DEMOCRACY. Privately printed, 1922.

Kelley, Leo Patrick — THE COUNTERFEITS. New York, Belmont, 1967.

Kelley, William Melvin — A DIFFERENT DRUMMER. New York, Doubleday, 1962; London, Hutchinson, 1963.

Kelly, Eric Philbrook — THE TRUMPETER OF KRAKOW. New York, Macmillan, 1928; London, Chatto & Windus, 1968.

Kelly, Mary Theresa — A COLD COMING. London, Secker & Warburg, 1956; New York, Walker, 1968.

Kelton, Elmer — HOT IRON. New York, Ballantine, 1956.

Kemelman, Harry — FRIDAY THE RABBI SLEPT LATE. New York, Crown, 1964; London, Hutchinson, 1965.

Kendall, Carol — THE BLACK SEVEN. New York, Harper, 1946; London, Lane, 1950.

Kendrick, Baynard Hardwick — BLOOD ON LAKE LOUISA. New York, Greenberg, 1934; London, Methuen, 1937.

Kennedy, John Pendleton — THE RED BOOK. 1818-19

Kennedy, Margaret — A CENTURY OF REVOLUTION 1789-1920. London, Methuen, 1922.

Kenrick, Tony — THE ONLY GOOD BODY'S A DEAD ONE. London, Cape, 1970; New York, Simon & Schuster, 1971.

Kenyon, Michael — MAY YOU DIE IN IRELAND. London, Collins, and New York, Morrow, 1965.

Keppel-Jones, Arthur Mervyn — DO WE GOVERN OURSELVES? Johannesburg, Society of Friends of Africa, 1945.

Kerr, Anne Judith — THE TIGER WHO CAME TO TEA. London, Collins, and New York, Coward McCann, 1968.

Kersh, Gerald — JEWS WITHOUT JEHOVAH. London, Wishart, 1934.

Kesey, Ken Elton — ONE FLEW OVER THE CUCKOO'S NEST. New York, Viking, 1962; London, Methuen, 1963.

Ketchum, Philip L. — DEATH IN THE LIBRARY. New York, Crowell, 1937.

Key, Alexander Hill — THE RED EAGLE. New York, Volland, 1930.

Keyes, Daniel — FLOWERS FOR ALGERNON. New York, Harcourt Brace, and London, Cassell, 1966.

Keyes, Frances Parkinson — THE OLD GRAY HOMESTEAD. Boston, Houghton Mifflin, and London, Hodder & Stoughton, 1919.

Kidd, Flora — VISIT TO ROWANBANK. London, Mills & Boon, 1966 — WHISTLE AND I'LL COME, London, Mills & Boon, 1966; Toronto, Harlequin, 1967 — NURSE AT ROWANBANK, Torornto, Harlequin, 1966; London, Mills & Boon, 1967.

Killough, Karen Lee — A VOICE OUT OF RAMAH. New York, Ballantine, 1979 — THE DOPPELGANGER GAMBIT. New York, Ballantine, 1979

Kimbro, John M. — THE HOUSE ON WINDSWEPT RIDGE, as Katheryn Kimbrough. New York, Popular, 1971; London, Sphere, 1973 — THE TWISTED CAMEO, as Katheryn Kimbrough. New York, Popular, 1971; London, Sphere, 1973.

Kimenye, Barbara — KALASANDA. Nairobi and London, Oxford Univ., 1965.

King, Gen. Charles — CAMPAIGNING WITH CROOK. Milwaukee, Sentinel, 1880.

King, Charles Daly — BEYOND BEHAVIORISM: THE FUTURE OF PSYCHOLOGY, as Robert Courtney. New York, Grant, 1927.

King, David Clive — HAMID OF ALEPPO. New York, Macmillan, 1958.

King, Rufus Frederick — NORTH STAR: A DOG STORY FOR THE CANADIAN NORTHWEST. New York, Watt, 1925.

King, Stephen — THINNER, as Richard Bachman.

Kingman, Mary Lee — PIERRE PIDGEON. Boston, Houghton Mifflin, 1943.

Kipling, Joseph Rudyard — SCHOOLBOY LYRICS. Lahore, privately printed, 1881.

Kirk, Russell Amos — RANDOLPH OF ROANOKE: A STUDY IN CONSERVATIVE THOUGHT. Chicago, Univ. of Chicago, 1951.

Kirst, Hans Hellmut — THE NIGHT OF THE GENERALS. 1963.

Kitchin, Clifford Henry Benn — CURTAINS. Oxford (ENG), Blackwell, 1919.

Kjelgaard, Jim (James Arthur) — FOREST PATROL.

New York, Holiday House, 1941; London, Sampson Low, 1948.

Klass, Philip — OF ALL POSSIBLE WORLDS, as William Tenn. New York, Ballantine, 1955; London, Joseph, 1956.

Klein, Norma — MOM, THE WOLF MAN, AND ME. New York, Pantheon, 1972.

Kline, Otis Adelbert — THE PLANET OF PERIL. Chicago, McClurg, 1929.

Klinger, Henry — WANTON FOR MURDER. New York, Doubleday, 1961.

Kneale, Thomas Nigel — TOMATO CAIN AND OTHER STORIES. London, Collins, 1949; New York, Knopf, 1950.

Knebel, Fletcher — NO HIGH GROUND, with Charles W. Bailey II, New York, Harper, and London, Weidenfeld & Nicolson, 1960.

Knibbs, Henry Herbert — FIRST POEMS, as Henry K. Herbert. Rochester (NY), Genesee Press, 1908.

Knight, Alanna — LEGEND OF THE LOCH. London, Hurst & Blackett, 1969; New York, Lancer, 1970.

Knight, Damon Francis — HELL'S PAVEMENT. New York, Lion, 1955; London, Banner, 1958.

Knight, Francis Edgar — THE ALBATROSS COMES HOME, as Frank Knight. London, Hollis & Carter, 1949.

Knight, Norman Louis — A TORRENT OF FACES, with James Blish. New York, Doubleday, 1967; London, Faber, 1968.

Knowles, Mabel Winifred — LOVE'S OBJECT; OR, SOME THOUGHTS FOR YOUNG GIRLS, as May Wynne. London, Nisbet, 1899.

Knox, William (Bill) — DEADLINE FOR A DREAM. London, Long, 1957; as IN AT THE KILL, New York, Doubleday, 1961.

Knox, Ronald Arbuthnott — SIGNA SEVERA. Privately printed, 1906.

Koestler, Arthur — VON WEISSEN NACHTEN UND ROTEN TAGEN. Kharkov, Ukrainian State, 1933.

Konigsburg, Elaine Lobl — FROM THE MIXED-UP FILES OF MRS. BASIL E. FRANKWEILER. New York, Atheneum, 1967; London, Macmillan, 1969.

Koontz, Dean Ray — STAR QUEST. New York, Ace, 1968.

Kornbluth, Cyril M. — GUNNER CADE, as Cyril M. Judd, with Judith Merril. New York, Simon & Schuster, 1952; London, Gollancz, 1964 — OUTPOST MARS, as Cyril M. Judd, with Judith Merril. New York, Abelard, 1952; London, New English Library, 1966 — TAKEOFF, as C.M. Kornbluth. New York, Doubleday, 1952 — THE NAKED STORM, as Simon Eisner. New York, Lion, 1952.

Krasilovsky, Phyliss — THE MAN WHO DIDN'T WASH HIS DISHES. New York, Doubleday, 1950; Kingswood (ENG), World's Work, 1962.

Kraus, Joanna Halpert — SEVEN SOUND AND MOTION STORIES. Rowayton (CT), New Plays, 1971.

Kraus, Robert — JUNIOR, THE SPILED CAT. New York and London, Oxford Univ., 1955.

Krause, Herbert — WIND WITHOUT RAIN. Indianapolis, Bobbs Merrill, 1939; NEIGHBOR BOY, Iowa City, Midland House, 1939.

Krauss, Ruth — A GOOD MAN AND HIS WIFE. New York, Harper, 1944.

Krumgold, Joseph Quincy — THANKS TO MURDER. New York, Vanguard, and London, Gollancz, 1935.

Kurland, Michael Joseph — TEN YEARS TO DOOMSDAY, with Chester Anderson. New York, Pyramid, 1964.

Kurnitz, Harry — FAST COMPANY, as Marco Page. New York, Dodd Mead, and London, Heinemann, 1938.

Kuskin, Karla — ROAR AND MORE. New York, Harper, 1956.

Kuttner, Henry — LAWLESS GUNS, as Will Garth. New York, Dodge, 1937.

Kyne, Peter Bernard — THE THREE GODFATHERS. New York, Doran, 1913; London, Hodder & Stoughton, 1914.

L

La Bern, Arthur Joseph — IT ALWAYS RAINS ON SUNDAY. London, Nicholson & Watson, 1945.

La Farge, Oliver Hazard Perry — TRIBES AND TEMPLES: A RECORD OF THE EXPEDITION TO MIDDLE AMERICA CONDUCTED BY THE TULANE UNIVERSITY OF LOUISIANA IN 1925. New Orleans, Tulane Univ., 2 vols., 1926-27.

La Moore, Louis Dearborn — SMOKE FROM THIS ALTAR, as Louis L'Amour. Oklahoma City, Lusk, 1939.

La Tourrette, Jacqueline — THE JOSEPH STONE. New York, Nordon, 1971.

Lafferty, Raphael Aloysius — PAST MASTER. New York, Ace, and London, Rapp & Whiting, 1968.

Lake, David John — JOHN MILTON: PARADISE LOST. Calcutta, Mukhopadhyay, 1967.

Lampman, Evelyn Sibley — CRAZY CREEK. New York, Doubleday, 1948.

Lane, Roumelia — ROSE OF THE DESERT. London, Mills & Boon, 1967; Toronto, Harlequin, 1968 — HIDEAWAY HEART. London, Mills & Boon, 1967; Toronto, Harlequin, 1968.

Lang, Andrew — BALLADS AND LYRICS OF OLD FRANCE, WITH OTHER POEMS. London, Longman, 1872.

Lange, Jr., John Frederick — TARNSMAN OF GOR, as John Norman. New York, Ballantine, 1966; London, Sidgwick & Jackson, 1969.

Langley, John — RUSTLER'S BRAND. London, Lane, 1954.

Langton, Jane Gillson — THE MAJESTY OF GRACE. New York, Harper, 1961.

Lanier, Sidney — TIGER-LILIES: A NOVEL. 1867.

Lanier, Sterling Edmund — THE WAR FOR THE LOT. Chicago, Follett, 1969.

Lardner, Ring — BIB BALLADS. 1915.

Latham, Jean Lee — 555 POINTERS FOR BEGINNING ACTORS AND DIRECTORS. Chicago, Dramatic Publishing, 1935.

Latimer, Jonathan Wyatt — MURDER IN THE MADHOUSE. New York, Doubleday, and London, Hurst & Blackett, 1935.

Latis, Mary J. — BANKING ON DEATH, as Emma Lathen, with Martha Hennissart. New York, Macmillan, 1961; London, Gollancz, 1962.

Lattimore, Eleanor Frances — LITTLE PEAR. New York, Harcourt Brace, 1931; London, Museum Press, 1947.

Laumer, John Keith — HOW TO DESIGN AND BUILD FLYING MODELS. New York, Harper, 1960; London, Hale, 1975.

Lawrence, Ann Margaret — TOM ASS; OR, THE SECOND GIFT. London, Macmillan, 1972; New York, Walck, 1973.

Lawrence, (Hilda) Hildegarde — BLOOD UPON THE SNOW. New York, Simon & Schuster, 1944; London, Chapman & Hall, 1946.

Lawrence, Mildred — SUSAN'S BEARS. New York, Grosset & Dunlap, 1945.

Lawson, Robert — COUNTRY COLIC. Boston, Little Brown, 1944.

Lazarus, Marguerite — IMAGES OF ROSE, as Anna Gilbert. London and New York, 1974.

Le Fanu, Joseph Sheridan — THE COCK AND THE ANCHOR. 1845.

Le Feuvre, Amy — ERIC'S GOOD NEWS. London, Religious Tract Society, 1894; Chicago, Revell, 1896.

LeFontaine, Joseph Raymond Hervé — A MANUAL FOR CRYOGENIC FLUID CONTROLS. Dayton, Koehler, 1958.

Le Guin, Ursula Kroeber — ROCANNON'S WORLD. New York, Ace, 1966; London, Tandem, 1972.

Le May, Alan — PAINTED PONIES. New York, Doran, and London, Cassell, 1927.

Le Queux, William Tufnell — GUILTY BONDS. London, Routledge, 1891; New York, Fenno, 1895.

Lea, Alec Richard — THE OUTWARD URGE. London, Rich & Cowan, 1944.

Lea, Tom — JOHN W. NORTON, AMERICAN PAINTER 1876-1934, with Thomas E. Tallmadge. Chicago, Lakeside Press, 1935.

Leaf, Wilbur Munro — LO, THE POOR INDIAN, as Mun. New York, Leaf Mahony Seidel & Stokes, 1934 — GRAMMAR CAN BE FUN. New York, Stokes, 1934; London, Ward Lock, 1951.

Lear, Edward — ILLUSTRATIONS OF THE FAMILY OF PSITTACIDAE, OR PARROTS, Privately printed, 1832.

Leasor, Thomas James — NOT SUCH A BAD DAY. Leicester (ENG), Blackfriars Press, 1946.

Leblanc, Maurice Marie Emile — ARSENE LUPIN, with Edgar Jepson. 1909.

Lee, Benjamin — PAGANINI STRIKES AGAIN. London, Hutchinson, 1970.

Lee, Dennis Beynon — KINGDOM OF ABSENCE. Toronto, House of Anansi, 1967.

Lee, Elsie — HOW TO GET THE MOST OUT OF YOUR TAPE RECORDING, as Lee Sheridan, with Michael Sheridan. Flushing (NY), Robins, 1958 — MORE FUN WITH YOUR TAPE RECORDERS AND STEREO, as Lee Sheridan, with Michael Sheridan. Los Angeles, Trend, 1958.

Lee, Manfred B. — THE ROMAN HAT MYSTERY, as Ellery Queen, with Frederic Dannay. New York, Stokes, and London, Gollancz, 1929.

Lee, Mildred — THE INVISIBLE SUN. Philadelphia, Westminster, 1946.

Lee, Tanith — THE BETROTHED. Sideup (ENG), Slughorn Press, 1968.

Lee, Wayne Cyril — PRAIRIE VENGEANCE. New York, Arcadia, 1954; London, Barker, 1955.

Leeson, Robert Arthur — UNITED WE STAND: AN IL-LUSTRATED ACCOUNT OF TRADE UNION EMBLEMS. Bath (ENG), Adams & Dart, 1971.

Lehman, Paul Evan — IDAHO. New York, Macauley, 1933; as COWBOY IDAHO, London, Ward Lock, 1933.

Leiber, Fritz Reuter Jr. — NIGHT'S BLACK AGENTS. Sauk City (WI), Arkham House, 1947; London, Spearman, 1975.

Leisk, David Johnson — BARNABY, as Crockett Johnson. New York, Holt, 1943.

Leitch, Adelaide — FLIGHTLINE NORTH. St. John's, Newfoundland, Guardian, 1952.

Lemarchand, Elizabeth Wharton — DEATH OF AN OLD GIRL. London, Hart Davis, 1967; New York, Award, 1970.

L'Engle, Madeleine — 18 WASHINGTON SQUARE, SOUTH. Boston, Baker, 1944.

Lenski, Lois Lenore — SKIPPING VILLAGE. New York, Stokes, 1927.

— THE MYSTERY OF THE YELLOW ROOM. 1908.

Leroux, Gaston — THE MYSTERY OF THE YELLOW ROOM. 1908.

Leslie, Doris — THE STARLING. London, Hurst & Blackett, and New York, Century, 1927.

Lesser, Milton — EARTHBOUND. Philadelphia, Winston, 1952; London, Hutchinson, 1955.

Lessing, Doris May — THE GRASS IS SINGING. London, Joseph, and New York, Crowell, 1950.

Levin, Ira — A KISS BEFORE DYING. New York, Simon & Schuster, 1953; London, Joseph, 1954.

Lewin, Michael Z. — HOW TO BEAT COLLEGE TESTS: A PRACTICAL GUIDE TO EASE THE BURDEN OF USELESS COURSES. New York, Dial, 1970.

Lewis, Alfred Henry — WOLFVILLE. New York, Stokes, and London, Lawrence & Bullen, 1897.

Lewis, Clive Staples — SPIRITS IN BONDAGE: A CYCLE OF LYRICS, as Clive Hamilton. London, Heinemann, 1919.

Lewis, Ernest Michael Roy — THE FUTURE OF AUSTRALIA, as Roy Lewis. New Delhi, Hindustan Times Press, 1944.

Lewis, Harry Sinclair — HIKE AND THE AEROPLANE, as Tom Graham. New York, Stokes, 1912.

Lewis, Hilda Winifred — PEGASUS YOKED. London, Hurst & Blackett, 1933.

Lewis, John Royston — CASES FOR DISCUSSION. Oxford (ENG), Pergamon Press, 1965.

Lewis, Maynah — NO PLACE FOR LOVE. London, Hurst & Blackett, 1963.

Lewisohn, Ludwig — THE BROKEN SNARE. 1908.

Lewty, Marjorie — NEVER IT CALL IT LOVING. London, Mills & Boon, 1958; Toronto, Harlequin, 1968.

Lexau, Joan M. — OLAF READS. New York, Dial, 1961.

Ley, Alice Chetwynd — THE JEWELLED SNUFF BOX. London, Hale, 1959; New York, Beagle, 1974.

Ley, Robert Arthur — TIME TRANSFER AND OTHER STORIES, as Arthur Sellings. London, Joseph, 1956.

Lichtenberg, Jacqueline — HOUSE OF ZEOR. New York, Doubleday, 1974.

Lifton, Betty Jean — JOJI AND THE DRAGON. New York, Morrow, 1957.

Lightner, Alice Martha — THE PILLAR AND THE FLAME, as Alice L. Hopf. New York, Vinal, 1928.

Lindsay, David — A VOYAGE TO ARCTURUS. London, Methuen, 1920; New York, Macmillan, 1963.

Lindsay, Norman Alfred William — A CURATE IN BOHEMIA. Sydney (AUS), Bookstall, 1913; London, Laurie, 1937.

Lindsay, Rachel — IN NAME ONLY, as Roberta Leigh. London, Falcon, 1951; Toronto, Harlequin, 1973.

Lindsay, Vachel — THE TRAMP'S EXCUSE AND OTHER POEMS. 1909.

Linebarger, Paul Myron Anthony — THE POLITICAL DOCTRINES OF SUN YAT-SEN, as P.M.A. Linebarger. Baltimore, John Hopkins Univ., 1937.

Lingard, Joan Amelia — LIAM'S DAUGHTER. London, Hodder & Stoughton, 1963.

Linington, Barbara Elizabeth — THE PROUD MAN. New York, Viking, 1955.

Linklater, Eric Robert Russell — POOBIE. Edinburgh, Porpoise Press, 1925.

Lionni, Leo — LITTLE BLUE AND LITTLE YELLOW. New York, McDowell Obolensky, 1959; Leicester (ENG), Brockhampton, 1962.

Lipkind, William — WINNEBAGO GRAMMAR. New York, Columbia Unov., 1945.

Lippincott, Joseph Wharton — BUN, A WILD RABBIT. Philadelphia, Penn, 1918.

Little, Constance And Gwyneth — THE GREY MIST MURDERS. New York, Doubleday, 1938.

Little, Flora Jean — IT'S A WONDERFUL WORLD. Guelph (CAN), privately printed, 1947.

Litvonov, Ivy — GROWING PAINS. London, Heinemann, and New York, Doran, 1913.

Lively, Penelope — ASTERCOTE. London, Heinemann, 1970; New York, Dutton, 1971.

Livingston, Myra Cohn — WHISPERS AND OTHER POEMS. New York, Harcourt Brace, 1958.

Llewellyn, David William Alun — BALLADS AND SONGS. London, Stockwell, 1921.

Lobel, Anita — SVEN'S BRIDGE. New York, Harper, 1965.

Lobel, Arnold — A ZOO FOR MISTER MUSTER. New York, Harper, 1962.

Locke, Elsie Violet — THE SHEPHERD AND THE SCUL-LERY-MAID. Christchurch (NZ), New Zealand Communist Party, 1950.

Lockridge, Frances — HOW TO ADOPT A CHILD. New York, New York Children, 1928.

Lockridge, Richard Orson — MR. AND MRS. NORTH. New York, Stokes, 1936; London, Joseph, 1937.

Lockridge, Richard Orson And Frances Louise — THE NORTHS MEET MURDER. New York, Stokes, and London, Joseph, 1940.

Lofting, Hugh John — THE STORY OF DR. DOLITTLE, BEING THE HISTORY OF HIS PECULIAR LIFE AND ASTONISHING ADVENTURES IN FOREIGN PARTS. New York, Stokes, and London, Cape, 1920.

Lofts, Norah — I MET A GYPSY. London, Methuen, and New York, Knopf, 1935.

London, John Griffith — THE SON OF THE WOLF: TALES OF THE FAR NORTH, as Jack London. Boston, Houghton Mifflin, 1900; London, Isbister, 1902.

Long, Charles Russell — THE INFINITE BRAIN. New York, Avalon, 1957.

Long, Frank Belknap — A MAN FROM GENOA AND OTHER POEMS. Athol (MA), Cook, 1926.

Longfellow, Henry Wadsworth — ELEMENTS OF FRENCH GRAMMAR. 1830

Loomis, Noel Miller — MURDER GOES TO PRESS. New York, Phoenix, 1937.

Loring, Emilie — FOR THE COMFORT OF THE FAMILY: A VACATION EXPERIMENT, as Josephine Story. New York, Doran, 1914.

Lott, Milton — THE LAST HUNT. Boston, Houghton Mifflin, 1954; London, Collins, 1955.

Lovecraft, Howard Phillips — THE MATERIALIST TODAY, as H.P. Lovecraft. Privately printed, 1926.

Lovesey, Peter — THE KINGS OF DISTANCE: A STUDY OF FIVE GREAT RUNNERS. London, Eyre & Spottiswoode, 1968.

Low, Lois Dorothea — ISLE FOR A STRANGER, as Dorothy Mackie Low. London, Hurst & Blackett, 1962; New York, Ace, 1968.

Lowell, Amy — DREAM DROPS; OR, STORIES FROM FAIRY LAND. 1887.

Lowell, James Russell — CLASS POEM. 1838.

Lowndes, Marie Adelaide Belloc — H.R.H. THE PRINCE OF WALES; AN ACCOUNT OF HIS CAREER, anonymously. London, Richards, and New York, Appleton, 1898.

Lowndes, Robert Augustine Ward — MYSTERY OF THE THIRD MINE. Philadelphia, Winston, 1953.

Ludlum, Robert — THE SCARLATTI INHERITANCE. Cleveland, World, and London, Hart Davis, 1971.

Lupoff, Richard Allen — EDGAR RICE BURROUGHS: MASTER OF ADVENTURE. New York, Canaveral Press, 1965.

Lustgarten, Edgar Marcus — A CASE TO ANSWER. London, Eyre & Spottiswoode, 1947; as ONE MORE UNFORTUNATE, New York, Scribner, 1947.

Lutyens, Mary — FORTHCOMING MARRIAGES. London, Murray, and New York, Dutton, 1933.

Lutz, Giles Alfred — FIGHT OR RUN. New York, Popular, 1954.

Lutz, John Thomas — THE TRUTH OF THE MATTER. New York, Pocket Books, 1971.

Lyall, Gavin Tudor — THE WRONG SIDE OF THE SKY. London, Hodder & Stoughton, and New York, Scribner, 1961.

Lynch, Patricia Nora — THE GREEN DRAGON. London, Harrap, 1925.

Lynn, Elizabeth A. — A DIFFERENT LIGHT. New York, Berkly, 1978; London, Gollancz, 1979.

M

Macardle, Dorothy Margaret Callan — EARTH-BOUND: NINE STORIES OF IRELAND. Worcester (MA), Harrigan Press, 1924 — TRAGEDIES OF KERRY 1922-1923. Dublin, Emton Press, 1924.

MacDonald, Allan William Colt — RESTLESS GUNS. New York, Chelsea, 1929; London, Collins, 1934.

MacDonald, George — PHANTASTES: A FAERIE ROMANCE FOR MEN AND WOMEN. London, Smith Elder, 1858; Boston, Loring, 1870.

MacDonald, John Dann — THE BRASS CUPCAKE. New York, Fawcett, 1950; London, Muller, 1955.

MacDonald, Philip — AMBROTOX AND LIMPING DICK, as Oliver Fleming, with Ronald MacDonald. London, Ward Lock, 1920.

MacGibbon, Jean — WHEN THE WEATHER'S CHANGING, as Jean Howard. London, Putnam, 1945.

MacGill, Mrs. Patrick Margaret — THE "GOOD-NIGHT" STORIES, as Margaret Gibbon. London, Year Book Press, 1912.

MacGregor, Ellen — TOMMY AND THE TELEPHONE. Chicago, Whitman, 1947.

MacGregor, James Murdoch — WORLD OUT OF MIND, as J.T. McIntosh. New York, Doubleday, 1953; London, Museum Press, 1955.

MacInnes, Helen Clark — ABOVE SUSPICION. Boston, Little Brown, and London, Harrap, 1941.

MacIntyre, Elisabeth — AMBROSE KANGAROO: A STORY THAT NEVER ENDS. Sydney (AUS), Consolidated, 1941; New York, Scribner, 1942.

Mackay, Constance D'Arcy — COSTUMES AND SCENERY FOR AMATEURS. New York, Holt, 1915.

MacKay, Mary — A ROMANCE OF TWO WORLDS, as Marie Corelli. 2 vols. London, 1886. — VENDETTA; OR, THE STORY OF OUR FORGOTTEN, as Marie Corelli. 3 vols. London, 1886.

Mackelworth, Ronald Walter — FIREMANTLE, as R.W. Mackelworth. London, Hale, 1968; as THE DIABOLS, New York, Paperback Library, 1969.

Macken, Walter — QUENCH THE MOON. London, Macmillan, and New York, Viking, 1948.

MacKenzie, Donald — OCCUPATION: THIEF. Indianapolis, Bobbs Merrill, 1955; as FUGITIVES, London, Elek, 1955.

MacKenzie, Jean — STORM ISLAND. Toronto, Macmillan, 1968.

Mackie, Doris — MARRIED MAN'S GIRL, as Susan Inglis. London, Mills & Boon, 1934.

Mackinlay, Leila Antionette Sterling — LITTLE MOUNTEBANK. London, Mills & Boon, 1930.

Mackintosh, Elizabeth — THE MAN IN THE QUEUE, as Gordon Daviot. London, Methuen, and New York, Dutton, 1929. KIF: AN UNVARNISHED HISTORY, London, Benn, and New York, Appleton, 1929.

MacLean, Alistair Stuart — H.M.S. ULYSSES. London, Collins, 1955; New York, Doubleday, 1956.

MacLean, Katherine Anne — COSMIC CHECKMATE, with Charles V. De Vet. New York, Ace, 1962 — THE DIPLOIDS AND OTHER FLIGHTS OF FANCY. New York, Avon, 1962.

MacLeish, Archibald — SONGS FOR A SUMMER'S DAY. 1915.

MacLeod, Charlotte Matilda — MYSTERY OF THE WHITE KNIGHT. New York, Avalon, 1965 — THE FOOD OF LOVE, as Matilda Hughes, New York, Avalon, 1965 — NEXT DOOR TO DANGER, New York, Avalon, 1965.

MacLeod, Jean S — LIFE FOR TWO. London, Mills & Boon, 1936.

MacLeod, Robert — THE APPALOOSA. Fawcett, 1966.

MacPherson, A.D.L. — BEGGARS MAY SING, as Sara Seale. London, 1932; Toronto, Harlequin, 1968.

MacPherson, Margaret — THE SHINTY BOYS. London, Collins, and New York, Harcourt Brace, 1963.

MacVicar, Angus — THE PURPLE ROCK. London, Paul, 1933.

Maddock, Reginald Bertram — CORRIGAN AND THE WHITE COBRA, TOMB OF OPI, YELLOW PERIL, BLACK RIDERS, GOLDEN PAGODA, DREAM-

MAKERS, BLUE CRATER, GREEN TIGER, RED LIONS, LITTLE PEOPLE, as R.B. Maddock. London, Nelson, 10 vols., 1956-63.

Maddocks, Margaret Kathleen Avern — COME LASSES AND LADS. London, Hurst & Blackett, 1944.

Mahy, Margaret — THE DRAGON OF AN ORDINARY FAMILY. New York, Watts, and London, Heinemann, 1969.

Maling, Arthur Gordon — DECOY. New York, Harper, 1969; London, Joseph, 1971.

Malzberg, Barry Norman — ORACLE OF THE THOUSAND HANDS. New York, Olympia, 1968.

Manfred, Frederick Feikema — THE GOLDEN BOWL. St. Paul (MN), Webb, 1944; London, Dobson, 1947.

Manley-Tucker, Audrie — LEONIE. London, Mills & Boon, 1958.

Mann, Edward Beverly — THE MAN FROM TEXAS. New York, Morrow, 1931; London, Hurst & Blackett, 1934.

Mann, Jessica — A CHARITABLE END. London, Collins, and New York, McKay, 1971.

Manning, Laurence Edward — THE HOW AND WHY OF BETTER GARDENING. New York, Van Nostrand, 1951.

Manning, Rosemary — FROM HOLST TO BRITTEN: A STUDY OF MODERN CHORAL MUSIC. London, Workers' Music, 1949.

Manning-Sanders, Ruth — THE PEDLAR AND OTHER POEMS. London, Selwyn & Blount, 1919.

Markoosie — HARPOON OF THE HUNTER. Montreal and London, McGill-Queen's University Press, 1970.

Marlowe, Dan James — DOORWAY TO DEATH. New York, Avon, and London, Digit, 1959.

Marlowe, Derek — A DANDY IN ASPIC. London, Gollancz, and New York, Putnam, 1966.

Marquand, John Phillips — PRINCE AND BOATSWAIN: SEA TALES FROM THE RECOLLECTIONS OF REAR-ADMIRAL CHARLES E. CLARK, with James Morgan. Greenfield (MA), Hall. 1915.

Marsh, Edith Ngaio — A MAN LAY DEAD. London, Bles, 1934; New York, Sheridan, 1942.

Marshall, Edison Tesla — THE VOICE OF THE PACK. Boston, Little Brown, and London, Hodder & Stoughton, 1920.

Marshall, Evelyn — THE SHORE HOUSE MYSTERY, as Jean Marsh. London, Hamilton, 1931.

Marshall, Rosamond Van Der Zee — L'ENFANT DU CIRQUE. 1930.

Martin, David — BATTLEFIELDS AND GIRLS: POEMS. Glasgow, Maclellan, 1942.

Martin, George Raymond Richard — A SONG FOR LYA AND OTHER STORIES. New York, Avon, 1976; London, Coronet, 1978.

Martin, Patricia Miles — SYLVESTER JONES AND THE VOICE OF THE FOREST. New York, Lothrop, 1958.

Martin, Rhona — GALLOWS WEDDING. London, Bodley Head, 1978; New York, Coward McCann, 1979.

Masefield, John — SALT-WATER BALLADS. London, Grant Richards, 1902; New York, Macmillan, 1913.

Mason, Alfred Edward Woodley — A ROMANCE OF WASTDALE. London, Mathews, and New York, Stokes, 1895.

Mason, Douglas Rankine — THE BLOCKADE OF SINITRON, as John Rankine. London, Nelson, 1966 — INTERSTELLAR TWO-FIVE, as John Rankine.

London, Dobson, 1966 — FROM CARTHAGE THEN I CAME, as Douglas R. Mason. New York, Doubleday, 1966;London,Hale,1968.

Mason, Francis Van Wyck — SEEDS OF MURDER. New York, Doubleday, 1930; London, Eldon, 1937.

Masson, David Irvine — HAND-LIST OF INCUNABULA IN THE UNIVERSITY LIBRARY, LIVERPOOL. Privately printed, 1948; supplement, 1955.

Masters, Edgar Lee — A BOOK OF VERSES. 1898.

Masur, Harold Q. — BURY ME DEEP. New York, Simon & Schuster, 1947; London, Boardman, 1948.

Mather, Anne — CAROLINE. London, Hale, 1965.

Matheson, Richard Burton — SOMEONE IS BLEEDING. New York, Lion, 1953.

Mathews, John Joseph — WAH 'KON-TAH: THE OSAGE AND THE WHITE MAN'S ROAD. Norman, Univ. of Oklahoma, 1932.

Mathis, Sharon Bell — BROOKLYN STORY. New York, Hill & Wang, 1970.

Matthews, Patricia Anne — HORROR AT GULL HOUSE, as Petty Brisco, with Clayton Matthews. New York, Belmont, 1970 — MERRY'S TREASURE, as Patty Brisco. New York, Avalon, 1970.

Mattingley, Christobel — THE PICNIC DOG. London, Hamish Hamilton, 1970.

Maugham, Robert Cecil Romer — THE 1946 MS, as Robin Maugham. London, War Facts Press, 1943.

Maugham, William Somerset — LIZA OF LAMBETH. London, Unwin, 1897; New York, Doran, 1921.

May, Winifred Jean — A CLUSTER OF PALMS, as Wynne May. London, Mills & Bboon, 1967.

Mayne, William — FOLLOW THE FOOTPRINTS. London, Oxford Univ., 1953.

McBain, Laurie Lee — DEVIL'S DESIRE. New York, Avon, 1975.

McCaffrey, Anne Inez — RESTOREE. New York, Ballantine, and London, Rapp & Whiting, 1967.

McCaig, Robert Jesse — TOLL MOUNTAIN. New York, Dodd Mead, 1953; London, Collins, 1954.

McCarry, Charles — CITIZEN NADER. New York, Saturday Review Press, 1972.

McCarthy, Gary — THE DERBY MAN. New York, Doubleday, 1976; London, Hale, 1978.

McClary, Thomas Calvert — REBIRTH, WHEN EVERYONE FORGOT. New York, Bartholomew House, 1944.

McCloskey, John Robert — LENTIL. New York, Viking, 1940.

McCloy, Helen Worrell Clarkson — DANCE OF DEATH. New York, Morrow, 1938; as DESIGN FOR DYING, London, Heinemann, 1938.

McClure, James Howe — THE STEAM PIG. London, Gollancz, 1971; New York, Harper, 1972.

McConnell, James Douglas Rutherford — COMES THE BLIND FURY, as Douglas Rutherford. London, Faber, 1950.

McCord, David Thompson Watson — ODDLY ENOUGH. Cambridge (MA), Washburn & Thomas, 1926.

McCoy, Horace — THEY SHOOT HORSES, DON'T THEY? New York, Simon & Schuster, and London, Barker, 1935.

McCulley, Johnston — BROADWAY BAB. New York, Watt, 1919; London, Hutchinson, 1926.

McCurtin, Peter — HANGTOWN. New York, Belmont, 1970; as ARIZONA HANGTOWN, London, Hale,

1972: MAFIOSA. New York, Belmont, 1970; London, New English Library, 1971.

McCutchan, Donald Philip — WHISTLE AND I'LL COME. London, Harrap, 1957.

McCutcheon, George Barr — GRAUSTARK: THE STORY OF A LOVE BEHIND THE THRONE. Chicago, Stone, 1901; London, Richards, 1902.

McDonald, Gregory — RUNNING SCARED. New York, Obolensky, 1964; London, Gollancz, 1977.

McElfresh, Elizabeth Adeline — MY HEART WENT DEAD. New York, Phoenix, 1949.

McEvoy, Marjorie — NO CASTLE OF DREAMS. London, Jenkins, 1960; New York, Lenox Hill, 1971 — A RED, RED ROSE. London, Jenkins, 1960.

McGaughy, Dudley Dean — GUNS TO THE SUNSET, as Dean Owen. New York, Phoenix, 1948; London, Wright & Brown, 1950.

McGerr, Patricia — PICK YOUR VICTIM. New York, Doubleday, 1946; London, Collins, 1947.

McGinley, Phyliss — ON THE CONTRARY. New York, Doubleday, 1934.

McGivern, William Peter — BUT DEATH RUNS FASTER. New York, Dodd Mead, 1948; London, Boardman, 1949.

McGraw, Eloise Jarvis — SAWDUST IN HIS SHOES. New York, Coward McCann, 1950.

McGregor, Iona — AN EDINBURGH REEL. London, Faber, 1968.

McGuane, Thomas Francis, III — THE SPORTING CLUB. New York, Simon & Schuster, 1968; London, Deutsch, 1969.

McGuire, Dominic Paul — MURDER IN BOSTALL. London, Skeffinton, 1931; as THE BLACK ROSE MURDER, New York, Brentano's, 1932.

McHugh, Vincent — TOUCH ME NOT. New York, Cape & Ssmith, 1930.

McIlwain, David — SPACEWAYS, as Charles Eric Maine. London, Hodder & Stoughton, 1953; as SPACEWAYS SATELLITE. New York, Avalon, 1958.

McIntyre, Vonda Neel — THE EXILE WAITING. New York, Doubleday, 1975; London, Gollancz, 1976.

McKee, David John — BRONTO'S WINGS. London, Dobson, 1964.

McKenna, Richard Milton — THE SAND PEBBLES. New York, Harper, 1962; London, Gollancz, 1963.

McLaughlin, Dean Benjamin Jr. — DOME WORLD. New York, Pyramid, 1962.

McLaughlin, Lorrie Bell — WEST TO THE CARIBOO. Toronto, Macmillan, 1962; New York, St. Martin's, and London, Macmillan, 1963.

McLean, Allan Campbell — THE HILL OF THE RED FOX. London, Collins, 1955; New York, Dutton, 1956.

McMullen, Mary — STRANGLEHOLD. New York, Harper, 1951; as DEATH OF MISS X. London, Collins, 1952.

McMurtry, Larry — HORSEMAN, PASS BY. New York, Harper, 1961; as HUD, New York, Popular, 1963; London, Sphere, 1971.

McNeile, Herman Cyril — THE LIEUTENANT AND OTHERS, as Sapper. London, Hodder New York Stoughton, 1915.

McNeill, Janet — MY FRIEND SPECS MCCANN. London, Faber, 1955 — A CHILD IN THE HOUSE. London, Hodder & Stoughton, 1955.

McNichols, Charles Longstreth — CRAZY WEATHER. New York, Macmillan, 1944; London, Gollancz, 1945: JAPAN: ITS RESOURCES AND INDUSTRIES, with Clayton D. Carus, New York, Harper, 1944.

McNickle, William D'Arcy — THE SURROUNDED. New York, Dodd Mead, 1936.

McShane, Mark — THE STRAIGHT AND THE CROOKED. London, Long, 1960.

Mead, Edward Shepherd — THE MAGNIFICENT MACINNES, as Shepherd Mead. New York, Farrar Straus, 1949.

Meade, Elizabeth Thomasina — LOTY'S LAST HOME, as L.T. Meade. London, Shaw, 1875.

Meader, Stephen Warren — THE BLACK BUCCANEER. New York, Harcourt Brace, 1920.

Meaker, Marijane — DINKY HOCKER SHOOTS SMACK!, as M.E. Kerr. New York, Harper, 1972; London, Gollancz, 1973.

Means, Florence Crannell — RAFAEL AND CONSUELO, with Harriet Louise Fullen. New York, Friendship Press, 1929.

Mears, Leonard F. — TROUBLE TOWN, as Johnny Nelson. Sydney (AUS), Cleveland, 1955 — DRIFT, as Marshall Grover. Sydney, Scripts, n.d. — COLORADO PURSUIT, as Marshall Grover. Sydney, Scripts, n.d. — BORN TO DRIFT, as Marshall Grover. Sydney, Scripts, n.d. — COLD TRAIL TO KIRBY, as Marshall Grover. Sydney, Scripts, n.d.

Meek, Sterner St. Paul — JERRY: THE ADVENTURES OF AN ARMY DOG, as S.P. Meek. New York, Morrow, 1932.

Meggs, Brown Moore — SATURDAY GAMES. New York, Random, 1974; London, Collins, 1975.

Meigs, Cornelia Lynde — THE KINGDOM OF THE WINDING ROAD. New York and London, Macmillan, 1915.

Meltzer, David — POEMS, with Donald Schenker. Privately printed, 1957.

Melville, Herman — TYPEE. 1846.

Melwood, Eileen Mary — NETTLEWOOD. London, Deutsch, 1974; New York, Seabury, 1975.

Mencken, H.L. — VENTURES INTO VERSE. 1903.

Mercer, Cecil William — THE BROTHER OF DAPHNE, as Dornford Yates. London, Ward Lock, 1914.

Meredith, Richard Carlton — THE SKY IS FILLED WITH SHIPS. New York, Ballantine, 1969 — WE ALL DIED AT BREAKAWAY STATION. New York, Ballantine, 1969.

Merriam, Eve — FAMILY CIRCLE. New Haven, Yale, 1946.

Merril, Josephine Judith — SHADOW ON THE HEARTH, as Judith Merril. New York, Doubleday, 1950; London, Sidgwick & Jackson, 1953.

Merrill, Jean — HENRY, THE HAND-PAINTED MOUSE. New York, Coward McCann, 1951.

Merritt, Abraham — THE MOON POOL, as A. Merritt. New York and London, Putnam, 1919.

Mertz, Barbara Louise Gross — TEMPLES, TOMBS, AND HIEROGLYPHS: THE STORY OF EGYPTOLOGY, as Barbara G. Mertz. New York, Coward McCann, and London, Gollancz, 1964.

Merwin, Samuel Kimball, Jr. — MURDER IN MINIATURES, as Sam Merwin, Jr. New York, Doubleday, 1940.

Meyer, Nicholas — TARGET PRACTICE. New York, Harcourt Brace, 1974; London, Hodder & Stoughton, 1975.

Meyers, Roy Lethbridge — DOLPHIN BOY. New York, Ballantine, 1967; as THE DOLPHIN RIDER. London, Rapp & Whiting, 1968.

Meynell, Laurence Walter — MOCKBEGGAR. London, Harrap, 1924; New York, Appleton, 1925.

Michener, James A. — THE UNIT IN THE SOCIAL STUDIES, with Harold M. Long. Cambridge (MA), Harvard, 1940.

Milburn, George — A HANDBOOK FOR AMATEUR MAGICIANS. Girard (KS), Haldeman Julius, 1926.

Miles, Favell Mary — THE RED FLAME, as Lady Miles. London, Hutchinson, 1921 — RED, WHITE, AND GREY, as Lady Miles. London, Hutchinson, 1921.

Milhous, Katherine — LOVINA. New York and London, Scribner, 1940.

Millar, Kenneth — THE DARK TUNNEL. New York, Dodd Mead, 1944; as I DIE SLOWLY, London, Lion, 1955.

Millar, Margaret Ellis — THE INVISIBLE WORM. New York, Doubleday, 1941; London, Long, 1943.

Millard, Joseph John — MANSION OF EVIL. New York, Fawcett, 1950.

Millay, Edna St. Vincent — RENASCENCE. 1917.

Miller, Bill — DEADLY WEAPON, as Wade Miller, with Robert Wade. New York, Farrar & Straus, 1946; London, Sampson Low, 1947.

Miller, Joaquin — SPECIMENS. 1868.

Miller, Peter Schuyler — GENUS HOMO, as P. Schuyler Miller, with L. Sprague de Camp. Reading (PA), Fantasy Press, 1950.

Miller, Walter Michael, Jr. — A CANTICLE FOR LEIBOWITZ. Philadelphia, Lippincott, and London, Weidenfeld & Nicolson, 1960.

Millhiser, Marlys Joy — MICHAEL'S WIFE. New York, Putnam, 1972.

Milne, Alan Alexander — LOVERS IN LONDON, as A.A. Milne. London, Alston Rivers, 1905.

Minarik, Else Holmelund — LITTLE BEAR. New York, Harper, 1957; Kingswood (ENG), World's Work, 1965.

Mitchell, Gladys Maude Winifred — SPEEDY DEATH. London, Gollancz, and New York, Dial, 1929.

Mitchell, Margaret Munnerlyn — GONE WITH THE WIND. New York and London, Macmillan, 1936.

Mitchell, Sibyl Elyne Keith — AUSTRALIA'S ALPS, as Elyne Mitchell. Sydney and London, Angus & Robertson, 1942.

Mitchison, Naomi Margaret — THE CONQUERED. London, Cape, and New York, Harcourt Brace, 1923.

Modell, Merriam — THE SOUND OF YEARS, as Evelyn Piper. New York, Simon & Schuster, 1946; London, Cassell, 1947.

Moffat, Gwen — SPACE BELOW MY FEET. London, Hodder & Stoughton, and New York, Houghton Mifflin, 1961.

Molesworth, Mary Louisa — LOVER AND HUSBAND, as Ennis Graham. London, Skeet, 3 vols., 1869.

Momaday, Navarre Scott — HOUSE MADE OF DAWN. New York, Harper, 1968; London, Gollancz, 1969.

Monjo, Ferdinand Nicolas, III — INDIAN SUMMER. New York, Harper, 1968; Kingswood (ENG), World's Work, 1969.

Monteilhet, Hubert — THE PRAYING MANTISES. 1962.

Monteleone, Thomas F. — SEEDS OF CHANGE. Toronto, Laser, 1975.

Montgomery, Lucy Maud — ANNE OF GREEN GABLES. Boston, Page, and London, Pitman, 1908.

Montgomery, Rutherford George — TROOPERS THREE. New York, Doubleday, 1932.

Moody, William Vaughn — THE MASQUE OF JUDGEMENT. 1900.

Moorcock, Michael — THE STEALER OF SOULS AND OTHER STORIES. London, Spearman, 1963; New York, Lancer, 1967.

Moore, Brian — THE EXECUTIONERS, as Michael Bryan. Toronto, Harlequin, 1951 — WREATH FOR A REDHEAD, as Michael Bryan. Toronto, Harlequin, 1951.

Moore, Catherine Lucille — THE BRASS RING, as Lewis Padgett, with Henry Kuttner. New York, Duell, 1946; London, Sampson Low, 1947.

Moore, Doris Elizabeth Langley — THE TECHNIQUE OF THE LOVE AFFAIR, as A Gentlewoman. London, Howe, and New York, Simon & Schuster, 1928.

Moore, Marianne — POEMS. 1921.

Moore, Patrick Alfred — THE MASTER OF THE MOON. London, Museum Press, 1952.

Moore, Ward — BREATHE IN THE AIR AGAIN. New York, Harper, 1942.

Moorhead, Diana — IN SEARCH OF MAGIC. Auckland (NZ) and Leicester (ENG), Brockhampton, 1971.

Morey, Walter Nelson — NORTH TO DANGER, with Virgil Burford. New York, Day, 1954.

Morgan, Alison Mary — FISH. London, Chatto & Windus, 1971; as A BOY CALLED FISH, New York, Harper, 1973.

Morgan, Dan — CEE TEE MAN. London, Panther, 1955.

Morland, Nigel — CACHEXIA: A COLLECTION OF PROSE POEMS, with Peggy Barwell. Paris, Barbier, 1930: PEOPLE WE HAVE NEVER MET: A BOOK OF SUPERFICIAL CAMEOS, with Peggy Barwell, Paris, Barbier, 1931.

Morressy, John — THE BLACKBOARD CAVALIER. New York, Doubleday, 1966; London, Gollancz, 1967.

Morris, Janet Ellen — HIGH COUCH ON SILISTRA. New York and London, Bantam, 1977 — THE GOLDEN SWORD. New York and London, Bantam, 1977.

Morris, William — THE EARTHLY PARADISE. 3 vols. 1868-70.

Morris, Wright Marion — MY UNCLE DUDLEY. New York, Harcourt Brace, 1942.

Morrison, Arthur — THE SHADOWS AROUND US: AUTHENTIC TALES OF THE SUPERNATURAL. London, Simpkin Marshall, 1891.

Morrissey, Joseph Lawrence — CITY OF THE HIDDEN EYES, as J.L. Morrissey. London, Consul, 1964.

Motley, Annette — MY LADY'S CRUSADE. London, Futura, 1977.

Motley, John Lothrop — MORTON'S HOPE; OR, THE MEMOIRS OF A PROVINCIAL. 1839.

Mowat, Farley McGill — PEOPLE OF THE DEER. Boston, Little Brown, and London, Joseph, 1952.

Mowery, William Byron — THE SILVER HAWK. New York, Doubleday, 1929.

Moyes, Patricia — DEAD MEN DON'T SKI. London, Collins, 1959; New York, Rinehart, 1960.

Muir, John — THE MOUNTAINS OF CALIFORNIA. 1894.

Mukerji, Dhan Gopal — RAJANI: SONGS OF THE NIGHT. San Francisco, Elder, 1916.

Mulford, Clarence Edward — BAR-20. New York, Outing, 1907; London, Hodder & Stoughton, 1914.

Murfree, Mary Noailles (Charles Egbert Craddock) — IN THE TENNESSEE MOUNTAINS. 1884

Murphy, Lawrence Agustus — THE NAKED RANGE, as Steven C. Lawrence. New York, Ace, 1956.

Murray, Max — THE WORLD'S BACK DOORS. London, Cape, 1927; New York, Cape & Smith, 1929.

Muskett, Netta Rachel — THE JADE SPIDER. London, Hutchinson, 1927.

Mussi, Mary — WINDIER SKIES, as Mary Howard. London, 1930.

Myers, John Myers — THE HARP AND THE BLADE. New York, Dutton, 1941.

N

Nebel, Louis Frederick — SLEEPERS EAST. Boston, Little Brown, 1933; London, Gollancz, 1934.

Neels, Betty — AMAZON IN AN APRON. London, Mills & Boon, 1969 — BLOW HOT, BLOW COLD. London, Mills & Boon, 1969; as SURGEON FROM HOLLAND, Toronto, Harlequin, 1970 — SISTER PETERS IN AMSTERDAM, London, Mills & Boon, 1969; Toronto, Harlequin, 1970.

Neihardt, John Gneisenau — THE DIVINE ENCHANTMENT: A MYSTICAL POEM. New York, White, 1900.

Neilan, Sarah — THE BRAGANZA PURSUIT. London, Hodder & Stoughton, and New York, Dutton, 1976

Nelson, Radell Faraday — THE GANYMEDE TAKEOVER, as Ray Nelson, with Philip K. Dick. New York, Ace, 1967; London, Arrow, 1971.

Nesbit, Edith — THE PROPHET'S MANTLE, as Fabian Bland, with Hubert Bland. London, Drane, 1885; Chicago, Belford Clarke, 1889.

Ness, Evaline — A GIFT FOR SULA SULA. New York, Scribner, 1963.

Neville, Emily Cheney — IT'S LIKE THIS, CAT. New York, Harper, 1963; London, Angus & Rrobertson, 1969.

Neville, Kris Ottman — EPOXY RESINS, with Henry Lee. New York, McGraw Hill, 1957.

Nevins, Francis Michael, Jr. — PUBLISH AND PERISH. New York, Putnam, 1975; London, Hale, 1977.

Newberry, Clare Turlay — HERBERT THE LION. New York, Brewer Warren and Putnam, 1931.

Newcomb, Simon — A CRITICAL EXAMINATION OF OUR FINANCIAL POLICY DURING THE SOUTHERN REBELLION. New York, Appleton, 1865.

Newman, Bernard — HOW TO RUN AN AMATEUR CONCERT PARTY. London, Reynolds, 1925.

Newton, Dwight Bennett — GUNS OF THE RIMROCK. New York, Phoenix, 1946; London, Sampson Low, 1947.

Nichols, John — THE STERILE CUCKOO. New York, McKay, 1965.

Nichols, John Beverly — PRELUDE. London, Chatto & Windus, 1920.

Nichols, Ruth — A WALK OUT OF THE WORLD. Toronto, Longman, and New York, Harcourt Brace, 1969 — CEREMONY OF INNOCENCE. London, Faber, 1969.

Nicholson, Margaret Beda — SUMMER FLIGHT, as Margaret Yorke. London, Hale, 1957.

Nickson, Arthur Thomas — TIN STAR SHERIFF, as Matt Winstan. London, Jenkins, 1956.

Nicole, Christopher Robin — WEST INDIAN CRICKET. London, Phoenix, 1957.

Nielsen, Helen Berniece — THE KIND MAN. New York, Washburn, and London, Gollancz, 1951.

Niven, Frederick John — THE LOST CABIN MINE. London, Lane, 1908; New York, Lane, 1909.

Niven, Laurence Van Cott — WORLD OF PTAVVS, as Larry Niven. New York, Ballantine, 1966; London, Macdonald, 1968.

Nolan, Frederick — THE LIFE AND DEATH OF JOHN HENRY TUNSTALL. Albuquerque, University of New Mexico, 1965.

Nolan, William Francis — ADVENTURE ON WHEELS: THE AUTOBIOGRAPHY OF A ROAD RACING CHAMPION, with John Fitch. New York, Putnam, 1959.

Norman, Lilith — THE CITY OF SYDNEY: OFFICIAL GUIDE. Sydney (AUS), City Council, 1959.

Norris, Benjamin Franklin — YVERNELLE: A LEGEND OF FUEDAL FRANCE. Philadelphia, Lippincott, 1891.

Norris, Kathleen Thompson — MOTHER. New York, Macmillan, 1911.

North, Sterling — (POEMS). Chicago, University of Chicago, 1925.

Norton, Alice Mary — THE PRINCE COMMANDS, as Andre Norton. New York and London, Appleton Century, 1934.

Norton, Mary — THE MAGIC BED-KNOB; OR, HOW TO BECOME A WITCH IN TEN EASY LESSONS. New York, Hyperion, 1943.

Norway, Kate — SISTER BROOKES OF BYND'S. London, Mills & Boon, 1957; as NURSE BROOKES, Toronto, Harlequin, 1958.

Norway, Nevil Shute — MARAZAN, as Nevil Shute. London, Cassell, 1926.

Nourse, Alan Edward — TROUBLE ON TITAN, as Alan E. Nourse. Philadelphia, Winston, 1954; London, Hutchinson, 1956.

Nowlan, Philip Francis — BUCK ROGERS ON THE MOON OF SATURN. Racine (WI), Whitman, 1934 — BUCK ROGERS IN THE DANGEROUS MISSION. New York, Blue Ribbon Press, 1934.

Nutt, Charles — THE HUNGER AND OTHER STORIES, as Charles Beaumont. New York, Putnam, 1957; as SHADOW PLAY, as Charles Beaumont, London, Panther, 1964 — RUN FROM THE HUNTER, as Keith Grantland, with John E. Tomerlin. New York, Fawcett, 1957; London, Boardman, 1959.

Nye, Nelson Coral — TWO-FISTED COWPOKE. New York, Greenberg, 1936; London, Nicholson & Watson, 1937.

Nye, Robert — JUVENILIA 1. Lowestoft (ENG), Scorpion Press, 1961.

O

Obets. Bob — BLOOD-MOON RANGE. New York, Pyramid, 1957.

O'Connor, John Woolf (Jack) — CONQUEST: A NOVEL OF THE OLD SOUTHWEST. New York, Harper, 1930.

O'Connor, Richard — THOMAS: ROCK OF CHICK-AMAUGA. New York, Prentice Hall, 1948.

O'Dell, Scott — REPRESENTATIVE PHOTOPLAYS ANALYZED. Hollywood, Palmer, 1924.

Odets, Clifford — AWAKE AND SING (play). 1935.

Odle, E.V. — THE HISTORY OF ALFRED RUDD. London, Collins, 1922.

O'Donnell, Lillian — DEATH ON THE GRASS. New York, Arcadia, 1960.

O'Donnell, Peter — MODESTY BLAISE. London, Souvenir Press, and New York, Doubleday, 1965.

Offord, Lenore Glen — MURDER ON RUSSIAN HILL. Philadelphia, Macrae Smith, 1938; as MURDER BEFORE BREAKFAST, London, Jarrolds, 1938.

Offutt, Andrew Jefferson — EVIL IS LIVE SPELLED BACKWARDS. New York, Paperback Library, 1970.

Ogilvie, Elisabeth May — HIGH TIDE AT NOON. New York, Crowell, 1944; London, Harrap, 1945.

O'Hara, John — APPOINTMENT IN SAMARRA. 1934.

Oliver, Symmes Chadwick — MISTS OF DAWN, as Chad Oliver. Philadelphia, Winston, 1952; London, Hutchinson, 1954.

Olsen, Alfred John, Jr. — RHYTHM RIDES THE ROCKET, as Bob Olsen. New York, Columbia, 1940.

Olsen, Theodore Victor — HAVEN OF THE HUNTED. New York, Ace, 1956.

O'Malley, Lady Mary Dolling — PEKING CIRCUS, as Ann Bridge. London and Boston, 1932.

Oman, Carola Mary Anima — THE MENIN ROAD AND OTHER POEMS. London, Hodder & Stoughton, 1919.

Onadipe, Nathaniel Kolawole — THE ADVENTURES OF SOUZA, THE VILLAGE LAD, as Kola Onadipe. Lagos, African Univ., 1963.

O'Neill, Eugene — THIRST AND OTHER ONE ACT PLAYS. 1914.

Onstott, Kyle — YOUR DOG AS A HOBBY, with Irving C. Ackerman. New York, 1940.

Oppenheim, Edward Phillips — THE PEER AND THE WOMAN. New York, Taylor, 1892; London, Ward Lock, 1895.

Orczy, Emma Magdalena Rosalia Maria Josefa Barbara — THE EMPEROR'S CANDLESTICKS, as Baroness Orczy. London, Pearson, 1899; New York, Doscher, 1908.

Orgel, Doris — THE TALE OF GOCKEL, HINKEL, AND GACKELIAH. New York, Random, 1961.

Ormerod, Roger — TIME TO KILL. London, Hale, 1974.

Ormondroyd, Edward — DAVID AND THE PHOENIX. Chicago, Follett, 1957.

O'Rourke, Frank — "E" COMPANY. New York, Simon & Schuster, 1945.

Ostenso, Martha — A FAR LAND. New York, Seltzer, 1924.

Ottley, Reginald Leslie — STAMPEDE. London, Laurie, 1961.

Overholser, Wayne D. — BUCKAROO'S CODE. New York, Macmillan, 1947; Redhill (ENG), Wells Gardner, 1948.

Overton, Jenny Margaret Mary — CREED COUNTRY. London, Faber, 1969; New York, Macmillan, 1970.

Ovstedal, Barbara — SOVEREIGN'S KEY, as Rosalind Laker. London, Hale, 1969

P

Packard, Frank Lucius — ON THE IRON AT BIG CLOUD. New York, Crowell, 1911.

Page, Thomas Nelson — IN OLE VIRGINIA. 1887.

Paine, Albert Bigelow — RHYMES BY TWO FRIENDS, with William Allen White. Privately printed, 1873.

Palmer, Charles Stuart — ACE OF JADES. New York, Mohawk, 1931.

Palmer, Cyril Everard — A BROKEN VESSEL. Kingston, Jamaica, Pioneer Press, 1960.

Pangborn, Edgar — A-100, as Bruce Harrison. New York, Dutton, 1930.

Panshin, Alexei — RITE OF PASSAGE. New York, Ace, 1968; London, Sidgwick & Jackson, 1969 — STAR WELL. New York, Ace, 1968 — THE THURB REVOLUTION. New York, Ace, 1968 — HEINLEIN IN DIMENSION: A CRITICAL ANALYSIS. Chicago, Advent, 1968.

Pargeter, Edith Mary — HORTENSIUS, FRIEND OF NERO. London, Lovat Dickson, 1936; New York, Greystone, 1937 — IRON-BOUND. London, Lovat Dickson, 1936..

Pargeter, Margaret — WINDS FROM THE SEA. London, Mills & Boon, and Toronto, Harlequin, 1975 — THE KILTED STRANGER. London, Mills & Boon, 1975; Toronto, Harlequin, 1976 — RIDE A BLACK HORSE. London, Mills & Boon, 1975; Toronto, Harlequin, 1976.

Parish, Margaret Cecile — GOOD HUNTING, LITTLE INDIAN, as Peggy Parish. New York, Scott, 1962 — MY BOOK OF MANNERS, as Peggy Parish. New York, Golden, 1962; London, Golden Pleasure, 1963.

Park, Rosina Ruth Lucia — THE HARP IN THE SOUTH. Sydney (AUS), Angus & Robertson; London, Joseph, and Boston, Houghton Mifflin, 1948.

Parker, Richard — ESCAPE FROM THE ZOO. London, Sylvan Press, 1945.

Parker, Robert Brown — THE GODWULF MANUSCRIPT. Boston, Houghton Mifflin, 1973; London, Deutsch, 1974.

Parkman, Francis — THE CALIFORNIA AND OREGON TRAIL. 1849.

Patchett, Mary Elwyn Osborne — AJAX, THE WARRIOR. London, Lutterworth, 1953; as AJAX, GOLDEN DOG OF THE AUSTRALIAN BUSH, Indianapolis, Bobbs Merrill, 1953.

Paton Walsh, (Jill) Gillian — HENGEST'S TALE. London, Macmillan, and New York, St. Martin's, 1966.

Patten, Brian — PORTRAITS. Liverpool (ENG), privately printed, 1962.

Patten, Lewis Byford — MASSACRE AT WHITE RIVER. New York, Ace, 1952; London, Ward Lock, 1961.

Patterson, Henry — SEVEN PILLARS TO HELL, as Hugh Marlowe. London and New York, Abelard Schuman, 1963.

Pattinson, Nancy Evelyn — MY DREAM IS YOURS, as Nan Asquith. London, 1954.

Pattullo, George — THE UNTAMED: RANGE LIFE IN THE SOUTHWEST. New York, Fitzgerald, 1911.

Paul, Elliot Harold — INDELIBLE. Boston, Houghton Mifflin, 1922; London, Jarrolds, 1924.

Paulding, James Kirke — SALMAGUNDI; OR, THE WHIM-WHAMS AND OPINIONS OF LAUNCELOT

LANGSTAFF, ESQ., AND OTHERS (with Washington and William Irving). 1807-08.

Pauley, Barbara Anne — BLOOD KIN. New York, Doubleday, 1972.

Payne, John Howard — JULIA; OR, THE WANDERER. 1806.

Peake, Lilian — MAN OF GRANITE. London, Mills & Boon, 1971; Toronto, Harlequin, 1975 — THIS MOMENT IN TIME. London, Mills & Boon, 1971; Toronto, Harlequin, 1972.

Pearce, Ann Philippa — MINNOW ON THE SAY. London, Oxford Univ., 1955; as THE MINNOW LEADS TO TREASURE, Cleveland, World, 1958.

Pease, Howard — THE TATTOOED MAN. New York, Doubleday, and London, Heinemann, 1926.

Peck, Richard — OLD TOWN: A COMPLEAT GUIDE, with Norman Strasma. Chicago, 1965.

Peck, Robert Newton — THE HAPPY SADIST. New York, Doubleday, 1962.

Pedler, Christopher Magnus Howard — MUTANT 59, THE PLASTIC EATER, as Kit Pedler, with Gerry Davis. London, Souvenir Press, 1971; New York, Viking, 1972.

Pedler, Margaret Bass — THIS SPLENDID FOLLY. London, Mills & Boon, 1918; New York, Doran, 1921

Peet, William Bartlett — HUBERT'S HAIR-RAISING ADVENTURE, as Bill Peet. Boston, Houghton Mifflin, 1959; London, Deutsch, 1960.

Pemberton, Max — THE DIARY OF A SCOUNDREL. London, Ward & Downey, 1891.

Pendelton, Donald Eugene — FRAME UP, as Stephen Gregory. Fresno (CA), Vega, 1960.

Pendower, Jacques — THE TERROR OF TORLANDS, as T.C.H. Jacobs. London, Stanley Paul, 1930.

Percy, Walker — ALPHA YES, TERRA NO! New York, Ace, 1965 — THE CAVES OF MARS. New York, Ace, 1965 — SAGA OF LOST EARTHS. New York, Ace, 1965 — THE STAR MILL. New York, Ace, 1965.

Perkins, Lucy Fitch — THE GOOSE GIRL: A MOTHER'S LAP-BOOK OF RHYMES AND PICTURES. Chicago, McClurg, 1906.

Perry, George Sessions — WALLS RISE UP. New York, Doubleday, 1939.

Perry, Ritchie John Allen — THE FALL GUY. London, Collins, and Boston, Houghton Mifflin, 1972.

Peter, Elizabeth O. — CONFIDENT TOMORROWS. London, Hurst & Blackett, 1931.

Peters, Maureen — ELIZABETH THE BELOVED. London, Hale, 1965; New York, Beagle, 1972.

Peters, Natasha — SAVAGE SURRENDER. New York, Ace, 1977; London, Arrow, 1978.

Petersham, Maud Sylvia Fuller And Miska — MIKI. New York, Doubleday, 1929.

Petry, Ann Lane — THE STREET. Boston, Houghton Mifflin, 1946; London, Joseph, 1947.

Peyton, Kathleen W. — SABRE, THE HORSE FROM THE SEA, as Kathleen Herald. London, Black, 1948; New York, Macmillan, 1963.

Philips, Judson Pentecost — RED WAR, as Judson Philips, with Thomas A. Johnson. New York, Doubleday, 1936: HOLD 'EM GIRLS: THE INTELLIGENT WOMAN'S GUIDE TO MEN AND FOOTBALL, with Robert W. Wood, Jr., New York, Putnam, 1936.

Philliphent, John Thomas — SPACE PUPPET, as John Rackham. London, Pearson, 1954 — JUPITER EQUILATERAL, as John Rackham. London, Pearson, 1954 — THE MASTER WEED, as John Rackham. London, Pearson, 1954.

Phillpotts, Eden — MY ADVENTURE IN THE FLYING SCOTSMAN: A ROMANCE OF LONDON AND NORTH-WESTERN RAILWAY SHARES. London, Hogg, 1888.

Phipson, Joan Margaret — CHRISTMAS IN THE SUN. Sydney and London, Angus & Robertson, 1951.

Picard, Barbara Leonie — THE MERMAID AND THE SIMPLETON. London, Oxford Univ., 1949; New York, Criterion, 1970.

Piercy, Marge — BREAKING CAMP. Middletown (CT), Wesleyan Univ., 1968.

Pilcher, Rosamunde — HALF-WAY TO THE MOON. London, Mills & Boon, 1949.

Piper, Henry Beam — MURDER IN THE GUNROOM, as H. Beam Piper. New York, Knopf, 1953.

Piserchia, Doris Elaine — MISTER JUSTICE. New York, ACE, 1973; London, Dobson, 1977.

Plagemann, Bentz — WILLIAM WALTER. New York, Greystone, 1941.

Platt, Charles — THE GARBAGE WORLD. New York, Berkley, 1967; London, Panther, 1968.

Plowman, Stephanie — NELSON. London, Methuen, 1955.

Plummer, Clare Emsley — PAINTED CLAY, as Clare Emsley. London, 1947.

Pocock, Henry Roger Ashwell — TALES OF WESTERN LIFE, LAKE SUPERIOR, AND THE CANADIAN PRIARIE, as H.R.A. Pocock. Ottawa, Mitchell, 1888.

Poe, Edgar Allan — TAMERLANE AND OTHER POEMS. 1827

Pohl, Frederik — THE SPACE MERCHANTS, with C.M. Kornbluth. New York, Ballantine, 1953; London, Heinemann, 1955 — DANGER MOON, as James MacCreigh. Sydney (AUS), American Science Fiction, 1953.

Politi, Leo — LITTLE PANCHO. New York, Viking, 1938.

Polland, Madeleine Angela — CHILDREN OF THE RED KING. London, Constable, 1960; New York, Holt Rinehart, 1961.

Ponsonby, Doris Almon — THE GAZEBO, as D.A. Ponsonby. London, Hutchinson, 1945; as IF MY ARMS COULD HOLD, as Doris Ponsonby. New York, Liveright, 1947.

Poole, Jane Penelope Josephine — A DREAM IN THE HOUSE. London, Hutchinson, 1961.

Popkin, Zelda — DEATH WEARS A WHITE GARDENIA. Philadelphia, Lippincott, 1938; London, Hutchinson, 1939.

Porter, Eleanor Hodgman — CROSS CURRENT: THE STORY OF MARGARET. Boston, Wilde, 1907; London, Harrap, 1928.

Porter, Geneva Grace Stratton — THE SONG OF THE CARDINAL: A LOVE STORY, as Gene Stratton Porter. Indianapolis, Bobbs Merrill, 1903; London, Hodder & Stoughton, 1913.

Porter, Joyce — DOVER ONE. London, Cape, and New York, Scribner, 1964.

Porter, Sheena — THE BRONZE CHRYSANTHEMUM. London, Oxford Univ., 1961; Princeton (NJ), Van Nostrand, 1965.

Porter, William Sydney (Or Sidney) — CABBAGES AND KINGS, as O. Henry. New York, McClure, 1904; London, Nash, 1912.

Portis, Charles McColl — NORWOOD. New York, Simon & Schuster, 1966; London, Cape, 1967.

Post, Melville Davisson — THE STRANGE SCHEMES OF RANDOLPH MASON. New York, Putnam, 1896.

Postgate, Raymond William — THE INTERNATIONAL (SOCIALIST BUREAU) DURING THE WAR. London, The Herald, 1918.

Potter, Helen Beatrix — THE TALE OF PETER RABBIT. Privately printed, 1900.

Potter, Joanna — ELIZA STANHOPE, as Joanna Trollope. London, Hutchinson, 1978; New York, Dutton, 1979.

Potter, Margaret Edith — MURDER TO MUSIC, as Margaret Newman. London, 1959.

Potts, Jean — SOMEONE TO REMEMBER. Philadelphia, Westminster, 1943.

Pound, Ezra — POETRY: A LUME SPENTO. 1908.

Pournelle, Jerry Eugene — RED HEROIN, as Wade Curtis. New York, Berkley, 1969.

Powell, James — A MAN MADE FOR TROUBLE. Canoga Park (CA), Major, 1976; London, Hale, 1981.

Power, Rhoda Dolores — UNDER COSSACK AND BOLSHEVIK. London, Methuen, 1919; as UNDER THE BOLSHEVIK REIGN OF TERROR, New York, McBride & Nast, 1919.

Powys, John Cowper — ODES AND OTHER POEMS. London, Rider, 1896.

Pragnell, Festus — THE GREEN MAN OF KILSONA. London, Allan, 1936; as THE GREEN MAN OF GRAYPEC. New York, Greenberg, 1950.

Prather, Richard Scott — CASE OF THE VANISHING BEAUTY. New York, Fawcett, 1950; London, Fawcett, 1957.

Pratt, Murray Fletcher — THE HEROIC YEARS: FOURTEEN YEARS OF THE REPUBLIC 1801-1815. New York, Smith & Haas, 1934.

Prebble, John Edward Curtis — WHERE THE SEA BREAKS. London, Secker & Warburg, 1944.

Prescott, John Brewster — THE BEAUTIFUL SHIP: A STORY OF THE GREAT LAKES. New York, Longman, 1952.

Prescott, William Hickling — HISTORY OF THE REIGN OF FERDINAND AND ISABELLA, THE CATHOLIC. 1837.

Preston, Ivy Alice — THE SILVER STREAM. Christchurch (NZ), Pegasus Press, 1959.

Price, Anthony — THE LABYRINTH MAKERS. London, Gollancz, 1970; New York, Doubleday, 1971.

Price, Susan — THE DEVIL'S PIPER. London, Faber, 1973; New York, Morrow, 1976.

Priest, Christopher — INDOCTRINAIRE. London, Faber, and New York, Harper, 1970.

Priestley, John Boynton — THE CHAPMAN OF RHYMES. London, Alexander Moring, 1918.

Prior, Allan — A FLAME IN THE AIR. London, Joseph, 1951.

Procter, Maurice — NO PROUD CHIVALRY. London, Longman, 1947.

Pronzini, Bill — THE STALKER. New York, Random, 1971; London, Hale, 1974.

Propper, Milton Morris — THE STRANGE DISAPPEARANCE OF MARY YOUNG. New York, Harper, 1929; London, Harrap, 1932.

Pudney, John Sleigh — SPRING ENCOUNTER. London, Methuen, 1933.

Purdom, Thomas Edward — I WANT THE STARS, as Tom Purdom. New York, Ace, 1964.

Purdum, Herbert R. — MY BROTHER JOHN. New York, Doubleday, 1966.

Pye, Virginia Frances Kennedy — ST. MARTIN'S HOLIDAY. London, Heinemann, 1930.

Pyle, Howard — THE MERRY ADVENTURES OF ROBIN HOOD OF GREAT RENOWN IN NOTTINGHAMSHIRE. New York, Scribner, and London, Sampson Low, 1883.

Pynchon, Thomas — V. Philadelphia, Lippincott, and London, Cape, 1963.

R

Radford, Edwin Isaac And Mona Augusta — MURDER JIGSAW, as E. and M.A. Radford. London, Melrose, 1944.

Rae, Gwynedd — MOSTLY MARY. London, Mathews & Marrot, 1930; New York, Morrow, 1931.

Rae, Hugh Crawford — SKINNER. London, Blond, and New York, Viking, 1965.

Raine, William McLeod — A DAUGHTER OF THE RAASAY: A TALE OF THE '45. New York, Stokes, 1902; as FOR LOVE AND HONOUR, London, Isbister, 1904.

Rand, Ayn — WE THE LIVING. New York, Macmillan, and London, Cassell, 1936.

Randall, Florence Engel — HEDGEROW. New York, Harcourt Brace, and London, Heinemann, 1967.

Randall, Marta — A CITY IN THE NORTH. New York, Warner, 1976.

Randall, Rona — THE MOON RETURNS. London, Collins, 1942

Randolph, Georgiana Ann — 8 FACES AT 3, as Craig Rice. New York, Simon & Schuster, and London, Eyre & Spottiswoode, 1939.

Ransome, Arthur Michell — THE SOULS OF THE STREETS AND OTHER LITTLE PAPERS. London, Langham, 1904.

Raphael, Rick — CODE THREE. New York, Simon & Schuster, 1965; London, Gollancz, 1966 — THE THIRSTY QUENCHERS. London, Gollancz, 1965.

Raskin, Ellen — NOTHING EVER HAPPENS ON MY BLOCK. New York, Atheneum, 1966.

Rathbone, Julian — DIAMONDS BID. London, Joseph, 1966; New York, Walker, 1967.

Rathbone, St. George Henry — OLD SHADOW, as Marline Manly. Chicago, Pictorial, 1871.

Rawlings, Marjorie Kinnan — SOUTH MOON UNDER. New York, Scribner, and London, Faber, 1933.

Rawson, Clayton — DEATH FROM A TOP HAT. New York, Putnam, and London, Collins, 1938.

Ray, Mary Eva Pedder — THE VOICE OF APOLLO. London, Cape, 1964; New York, Farrar Straus, 1965.

Rayer, Francis George — LADY IN DANGER. Dublin, Grafton, 1948.

Rayner, Claire Berenice — THE FINAL YEAR. London, Corgi, 1962 — MOTHERS AND MIDWIVES. London, Allen & Unwin, 1962.

Rayner, William — THE REAPERS. London, Faber, 1961.

Read, Herbert Edward — SONGS OF CHAOS. London, Elkin Mathews, 1915; New York, St. Martin's, 1975.

Reamy, Tom — BLIND VOICES. New York, Berkley, 1978; London, Sidgwick & Jackson, 1979.

Reaney, James Crerar — THE RED HEART. Toronto, McClelland & Stewart, 1949.

Reed, Ishmael — THE FREE-LANCE PALLBEARERS. New York, Doubleday, 1967; London, MacGibbon & Kee, 1968.

Reed, Lillian — ARMED CAMPS, as Kit Reed. London, Faber, 1959; New York, Dutton, 1970.

Reed, Talbot Baines — THE ADVENTURES OF A THREE-GUINEA WATCH. London, Religious Tract Society, 1883.

Rees, George Leslie Clarke — DIGIT DICK ON THE GREAT BARRIER REEF, AND THE TASMANIAN DEVIL, IN BLACK SWAN LAND, AND THE LOST OPALS. 4 vols. Sydney (AUS), Sands, 1942-57.

Reese, John — SHEEHAN'S MILL. New York, Doubleday, 1943.

Reeve, Arthur Benjamin — THE SILENT BULLET: ADVENTURES OF CRAIG KENNEDY, SCIENTIFIC DETECTIVE. New York, Dodd Mead, 1912; as THE BLACK HAND, London, Nash, 1912.

Reeves, James — THE NATURAL NEED. Deya, Mallorca, Seizin Press, and London, Constable, 1936.

Reid, Henrietta — ISLAND OF SECRETS. London, Mills & Boon, 1965.

Reid, Meta Mayne — THE LAND IS DEAR. London, Melrose, 1936.

Reilly, Helen — THE THIRTY-FIRST BULLFINCH. New York, Doubleday, 1930.

Reitci, John George — A NEW LEAF AND OTHER STORIES, as Jack Ritchie. New York, Dell, 1971.

Rendell, Ruth — FROM DOON WITH DEATH. London, Hutchinson, 1964; New York, Doubleday, 1965.

Repp, Edward Earl — CYCLONE JIM, as E. Earl Repp. New York, Godwin, 1935; London, Wright & Brown, 1936 — HELL ON THE PECOS, as E. Earl Repp. New York, Godwin, 1935; London, Wright & Brown, 1936.

Rey, Hans Augusto — ZEBROLOGY. London, Chatto & Windus, 1937.

Rey, Margret — HOW THE FLYING FISHES CAME INTO BEING, with H.A. Rey. London, Chatto & Windus, 1938.

Reynolds, Dallas McCord — THE CASE OF THE LITTLE GREEN MEN, as Mack Reynolds. New York, Phoenix, 1951.

Rhodes, Eugene Manlove — GOOD MEN AND TRUE. New York, Holt, 1910.

Rice, Elmer — ON TRIAL (play). 1914.

Richards, Laura Elizabeth — FIVE MICE IN A MOUSE-TRAP, BY THE MAN IN THE MOON, DONE IN VERNACULAR, FROM THE LUNACULAR. Boston, Estes, 1880.

Richmond, Walter And Leigh — SHOCK WAVES, as Walt and Leigh Richmond. New York, Ace, 1967 — THE LOST MILLENNIUM, as Walt and Leigh Richmond. New York, Ace, 1967.

Richardson, Robert Shirley — PRELIMINARY ELEMENTS OF OBJECT COMAS SOLA (1927AA), with others. Berkeley, Univ. of California, 1927.

Richmond, Roaldus Frederick — CONESTOGA WAGON, as Roe Richmond. New York, PHOENIX,

1949; London, CLERKE & COCKERAN, 1951.

Richter, Conrad Michael — BROTHERS OF NO KIN AND OTHER STORIES. New York, Hinds, 1924.

Riddle, Betsy — MISS CARMICHAEL'S CONSCIENCE: A STUDY IN FLUCTUATIONS, as Baroness von Hutten. Philadelphia, 1900.

Ridge, Antonia — THE HANDY ELEPHANT AND OTHER STORIES. London, Faber, 1946.

Riefe, Alan — TALES OF HORROR. New York, Pocket Books, 1965.

Rigsby, Vechel Howard — VOYAGE TO LEANDRO. New York, Harper, 1939.

Riley, James Whitcomb — "THE OLD SWIMMIN-HOLE," AND 'LEVEN MORE POEMS. 1883.

Riley, Louise — THE MYSTERY HORSE. Toronto, Copp Clark, and New York, Messner, 1950; Oxford, Blackwell, 1957.

Rinehart, Mary Roberts — THE CIRCULAR STAIRCASE. Indianapolis, Bobbs Merrill, 1908; London, Cassell, 1909.

Ritchie, Claire — THE SHELTERED FLAME. London, Hodder & Stoughton, 1949.

Roan, Tom — WHISPERING RANGE. New York, King, 1934; London, Nicholson & Watson, 1935.

Roark, Garland — WAKE OF THE RED WITCH. Boston, Little Brown, 1946.

Robbe-Grillet, Alain — THE VOYEUR. 1958.

Roberts, Charles George Douglas — ORION AND OTHER POEMS, as Charles G.D. Roberts. Philadelphia, Lippincott, 1880.

Roberts, Elizabeth Madox — IN THE GREAT STEEP'S GARDEN: POEMS. Colorado Springs, Gowdy Simmons, 1915.

Roberts, Irene — LOVE SONG OF THE SEA. London, Fleetway, 1960 — JUMP INTO HELL! London, Brown Watson, 1960.

Roberts, Janet Louise — JEWELS OF TERROR. New York, Lancer, 1970 — LOVE SONG. New York, Pinnacle, 1970.

Roberts, Keith John Kingston — THE FURIES. London, Hart Davis, and New York, Berkley, 1966.

Roberts, Willo Davis — MURDER AT GRAND BAY. New York, Arcadia, 1955.

Robertson, Frank Chester — THE FOREMAN OF THE FORTY-BAR. New York, Barse & Hopkins, 1925; London, Collins, 1927.

Robertson, Keith Carlton — TICKTOCK AND JIM. Philadelphia, Winston, 1948; as WATCH FOR A PONY, London, Heinemann, 1949.

Robinett, Stephen — STARGATE. New York, St. Martin's, 1976; London, Hale, 1978.

Robins, Denise Naomi — THE MARRIAGE BOND. London, Hodder & Stoughton, 1924 — SEALED LIPS. London, Hodder & Stoughton, 1924.

Robinson, Edwin Arlington — THE TORRENT AND THE NIGHT BEFORE. 1896.

Robinson, Frank Malcolm — THE POWER. Philadelphia, Lippincott, 1956; London, Eyre & Spottiswoode, 1957.

Robinson, Joan Mary Gale — A STANDS FOR ANGEL. London, Mowbray, 1939; as A IS FOR ANGEL, New York, Lothrop, 1953.

Robinson, Spider — TELEMPATH. New York, Berkley, 1976; London, Macdonald & Jane's, 1978.

Roby, Mary Linn — STILL AS THE GRAVE. New York, Dodd Mead, 1964; London, Collins, 1965.

Rocklin, Ross Louis — THE MEN AND THE MIRROR, as Ross Rocklynne. New York, Ace, 1973 — THE SUN DESTROYERS, as Ross Rocklynne. New York, Ace, 1973.

Rodell, Marie Freid — BREATHE NO MORE, as Marion Randolph. New York, Holt, and London, Heinemann, 1940.

Roderus, Frank — JOURNEY TO UTAH. New York, Doubleday, 1977; London, Hale, 1978: DUSTER. Independence (MO), Independence Press, 1977.

Rodgers, Mary — THE ROTTEN BOOK. New York, Harper, 1969.

Rogers, Joel Townsley — ONCE IN A RED MOON. New York, Brentano's, 1923.

Rogers, Rosemary — SWEET SAVAGE LOVE. New York, Avon, 1974; London, Futura, 1977. — THE WILDEST HEART. New York, Avon, 1974; London, Futura, 1978.

Rohmer, Richard — THE GREEN NORTH. Toronto, Maclean Hunter, 1970.

Rolvaag, Olle Edvart — ORDFORKLARING TIL NORDAHL ROLFSENS LAESEBOK FOR FOLKESKOLEN II. Minneapolis, Augsburg, 1909.

Rome, Margaret — THE LOTTERY OF MATTHEW DEVLIN. London, Mills & Boon, 1968 — THE MARRIAGE OF CAROLINE LINDSAY. London, Mills & Boon, 1968; Toronto, Harlequin, 1974.

Roos, Audrey And William — MADE UP TO KILL, as Kelley Roos. New York, Dodd Mead, 1940; as MADE UP FOR MURDER, London, Jarrolds, 1941.

Roose-Evans, James — DIRECTING A PLAY: JAMES ROOSE-EVANS ON THE ART OF DIRECTING AND ACTING. London, Studio Vista, and New York, Theatre Arts, 1968.

Roshwald, Mordecai Marceli — ADAM VE'HINUKNO (Man and Education). Tel-Aviv, Dvir, 1954.

Ross, Diana — THE WORLD AT WORK, GETTING YOU THINGS, MAKING YOU THINGS. 2 vols. London, Country Life, 1939.

Ross, Sinclair — AS FOR ME AND MY HOUSE. New York, Reynal, 1941.

Ross, Zola Helen — THREE DOWN VULNERABLE, as Z.H. Ross. Indianapolis, Bobbs Merrill, 1946.

Rossi, Jean Baptiste — THE 10:30 FROM MARSEILLES, as Sebastien Japrisot. 1963.

Rossiter, John — THE BLOOD RUNNING COLD, as Jonathan Ross. London, Cassell, 1968.

Roth, Holly — THE CONTENT ASSIGNMENT. New York, Simon & Schuster, and London, Hamish Hamilton, 1954.

Rotsler, William — CONTEMPORARY EROTIC CINEMA. New York, Ballantine, 1973.

Rounds, Glen Harold — OL' PAUL, THE MIGHTY LOGGER. New York, Holiday House, 1936.

Rowland, Donald Sydney — THE BATTLE DONE, as Donald S. Rowland. London, Brown Watson, 1958.

Rubel, James Lyon — THE MEDICO OF PAINTED SPRINGS, as Mason Macrae. New York, Phoenix, 1934; London, Mills & Boon, 1935.

Ruck, Amy Roberta — HIS OFFICIAL FIANCEE, as Berta Ruck. London, Hutchinson, and New York, Dodd Mead, 1914.

Rundle, Anne — THE MOON MARRIAGE. London, Hurst & Blackett, 1967.

Rush, Philip — ROGUE'S LUTE. London, Dakars, 1944.

Rushing, Jane Gilmore — WALNUT GROVE. New York, Doubleday, 1964.

Russ, Joanna — PICNIC ON PARADISE. New York, Ace, 1968; London, Macdonald, 1969.

Russell, Bertrand Arthur William — GERMAN SOCIAL DEMOCRACY. London, Longman, 1896; New York, Simon & Schuster, 1965.

Russell, Charles Marion — RAWHIDE RAWLINS STORIES. Great Falls, Montana Newspaper Association, 1921.

Russell. Eric Frank — SINISTER BARRIER. Kingswood (ENG), World's Work, 1943; Reading (PA), Fantasy Press, 1948.

Russell, Martin James — NO THROUGH ROAD. London, Collins, 1965; New York, Coward McCann, 1966.

Russell, Ray — THE CASE AGAINST SATAN. New York, Obolensky, 1962; London, Souvenir, 1963 — SARDONICUS AND OTHER STORIES, New York, Ballantine, 1962.

Ryan, Marah Ellis — MERZE: THE STORY OF AN ACTRESS. Chicago, Rand McNally, 1889.

S

Sabatini, Rafael — THE LOVERS OF YVONNE. London, Pearson, 1902; as THE SUITORS OF YVONNE. New York, Putnam, 1902.

Saberhagen, Frederick Thomas — THE GOLDEN PEOPLE, as Fred Saberhagen. New York, Ace, 1964.

Sachs, Marilyn — AMY MOVES IN. New York, Doubleday, 1964.

St. Clair, Margaret — AGENT OF THE UNKNOWN. New York, Ace, 1956 — THE GREEN QUEEN. New York, Ace, 1956.

Saltus, Edgar — BALZAC. 1884.

Sandburg, Carl — IN RECKLESS ECSTASY. 1904.

Sanders, Dorothy Lucy — FAIRIES ON THE DOORSTEP, as Dorothy Lucie Sanders. Sydney (AUS), Australasian, 1948; as POOL OF DREAMS, as Lucy Walker. New York, Ballantine, 1973 — THE RANDY, as Dorothy Lucie Sanders. Sydney, Australasian, 1948.

Sandoz, Mari Susette — OLD JULES. Boston, Little Brown, 1935; London, Chapman & Hall, 1937.

Santayana, George — SONNETS AND OTHER VERSES. 1894.

Sale, Richard Bernard — NOT TOO NARROW, NOT TOO DEEP. New York, Simon & Schuster, and London, Cassell, 1936.

Salkey, Felix Andrew Alexander — A QUALITY OF VIOLENCE, as Andrew Salkey. London, Hutchinson, 1959.

Sallis, James — A FEW LAST WORDS. London, Hart Davis, 1969; New York, Macmillan, 1970.

Sanders, Lawrence — HANDBOOK OF CREATIVE CRAFTS, with Richard Carol. New York, Pyramid, 1968.

Santee, Ross — MEN AND HORSES. New York, Century, 1926.

Sargent, Pamela — CLONED LIVES. New York, Fawcett, 1976.

Saroyan, William — THE DARING YOUNG MAN ON THE FLYING TRAPEZE, AND OTHER STORIES. 1934.

Saville, Leonard Malcolm — MYSTERY AT WITCHEND. London, Newnes, 1943; as SPY IN THE HILLS, New York, Farrar & Rinehart, 1945.

Sawley, Petra — NO TIME FOR LOVE. London, Gresham, 1967 — NO PLACE FOR LOVE. London, Gresham, 1967 — LOVE ON ICE. London, Gresham, 1967.

Sawyer, John And Nancy — VICTIM OF LOVE, as Nancy Buckingham. London, 1967.

Sawyer, Ruth — THE PRIMROSE RING. New York and London, Harper, 1915.

Saxton, Josephine — THE HIEROS GAMOS OF SAM AND AN SMITH. New York, Doubleday, 1969.

Sayers, Dorothy Leigh — OP.1. Oxford (ENG), Blackwell, 1918.

Sayers, James Denson — CAN THE WHITE RACE SURVIVE? Washington (DC), Independent, 1929.

Scarborough, Dorothy — FUGITIVE VERSES. Waco (TX), Baylor Univ., 1912.

Scarry, Richard McClure — THE GREAT BIG CAR AND TRUCK BOOK. New York, Simon & Schuster, 1951.

Schachner, Nathan — AARON BURR, as Nat Schachner. New York, Stokes, 1937.

Schaefer, Jack Warner — SHANE. Boston, Houghton Mifflin, 1949; London, Deutsch, 1954.

Scherf, Margaret Louise — THE CORPSE GROWS A BEARD. New York, Putnam, 1940; London, Patridge, 1946.

Schlee, Ann — THE STRANGERS. London, Macmillan, 1971; New York, Atheneum, 1972.

Schlein, Miriam — A DAY AT THE PLAYGROUND. New York, Simon & Schuster, 1951.

Schmidt, James Norman — MURDER, CHOP CHOP, as James Norman. New York, Morrow, 1942; London, Joseph, 1943.

Schmidt, Stanley Albert — NEWTON AND THE QUASI-APPLE. New York, Doubleday, 1975.

Schmitz, James Henry — AGENT OF VEGA. New York, Gnome, 1960.

Schoepflin, Harold Vincent — THE DOOMSDAY PLANET, as Vincent Harl. New York, Belmont, 1966.

Scortia, Thomas Nicholas — WHAT MAD ORACLE? Evanston (IL), Regency, 1961.

Scott, Reginald Thomas Maitland — SECRET SERVICE SMITH. New York, Dutton, 1923; London, Hodder & Stoughton, 1924.

Searls, Henry Hunt, Jr. — THE BIG X, as Hank Searls. New York, Harper, and London, Heinemann, 1959.

Seed, Cecile Eugenie — THE DANCING MULE, as Jenny Seed. London, Nelson, 1964.

Seeley, Mabel — THE LISTENING HOUSE. New York, Doubleday, 1938; London, Collins, 1939.

Seelye, John Douglas — THE TRUE ADVENTURES OF HUCKLEBERRY FINN, AS TOLD TO JOHN SEELYE. Evanston (IL), Northwestern Univ., 1970.

Seifert, Elizabeth — YOUNG DOCTOR GALAHAD. New York, Dodd Mead, 1938; as YOUNG DOCTOR, London, Collins, 1939.

Seltzer, Charles Alden — THE COUNCIL OF THREE. New York, Abbey, 1900.

Selwyn, Francis — CRACKSMAN ON VELVET. London, Deitsch, and New York, Stein & Day, 1974.

Senarens, Luis Philip — A.D.T.; OR, THE MESSENGER BOY DETECTIVE, as Police Captain Howard. New York, Champion, 1882 — THE GIRL DETECTIVE, as Police Captain Howard. New York, Champion, 1882 — THE MYSTERY OF ONE NIGHT, as Police Captain Howard. New York, Champion, 1882 — YOUNG VIDOCQ, as Police Captain Howard. New York, Champion, 1882.

Sendak, Maurice Bernard — KENNY'S WINDOW. New York, Harper, 1956.

Seredy, Kate — THE GOOD MASTER. New York, Viking, 1935; London, Harrap, 1937.

Serling, Edward Rodman — STORIES FROM THE TWILIGHT ZONE, as Rod Serling. New York, Bantam, 1960.

Serraillier, Ian Lucien — THREE NEW POETS, with others. Billericay (ENG), Grey Walls Press, 1942.

Serviss, Garrett Putman — ASTRONOMY WITH AN OPERA-GLASS. New York, Appleton, 1888.

Seton, Anya — MY THEODOSIA. Boston, Houghton Mifflin, 1941; London, Hodder & Stoughton, 1945.

Seton, Ernest Evan Thompson — A LIST OF ANIMALS IN MANITOBA. Toronto, Oxford Univ., 1886.

Sewell, Anna — BLACK BEAUTY, HIS GROOMS AND COMPANIONS: THE AUTOBIOGRAPHY OF A HORSE, TRANSLATED FROM THE ORIGINAL EQUINE. London, Jarrolds, 1877; New York, Angell, 1878.

Sewell, Helen Moore — A HEAD FOR HAPPY. New York, Macmillan, 1931.

Seymour, Alan — THE ONE DAY OF THE YEAR. London, Souvenir, 1967.

Shannon, Monica — CALIFORNIA FAIRY TALES. New York, Doubleday, and London, Heinemann, 1926.

Shappiro, Herbert Arthur — THE BLACK RIDER. New York, Arcadia, 1941 — THE VALLEY OF DEATH. New York, Arcadia, 1941.

Sharkey, John Michael — THE SECRET MARTIANS, as Jack Sharkey. New York, Ace, 1960 — MURDER, MAESTRO, PLEASE, as Jack Sharkey. New York and London, Abelard Schuman, 1960.

Sharmat, Marjorie Weinman — REX. New York, Harper, 1967.

Sharp, Edith Lambert — NKWALA. Boston, Little Brown, 1958; London, Dent, 1959.

Sharp, Margery — RHODODENDRON PIE. London, Chatto & Windus, and New York, Appleton, 1930.

Shaver, Richard Sharpe — I REMEMBER LEMURIA, AND THE RETURN OF SATHANAS. Evanston (IL), Venture, 1948.

Shaw, Robert — NIGHT WALK, as Bob Shaw. New York, Banner, 1967; London, New English Library, 1970.

Shaw, Felicity — THE HAPPY EXILES. London, Hamish Hamilton, and New York, Harper, 1956.

Shea, Cornelius — LOVE AND LURE; OR, THE HEART OF A "BAD" MAN: A ROMANCE OF ARIZONA. New York, Broadway, 1912: LOOK OUT FOR PAINT. Boston, Baker, 1912.

Sheckley, Robert — UNTOUCHED BY HUMAN HANDS. New York, Ballantine, 1954; London, Joseph, 1955.

Sheldon, Alice Hastings — TEN THOUSAND LIGHT-YEARS FROM HOME, as James Tiptree Jr. London, Eyre Methuen, 1975.

Shellabarger, Samuel — THE DOOR OF DEATH. New York, Century, 1928; London, Methuen, 1929 —

THE CHEVALIER BAYARD: A STUDY IN FADING CHIVALRY. New York, Century, 1928.

Shelley, John Lascola — GUNPOINT! New York, Graphic, 1956; London, Hale, 1959.

Shelley, Noreen — PIGGY GRUNTER'S RED UMBRELLA, NURSERY RHYMES, AT THE FIRE, AT THE CIRCUS, 4 vols. Sydney (AUS), Johnson, 1944.

Shepherd, Donald Lee — DARK EDEN, as Barbara Kevern. New York, Pocket Books, 1973.

Sherriff, Robert Charles — JOURNEY'S END, as R.C. Sherriff, with Vernon Bartlett. London, Gollancz, and New York, Stokes, 1930 — Play version. London, Gollancz, and New York, Brentano's, 1929.

Sherry, Sylvia — STREET OF THE SMALL NIGHT MARKET. London, Cape, 1966; as SECRET OF THE JADE PAVILION, Philadelphia, Lippincott, 1967.

Sherwood, Robert — THE BEST MOVING PICTURES OF 1922-23; WHO'S WHO IN THE MOVIES AND THE YEAR BOOK OF THE AMERICAN SCREEN. 1923.

Shiel, Matthew Phipps — PRINCE ZALESKI, as M.P. Shiel. London, Lane, and Boston, Roberts, 1895.

Shiras, Wilmar House — SLOW DAWNING, as Jane Howes. St. Louis, Herder, 1946.

Shotwell, Louisa Rossiter — THIS IS THE INDIAN AMERICAN, YOUR NEIGHBOR, THE MIGRANT, 3 vols. New York, Friendship Press, 1955-58.

Shrake, Edwin — BLOOD RECKONING. New York, Bantam, 1962.

Silko, Leslie — LAGUNA WOMAN: POEMS. Greenfield Center (NY), Greenfield Review Press, 1974.

Sillitoe, Alan — WITHOUT BEER OR BREAD. London, Outposts, 1957.

Silverberg, Robert — REVOLT ON ALPHA C. New York, Crowell, 1955.

Simak, Clifford Donald — THE CREATOR. Los Angeles, Crawford, 1946.

Simenon, Georges — THE STRANGE CASE OF PETER THE LETT. 1933.

Simms, William Gilmore — MONODY ON THE DEATH OF GEN. CHARLES COTESWORTH PINCKNEY. 1825.

Simon, Roger Lichtenberg — HEIR. New York, Macmillan, 1968.

Simpson, Helen De Guerry — PHILOSOPHIES IN LITTLE. Sydney (AUS), Angus & Robertson, 1921.

Sims, George Frederick Robert — THE SWALLOW LOVERS. London, privately printed, 1942.

Sinclair, Olga Ellen — THE MAN AT THE MANOR. London, Gresham, 1967; New York, Dell, 1972 — GYPSIES. Oxford (ENG), Blackwell, 1967.

Sinclair, Upton — SPRINGTIME AND HARVEST: A ROMANCE. New York, Sinclair Press, 1901; as KING MIDAS. New York and London, Funk & Wagnalls, 1901.

Singer, Isaac Bashevis — THE FAMILY MOSKAT. New York, Knopf, 1950; London, Secker & Warburg, 1966.

Siodmak, Kurt — SCHLUSS IN TONFILMATELIER. Berlin, Scherl, 1930.

Skinner, Burrhus Frederic — THE BEHAVIOR OF ORGANISMS: AN EXPERIMENTAL ANALYSIS, as B.F. Skinner. New York, Appleton, 1938.

Skinner, June O'Grady — O'HOULIHAN'S JEST: A LAMENT FOR THE IRISH, as Rohan O'Grady. New York, Macmillan, and London, Gollancz, 1961.

Sky, Kathleen — BIRTHRIGHT. Toronto, Laser, 1975.

Sladek John Thomas — THE HOUSE THAT FEAR BUILT, as Cassandra Knye, with Thomas M. Disch. New York, Paperback Library, 1966.

Slaughter, Frank Gill — THAT NONE SHOULD DIE. New York, Doubleday, 1941; London, Jarrolds, 1942.

Sleigh, Barbara — CARBONEL. London, Parrish, 1955; Indianapolis, Bobbs Merrill, 1957.

Slesar, Henry — THE GRAY FLANNEL SHROUD. New York, Random, 1959; London, Deutsch, 1960.

Sloane, William Milligan, III — BACK HOME: A GHOST PLAY. New York, Longman, 1931.

Slobodkin, Louis — THE FRIENDLY ANIMALS. New York, Vanguard, 1944 — MAGIC MICHAEL. New York, Macmillan, 1944.

Slobodkina, Esphyr — CAPS FOR SALE. New York, Scott, 1940; Kingswood (ENG), World's Work, 1959.

Smith, Cicely Fox — SONGS OF GREATER BRITAIN AND OTHER POEMS. London, Simpkin, 1899 — THE FOREMOST TRAIL, London, Sampson Low, 1899.

Smith, Clark Ashton — THE STAR-TREADER AND OTHER POEMS. San Francisco, Robertson, 1912.

Smith, Doris Edna Elliott — STAR TO MY BARQUE. London, Ward Lock, 1964.

Smith, Edward Elmer — THE SKYLARK OF SPACE, as E.E. Smith, with Mrs. Lee Hawkins Garby. Providence (RI), Buffalo, 1946; London, Digit, 1959.

Smith, Lady Eleanor Furneaux — RED WAGON: A STUDY OF THE TOBER. London, Gollancz, and Indianapolis, Bobbs Merrill, 1930.

Smith, Emma — MAIDENS' TRIP. London, Putnam, 1948.

Smith, Ernest Bramah — ENGLISH FARMING AND WHY I TURNED IT UP. London, 1894.

Smith, Evelyn E. — THE BUILDING BOOK. New York, Howell Soskin, 1947.

Smith, George Henry — 1976: YEAR OF TERROR. New York, Epic, 1961 — SCOURGE OF THE BLOOD CULT. New York, Epic, 1976 — THE COMING OF THE RATS. New York, Pike, 1961; London, Digit, 1964.

Smith, George Oliver — VENUS EQUILALATERAL. Philadelphia, Prime Press, 1947; London, Futura, 1975.

Smith, Helen Zenna — JUST JANE, as Evadne Price. London, Hamilton, 1928.

Smith, Joan — AN AFFAIR OF THE HEART. New York, Fawcett, 1977 — ESCAPADE. New York, Fawcett, 1977.

Smith, Sarah — THE STORY OF OLD — LONDON, as Hesba Stretton. London, Religious Tract Society, 1869; New York, Whittaker, 1886.

Smith, William Jay — POEMS. Pawlet (VT), Banyan Press, 1947.

Snedeker, Caroline Dale — THE COWARD OF THERMOPYLAE. New York, Doubleday, 1911; as THE SPARTAN, London, Hodder & Stoughton, 1913.

Snow, Charles Horace — DUST OF GOLD. London, Methuen, 1928

Snyder, Zilpha Keatley — SEASON OF PONIES. New York, Atheneum, 1964.

Sobol, Donald J. — THE DOUBLE QUEST. New York, Watts, 1957.

Stolz, Mary Slattery — TO TELL YOUR LOVE. New York, Harper, 1950.

Stong, Philip Duffield — STATE FAIR. New York, Century, and London, Barker, 1932.

Storey, Margaret — KATE AND THE FAMILY TREE. London, Bodley Head, 1965; as THE FAMILY TREE, Nashville (TN), Nelson, 1973.

Storr, Catherine — INGEBORG AND RUTHY. London, Harrap, 1940.

Stout, Rex Todhunter — FER-DE-LANCE. New York, Farrar & Rinehart, 1934; London, Cassell, 1935.

Stover, Leon Eugene — STONEHENGE, with Harry Harrison. New York, Scribner, and London, Davies, 1972 — LA SCIENCE-FICTION AMERICAINE: ESSAI D'ANTHROPOLOGIE CULTURELLE. Paris, Aubier Montaigne, 1972.

Straight, Michael Whitney — MAKE THIS THE LAST WAR: THE FUTURE OF THE UNITED NATIONS. New York, Harcourt Brace, and London, Allen & Unwin, 1943.

Straker, John Foster — POSTMAN'S KNOCK. London, Harrap, 1954.

Stratton, Rebecca — THE ROSS INHERITANCE. London, Mills New York Boon, 1969 — GOOD MORNING, DOCTOR HOUSTON. London, Mills & Boon, 1969; Toronto, Harlequin, 1970 — THE SILVER FISHES. London, Mills & Boon, 1969; Toronto, Harlequin, 1970 — A WIFE FOR ANDREW. London, Mills & Boon, 1969; Toronto, Harlequin, 1970. All as Lucy Gillen.

Streatfeild, Noel — THE WHICHARTS. London, Heinemann, 1931; New York, Coward McCann, 1932.

Street, Cecil John Charles — WITH THE GUNS, as F.O.O. London, Nash, 1916.

Stribling, Theodore Sigismund — THE CRUISE OF THE DRY DOCK. Chicago, Reilly & Britton, 1917.

Strong, Leonard Alfred George — DALLINGTON RHYMES, as L.A.G. Strong. Oxford (ENG), Holywell, 1919.

Stubbs, Jean — THE ROSE-GROWER. London, Macmillan, 1962; New York, St. Martin's, 1963.

Stucley, Elizabeth Florence — POLLYCON: A BOOK FOR THE YOUNG ECONOMIST. Oxford (ENG), Blackwell, 1933.

Sublette, Clifford MacClellan — THE SCARLET COCKEREL. Boston, Atlantic Monthly Press, 1925; London, Hodder New York Stoughton, 1926.

Sudbery, Rodie — THE HOUSE IN THE WOOD. London, Deutsch, 1968; as A SOUND OF CRYING, New York, McCall, 1970.

Suddaby, Donald — SCARLET-DRAGON: A LITTLE CHINESE PHANTASY. Blackburn (ENG), privately printed, 1923.

Summers, Ethel Snelson — NEW ZEALAND INHERITANCE, as Essie Summers. London, Mills & Boon, 1957; as HEATHERLEIGH, Toronto, Harlequin, 1963.

Summerton, Margaret — THE SUNSET HOUR. London, Hodder & Stoughton, 1957.

Sutcliffe, Rosemary — THE ARMOURER'S HOUSE. London and New York, Oxford Univ., 1951.

Sutherland, Efua Theodora — PLAYTIME IN AFRICA. London, Brown Knight & Truscott, 1960; New York, Atheneum, 1962.

Sutton, Evelyn Mary — MY CAT LIKES TO HIDE IN BOXES. London, Hamish Hamilton, 1973; New York, Parents Magazine, 1974.

Sutton, Jefferson H. — FIRST ON THE MOON, as Jeff Sutton. New York, Ace, 1958.

Sutton, Jefferson H. And Eugenia Geneva Sutton — THE RIVER, as Jeff and Jean Sutton. New York, Belmont, 1966.

Swan, Annie S. — UPS AND DOWNS: A FAMILY CHRONICLE. London, Charing Cross, 1878.

Swarthout, Glendon Fred — WILLOW RUN. New York, Crowell, 1943.

Swatridge, Irene Maude — WELL PLAYED, JULIANA! as Irene Mossop. London, 1928.

Syme, Neville Ronald — FULL FATHOM FIVE. London, Lunn, 1946.

Symonds, John — WILLIAM WASTE. London, Low & Marston, 1947.

Symons, Dorothy Geraldine — ALL SOULS. London and New York, Longman, 1950.

Symons, Julian Gustave — CONFUSIONS ABOUT X. London, Fortune Press, 1939.

Szilard, Leo — THE VOICE OF THE DOLPHINS AND OTHER STORIES. New York, Simon & Schuster, and London, Gollancz, 1961.

T

Tarkington, Booth — THE GENTLEMAN FROM INDIANA. 1899.

Tate, Allen — POETRY: MR. POPE AND OTHER POEMS. 1928.

Tate, Joan — JENNY. London, Heinemann, 1964.

Tate, Peter — THE THINKING SEAT. New York, Doubleday, 1969; London, Faber, 1970.

Tattersall, Honor Jill — A SUMMER'S CLOUD. London, Collins, 1965.

Taylor, Bayard — XIMENA; OR, THE BATTLE OF THE SIERRA MORENA AND OTHER POEMS. 1844.

Taylor, Lois Dwight — SPANIARD'S MARK, as Anne Eliot. New York, 1933.

Taylor, Phoebe Atwood — THE CAPE COD MYSTERY. Indianapolis, Bobbs Merrill, 1931.

Taylor, Robert Lewis — ADRIFT IN A BONEYARD. New York, Doubleday, 1947.

Taylor, Sydney Brenner — ALL-OF-A-KIND FAMILY. Chicago, Wilcox & Follett, 1951; London, Blackie, 1961.

Taylor, Theodore — THE MAGNIFICENT MITSCHER. New York, Norton, 1954.

Teasdale, Sara — SONNETS TO DUSE AND OTHER POEMS. 1907.

Telfair, Richard — WYOMING JONES. New York, Fawcett, 1958; London, Fawcett, 1959.

Temple, William Frederick — FOUR-SIDED TRIANGLE. London, Long, 1949; New York, Fell, 1951.

Tennant, Emma Christina — THE COLOUR OF RAIN, as Catherine Aydy. London, Weidenfeld & Nicolson, 1964.

Tevis, Walter Stone — THE HUSTLER. New York, Harper, 1959; London, Joseph, 1960.

Thane, Elswyth — RIDERS OF THE WIND. New York, Stokes, 1926; London, Murray, 1928.

Thayer, Emma Redington — ALICE AND THE WONDERLAND PEOPLE, as Lee Thayer. New York, Bungalow Book and Toy, 1914.

Thiele, Colin Milton — PROGRESS TO DENIAL. Adelaide (AUS), Jindyworobak, 1945 — SPLINTERS AND SHARDS, Adelaide, Jindyworobak, 1945.

Thimblethorpe, June Sylvia — THE SCANDALOUS LADY ROBIN, as Sylvia Thorpe. London, Hutchinson, 1950; New York, Fawcett, 1975.

Thomas, Donald Michael — PERSONAL AND POSSESSIVE, as D.M. Thomas. London, Outposts, 1964.

Thomas, Ross — THE COLD WAR SWAP. New York, Morrow, 1966; as SPY IN THE VODKA, London, Hodder & Stoughton, 1967.

Thomason, John William Jr. — FIX BAYONETS! New York, Scribner, 1926.

Thompson, Edward Anthony — CROWDED AND DANGEROUS, as Anthony Lejeune. London, Macdonald, 1959.

Thompson, George Selden — THE DOG THAT COULD SWIM UNDER WATER, as George Selden. New York, Viking, 1956.

Thompson, Thomas — RANGE DRIFTER. New York, Doubleday, 1949; London, Hodder & Stoughton, 1950.

Thomson, Basil Home — THE DIVERSIONS OF A PRIME MINISTER. Edinburgh, Blackwood, 1894.

Thomson, June — NOT ONE OF US. New York, Harper, 1971; London, Constable, 1972.

Thoreau, Henry David — A WEEK ON THE CONCORD AND MERRIMACK RIVERS. 1849.

Thorpe, Kay — DEVON INTERLUDE. London, Mills & Boon, 1968; Toronto, Harlequin, 1969 — THE LAST OF THE MALLORYS. London, Mills & Boon, and Toronto, Harlequin, 1968 — OPPORTUNE MARRIAGE. London, Mills & Boon, 1968; Toronto, Harlequin, 1975.

Tourgee, Albion — THE VETERAN AND HIS PIPE. 1886.

Thurber, James Grover — IS SEX NECESSARY? OR, WHY YOU FEEL THE WAY YOU DO, with E.B. White. New York, Harper, 1929; London, Heinemann, 1930.

Thurston, Robert Donald — ALICIA II. New York, Putnam, 1978 — BATTLESTAR, with Glen A. Larson. New York, Berkley, and London, Futura, 1978.

Thwaite, Ann — THE YOUNG TRAVELLERS IN JAPAN. London, Phoenix, 1958.

Tidyman, Ernest — FLOWER POWER. New York, Paperback Library, 1968. THE ANZIO DEATH TRAP, New York, Belmont, 1968.

Tillett, Dorothy Stockbridge — PATHS OF JUNE, as Dorothy Stockbridge. New York, Dutton, 1920.

Tippette, Giles — THE BANK ROBBER. New York, Macmillan, 1970.

Tirbutt, Honoria — IN LOVING MEMORY, as Emma Page. London, Collins, 1970.

Titus, Eve — ANATOLE. New York, McGraw Hill, 1956; London, Lane, 1957.

Todd, Barbara Euphan — THE 'NORMOUS SATURDAY FAIRY BOOK, with Marjory Royce and Moira Meighn. London, Paul, 1924.

Todd, Herbert Eatton — BOBBY BREWSTER AND THE WINKERS' CLUB. Leicester (ENG), Ward, 1949.

Tolbert, Frank Xavier, Sr. — NIEMAN-MARCUS: THE STORY OF THE PROUD DALLAS STORE. New York, Holt, 1953.

Tolkien, John Ronald Reuel — A MIDDLE ENGLISH VOCABULARY, as J.R.R. Tolkien. London, and New York, Oxford Univ., 1922.

Tomalin, Ruth — THRENODY FOR DORMICE. London, Fortune Press, 1947.

Tompkins, Walker Allison — OZAR, THE AZTEC. London, Gramol, 1935.

Torday, Ursula — THE BALLAD-MAKER OF PARIS. London, 1935.

Townsend, John Rowe — GUMBLE'S YARD. London, Hutchinson, 1961; as TROUBLE IN THE JUNGLE, Philadelphia, Lippincott, 1969.

Train, Arthur Cheney — MCALLISTER AND HIS DOUBLE. New York, Scribner, and London, Newnes, 1905.

Tranter, Nigel Godwin — THE FORTALICES AND EARLY MANSIONS OF SOUTHERN SCOTLAND 1400-1650. Edinburgh, Moray Press, 1935.

Travers, Pamela Lyndon — MARY POPPINS. London, Howe, and New York, Reynal & Hitchcock, 1934.

Treadgold, Mary — WE COULDN'T LEAVE DINAH. London, Cape, 1941; as LEFT TILL CALLED FOR, New York, Doubleday, 1941.

Trease, Robert Geoffrey — THE SUPREME PRIZE AND OTHER POEMS. London, Stockwell, 1926.

Treece, Henry — 38 POEMS. London, Fortune Press, 1940.

Trench, John Chenevix — DOCKEN DEAD. London, Macdonald, 1953; New York, Macmillan, 1954.

Tresselt, Alvin — RAIN DROP SPLASH. New York, Lothrop, 1946.

Trevor, Elleston — INTO THE HAPPY GLADE, as T. Dudley-Smith. London, Swan, 1943. — OVER THE WALL, as T. Dudley-Smith, London, Swan, 1943 — ANIMAL LIFE STORIES: RIPPLESWIM THE OTTER, SCAMPER-FOOT THE PINE MARTEN, SHADOW THE FOX, London, Swan, 3 vols., 1943-45.

Trevor, Lucy Meriol — THE FOREST AND THE KINGDOM. London, Faber, 1949.

Trimble, Louis Preston — SPORTS OF THE WORLD. Los Angeles, Golden West, 1939.

Tripp, Miles Barton — FAITH IS A WINDSOCK. London, Davies, 1952.

Tubb, Edwin Charles — SATURN PATROL, as King Lang. London, Warren, 1951 — PLANETFALL, as Gill Hunt. London, Warren, 1951.

Tucker, Arthur Wilson "Bob" — THE CHINESE DOLL, as Wilson Tucker. New York, Rinehart, 1946; London, Cassell, 1948.

Tudor, Tasha — PUMPKIN MOONSHINE. New York and London, Oxford Univ., 1938.

Tunis, John Roberts — $PORT, HEROES, AND HYSTERICS. New York, Day, 1928.

Turkle, Brinton — OBADIAH THE BOLD. New York, Viking, 1965.

Turner, Ethel Sybil — SEVEN LITTLE AUSTRALIANS. London, Ward Lock, 1894.; Philadelphia, McKay, 1904.

Turner, George Reginald — YOUNG MAN OF TALENT. London, Cassell, 1959; as SCOBIE. New York, Simon & Schuster, 1959.

Turner, Philip William — THE CHRISTMAS STORY: A CAROL SERVICE FOR CHILDREN. London, Church Information Office, 1964.

Tuttle, Lisa — WINDHAVEN, with George R.R. Martin. New York, Simon & Schuster, 1980.

Tuttle, Wilbur Coleman — REDDY BRANT, HIS ADVENTURES. New York, Century, 1920.

Tyre, Nedra — RED WINE FIRST. New York, Simon & Schuster, 1947.

U

Ude, Wayne — BUFFALO AND OTHER STORIES. Amherst (MA), Lynx House, 1979.

Uchida, Yoshiko — THE DANCING KETTLE AND OTHER JAPANESE FOLK TALES. New York, Harcourt Brace, 1949.

Udry, Janice May — LITTLE BEAR AND THE BEAUTIFUL KITE. Racine (WI), Whitman, 1955.

Uhnak, Dorothy — POLICEWOMAN: A YOUNG WOMAN'S INITIATION INTO THE REALITIES OF JUSTICE. New York, Simon & Schuster, 1964.

Ungerer, Jean Thomas — THE MELLOPS GO FLYING, as Tomi Ungerer. New York, Harper, 1957; London, Methuen, 1957 — THE MELLOPS GO DIVING FOR TREASURE. New York, Harper, 1957.

Unwin, David Storr — RICK AFIRE!, as David Severn. London, Lane, 1942.

Unwin, Nora Spicer — ROUND THE YEAR: VERSES AND PICTURES. London, Chatto & Windus, 1939; New York, Holiday House, 1940.

Upchurch, Boyd Bradfield — THE LAST STARSHIP FROM EARTH, as John Boyd. New York, Weybright & Talley, 1965; London, Gollancz, 1969 — THE SLAVE STEALER, as John Boyd. New York, Weybright & Talley, 1968; London, Jenkins, 1969.

Upfield, Arthur William — THE HOUSE OF CAIN. London, Hutchinson, 1928; New York, Dorrance, 1929.

Upton, Bertha Hudson — THE ADVENTURES OF TWO DUTCH DOLLS -- AND A GOLLIWOGG. London and New York, Longman, 1895.

Uttley, Alice Jane — THE SQUIRREL, THE HARE, AND THE LITTLE GREY RABBIT, as Alison Uttley. London, Heinemann, 1929.

V

Vaizey, Jessie Bell — A ROSE-COLOURED THREAD, as Mrs. George de Horne Vaizey. London, Bowden, 1898.

Van De Wetering, Janwillem — OUTSIDER IN AMSTERDAM. 1974.

Van Gulik, Robert H. — DEE GOONG AN. 1949.

Van Scyoc, Sydney Joyce — SALTFLOWER. New York, Avon, 1971.

Van Siller, Hilda — ECHO OF A BOMB, as Van Siller. New York, Doubleday, 1943; London, Jarrolds, 1944.

Van Slyke, Helen Lenore — THE RICH AND THE RIGHTEOUS. New York, Doubleday, 1971; London, Cassell, 1972.

Van Stockum, Hilda — A DAY ON SKATES. New York and London, Harper, 1934.

Van Vechten, Carl — FINE OLD ENGLISH DITTIES, WITH MUSIC. 1904.

Van Vogt, Alfred Elton — SLAN, as A.E. van Vogt. Sauk City (WI), Arkham House, 1946; London, Weidenfeld & Nicolson, 1953.

Vance, John Holbrook — THE DYING EARTH, as Jack Vance. New York, Curl, 1950; London, Mayfloer, 1972.

Vance, Louis Joseph — TERENCE O'ROURKE, GENTLEMAN ADVENTURER. New York, Wessels, 1905; London, Richards, 1906.

Vance, William E. — THE BRANDED LAWMAN. New York, Ace, 1952.

Varley, John — THE OPHIUCHI HOTLINE. New York, Dial, 1977; London, Sidgwick & Jackson, 1978.

Venables, Terry — HAZELL PLAYS SOLOMON, as P.B. Yuill, with Gordon Williams. London, Macmillan, 1975; New York, Walker, 1975.

Verney, John — VERNEY ABROAD. London, Collins, 1954.

Vernon, Roger Lee — THE SPACE FRONTIER. New York, New American Library, 1955.

Verrill, Alpheus Hyatt — GASOLENE ENGINES: THEIR OPERATION, USE , AND CARE, as A. Hyatt Verrill. New York, Henley, 1912 — KNOTS, SPLICES, AND ROPE WORK, as A. Hyatt Verrill. New York, Henley, 1912.

Vickers, Roy C. — LORD ROBERTS: THE STORY OF HIS LIFE. London, Pearson, 1914.

Vidal, Eugene Luther Gore — WILLIWAW. New York, Dutton, 1946; London, Panther, 1965.

Vinge, Joan Carol Dennison — THE OUTCASTS OF HEAVEN BELT. New York, New American Library, 1978 — FIRESHIP. New York, Dell, 1978; London, Sidgwick & Jjackson, 1981.

Vinge, Vernor Steffen — GRIMM'S WORLD. New York, Berkley, 1976; London, Hamlyn, 1978 — THE WITLING. New York, DAW, and London, Dobson, 1976.

Vining, Elizabeth Gray — MEREDITHS' ANN. New York, Doubleday, and London, Heinemann, 1927.

Vinson, Rex Thomas — LIGHT A LAST CANDLE, as Vincent King. New York, Ballantine, 1969; London, Rapp & Whiting, 1970.

Viorst, Judith Stahl — PROJECTS: SPACE. New York, Washington Square Press, 1962.

Vipont, Elfrida — QUAKERISM: AN INTERNATIONAL WAY OF LIFE, as E.V. Foulds. Manchester (ENG), 1930 Committee, 1930.

Von Arnim, Mary Annette, Countess — ELIZABETH AND HER GERMAN GARDEN, as Elizabeth. London and New York, 1898.

Vonnegut, Kurt, Jr. — PLAYER PIANO. New York, Scribner, 1952; London, Macmillan, 1953.

Vulliamy, Colwyn Edward — CHARLES KINGSLEY AND CHRISTIAN SOCIALISM. London, Fabian Society, 1914.

W

Waber, Bernard — LORENZO. Boston, Houghton Mifflin, 1961.

Wade, Robert — DEADLY WEAPON, as Wade Miller, with Bill Miller. New York, Farrar & Straus, 1946; London, Sampson Low, 1947.

Wagoner, David Russell — DRY SUN, DRY WIND. Bloomington (IN), Indiana Univ., 1953.

Wahl, Jan — PLEASANT FIELDMOUSE. New York, Harper, 1964; Kingswood (ENG), World's Work, 1969 — THE BEAST BOOK, New York, Harper, 1964.

Wahloo, Per And Maj Sjowall — ROSEANNA. 1967.

Wainwright, John — DEATH IN A SLEEPING CITY. London, Collins, 1965.

Waldo, Edward Hamilton — "IT," as Theodore Sturgeon. Philadelphia, Prime Press, 1948 — WITHOUT SORCERY, as Theodore Sturgeon. Philadelphia, Prime Press, 1948.

Walker, David Harry — THE STORM AND THE SILENCE. Boston, Houghton Mifflin, 1949; London, Cape, 1950.

Wall, John W. — RINGSTONES AND OTHER CURIOUS TALES, as Sarban. London, Davies, and New York, Coward McCann, 1951.

Wallace, Floyd — ADDRESS: CENTAURI. New York, Gnome, 1955.

Wallace, Richard Horatio Edgar — THE MISSION THAT FAILED! A TALE OF THE RAID AND OTHER POEMS, as Edgar Wallace. Cape Town (SAFR), Maskew Miller, 1898.

Walling, Robert Alfred John — FLAUNTING MOLL AND OTHER STORIES. London, Harper, 1898.

Wallis, George C. — THE CHILDREN OF THE SPHINX, as G.C. Wallis. London, Simpkin Marshall, 1924.

Walsh, James Morgan — THE BRETHREN OF THE COMPASS, as J.M. Walsh, with E.J. Blythe. London, Jarrolds, 1925 — THE WHITE MASK, as J. M. Walsh. London, Hamilton, 1925; New York, Doran, 1927.

Walsh, Sheila — THE GOLDEN SONGBIRD. London, Hurst & Blackett, and New York, New American Library, 1975.

Walsh, Thomas Francis Morgan — NIGHTMARE IN MANHATTAN. Boston, Little Brown, 1950; London, Hamish Hamilton, 1951.

Wambaugh, Joseph Aloysius Jr. — THE NEW CENTURIONS. Boston, Little Brown, 1970; London, Joseph, 1971.

Wandrei, Donald — ECSTASY AND OTHER POEMS. Athol (MA), Cook, 1928.

Ward, Arthur Sarsfield — PAUSE!, anonymously. London, Greening, 1910.

Ward-Thomas, Evelyn Bridget Patricia — IMPERIAL HIGHNESS, as Evelyn Anthony. London, 1953.

Warren, Charles Marquis — ONLY THE VALIANT. New York, Macmillan, 1943; London, Corgi, 1953.

Warren, Robert Penn — JOHN BROWN, THE MAKING OF A MARTYR. 1929.

Warriner, Thurman — METHOD IN HIS MURDER. London, Hodder & Stoughton, and New York, Macmillan, 1950.

Waterloo, Stanley — HOW IT LOOKS. New York, Brentano's, 1888.

Waters, Frank Joseph — FEVER PITCH. New York, Liveright, 1930.

Watkins, William Jon — FIVE POEMS. Chula Vista (CA), Word Press, 1968.

Watkins-Pitchford, Denys James — WILD LONE. London, Eyre & Spottiswoode, and New York, Scribner, 1938.

Watson, Clyde — FATHER FOX'S PENNYRHYMES. New York, Crowell, 1971.

Watson, Colin — COFFIN, SCARCELY USED. London, Eyre & Spottiswoode, 1958; New York, Putnam, 1967.

Watson, Ian — JAPAN: A CAT'S EYE VIEW. Osaka, Bunken, 1969.

Watson, Julia — THE LOVECHILD, as Julia Fitzgerald. London, 1967.

Watts, Peter Christopher — OUT OF YESTERDAY. London, Hodder & Stoughton, 1950.

Waugh, Hillary Baldwin — MADAM WILL NOT DINE TONIGHT. New York, Coward McCann, 1947; London, Boardman, 1949; as IF I LIVE TO DINE, Hasbrouck Heights (NJ), Graphic, 1949.

Way, Margaret — BLAZE OF SILK. London, Mills & Boon, 1970; Toronto, Harlequin, 1971 — KING COUNTRY. London, Mills & Boon, 1970; Toronto, Harlequin, 1971 — THE TIME OF THE JACARANDA. London, Mills & Boon, and Toronto, Harlequin, 1970.

Wayne, Anne Jenifer — THIS IS THE LAW: STORIES OF WRONGDOERS BY FAULT OR FOLLY. London, Sylvan Press, 1948.

Webb, Jack — THE BIG SIN. New York, Rinehart, 1952; London, Boardman, 1953. HIGH MESA, as Tex Grady, New York, Dutton, 1952; London, Foulsham, 1954.

Webb, Jean Francis — LOVE THEY MUST. New York, Washburn, 1933.

Webster, Alice Jane Chandler — WHEN PATTY WENT TO COLLEGE, as Jean Webster. New York, Century, 1903; as PATTY AND PRISCILLA. London, Hodder & Stoughton, 1915.

Weinbaum, Stanley Grauman — DAWN OF FLAME. New York, Ruppert, 1936.

Weir, Rosemary — THE SECRET JOURNEY. London, Parrish, 1957.

Welch, James — RIDING THE EARTHBOY 40. Cleveland, World, 1971.

Wellman, Manly Wade — THE INVADING ASTEROID. New York, Stellar, 1932.

Wellman, Paul Iselin — BRONCHO APACHE. New York and London, Macmillan, 1936.

Wells, Carolyn — THE STORY OF BETTY. New York, Century, 1899.

Wells, Herbert George — TEXT-BOOK OF BIOLOGY, as H.G. Wells, 2 vols. London, Clive, 1893 — HONOURS PHYSIOGRAPHY, as H. G. Wells, with R.A. Gregory. London, Hughes, 1893.

Wersba, Barbara — THE BOY WHO LOVED THE SEA. New York, Coward McCann, 1961.

West, Joyce Tarlton — SHEEP KINGS. Wellington (NZ), Tombs, 1936.

West, Kingsley — A TIME FOR VENGEANCE. New York, Doubleday, 1961.

West, Wallace George — BETTY BOOP IN SNOW-WHITE. Racine (WI), Whitman, 1934 — ALICE IN WONDERLAND. Racine, Whitman, 1934 — PARAMOUNT NEWSREEL MEN WITH ADMIRAL BYRD IN LITTLE AMERICA. Racine, Whitman, 1934.

Westall, Robert — THE MACHINE-GUNNERS. London, Macmillan, 1975; New York, Morrow, 1976.

Westerman, Percy Francis — A LAD OF GRIT. London, Blackie, 1908.

Westlake, Donald Edwin — THE MERCENARIES. New York, Random, 1960; London, Boardman, 1961.

Weston, Carolyn — TORMENTED. New York, Surrey House, 1956.

Westwood, Gwen — MONKEY BUSINESS. London, Hamish Hamilton, 1965.

Wharton, Edith — THE DECORATION OF HOUSES (with Ogden Codman, Jr.). 1897.

White, Ethel Lina — THE WISH-BONE. London, Ward Lock, 1927.

White, James — THE SECRET VISITOR. New York, Ace, 1957; London, Digit, 1961.

White, Jon Ewbank Manchip — DRAGON AND OTHER POEMS. London, Fortune Press, 1943.

White, Lionel — THE SNATCHERS. New York, Fawcett, 1953; London, Miller, 1958.

White, Stewart Edward — THE CLAIM JUMPERS: A ROMANCE. New York, Appleton, 1901; London, Hodder & Stoughton, 1905.

White, Theodore Edwin — INVASION FROM 2500, as Norman Edwards, with Terry Carr. Derby (CT), Monarch, 1964.

White, Terence Hanbury — LOVED HELEN AND OTHER POEMS, as T.H. White. London, Chatto & Windus, and New York, Viking, 1929 — THE GREEN BAY TREE; OR, THE WICKED MAN TOUCHES WOOD, as T.H. White. Cambridge (ENG), Heffer, 1929.

White, William Anthony Parker — THE CASE OF THE SEVEN OF CALVARY, as Anthony Boucher. New York, Simon & Schuster, and London, Hamish Hamilton, 1937.

Whitechurch, Victor Lorenzo — THE COURSE OF JUSTICE. London, Isbister, 1903.

Whitfield, Raoul — GREEN ICE. New York, Knopf, 1930; as THE GREEN ICE MURDERS, New York, Avon, 1947. WINGS OF GOLD, New York, Knopf, 1930.

Whitman, Walt — FRANKLIN EVANS. 1842.

Whitney, Phyliss Ayame — A PLACE FOR ANN. Boston, Houghton Mifflin, 1941.

Whitson, John Harvey — CAPTAIN CACTUS. New York, Beadle & Adams, 1888.

Whittier, John Greenleaf — LEGENDS OF NEW-ENGLAND. 1831.

Whittington, Harry — VENGEANCE VALLEY. New York, Phoenix, 1945; London, Ward Lock, 1947.

Wibberley, Leonard Patrick O'Connor — THE LOST HARPOONER, as Patrick O'Connor. New York, Washburn, 1947; London, Harrap, 1959.

Wiegand, William George — AT LAST, MR. TOLLIVER. New York, Rinehart, 1950; London, Hodder & Stoughton, New York 1951.

Wier, Ester Alberti — THE ANSWER BOOK ON NAVAL SOCIAL CUSTOMS AND AIR FORCE SOCIAL CUSTOMS, with Dorothy Hickey, 2 vols. Harrisburg, Military Services Publishing, 1956-57.

Wiese, Kurt — KAROO THE KANGAROO. New York, Coward McCann, 1929 — THE CHINESE INK STICK. New York, Doubleday, 1929.

Wiggin, Kate Douglas — THE STORY OF PATSY: A REMINISCENCE. San Francisco, Murdock, 1883; London, Gay & Bird, 1889.

Wilcox, Collin — THE BLACK DOOR. New York, Dodd Mead, 1967; London, Cassell, 1968.

Wilder, Laura Ingalls — LITTLE HOUSE IN THE BIG WOODS. New York, Harper, 1932; London, Methuen, 1956.

Wilder, Thornton — THE CABALA. 1926.

Wilhelm, Kate — THE MILE-LONG SPACESHIP. New York, Berkley, 1963; as ANDOVER AND THE ANDROID. London, Dobson, 1966 — MORE BITTER THAN DEATH. New York, Simon & Schuster, 1963; London, Hale, 1965.

Wilkinson, Anne Cochran Boyd — COUNTERPOINT TO SLEEP. Montreal, First Statement Press, 1951.

Willard, Barbara — LOVE IN AMBUSH, with Elizabeth Helen Devas. London, Howe, 1930.

Williams, Charles — HILL GIRL. New York, Fawcett, 1951; London, Red Seal, 1958.

Williams, Claudette — SPRING GAMBIT. New York, Fawcett, 1976.

Williams, Dorothy Jeanne — TAME THE WILD STALLION, as J.R. Williams. Englewood Cliffs, Prentice Hall, 1957; Kingswood (ENG), World's Work, 1958.

Williams, George Valentine — WITH OUR ARMY IN FLANDERS. London, Arnold, 1915.

Williams, Gordon — THE LAST DAY OF LINCOLN CHARLES. London, Secker & Warburg, 1965; New York, Stein & Day, 1966.

Williams, Jay — THE STOLEN ORACLE. New York, Oxford Univ., 1943.

Williams, John Alfred — THE ANGRY ONES. New York, Ace, 1960.

Williams, John Edward — NOTHING BUT THE NIGHT. Denver, Swallow, 1948.

Williams, Robert Moore — THE CHAOS FIGHTERS. New York, Ace, 1955 — CONQUEST OF THE SPACE SEA. New York, Ace, 1955.

Williams, Ursula Moray — JEAN-PIERRE. London, Black, 1931.

Williams, William Carlos — POEMS. 1909.

Williamson, Alice Muriel — THE BARN STORMERS, BEING THE TRAGICAL SIDE OF A COMEDY, as Mrs. Harcourt Williamson. New York, Stokes, 1897.

Williamson, Charles Norris — MEMOIRS OF THE LIFE AND WRITINGS OF THOMAS CARLYLE, as C.N. Williamson, with Richard Herne Shepherd. London, Allen, 1881.

Williamson, C.N. and A.M. — THE LIGHTNING CONDUCTOR: THE STRANGE ADVENTURES OF A MOTOR-CAR. London, Methuen, 1902; New York, Holt, 1903.

Williamson, John Stewart — THE GIRL FROM MARS, as Jack Williamson, with Miles J. Breuer. New York, Stellar, 1929.

Willis, Edward Henry — FIGHTING YOUTH OF RUSSIA, as Ted Willis. London, Russia Today Society, 1942.

Willis, Nathaniel Parker — SKETCHES. 1827.

Wills, Maitland Cecil Melville — AUTHOR IN DISTRESS. London, Heritage, 1934; as NUMBER 18, London, Lane, 1934.

Wilson, Barbara Ker — SCOTTISH FOLK TALES AND LEGENDS. London, Oxford Univ., and New York, Walck, 1954.

Wilson, Colin Henry — THE OUTSIDER. London, Gollancz, and Boston, Houghton Mifflin, 1956.

Wilson, Edmund — THE UNDERTAKER'S GARLAND (with John Peale Bishop). 1922.

Wilson, Harry Leon — ZIGZAG TALES FROM THE EAST TO THE WEST. New York, Keppler & Schwarzmann, 1894.

Wilson, John Anthony Burgess — TIME FOR A TIGER, as Anthony Burgess. London, Heinemann, 1956.

Wilson, Joyce Muriel — WILD CAT ISLAND, as Joyce Stranger. London, Methuen, 1961.

Wilson, Richard — THE GIRLS FROM PLANET 5. New York, Ballantine, 1955; London, Hale, 1968.

Wilson, Robert Anton — PLAYBOY'S BOOK OF FORBIDDEN WORDS. Chicago, Playboy Press, 1972.

Wilson, Woodrow — CONGRESSIONAL GOVERNMENT. 1885.

Winsor, Kathleen — FOREVER AMBER. New York, Macmillan, 1944; London, Macdonald, 1945.

Winsper, Violet — LUCIFER'S ANGEL. London, Mills & Boon, and Toronto, Harlequin, 1961 — WIFE WITHOUT KISSES. London, Mills & Boon, 1961; Toronto, Harleqion, 1973.

Winston, Daoma — TORMENTED LOVERS. Derby (CT), Monarch, 1962.

Winther, Sophus Keith — THE REALISTIC WAR NOVEL. Seattle, Univ. of Washington, 1930.

Wister, Owen — THE NEW SWISS FAMILY ROBINSON. Cambridge (MA), Sever, 1882.

Witting, Clifford — MURDER IN BLUE. London, Hodder & Stoughton, and New York, Scribner, 1937.

Wodhams, Jack — THE AUTHENTIC TOUCH. New York, Curtis, 1971.

Wojciechowska, Maia Teresa — MARKET DAY FOR TI ANDRE. New York, Viking, 1952.

Wolf, Gary K. — KILLERBOWL. New York, Doubleday, 1975; London, Sphere, 1976.

Wolfe, Bernard — HOW TO GET A JOB IN THE AIRCRAFT INDUSTRY. Mount Vernon (NY), Wallach, 1943.

Wolfe, Gene Rodman — OPERATION ARES. New York, Berkley, 1970; London, Dobson, 1977.

Wolfe, Thomas — LOOK HOMEWARD, ANGEL: A STORY OF THE BURIED LIFE. 1929.

Wollheim, Donald Allen — THE SECRET OF SATURN'S RINGS, THE MARTIAN MOONS, THE NINTH PLANET, 3 vols. Philadelphia, Winston, 1954-59.

Wood, Mrs. Henry — EAST LYNNE. 1861.

Wood, Edgar Allardyce — THE MAGPIE MENACE, as Kerry Wood. Red Deer (CAN), Kerry Wood, 1936.

Wood, Lorna — THE CRUMB-SNATCHERS. London, Cape, 1933.

Woodberry, George Edward — A HISTORY OF WOODENGRAVING. 1883.

Woodiwiss, Kathleen E. — THE FLAME AND THE FLOWER. New York, Avon, 1972; London, Futura, 1975.

Woods, Helen — A CHARMED CIRCLE, as Helen Ferguson. London, Cape, 1929.

Woolf, Douglas — THE HYPOCRITIC DAYS. Majorca, Divers Press, 1955.

Woolman, John — SOME CONSIDERATIONS ON THE KEEPING OF NEGROES. 1754.

Worboys, Annette Isobel — DREAM OF PETALS WHIM, as Anne Eyre Worboys. London, Ward Lock, 1961 — PALM ROCK AND PARADISE, as Anne Eyre Worboys. London, Ward Lock, 1961.

Wormser, Richard Edward — THE MAN WITH THE WAX FACE. New York, Smith & Haas, 1934.

Wren, Percival Christopher — THE INDIAN TEACHER'S GUIDE TO THE THEORY AND PRACTICE OF MENTAL, MORAL, AND PHYSICAL EDUCATION, as P.C. Wren. Bombay, India, Longman, 1910.

Wright, Austin Tappan — ISLANDIA. New York, Rinehart, 1942.

Wright, Harold Bell — THAT PRINTER OF UDELL'S: A STORY OF THE MIDDLE WEST. Chicago, Book Supply, 1903; London, Hodder & Stoughton, 1910.

Wright, Richard — UNCLE TOM'S CHILDREN: FOUR NOVELLAS. 1938.

Wright, Sydney Fowler — SCENES FROM THE MORTE D'ARTHUR, as Alan Seymour. London, Erskine MacDonald, 1919.

Wright, Willard Huntington — EUROPE AFTER 8:15, with H.L. Mencken and George Jean Nathan. New York, Lane, 1914.

Wrightson, Alice Patricia — THE CROOKED SNAKE. Sydney and London, Angus & Robertson, 1955.

Wylie, Philip Gordon — HEAVY LADEN. New York, Knopf, 1928.

Wylie, Elinor Hoyt — INCIDENTAL NUMBERS. 1912.

Y

Yarbro, Chelsea Quinn — OGILVIE, TALLANT, AND MOON. New York, Putnam, 1976 — TIME OF THE FOURTH HORSEMAN. New York, Doubleday, 1976; London, Sidgwick & Jackson, 1980.

Yates, Elizabeth — HIGH HOLIDAY. London, Black, 1938.

Yep, Laurence Michael — SWEETWATER. New York, Harper, 1973; London, Faber, 1976.

Yerby, Frank Garvin — THE FOXES OF HARROW. New York, Dial, 1946; London, Heinemann, 1947.

Yolen, Jane — SEE THIS LITTLE LINE? New York, McKay, 1963 — PIRATES IN PETTICOATS. New York, McKay, 1963.

Yonge, Charlotte Mary — LE CHATEAU DE MELVILLE; OU, RECREATIONS DU CABINET D'ETUDE. London, Simkin, 1838.

Young, Delbert Alton — MUTINY ON HUDSON BAY. Toronto, Gage, 1964.

Young, Gordon Ray — SAVAGES. New York, Doubleday, 1921; London, Cape, 1922.

Young, Michael Dunlop — WILL THE WAR MAKE US POORER?, with Henry Bunbury. London, Oxford Univ., 1943.

Young, Robert Franklin — THE WORLDS OF ROBERT F. YOUNG. New York, Simon & Schuster, 1965; London, Gollancz, 1966.

Young, Scott Alexander — RED SHIELD IN ACTION: A RECORD OF CANADIAN SALVATION ARMY WAR SERVICES IN THE SECOND GREAT WAR. Toronto, Clarke, 1949.

Z

Zagat, Arthur Leo — SEVEN OUT OF TIME. Reading (PA), Fantasy, 1949.

Zangwill, Israel — MOTZA KLEIS, anonymously, with Louis Cowen. London, privately printed, 1882.

Zebrowski, George — THE OMEGA POINT. New York, Ace, 1972; London, New English Library, 1974.

Zelazny, Roger Joseph — THIS IMMORTAL. New York, Ace, 1966; London, Hart Davis, 1967 — THE DREAM MASTER. New York, Ace, 1966; London, Hart Davis, 1968.

Zinberg, Leonard S. — WALK HARD — TALK LOUD, as Len Zinberg. Indianapolis, Bobbs Merrill, 1940.

Zindel, Paul — THE PIGMAN. New York, Harper, 1968; London, Bodley Head, 1969.

Zion, Eugene — ALL FALLING DOWN, as Gene Zion. New York, Harper, 1951; Kingswood (ENG), World's Work, 1969.

Zolotow, Charlotte — THE PARK BOOK. New York, Harper, 1944 — BUT NOT BILLY. New York and London, Harper, 1944.

Appendix 3
IMPORTANT ILLUSTRATORS

Presented here is a comprehensive, but by no means complete, list of illustrators of all types of works: novels, biographies, essays, poetry, science fiction, mystery and detective, histories, narratives, the entire gamut of writing. Use this list along with the First Books List (Appendix 2) and the True Names-Pseudonyms List (Appendix 1). In many cases you will find authors and illustrators combined. For example; TOM SAWYER by Mark Twain and illustrated by Norman Rockwell. This particular book would be collectible for the illustrator only since Rockwell was not yet born when TOM SAWYER was first published.

ILLUSTRATORS TO WATCH FOR - BOOKS, MAGAZINE COVERS, PRINTS, POSTERS, POSTCARDS, ADVERTISEMENTS, ETC.

Abbey, Edwin Austin
Armstrong, Rolf
Artzybasheff, Boris
Audubon, John J.

Bacon, John R.
Bacon, Peggy
Beardsley, Aubrey

"Beggarstaffs, The" (James Pryde & Wm. Nicholson)
Beneker, Gerrit A.
Benton, Thomas Hart
Bernard, Edouard
Bird, Elisha Brown
Blaine, Mahlon
Blake, William
Boileau, Philip
Bonnard, Paul
Bonnard, Pierre
Bonte, B. Willard
Bradley, Will
Bragdon, Claude Fayette
Brangwyn, Frank
Britton, L.N.
Bull, Charles Livingston
Byrd, David

Carleton, B.
Carlu, Jean
Carqueville, Will
Carre, Jean
Chagall, Marc
Chambers, C.E.
Chambers, Robert William
Cheret, Jules

Christy, Howard Chandler
Clarke, Harry
Coughlin, John C.
Cox, Charles H.
Cox, Palmer
Crane, Walter
Cruikshank, George

Dali, Salvador
Darly, F.O.A.C.
Davis, Paul
Day, Francis
Deland, Francis
Denslow, W.W.
Dimitri, Ivan
Dixon, (Lafayette) Maynard
Doré, Gustav
Dougherty, James
Dow, Arthur Wesley
Downe, Albro
Dulac, Edmund
Dunn, Harvey
Durer, A.

Eddy, Henry B.
Edwards, George Wharton

Ellis, Harvey
Emerson, R.L.

Erte
Falls, C.B.
Falter, John
Fischer, Anton Otto
Fisher, Harrison
Flag, James Montgomery
Forsythe, Clyde
Fox, R. Atkinson
Frost, A.B.

Gibson, Charles Dana
Gilbert, F. Allan
Gill, Eric
Greenaway, Kate
Greenough, W.C.
Greulle, Johnny
Goff, Seymour
Grohe, Glenn
Gurvin, Abe
Gutmann, Bessie Pease

Haeberle, R.L.
Held Jr., John
Hendee, A.

Hirsch, Joseph
Hogarth, William
Homer, Winslow

Icart, Louis

James, Will
Jansen, R.H.

Kenney, Clayton
Kent, Rockwell
King, Alexander
Kyd

Leyendecker, J.C.
Lindsay, Norman

Martin, David Stone
Mayer, Hy
Mc Creary, Harrison
Mc Vicker, Harry W.
Michaelson, J.
Miro, Joan
Mora, F. Luis
Morgan, Wallace
Morse, Alice C.
Mucha, Alphonse

Nankivell, Frank Arthur
Neal, John R.
Newell, Peter (Sheaf Hersey)
Nielsen, Kay
Norton, M.E.
Nutting, Wallace

O'Neill, Rose
Orr, A.E.
Ottman, Chic
Outcault, Richard Fulton

Parrish, Maxfield
Paus, Herbert
Peixotto, Ernest
Pendergast, Maurice
Penfield, Edward
Pennell, Joseph
Perlin, Bernard
Phillips, S. Coles
Picasso, Pablo
Podwal, Marc
Pogany, Willie
Porter, Bruce
Potthast, Edward Henry
Prang, Louis
Pyle, Howard

Rackham, Arthur
Raemakers, Louis
Raleigh, Henry
Reed, Ethel
Remington, Frederic
Reuterdahl, H.
Rhead, Louis J.
Richardson, Frederick
Riesenberg, Sidney
Riquer, Aljandro De
Robinson, W. Heath
Rockwell, Norman
Rogers, A.P.
Rogers, Bruce
Rosenberg, Henry M.
Russell, Charles M.

St. John, J. Allen
Sarg, Tony
Sattler, Joseph
Scotson-Clark, George Frederick
Schoonover, Frank
Schweinfurth, J.A.
Shahn, Ben

Shepard, Ernest
Sheridan, J.E.

Sloan, John
Smith, Dan V.
Smith, F. Berkeley
Smith, Jessie Wilcox
Smith, Lawrence D.
Spy
Steinlen, Theophile-Alexandre
Sterner, Albert
Stewardson, John
Strathman, F.
Szyk, Arthur

Tenniel, John
Toulouse-Lautrec, Henri De
Treidler, Adolph
Twachtman, John

Underwood, Clarence F.

Verrees, J. Paul

Wagner, Robert Leicester
Walton, Tony
Warren, Ferdinand
Watson, Henry Sumner
Wells, E.B.

Whitehead, Walter
Williams, John Scott
Wood, Page
Woodbury, Charles Herbert
Wyeth, N.C.

Young, Ellsworth

Zagat, A.L.

Appendix 4

COLLECTIBLE AMERICANA BOOKS AND THEIR VALUES

This is another important collecting category. An inspection of the titles listed here will illustrate the gamut of the subject.

The authors and titles I have selected are those which are best known to the general public. Only titles having a current nominal market value of at least $25 are listed. It is reasonable to assume that all first edition books by any of the authors listed will have value — do not assume that all books by the same author will have comparable values.

The titles listed are all first editions, and first impressions if pertinent. The values noted are for books in very good to fine condition with dust jackets (if the book was originally issued with one). "Points" are associated with properly identifying many of these books and a library should be checked for a bibliography of the author or subject in question. Alternatively, a rare book dealer should be consulted for final determination as to the correct state and current value.

A

Abbey, James — CALIFORNIA. A TRIP ACROSS THE PLAINS IN THE SPRING OF 1850. New Albany, 1850. 64pp., wraps. $3,000-4,000

Abbott, E.C. & Helena Huntington Smith — WE POINTED THEM NORTH. NY, (1939). $85-100

Adams, Ramon — THE RAMPAGING HERD. Norman, 1959. $225-275

Aken, David — PIONEERS OF THE BLACK HILLS. (Milwaukee, ca.1920). $100-125

Aldridge, Reginald — LIFE ON A RANCH. NY, 1884. Wraps. $250-500

Alexander, E.P. — MILITARY MEMOIRS OF A CONFEDERATE. NY, 1907. $135-160

Allan, J.T. — CENTRAL AND WESTERN NEBRASKA, AND THE EXPERIENCES OF ITS STOCK GROWERS. Omaha, 1883, wraps. $225-275

Allen, J.A. — NOTES ON THE NATURAL HISTORY OF PORTIONS OF MONTANA AND DAKOTA. Boston, 1874, wraps. $110-135

Allen, William A. — ADVENTURES WITH INDIANS AND GAME. Chicago, 1903. $175-225

Alter, J. — JAMES BRIDGER: TRAPPER, FRONTIERSMAN, SCOUT, AND GUIDE. Salt Lake City, (1925) — $150-200

Andreas, A.T. — ATLAS MAP OF PEORIA COUNTY, ILLINOIS. Chicago, 1873. $350-425

Andreas, A.T. — HISTORY OF CHICAGO. Chicago, 1884-86, 3 vols. $375-425

Andreas, A.T. — HISTORY OF THE STATE OF KANSAS. Chicago, 1883. $450-550

Andreas, A.T. — ILLUSTRATED HISTORICAL ATLAS OF THE STATE OF IOWA. Chicago, 1875. $450 or more

Applegate, Jesse — A DAY WITH THE COW COLUMN IN 1843. Chicago, 1934 — $85-110

Armour, Samuel — HISTORY OF ORANGE COUNTY, CALIFORNIA. Los Angeles, 1921 — $125-145

Armstrong, Moses K. — HISTORY AND RESOURCES OF DAKOTA, MONTANA AND IDAHO. Yanktown (Dakota Territory), 1866, wraps. $3,750-4,250

Ashley, Clifford W. — THE YANKEE WHALER. Boston, 1926, trade edition. $225-300

Atwater, Caleb — A HISTORY OF THE STATE OF OHIO. Cincinnati, (1838). $175-200

Atwater, Caleb — MYSTERIES OF WASHINGTON CITY. Washington, 1844. $135-160

B

Babbitt, E.L. — THE ALLEGHENY PILOT. Freeport (PA), 1855, wraps. $175-225

Bailey, Washington — A TRIP TO CALIFORNIA IN 1853. LeRoy (IL), 1915, wraps. $350-450

Baily, Francis — JOURNAL OF A TOUR IN UNSETTLED PARTS OF NORTH AMERICA IN 1796 & 1797. London, 1856. $600-750

Balme, J.R. — AMERICAN STATES, CHURCHES AND SLAVERY. London, 1863. $45-65

Bandini, Joseph — A DESCRIPTION OF CALIFORNIA IN 1828. Berkeley, 1951. $85-100

Banta, William & J.W. Caldwell, Jr. — TWENTY-SEVEN YEARS ON THE FRONTIER, OR FIFTY YEARS IN TEXAS. Austin, 1893. $1800 or more

Barbe-Marbois, Francois — THE HISTORY OF LOUISIANA, PARTICULARLY THE CESSION OF THAT COLONY TO THE U.S.A. Philadelphia, 1830. $375-425

Barnard, George N. — PHOTOGRAPHIC VIEW OF SHERMAN'S CAMPAIGN. 61 gold-tone albumen prints. NY, (1866). $10,000 or more

Barnes, David M. — THE DRAFT RIOTS IN NEW YORK, JULY, 1863. NY, 1863, wraps. $175-225

Barreiro, Antonio — OJEADA SOBRE NUEVO-MEXICO. Puebla (Mexico), 1832. $850-1,100

Barrows, R.M. — THE KITBOOK FOR SOLDIERS, SAILORS, AND MARINES. Chicago, (1943). $75-125

Barrows, Willard — NOTES ON IOWA TERRITORY. Cincinnati, 1845. $1,500 or more

Bartlett, John Russell — PERSONAL NARRATIVE OF EXPLORATIONS AND INCIDENTS IN TEXAS, NEW MEXICO, CALIFORNIA, ETC. NY, 1854. Fldg map, 44 plates. $550-750

Barton, James L. — COMMERCE OF THE LAKES. Buffalo, 1847, wraps. $125-150

Bass, W.W. — EDITOR — ADVENTURES IN THE CANYONS OF THE COLORADO BY TWO OF ITS EARLIEST EXPLORERS, JAMES WHITE AND H.W. HAWKINS. Grand Canyon, 1920, wraps. $175-225

Bates, Finis L. — ESCAPE AND SUICIDE OF JOHN WILKES BOOTH. Memphis, 1907. $85-100

Baylies, Francis — A NARRATIVE OF GENERAL WOOL'S CAMPAIGN IN MEXICO. Albany, 1851. $350-500

Beard, Charles A. — AN ECONOMIC INTERPRETATION OF THE CONSTITUTION OF THE UNITED STATES. NY, 1913. $225-275

Beck, Lewis C. — A GAZETEER OF THE STATES OF ILLINOIS AND MISSOURI. Albany (NY), 1823. $850 or more

Becker, Robert H. — DESIGNS ON THE LAND: DISENOS OF CALIFORNIA RANCHOS. San Francisco, 1964. $175-450

Beechey, F.W. — AN ACCOUNT OF A VISIT TO CALIFORNIA. (SF, 1941). $175-225

Benedict, Carl Peters — A TENDERFOOT KID ON GYP WATER. Austin, 1943. $175-225

Benson, Henry C. — LIFE AMONG THE CHOCTAW INDIANS. Cincinnati, 1860. $225-300

Benton, Frank — COWBOY LIFE ON THE SIDETRACK. Denver, (1903). $125-175

Bevier, Robert S. — HISTORY OF THE FIRST AND SECOND MISSOURI CONFEDERATE BRIGADES., 1861-65. St. Louis, 1879. $175-225

Bickerstaff, Isaac — THE RHODE-ISLAND ALMANAC FOR 1842. Providence, (1841), wraps. $175-225

Biggers, Don H. — FROM CATTLE RANGE TO COTTON PATCH. Abilene, (ca.1908), wraps. $450-600

Bingham, Helen M. — HISTORY OF GREEN COUNTY, WISCONSIN. Milwaukee, 1877. $85-100

BIOGRAPHICAL SOUVENIR OF THE STATE OF TEXAS. Chicago, 1889. $1,200 or more

Birkbeck, Morris — AN APPEAL TO THE PEOPLE OF ILLINOIS, ON THE QUESTION OF A CONVENTION. Shawneetown (IL), 1823, wraps. $550-750

Birkbeck, Morris — NOTES ON A JOURNEY IN AMERICA FROM THE COAST OF VIRGINIA TO THE TERRITORY OF ILLINOIS. Philadelphia, 1817. $300-375

Blackbird, Andrew J. — HISTORY OF THE OTTAWA AND CHIPPEWA INDIANS OF MICHIGAN. Ypsilanti (MI), 1887. $175-225

Blanchard, Rufus (Publisher) — CITIZEN'S GUIDE FOR THE CITY OF CHICAGO: COMPANION TO BLANCHARD'S MAP OF CHICAGO. Chicago, (1868), wraps, map bound in. $750 or more

Blowe, Daniel — A GEOGRAPHICAL, COMMERCIAL, AND AGRICULTURAL VIEW OF THE UNITED STATES OF AMERICA. Liverpool (Eng), (1820). $250-325

Bond, J. Wesley — MINNESOTA AND ITS RESOURCES. Chicago, 1856. $125-175

Bonnell, George W. — TOPOGRAPHICAL DESCRIPTION OF TEXAS. Austin, 1840. $2,200-3,500

Bonner, T.D. — THE LIFE AND ADVENTURES OF JAMES P. BECKWOURTH, MOUNTAINEER, SCOUT AND PIONEER, ETC. NY, 1856. $225-275

Bonney, Edward — BANDITTI OF THE PRAIRIES; OR, THE MURDERER'S DOOM! Chicago, 1850, wraps. $4,200 or more

Bosworth, Newton — HOCHELAGA DEPICTA: THE EARLY HISTORY AND PRESENT STATE OF THE CITY AND ISLAND OF MONTREAL. Montreal, 1839. $225-275

Bouchette, Joseph — A TOPOGRAPHICAL DESCRIPTION OF THE PROVINCE OF LOWER CANADA, WITH REMARKS UPON UPPER CANADA. London (Eng), 1815. $325-375

Bourke, John G. — ON THE BORDER WITH CROOK. NY, 1891. $175-225

Bowditch, Nathaniel — THE NEW AMERICAN PRACTICAL NAVIGATOR. Newburyport (MA), 1802. $1,500 or more

Brackenridge, H.M. — JOURNAL OF A VOYAGE UP THE MISSOURI. Baltimore, 1815. $350 or more

Bradbury, John — TRAVELS IN THE INTERIOR OF AMERICA. Liverpool, 1817. $1,100-1,500

Bradley, Joshua — ACCOUNTS OF RELIGIOUS REVIVALS IN MANY PARTS OF THE UNITED STATES FROM 1815 TO 1818. Albany (NY), 1819. $60-75

Brady, William — GLIMPSES OF TEXAS. Houston, 1871, wraps or cloth. $1,200-1,500

Braman, D.E.E. — INFORMATION ABOUT TEXAS. Philadelphia, 1857. $450-600

BRAND BOOK OF THE WESTERN SOUTH DAKOTA STOCK GROWERS' ASSOCIATION. Omaha, (1901). $275-325

Brice, Wallace — A HISTORY OF FORT WAYNE. Fort Wayne (IN), 1868. $110-135

BRIEF DESCRIPTION OF WESTERN TEXAS, A (by W.G. Kingsbury). San Antonio, 1873. $650-800

Briggs, L.Vernon — HISTORY OF SHIPBUILDING ON NORTH RIVER, PLYMOUTH COUNTY, MASSACHUSETTS. Boston, 1889. $175-225

Britton, Wiley — MEMOIRS OF THE REBELLION ON THE BORDER. Chicago, 1882. $85-100

Brower, Jacob V. — MEMOIRS OF EXPLORATIONS IN THE BASIN OF THE MISSISSIPPI. St. Paul (MN), 1898-1904, 8 vols. $450 or more

Brown, Henry — HISTORY OF ILLINOIS. NY, 1844. $175-225

Brown, Jesse & A.M. Willard — THE BLACK HILLS TRAILS. Rapid City (SD), 1924. $125-150

Brown, Samuel R. — THE WESTERN GAZETTEER, OR EMIGRANT'S DIRECTORY. Auburn, 1817. $500-750

Brown, William C. — THE SHEEPEATER CAMPAIGN IN IDAHO. Boise, 1926, map, wraps. $250-325

Brown, William H. — THE EARLY HISTORY OF THE STATE OF ILLINOIS. Chicago, 1840, wraps. $1,100-1,400

Browne, J. Ross — ETCHINGS OF A WHALING CRUISE. NY, 1846. $350-425

Browne, J. Ross — ADVENTURES IN THE APACHE COUNTRY. NY, 1869. $175-250

Bruffey, George A. — EIGHTY-ONE YEARS IN THE WEST. Butte, 1925, wraps. $85-100

Brunson, Edward — PROFITS IN SHEEP AND CATTLE IN CENTRAL AND WESTERN KANSAS. Kansas City, 1883, wraps. $225-275

Bryant, Edwin — WHAT I SAW IN CALIFORNIA. NY, 1848. $300-400

Buffum, E. Gould — SIX MONTHS IN THE GOLD MINES. Philadelphia, 1850, cloth or wraps. $350-500

Burney, James — HISTORY OF THE BUCCANEERS OF AMERICA. London, 1816. $375-450

Burnham, Daniel H. & Edward H. Bennett — PLAN OF CHICAGO. Chicago, 1909. $325-375

Burns, John H. — MEMOIRS OF A COW PONY. Boston, (1906). $275-350

Burton, Harley — A HISTORY OF THE JA RANCH. Austin, 1928. $450-600

Butcher, S.D. — S.D. BUTCHER'S PIONEER HISTORY OF CUSTER COUNTRY. Broken Bow (NB), 1901. $125-150

Butler, Mann — A HISTORY OF THE COMMONWEALTH OF KENTUCKY. LOUISVILLE, 1834. $325-375

Butterfield, C.W. — AN HISTORICAL ACCOUNT OF THE EXPEDITION AGAINST SANDUSKY. Cincinnati, 1873. $125-150

Butterfield, C.W. — HISTORY OF SENECA COUNTY, OHIO. Sandusky (OH), 1848. $125-150

Byers, William N. & John H. Kellom — A HAND BOOK TO THE GOLD FIELDS OF NEBRASKA AND KANSAS. Chicago, 1859, wraps. $5,250 or more

Byrd, William (Of Westover) — THE WRITINGS OF "COLONEL WILLIAM BYRD OF WESTOVER IN VIRGINIA, ESQ." NY, 1901. $125-150

Byrne, B.M. — LETTERS ON THE CLIMATE, SOILS, AND PRODUCTIONS OF FLORIDA. Jacksonville (FL), 1851, wraps. $325-375

C

CABINET OF NATURAL HISTORY AND AMERICAN RURAL SPORT, THE — Philadelphia, 1830-32-33, 3 vols. $17,000 or more

Cable, George W. — THE CREOLES OF LOUISIANA. NY, 1884. $85-100

Caldwell, J.A. — HISTORY OF BELMONT AND JEFFERSON COUNTIES, OHIO. Wheeling (OH), 1880. $125-175

Caldwell, J.F.J. — HISTORY OF A BRIGADE OF SOUTH CAROLINIANS. Philadelphia, 1866. $225-275

Calhoun, James S. — OFFICIAL CORRESPONDENCE OF JAMES S. CALHOUN WHILE INDIAN AGENT AT SANTA FE. Washington, 1915. $125-150

Campbell, J.L. — IDAHO AND MONTANA GOLD REGIONS. Chicago, 1965. $1,700 or more

Campbell, J.L. — THE GREAT AGRICULTURAL & MINERAL WEST. Chicago, 1866, wraps. $1,700 or more

Campbell, Patrick — TRAVELS IN THE INTERIOR INHABITED PARTS OF NORTH AMERICA. Toronto, 1937. $135-160

Canfield, Chauncey L. - Editor — THE DIARY OF A FORTY-NINER. San Francisco, 1906. $125-175

Cannon, George Q. — WRITINGS FROM THE "WESTERN STANDARD." PUBLISHED IN SAN FRANCISCO. Liverpool (Eng), 1864. $125-175

Cannon, J.P. — INSIDE OF REBELDOM: THE DAILY LIFE OF A PRIVATE IN THE CONFEDERATE ARMY. Washington, 1900. $100-150

Canova, Andrew P. — LIFE AND ADVENTURES IN SOUTH FLORIDA. Palatka (FL), 1885, wraps. $225-275

Capron, Elisha S. — HISTORY OF CALIFORNIA. Boston, 1854. $85-125

Carey, C.H. — HISTORY OF OREGON. Chicago, 1922. $60-85

Carlyle, Thomas — OCCASIONAL DISCOURSE ON THE NIGGER QUESTION. London, 1853, wraps. $350-425

Carr, John — EARLY TIMES IN MIDDLE TENNESSEE. Nashville (TN), 1857. $175-225

Carr, John — PIONEER DAYS IN CALIFORNIA. Eureka (CA), 1891. $125-150

Carr, Spencer — A BRIEF SKETCH OF LA CROSSE, WISCONSIN. La Crosse, 1854, wraps. $275-325

Carroll, H. Bailey — THE TEXAN SANTA FE TRAIL. Canyon (TX), 1951, boxed. $85-100

Carson, James H. — LIFE IN CALIFORNIA. Tarrytown (NY), 1931. $50-65

Carstarphen, J.E. — MY TRIP TO CALIFORNIA. Louisiana (MO), 1914. $100-125

Carter, Robert G. — MASSACRE OF SALT CREEK PRAIRIE AND THE COW-BOY'S VERDICT. Washington, 1919, wraps. $350 or more

Carter, Robert G. — PURSUIT OF KICKING BIRD: A CAMPAIGN IN THE TEXAS "BAD LANDS." Washington, 1920, wraps. $300 or more

Carter, W.A. — HISTORY OF FANNIN COUNTY, TEXAS. Bonham (TX), 1885. $900 or more

Casler, John — FOUR YEARS IN THE STONEWALL BRIGADE. Guthrie (OK), 1893. $125-150

Castenada, Carlos E. — OUR CATHOLIC HERITAGE IN TEXAS, 1519-1810. Austin (TX), 1936-42, 5 vols. $750 or more

Castleman, Alfred L. — ARMY OF THE POTOMAC: BEHIND THE SCENES. Milwaukee, 1863. $85-100

Cates, Cliff D. — PIONEER HISTORY OF WISE COUNTY, TEXAS. Decatur (TX), 1907, wraps. $225-300

Catlin, George — LETTERS AND NOTES ON THE MANNERS, CUSTOMS, AND CONDITIONS OF THE NORTH AMERICAN INDIANS. London, 1841, 2 vols. $1,000 or more

Catlin, George — O-KEE-PA, A RELIGIOUS CEREMONY. London, 1867. $1,500 or more

Catlin, George — NORTH AMERICAN INDIAN PORTFOLIO. London, 1844, large folio. $15,000 or more

CATTLE RAISING IN SOUTH DAKOTA — (Forest City, 1904), wraps. $125-135

CELEBRATION OF THE 73RD ANNIVERSARY OF THE DECLARATION OF INDEPENDENCE — ON BOARD THE BARQUE "HANNAH SPRAGUE," ETC. NY, 1849, wraps. $100-125

Celiz, Fray Francisco — DIARY OF THE ALARCON EXPEDITION INTO TEXAS, 1718-1719. Los Angeles, 1935. $150-200

Chadwick, Henry — THE GAME OF BASE BALL: HOW TO LEARN IT, HOW TO PLAY IT, AND HOW TO TEACH IT. NY, (1868). $85-100

Chamisso, Adelbert Von — A SOJOURN AT SAN FRANCISCO BAY 1816. San Francisco, 1936. $150-175

Charlevoix, Pierre F.X. — JOURNAL OF A VOYAGE TO NORTH AMERICA. Chicago, 1923, 2 vols. $175-225

Chase, Charles M. — THE EDITOR'S RUN IN NEW MEXICO AND COLORADO. Lyndon, (VT), 1882, wraps. $225-300

Child, Andrew — OVERLAND ROUTE TO CALIFORNIA. Milwaukee, 1852. $5,000 or more

Childs, C.G. (Engraver) — VIEWS IN PHILADELPHIA AND ITS VICINITY. Philadelphia, 1827-(30). $2,000 or more

Chittenden, Hiram M. — HISTORY OF EARLY STEAMBOAT NAVIGATION ON THE MISSOURI RIVER. NY, 1903, 2 vols. $175-225

Chittenden, Hiram — THE AMERICAN FUR TRADE OF THE FAR WEST. NY, 1902, 3 vols. $375-450

Claiborne, John Herbert — SEVENTY-FIVE YEARS IN OLD VIRGINIA. NY, 1905. $60-75

Clappe, Louise A.K.S. — CALIFORNIA IN 1851; 1852: THE DAME SHIRLEY LETTERS. San Francisco, 1933, 2 vols. $100-150

Clark, Charles M. — A TRIP TO PIKE'S PEAK AND NOTES BY THE WAY. Chicago, 1861. $650 or more

Clark, Stanley — THE LIFE AND ADVENTURES OF THE AMERICAN COWBOY. (Providence), 1897. $150-175

Clark, Walter (Editor) — HISTORIES OF THE SEVERAL REGIMENTS AND BATTALIONS FROM NORTH CAROLINA IN THE GREAT WAR, 1861-1865. Raleigh (NC), 1901, 5 vols. $200-250

Clarke, A.B. — TRAVELS IN MEXICO AND CALIFORNIA. Boston, 1852, wraps. $800 or more

Clarke, Lewis — NARRATIVE OF THE SUFFERINGS OF LEWIS CLARKE DURING A CAPTIVITY OF MORE THAN TWENTY-FIVE YEARS. Boston, 1845, wraps. $125-150

Clay, John — MY LIFE ON THE RANGE. Chicago, (1924). $200-250

Clayton, William — THE LATTER-DAY SAINTS' EMIGRANTS' GUIDE. St. Louis, 1848, wraps. $3,500 or more

Clum, Woodworth — APACHE AGENT: THE STORY OF JOHN P. CLUM. Boston, 1936. $60-85

Cobbett, Thomas B. — COLORADO MINING DIRECTORY. Denver, 1879. $450 or more

Coffin, Joshua — A SKETCH OF THE HISTORY OF NEWBURY, NEWBURYPORT, AND WEST NEWBURYPORT. Boston, 1845. $125-175

Cohn, David L. — NEW ORLEANS AND ITS LIVING PAST. Boston, 1941, limited and signed. $85-100

Coke, Henry J. — A RIDE OVER THE ROCKY MOUNTAINS TO OREGON AND CALIFORNIA. London, 1852. $175-225

Colbert, E. — CHICAGO: HISTORICAL AND STATISTICAL SKETCH OF THE GARDEN CITY. Chicago, 1868, wraps. $125-150

Collins, Charles — COLLINS' HISTORY AND DIRECTORY OF THE BLACK HILLS. Central City, Dakota Territory, 1878, wraps. $2,000 or more

Collins, Charles (Compiler) — COLLINS' OMAHA DIRECTORY. (Omaha, 1866). $800 or more

Collins, Mrs. Nat — THE CATTLE QUEEN OF MONTANA. St. James (MN), 1893, wraps. $1,100 or more

Collins, Lieut. R.M. — CHAPTERS FROM THE UNWRITTEN HISTORY OF THE WAR BETWEEN THE STATES. St. Louis, 1893. $225-2775

Colt, Mirian Davis — WENT TO KANSAS. Watertown (NY), 1862. $375-450

Colton, Calvin — TOUR OF THE AMERICAN LAKES. London, 1853, 2 vols. $175-225

Colton, Walter — THREE YEARS IN CALIFORNIA. NY, 1850. $175-225

Conclin, George — CONCLIN'S NEW RIVER GUIDE, OR A GAZETEER OF ALL THE TOWNS ON THE WESTERN WATERS. Cincinnati, 1850, wraps, 44 full-page maps. $125-175

CONFEDERATE RECEIPT BOOK. RICHMOND, 1963, wraps. $350-450

Conklin, E. — PICTURESQUE ARIZONA. NY, 1878. $200-250

Connelley, William E. — WILD BILL AND HIS ERA. NY, 1933. $85-100

Connelley, William E. — QUANTRILL AND THE BORDER WARS. Cedar Rapids (IA), 1910. $100-125

Connolly, A.P. — THRILLING NARRATIVE OF THE MINNESOTA MASSACRE AND THE SIOUX WAR OF 1862-1863. Chicago, (1896). $175-225

CONSTITUTION AND LAWS OF THE CHEROKEE NATION. St. Louis, 1875. $375-425

CONSTITUTION AND LAWS OF THE MUSKOGEE NATION. St. Louis, 1880. $225-275

CONSTITUTION AND PLAYING RULES OF THE INTERNATIONAL BASEBALL ASSOCIATION — AND THE CHAMPIONSHIP RECORD FOR 1877. Jamaica Plain (MA), 1878, wraps. $125-175

CONSTITUTION OF THE REPUBLIC OF MEXICO AND THE STATE OF COAHUILA AND TEXAS, THE. NY, 1832. $1,100 or more

CONSTITUTION OF THE STATE OF WEST TEXAS. Austin, (1868), wraps. $650 or more

CONSTITUTION OF THE STATE OF SEQUOYAH. (Muscogee (Indian Territory, 1905), wraps. $3,500 or more. Second edition. $3,000 or more

Cook, D.J. — HANDS UP, OR 20 YEARS OF DETECTIVE LIFE IN THE MOUNTAINS AND ON THE PLAINS. Denver, 1882. $275-325

Cook, James H. — FIFTY YEARS ON THE OLD FRONTIER. New Haven, 1923. $60-75

Cook, John R. — THE BORDER AND THE BUFFALO. Topeka (KS), 1907. $50-65

Cooke, Philip St. George — THE CONQUEST OF NEW MEXICO AND CALIFORNIA. NY, 1878. $175-250

Coon, James Churchill — LOG OF THE CRUISE OF 1889 D.T.S.C., NEW SMYRNA TO LAKE WORTH, EAST COAST OF FLORIDA. Lake Helen (FL), 1889,

wraps. $125-175

Costanso, Miguel — THE SPANISH OCCUPATION OF CALIFORNIA. SF, 1934. $175-225

Coulter, E. Merton — TRAVELS IN THE CONFEDERATE STATES: A BIBLIOGRAPHY. Norman (OK), 1948. $65-90

Courtauld, George — ADDRESS TO THOSE WHO MAY BE DISPOSED TO REMOVE TO THE UNITED STATES OF AMERICA. Sudbury (Canada), 1820, wraps. $1,350 or more

Couts, Cave J. — FROM SAN DIEGO TO THE COLORADO IN 1849. LA, 1932. $125-175

Cowan, Robert E. — A BIBLIOGRAPHY OF THE HISTORY OF CALIFORNIA AND THE PACIFIC WEST, 1510-1906. SF, 1914. $350 or more

Cox, Isaac — THE ANNALS OF TRINITY COUNTY. SF, 1940. $65-85

Cox, James — HISTORICAL AND BIOGRAPHICAL RECORD OF THE CATTLE INDUSTRY AND THE CATTLEMAN OF TEXAS AND ADJACENT TERRITORY. St. Louis, 1895. $3,200 or more

Cox, Ross — ADVENTURES ON THE COLUMBIA RIVER. London, 1831, 2 vols. $800 or more

Cox, Sandford C. — RECOLLECTIONS OF THE EARLY SETTLEMENT OF THE WABASH VALLEY. Lafayette (IN), 1860. $115-135

Coy, Owen C. — PICTORIAL HISTORY OF CALIFORNIA. Berkeley, 1925. $110-125

Crakes, Sylvester — FIVE YEARS A CAPTIVE AMONG THE BLACK-FEET INDIANS. Columbus (OH), 1858. $325-375

Crawford, Lucy — THE HISTORY OF THE WHITE MOUNTAINS. Portland (ME), 1846. $110-135

Cremony, John C. — LIFE AMONG THE APACHES. SF, 1868. $225-250

Creuzbaur, Robert - Compiler — ROUTE FROM THE GULF OF MEXICO AND THE LOWER MISSISSIPPI VALLEY TO CALIFORNIA AND THE PACIFIC OCEAN. NY, 1849. $4,500 or more

Crocket, George L. — TWO CENTURIES IN EAST TEXAS. Dallas (ca.1932). $175-225

Crotty, D.G. — FOUR YEARS CAMPAIGNING IN THE ARMY OF THE POTOMAC. Grand Rapids (MI), 1894. $85-100

Cuffe, Paul — NARRATIVE OF THE LIFE AND ADVENTURES OF PAUL CUFFE, A PEQUOT INDIAN. NY, 1838, wraps. $200-250

Cuming, F. — SKETCHES OF A TOUR TO THE WESTERN COUNTRY. Pittsburgh, 1810. $350-450

Cumings, Samuel — THE WESTERN PILOT. Cincinnati, 1825. $750 or more

Cunningham, Eugene — FAMOUS IN THE WEST. El Paso, 1926, wraps. $175-225

Cunningham, Eugene — TRIGGERNOMETRY: A GALLERY OF GUNFIGHTERS. NY, 1934. $100-150

Curley, Edwin A. — NEBRASKA: ITS ADVANTAGES AND DRAWBACKS. London, 1875. $100-150

Curtis, Edward S. — THE NORTH AMERICAN INDIAN. Cambridge (MA), 1907-30, 20 vols., and 20 portfolios, limited & signed. $60,000 — perhaps much more

Curtiss, Daniel S. — WESTERN PORTRAITURE, AND EMIGRANTS' GUIDE. NY, 1852. $225-275

Cushman, H.B. — A HISTORY OF THE CHOCTAW, CHICKSAW AND NATCHEZ INDIANS. Greenville (TX), 1899. $275-325

Custer, Elizabeth B. — "BOOTS AND SADDLES" OR LIFE IN DAKOTA WITH GENERAL CUSTER. NY, 1885. $50-65

Custer, Elizabeth B. — TENTING ON THE PLAINS. NY, 1887. $45-60

Custer, George A. — MY LIFE ON THE PLAINS. NY, 1874. $175-200

Cutts, James M. — THE CONQUEST OF CALIFORNIA AND NEW MEXICO. Philadelphia, 1847. $175-225

D

Dacus, J.A. — LIFE AND ADVENTURES OF FRANK AND JESSE JAMES. St. Louis, 1880. $325-375

Dale, Edward Everett — THE RANGE CATTLE INDUSTRY. Norman (OK), 1930. $175-225

Dalton, Emmett — WHEN THE DALTONS RODE. Garden City (NY), 1931. $60-75

Damon, Samuel C. — A JOURNEY TO LOWER OREGON AND UPPER CALIFORNIA, 1848-49. SF, 1927. $150-200

Dana, Edmund — GEOGRAPHICAL SKETCHES ON THE WESTERN COUNTRY; DESIGNED FOR EMIGRANTS AND SETTLERS. Cincinnati, 1819. $450-600

Daniels, William M. — A CORRECT ACCOUNT OF THE MURDER OF GENERALS JOSEPH AND HYRUM SMITH, AT CARTHAGE, ON THE 27TH DAY OF JUNE, 1944. Nauvoo (IL), 1845, wraps. $2,750-3,250

Darby, William — THE EMIGRANT'S GUIDE TO THE WESTERN AND SOUTHWESTERN STATES AND TERRITORIES. NY, 1818. $350-450

Darby, William — A GEOGRAPHICAL DESCRIPTION OF THE STATE OF LOUISIANA. Philadelphia, 1816. $325-375

Darby, William — A TOUR FROM THE CITY OF NEW YORK, TO DETROIT, IN THE MICHIGAN TERRITORY. NY, 1819. $225-275

Darlington, Mary Carson - Editor — FORT PITT AND LETTERS FROM THE FRONTIER. Pittsburgh, 1892, limited large paper edition. $175-225

Daubeny, Charles — JOURNAL OF A TOUR THROUGH THE UNITED STATES AND CANADA — 1837-1838. Oxford, 1843. $175-250

Davidson, Gordon Charles — THE NORTH WEST COMPANY. Berkeley, 1918. $125-150

David, Ellis — A COMMERCIAL ENCYCLOPEDIA OF THE PACIFIC SOUTHWEST. Oakland, 1915. $125-150

Davis, Paris M. — AN AUTHENTICK HISTORY OF THE LATE WAR BETWEEN THE UNITED STATES AND GREAT BRITAIN. Ithaca (NY), 1829. $125-150

Davis, William Heath — SIXTY YEARS IN CALIFORNIA. SF, 1889. $250-300

Davis, William W.H. — EL GRINGO; OR NEW MEXICO AND HER PEOPLE. NY, 1857. $150-225

Davis, William W.H. — THE SPANISH CONQUEST OF NEW MEXICO: 1527-1703. Doylestown, 1869. $175-225

Davis, William J. - Editor (By Adam R. Johnson) — THE PARTISAN RANGERS OF THE CONFEDERATE STATES ARMY. Louisville (KY), 1904. $125-175

Dawson, Nicholas — CALIFORNIA IN '41. TEXAS IN '51. MEMOIRS. (Austin, Texas, ca.1910). $600-750

Dawson, Simon J. — REPORT ON THE EXPLORATION OF THE COUNTRY BETWEEN LAKE SUPERIOR AND THE RED RIVER SETTLEMENT AND THE ASSINIBOINE AND SASKATCHEWAN. Toronto, 1859. $225-275

Dawson, Thomas F. & F.J.V. Skiff — THE UTE WAR: A HISTORY OF THE WHITE RIVER MASSACRE, ETC. Denver, 1879, wraps. $2,000 or more

Day, Sherman — REPORT OF THE COMMITTEE ON INTERNAL IMPROVEMENTS, ON THE USE OF THE CAMELS ON THE PLAINS, MAY 30, 1885. (Sacramento), 1885, unbound. $60-75

De Barthe, Joe — THE LIFE AND ADVENTURES OF FRANK GROUARD, CHIEF OF SCOUTS. St. Joseph (MO), (1894). $275-325

De Cordova, J. — TEXAS: HER RESOURCES AND HER PUBLIC MEN. Philadelphia, 1858. $400-500

De Cordova, J. — THE TEXAS IMMIGRANT AND TRAVELLER'S GUIDE BOOK. Austin, 1856. $400 or more

De Hass, Wills — HISTORY OF THE EARLY SETTLEMENT AND INDIAN WARS OF WESTERN VIRGINIA. Wheeling (WV), 1851. $225-275

De Quille, Dan (William Wright) — HISTORY OF THE BIG BONANZA. Hartford, 1876. $125-150

De Quille, Dan (William Wright) — A HISTORY OF THE COMSTOCK SILVER LODE AND MINES. Virginia City (Nevada), (1889). $175-225

De Roos, Fred F. — PERSONAL NARRATIVE OF TRAVELS IN THE UNITED STATES AND CANADA IN 1826. London, 1827. $350-425

De Tonty, Henri — RELATION OF HENRI DE TONTY CONCERNING THE EXPLORATIONS OF LA SALLE. Chicago, 1898, limited, text in French and English. $225-275

De Voto, Bernard — ACROSS THE WIDE MISSOURI. Boston, 1947, limited and boxed. $125-150

De Wolff, J.H. — PAWNEE BILL (MAJ. GORDON W. LILLIE): HIS EXPERIENCE AND ADVENTURES ON THE WESTERN PLAINS. n.p., 1902 — $150-175

Debar, J.H. — THE WEST VIRGINIA HANDBOOK AND IMMIGRANT'S GUIDE. Parkersburg (WV), 1870. $125-175

DECLARATION OF THE IMMEDIATE CAUSE WHICH INDUCE AND JUSTIFY THE SECESSION OF SOUTH CAROLINA FROM THE FEDERAL UNION, AND THE ORDINANCE OF SECESSION. Charleston (SC), 1869, wraps. $450-550

Delafield, Jr., John — AN INQUIRY INTO THE ORIGIN OF THE ANTIQUITIES OF AMERICA. NY, 1839, includes an 18-foot long folding plate. $175-225

Delano, Alonzo — LIFE ON THE PLAINS AND AMONG THE DIGGINGS. Auburn (NY), 1854. $450 or more

Delano, Amasa — A NARRATIVE OF VOYAGES AND TRAVELS, IN THE NORTHERN AND SOUTHERN HEMISPHERES. Boston, 1817. $500 or more

Delano, Judah — WASHINGTON (D.C.) DIRECTORY. Washington, 1822. $550 or more

Delay, Peter J. — HISTORY OF YUBA AND SUTTER COUNTIES, CALIFORNIA. LA, 1924. $125-175

Denny, Arthur — PIONEER DAYS ON PUGET SOUND. Seattle, 1888. $100 or more

DEPREDATIONS AND MASSACRE BY THE SNAKE RIVER INDIANS. (Washington), 1861. $125-150

DESCRIPTION OF CENTRAL IOWA, WITH SPECIAL REFERENCE TO POLK COUNTY AND DES MOINES, THE STATE CAPITAL, A. Des Moines, 1858, wraps. $450-525

DESCRIPTIVE ACCOUNT OF THE CITY OF PEORIA, A. Peoria, 1859, wraps. $150-175

Dexter, A. Hersey — EARLY DAYS IN CALIFORNIA. (Denver), 1886. $225-275

Dickins, James — 1861 TO 1865, BY AN OLD JOHNNIE: PERSONAL RECOLLECTIONS AND EXPERIENCES OF THE CONFEDERATE ARMY. Cincinatti, 1897. $125-175

Dietz, August — THE POSTAL SERVICE OF THE CONFEDERATE STATES OF AMERICA. Richmond (VA), 1929. $125-175

Dimsdale, Thomas J. — THE VIGILANTES OF MONTANA. Virginia City (MT), 1866. $1,700 or more

Diomedi, Alexander — SKETCHES OF MODERN INDIAN LIFE. (Woodstock, MD, ca. 1894), wraps. $140-170

DIRECTORY OF THE CITY OF MINERAL POINT FOR THE YEAR 1859. Mineral Point (WI), 1859. $225-275

Disturnell, John — THE INFLUENCE OF CLIMATE IN NORTH AND SOUTH AMERICA. NY, 1867. $125-150

Disturnell, John - Publisher — DISTURNELL'S GUIDE THROUGH THE MIDDLE, NORTHERN, AND EASTERN STATES. NY, 1847, maps. $75-100

Disturnell, John (Publisher) — THE EMIGRANT'S GUIDE TO NEW MEXICO, CALIFORNIA, AND OREGON. NY, 1849. $800 or more

Disturnell, John - Publisher — THE GREAT LAKES OR INLAND SEAS OF AMERICA. NY, 186?. $175-225

Disturnell, John - Publisher — THE UPPER LAKES OF NORTH AMERICA: A GUIDE. NY, 1857. $125-150

Dobie, J. Frank — THE FIRST CATTLE IN TEXAS AND THE SOUTHWEST. Austin, 1939. $100-125

Dobie, J. Frank — GUIDE TO LIFE AND LITERATURE OF THE SOUTHWEST. Austin, 1943, wraps. $45-75

Doddridge, Joseph — NOTES, ON THE SETTLEMENT AND INDIAN WARS, OF THE WESTERN PARTS OF VIRGINIA AND PENNSYLVANIA, ETC. Wellsburgh (VA), 1924. $500 or more

Dodge, Grenville M. — HOW WE BUILT THE UNION PACIFIC RAILWAY. Council Bluffs (IA), (ca.1908), wraps. $125-175

Dodge, Grenville M. — UNION PACIFIC RAILROAD, REPORT OF G.M. DODGE, CHIEF ENGINEER, TO THE BOARD OF DIRECTORS — TO IDAHO, MONTANA, OREGON, AND PUGET'S SOUND. Washington, 1869, wraps. $350 or more

Dodge, Richard Irving — THE BLACK HILLS. NY, 1876. $125-150

Dodge, Richard Irving — OUR WILD INDIANS. Hartford, 1882. $100-125

Dodge, Richard Irving — THE PLAINS OF THE GREAT WEST AND THEIR INHABITANTS. NY, 1877. $100-125

Dodge, William Sumner — A WAIF OF THE WAR; OR, THE HISTORY OF THE 75TH ILLINOIS INFANTRY. Chicago, 1866. $165-200

DOMESTIC COOKERY: THE EXPERIENCED AMERICAN HOUSEKEEPER. NY, 1823. $150-175

Donoho, M.H. — CIRCLE-DOT, A TRUE STORY OF COWBOY LIFE 40 YEARS AGO. Topeka, 1907. $85-100

Douglas, C.L. — CATTLE KINGS OF TEXAS. Dallas, (1939). $100 or more (also a limited edition — $350 or more)

Douglas, C.L. — FAMOUS TEXAS FEUDS. Dallas, (1936). $125-150

Douglas, James — THE GOLD FIELDS OF CANADA. Quebec, 1863, wraps. $150-175

Dow, George Francis — THE ARTS AND CRAFTS IN NEW ENGLAND. Topsfield (MA), 1927. $175-225

Dow, George Francis — WHALE SHIPS AND WHALING. Salem, 1925, limited. $150-175

Dow, George Francis & John H. Edmonds — THE PIRATES OF THE NEW ENGLAND COAST. Salem, 1923. $90-125

Downie, William — HUNTING FOR GOLD: PERSONAL EXPERIENCES IN THE EARLY DAYS ON THE PACIFIC COAST. SF, 1893. $175-225

DRAFT OF A CONSTITUTION PUBLISHED UNDER THE DIRECTION OF A COMMITTEE OF CITIZENS OF COLORADO. Denver, 1875. $175 or more

DRAGOON CAMPAIGNS TO THE ROCKY MOUNTAINS. BY A DRAGOON (James Hildreth) — NY, 1836. $350-450

Drake, Benjamin — THE LIFE AND ADVENTURES OF BLACK HAWK. Cincinnati, 1838. $175-225

Drake, Benjamin — TALES AND SKETCHES OF THE QUEEN CITY. Cincinnati, 1838. $90-125

Drake, Benjamin & E.D. Mansfield — CINCINATTI IN 1826. Cincinnati, 1827. $125-175

Drake, Daniel — AN ACCOUNT OF EPIDEMIC CHOLERA, AS IT APPEARED IN CINCINNATI. Cincinnati, 1832, wraps. $250-300

Drake, Daniel — NATURAL AND STATISTICAL VIEW, OR PICTURE OF CINCINNATI AND THE MIAMI COUNTRY. Cincinnati, 1815. $400 or more

Drake, Morgan — LAKE SUPERIOR RAILROAD: LETTER TO THE HON. LEWIS CASS. Pontiac (MI), 1853, wraps. $275-325

Drannan, Capt. William F. — THIRTY-ONE YEARS ON THE PLAINS AND IN THE MOUNTAINS. Chicago, 1899. $175-225

Drayton, John — MEMOIRS OF THE AMERICAN REVOLUTION. Charleston (SC), 1821, 2 vols. $650-725

Drayton, John — A VIEW OF SOUTH-CAROLINA. Charleston, 1802. $850 or more

Driggs, George W. — OPENING OF THE MISSISSIPPI; OR TWO YEARS' CAMPAIGNING IN THE SOUTHWEST. Madison (WI), 1864. $175-225

Drips, Joseph H. — THREE YEARS AMONG THE INDIANS IN DAKOTA. Kimball (SD), 1894, wraps. $800 or more

Drysdale, Isabel — SCENES IN GEORGIA. Philadelphia, (1827). $100-125

Duflot De Mofras, Eugene — EXPLORATION DU TERRITOIRE DE L'OREGON. Paris, 1844, 2 vols. at least $3,750

Duflot De Mofras, Eugene — TRAVELS ON THE PACIFIC COAST. Santa Ana, 1937, 2 vols. $175-225

Duncan, John M. — TRAVELS THROUGH PART OF THE UNITED STATES AND CANADA IN 1818 AND

1819. Glasgow, Scotland, 1823, 2 vols. $400 or more; NY, 1823, 2 vols. $125-175

Duncan, L. Wallace — HISTORY OF MONTGOMERY COUNTY, KANSAS. Iola (KS), 1903. $125-175

Duncan, L. Wallace — HISTORY OF WILSON AND NEOSHO COUNTIES, KANSAS. Fort Scott (KS), 1902. $125-175

Dunlap, William — A HISTORY OF THE AMERICAN THEATRE. NY, 1832. $125-175

Dunlap, William — A HISTORY OF THE NEW NETHERLANDS. NY, 1839-40, 2 vols. $225-275

Dunlap, William — HISTORY OF THE RISE AND PROGRESS OF THE ARTS OF DESIGN IN THE UNITED STATES. NY, 1834, 2 vols. $225-275

Dunn, John — HISTORY OF THE OREGON TERRITORY AND BRITISH NORTH-AMERICAN FUR TRADE. London, 1844. $500 or more

Dunn, John — THE OREGON TERRITORY AND THE BRITISH NORTH-AMERICAN FUR TRADE. Philaddelphia, 1845, wraps. $350

Dustin, Fred — THE CUSTER TRAGEDY. Ann Arbor (MI), 1939, 3 folding maps, limited. $350-425

Duval, John C. — EARLY TIMES IN TEXAS. Austin, 1892. $175-225

Dwight, Timothy — TRAVELS IN NEW-ENGLAND AND NEW YORK. New Haven (CT), 1821-22, 4 vols., 3 maps. $225-275

Dwinelle, John W. — THE COLONIAL HISTORY OF THE CITY OF SAN FRANCISCO. SF, 1863. $675 or more

Dyer, Mrs. D.B. — "FORT RENO," OR PICTURESQUE "CHEYENNE AND ARRAPAHOE ARMY LIFE," BEFORE THE OPENING OF OKLAHOMA. NY, 1896. $175-225

Dyer, Frederick H. — A COMPENDIUM OF THE WAR OF THE REBELLION. Des Moines, 1908. $90-120

E

Early, Lieut. Gen. Jubal A. — A MEMOIR OF THE LAST YEAR OF THE WAR FOR INDEPENDENCE IN THE CONFEDERATE STATES OF AMERICA. Toronto, 1866. $175-225

Eastman, Mary H. — THE AMERICAN ABORIGINAL PORTFOLIO. Philadelphia, (1853), 26 plates. $550-650

Easton, John — A NARRATIVE OF THE CAUSES WHICH LED TO PHILLIP'S INDIAN WAR. Albany (NY), 1858, map. $75-100

Eaton, Rachel Caroline — JOHN ROSS AND THE CHEROKEE INDIANS. Menasha, (WI), 1914. $175-225

Eckenrode, Hamilton J. — THE REVOLUTION IN VIRGINIA. Boston, 1916. $60-75

Edelman, George W. — A GUIDE TO THE VALUE OF CALIFORNIA GOLD. Philadelphia, 1850. $1,500 or more

Edward, David B. — THE HISTORY OF TEXAS. Cincinnati, 1836. $450 or more

Edwards, Billy — GLADIATORS OF THE PRIZE RING, OR PUGILISTS OF AMERICA. Chicago, (1895), folio. $125-175

Edwards, Frank S. — A CAMPAIGN IN NEW MEXICO WITH COL. DONIPHAN. Philadelphia, 1847, wraps. $350-450

Edwards, J.C. — SPEECH IN RELATION TO THE TERRITORY IN DISPUTE BETWEEN THE STATE OF MISSOURI AND THE UNITED STATES. Washington, 1843, 20 pp., sewed. $125-175

Edwards, John N. — NOTED GUERRILLAS. St. Louis, 1877. $125-150

Edwards, John N. — SHELBY AND HIS MEN, OR THE WAR IN THE WEST. Cincinnati, 1867. $60-75

Edwards, John N. — SHELBY'S EXPEDITION TO MEXICO. Kansas City, 1872. $100-125

Edwards, Philip Leget — CALIFORNIA IN 1837. Sacramento, 1890, wraps. $175-225

Edwards, Philip Leget — SKETCH OF THE OREGON TERRITORY; OR, THE EMIGRANT'S GUIDE. Liberty (MO), 1842, wraps. $5,500 — perhaps much more

Edwards, Samuel E. — THE OHIO HUNTER. Battle Creek (MI), 1866. $600-700

Edwards, W.F. (Publisher) — W.F. EDWARDS' TOURISTS' GUIDE AND DIRECTORY OF THE TRUCKEE BASIN. Truckee (CA), 1883. $500 or more

Egle, William H. — HISTORY OF DAUPHINE AND LEBANON COUNTIES (PENNSYLVANIA) — Philadelphia, 1883. $100-125

Egle, William H. — AN ILLUSTRATED HISTORY OF THE COMMONWEALTH OF PENNSYLVANIA. Harrisburg (PA), 1876. $60-75

Elliott, David Stewart — LAST RAID OF THE DALTONS. Coffeyville, (KS), 1892, wraps. $375-450

Elliott, W.W. — HISTORY OF THE ARIZONA TERRITORY. SF, 1884. $850-1000

Ellis, Edward S. — THE LIFE AND TIMES OF CHRISTOPHER CARSON. NY, (1861). $100-125

Ellis, Edward S. — THE LIFE AND ADVENTURES OF COL. DAVID CROCKETT. NY, 1861. $100-125

Ellis, William — THE AMERICAN MISSION IN THE SANDWICH ISLANDS. Honolulu, 1866. $225-275

Ellsworth, Henry W. — VALLEY OF THE UPPER WABASH, INDIANA. NY, 1838, 3 folding lithographs and a map. $225-275

Ellsworth, Lincoln — THE LAST WILD BUFFALO HUNT. NY, 1916. $60-75

Emerson, Charles L. — RISE AND PROGRESS OF MINNESOTA TERRITORY. St. Paul (MN), 1855, wraps. $375-425

Emmons, Samuel Franklin — GEOLOGY AND MINING INDUSTRY OF LEADVILLE, COLORADO. Washington, 1883, 2 vols. $350-425

Emory, William H. — NOTES OF A MILITARY RECONNAISSANCE. Washington, 1848, 68 plates, maps and plans. $175-225

Englehardt, Zephyrin — THE FRANCISCANS OF ARIZONA. Harbor Springs (MI), 1899, wraps. $225-275

Englehardt, Zephyrin — THE FRANCISCANS IN CALIFORNIA. Harbor Springs, 1897, wraps. $225-275

Erwin, Milo — THE HISTORY OF WILLIAMSON COUNTY, ILLINOIS. Marion (IL), 1876. $125-175

Esshom, Frank — PIONEERS AND PROMINENT MEN OF UTAH. Salt Lake City, 1913. $110-135

Ethell, Henry C. — THE RISE AND PROGRESS OF CIVILIZATION IN THE HAIRY NATION AND THE HISTORY OF DAVIS COUNTY. Bloomfield, (IA), 1883. $125-175

ETHNOLOGIC DICTIONARY OF THE NAVAJO LANGUAGE, AN. BY THE FRANCISCAN FATHERS. St. Michaels (AZ), 1910, wraps. $600-750

Etzenhouser, R. — FROM PALMYRA, NEW YORK, 1839, TO INDEPENDENCE, MISSOURI, 1894. Independence, 1894, wraps. $125-150

Evans, Elwood — PUGET SOUND: ITS PAST, PRESENT AND FUTURE. Olympia, 1869, wraps. $225-275

Evans, Elwood — WASHINGTON TERRITORY. Olympia, 1877, wraps. $275-325

Evans, Estwick — A PEDESTRIOUS TOUR, OF 4,000 MILES, THROUGH THE WESTERN STATES AND TERRITORIES. Concord (NH), 1819. $650 or more

Everett, Horace — REGULATING THE INDIAN DEPARTMENT. (Washington, 1834). $225-275

Everts And Kirk — THE OFFICIAL STATE ATLAS OF NEBRASKA. Philadelphia, 1885, 207 colored maps, plates. $450 or more

EVIDENCE CONCERNING PROJECTED RAILWAYS ACROSS THE SIERRA NEVADA MOUNTAINS. Carson City, 1865. $800 or more

Evjen, John O. — SCANDINAVIAN IMMIGRANTS IN NEW YORK, 1639-1674. Minneapolis (MN), 1916. $100-125

Ewell, Thomas T. — A HISTORY OF HOOD COUNTY, TEXAS. Granbury (TX), 1895. $600-800

F

FACTS CONCERNING THE CITY OF SAN DIEGO, THE GREAT SOUTHWESTERN SEA-PORT OF THE UNITED STATES, WITH A MAP SHOWING THE CITY AND ITS SURROUNDINGS. San Diego, (1888), wraps. $225-300

Fairbanks, George R. — EARLY HISTORY OF FLORIDA. St. Augustine (FL), 1857, 82pp., sewed. $250-325

Fairbanks, George R. — THE SPANIARDS IN FLORIDA. Jacksonville (FL), 1868, wraps. $175-250

Fairchild, T.B. — A HISTORY OF THE TOWN OF CUYAHOGA FALLS, SUMMIT COUNTY. Cleveland, 1876. $125-175

Fairfield, Asa Merrill — FAIRFIELD'S PIONEER HISTORY OF LASSEN COUNTY, CALIFORNIA. SF, (1916). $175-225

Falconer, Thomas — LETTERS AND NOTES ON THE TEXAN SANTA FE EXPEDITION, 1841-42. NY, 1930. $175-225

Falconer, Thomas — ON THE DISCOVERY OF THE MISSISSIPPI, AND ON , OREGON, AND NORTHWESTERN BOUNDARY OF THE UNITED STATES. London, 1844. $575-750

Farnham, S.B. — THE NEW YORK AND IDAHO GOLD MINING CO. NY, 1864. $225-300

Farnham, Thomas J. — HISTORY OF OREGON TERRITORY. NY, 1844, wraps. $225-300

Farnham, Thomas J. — TRAVELS IN THE CALIFORNIAS. NY, 1844. $1,750 or more

Farnham, Thomas J. — TRAVELS IN THE GREAT WESTERN PRAIRIES. Poughkeepsie (NY), 1841. $550-650

Finley, Ernest L. — HISTORY OF SONOMA COUNTY. Santa Rosa (CA), 1937. $85-100

Finney & Davis - Publishers — BIOGRAPHICAL AND STATISTICAL HISTORY OF THE CITY OF OSHKOSH. Oshkosh, 1867. $100-125

FIRST ANNUAL REPORT OF THE DIRECTORS OF THE CENTRAL MINING CO. Detroit, 1855. wraps. $100-125

FIRST ANNUAL REVIEW OF PIERCE COUNTY. Prescott (WI), 1855, wraps. $125-150

FIRST SETTLEMENT AND EARLY HISTORY OF PALMYRA, WAYNE COUNTY; NEW YORK, THE. Palmyra, 1858, wraps, 10 pp. $125-175

Fisher, Richard S. — INDIANA: ITS GEOGRAPHY, STATISTICS, COUNTY TOPOGRAPHY. NY, 1852, fldg. map. $175-225

Fleming, E.B. — EARLY HISTORY OF HOPKINS COUNTY, TEXAS. n.p., 1902. $400-500

Fletcher, Charles H. — JEFFERSON COUNTY, IOWA, CENTENNIAL HISTORY. Fairfield (IA), 1876, wraps. $100-125

Flickinger, Robert E. — PIONEER HISTORY OF POCAHONTAS COUNTY, IOWA. Fonda (IA), 1904. $85-100

Flint, Timothy — INDIAN WARS OF THE WEST. Cincinnati, 1833. $225-300

Flower, Richard — LETTERS FROM ILLINOIS, 1820-1821. London, 1822, wraps. $750-850

Foote, Henry Stuart — TEXAS AND THE TEXANS. Philadelphia, 1841, 2 vols. $500-650

Forbes, Alexander — CALIFORNIA: A HISTORY. London, 1839. $550-650

Forbes, James Grant — SKETCHES, HISTORICAL AND TOPOGRAPHICAL, OF THE FLORIDAS. NY, 1821, map. $550 or more

Foreman, Grant — PIONEER DAYS IN THE EARLY SOUTHWEST. Cleveland, 1926. $125-175

Forney, Col. John W. — WHAT I SAW IN TEXAS. Philadelphia, (1872), wraps. $275-350

Forrest, Earle R. — MISSIONS AND PUEBLOS OF THE OLD SOUTHWEST. Cleveland, 1929. $175-225

Foster, Charles — THE GOLD PLACERS OF CALIFORNIA. Akron (OH), 1849, wraps. $3,000-3,750

Foster, George G. - Editor — THE GOLD REGIONS OF CALIFORNIA. NY, 1848, wraps. $350-500

Foster, Isaac — THE FOSTER FAMILY, CALIFORNIA PIONEERS. (Santa Barbara, 1925). $125-150

Foster, James S. — ADVANTAGES OF DAKOTA TERRITORY. Yankton, 1873, wraps. $1,200 or more

Foster, James S. — OUTLINES OF HISTORY OF THE TERRITORY OF DAKOTA AND EMIGRANT'S GUIDE TO THE FREE LANDS OF THE NORTHWEST. Yankton, 1870, map, wraps. $2,750 or more

Fountain, Albert J. — BUREAU OF IMMIGRATION OF THE TERRITORY OF NEW MEXICO: REPORT OF DONA ANA COUNTY. Santa Fe (NM), 1882, wraps. $175-225

Fox, Lady Mary — ACCOUNT OF AN EXPEDITION TO THE INTERIOR OF NEW HOLLAND. London, 1837. $325 or more

Franks, David — THE NEW-YORK DIRECTORY. NY, 1786, 82 pp. $3,500 or more

Fremont, John Charles — OREGON AND CALIFORNIA: THE EXPLORING EXPEDITION TO THE ROCKY MOUNTAINS, OREGON, AND CALIFORNIA. Buffalo, 1849. $85

French, Capt. W.J. — WILD JIM, THE TEXAS COWBOY AND SADDLE KING. Antioch (IL), 1890, wraps. $450-600

French, William — SOME RECOLLECTIONS OF A WESTERN RANCHMAN. London, (1927). $400-450

Fridge, Ike — HISTORY OF THE CHISUM WAR — COWBOY LIFE ON THE FRONTIER. Electra (TX), (1927), wraps. $450 or more

Frink, Margaret A. — JOURNAL OF THE ADVENTURES OF A PARTY OF CALIFORNIA GOLD-SEEKERS. (Oakland, 1897). $450-600

Frink, F.W. — A RECORD OF RICE COUNTY, MINNESOTA, IN 1868. Faribault (MN), 1868, wraps. $125-175

Frost, John — HISTORY OF THE STATE OF CALIFORNIA. Auburn (CA), 1850. $175-225

Frost, John — THE MEXICAN WAR AND ITS WARRIORS. New Haven, 1849. $250-300

Fry, Frederick — FRY'S TRAVELER'S GUIDE, AND DESCRIPTIVE JOURNAL OF THE GREAT NORTH WESTERN TERRITORIES. Cincinnati, 1865. $550-650

Fulkerson, H.S. — RANDOM RECOLLECTIONS OF EARLY DAYS IN MISSISSIPPI. Vicksburg (MS), 1885, wraps. $450-525

Fuller, C.L. — POCKET MAP AND DESCRIPTIVE OUTLINE HISTORY OF THE BLACK HILLS OF DAKOTA AND WYOMING. Rapid City, 1887, wraps, fldg. map. $700-850

Fuller, Emeline — LEFT BY THE INDIANS, OR RAPINE, MASSACRE AND CANNIBALISM ON THE OVERLAND TRAIL IN 1860. Mt. Vernon (IA), 1892, wraps. $250-325

Fullmer, John S. — ASSASSINATION OF JOSEPH AND HYRUM SMITH, THE PROPHET AND THE PATRIARCH OF THE CHURCH OF JESUS CHRIST OF LATTER-DAY SAINTS. Liverpool, 1855. $600-750

Fulmore, Z.T. — THE HISTORY AND GEOGRAPHY OF TEXAS AS TOLD IN COUNTY NAMES. (Austin, 1915). $125-175

G

Gale, George — UPPER MISSISSIPPI. Chicago, 1867. $125-150

Gallaher, James — THE WESTERN SKETCH-BOOK. Boston, 1850. $175-225

Gallatin, Albert — LETTERS OF ALBERT GALLATIN ON THE OREGON QUESTION. Washington, 1846. $100-125

Gard, Wayne — ALONG THE EARLY TRAILS OF THE SOUTHWEST. Austin, 1969, Limited and signed edition. $175-225

Garden, Alexander — ANECDOTES OF THE REVOLUTIONARY WAR IN AMERICA. Charleston, 1822, First & Second Series, 2 vols. $325-400

Garland, Hamlin — THE BOOK OF THE AMERICAN INDIAN. NY, 1923, 34 plates by Frederic Remington. $175-250

Garneau Jr., Joseph — NEBRASKA: HER RESOURCES, ADVANTAGES AND DEVELOPMENT. Omaha (NE), 1893, wraps. $225-275

Garner, James W. — RECONSTRUCTION IN MISSISSIPPI. NY, 1901. $175-225

Garrard, Lewis H. — WAH-TO-YAH, AND THE TAOS TRAIL. Cincinnati, 1850. $650-800

Garrett, Pat F. — THE AUTHENTIC LIFE OF BILLY, THE KID. Santa Fe, 1882, wraps. $4,250 or more

Gass, Patrick — A JOURNAL OF THE VOYAGES AND TRAVELS OF A CORPS OF DISCOVERY, UNDER THE COMMAND OF CAPT. LEWIS AND CAPT. CLARK, ETC. Pittsburgh, 1807. $850-1,000

GEM, A: "THE CITY OF THE PLAINS." ABILENE: THE CENTRE OF THE "GOLDEN BELT." Burlington (IA), 1887, wraps. $100-125

GENERAL AND STATISTICAL DESCRIPTION OF PIERCE COUNTY (WISCONSIN). (Prescott, Wis., 1854), 9 pp., sewed. $125-150

GENERAL ORDERS AFFECTING THE VOLUNTEER FORCE: ADJUTANT GENERAL'S OFFICE, 1863. Washington, 1864. $175-225

GEOLOGICAL SURVEY OF TEXAS: FIRST ANNUAL REPORT. Austin, 1890. $350 or more

Gerhard, Fred — ILLINOIS AS IT IS. Chicago, 1857, 3 fldg. maps. $175-225

Gerstaecker, Friedrich — CALIFORNIA GOLD MINES. Oakland, 1946, signed. $100-125

Gerstaecker, Friedrich — SCENES OF LIFE IN CALIFORNIA. SF, 1942, limited. $85-110

Giddings, Marsh — FIRST ANNUAL MESSAGE TO THE LEGISLATIVE ASSEMBLY OF THE TERRITORY OF NEW MEXICO. Santa Fe, 1871, wraps. $150-200

Gilbert, Paul T. & Charles L. Bryglenn, Allen — HISTORY OF CASS COUNTY (MISSOURI). Topeka (KS), 1917. $125-175

GOLD, SILVER, LEAD, AND COPPER MINES OF ARIZONA — (Philadelphia, 1867), wraps. $550 or more

Goldsborough, Charles W. — THE UNITED STATES' NAVAL CHRONICLE. VOL 1. Washington City, 1824. $175-225

Goldsmith, Oliver — OVERLAND IN FORTY-NINE. Detroit, 1896. $950 or more

Goodnight, Charles, III — THE LOVING BRAND BOOK. Austin, 1965, limited. $275

Goodwin, H.C. — PIONEER HISTORY; OR CORTLAND COUNTY AND THE BORDER WARS OF NEW YORK. NY, 1859. $100-125

Goodyear, W.A. — THE COAL MINES OF THE WESTERN COAST OF THE UNITED STATES. SF, 1877. $125-150

Gordon, Samuel — RECOLLECTIONS OF OLD MILESTOWN, MONTANA. Miles City (MT), 1918. $175-200

Gouge, William M. — THE FISCAL HISTORY OF TEXAS. Philadelphia, 1852. $175-225

Gould, E.W. — FIFTY YEARS ON THE MISSISSIPPI. St. Louis, 1889. $200-250

Gould, Stephen — THE ALAMO CITY GUIDE. (San Antonio), 1882, wraps. $1,000 or more

Gove, Capt. Jesse A. — THE UTAH EXPEDITION, 1857-58. Concord, 1928. $65-80

Graham, W.A. — MAJOR RENO VINDICATED. Hollywood, 1935, wraps. $85-100

Graham, W.A. - Editor — THE OFFICIAL RECORD OF A COURT OF INQUIRY CONVENED — REQUEST OF MAJOR MARCUS A. RENO TO INVESTIGATE HIS CONDUCT AT THE BATTLE OF THE LITTLE BIG HORN, ETC. Pacific Palisades (CA), 1951, 2 vols., folio, limited. $400 or more

Grant, Blanche C. - Editor — KIT CARSON'S OWN STORY. Taos (NM), 1926, wraps. $85-100

Grant, U.S. — GENERAL ORDERS, NO. 67 — Washington, 1868, sewed. $100-125

Graves, Richard S. — OKLAHOMA OUTLAWS. (Oklahoma City, 1915), wraps. $65-80

Graydon, Alexander — MEMOIRS OF A LIFE, CHIEFLY PASSED IN PENNSYLVANIA, WITHIN THE LAST 60 YEARS. Harrisburg (PA), 1811. $175-200

GREAT EASTERN GOLD MINING CO., THE — NY, 1880, wraps. $175-225

GREAT TRANS-CONTINENTAL RAILROAD GUIDE. Chicago, 1869, wraps. $225-275

Grece, Charles F. — FACTS AND OBSERVATIONS RESPECTING CANADA, AND THE UNITED STATES OF AMERICA. London, 1819. $250-325

Greeley, Horace — AN OVERLAND JOURNEY FROM NEW YORK TO SAN FRANCISCO. NY, 1860. $85-100

Green, Ben K. — THE COLOR OF HORSES. Flagstaff (AZ), (1974), trade edition. $40-50

Green, Ben K. — THE LAST TRAIL DRIVE THROUGH DOWNTOWN DALLAS. Flagstaff, (1971), trade edition. $30-35

Green, Jonathan S. — JOURNAL OF A TOUR ON THE NORTHWEST COAST OF AMERICA IN THE YEAR 1829. NY, 1915, limited. $325-375

Green, Max — THE KANZAS REGION. NY, 1856, wraps, 2 maps. $175-225

Green, Thomas J. — JOURNAL OF THE TEXIAN EXPEDITION AGAINST MIER. NY, 1845. $400-500

Greenhow, Robert — THE GEOGRAPHY OF OREGON AND CALIFORNIA. Boston, 1845, wraps. $350-400

Greenhow, Robert — THE HISTORY OF OREGON AND CALIFORNIA. Boston, 1844. $200-250

Greer, James K. — BOIS D'ARC TO BARB'D WIRE. Dallas, 1936. $175-225

Greer, James K. — COLONEL JACK HAYES: TEXAS FRONTIER LEADER AND CALIFORNIA BUILDER. NY, 1952. $125-150

Greer, James K. - Editor — A TEXAS RANGER AND FRONTIERSMAN. Dallas, 1932. $110-135

Gregory, Joseph W. — GREGORY'S GUIDE FOR CALIFORNIA TRAVELLERS VIA THE ISTHMUS OF PANAMA. NY, 1850, wraps. $1,750 or more

Gregory, Samuel — HISTORY OF MEXICO; WITH AN ACCOUNT OF THE TEXAN REVOLUTION. Boston, 1847, wraps. $175-225

Grinnell, George Bird — TWO GREAT SCOUTS AND THEIR PAWNEE BATTALION. Cleveland, 1928. $75-100

Griswold, N.W. — BEAUTIES OF CALIFORNIA. SF, 1883, wraps. $175-225

Grover, La Fayette - Editor — THE OREGON ARCHIVES. Salem (OR), 1853. $850-1,000

Gunn, Douglas — SAN DIEGO: CLIMATE, RESOURCES, TOPOGRAPHY, PRODUCTION, ETC. San Diego, 1886, wraps. $450 or more

H

Hafen, Le Roy R. - Editor — THE MOUNTAIN MEN AND THE FUR TRADE OF THE FAR WEST. Glendale (CA), 1965-72, 10 vols. $400-500

Hafen, Le Roy R. — THE OVERLAND MAIL, 1849-1869. Cleveland, 1926. $75-100

Hafen, Le Roy R. — OVERLAND ROUTES TO THE GOLD FIELDS. Glendale, 1942. $60-75

Hafen, Le Roy R. — THE OLD SPANISH TRAIL. Glendale, 1954. $30-40

Hafen, Le Roy R. & Ann W. - Editors — THE FAR WEST AND THE ROCKIES, 1820-75. Glendale, 1954-61, 15 vols. $400-500

Hafen, Le Roy R. & W.J. Ghent — BROKEN HAND: THE LIFE STORY OF THOMAS FITZPATRICK, CHIEF OF THE MOUNTAIN MEN. Denver, 1931, limited and signed. $275-325

Hafen, Le Roy R. & Francis Marion Young — FORT LARAMIE AND THE PAGEANT OF THE WEST, 1834-1890. Glendale, 1938. $60-75

Hale, Edward Everett — A TRACT FOR THE DAY: HOW TO CONQUER TEXAS BEFORE TEXAS CONQUERS US. Boston, 1845, wraps. $175 or more

Hale, John — CALIFORNIA AS IT IS. SF, 1954, limited. $200-225

Hale, Will (William Hale Stone) — TWENTY-FOUR YEARS A COWBOY AND RANCHMAN IN SOUTHERN TEXAS AND OLD MEXICO. Hedrick (Oklahoma Territory), (1905), wraps. $4,500 or more

Haley, J. Evetts — FORT CONCHO ON THE TEXAS FRONTIER. San Angelo (TX), 1952, trade edition. $85-100

Haley, J. Evetts — THE HERALDRY OF THE RANGE. Canyon (TX), 1949. $425-500

Haley, J. Evetts — JEFF MILTON: A GOOD MAN WITH A GUN. Norman (OK), 1948. $85-100

Haley, J. Evetts — LIFE ON THE TEXAS RANGE. Austin, 1952. $85-100

Haley, J. Evetts — THE XIT RANCH OF TEXAS. Chicago, 1929. $225 or more

Hall, Edward H. — THE GREAT WEST. NY, 1864, wraps. $225-300

Hall, Frederic — THE HISTORY OF SAN JOSE AND SURROUNDINGS. SF, 1871. $150-175

Hall, J. — SONORA: TRAVELS AND ADVENTURES IN SONORA. Chicago, 1881. $1,500 or more

Hall, James — THE ROMANCE OF WESTERN HISTORY. Cincinnati, 1857. $60-75

Hall, James — SKETCHES OF HISTORY, LIFE, AND MANNERS IN THE WEST. Cincinnati, 1834. $175-225

Hall, James — STATISTICS OF THE WEST. Cincinnati, 1836. $125-165

Halley, William — CENTENNIAL YEAR BOOK OF DESCRIPTION OF THE CONTRA COSTA UNDER SPANISH, MEXICAN, AND AMERICAN RULE. Oakland, 1876. $100-150

Hamilton, Patrick — THE RESOURCES OF ARIZONA. Prescott (AZ), 1881, wraps. $225 or more

Hamilton, W.T. — MY SIXTY YEARS ON THE PLAINS. NY, 1905. $125-150

HAND-BOOK OF NESS COUNTY, THE BANNER COUNTY OF WESTERN KANSAS. Chicago, 1887, wraps. $200-250

Hardin, John Wesley — THE LIFE OF JOHN WESLEY HARDIN. Seguin (TX), 1896, wraps. $125-150

Hare, George H. — GUIDE TO SAN JOSE AND VICINITY. San Jose (CA), 1872, wraps. $175-225

Harlan, Jacob Wright — CALIFORNIA, '46 TO '88. SF, 1888. $125-150

Harlow, Neal — THE MAPS OF SAN FRANCISCO BAY. SF, 1950, limited. $550 or more

Harman, S.W. — HELL ON THE BORDER. Fort Smith, (AR), (1898), wraps. $550-625

Harris, Sarah Hollister — AN UNWRITTEN CHAPTER OF SALT LAKE, 1851-1901. New York, 1901. $225-275

Harris, W.B. — PIONEER LIFE IN CALIFORNIA. Stockton (CA), 1884, wraps. $275+

Hart, John A. Et Al — HISTORY OF PIONEER DAYS IN TEXAS AND OKLAHOMA. (Guthrie, 1906). $175-225

Hartley, Oliver C. — DIGEST OF THE LAWS OF TEXAS. Philadelphia, 1850. $175-225

Harvey, Henry — HISTORY OF THE SHAWNEE INDIANS. Cincinnati, 1855. $150+

Haskins, C.W. — THE ARGONAUTS OF CALIFORNIA. New York, 1890. $250+

Hastain, E. — TOWNSHIP PLATS OF THE CREEK NATION. Muskogee (OK), 1910. $300+

Hastings, Frank S. — A RANCHMAN'S RECOLLECTIONS. Chicago, 1921. $125+

Hastings, Lansford W. — THE EMIGRANT'S GUIDE TO OREGON AND CALIFORNIA. Cincinnati, 1845, wraps or boards. At least $11,000

Hastings, Lansford W. — A NEW HISTORY OF OREGON AND CALIFORNIA. Cincinnati, 1849. $450+

Hawley, A.T. — THE CLIMATE, RESOURCES, AND ADVANTAGES OF HUMBOLDT COUNTY. Eureka (CA), 1879, wraps. $500+

Hawley, A.T. — THE PRESENT CONDITION, GROWTH, PROGRESS AND ADVANTAGES OF LOS ANGELES CITY AND COUNTY, SOUTHERN CALIFORNIA. Los Angeles, 1876, map, wraps. $500+

Hawley, W.A. — THE EARLY DAYS OF SANTA BARBARA. New York, 1910, wraps. $125+

Hayden, Ferdinand V. — GEOLOGICAL AND GEOGRAPHICAL ATLAS OF COLORADO. (Washington), 1877. 20 2-page maps. $225+

Hayden, Ferdinand V. — SUN PICTURES OF ROCKY MOUNTAIN SCENERY. New York 1870, 30 mounted photos. $2500+

Hayden, Ferdinand V. — THE YELLOWSTONE NATIONAL PARK. Boston, 1876. Illustrated by Thomas Moran, 2 maps. $3500+

Heckendorn & Wilson — MINERS AND BUSINESS MEN'S DIRECTORY (for Toulumne, California). Columbia (CA), 1856, wraps. $1700+

Helm, Mary S. — SCRAPS OF EARLY TEXAS HISTORY. Austin, 1884. $375+

Herndon, William H. & Jesse W. Weik — HERNDON'S LINCOLN: THE TRUE STORY OF A GREAT LIFE. Chicago, (1889), 3 volumes, 63 plates. $250+

Hewitt, Randall H. — ACROSS THE PLAINS AND OVER THE DIVIDE. New York, (1906), 58 plates and folding map. $125-150

Hewitt, Randall H. — NOTES BY THE WAY: MEMORANDA OF A JOURNEY ACROSS THE PLAINS, FROM DUNDEE, ILL., TO OLYMPIA, W.T. MAY 7 TO NOVEMBER 3, 1862. Olympia (WA), 1863, wraps. $3,500+

Hilton, A. — OKLAHOMA AND INDIAN TERRITORY ALONG THE FRISCO. St. Louis, 1905, wraps, 2 maps. $125-175

Hind, Henry Youle. — NORTH-WEST TERRITORY. Toronto, 1859, folding maps, plans. $350-425

Hinkle, James F. — EARLY DAYS OF A COWBOY ON THE PECOS. Roswell (NM), 1937, wraps. $50-525

Hinton, Richard J. — THE HAND-BOOK OF ARIZONA. San Francisco, 1878, maps. $125-150

HISTORICAL AND DESCRIPTIVE REVIEW OF THE INDUSTRIES OF TACOMA, 1887. Los Angeles, 1887, unbound. $125-150

HISTORICAL AND DESCRIPTIVE REVIEW OF THE INDUSTRIES OF WALLA WALLA. N.p., 1891, wraps. $175-225

HISTORY OF ALAMEDA COUNTY, CALIFORNIA By J.P. Munro-Fraser. Oakland, 1883. $275-350

HISTORY OF AMADOR COUNTY, CALIFORNIA. Oakland, 1881. $200-250

HISTORY OF THE ARKANSAS VALLEY, COLORADO. Chicago, 1881. $140

HISTORY OF THE CITY OF DENVER, ARAPAHOE COUNTY, AND COLORADO. Chicago, 1880. $275

HISTORY OF IDAHO TERRITORY. San Francisco, 1884, maps. $300

HISTORY OF LOS ANGELES COUNTY, CALIFORNIA. Oakland, 1880, folding map. $500

HISTORY OF MARIN COUNTY, CALIFORNIA By J.P. Munro-Fraser. San Francisco, 1880. $400

HISTORY OF MENDOCINO COUNTY, CALIFORNIA. San Francisco, 1880. $350

HISTORY OF MILAM, WILLIAMSON, BASTROP, TRAVIS, LEE AND BURLESON COUNTIES, TEXAS. Chicago, 1893. $400

HISTORY OF MONTANA, 1739-1885. Chicago, 1885, folding map. $325

HISTORY OF NAPA AND LAKE COUNTIES, CALIFORNIA. San Francisco, 1881. $350

HISTORY OF NEVADA. Oakland, 1881, 116 plates. $575

HISTORY OF NEVADA COUNTY, CALIFORNIA By Frank L. Wells. Oakland, 1880, folio. $500

HISTORY OF SAN JOAQUIN COUNTY, CALIFORNIA By Frank T. Gilbert. Oakland, 1879. $475

HISTORY OF SAN LUIS OBISPO COUNTY, CALIFORNIA By Myron Angel. Oakland, 1883. $400

HISTORY OF SANTA BARBARA AND VENTURA COUNTIES, CALIFORNIA By Jesse D. Mason. Oakland, 1883. $175

HISTORY OF SONOMA COUNTY, CALIFORNIA. San Francisco, 1880. $175

HISTORY OF TEXAS, OR THE EMIGRANT'S GUIDE TO THE NEW REPUBLIC. BY A RESIDENT EMIGRANT, A. New York, 1844, with color plate. $450

Hittell, John S. — THE COMMERCE AND INDUSTRIES OF THE PACIFIC COAST OF NORTH AMERICA. San Francisco, 1882, folding map in color. $145

Hittell, John S. — A HISTORY OF THE CITY OF SAN FRANCISCO. San Francisco, 1878. $140

Hittell, John S. — THE RESOURCES OF VALLEJO. (Vallejo, CA, 1869), folding map, wraps. $350

Hittell, John S. — YOSEMITE: ITS WONDERS AND ITS BEAUTIES. San Francisco, 1868, 20 mounted photo views by "Helios" (Eadweard Muybridge). At least $1500

Hittell, Theodore H. (Editor) — ADVENTURES OF JAMES CAPEN ADAMS, MOUNTAINEER AND GRIZZLY BEAR HUNTER, OF CALIFORNIA. San Francisco, 1869. $225

Hodge, Hiram C. — ARIZONA AS IT IS. New York, 1877, map. $175

Holden, W.C. — ALKALI TRAILS. Dallas, (1930), maps. $135

Holden, W.C. — ROLLIE BURNS; OR, AN ACCOUNT OF THE RANCHING INDUSTRY ON THE SOUTH PLAINS. Dallas, (1932), maps. $140

Holden, W.C. — THE SPUR RANCH. Boston, (1934). $175

Holder, Charles F. — ALL ABOUT PASADENA AND ITS VICINITY. Boston, 1889, wraps. $125

Holder, Charles F. — THE CHANNEL ISLANDS OF CALIFORNIA. Chicago, 1910. $90

Holley, Mary Austin — TEXAS: OBSERVATIONS, HISTORICAL, GEOGRAPHICAL AND DESCRIPTIVE. Baltimore, 1833, folding map. At least $1500

Hollister, Ovando J. — THE SILVER MINES OF COLORADO. Central City (CO), 1867, wraps. $550

Hollister, Uriah S. — THE NAVAJO AND HIS BLANKET. Denver, 1903, color plates. $175

Honig, Louis O. — THE PATHFINDER OF THE WEST: JAMES BRIDGER. Kansas City, 1951. $65

Hopkins, Harry C. — HISTORY OF SAN DIEGO: ITS PUEBLO LANDS AND WATER. San Diego, (1929). $75

Horgan, Paul — GREAT RIVER: THE RIO GRANDE IN AMERICAN HISTORY. New York, 1954, 2 vols. $45

Houstoun, Mrs. Matilda C. — TEXAS AND THE GULF OF MEXICO. London, 1844, 2 vols. $450

Howard, Oliver Otis — NEZ PERCE JOSEPH. Boston, 1881, maps. $175

Hughes, John T. — CALIFORNIA: ITS HISTORY, POPULATION, CLIMATE, SOIL, PRODUCTIONS, AND HARBORS. Cincinnati, 1848, wraps. $225

Hulaniski, F.J. (Editor) — HISTORY OF CONTRA COSTA COUNTY, CALIFORNIA. Berkeley (CA), 1917. $175

Hunt, George M. — EARLY DAYS UPON THE PLAINS OF TEXAS. Lubbock (TX), (1919). $250

Hunt, Richard S. & Jesse F. Randel — GUIDE TO THE REPUBLIC OF TEXAS. New York, 1839, folding map. $875

Hunt, Richard S. & Jesse F. Randel — A NEW GUIDE TO TEXAS. New York, 1845, folding map. $675

Hunter, J. Marvin — THE TRAIL DRIVERS OF TEXAS. (San Antonio, 1920-23), 2 vols. $200

Hunter, J. Marvin & Noah H. Rose — THE ALBUM OF GUN-FIGHTERS. (Bandera, TX, 1951). $85

Hunter, John D. — MANNERS AND CUSTOMS OF SEVERAL INDIAN TRIBES LOCATED WEST OF THE MISSISSIPPI. Philadelphia, 1823. $225

Huntington, D.B. — VOCABULARY OF THE UTAH AND SHO-SHO-NE, OR SNAKE DIALECT, WITH INDIAN LEGENDS AND TRADITIONS. Salt Lake City, 1872, sewed. $140

Hutchings, James M. — SCENES OF WONDER AND CURIOSITY IN CALIFORNIA. San Francisco, (1860). $125

Hyde, George E. — THE EARLY BLACKFEET AND THEIR NEIGHBORS. Denver, 1933, wraps. $125

Hyde, George E. — THE PAWNEE INDIANS. Denver, 1934, 2 vols., wraps. $125

Hyde, George E. — RED CLOUD'S FOLK. Norman (OK), 1937. $65

Hyde, George E. — RANGERS AND REGULARS. Denver, 1933, wraps. $100

I

IDAHO: A GUIDE IN WORD AND PICTURE. Caldwell, 1937. $200

Ide, Simeon — THE CONQUEST OF CALIFORNIA: A BIOGRAPHY OF WILLIAM B. IDE. Oakland, 1944. $70

Ide, William Brown — WHO CONQUERED CALIFORNIA? By Simeon Ide. Claremont (NH), (1880 or 1885?). $325

ILLUSTRATED ALBUM OF BIOGRAPHY OF POPE AND STEVENS COUNTIES, MINNESOTA. Chicago, 1888. $175

ILLUSTRATED ATLAS AND HISTORY OF YOLO COUNTY, CALIFORNIA, THE. San Francisco, 1879, map, and 50 plates, large folio. $400

ILLUSTRATED HISTORICAL ATLAS OF THE STATE OF INDIANA. Chicago, 1876. $275

ILLUSTRATED HISTORY OF LOS ANGELES COUNTY, AN. Chicago, 1889. $300

ILLUSTRATED HISTORY OF SAN JOAQUIN COUNTY, AN. Chicago, 1890. $300

INDIAN COUNCIL IN THE VALLEY OF THE WALLA-WALLA, 1855, THE By Lawrence Kip. San Francisco, 1855, wraps. $850

INDIAN MISSION IN THE UNITED STATES, THE. Philadelphia, 1841, wraps. At least $1750

INDUSTRIAL PRODIGY OF THE NEW SOUTHWEST, THE. Muskogee, Indian Territory (ca. 1902), wraps. $100

Ingersoll, Luther A. — CENTURY ANNALS OF SAN BERNARDINO COUNTY. Los Angeles, 1904. $125

Inman, Col. Henry — THE OLD SANTA FE TRAIL. New York, 1897, map and 8 plates by Frederic Remington. $175

Inman, Col. Henry — STORIES OF THE OLD SANTA FE TRAIL. Kansas City, 1881. $135

Inman, Col. Henry (Editor) — BUFFALO JONES' 40 YEARS OF ADVENTURE. Topeka, 1899, 43 plates. $185

Inman, Col. Henry & William F. Cody — THE GREAT SALT LAKE TRAIL. New York, 1898, map and 8 plates. $185

Irving, John Treat, Jr. — INDIAN SKETCHES, TAKEN DURING AN EXPEDITION TO THE PAWNEE TRIBES. Philadelphia, 1835, 2 vols. $300

Ives, Joseph C. — REPORT UPON THE COLORADO RIVER OF THE WEST. Washington, 1861, 4 folding maps, plates. $225

Ivins, Virginia W. — PEN PICTURES OF EARLY WESTERN DAYS. (Keokuk, IA), 1905. $115

J

Jackson, A.P. And Cole, E.C. — OKLAHOMA! POLITICALLY AND TOPOGRAPHICALLY DESCRIBED. Kansas City, (1885), wraps. $525-600

Jackson, A.W. — BARBARIANA: OR SCENERY, CLIMATE, SOILS AND SOCIAL CONDITIONS OF SANTA BARBARA CITY AND COUNTY. San Francisco, 1888, wraps. $90-125

Jackson, Andrew — MESSAGE FROM THE PRESIDENT OF THE UNITED STATES, IN COMPLIANCE WITH A RESOLUTION OF THE SENATE CONCERNING THE

FUR TRADE AND INLAND TRADE TO MEXICO. (Washington, 1832), unbound. $275-325

Jackson, George — SIXTY YEARS IN TEXAS. (Dallas, 1908). $175-200

James, Edwin - Editor — ACCOUNT OF AN EXPEDITION FROM PITTSBURGH TO THE ROCKY MOUNTAINS. 3 vols. Philadelphia, 1822-23. $1300-1500

James, Edwin - Editor — A NARRATIVE OF THE CAPTIVITY AND ADVENTURES OF JOHN TANNER. New York, 1830. $650-750

James, Fred — THE KLONDIKE GOLDFIELDS AND HOW TO GET THERE. London, 1897, wraps. $450--525

James, W.S. — COW-BOY LIFE IN TEXAS. Chicago, (1893), 34 plates, wraps. $275

James, William F. And Mc Murry, George H. — HISTORY OF SAN JOSE, CALIFORNIA. San Jose, 1933. $75-90

Jefferson, H.E. — OKLAHOMA: THE BEAUTIFUL LAND. Chicago, 1889, wraps. $550+

Jennings, N.A. — A TEXAS RANGER. New York, 1899. $300

Jerome, Chauncey — HISTORY OF THE AMERICAN CLOCK BUSINESS FOR THE PAST 60 YEARS. New Haven, 1860, wraps. $175

Jocknick, Sidney — EARLY DAYS ON THE WESTERN SLOPE OF COLORADO. Denver, 1913. $175

Johnson, Crisfield — THE HISTORY OF CUYAHOGA COUNTY, OHIO. Cleveland (OH), 1879. $100

Johnson, Edwin F. — RAILROAD TO THE PACIFIC, NORTHERN ROUTE. New York, 1854, 3 maps. $350

Johnson, Harrison — JOHNSON'S HISTORY OF NEBRASKA. Omaha (NE), 1880, folding map. $150

Johnson, Don Carlos — A BRIEF HISTORY OF SPRINGVILLE, UTAH. Springville, 1900, wraps. $225.

Johnson, Overton & William H. Winter — ROUTE ACROSS THE ROCKY MOUNTAINS, ETC. Lafayette (IN), 1846. $1700+

Johnson, Sidney S. — TEXANS WHO WORE THE GRAY. Tyler (TX), ca.1907. $375

Johnston, Carrier Polk & W.H.S. Mc Glumphy — HISTORY OF CLINTON AND CALDWELL COUNTIES, MISSOURI. Topeka (KS), 1923. $100

Johnston, Charles — A NARRATIVE OF THE INCIDENTS ATTENDING THE CAPTURE, DETENTION, AND RANSOM OF —. New York, 1827. $235

Jones, A.D. — ILLINOIS AND THE WEST. Boston, 1838, folding map. $125

Jones, Anson B. — MEMORANDA AND OFFICIAL CORRESPONDENCE RELATING TO THE REPUBLIC OF TEXAS, ITS HISTORY AND ANNEXATION. New York, 1859. $175

Jones, Charles C., Jr. — THE DEAD TOWNS OF GEORGIA. Savannah (GA), 1878, maps. $125

Jones, Charles C., Jr. — THE HISTORY OF GEORGIA. Boston, 1883, maps and plates, 2 vols. $200

Jones, Charles C., Jr. — THE HISTORY OF SAVANNAH. Syracuse (NY), 1890. $200

Jones, David — A JOURNAL OF TWO VISITS MADE TO SOME NATIONS OF INDIANS ON THE WEST SIDE OF THE RIVER OHIO, IN THE YEARS 1772 AND 1773. Burlington (NJ), 1774. At least $7500

Jones, Herschel — ADVENTURES IN AMERICANA. New York, 1928, 2 vols., 300 plates. $350

Jones, Jonathan H. — A CONDENSED HISTORY OF THE APACHE AND COMANCHE INDIAN TRIBES. San Antonio, 1899. $500

Jones, Samuel — PITTSBURGH IN THE YEAR EIGHTEEN-HUNDRED AND TWENTY-SIX. Pittsburgh, 1826. At least $1200

Jones, William Carey — LAND TITLES IN CALIFORNIA. San Francisco, 1852, wraps. $725

JOURNAL OF THE CONVENTION TO FORM A CONSTITUTION FOR THE STATE OF WISCONSIN: BEGUN AND HELD AT MADISON ON THE 5TH DAY OF OCTOBER, 1846. Madison (WI), 1847. $175

JOURNAL OF AN EXCURSION MADE BY THE CORPS OF CADETS UNDER CAPT. PATRIDGE. Concord (NH), 1822, wraps. $100

Judd, A.N. — CAMPAIGNING AGAINST THE SIOUX. (Watsonville, CA, 1906), wraps. At least $825

K

Kane, Paul — WANDERINGS OF AN ARTIST AMONG THE INDIANS OF NORTH AMERICA. London, 1859. $1200-1500

Kane, Thomas Leiper — THE MORMONS. Philadelphia, 1850, wraps. $275-325

Keating, William H. — NARRATIVE OF AN EXPEDITION TO THE SOURCE OF ST. PETER'S RIVER, LAKE WINNEPEEK — 2 vols. Philadelphia, 1824. $325-375

Keleher, William A. — THE FABULOUS FRONTIER. Santa Fe, (1945). $115

Keleher, William A. — THE MAXWELL LAND GRANT. Santa Fe, (1942). $200-250

Keller, George — A TRIP ACROSS THE PLAINS. (Masillon, Ohio, 1851). $3000-5000

Kelley, Hall J. — GENERAL CIRCULAR TO ALL PERSONS OF GOOD CHARACTER WHO WISH TO EMIGRATE TO THE OREGON TERRITORY. Charlestown (MA), 1831, wraps. $675

Kelley, Hall J. — A GEOGRAPHICAL SKETCH OF THAT PART OF NORTH AMERICA CALLED OREGON. Boston, 1830, folding map, wraps. $1500+

Kelley, Hall J. — HISTORY OF THE COLONIZATION OF THE OREGON TERRITORY. Worcester (MA), 1850, sewn. $1200+

Kelley, Hall J. — A HISTORY OF THE SETTLEMENT OF OREGON AND THE INTERIOR OF UPPER CALIFORNIA. Springfield (MA), 1868, wraps. $5500+

Kelly, Charles — OLD GREENWOOD: THE STORY OF CALEB GREENWOOD, TRAPPER, PATHFINDER AND EARLY PIONEER OF THE WEST. Salt Lake City, 1936. $160

Kelly, Charles — THE OUTLAW TRAIL: A HISTORY OF BUTCH CASSIDY AND HIS WILD BUNCH. Salt Lake City, 1938. $140

Kelly, Charles & Maurice L. Howe — MILES L. GOODYEAR, FIRST CITIZEN OF UTAH. Salt Lake City, 1937. $80

Kelly, George Fox — LAND FRAUDS OF CALIFORNIA. Np., 1864, wraps. $550+

Kelly, L.V. — THE RANGE MEN: THE STORY OF THE RANCHERS AND INDIANS OF ALBERTA. Toronto, 1913. $325

Kelly, William — AN EXCURSION TO CALIFORNIA OVER THE PRAIRIES, ROCKY MOUNTAINS, AND

GREAT SIERRA NEVADA. 2 vols. London, 1851. $450-525

Kendall, George Wilkins — NARRATIVE OF THE TEXAN SANTA FE EXPEDITION, New York, 1844, 2 vols., folding map, plates. $500

Kendall, George Wilkins — THE WAR BETWEEN THE UNITED STATES AND MEXICO. New York, 1841. $1800-2500

Kennedy, William — TEXAS: ITS GEOGRAPHY, NATURAL HISTORY, AND TOPOGRAPHY. New York, 1844, wraps. $225

Kennedy, William — TEXAS: THE RISE, PROGRESS AND PROSPECTS OF THE REPUBLIC OF TEXAS. London, 1841, 2 vols., charts, maps. $550

Kercheval, Samuel — A HISTORY OF THE VALLEY OF VIRGINIA. Winchester, Virginia, 1833. $675-750

King, Charles — THE FIFTH CAVALRY IN THE SIOUX WAR TO 1876: CAMPAIGNING WITH CROOK. Milwaukee, 1880, wraps. $275

King, Frank M. — LONGHORN TRAIL DRIVERS. (Los Angeles, 1940). $115

King, Frank M. — WRANGLIN' IN THE PAST. (Los Angeles, 1935). $115

King, Richard — NARRATIVE OF A JOURNEY TO THE SHORES OF THE ARCTIC OCEAN, IN 1833, 1834, AND 1835. London, 1836, 2 vols., maps. $500

Kinzie, Mrs. Juliette A. — WAU-BUN, THE "EARLY DAY" IN THE NORTH-WEST. New York, 1856. $125

Kip, Lawrence — ARMY LIFE IN THE PACIFIC. New York, 1859. $400

KLONDYKE MINES AND THE GOLDEN VALLEY OF THE YUKON, THE. N.p, 1897, wraps. $125

Kneedler, H.S. — THE COAST COUNTRY OF TEXAS. Cincinnati, 1896, wraps. $175

Knight, Dr. & John Slover — INDIAN ATROCITIES. Nashville, 1843. At least $1750

Knoblock, Byron W. — BANNERSTONES OF THE NORTH AMERICAN INDIAN. La Grange (IL), 1939, 270 plates. $225

Knox, Dudley W. — NAVAL SKETCHES OF THE WAR IN CALIFORNIA. New York, 1939. $200

Kohl, L.G. — KITCHI-GAMI: WANDERINGS ROUND LAKE SUPERIOR. London, 1860. $325

Kroeber, Alfred L. — HANDBOOK OF THE INDIANS OF CALIFORNIA. Washington, 1925, maps, plates. $175

Kuykendall, Ivan Lee — GHOST RIDERS OF THE MOGOLLON. San Antonio, (1954). $375

Kuykendall, Judge W.L. — FRONTIER DAYS. N.p., 1917. $85

L

La Bree, Ben (Editor) — THE CONFEDERATE SOLDIER IN THE CIVIL WAR, 1861-1865. Louisville, 1895, folio. $250

La Frentz, F.W. — COWBOY STUFF. *, 1922. Limited to 500. $550-650

La Salle, Charles E. — COLONEL CROCKET, THE TEXAS TRAILER. New York, (1871), wraps. $125

La Salle, Nicolas De — RELATIONS OF THE DISCOVERY OF THE MISSISSIPPI RIVER. Chicago, 1898, French and English text. $350

Lamson, David R. — TWO YEARS' EXPERIENCE AMONG THE SHAKERS. West Boylston (MA), 1848.

$125

Lancaster, Robert A., Jr. — HISTORIC VIRGINIA HOMES AND CHURCHES. Philadelphia, 1915. $110

Lane, Walter P. — ADVENTURES AND RECOLLECTIONS OF GEN. WALTER WALTER P. LANE. Marshall (TX), 1887, wraps. $1000

Lang, H.O.(Editor) — HISTORY OF THE WILLAMETTE VALLEY. Portland (OR), 1885. $90

Lang, William W. — A PAPER ON THE RESOURCES AND CAPABILITIES OF TEXAS. (New York), 1881, wraps. $135-160

Langley, Henry G. — THE SAN FRANCISCO DIRECTORY FOR THE YEAR 1858. San Francisco, 1858. $400

Langston, Mrs. George — HISTORY OF EASTLAND COUNTY, TEXAS. Dallas, 1904. $250

LAWS AND DECREES OF THE STATE OF COAHUILA AND TEXAS, IN SPANISH AND ENGLISH. Houston, 1839. $600-700

Langworthy, Lucius H. — DUBUQUE: ITS HISTORY, MINES, INDIAN LEGENDS. Dubuque (IA), (1855), wraps. $250

Lanier, Sidney — FLORIDA: ITS SCENERY, CLIMATE, AND HISTORY. Philadelphia, 1876. $250

Lanman, Charles — ADVENTURES IN THE WILDS OF THE UNITED STATES AND BRITISH AMERICAN PROVINCES. Philadelphia, 1856, 2 vols. $675

Lanman, Charles — HAW-HO-NOO, OR RECORDS OF A TOURIST. Philadelphia, 1850. $350

Lanman, Charles — A SUMMER IN THE WILDNERNESS. New York, 1847. $350

Lanman, Charles — A TOUR TO THE RIVER SAGUENAY. Philadelphia, 1848, wraps. $300

Lapham, I.A. — A GEOGRAPHICAL AND TOPOGRAPHICAL DESCRIPTION OF WISCONSIN. Milwaukee, 1844, folding map. $450

LARAMIE, HAHN'S PEAK AND PACIFIC RAILWAY SYSTEM: THE DIRECT GATEWAY TO SOUTHERN WYOMING, NORTHERN COLORADO, AND EASTERN UTAH. N.p, ca.1910, wraps, folio. $250

Larimer, Mrs. Sarah L. — THE CAPTURE AND ESCAPE; OR, LIFE AMONG THE SIOUX. Phladelphia, 1870. $125

Larimer, William — REMINISCENCES OF GEN. WILLIAM LARIMER AND OF HIS SON WILLIAM H.H. LARIMER. Lancaster (PA), 1918, folding chart. $450

Laroque, Francois — A JOURNAL OF FRANCOIS A. LAROQUE FROM THE ASSINIBOINE TO THE YELLOWSTONE, 1805. Ottawa (Canada), 1910, wraps. $275

Larpenteur, Charles — FORTY YEARS A FUR TRADER OF THE UPPER MISSISSIPPI. New York, 1898, 6 maps, 2 vols. $135

Latham, H. — TRANS-MISSOURI STOCK RAISING. Omaha, 1871, map, wraps. At least $550

Latour, A. Lacarriere — HISTORICAL MEMOIR OF THE WAR IN WEST FLORIDA AND LOUISIANA IN 1814-15. Philadelphia, 1816, 2 vols, atlas. $1800

Latrobe, Charles Joseph — THE RAMBLER IN MEXICO. London, 1836. $275

LAWS AND DECREES OF THE STATE OF COAHUILA AND TEXAS, IN SPANISH AND ENGLISH. Houston, 1839. $625

LAWS AND REGULATIONS OF UNION DISTRICT, CLEAR CREEK COUNTY, C.T. Central, C.T. (Colorado Territory), 1864, wraps. $675

LAWS FOR THE BETTER GOVERNMENT OF CALIFORNIA. San Francisco, 1848. The first English book printed in California. At least $5500

LAWS OF THE CHEROKEE NATION. Tahlequah, Indian Territory, 1852. $1500

LAWS OF THE CHOCTAW NATION, MADE AND ENACTED BY THE GENERAL COUNCIL FROM 1886 TO 1890. Atoka, Indian Territory. In Choctaw and English. $300

LAW OF DESCENT AND DISTRIBUTION GOVERNING LANDS OF THE CREEK NATION, AS HELD BY C. W. RAYMOND, JUDGE OF THE U.S. COURT FOR THE INDIAN TERRITORY. N.p, 1903, wraps. $250

LAWS OF THE GREGORY DISTRICT, FEBRUARY 18 & 20, 1860. Denver, 1860, wraps. $1200

LAWS OF THE TERRITORY OF NEW MEXICO. Santa Fe (NM), 1862, wraps. $300

LAWS OF THE TOWN OF SAN FRANCISCO. San Francisco, 1847, wraps. $1250

Layne, J. Gregg — ANNALS OF LOS ANGELES. San Francisco, 1935. $60-75

Le Conte, Joseph. — A JOURNAL OF RAMBLINGS THROUGH THE HIGH SIERRAS OF CALIFORNIA. San Francisco, 1875, photos. At least $1800

Lea, Pryor — AN OUTLINE OF THE CENTRAL TRANSIT, IN A SERIES OF SIX LETTERS TO HON. JOHN HEMPHILL. Galveston (TX), 1859, wraps. $125

Lea, Tom — THE KING RANCH. 2 vols. Boston, (1957). $135-160. Also a special limited edition, $500 or more.

LEADVILLE CHRONICLE ANNUAL. Leadville (CO), 1881, wraps. $175

LEADVILLE, COLORADO: THE MOST WONDERFUL MINING CAMP IN THE WORLD By John L. Loomis. Colorado Springs, 1879, wraps. $325-375

LEE TRIAL! AN EXPOSE OF THE MOUNTAIN MEADOWS MASSACRE, THE. Salt Lake City, 1875, wraps. $950

Leeper, David Rohrer — THE ARGONAUTS OF FORTY-NINE. South Bend, 1894. $85-110

Leese, Jacob P. — HISTORICAL OUTLINE OF LOWER CALIFORNIA. New York, 1865, wraps. $175

Leigh, William R. — THE WESTERN PONY. New York, (1933), color plates. $500

Leonard, H.L.W. — OREGON TERRITORY. Cleveland, 1846, wraps. At least $3000

Lester, C. Edwards — SAM HOUSTON AND HIS REPUBLIC. New York, 1846, maps. $350

LETTER FROM THE SECRETARY OF STATE, ACCOMPANYING CERTAIN LAWS OF THE NORTHWESTERN AND INDIAN TERRITORIES OF THE UNITED STATES (Washington), 1902, sewn. $150

Levy, Daniel — LES FRANCAIS EN CALIFORNIE. San Francisco, 1884, wraps. $175

Lewis, Meriwether & William Clark — HISTORY OF THE EXPEDITION UNDER THE COMMAND OF CAPTAINS LEWIS AND CLARK. Philadelphia, 1814, 2 vols., folding map and charts. Possibly as much as $50,000 — see a specialist.

Lewis, Meriwether & William Clark — ORIGINAL JOURNALS OF THE LEWIS AND CLARK EXPEDITION, 1804-1806. New York, 1904-05, 8 vols., atlas. $1500

Lewis, Meriwether & William Clark — TRAVELS TO THE SOURCE OF THE MISSOURI RIVER AND ACROSS THE AMERICAN CONTINENT TO THE PACIFIC OCEAN. London, 1814, map and charts. $3000

Lockwood, Frank C. — THE APACHE INDIANS. New York, 1938. $85

Lockwood, Frank C. — ARIZONA CHARACTERS. Los Angeles, 1928. $125

Lockwood, Frank C. — PIONEER DAYS IN ARIZONA. New York, 1932. $90

LONE STAR GUIDE DESCRIPTIVE OF COUNTRIES ON THE LINE OF THE INTERNATIONAL AND GREAT NORTHERN RAILROAD OF TEXAS, THE By H.M. Hoxie. St. Louis, ca. 1877, folding map, table, wraps. $225

Loughborough, John — THE PACIFIC TELEGRAPH AND RAILWAY. St. Louis, 1849, folding maps, not bound. $750

Lowman, Al — THIS BITTERLY BEAUTIFUL LAND: A TEXAS COMMONPLACE BOOK. (Austin, 1972), folio. $500

Luhan, Mabel Dodge — TAOS AND ITS ARTISTS. New York, 1947. $175

Luke, L.D. — ADVENTURES AND TRAVELS IN THE NEW WONDER LAND OF YELLOWSTONE PARK. Utica (NY), 1886. $85

Lyman, Albert — JOURNAL OF A VOYAGE TO CALIFORNIA, AND LIFE IN THE GOLD DIGGINGS. Hartford (CT), 1852, wraps. $1500

M

M'Clung, John A. — SKETCHES OF WESTERN ADVENTURE. Maysville (KY), 1832. $875

M'Donell, Alexander — A NARRATIVE OF TRANSACTIONS IN THE RED RIVER COUNTRY. London, 1819, folding map. At least $1500

MacCabe, Julius P. Bolivar — A DIRECTORY OF CLEVELAND AND THE CITIES OF OHIO FOR THE YEARS 1837-1838. Cleveland, 1837. $875

MacCabe, Julius P. Bolivar — DIRECTORY OF THE CITY OF DETROIT. Detroit, 1837. $850

MacCabe, Julius P. Bolivar — DIRECTORY OF THE CITY OF MILWAUKEE. Milwaukee, 1847. $450

Mack, Effie — NEVADA: A HISTORY OF THE STATE. Glendale, 1936, map. $85

Mackay, Malcolm S. — COW-RANGE AND HUNTING TRAIL. New York, 1925. $225

Magoffin, Susan Shelby — DOWN THE SANTA FE TRAIL AND INTO MEXICO. New Haven, 1926, maps. $150

Maillard, N. Doran — THE HISTORY OF THE REPUBLIC OF TEXAS, FROM THE DISCOVERY OF THE COUNTRY TO THE PRESENT TIME. London, 1842, folding map. $475

Mangam, William D. — THE CLARKS OF MONTANA. (New York, 1939), wraps. $350

Manly, William Lewis — DEATH VALLEY IN '49. San Jose (CA), 1894. $125

MARCH OF THE FIRST, THE. Denver, 1863, sewn. At least $3500

Marcy, Randolph B. — THE PRAIRIE TRAVELER: A HAND-BOOK FOR OVERLAND EXPEDITIONS. New York, 1859, map. $375

Marks, B. — SMALL SCALE FARMING IN CENTRAL CALIFORNIA. San Francisco, 1888, wraps. $125

Marsh, James B. — FOUR YEARS IN THE ROCKIES. New Castle (PA), 1884. $400

Marshall, William I. — ACQUISITION OF OREGON, AND THE LONG SUPPRESSED EVIDENCE ABOUT MARCUS WHITMAN. (Seattle), 1905, 2 vols. $200

Martin, Aaron — AN ATTEMPT TO SHOW THE INCONSISTENCY OF SLAVE-HOLDING, WITH THE RELIGION OF THE GOSPEL. Lexington (KY), 1807, sewn. At least $2000

Martineau, Harriet — SOCIETY IN AMERICA. London, 1837, 3 vols. $625

Mason, Emily V. (Editor) — THE SOUTHERN POEMS OF THE WAR. Baltimore, 1867. $125

Mason, Z.H. — A GENERAL DESCRIPTION OF ORANGE COUNTY, FLORIDA. Orlando (FL) (1881), map, wraps. $325

Mathews, A.E. — CANYON CITY, COLORADO, AND ITS SURROUNDINGS. New York, 1870, map. At least $3500

Mathews, A.E. — PENCIL SKETCHES OF COLORADO. (New York), 1866. At least $4500

Mathews, A.E. — PENCIL SKETCHES OF MONTANA. New York, 1868. At least $3500

Mathews, Alfred E. — GEMS OF ROCKY MOUNTAIN SCENERY. New York, 1869. $1750

Mathews, Alfred E. — INTERESTING NARRATIVE; BEING A JOURNAL OF THE FLIGHT OF ALFRED E. MATHEWS, OF STARK CO., OHIO, FROM THE STATE OF TEXAS —. (New Philadelphia, OH), 1861, sewn. $1250

Mathews, Mrs. M.M. — TEN YEARS IN NEVADA. Buffalo (NY), 1880. $225

Matson, N. — REMINISCENCES OF BUREAU COUNTY. Princeton (IL), 1872. $90

Maynard, G.W. — REPORT ON THE PROPERTY OF THE ALICE GOLD AND SILVER MINING CO., BUTTE. New York, 1882, maps, wraps. $125

McAdam, R.W. — CHICKASAWS AND CHOCTAWS. COMPRISING THE TREATIES OF 1855 AND 1866. Ardmore (OK), 1891, wraps. $350

McCall, Ansel J. — PICK AND PAN: A TRIP TO THE DIGGINGS IN 1849. Bath (NY), 1889, wraps. $725

McCall, George A. — LETTERS FROM THE FRONTIERS. Philadelphia, 1868. $300

McCall, Hugh — THE HISTORY OF GEORGIA. Savannah (GA), 1811-16, 2 vols. $450

McCalla, William L. — ADVENTURES IN TEXAS. Philadelphia, 1841. $625

McClintock, John S. — PIONEER DAYS IN THE BLACK HILLS. Deadwood, (1939). $125

McClintock, Walter — OLD INDIAN TRAILS. Boston, 1923. $60

McClintock, Walter — THE OLD NORTH TRAIL. London, 1910, folding map. $100

McCollum, William — CALIFORNIA AS I SAW IT. Buffalo (NY), 1850, wraps. At least $8000

McConkey, Mrs. Harriet E. — DAKOTA WAR; OR, INDIAN MASSACRE AND WAR IN MINNESOTA. St. Paul (MN), 1863. $350

McConnell, Joseph Carroll — THE WEST TEXAS FRONTIER. Jacksboro (TX), 1933. $125

McConnell, W.J. — EARLY HISTORY OF IDAHO. Caldwell, 1913. $85

McCorkle, John & O.S. Barton — THREE YEARS WITH QUANTRELL. Armstrong (MO), (1914), wraps. $250

McCormick, Richard C. — ARIZONA: ITS RESOURCES AND PROSPECTS. New York, 1865, folding map, wraps. $125

McCormick, S.J. — ALMANAC FOR THE YEAR 1864; CONTAINING USEFUL INFORMATION RELATIVE TO THE POPULATION, PROGRESS AND RESOURCES OF OREGON, WASHINGTON AND IDAHO. Portland, (1863), wraps. $225+

McCoy, Isaac — HISTORY OF BAPTIST INDIAN MISSIONS. Washington, 1840. $300

McCoy, Isaac — REMARKS ON THE PRACTICABILITY OF INDIAN REFORM. Boston, 1827, wraps. $350

McCoy, Isaac — REMOVE INDIANS WESTWARD. (Washington), 1829, sewn. $125

McCoy, Joseph G. — HISTORIC SKETCHES OF THE CATTLE TRADE OF THE WEST AND SOUTHWEST. Kansas City, 1874. $1000

McDanield, H.F. & N.A. Taylor. — THE COMING EMPIRE; OR, 2,000 MILES IN TEXAS ON HORSEBACK. New York, (1877). $125

McEachran, D. — NOTES OF A TRIP TO BOW RIVER, NORTH-WEST TERRITORIES. Montreal, 1881. $225

McGee, Joseph H. — STORY OF THE GRAND RIVER COUNTRY, 1821-1905. (Gallatin, MO, 1909), wraps. $125

McGlashan, C.F. — HISTORY OF THE DONNER PARTY: A TRAGEDY OF THE SIERRAS. Truckee (CA), (1879). $700

McIlvaine, William, Jr. — SKETCHES OF SCENERY AND NOTES OF PERSONAL ADVENTURE, IN CALIFORNIA AND MEXICO. Philadelphia, 1850, plates. $1800

McIntire, Jim — EARLY DAYS IN TEXAS: A TRIP TO HELL AND HEAVEN. Kansas City (MO), (1902), plates. $300

McKay, Richard C. — SOUTH STREET: A MARITIME HISTORY OF NEW YORK. New York, (1934), 48 illus. $175

McKee, Dr. W.H. — THE TERRITORY OF NEW MEXICO AND ITS RESOURCES. New York, 1866, wraps. At least $2500

McKee, James Cooper — NARRATIVE OF THE SURRENDER OF A COMMAND OF U.S. FORCES AT FORT FILLMORE, N.M., IN JULY A.D. 1861. New York, 1881, wraps, (2nd edition). $225

McKim, Randolph H. — A SOLDIER'S RECOLLECTIONS: LEAVES FROM THE DIARY OF A YOUNG CONFEDERATE. New York, 1911. $75

McKnight, George S. — CALIFORNIA 49ER: TRAVELS FROM PERRYSBURG TO CALIFORNIA. Perrysburg (OH), 1903, wraps. $175

McLeod, Donald — HISTORY OF WISKONSAN, FROM ITS FIRST DISCOVERY TO THE PRESENT PERIOD. Buffalo (NY), 1846, folding map, plates. $325

McMurtrie, Douglas C. & Albert H. Allen — EARLY PRINTING IN COLORADO. Denver, 1935. $100

McMurtrie, Douglas C. — PIONEER PRINTING IN TEXAS. Austin, 1932, wraps. $100

McMurtrie, Douglas C. — THE BEGINNINGS OF PRINTING IN UTAH. Chicago, 1931. $100

McNeil, Samuel — MCNEILS TRAVELS IN 1849, TO, THROUGH AND FROM THE GOLD REGIONS. Columbus (OH), 1850, wraps. At least $6000

Meeker, Ezra — WASHINGTON TERRITORY WEST OF THE CASCADE MOUNTAINS. Olympia (WA), 1870, wraps. $825

MEMORIAL AND BIOGRAPHICAL HISTORY OF JOHNSON AND HILL COUNTIES, TEXAS. Chicago, 1892. $350

MEMORIAL AND BIOGRAPHICAL HISTORY OF MCLENNAN, FALLS, BELL AND CORYELL COUNTIES, TEXAS. Chicago, 1893. $425

MEMORIAL TO THE PRESIDENT AND CONGRESS FOR THE ADMISSION OF WYOMING TERRITORY TO THE UNION. Cheyenne (WY), 1889, wraps. $135

Mercer, A.S. — THE BANDITTI OF THE PLAINS. (Cheyenne, WY, 1894), map. At least $3500

Mercer, A.S. — WASHINGTON TERRITORY: THE GREAT NORTH-WEST. Utica (NY), 1865, wraps. $950

MEXICAN TREACHERIES AND CRUELTIES By Lieut. G.N. Allen. Boston, 1847, wraps. $100

MEXICO AND THE UNITED STATES: AN AMERICAN VIEW OF THE MEXICAN QUESTION. BY A CITIZEN OF CALIFORNIA. San Francisco, 1866, wraps. $125

MEXICO IN 1842 — TO WHICH IS ADDED, AN ACCOUNT OF TEXAS AND YUCATAN, AND OF THE SANTA FE EXPEDITION By George F. Folsom?. New York, 1842, folding map. $400

Miles, William — JOURNAL OF THE SUFFERINGS AND HARDSHIPS OF CAPT. PARKER H. FRENCH'S OVERLAND EXPEDITION TO CALIFORNIA. Chambersburg (PA), 1851, wraps. At least $4000

Miller, Joaquin — AN ILLUSTRATED HISTORY OF MONTANA. Chicago, 1894, 2 vols. $200

Mills, William W. — FORTY YEARS AT EL PASO, 1858-1898. (Chicago, 1901). $225

Mitchell, G.R. — THE PACIFIC GOLD COMPANY OF GILPIN COUNTY, COLORADO. Boston, 1866, wraps. $150

Mitchell, John D. — LOST MINES OF THE GREAT SOUTHWEST. (Phoenix, 1933). $100

Mitchell, S. Augustus (Publisher) — ACCOMPANIMENT TO MITCHELL'S NEW MAP OF TEXAS, OREGON AND CALIFORNIA, WITH THE REGIONS ADJOINING. Philadelphia, 1846, folding map. $650

Mitchell, S. Augustus (Publisher) — DESCRIPTION OF OREGON AND CALIFORNIA, EMBRACING AN ACCOUNT OF THE GOLD REGIONS. Philadelphia, 1849, folding map. $725

Moellhausen, Baldwin — DIARY OF A JOURNEY FROM THE MISSISSIPPI TO THE COASTS OF THE PACIFIC WITH A UNITED STATES GOVERNMENT EXPEDITION. London, 1858, 2 vols, folding map. $1250

Mokler, A.J. — A HISTORY OF NATRONA COUNTY, WYOMING. Chicago, 1923. $175

MONTANA, ITS CLIMATE, INDUSTRIES AND RESOURCES. Helena (MT), 1884, wraps. $175

MONTANA TERRITORY, HISTORY AND BUSINESS DIRECTORY 1879 By F.W. Warner. Helena (MT), (1879), map. $450

Morfi, Juan Agustin — HISTORY OF TEXAS, 1673-1779. Albuquerque (NM), 1935, map. $225

Morgan, Dale L. — JEDEDIAH SMITH AND THE OPENING OF THE WEST. Indianapolis (IN), (1953). $65

Morgan, Dale L. & Carl I. Wheat — JEDEDIAH SMITH AND HIS MAPS OF THE AMERICAN WEST. San Francisco, 1954, 7 folding maps. $650

Morgan, Dick T. — MORGAN'S MANUAL OF THE U.S. HOMESTEAD AND TOWNSITE LAWS. Guthrie (OK), 1893, wraps. $250

Morgan, Martha M. (Editor) — A TRIP ACROSS THE PLAINS IN THE YEAR 1849. San Francisco, 1864, wraps. At least $6500

Morgan, Thomas J. — A GLANCE AT TEXAS. Columbus, 1844. $1750

Morphis, J.M. — HISTORY OF TEXAS. New York, 1874, folding map. $175

Morrell, Z.N. — FLOWERS AND FRUITS FROM THE WILDERNESS; OR 36 YEARS IN TEXAS. Boston, 1872. $150

Morse, John F. & Samuel Colville — ILLUSTRATED HISTORICAL SKETCHES OF CALIFORNIA. Sacramento (CA), 1854, wraps. $750

Mowry, Sylvester — MEMOIR OF THE PROPOSED TERRITORY OF ARIZONA. Washington, 1857, map, wraps. At least $2500

Muir, John — THE MOUNTAINS OF CALIFORNIA. New York, 1894. $300

Muir, John (Editor) — PICTURESQUE CALIFORNIA. San Francisco, (1888), 2 vols., 130 plates, folio. $850

Mullan, John — MINERS' AND TRAVELERS' GUIDE TO OREGON. New York, 1865, folding map. $425

Mullan, John — REPORT ON THE CONSTRUCTION OF A MILITARY ROAD FROM FORT WALLA-WALLA TO FORT BENTON. Washington, 1863, 4 folding maps, 11 plates. $300

Mumey, Nolie — BLOODY TRAILS ALONG THE RIO GRANDE. Denver, 1938, map. $50

Mumey, Nolie — CALAMITY JANE. Denver, 1950, folding map, 2 pamphlets, signed. $200

Mumey, Nolie — CREEDE: HISTORY OF A COLORADO MINING TOWN. Denver, 1949. $75

Mumey, Nolie — HISTORY OF THE EARLY SETTLEMENTS OF DENVER. Glendale, 1942, map. $75

Mumey, Nolie — MARCH OF THE FIRST DRAGOONS TO THE ROCKY MOUNTAINS IN 1835. Denver, 1957, folding map. $75

Mumey, Nolie — OLD FORTS AND TRADING POSTS OF THE WEST. Denver, 1956. $75

Mumey, Nolie — PIONEER DENVER, INCLUDING SCENES OF CENTRAL CITY, COLORADO CITY, AND NEVADA CITY. Denver, 1948, folding plate. $90

Mumey, Nolie — POKER ALICE. Denver, 1951, folding map, wraps. $75

Mumey, Nolie — THE TETON MOUNTAINS. Denver, 1947. $75

MURDER BY DEPUTY U.S. MARSHALL E.M. THORNTON OF E.M. DALTON WAYLAID AND ASSASSINATED IN COLD BLOOD. Salt Lake City, 1886, wraps. $150

N

Napton, William B. — OVER THE SANTA FE TRAIL. Kansas City, 1905, wraps. $175

NARRATIVE AND REPORT OF THE CAUSES AND CIRCUMSTANCES OF THE DEPLORABLE CONFLAGARATION AT RICHMOND. N.p., 1812. $150

NARRATIVE OF THE ADVENTURES AND SUFFERINGS OF CAPT. DANIEL D. HEUSTIS, A. Boston, 1847, wraps. $1200

NARRATIVE OF THE CAPTIVITY AND PROVIDENTIAL ESCAPE OF MRS. JANE LEWIS By William P. Edwards. (New York), 1833, wraps. $325

NARRATIVE OF THE CAPTURE AND BURNING OF FORT MASSACHUSETTS By Rev. John Norton. Albany (NY), 1870. $110

NARRATIVE OF THE FACTS AND CIRCUMSTANCES RELATING TO THE KIDNAPPING AND PRESUMED MURDER OF WILLIAM MORGAN, A. Batavia (NY), 1827, sewn. $275

NARRATIVE OF THE MASSACRE AT CHICAGO, AUGUST 15, 1812, AND SOME PRECEDING EVENTS By Mrs. Juliette A. Kinzie. Chicago, 1844, map, wraps. At least $3000

NARRATIVE OF OCCURRENCES IN THE INDIAN COUNTRY OF NORTH AMERICA, A By Samuel Hull Wilcocke. London, 1807, wraps. $850

NARRATIVE OF THE SUPPRESSION BY COL. BURR OF THE "HISTORY OF THE ADMINISTRATION OF JOHN ADAMS," A By James Cheetham. New York 1802, sewn. $250

NECESSITY OF A SHIP-CANAL BETWEEN THE EAST AND WEST, THE By J.W. Foster. Chicago, 1863, wraps. $145

Neese, George M. — THREE YEARS IN THE CONFEDERATE HORSE ARTILLERY. New York, 1911. $90

Neil, John B. — BIENNIAL MESSAGE OF THE GOVERNOR OF IDAHO TO THE 11TH SESSION OF THE LEGISLATURE OF IDAHO TERRITORY. Boise City (ID), 1880, wraps. $140

NEW EMPIRE: OREGON, WASHINGTON, IDAHO, THE. Portland (OR), 1888, folding map, wraps. $85

NEW TEXAS SPELLING BOOK, THE By E.H. Cushing. Houston, 1863. $1200

NEW YORK AND ORO-FINO GOLD AND SILVER MINING CO. OF IDAHO. New York, 1865, wraps. $140

Newberry, J.S. — REPORT ON THE PROPERTIES OF THE RAMSHORN CONSOLIDATED SILVER MINING COMPANY AT BAY HORSE, IDAHO. New York, (1881), wraps. $140

Newell, Rev. Chester — HISTORY OF THE REVOLUTION IN TEXAS. New York, 1838, folding map. $500

Newmark, Harris — SIXTY YEARS IN SOUTHERN CALIFORNIA, 1853-1913. New York, 1916. $60

Nimmo, Joseph, Jr. — RANGE AND RANCH CATTLE TRAFFIC. (Washington, 1884), 4 folding maps, wraps. $1800

Nordhoff, Charles — CALIFORNIA FOR HEALTH, PLEASURE AND RESIDENCE. New York, 1872, map. $125

North, Thomas — FIVE YEARS IN TEXAS; OR, WHAT YOU DID NOT HEAR DURING THE WAR. Cincinnati, 1879. $125

NORTHERN ROUTE TO IDAHO, THE By D.D. Merrill. St. Paul (NM), (1864), folding map. At least $1500

NOTES ON CALIFORNIA AND THE PLACERS By James Delavan. New York, 1850, wraps. At least $2000

O

O'Bryan, William — A NARRATIVE OF TRAVELS IN THE UNITED STATES — AND ADVICE TO EMIGRANTS AND TRAVELLERS GOING TO THAT INTERESTING COUNTRY. London, 1836. $350

OBSERVATIONS ON THE WISCONSIN TERRITORY By William Rudolph Smith. Philadelphia, 1835, folding map. $525

OFFICIAL HISTORICAL ATLAS OF ALAMEDA COUNTY. Oakland, 1878. Folding maps, folio. $375

Ogden, George — LETTERS FROM THE WEST. New Bedford (MA), 1823. $675

Older, Mr. & Mrs. Fremont — THE LIFE OF GEORGE HEARST, CALIFORNIA PIONEER. San Francisco, 1933. $450

Oldham, Williamson S. & George W. White — DIGEST OF THE GENERAL STATUTE LAWS OF THE STATE OF TEXAS. Austin (TX), 1859. $200

Oliphant, Laurence — MINNESOTA AND THE FAR WEST. Edinburgh (Scotland), 1855, folding map, plates. $175

Oliver, John W. (Publisher) — GUIDE TO THE NEW GOLD REGION OF WESTERN KANSAS AND NEBRASKA. New York, 1859, folding map, wraps. At least $5000

Olmsted, Frederick Law — A JOURNEY THROUGH TEXAS. New York, 1857, folding map. $175

Onderdonk, James L. — IDAHO: FACTS AND STATISTICS. San Francisco, 1885, wraps. $225

ONLY AUTHENTIC LIFE OF ABRAHAM LINCOLN, ALIAS "OLD ABE," A SON OF THE WEST. (New York, 1864), wraps. $450

ORDNANCE MANUAL FOR THE USE OF THE OFFICERS OF THE CONFEDERATE STATES OF AMERICA. Charleston, 1863. $650

OREGON: AGRICULTURAL, STOCK RAISING, MINERAL RESOURCES, CLIMATE, ETC. By Union Pacific Rail Road. Council Bluffs (IA), 1888, wraps. $200

ORIGIN AND TRADITIONAL HISTORY OF THE WYANDOTTS by Peter D. Clarke. Toronto, 1870. $90

Orr, George — THE POSSESSION OF LOUISIANA BY THE FRENCH. London, 1803. $175

Orr, N.M. — THE CITY OF STOCKTON. Stockton (CA), 1874, wraps. $160

Orr & Ruggles — SAN JOAQUIN COUNTY. Stockton, 1887, map, wraps. $175

Osgood, Ernest Staples — THE DAY OF THE CATTLEMAN. Minneapolis, 1929, maps. $175

Otero, Miguel Antonio — THE REAL BILLY THE KID. New York, 1936. $60

P

Packard, Wellman & G. Larison — EARLY EMIGRATION TO CALIFORNIA. Bloomington (IL), 1928, wraps. $450

Palladino, Lawrence B. — INDIAN AND WHITE IN THE NORTHWEST. Baltimore, 1894. $200

Palmer, H.E. — THE POWDER RIVER INDIAN EXPEDI- TION, 1865. Omaha (NE), 1887, wraps. $325

Palmer, Joel — JOURNAL OF TRAVELS OVER THE ROCKY MOUNTAINS, TO THE MOUTH OF THE COLUMBIA RIVER. Cincinnati, 1847, wraps. $2300 or more

Palmer, William J. — REPORT OF SURVEYS ACROSS THE CONTINENT. Philadelphia, 1869, 3 maps, photo plates, wraps. $850

Parker, A.A. — A TRIP TO THE WEST AND TEXAS. Con- cord (NH), 1835. $450

Parker, Aaron — FORGOTTEN TRAGEDIES OF INDIAN WARFARE IN IDAHO. Grangeville (ID), 1925, wraps. $125

Parker, Frank (Editor) — WASHINGTON TERRITORY! THE PRESENT AND PROSPECTIVE FUTURE OF THE UPPER COLUMBIA COUNTRY. Walla Walla (WA), 1881, wraps. $450

Parker, Henry W. — HOW OREGON WAS SAVED TO THE U.S. New York, 1901, wraps. $45

Parker, J.M. — AN AGED WANDERER: A LIFE SKETCH OF A COWBOY ON THE WESTERN PLAINS IN EARLY DAYS. San Angelo (TX), n.d., wraps. $450

Parker, Samuel — JOURNAL OF AN EXPLORING TOUR BEYOND THE ROCKY MOUNTAINS. Ithaca (NY), 1838. $550

Parker (Nathan H.) & (D.H.) Huyett — THE IL- LUSTRATED MINERS' HAND-BOOK AND GUIDE TO PIKE'S PEAK. St. Louis, 1859, 2 folding maps. At least $6500

Parker, Solomon — PARKER'S AMERICAN CITIZEN'S SURE GUIDE. Sag Harbor (NY), 1808. $185

Parkman, Francis — THE CALIFORNIA AND OREGON TRAIL. New York, 1849, 2 vols., wraps, or 1 vol., cloth. At least $10,000

Parkman, Francis — HISTORY OF THE CONSPIRACY OF PONTIAC AND THE WAR OF THE NORTH AMERICAN TRIBES. Boston, 1851, 4 maps. $165

Parkman, Francis — THE OLD REGIME IN CANADA. Boston, 1874, large paper. $165

Parsons, George Frederic — THE LIFE AND ADVEN- TURES OF JAMES W. MARSHALL. Sacramento, 1870. $175

PASADENA AS IT IS TODAY FROM A BUSINESS STANDPOINT. (Pasadena, 1886), wraps. $175

PASADENA, LOS ANGELES COUNTY, SOUTHERN CALIFORNIA. Los Angeles, 1898, wraps. $125

Patterson, A.W. — HISTORY OF THE BACKWOODS; OR, THE REGION OF THE OHIO. Pittsburgh, 1843, folding map. $450

Patterson, Lawson B. — TWELVE YEARS IN THE MINES OF CALIFORNIA. CAMBRIDGE (MA), 1862. $175

Pattie, James O. — THE PERSONAL NARRATIVE OF JAMES O. PATTIE, OF KENTUCKY. Cincinnati, 1831, plates. At least $10,000

Patton, The Rev. W.W. & R.N. Isham — U.S. SANITARY COMMISSION, NO.38: REPORT ON THE CONDI- TION OF CAMPS AND HOSPITALS AT CAIRO — PADAUCAH AND ST. LOUIS. Chicago, 1861, sewn. $125

Paulding, James Kirke — SLAVERY IN THE UNITED STATES. New York, 1836. $85

Paulison, C.M.K. — ARIZONA: THE WONDERFUL COUNTRY. Tucson (AZ), 1881, wraps. $3000

Payne, John Howard — INDIAN JUSTICE: A CHEROKEE MURDER TRAIL AT TAHLEQUAH IN 1840. Oklahoma City, 1934. $175

Peters, De Witt C. — KIT CARSON'S LIFE. Hartford, 1874. $135

Peters, De Witt C. — THE LIFE AND ADVENTURES OF KIT CARSON, THE NESTOR OF THE ROCKY MOUN- TAINS. New York, 1858. $175

Petter, Rodolphe — ENGLISH-CHEYENNE DICTION- ARY. Kettle Falls (WA), 1913-15, folio. $250

Phillips, D.L. — LETTERS FROM CALIFORNIA. Springfield (IL), 1877. $165

PIONEERING ON THE PLAINS. JOURNEYS TO MEXICO IN 1848. THE OVERLAND TRIP TO CALIFORNIA By Alexander W. Mccoy, Et Al. (Kaukauna, WI, 1924), wraps. $200

Platt, P.L. & N. Slater — THE TRAVELERS' GUIDE ACROSS THE PLAINS, UPON THE OVERLAND ROUTE TO CALIFORNIA. Chicago, 1852, folding map, wraps. At least $9500

Pleasants, W.J. — TWICE ACROSS THE PLAINS, 1849- 1856. San Francisco, 1906. $500

Polley, J.B. — HOOD'S TEXAS BRIGADE. New York, 1910. $400

Pollock, J.M. — THE UNVARNISHED WEST: RANCH- ING AS I FOUND IT. London, (1911). $350

Poor, M.C. — DENVER, SOUTH PARK AND PACIFIC. Denver, 1949. map. $375

Porter, Lavinia Honeyman — BY OX TEAM TO CALIFORNIA. Oakland, 1910. $525

PORTRAIT AND BIOGRAPHICAL RECORD OF DENVER AND VICINITY. Chicago, 1898. $400

Poston, Charles D. — APACHE LAND. San Francisco, 1878. $150

Poston, Charles D. — SPEECH OF THE HON. CHAR- LES D. POSTON, OF ARIZONA, ON INDIAN AF- FAIRS. New York, 1865, wraps. $800

Powell, H.M.T. — THE SANTA FE TRAIL TO CALIFOR- NIA, 1849-1852. San Francisco, (1931), maps. At least $1500

Powell, J.W. — CANYONS OF THE COLORADO. Mead- ville (PA), 1895, 10 folding plates. $1500

Prescott, William H. — THE HISTORY OF THE CON- QUEST OF MEXICO. New York, 1843, maps, 3 vols. $250

PROCEEDINGS OF THE FIRST ANNUAL SESSION OF THE TERRITORIAL GRANGE OF MONTANA. Diamond City (MT), 1875. $350

PROGRESSIVE MEN OF SOUTHERN IDAHO. Chicago, 1904. $375

Prosch, J.W. — MCCARVER AND TACOMA. Seattle, (1906). $100

PROSPECTUS OF HOPE GOLD COMPANY. New York, 1864, wraps. $150

PROSPECTUS OF THE LEADVILLE & TEN MILE NAR- ROW GAUGE RAILWAY COMPANY OF LEADVILLE, COL. Leadville, 1880, wraps. $275

PUGET SOUND BUSINESS DIRECTORY AND GUIDE TO WASHINGTON TERRITORY, 1872. Olympia (WA),(1872). $650

PUGET SOUND DIRECTORY, 1887 By R.L. Polk. N.p., 1887. $650

Q

Quickfall — WESTERN LIFE, AND HOW I BECAME A BRONCO BUSTER by Bob Grantham. London, (1890), wraps. $550

R

Raht, Carlysle Graham — THE ROMANCE OF DAVIS MOUNTAINS AND BIG BEND COUNTRY. El Paso, (1919). $90

Raine, William Macleod — CATTLE BRANDS: A SKETCH OF BYGONE DAYS IN THE COW-COUNTRY. Boston, (1920), wraps. $125

Raines, C.W. — A BIBLIOGRAPHY OF TEXAS. Austin, 1896. $150

Ramsay, David — THE HISTORY OF SOUTH CAROLINA. Charleston, 1809, 2 vols., 2 folding maps. $575

Ramsdell, Charles W. — RECONSTRUCTION IN TEXAS. New York, 1910, wraps. $125

Ramsey, J.G.M. — THE ANNALS OF TENNESSEE. Charleston, 1853, folding map. $300

Ranck, George W. — HISTORY OF LEXINGTON, KENTUCKY. Cincinnati, 1872. $85

Randall, Thomas E. — HISTORY OF THE CHIPPEWA VALLEY. Eau Claire (WI), 1875. $85

Rankin, M. Wilson — REMINISCENCES OF FRONTIER DAYS. Denver, (1938). $125

Rankin, Melinda — TEXAS IN 1850. Boston, 1850. $325

Raymond, Dora Neill — CAPTAIN LEE HALL OF TEXAS. Norman (OK), 1940. $45

Reagan, John H. — MEMOIRS, WITH SPECIAL REFERENCE TO SECESSION AND THE CIVIL WAR. New York, 1906. $225

Recio, Jesus T. — TOMOCHIE! EPISODIOS DE LA COMPANIA DE CHIHUAHUA, 1893. Rio Grande City (TX), 1894. $400

Redmond, Pat. H. — HISTORY OF QUINCY (ILL.) AND ITS MEN OF MARK. Quincy, 1869. $125

Reed, J.W. — MAP OF AND GUIDE TO THE KANSAS GOLD REGIONS. New York, 1859, wraps. At least $3500

Reed, Nathaniel — THE LIFE OF TEXAS JACK. (Tulsa, 1936), wraps. $825

Reed, S.G. — A HISTORY OF THE TEXAS RAILROADS. Houston, (1941). $225

Reed, Wallace P. — HISTORY OF ATLANTA, GEORGIA. Syracuse (NY), 1889, portraits. $85

Reed, William — LIFE ON THE BORDER, SIXTY YEARS AGO. Fall River (MA), 1882, wraps. $65

Rees, William — DESCRIPTION OF THE CITY OF KEOKUK. Keokuk (IA), 1854, wraps. $275

Rees, William — THE MISSISSIPPI BRIDGE CITIES: DAVENPORT, ROCK ISLAND AND MOLINE. (Rock Island, IL), 1854, sewn. $175

REGULATIONS FOR THE UNIFORM AND DRESS OF THE ARMY OF THE UNITED STATES. Philadelphia, 1851, 25 chromolitho's. $575

Reid, A.J. — THE RESOURCES AND MANUFACTURING CAPACITY OF THE LOWER FOX RIVER VALLEY. Appleton (WI), 1874, foldong map, panorama, wraps. $85

Reid, John C. — REID'S TRAMP, OR A JOURNAL OF THE INCIDENTS OF TEN MONTHS TRAVEL THROUGH TEXAS, NEW MEXICO, ARIZONA, SONORA, AND CALIFORNIA. Selma (AL), 1858. At least $9000

Reid, Samuel C., Jr. — THE SCOUTING EXPEDITIONS OF MCCULLOCH'S TEXAS RANGERS. Philadelphia, 1847. $325

REIGN OF TERROR IN KANSAS, THE By Charles W. Briggs. Boston, 1856, wraps. $675

RELIEF BUSINESS DIRECTORY, NAMES AND NEW LOCATIONS IN SAN FRANCISCO, OAKLAND, BERKELEY AND ALAMEDA OF 4,000 SAN FRANCISCO FIRMS AND BUSINESS MEN. Berkeley, 1906, wraps. $250

REMARKS ADDRESSED TO THE CITIZENS OF ILLINOIS, ON THE PROPOSED INTRODUCTION OF SLAVERY By Morris Birkbeck. N.p., ca. 1824. At least $3500

REMINISCENCES OF A CAMPAIGN IN MEXICO By John B. Robertson. Nashville (TN), 1849. $275

Remy, Jules & Julius L. Brenchley — A JOURNEY TO GREAT SALT LAKE CITY. London, 1861, map, 2 vols. $600

Renfrow, W.C. — OKLAHOMA AND THE CHEROKEE STRIP. Chicago, 1893, folding map, wraps. $100

REPORT FROM A SELECT COMMITTEE OF THE HOUSE OF REPRESENTATIVES, ON THE OVERLAND EMIGRATION ROUTE FROM MINNESOTA TO BRITISH OREGON. St. Paul (MN), 1858, wraps. $750

REPORT OF A COMMITTEE APPOINTED BY THE TRUSTEES OF THE TOWN OF MILWAUKEE, RELATIVE TO THE COMMERCE OF THAT TOWN AND THE NAVIGATION OF LAKE MICHIGAN By I.A. Lapham And F. Randall. Milwaukee (WI), 1842, sewn. $375

REPORT OF THE BOARD OF CANAL COMMISSIONERS, TO THE GENERAL ASSEMBLY OF OHIO. Columbus (OH), 1824, sewn. $175

REPORT OF THE BOARD OF INTERNAL IMPROVEMENTS FOR THE STATE OF KENTUCKY, AND REPORTS OF THE ENGINEERS. (Frankfort, KY, 1836), sewn. $125

Report Of The Secretary Of The Interior, Communicating — THE REPORT OF J. ROSS BROWNE, ON THE LATE INDIAN WAR IN OREGON AND WASHINGTON TERRITORIES. Washington, 1858, sewn. $150

REPORT ON THE GOVERNOR'S MESSAGE, RELATING TO THE "POLITICAL SITUATION," "POLYGAMY," AND "GOVERNMENTAL ACTION." Salt Lake, 1882, wraps. $150

REPORTS OF THE COMMITTEE SENT IN 1873, BY THE MEXICAN GOVERNMENT, TO THE FRONTIER OF TEXAS. New York, 1875, 3 folding maps. $250

REPORTS OF TERRITORIAL OFFICERS OF THE TERRITORY OF COLORADO. Central City (CO), 1871, wraps. $125

RESOURCES AND DEVELOPMENT OF THE TERRITORY OF WASHINGTON. Seattle, 1886, sewn. $125

Revere, Joseph W. — A TOUR OF DUTY IN CALIFORNIA. New York, 1849, folding map. $450

Reynolds, John — THE PIONEER HISTORY OF ILLINOIS. Belleville (IL), 1852. $350

Reynolds, John — SKETCHES OF THE COUNTRY ON THE NORTHERN ROUTE FROM BELLEVILLE, ILL.,

TO THE CITY OF NEW YORK, AND BACK BY THE OHIO VALLEY. Belleville, 1854. $675

Richardson, Rupert N. & C.C. Rister — THE GREATER SOUTHWEST. Glendale, 1934. $65

Ridge, John R. — JOAQUIN MURIETA, THE BRIGAND CHIEF OF CALIFORNIA. San Francisco, 1932, folding poster. $95

Ridings, Sam P. — THE CHISHOLM TRAIL. Guthrie (OK), (1936), folding map. $100

Ripley, R.S. — THE WAR WITH MEXICO. New York, 1849. $250

Rister, Carl Coke — THE SOUTHWESTERN FRONTIER, 1865-1881. Cleveland, 1928, maps. $185

Roberts, Mrs. D.W. — A WOMAN'S REMINISCENCES OF SIX YEARS IN CAMP WITH THE TEXAS RANGERS. Austin, (1928), wraps. $85

Roberts, Oran M. — DESCRIPTION OF TEXAS. St. Louis, 1881, five 2-page maps. $225

Roberts, W.H. — NORTHWESTERN WASHINGTON. Port Townsend (WA), 1880, folding map, wraps. $450

Robertson, John W. — FRANCIS DRAKE AND OTHER EARLY EXPLORERS ALONG THE PACIFIC COAST. San Francisco, 1927, 28 maps. $225

Robertson, Wyndham, Jr. — OREGON, OUT RIGHT AND TITLE. Washington, 1846, folding map, wraps or boards. $1300

Robinson, Jacob — SKETCHES OF THE GREAT WEST. Portsmouth (NH), 1848, wraps. At least $5000

Robinson, William Davis — MEMOIRS OF THE MEXICAN REVOLUTION. Philadelphia, 1820. $350

Rock, Marion Tuttle — ILLUSTRATED HISTORY OF OKLAHOMA. Topeka, 1890, 90 plates. $525

ROCKY MOUNTAIN DIRECTORY AND COLORADO GAZETTEER FOR 1871. Denver, (1870). $275

Rogers, A.N. — COMMUNICATION RELATIVE TO THE LOCATION OF THE U.P.R.R. ACROSS THE ROCKY MOUNTAINS THROUGH COLORADO TERRITORY. Central City (CO), 1867, wraps. $550

Rollinson, John K. — HISTORY OF THE MIGRATION OF OREGON-RAISED HERDS TO MIDWESTERN MARKETS: WYOMING CATTLE TRAILS. Caldwell (ID), 1948. $150

Rollinson, John K. — HOOFPRINTS OF A COWBOY AND A U.S. RANGER. Caldwell, 1941. $85

Roosevelt, Theodore — THE WINNING OF THE WEST. New York, 1889-96, 4 vols. $450

Root, Frank A. & William E. Connelley — THE OVERLAND STAGE TO CALIFORNIA. Topeka (KS), 1901, map. $175

Root, Riley — JOURNAL OF TRAVELS FROM ST. JOSEPH TO OREGON. Galesburg (IL), 1850, wraps. At least $5000

Rose, Victor M. — ROSS' TEXAS BRIGADE. Louisville (KY), 1881. $1000

Ross, Alexander — ADVENTURES OF THE FIRST SETTLERS ON THE OREGON OR COLUMBIA RIVER. London, 1949, folding map. $1300

Ross, Alexander — THE FUR HUNTERS OF THE FAR WEST. London, 1855, 2 vols., map. $650

RULES AND ORDERS OF THE HOUSE OF REPRESENTATIVES OF THE TERRITORY OF WASHINGTON, 1864-5. Olympia, Washington Territory, 1864. wraps. $225

RULES AND REGULATIONS OF THE UTAH AND NORTHERN RAILWAY, FOR THE GOVERNMENT OF EMPLOYEES. Salt Lake City, 1879. $150

RULES, REGULATIONS, AND BY-LAWS OF THE BOARD OF COMMISSIONERS TO MANAGE THE YOSEMITE VALLEY AND MARIPOSA BIG TREE GROVE. Sacramento, 1885, wraps. $175

Russell, Alex J. — THE RED RIVER COUNTRY, HUDSON'S BAY AND NORTH-WEST TERRITORIES. Ottawa (CAN), 1869, folding map, wraps. $175

Russell, Osborne — JOURNAL OF A TRAPPER, OR NINE YEARS IN THE ROCKY MOUNTAINS. (Boise, ID, 1914). $450

Ruxton, George E. — LIFE IN THE FAR WEST. Edinburgh (SCOTLAND), 1849. $250

Ryan, William R. — PERSONAL ADVENTURES IN UPPER AND LOWER CALIFORNIA IN 1848-49. London, 1850, 23 plates. $350

S

Sabin, Edwin L. — BUILDING THE PACIFIC RAILWAY. Philadelphia, 1919. $65

Sabin, Edwin L. — KIT CARSON DAYS (1809-1868). Chicago, 1914. $100

St. Clair, Maj. Gen. — A NARRATIVE OF THE MANNER IN WHICH THE CAMPAIGN AGAINST THE INDIANS, IN THE YEAR 1791, WAS CONDUCTED. Philadelphia, 1812. $400

St. John, John R. — A TRUE DESCRIPTION OF THE LAKE SUPERIOR COUNTRY. New York, 1846, 2 folding maps. $325

Sale, Edith Tunis — MANORS OF VIRGINIA IN COLONIAL TIMES. Philadelphia, 1909, 49 plates. $135

Salpointe, John B. — A BRIEF SKETCH OF THE MISSION OF SAN XAVIER DEL BAC WITH A DESCRIPTION OF ITS CHURCH. San Francisco, 1880, wraps. $200

SALT LAKE CITY DIRECTORY AND BUSINESS GUIDE, THE By Edward L. Sloan. Salt Lake City, 1869. $200

SAN BERNARDINO COUNTY, CALIFORNIA, ILLUSTRATED DESCRIPTION OF. San Bernardino, 1881, wraps. $200

SAN BERNARDINO COUNTY, CALIFORNIA. INGERSOLL'S CENTURY ANNALS OF SAN BERNARDINO COUNTY, 1769-1904. Los Angeles, 1904. $125

SAN FRANCISCO BAY AND CALIFORNIA IN 1776 By Pedro Font. Providence (RI), 1911. $250

SAN FRANCISCO BOARD OF ENGINEERS: REPORT UPON CITY GRADES. San Francisco, 1854, wraps. $185

SAN FRANCISCO DIRECTORY FOR THE YEAR 1852-53. San Francisco, 1852. $875

Sandburg, Carl — ABRAHAM LINCOLN: THE PRAIRIE YEARS. New York, (1926), 2 vols., boxed, signed, large paper. $475

Sandburg, Carl — ABRAHAM LINCOLN: THE WAR YEARS. New York, (1939-41), 4 vols., boxed, signed, large paper. $475

Sanders, Daniel C. — A HISTORY OF THE INDIAN WARS WITH THE FIRST SETTLERS OF THE UNITED STATES. Montpelier (VT), 1812. $650

Sanders, Capt. John — MEMOIR ON THE MILITARY RESOURCES OF THE VALLEY OF THE OHIO. Pittsburgh, 1845, unbound. $185

Sanford, Nettle — HISTORY OF MARSHALL COUNTY, IOWA. Clinton (IA), 1867. $165

Sansom, Joseph — SKETCHES OF LOWER CANADA, HISTORICAL AND DESCRIPTIVE. New York, 1817. $225

Santee, Ross — MEN AND HORSES. New York, (1926). $125

Santleben, August — A TEXAS PIONEER. New York, 1910. $300

Sargent, George B. — NOTES ON IOWA. New York, 1848, map. $900

Satterlee, M.P. — A DETAILED ACCOUNT OF THE MASSACRE BY THE DAKOTA INDIANS OF MINNESOTA IN 1862. Minneapolis, 1923, wraps. $175

Saunders, James E. — EARLY SETTLERS OF ALABAMA. New Orleans, 1899. $200

Sawyer, Eugene T. — THE LIFE AND CAREER OF TIBURCIO VASQUEZ. (San Jose, CA, 1875), wraps. $350

Saxton, Charles — THE OREGONIAN; OR HISTORY OF THE OREGON TERRITORY. Oregon City (OR), 1846, wraps. At least $1800

SCENES IN THE ROCKY MOUNTAINS, OREGON, CALIFORNIA, NEW MEXICO AND GRAND PRAIRIES. BY A NEW ENGLANDER By Rufus B. Sage. Philadelphia, 1846, wraps. $850

Scharf, John Thomas — HISTORY OF THE CONFEDERATE STATES NAVY. New York, 1887, 42 plates. $165

Scharf, John Thomas — HISTORY OF DELAWARE. Philadelphia, 1888, 2 vols. $175

Scharf, John Thomas — HISTORY OF MARYLAND. Baltimore, 1879, 3 vols., folding maps and charts. $225

Scharf, John Thomas — HISTORY OF WESTCHESTER COUNTY, NEW YORK. Philadelphia, 1886, 2 vols. $325

Scharf, John Thomas — HISTORY OF WESTERN MARYLAND. Philadelphia, 1882, 2 vols., map, 109 plates. $175

Scharmann, H.B. — OVERLAND JOURNEY TO CALIFORNIA. (New York, 1918). $175

Schmitz, Joseph M. — TEXAN STATECRAFT, 1836-1845. San Antonio, 1941. $65

Schoolcraft, Henry R. — HISTORICAL AND STATISTICAL INFORMATION RESPECTING THE INDIAN TRIBES, —. Philadelphia, 1851-57, 6 vols., maps, table. At least $2250

Schoolcraft, Henry R. — INFORMATION RESPECTING THE HISTORY, CONDITIONS, AND PROSPECTS OF THE INDIAN TRIBES OF THE UNITED STATES. Philadelphia, 1853-57, 6 vols. At least $1750

Schoolcraft, Henry R. — THE INDIAN TRIBES OF THE UNITED STATES. Philadelphia, 1884, 2 vols., 100 plates. $225

Schoolcraft, Henry R. — INQUIRIES RESPECTING THE HISTORY OF THE INDIAN TRIBES OF THE UNITED STATES. (Washington, ca. 1847-50), wraps. $575

Schoolcraft, Henry R. — JOURNAL OF A TOUR INTO THE INTERIOR OF THE MISSOURI AND ARKANSAW. London, 1821, folding map. $275

Schoolcraft, Henry R. — NARRATIVE JOURNAL OF TRAVELS THROUGH THE NORTHWESTERN REGIONS OF THE U.S. —. Albany (NY), 1821, folding map, 7 plates. $250

Schoolcraft, Henry R. & James Allen — EXPEDITION TO NORTH-WEST INDIANS. (Washington, 1834), wraps. $225

Schwettman, Martin W. — SANTA RITA, THE UNIVERSITY OF TEXAS OIL DISCOVERY. N.p., 1943, wraps. $75

Sealsfield. Charles Karl Postl — THE CABIN BOOK; or, SKETCHES OF LIFE IN TEXAS. New York, 1844, 3 parts, wraps. $750

Seyd, Ernest — CALIFORNIA AND ITS RESOURCES. London, 1858, 2 folding maps. $575

Seymour, E.S. — EMIGRANT'S GUIDE TO THE GOLD MINES OF UPPER CALIFORNIA. Chicago, 1849, wraps. At least $2500

Sherwood, J. Ely — CALIFORNIA: HER WEALTH AND RESOURCES. New York, 1848, wraps. $1350

Shields, G.O. — CRUISING IN THE CASCADES. Chicago, 1889. $125

Shinn, Charles Howard — GRAPHIC DESCRIPTION OF PACIFIC COAST OUTLAWS. (San Francisco, ca.1890-95), wraps. $425

Shinn, Charles Howard — MINING CAMPS. New York, 1885. $175

Shinn, Charles Howard — PACIFIC RURAL HANDBOOK. San Francisco, 1879. $135

Shipley, Conway — SKETCHES IN THE PACIFIC. London, 1851, plates, folio. At least $5500

Shipman, Mrs. O.L. — TAMING THE BIG BEND. (Marfa, TX) 1926, folding map. $275

Silliman, Benjamin — A DESCRIPTION OF THE RECENTLY DISCOVERED PETROLEUM REGION IN CALIFORNIA. New York, 1864, wraps. $850

SILVER MINES OF VIRGINIA AND AUSTIN, NEVADA. Boston, 1865, wraps. $375

Simpson, James H. — REPORT OF THE SECRETARY OF WAR — AND MAP OF WAGON ROADS IN UTAH. (Washington, 1859), folding map. $175

Simpson, Thomas — NARRATIVE OF THE DISCOVERIES ON THE NORTHWEST COAST OF AMERICA. London, 1843, maps. $450

Siringo, Charles — A HISTORY OF "BILLY THE KID." (Santa Fe, NM, 1920), wraps. $850

Siringo, Charles A. — RIATA AND SPURS. Boston, 1927, plates. $375

Siringo, Charles A. — TEXAS COWBOY, OR FIFTEEN YEARS ON THE HURRICANE DECK OF A SPANISH PONY. Chicago, 1885, wraps or cloth. At least $5500

Sitgreaves, Lorenzo — REPORT OF AN EXPEDITION DOWN THE ZUNI AND COLORADO RIVERS. Washington, 1853, folding map, 79 plates. $400

SKETCHES OF MISSION LIFE AMONG THE INDIANS OF OREGON. New York, 1854. $275

Sloan, Edward L. (Editor) — SALT LAKE CITY: GAZETTEER AND DIRECTORY. Salt Lake City, 1874. $250

Sloan, Robert W. — UTAH GAZETTEER AND DIRECTORY OF LOGAN, OGDEN, PROVO AND SALT LAKE CITIES. Salt Lake City, 1884. $250

Smart, Stephen F. — LEADVILLE, TEN MILE — AND ALL OTHER NOTED COLORADO MINING CAMPS. Kansas City, 1879, 2 folding maps, wraps. $500

Smith, Ashbel — REMINISCENCES OF THE TEXAS REPUBLIC. Galveston (TX), 1876. $275

Smith, Frank Meriweather (Editor) — SAN FRANCISCO VIGILANCE COMMITTEE OF '56. San Francisco, 1883, wraps. $200

Smith, James F. — THE CHEROKEE LAND LOTTERY, ETC. New York, 1838. $275

Smith, Jodie (Editor) — HISTORY OF THE CHISUM WAR By Ike Fridge. (Electra, TX, 1927), wraps. $125

T

Taft, Robert — ARTISTS AND ILLUSTRATORS OF THE OLD WEST. New York, 1953. $65

TALLAPOOSA LAND, MINING AND MANUFACTURING CO., HARALSON COUNTY. Tallapoosa (GA), 1887, map, wraps. $125

Tallent, Annie D. — THE BLACK HILLS; OR THE LAST HUNTING GROUNDS OF THE DAKOTAHS. St. Louis (MO), 1899, 50 plates. $150

Tanner, Henry S. — A BRIEF DESCRIPTION OF THE CANALS AND RAILROADS OF THE UNITED STATES. Philadelphia, 1834, maps. $225

Tanner, Henry S. — A NEW AMERICAN ATLAS. Philadelphia, 1823, 2 folding and 16 2-page maps. At least $3500

Tarascon, Louis A. — AN ADDRESS TO THE CITIZENS OF PHILADELPHIA, ON THE GREAT ADVANTAGES WHICH ARISE FROM THE TRADE OF THE WESTERN COUNTRY. Philadelphia, 1806, wraps. $875

Tarascon, Louis A., Et Al. — PETITION — PRAYING THE OPENING OF A WAGON ROAD FROM THE RIVER MISSOURI, NORTH OF THE RIVER KANSAS, TO THE RIVER COLUMBIA. Washington, 1824, sewn. $275

Taylor, Bayard — ELDORADO, OR, ADVENTURES IN THE PATH OF EMPIRE. New York, 1850, 2 vols. $700

Taylor, F. — A SKETCH OF THE MILITARY BOUNTY TRACT OF ILLINOIS. Philadelphia, 1839. $225

Taylor, James W. — NORTHWEST BRITISH AMERICA AND ITS RELATIONS TO THE STATE OF MINNESOTA. St. Paul (MN), 1860, map. At least $2500

Taylor, James W. — THE SIOUX WAR. St. Paul (MN), 1862. $1200

Taylor, John W. — IOWA, THE "GREAT HUNTING GROUND" OF THE INDIANS; AND THE "BEAUTIFUL LAND" OF THE WHITE MAN. Dubuque (IA), 1860, wraps. $275

Taylor, Joseph Henry — TWENTY YEARS ON THE TRAP LINE. Bismarck (ND), 1891, plates. $250

Taylor, Oliver I. — DIRECTORY OF WHEELING AND OHIO COUNTY. Wheeling (WV), 1851. $175

Taylor, Thomas U. — JESSE CHISHOLM. Bandera (TX), (1939). $125

TERRITORY OF WYOMING: ITS HISTORY, SOIL, CLIMATE, RESOURCES, ETC., THE By J.K. Jeffrey. Laramie City (Wyoming Territory), 1874, wraps. $625

TEXAS IN 1840, OR THE EMIGRANT'S GUIDE TO THE NEW REPUBLIC By A.B. Lawrence & C.J. Stille. New York, 1840. $550

TEXAS, THE HOME FOR THE EMIGRANT FROM EVERYWHERE By J.B. Robertson. Houston, 1875, wraps. $250

Thom, Adam — THE CLAIMS TO THE OREGON TERRITORY CONSIDERED. London, 1844, wraps. $225

Thomas, David — TRAVELS THROUGH THE WESTERN COUNTRY IN THE SUMMER OF 1816. Auburn (NY), 1819, folding map. $350

Thomas, Henry W. — HISTORY OF THE DOLES-COOK BRIGADE, ARMY OF NORTHERN VIRGINIA. Atlanta, 1903. $125

Thompson, Capt. B.F. — HISTORY OF THE 112TH REGIMENT OF ILLINOIS VOLUNTEER INFANTRY, 1862-1865. Toulon (IL), 1885. $125

Thompson, Daniel Pierce (Editor) — THE LAWS OF VERMONT, 1824-34, inclusive. Montpelier (VT), 1835. $350

Thompson, David — HISTORY OF THE LATE WAR, BETWEEN GREAT BRITAIN AND THE U.S.A. Niagara (Canada), 1832. $275

Thompson, Maurice — THE STORY OF LOUISIANA. Boston, (1888). $65

Thompson, R.A. — CENTRAL SONOMA: A BRIEF DESCRIPTION OF THE TOWNSHIP AND TOWN OF SANTA ROSA, SONOMA COUNTY, CALIFORNIA. Santa Rosa, 1884, wraps. $250

Thompson, R.A. — CONQUEST OF CALIFORNIA. Santa Rosa, 1896, wraps. $110

Thwaites, Reuben Gold — HISTORIC WATERWAYS: SIX HUNDRED MILES OF CANOEING DOWN THE ROCK, FOX, AND WISCONSIN RIVERS. Chicago, 1888. $175

Tierney, Luke — HISTORY OF THE GOLD DISCOVERIES ON THE SOUTH PLATTE RIVER. Pacific City (IA), 1859, wraps. At least $17,500

Todd, Frederick P. — SOLDIERS OF THE AMERICAN ARMY, 1775-1941. New York, 1941, 24 hand-colored plates, signed. $575

Tower, Col. Reuben — AN APPEAL TO THE PEOPLE OF NEW YORK IN FAVOR OF THE CONSTRUCTION OF THE CHENANGO CANAL. Utica (NY), 1830, sewed. $125

U

Udell, John — INCIDENTS OF TRAVEL TO CALIFORNIA, ACROSS THE GREAT PLAINS. Jefferson (OH), 1856. $450

UNIFORM AND DRESS OF THE ARMY OF THE CONFEDERATE STATES. Richmond, 1861, 15 plates. $500

UNITED STATES ENROLLMENT LAWS FOR CALLING OUT THE NATIONAL FORCES, THE. New York, 1864, wraps. $85

UNITED STATES "HISTORY" AS THE YANKEE MAKES IT AND TAKES IT. BY A CONFEDERATE SOLDIER By John Cussons. Glen Allen, 1900, wraps. $125

Upham, Samuel C. — NOTES FROM SUNLAND, ON THE MANATEE RIVER, GULF COAST OF SOUTH FLORIDA. Braidentown (FL), 1881, wraps. $175

V

Van Buren, A.D. — JOTTINGS OF A YEAR'S SOJOURN IN THE SOUTH. Battle Creek (MI), 1859. $125

Van Cleve, Mrs. Charlotte O.C. — "THREE SCORE YEARS AND TEN"; LIFE-LONG MEMORIES OF FORT SNELLING, MINN., AND OTHER PARTS OF THE WEST. (Minneapolis), 1888. $85

Van Tramp, John C. — PRAIRIE AND ROCKY MOUNTAIN ADVENTURES. Columbus (OH), 1858. $140

Van Zandt, Nicholas Biddle — A FULL DESCRIPTION OF THE SOIL, WATER, TIMBER, AND PRAIRIES OF EACH LOT, OR QUARTER SECTION OF THE MILITARY LANDS BETWEEN THE MISSISSIPPI AND ILLINOIS RIVERS. Washington, 1818, folding map. At least $4250

Vaughn, Robert — THEN AND NOW, OR 36 YEARS IN THE ROCKIES. Minneapolis, 1900. $165

Velasco, Jose Francisco — SONORA: ITS EXTENT, POPULATION, NATURAL PRODUCTIONS, INDIAN TRIBES, MINES, MINERAL LANDS, —. San Francisco, 1861. $225

VINDICATION OF THE RECENT AND PREVAILING POLICY OF GEORGIA IN ITS INTERNAL AFFAIRS, — By Augustin S. Clayton. Athens (GA), 1827, wraps. $275

Vischer, Edward — SKETCHES OF THE WASHOE MINING REGION. San Francisco, 1862, portfolio with 29 plates, wraps. $1800

VISIT TO TEXAS, A. New York, 1834, folding color map. $700

Volney, C.F. — A VIEW OF THE SOIL AND CLIMATE OF THE UNITED STATES. Philadelphia, 1804, 2 folding maps, 2 folding plates. $225

Voorhees, Luke — PERSONAL RECOLLECTIONS OF PIONEER LIFE ON THE MOUNTAINS AND PLAINS OF THE GREAT WEST. Cheyenne (WY), (1920). $140

W

Wagner, Lieut. Col. A.L. & Comm. J.D. Kelley — THE UNITED STATES ARMY AND NAVY: THEIR HISTORIES, —. Akron (OH), 1899, 43 plates, folio. $225

Wagner, Henry R. — THE CARTOGRAPHY OF THE NORTHWEST COAST OF AMERICA TO THE YEAR 1800. Berkeley (CA), 1937, 2 vols, folio, boxed. $575

Wagner, Henry R. — THE PLAINS AND THE ROCKIES. San Francisco, 1920. $350; San Francisco, 1921. $125

Wagner, Henry R. — SPANISH EXPLORATIONS IN THE STRAIT OF JUAN DE FUCA. Santa Ana (CA), 1933, maps. $250

Wagner, Henry R. — THE SPANISH SOUTHWEST, 1542-1794. Berkeley (CA), 1924. $400

Wagner, Henry R. — THE SPANISH VOYAGES TO THE NORTHWEST COAST OF AMERICA. San Francisco, 1929, maps. $225

Wakefield, John A. — HISTORY OF THE WAR BETWEEN THE UNITED STATES AND THE SAC AND FOX NATIONS OF INDIANS. Jacksonville (IL), 1834. $725

Walker, Judson E. — CAMPAIGNS OF GENERAL CUSTER IN THE NORTH-WEST, AND THE FINAL SURRENDER OF SITTING BULL. New York, 1881, wraps. $275

Walker, Tacetta — STORIES OF EARLY DAYS IN WYOMING: BIG HORN BASIN. Casper (WY), (1936). $40

Wall, W.G. — WALL'S HUDSON RIVER PORTFOLIO. New York, ca. 1826, 21 color plates, folio. At least $5000

Wallace, Ed. R. — PARSON HANKS: 14 YEARS IN THE WEST. Arlington (TX), ca. 1906. $175

Walters, Lorenzo D. — TOMBSTONE'S YESTERDAY. Tucson (AZ), 1928. $125

Walther, C.F. & I.N. Taylor. — THE RESOURCES AND ADVANTAGES OF THE STATE OF NEBRASKA. (Omaha, NE, 1871), folding map, wraps. $225

Walton, W.M. — LIFE AND ADVENTURES OF BEN THOMPSON, THE FAMOUS TEXAN. Austin (TX), 1884, wraps. $1800

WAR IN FLORIDA. BY A LATE STAFF OFFICER, THE By Woodburn Potter. Baltimore, 1836, folding map. $375

Warder, T.B. & J.M. Catlett — BATTLE OF YOUNG'S BRANCH, OR, MANASSAS PLAIN. Richmond (VA), 1862, 2 folding maps, wraps or leather. $675

Ware, Eugene — THE INDIAN WAR OF 1864. Topeka (KS), 1911. $175

Ware, Eugene — THE LYON CAMPAIGN IN MISSOURI. Topeka, 1907. $135

Ware, Joseph E. — THE EMIGRANT'S GUIDE TO CALIFORNIA. St. Louis, (1849), folding map. $2800

Warre, Henry J. — SKETCHES IN NORTH AMERICA AND THE OREGON TERRITORY. (London, 1848), maps, plates, folio. At least $12,000

Waters, Frank — MASKED GODS: NAVAHO AND PUEBLO CEREMONIALISM. Albuquerque (NM), 1950. $85

Watkins, C.L. — PHOTOGRAPHIC VIEWS OF THE FALLS AND VALLEY OF YOSEMITE. San Francisco, 1863, map and mounted photographs, folio. At least $12,000

Watkins, C.L. — PHOTOGRAPHS OF THE COLUMBIA RIVER AND OREGON. San Francisco, ca. 1873, 51 mounted albumen prints, large folio. At least $125,000

Watkins, C.L. — PHOTOGRAPHS OF THE PACIFIC COAST. San Francisco, ca. 1873, 49 mounted albumen prints, large folio. At least $125,000

Watkins, C.L. — WATKINS NEW SERIES COLUMBIA RIVER SCENERY, OREGON. N.p. ca. 1880, 40 plates. At least $10,000

Watson, Douglas S. (Editor) — CALIFORNIA IN THE FIFTIES. San Francisco, 1936, 50 views, folio. $450

Watson, Douglas S. (Editor) — THE SPANISH OCCUPATION OF CALIFORNIA. San Francisco, 1934. $125

Watts, J.L. — CHEROKEE CITIZENSHIP AND A BRIEF HISTORY OF INTERNAL AFFAIRS IN THE CHEROKEE NATION. Muldrow, Indian Territory (OK), 1895, wraps. $175

Wayland, John W. — HISTORY OF ROCKINGHAM COUNTY. Dayton (VA), 1912. $140

Wayland, John W. — HISTORIC HOMES OF NORTHERN VIRGINIA AND THE EASTERN PANHANDLE OF WESTERN VIRGINIA. Staunton (VA), 1937. $95

Webb, Walter Prescott — THE GREAT PLAINS. Boston, (1931). $125

Webb, Walter Prescott — THE TEXAS RANGERS. Boston, 1935. $100

Wells, William & Otto Onken — WESTERN SCENERY; OR, LAND AND RIVER, HILL AND DALE, IN THE MISSISSIPPI VALLEY. Cincinnati, 1851, 19 views. At least $3500

Werth, John J. — A DISSERTATION ON THE RESOURCES AND POLICY OF CALIFORNIA. Benicia (CA), 1851. $1300

Weston, Edward — CALIFORNIA AND THE WEST. New York, 1940. $250

Weston, Edward — MY CAMERA ON POINT LOBOS. Yosemite National Park and Boston, 1950, folio, spiral bound. $450

Weston, Silas — FOUR MONTHS IN THE MINES OF CALIFORNIA; OR, LIFE IN THE MOUNTAINS. Providence (RI), 1854, 24 pp., wraps. $375. Second edition of following item.

Weston, Silas — LIFE IN THE MOUNTAINS; OR, FOUR MONTHS IN THE MINES OF CALIFORNIA. Providence (RI), 1854, 36 pp., wraps. $425. First edition of previous item.

Wetherbee, J., Jr. — A BRIEF SKETCH OF COLORADO TERRITORY AND THE GOLD MINES OF THAT REGION. Boston, 1863, wraps. At least $2000

Wetmore, Alphonso — GAZETTEER OF THE STATE OF MISSOURI. St. Louis (MO), 1837, folding map. $50

Wetmore, Helen Cody — LAST OF THE GREAT SCOUTS: THE LIFE STORY OF COL. WILLIAM F. CODY, "BUFFALO BILL." (Duluth, MN, 1899), with 276 pages. $225

Wheat, Carl I. — BOOKS OF THE GOLD RUSH. San Francisco, 1949. $275

Wheat, Carl I. — THE MAPS OF THE CALIFORNIA GOLD REGION, 1848. San Francisco, 1942, 26 maps, folio. $1,200

Wheat, Carl I. — THE PIONEER PRESS OF CALIFORNIA. Oakland, 1948. $200

Whilldin, M.A. — DESCRIPTION OF WESTERN TEXAS. Galveston (TX), 1876, folding map, plates, wraps. $600

Whitaker, Arthur Preston (Editor) — DOCUMENTS RELATING TO THE COMMERCIAL POLICY OF SPAIN IN THE FLORIDAS. DeLand (FL), 1931, maps. $85

White, Philo — AGRICULTURAL STATISTICS OF RACINE COUNTY. Racine (WI), 1852, wraps. $125

Whitely, Ike — RURAL LIFE IN TEXAS. Atlanta (GA), 1891, wraps. $325

Whitney, J.D. — THE AURIFEROUS GRAVELS OF THE SIERRA NEVADA OF CALIFORNIA. Cambridge (MA), 1880, folding map and plates. $150

Whitney, J.D. — THE YOSEMITE BOOK. New York, 1868, 28 photo plates, 2 maps. $3500

Wilbarger, J.W. — INDIAN DEPREDATIONS IN TEXAS. Austin (TX), 1889, plates. $725

Wilkes, Charles — WESTERN AMERICA, INCLUDING CALIFORNIA AND OREGON. Philadelphia, 1949, 3 folding maps, wraps. $875

Wilkes, George — THE HISTORY OF OREGON, GEOGRAPHICAL AND POLITICAL. New York, 1845, folding map, wraps. $1750

Wilkeson, Samuel — WILKESON'S NOTES ON PUGET SOUND. (New York, ca. 1870), wraps. $350

Willcox, R.N. — REMINISCENCES OF CALIFORNIA LIFE. (Avery, OH), 1897. $225

Willey, S.H. — AN HISTORICAL PAPER RELATING TO SANTA CRUZ, CALIFORNIA. San Francisco, 1876, wraps. $165

Williams, G.T. — RECEIPTS AND SHIPMENTS OF LIVESTOCK AT UNION STOCK YARDS FOR 1890. Chicago, 1891, wraps. $350

Williams, Jesse — A DESCRIPTION OF THE UNITED STATES LANDS OF IOWA. New York, 1840, folding map. $750

Williams, John Lee — THE TERRITORY OF FLORIDA. New York, 1837, folding map. $300

Williams, John Lee — A VIEW OF WEST FLORIDA. Philadelphia, 1827, folding map. $175

Williams, Joseph — NARRATIVE OF A TOUR FROM THE STATE OF INDIANA TO THE OREGON TERRITORY. Cincinnati, 1843, wraps. $6500

Williams, O.W. — IN OLD NEW MEXICO, 1879-1880: REMINISCENCES OF JUDGE O.W. WILLIAMS. N.p., n.d., wraps. $125

Williams, Thomas J.C. — A HISTORY OF WASHINGTON COUNTY. Hagerstown (MD), 1906, 2 vols. $95

Williamson, Hugh — THE HISTORY OF NORTH CAROLINA. Philadelphia, 1812, 2 vols., folding map. $425

Williamson, James J. — MOSBY'S RANGERS. New York, 1896. $125

Willis, Nathaniel Parker — AMERICAN SCENERY. London, 1840, 2 vols., 117 views by W. H. Bartlett. At least $1000

Wilson, John Albert — HISTORY OF LOS ANGELES COUNTY, CALIFORNIA. Oakland, 1880. $500

Wilson, Obed G. — MY ADVENTURES IN THE SIERRAS. Franklin (OH), 1902. $85

Wilson, Woodrow — GEORGE WASHINGTON. New York, 1897. $125

Wiltsee, Ernest A. — GOLD RUSH STEAMERS —. San Francisco, 1938. $125

Winkler, A.V. — THE CONFEDERATE CAPITAL AND HOOD'S TEXAS BRIGADE. Austin (TX), 1894. $225

Wise, George — CAMPAIGNS AND BATTLES OF THE ARMY OF NORTHERN VIRGINIA. New York, 1916. $125

Wislizenus, Frederick A. — MEMOIR OF A TOUR TO NORTHERN MEXICO. Washington, 1848, 3 folding maps. $250

Wood, James H. — THE WAR, STONEWALL JACKSON, HIS CAMPAIGNS AND BATTLES, THE REGIMENT, AS I SAW THEM. Cumberland (MD), ca. 1910. $125

Wood, Silas — A SKETCH OF THE FIRST SETTLEMENT OF THE SEVERAL TOWNS ON LONG ISLAND. Brooklyn, 1824. $275

Wood, W.D. — REMINISCENCES OF RECONSTRUCTION IN TEXAS. (San Marcos, TX), 1902, wraps. $150

Woodman, David, Jr. — GUIDE TO TEXAS EMIGRANTS. Boston, 1835, map. At least $2500

Woodruff, W.E. — WITH THE LIGHT GUNS IN '61-'65. Little Rock, 1903. $200

Woods, Daniel B. — SIXTEEN MONTHS AT THE GOLD DIGGINGS. New York, 1851. $300

Woods, John — TWO YEARS' RESIDENCE — ON THE ENGLISH PRAIRIE, IN THE ILLINOIS COUNTRY. London, 1822, 2 maps. At least $1250

Woodson, W.H. — HISTORY OF CLAY COUNTY, MISSOURI. Topeka (KS), 1920. $75

Woolworth, James M. — NEBRASKA IN 1857. Omaha (ne), 1857, color folding map. $650

Wooten, Dudley G. (Editor) — A COMPREHENSIVE HISTORY OF TEXAS, 1865 TO 1897. Dallas, 1898, 2 vols., 23 plates. $350

Wright, E.W. (Editor) — LEWIS AND DRYDEN'S MARINE HISTORY OF THE PACIFIC NORTHWEST. Portland, 1895. $550

Wright, William — THE OIL REGIONS OF PENNSYLVANIA. New York, 1865. $225

Wyeth, John B. — OREGON; OR A SHORT HISTORY OF A LONG JOURNEY. Cambridge (MA), 1833, wraps. $1800

Y

Yoakum, Henderson K. — HISTORY OF TEXAS. NY, 1855, 2 vols. Fldg. document, maps, plates. $750

Yeary, Mamie — REMINISCENCES OF THE BOYS IN GRAY, 1861-1965. Dallas, 1912. $175

YELLOW BIRD. THE LIFE AND ADVENTURES OF JOAQUIN MURIETA (by John R. Ridge). San Francisco, 1854. Wraps. $25,000+

Young, Andrew W. — HISTORY OF CHAUTAUQUA COUNTY, NEW YORK. Buffalo, 1875. $135

Young, Ansel — THE WESTERN RESERVE ALMANAC FOR THE YEAR 1844. Cleveland, (1843), wraps. $150

Young, Harry — HARD KNOCKS: A LIFE STORY OF THE VANISHING WEST. Portland, 1915. $135

Young, John R. — MEMOIRS. Salt Lake City, 1920. $125

Youngblood, Charles L. — ADVENTURES OF CHAS. L. YOUNGBLOOD DURING TEN YEARS ON THE PLAINS. Boonville (IN), 1882. $235

Z

Zaccarelli, John — ZACCARELLI'S PICTORIAL SOUVENIR BOOK OF THE GOLDEN NORTHLAND. Dawson, (1908), wraps. $135

Zogbaum, Rufus F. — HORSE, FOOT AND DRAGOONS. New York, 1888. $90

Appendix 5

COLLECTIBLE FICTION BOOKS AND THEIR VALUES

The authors and titles selected here are those which are best known to the general public. Only titles having a current nominal market value of at least $25 are listed. It is reasonable to assume that all first edition books by any of the authors listed will have some value — do not assume that all books by the same author will have comparable values.

Some of the author names listed here are pseudonyms. Checking any name you find here with the names in Appendix 1 might lead you to other names which the author may have used, and thus to other valuable book titles.

The title's listed are all first editions and first impressions if pertinent. The values noted are for books in very good to fine condition with dust jackets (if the book was originally issued with one). "Points" are associated with properly identifying many of these books and a library should be checked for a bibliography of the author in question. Alternatively, a rare book dealer should be consulted for final determination as to the correct state and current value.

A

Abbey, Edward — THE BRAVE COWBOY. NY, 1956.
$75-100

Adams, Andy — THE LOG OF A COWBOY. Boston,
1903. $85-100

Adams, Clifton — THE DESPERADO. NY, 1950. $65-80

Adams, Richard — WATERSHIP DOWN. London, 1972.
$175-225

Aiken, Conrad — BLUE VOYAGE. NY, 1927. $110-135

Ainsworth, W. Harrison — THE MISER'S DAUGHTER.
London, 1842, 3 vols. $300-350

Albert, Marvin H. — THE LAW AND JAKE WADE. NY,
1956. $50-65

Alcott, Louisa May — LITTLE MEN. Boston, 1871.
$275-325

Alcott, Louisa May — LITTLE WOMEN. Boston, 1868-
69, 2 vols. $1,700-2,200

Alcott, Louisa May — AN OLD-FASHIONED GIRL. Boston, 1870. $85-125

Aldiss, Brian — THE BRIGHTFOUNT DIARIES. London,
(1955). $65-90

Aldrich, Thomas Bailey — THE STORY OF A BAD BOY.
Boston, 1870. $450-525

Alger, Horatio, Jr. — ABRAHAM LINCOLN, THE BACK-
WOODS BOY. NY, 1883. $85-110

Alger, Horatio, Jr. — BERTHA'S CHRISTMAS VISION:
AN AUTUMN SHEAF. Boston, 1856. $375-450

Alger, Horatio, Jr. — DAN THE DETECTIVE. NY, 1884.
$350-425

Alger, Horatio, Jr. — DEAN DUNHAM. NY, 1890, wraps.
$110-135

Alger, Horatio, Jr. — THE FIVE HUNDRED DOLLAR
CHECK. NY, (1891). $425-475

Alger, Horatio, Jr. — FROM CANAL BOY TO PRESI-
DENT. NY, 1881. $50-75

Alger, Horatio, Jr. — GRAND'THER BALDWIN'S
THANKSGIVING. Boston, (1875). $110-135

Alger, Horatio, Jr. — LUKE WALTON, OR THE
CHICAGO NEWSBOY. Philadelphia, (1889). $60-75

Alger, Horatio, Jr. — MARK STANTON. NY, 1890. $110-
-135

Alger, Horatio, Jr. — RAGGED DICK; OR STREET LIFE
IN NEW YORK WITH THE BOOT-BLACKS. Boston,
(1868). $800-1,000

Alger, Horatio, Jr. — RALPH RAYMOND'S HEIR. NY,
(1892), wraps. $60-75

Alger, Horatio, Jr. — ROBERT COVERDALE'S STRUG-
GLE. NY, (1910). $550 or more

Alger, Horatio, Jr. — THE WESTERN BOY — (NY, 1878).
$375-450

Alger, Horatio, Jr. — THE YOUNG MINER; OR TOM
NELSON IN CALIFORNIA. San Francisco, 1965.
$85-100

Alger, Horatio Jr., & O. Augusta Cheney — SEEKING
HIS FORTUNE AND OTHER DIALOGUES. Boston,
(1875). $575-750

Allan, Luke (William Lacey Amy) — THE BLUE WOLF:
A TALE OF THE CYPRESS HILLS. London, 1913.
$125-150

Ambler, Eric — A COFFIN FOR DIMITRIOS. NY, 1939.
$175-225

Andersen, Hans Christian — FAIRY TALES. Illustrated
by Arthur Rackham. London, (1932), signed by
Rackham. $800-1,000

Anderson, Poul — THE BROKEN SWORD. NY, (1954).
$85-100

Anderson, Poul — VAULTS OF THE AGES. Philadelphia, (1952). $80-100

Anderson, Sherwood — MARCHING MEN. NY, 1917.
$225-275

Anderson, Sherwood — WINDY MC PHERSON'S SON.
NY, 1916. $800 or more

Anderson, Sherwood — WINESBURG, OHIO. NY, 1919.
$500 or more

Anon — ADVENTURES OF A BROWNIE, AS TOLD TO
MY CHILD, THE (by Dinah M. Craik) — London,
1872. $275-325

Anon — CHILD'S BOOK ABOUT WHALES, THE. Concord (NH), 1843, wraps. $140-175

Anon — CHILD'S BOTANY, THE (by Samuel Griswold
Goodrich). Boston, 1828. $85-100

Anon — CINDERELLA. Retold by C.S. Evans. London,
1919, illustrated By Arthur Rackham, limited &
signed by Rackham. $500 or more

Anon — DREAM DROPS, OR STORIES FROM FAIRY
LAND (by Amy Lowell). Boston, (1887), wraps.
$1,200 or more

Anon — FAIRY BOOK, THE (by Dinah M. Craik). NY,
1837. $150-175

Anon — FAIRY GARLAND, A. London, (1928), illustrated by Edmund Dulac, limited & signed by
Dulac. $450-525

Anon — FAITH GARTNEY'S GIRLHOOD (by Mrs. A.D.T.
Whitney). Boston, 1863. $85-100

Anon — FAMILY ROBINSON CRUSOE, THE (translated
by Johann David Wyss). London, 1814, 2 vols.
$4,250 or more

Anon — HANDBOOK FOR BOYS. NY, 1911 (BSA).
$125-150

Anon — HANDBOOK FOR SCOUTMASTERS: BOY
SCOUTS OF AMERICA. NY, (1914). $85-100

Arthur, T.S. — TEN NIGHTS IN A BAR-ROOM, AND
WHAT I SAW THERE. Philadelphia, 1854. $175-225

Asimov, Isaac — THE END OF ETERNITY. Garden City,
1955. $80-100

Asimov, Isaac — FOUNDATION. NY, (1951). $125-175

Asimov, Isaac — FOUNDATION AND EMPIRE. NY,
(1952). $135-160

Asimov, Isaac — I, ROBOT. NY, (1950). $175-225

Asimov, Isaaac — PEBBLE IN THE SKY. GC, 1950.
$135-160

Asimov, Isaac — SECOND FOUNDATION, (NY, 1953).
$135-160

Atherton, Gertrude — WHAT DREAMS MAY COME, as
Frank Lin. Chicago, (1888), wraps. $140-175

Atterley, Joseph (George Tucker) — A VOYAGE TO THE
MOON. NY, 1827. $425-475

B

Bacheller, Irving — EBEN HOLDEN. Boston, (1900).
$125-150

Baldwin, James — GIOVANNI'S ROOM. NY, 1956.
$325-375

Bangs, John Kendrick — A HOUSE-BOAT ON THE
RIVER STYX. NY, 1896. $60-75

Bannerman, Helen — THE STORY OF LITTLE BLACK
SAMBO. London, 1899. $850 or more

Bardwell, Denver (James Denson Sayers) — GUN-SMOKE IN SUNSET VALLEY. NY & London, 1935. $50-65

Barrie, Sir James M. — THE LITTLE MINISTER. London, 1891, 3 vols. $650-750

Barrie, Sir James M. — PETER AND WENDY. London, 1911. $135-150; NY, (1911). $60-75

Barrie, Sir James M. — PETER PAN IN KENSINGTON GARDENS. NY, 1906. $275-350

Barth, John — THE FLOATING OPERA. NY, (1956). $225-275

Barth, John — THE SOT-WEED FACTOR. Garden City, 1960. $225-275

Barthelme, Donald — COME BACK, DR. CALIGARI. Boston, (1964). $175-200

Bates, H.E. — THE BEAUTY OF THE DEAD AND ONE OTHER STORY. London, 1941, Limited. $275-325

Baum, L. Frank — AMERICAN FAIRY TALES. Chicago, 1901. $175-225

Baum, L. Frank — THE ARMY ALPHABET. CHICAGO, 1900. $800 or more

Baum, L. Frank — THE COWARDLY LION AND THE HUNGRY TIGER. Chicago, (1913). $225-275

Baum, L. Frank — DOROTHY AND THE WIZARD OF OZ. Chicago, (1908). $325-375

Baum, L. Frank — THE ENCHANTED ISLAND OF YEW. Indianapolis, (1903). $275-325

Baum, L. Frank — FATHER GOOSE'S YEAR BOOK. Chicago, (1907). $175-225

Baum, L. Frank — THE LIFE AND ADVENTURES OF SANTA CLAUS. Indianapolis, 1902. $325-375

Baum, L. Frank — THE MARVELOUS LAND OF OZ. Chicago, 1904. $25-475

Baum, L. Frank — THE MASTER KEY. Indianapolis, (1901). $325-375

Baum, L. Frank — MOTHER GOOSE IN PROSE. Chicago, (1897), illustrated by Maxfield Parrish. $850-1,000

Baum, L. Frank — A NEW WONDERLAND. NY, 1900. $425-475

Baum, L. Frank — OZMA OF OZ. CHICAGO, (1907). $600 or more

Baum, L. Frank — THE PATCHWORK GIRL OF OZ. Chicago, (1913). $350-425

Baum, L. Frank — QUEEN ZIXI OF IX. NY, 1905. $325-375

Baum, L. Frank — THE ROAD TO OZ. Chicago, (1909). $275-325

Baum, L. Frank — THE SEA FAIRIES. Chicago, (1911). $175-225

Baum, L. Frank — THE SONGS OF FATHER GOOSE. Chicago, 1900. $225-275

Baum, L. Frank — THE WONDERFUL WIZARD OF OZ. Chicago & NY, 1900. $2,750 or more

Baum, L. Frank — THE YELLOW HEN. Chicago, (1916). $175-225

Beach, Rex — THE SILVER HORDE. NY, 1909. $30-45

Beach, Rex — THE SPOILERS. NY, 1906. $75-90

Beard, Daniel C. — AMERICAN BOY'S HANDY BOOK: WHAT TO DO AND HOW TO DO IT. NY, 1882. $85-125

Bell, Currer (Charlotte Bronte) — JANE EYRE: AN AUTOBIOGRAPHY. London, 1847, 3 vols. $5,500 or more

Bell, Currer — THE PROFESSOR. London, 1857, 2 vols. $1,100 or more

Bell, Ellis & Acton (Emily & Anne Bronte) — WUTHERING HEIGHTS. London, 1847, 3 vols. $15,000 or more

Bellah, James Warner — MASSACRE. NY, 1950. $35-50

Bellah, James Warner — THE MAN WHO SHOT LIBERTY VALANCE. NY, 1962, wraps. $35-50

Bellamy, Edward — LOOKING BACKWARD, 2000-1887. Boston, 1888. $375-425

Belloc, Hilaire — THE BAD CHILD'S BOOK OF BEASTS, by H. B. — Oxford (Eng), (1896). $175-225

Belloc, Hilaire — CAUTIONARY TALES FOR CHILDREN. London, (1908). $100-125

Bellow, Saul — THE ADVENTURES OF AUGIE MARCH. NY, 1953. $135-150

Bellow, Saul — DANGLING MAN. NY, (1944). $375-425

Bellow, Saul — THE VICTIM. NY, (1947). $275-325

Bennett, Emerson — CLARA MORELAND; OR, ADVENTURES IN THE FAR SOUTH-WEST. Philadelphia, 1963, wraps. $275-325

Bennett, Emerson — LENI-LEOTI; OR, ADVENTURES IN THE FAR WEST. Cincinnati, 1849, wraps. $550-650

Bennett, Emerson — THE PRAIRIE FLOWER; OR, ADVENTURES IN THE FAR WEST. Cincinnati, 1849, wraps. $450-550

Berger, Thomas Louis — LITTLE BIG MAN. NY, 1964. $50-65

Bishop, Zealia — THE CURSE OF YIG. Sauk City (WI), 1953. $60-75

Blackwood, Algernon — THE EMPTY HOUSE AND OTHER GHOST STORIES. London, 1906. $140-175

Blackwood, Algernon — INCREDIBLE ADVENTURES. London, 1914. $140-165

Blackwood, Algernon — THE LOST VALLEY. NY, 1914. $140-165

Blavatsky, H.P. — NIGHTMARE TALES. London, 1892. $175-225

Box, Edgar (Gore Vidal) — DEATH BEFORE BEDTIME. NY, 1953. $60-75

Box, Edgar — DEATH IN THE FIFTH POSITION. NY, 1952. $75-90

Box, Edgar — DEATH LIKES IT HOT. NY, 1954. $60-75

Bradbury, Ray — THE ANTHEM SPRINTERS. NY, 1963. $85-110

Bradbury, Ray — DANDELION WINE. Garden City, 1957. $125-150

Bradbury, Ray — DARK CARNIVAL. Sauk City, 1947. $425-475

Bradbury, Ray — FAHRENHEIT 451. NY, (1953). $165-190; same, wraps. $45-60

Bradbury, Ray — THE GOLDEN APPLES OF THE SUN. Garden City, 1953. $60-75

Bradbury, Ray — THE ILLUSTRATED MAN. GC, 1951. $125-150

Bradbury, Ray — THE MACHINERIES OF JOY. NY, 1964. $90-125

Bradbury, Ray — THE MARTIAN CHRONICLES. GC, 1950. $225-275

Bradbury, Ray — A MEDICINE FOR MELANCHOLY. GC, 1959. $60-75

Bradbury, Ray — THE OCTOBER COUNTRY. NY, (1955). $135-160

Bradbury, Ray — SWITCH ON THE NIGHT. NY, 1955. $60-75

Bramah, Ernest — THE EYES OF MAX CARRADOS. London, 1923. $450-550

Bramah, Ernest — MAX CARRADOS. London, 1914. $450-550

BRAND, MAX (Frederick Schiller Faust) — CALL OF THE BLOOD. NY, (1934). $175-225

Brand, Max — THE FALSE RIDER. NY, (1947). $35-50

Brand, Max — FLAMING IRONS. NY, (1948). $25-35

Brand, Max — HUNTED RIDERS. NY, 1935. $140-175

Brand, Max — MONTANA RIDES AGAIN. NY, 1934. $175-250

Brand, Max — THE RANCHER'S REVENGE. NY, 1934. $140-175

Brand, Max — WINE ON THE DESERT. NY, 1940. $140-175

Brand, Max — TIMBAL GULCH TRAIL. NY, 1934. $75-125

Browning, Robert — THE PIED PIPER OF HAMLIN. London, (1888), illustrated by Kate Greenaway. $275-325

Buchan, John — THE THIRTY-NINE STEPS. Edinburgh, 1915. $225-275

Buechner, Frederick — A LONG DAY'S DYING. NY, 1950. $60-75

Burgess, Anthony — A CLOCKWORK ORANGE. London, (1962). $500 or more

Burgess, Gelett — GOOPS AND HOW TO BE THEM. NY, (1900). $275-325

Burgess, Gelett — THE NONSENSE ALMANACK FOR 1900. NY, (1899). $125-150

Burgess, Gelett — THE PURPLE COW! (San Francisco, 1895), 8 leaves. $325-375

Burnett, Frances Hodgson — EDITHA'S BURGLAR. Boston, 1888. $60-75

Burnett, Frances Hodgson — LITTLE LORD FAUNTLEROY. NY, 1886. $325-375

Burnett, Frances Hodgson — THE SECRET GARDEN. NY, (1911). $125-150

Burnett, Frances Hodgson — THAT LASS O'LOWRIE'S. NY, 1877. $125-150

Burnett, W.R. — LITTLE CAESAR. NY, 1929. $125-150

Burroughs, Edgar Rice — AT THE EARTH'S CORE. Chicago, 1922. $550-650

Burroughs, Edgar Rice — BACK TO THE STONE AGE. Tarzana (CA), (1937). $275-325

Burroughs, Edgar Rice — THE CHESSMEN OF MARS. Chicago, 1922. $375-425

Burroughs, Edgar Rice — A FIGHTING MAN OF MARS. NY, (1931). $125-150

Burroughs, Edgar Rice — THE MASTER MIND OF MARS. Chicago, 1928. $125-175

Burroughs, Edgar Rice — A PRINCESS OF MARS. Chicago, 1917. $550-650

Burroughs, Edgar Rice — THUVIA, MAID OF MARS. Chicago, 1920. $400 or more

Burroughs, Edgar Rice — THE WARLORD OF MARS. Chicago, 1919. $400 or more

C

Cabell, James Branch — JURGEN. NY, 1919. $350 or more

Cain, James M. — THE MOTH. NY, 1948. $30-45

Cain, James M. — THE POSTMAN ALWAYS RINGS TWICE. NY, 1934. $550 or more

Caldwell, Erskine — GOD'S LITTLE ACRE. NY, 1933. $175-225

Caldwell, Erskine — TOBACCO ROAD. NY, 1932. $225-275

Callaghan, Morley — STRANGE FUGITIVE. NY, 1928. $225-275

Campbell, John W. — INVADERS FROM THE INFINITE. Hicksville (NY), (1961). $60-85

Capote, Truman — OTHER VOICES, OTHER ROOMS. NY, (1948). $125-150

Capote, Truman — IN COLD BLOOD. NY, (1965), Trade Edition. $30-40

Carr, John Dickson — DEATH TURNS THE TABLES. NY, 1941. $60-80

Carroll, Lewis — ALICE'S ADVENTURES IN WONDERLAND. NY, 1866. $2,500 or more

Carroll, Lewis — ALICE'S ADVENTURES UNDER GROUND. London, 1886. $175-225

Carroll, Lewis — THE HUNTING OF THE SNARK. London, 1876. $275-325

Carroll, Lewis — THROUGH THE LOOKING GLASS, AND WHAT ALICE FOUND THERE. London, 1872. $800 or more

Carter, Forrest — THE REBEL OUTLAW, JOSEY WALES. Gantt (AL), 1973. $60-75

Castelemon, H.C. (Harry) — FRANK ON THE LOWER MISSISSIPPI. Cincinnati, 1867. $60-75

Castlemon, Harry — GUY HARRIS, THE RUNAWAY. NY, 1887. $75-90

Castlemon, Harry — THE SPORTSMAN'S CLUB AMONG THE TRAPPERS. Philadelphia, 1874. $60-75

Cather, Willa — ALEXANDER'S BRIDGE. Boston, 1912. $350-425

Cather, Willa — APRIL TWILIGHTS. Boston, 1903, issued w/o dust jacket. $850 or more

Cather, Willa — DEATH COMES FOR THE ARCHBISHOP. NY, 1927. $60-75

Cather, Willa — A LOST LADY. NY, 1923. $60-75

Cather, Willa — MY ANTONIA. Boston, 1918. $475-550

Cather, Willa — O PIONEERS! Boston, 1913. $275-325

Cather, Willa — OBSCURE DESTINIES. NY, 1932. $35-50

Cather, Willa — ONE OF OURS. NY, 1932. $60-75

Cather, Willa — THE PROFESSOR'S HOUSE. NY, 1925. $75-100

Cather, Willa — THE SONG OF THE LARK. Boston, 1915. $225-275

Cather, Willa — THE TROLL GARDEN. NY, 1905. $325-375

Cather, Willa — YOUTH AND THE BRIGHT MEDUSA. NY, 1920. $45-60

Cather, Willa, With Dorothy Canfield — THE FEAR THAT WALKS BY NOONDAY. NY, 1931, limited to 30 copies. $750 or more

Chandler, Raymond — THE BIG SLEEP. NY, 1939. $850 or more

Chandler, Raymond — FAREWELL, MY LOVELY. NY, 1940. $2,250 or more

Chandler, Raymond — KILLER IN THE RAIN. Boston, 1964. $135-175

Chandler, Raymond — THE LADY IN THE LAKE. NY, 1943. $550 or more

Chandler, Raymond — THE LITTLE SISTER. London, (1949). $175-225

Chandler, Raymond — THE LONG GOOD-BYE. London, (1953). $275-325

Chandler, Raymond — THE LONG GOOD-BYE. Boston, (1954). $275-325

Chandler, Raymond — PLAYBACK. London, (1958). $125-175

Chandler, Raymond — SPANISH BLOOD. Cleveland & NY, 1946. $35-50

Cheever, John — THE WAY SOME PEOPLE LIVE. NY, (1943). $275-325

Chesterton, G.K. — THE MAN WHO WAS THURSDAY. London, 1908. $275-325

Chesterton, G.K. — FOUR FAULTLESS FELONS. London, (1930). $135-160

Chesterton, G.K. — THE INNOCENCE OF FATHER BROWN. London, 1911. $350 or more

Chesterton, G.K. — THE SCANDAL OF FATHER BROWN. NY, 1935. $60-75

Chesterton, G.K. — THE SECRET OF FATHER BROWN. London, (1927). $325-375

Chesterton, G.K. — THE WISDOM OF FATHER BROWN. London, 1914. $325-375

Christie, Agatha — CROOKED HOUSE. NY, (1949). $175-225

Christie, Agatha — DEAD MAN'S FOLLY. NY, (1956). $85-100

Christie, Agatha — DEATH COMES AS THE END. London, 1945. $135-175

Christie, Agatha — HERCULE POIROT'S CHRISTMAS. London, (1939). $175-225

Christie, Agatha — THE HOUND OF DEATH AND OTHER STORIES. London, 1933. $225-275

Christie, Agatha — THE MAN IN THE BROWN SUIT. London, 1924. $275-325

Christie, Agatha — MR. PARKER PYNE, DETECTIVE. NY, 1934. $650-750

Christie, Agatha — MURDER FOR CHRISTMAS. NY, 1939. $650-750

Christie, Agatha — MURDER IN MESOPOTOMIA. London, (1936). $325-375

Christie, Agatha — THE MYSTERIOUS AFFAIR AT STYLES. London, 1920. $2,250 or more

Christie, Agatha — THE PATRIOTIC MURDERS. NY, 1941. $650-750

Christie, Agatha — POIROT LOSES A CLIENT. NY, 1937. $625-675

Christie, Agatha — SAD CYPRESS. London, (1940). $275-325

Clark, Walter Van Tilburg — CHRISTMAS COMES TO HJALSEN. Reno (NV), 1930, wraps. $325-375

Clark, Walter Van Tilburg — THE OX-BOW INCIDENT. NY, (1940). $60-75

Clarke, Arthur C. — CHILDHOOD'S END. NY, (1953). $100-125

Clarke, Arthur C. — EARTHLIGHT. NY, (1955). $85-100

Clarke, Arthur C. — INTERPLANETARY FLIGHT. London, (1950). $85-100

Collins, Wilkie — THE WOMAN IN WHITE. NY, 1860. $350 or more

Cox, Palmer — THE BROWNIES AROUND THE WORLD. NY, (1894). $150-200

Cox, Palmer — THE BROWNIES AT HOME. NY, (1893). $75-90

Cox, Palmer — THE BROWNIES: THEIR BOOK. NY, (1887). $550 OR MORE

Cox, Palmer — QUEER PEOPLE WITH WINGS AND STINGS AND THEIR KWEER KAPERS. Philadelphia, (1888). $85-125

Cox, Palmer — QUEERIE QUEERS WITH HANDS, WINGS AND CLAWS. Buffalo, ca. 1887. $85-125

Crofts, Freeman Wills — THE GROOTE PARK MURDER. London, (1923). $200-250

Crofts, Freeman Wills — THE PIT-PROP SYNDICATE. London, (1922). $225-275

Crothers, Samuel Mc Cord — MISS MUFFET'S CHRISTMAS PARTY. St. Paul (MN), 1892. $60-75

Cummings, Ray — THE GIRL IN THE GOLDEN ATOM. NY, 1923. $100-125

D

Davis, Richard Harding — GALLEGHER AND OTHER STORIES. NY, 1891, wraps. $175-225

De Camp, L. Sprague — DEMONS AND DINOSAURS. Sauk City, 1970. $60-75

De Camp, L. Sprague & Fletcher Pratt — LAND OF UN-REASON. NY, (1942). $110-135

De La Mare, Walter — BROOMSTICKS AND OTHER TALES. London, 1925, signed. $85-100

De La Mare, Walter — CROSSINGS: A FAIRY PLAY. (London, 1921), limited, boxed. $85-100

Derleth, August — THE MEMOIRS OF SOLAR PONS. Sauk City (WI), 1951. $85-100

Derleth, August — THE REMINISCENCES OF SOLAR PONS. Sauk City, 1961. $85-100

Derleth, August — THE RETURN OF SOLAR PONS. Sauk City, 1958. $85-100

Dickens, Charles — A CHILD'S HISTORY OF ENGLAND. London, 1852-53-54, 3 vols. $450 or more

Dickens, Charles — A CHRISTMAS CAROL. London, 1843. $1,750 or more

Dickens, Charles — THE PERSONAL HISTORY OF DAVID COPPERFIELD. London, 1850. $350 or more

Dickens, Charles — GREAT EXPECTATIONS. London, 1861, 3 vols. $5,000 or more

Dickens, Charles — MASTER HUMPHREY'S CLOCK. London, 1840-41, 3 vols. $500 or more

Dickens, Charles — THE PERSONAL HISTORY OF DAVID COPPERFIELD. London, 1850. $350 or more

Dickens, Charles — A TALE OF TWO CITIES. London, 1859. $1,500 or more

Didion, Joan — RUN RIVER. NY, (1963). $110-125

Disney, Walt — THE ADVENTURES OF MICKEY MOUSE: BOOK I. Philadelphia, (1931). $325-375

Disney, Walt — THE GOLDEN TOUCH. London, 1935. $175-225

Disney, Walt — HONEST JOHN AND GIDDY. NY, (1940). $125-150

Disney, Walt — LITTLE RED RIDING HOOD AND THE BIG BAD WOLF. Philadelphia, (1934). $135-165

Disney, Walt — MICKEY MOUSE. Racine (WI), (1933), wraps. $175-225

Disney, Walt — MICKEY MOUSE IN KING ARTHUR'S COURT. London, ca. 1932. $325-375

Disney, Walt — MICKEY MOUSE STORY BOOK. Philadelphia, (1931). $175-225

Disney, Walt — THE POP-UP MINNIE MOUSE. NY, (1933). $225-275

Disney, Walt — STORIES FROM WALT DISNEY'S FANTASIA. NY, (1940). $175-225

Doctorow, E.L. — WELCOME TO HARD TIMES. NY, 1960. $100-125

Dodge, M.E. (Mary Mapes Dodge) — HANS BRINKER; OR, THE SILVER SKATES. NY, 1866. $375-425

Donleavy, J.P. — THE GINGER MAN. Paris, (1955). $450 or more

Dos Passos, John — THREE SOLDIERS. NY, (1921). $450-500

Doyle, A. Conan — THE ADVENTURES OF SHERLOCK HOLMES. London, 1892. $550 or more

Doyle, A. Conan — THE CASE-BOOK OF SHERLOCK HOLMES. London, (1927). $550 or more

Doyle, A. Conan — THE DOINGS OF RAFFLES HAW. London, 1892. $225-275

Doyle, A. Conan — THE FIRM OF GIRDLESTONE. London, 1890. $60-75

Doyle, A. Conan — THE GREAT SHADOW. Bristol (Eng), 1892. $175-225

Doyle, A. Conan — THE GREAT SHADOW AND BEYOND THE CITY. Bristol, (1893). $85-100

Doyle, A. Conan — HIS LAST BOW. London, 1917. $175-225

Doyle, A. Conan — THE HOUND OF THE BASKERVILLES. London, 1902. $450 or more

Doyle, A. Conan — THE MEMOIRS OF SHERLOCK HOLMES. London, 1894. $550 or more

Doyle, A. Conan — MY FRIEND THE MURDERER. NY, (1893). $225-275

Doyle, A. Conan — THE RETURN OF SHERLOCK HOLMES. London, 1905. $350 or more

Doyle, A. Conan — THE SIGN OF FOUR. London, 1890. $1,750 or more

Doyle, A. Conan — THE SPECKLED BAND. London, 1912. $350 or more

Doyle, A. Conan — A STUDY IN SCARLET. London, 1888, wraps. $15,000 or more

Drake, Leah Bodine — A HORNBOOK FOR WITCHES. Sauk City, 1950. $650-750

Dreiser, Theodore — JENNIE GERHARDT. NY, 1911. $225-275

Dulac, Edmund — SINBAD THE SAILOR AND OTHER STORIES FROM THE ARABIAN NIGHTS. London, (1911), limited & signed. $800 or more

E

Edmonds, Walter D. — ROME HAUL. Boston, 1929, limited. $175-225

Eggleston, Edward — THE BOOK OF QUEER STORIES, AND STORIES TOLD ON A CELLAR DOOR. Chicago, 1871. $225-275

Eggleston, Edward — THE HOOSIER SCHOOLMASTER. NY, (1871). $225-275

Eggleston, Edward — MR. BLAKE'S WALKING-STICK. Chicago, 1870. $325-375

Eliot, T.S. — OLD POSSUM'S BOOK OF PRACTICAL CATS. London, (1939). $175-200

Ellin, Stanley — MYSTERY STORIES. NY, 1956. $85-100

Ellison, Harlan — RUMBLE. NY, (1958), wraps. $60-75

F

Farquharson, Martha (Martha Finley) — ELSIE DINSMORE. NY, 1867. $2,500 OR MORE

Farrell, James T. — CALICO SHOES AND OTHER STORIES. NY, (1934). $175-225

Farrell, James T. — YOUNG LONIGAN: A BOYHOOD IN CHICAGO STREETS. NY, 1932. $225-275

Farrell, James T. — THE YOUNG MANHOOD OF STUDS LONIGAN. NY, (1934). $175-225

Faulkner, William — AS I LAY DYING. NY, (1930). $800 or more

Faulkner, William — DOCTOR MARTINO AND OTHER STORIES. NY, 1934, trade edition. $500 or more

Faulkner, William — THE MANSION. NY, (1959), limited & signed. $450 or more

Faulkner, William — MISS ZILPHIA GANT. (Dallas), 1932, limited. $1,000 or more

Faulkner, William — MOSQUITOES. NY, 1927. $1,000 or more

Faulkner, William — PYLON. NY, 1935, trade edition. $275-325

Faulkner, William — REQUIEM FOR A NUN. NY, (1951), Trade Edition. $175-225

Faulkner, William — SANCTUARY. NY, (1931). $850 or more

Faulkner, William — SARTORIS. NY, (1929). $800 or more

Faulkner, William — SOLDIER'S PAY. NY, 1926. $1,750 or more

Faulkner, William — THE SOUND AND THE FURY. NY, (1929). $1,000 or more

Faulkner, William — ABSALOM, ABSALOM! NY, 1936, trade edition. $275-325

Faulkner, William — INTRUDER IN THE DUST. NY, (1948). $175 or more

Faulkner, William — KNIGHT'S GAMBIT. NY, (1949). $175-225

Faulkner, William — LIGHT IN AUGUST. (NY, 1932). $600 or more

Faulkner, William — SANCTUARY. NY, (1931). $950 or more

Fearing, Kenneth — THE BIG CLOCK. NY, (1946). $60-75

Fellows-Johnston, Annie — THE LITTLE COLONEL. Boston, 1896. $85-100

Ferber, Edna — DAWN O'HARA: THE GIRL WHO LAUGHED. NY, (1911). $125-150

Field, Eugene — LOVE-SONGS OF CHILDHOOD. NY, 1894, trade edition. $25-35

Field, Eugene — POEMS OF CHILDHOOD. NY, 1904, illustrated by Maxfield Parrish. $135-159

Finney, Charles G. — THE CIRCUS OF DR. LAO. NY, 1935. $125-150

Fisher, Harry C. — THE MUTT AND JEFF CARTOONS. Boston, 1910. $85-125

Fisher, Vardis — APRIL: A FABLE OF LOVE. Caldwell (ID) & Garden City, 1937. $60-75

Fisher, Vardis — CHILDREN OF GOD, AN AMERICAN EPIC. Caldwell, 1939. $50-65

Fisher, Vardis — CITY OF ILLLUSION. Caldwell, or NY, (1941). $45-60

Fisher, Vardis — DARK BRIDWELL. Boston, 1931. $60-75

Fisher, Vardis — IN TRAGIC LIFE. Caldwell, 1932. $60-75

Fisher, Vardis — NO VILLAIN NEED BE. Caldwell, 1936. $60-75

Fisher, Vardis — ODYSSEY OF A HERO. Philadelphia, 1937. $60-75

Fisher, Vardis — PASSIONS SPIN THE PLOT. Caldwell, 1933. $125-150

Fisher, Vardis — WE ARE THE BETRAYED. Caldwell, (1935). $60-75

Fitzgerald, F. Scott — ALL THE SAD YOUNG MEN. NY, 1926. $1,000 or more

Fitzgerald, F. Scott — THE BEAUTIFUL AND THE DAMNED. NY, 1922. $1,250 or more

Fitzgerald, F. Scott — FLAPPERS AND PHILOSOPHERS. NY, 1920. $500 or more

Fitzgerald, F. Scott — THE GREAT GATSBY. NY, 1925. $3,000 or more (without a jacket — $100-150)

Fitzgerald, F. Scott — TALES OF THE JAZZ AGE. NY, 1922. $500 or more

Fitzgerald, F. Scott — TENDER IS THE NIGHT. NY, 1934. $650-750

Fitzgerald, F. Scott — THIS SIDE OF PARADISE. NY, 1920. $1,500 or more

Fitzgerald, F. Scott — THE VEGETABLE. NY, 1923. $650-750

Fitzgerald, Zelda — SAVE ME THE WALTZ. NY, 1932. $475-550

Fleming, Ian — CASINO ROYALE. London, (1953). $1,500 or more

Fleming, Ian — DR. NO. London, (1958). $125-150

Fleming, Ian — LIVE AND LET DIE — London, (1954). $600 or more

Fleming, Ian — ON HER MAJESTY'S SECRET SERVICE. London, (1963), trade edition. $60-75

Ford, Paul Leicester — THE HONORABLE PETER STIRLING AND WHAT PEOPLE THOUGHT OF HIM. NY, 1894. $135-160

Forester, C.S. — THE AFRICAN QUEEN. Boston, 1935. $225-275

Forester, C.S. — A PAWN AMONG KINGS. London, (1924). $550-650

Forester, C.S. — PLAIN MURDER. London, (1930). $175-225

Forster, E.M. — A ROOM WITH A VIEW. London, 1908. $250-300

Fowles, John — THE COLLECTOR. London, (1963). $700 or more

Fowles, John — THE FRENCH LIEUTENANT'S WOMAN. London, (1969). $175-225

Francis, Dick — BLOOD SPORT. London, (1967). $60-75

FRANKENSTEIN; OR THE MODERN PROMETHEUS (By Mary Wollstonecraft Shelley) — London, 1818, 3 vols. $8,500 or more

Freeman, R. Austin — THE ADVENTURES OF ROMNEY PRINGLE, as Clifford Ashdown, with J.J. Pitcairn. London, 1902. $1,200 or more

Freeman, R. Austin — THE CAT'S EYE. London, (1923). $225-275

Freeman, R. Austin — FELO DE SE? London, (1937). $225-275

Freeman, R. Austin — FOR THE DEFENCE: DR. THORNDYKE. London, 1934. $225-275

Freeman, R. Austin — MR. POLTON EXPLAINS. London, 1940. $225-275

Freeman, R. Austin — THE RED THUMB MARK. London, 1907. $550 or more

Freeman, R. Austin — THE SINGING BONE. London, 1912. $450 or more

G

Gag, Wanda — MILLIONS OF CATS. NY, 1928. $110-135

Garland, Hamlin — THE BOOK OF THE AMERICAN INDIAN. NY, 1923, 34 plates by Frederic Remington. $175-225

Garland, Hamlin — CAVANAGH, FOREST RANGER. NY, 1910. $60-75

Garland, Hamlin — MAIN-TRAVELLED ROADS. Boston, 1891, wraps. $175-225

Gernsback, Hugo — RALPH 124C41: A ROMANCE OF THE YEAR 2660. Boston, 1925. $550 or more

Gilbert, W.S. — THE "BAB" BALLADS: MUCH SOUND AND LITTLE SENSE.London, 1869. $225-250

Gilbert, W.S. — MORE "BAB" BALLADS. London, (1873). $125-150

Gissing, George — THYRZA: A TALE. London, 1887, 3 vols. $450-550

Gissing, George — WORKERS IN THE DAWN. London, 1880, 3 vols. $2,200 or more

Golding, William — LORD OF THE FLIES. London, (1954). $500 or more

Goulding, F.R. — ROBERT AND HAROLD; OR, THE YOUNG MAROONERS ON THE FLORIDA COAST. Philadelphia, 1852. $225-275

Graham, Tom (Sinclair Lewis) — HIKE AND THE AEROPLANE. NY, (1912). $800 or more

Grahame, Kenneth — DREAM DAYS. NY, 1899. $85-125; London & NY, 1902, illustrated by Maxfield Parrish. $85-125

Grahame, Kenneth — THE GOLDEN AGE. London, 1900, illustrated by Maxfield Parrish. $110-135

Grant, Robert — JACK HALL, OR THE SCHOOL DAYS OF AN AMERICAN BOY. Boston, 1888. $40-50

Green, Anna Katharine — THE CIRCULAR STUDY. NY, 1900. $225-275

Green, Anna Katharine — THE LEAVENWORTH CASE: A LAWYER'S STORY. NY, 1878, cloth or wraps. $1,000 or more

Greenaway, Kate — A APPLE PIE. London, (1886). $175-225

Greenaway, Kate — KATE GREENAWAY'S ALPHABET. London, (ca.1885). $175-225

Greenaway, Kate — KATE GREENAWAY'S BIRTHDAY BOOK FOR CHILDREN. London, (1880). $225-275

Greenaway, Kate — KATE GREENAWAY'S BOOK OF GAMES. London, (1889). $225-275

Greenaway, Kate — KATE GREENAWAY PICTURES. London, 1921. $175-225

Greenaway, Kate — MARIGOLD GARDEN. (London, 1885). $225-275

Greenaway, Kate — UNDER THE WINDOW: PICTURES AND RHYMES FOR CHILDREN. London, (1878). $450 or more

Greenaway, Kate (As Illustrator) — DAME WIGGINS OF LEE AND HER SEVEN WONDERFUL CATS. London, (1885). $225-275

Greenaway, Kate (As Illustrator) — A DAY IN A CHILD'S LIFE. London, (1881). $175-225

Greenaway, Kate (As Illustrator) — LANGUAGE OF FLOWERS. London, (1884). $175-225

Greenaway, Kate (As Illustrator) — THE "LITTLE FOLKS" PAINTING BOOK. London, (1879). $175-225

Greenaway, Kate (As Illustrator) — MOTHER GOOSE OR THE OLD NURSERY RHYMES. London, (1881). $275-325

Greene, Graham — THE BEAR FELL FREE. (London, 1935), limited & signed. $225-275

Greene, Graham — BRIGHTON ROCK. London, (1938). $150-200

Greene, Graham — CONFIDENTIAL AGENT. London, 1939. $175-225

Greene, Graham — A GUN FOR SALE. London, (1936). $225-275

Greene, Graham — THE HEART OF THE MATTER. NY, 1948. $100-125

Greene, Graham — IT'S A BATTLEFIELD. London, (1934). $275-325

Greene, Graham — THE LAWLESS ROADS. London, 1939. $1,000 or more

Greene, Graham — THE MAN WITHIN. London, (1929). $1,100 or more

Greene, Graham — MAY WE BORROW YOUR HUSBAND? London, (1967), limited & signed. $175-225

Greene, Graham — THE NAME OF ACTION. London, (1930). $175-225

Greene, Graham — OUR MAN IN HAVANA. London, (1958). $150-175

Greene, Graham — THE POWER AND THE GLORY. London, 1940. $175-225

Greene, Graham — THE QUIET AMERICAN. London, (1955). $85-125

Greene, Graham — RUMOUR AT NIGHTFALL. London, 1931. $150-200

Greene, Graham — STAMBOUL TRAIN. London, (1932). $675-800

Greene, Graham — THE THIRD MAN. London, (1950). $175-225

Grey, Zane (Pearl Zane Gray) — ARIZONA AMES. NY, 1932. $175-225

Grey, Zane — BETTY ZANE. NY, (1903). $450-525

Grey, Zane — BOULDER DAM. NY, (1963). $100-125

Grey, Zane — CAPTIVES OF THE DESERT. NY, (1952). $100-125

Grey, Zane — THE DESERT OF WHEAT. NY, (1919). $150-200

Grey, Zane — THE DUDE RANGER. NY, (1951). $200-250

Grey, Zane — FIGHTING CARAVANS. NY, 1929. $150-200

Grey, Zane — FORLORN RIVER. NY, 1927. $75-100

Grey, Zane — THE HASH KNIFE OUTFIT. NY, 1933. $175-225

Grey, Zane — HORSE HEAVEN HILL. NY, (1959). $100-150

Grey, Zane — KNIGHTS OF THE RANGE. NY, 1939. $100-125

Grey, Zane — LAST OF THE PLAINSMEN. NY, 1908. $275-375

Grey, Zane — LOST PUEBLO. NY, (1954). $100-125

Grey, Zane — THE LOST WAGON TRAIN. NY & London, 1936. $175-225

Grey, Zane — MAJESTY'S RANCHO. London, (1942). $75-100

Grey, Zane — THE MAVERICK QUEEN. NY, (1960). $150-175

Grey, Zane — RAIDERS OF THE SPANISH PEAKS. NY, 1938. $175-225

Grey, Zane — THE RAINBOW TRAIL. NY, 1915. $100-125

Grey, Zane — THE RANGER AND OTHER STORIES. NY, (1960). $150-175

Grey, Zane — RIDERS OF THE PURPLE SAGE. NY, 1912. $250-325

Grey, Zane — ROBBER'S ROOST. NY & London, 1932. $30-45

Grey, Zane — STRANGER FROM THE TONTO. NY, (1956). $50-65

Grey, Zane — SUNSET PASS. NY & London, 1931. $35-50

Grey, Zane — TEX THORNE COMES OUT OF THE WEST. Racine (WI), (1937). $140-165

Grey, Zane — THUNDERING HERD. NY, 1925. $175-225

Grey, Zane — TO THE LAST MAN. NY, (1922). $125-175

Grey, Zane — THE TRAIL DRIVER. NY, 1936. $275-325

Grey, Zane — THE VANISHING AMERICAN. NY, 1925. $35-45 (no dust jacket)

Grey, Zane — WANDERER OF THE WASTELAND. NY, (1923). $275-325

Grey, Zane — WEST OF THE PECOS. NY, 1937. $275-325

Grey, Zane — WESTERN UNION. NY, 1939. $100-125

Grey, Zane — WILD HORSE MESA. NY, 1928, signed. $500 or more

Grey, Zane — WYOMING. NY, (1953). $125-150

Griffith, George — A HONEYMOON IN SPACE. London, 1901. $125-150

Grile, Dod (Ambrose Bierce) — COBWEBS FROM AN EMPTY SKULL. London, 1874. $275-325

Grile, Dod — THE FIEND'S DELIGHT. London, (1872). $325-375

Grimm, Jacob L.K. & W.K. — THE FAIRY TALES OF THE BROTHERS GRIMM. London, 1909, illustrated by Arthur Rackham, trade edition. $350-425

Grimm, Jacob L.K. & W.K. — HANSEL AND GRETEL AND OTHER STORIES. NY, 1925, illustrated by Kay Nielsen. $525-575

Grimm, Jacob L.K. & W.K. — LITTLE BROTHER AND LITTLE SISTER. London, (1917), trade edition. $250-275

H

Haggard, H. Rider — ALLAN QUATERMAIN. London, 1887. $175-225

Haggard, H. Rider — AYESHA: THE RETURN OF SHE. London, 1905. $110-135

Haggard, H. Rider — HEART OF THE WORLD. London, 1896. $135-160

Haggard, H. Rider — SHE: A HISTORY OF ADVENTURE. NY, 1886, wraps. $225-275

Haggard, H. Rider — STELLA FREGELIUS: A TALE OF THREE DESTINIES. NY, 1903. $135-160

Hale, Lucretia — THE PETERKIN PAPERS. Boston, 1880. $225-275

Hale, Sarah Josepha - Editor — THE GOOD LITTLE BOY'S BOOK. NY, ca.1848. $60-75

Hammett, Dashiell — THE DAIN CURSE. NY, 1929. $1,200 or more

Hammett, Dashiell — THE GLASS KEY. NY, 1931. $1,200 or more

Hammett, Dashiell — THE MALTESE FALCON. NY, 1930. $2,200 or more

Hammett, Dashiell — RED HARVEST. NY, 1929. $2,200 or more

Hammett, Dashiell — SECRET AGENT X-9. Philadelphia, (1934). $400-500

Hammett, Dashiell — THE THIN MAN. NY, 1934. $800-1,000

Harris, Joel Chandler — THE TAR-BABY AND OTHER RHYMES OF UNCLE REMUS. NY, 1904. $175-225

Harris, Joel Chandler — UNCLE REMUS AND BRER RABBIT. NY, (1906). $275-325

Harris, Joel Chandler — DADDY JAKE THE RUNAWAY. NY, (1889). $225-275

Harris, Joel Chandler — TALES OF THE HOME FOLKS IN PEACE AND WAR. Boston, 1898. $175-225

Harris, Joel Chandler — UNCLE REMUS: HIS SONGS AND HIS SAYINGS. NY, 1881. $550-650

Harris, Joel Chandler — UNCLE REMUS RETURNS. Boston, 1918. $325-375

Harte, Bret — THE QUEEN OF THE PIRATE ISLE. London, 1886, illustrated by Kate Greenaway. $50-550

Harte, Bret — CONDENSED NOVELS AND OTHER PAPERS. NY, 1867. $175-225

Harte, Bret — GABRIEL CONROY. Hartford, 1876. $175-225

Harte, Bret — THE LOST GALLEON AND OTHER TALES. San Francisco, 1867. $325-375

Harte, Bret — THE LUCK OF ROARING CAMP AND OTHER SKETCHES. Boston, 1870. $425-475

Hawthorne, Nathaniel — THE CELESTIAL RAIL-ROAD. Boston, 1843, wraps. $1,500 or more

Hawthorne, Nathaniel — THE GENTLE BOY: A THRICE-TOLD TALE. Boston, 1839, wraps. $500 or more

Hawthorne, Nathaniel — GRANDFATHER'S CHAIR: A HISTORY. Boston, 1841. $225-275

Hawthorne, Nathaniel — THE HOUSE OF THE SEVEN GABLES. Boston, 1851. $650-725

Hawthorne, Nathaniel — THE MARBLE FAUN; OR, THE ROMANCE OF MONTE BENI. Boston, 1860, 2 vols. $550 or more

Hawthorne, Nathaniel — THE SCARLET LETTER. Boston, 1850. $900 or more

Hawthorne, Nathaniel — TWICE-TOLD TALES. Boston, 1837. $1,500 or more

Hawthorne, Nathaniel — BIOGRAPHICAL STORIES FOR CHILDREN. Boston, 1842. $125-150

Hawthorne, Nathaniel — TANGLEWOOD TALES, FOR GIRLS AND BOYS. Boston, 1853. $225-275

Hawthorne, Nathaniel — A WONDER-BOOK FOR GIRLS AND BOYS. Boston, 1852. $650-750

Hazel, Harry (Justin Jones) — THE WEST POINT CADET. Boston, 1845, wraps. $150-175

Hearn, Lafcadio — JAPANESE FAIRY TALES. Tokyo, (1898-1903), 5 vols., wraps. $600-750

Hegan, Alice Caldwell — MRS. WIGGS OF THE CABBAGE PATCH. NY, 1901. $60-75

Heinlein, Robert — ASSIGNMENT IN ETERNITY. Reading (PA), (1953). $85-100

Hemingway, Ernest — DEATH IN THE AFTERNOON. NY, 1932. $325-375

Hemingway, Ernest — A FAREWELL TO ARMS. NY, 1929. $550 or more

Hemingway, Ernest — THE FIFTH COLUMN AND THE FIRST FORTY-NINE STORIES. NY, 1938. $225-275

Hemingway, Ernest — IN OUR TIME. NY, 1925. $800 or more

Hemingway, Ernest — MEN WITHOUT WOMEN. NY, 1927. $500 or more

Hemingway, Ernest — THE SUN ALSO RISES. NY, 1926. $1,750 or more

Hemingway, Ernest — THREE STORIES AND AND TEN POEMS. (Paris, 1923). $4,500 or more

Hemingway, Ernest — TO HAVE AND HAVE NOT. NY, 1937. $325-375

Hemingway, Ernest — THE TORRENTS OF SPRING. NY, 1926. $750 or more

Henry, O. (William Sidney Porter) — HEART OF THE WEST. NY, 1907. $275-325

Henry, O. — ROADS OF DESTINY. NY, 1909. $225-275

Henry, O. — THE VOICE OF THE CITY. NY, 1908. $275-325

Henty, G.A. — A SEARCH FOR A SECRET. London, 1867, 3 vols. $1,500 or more

Henty, G.A. — ALL BUT LOST. London, 1869, 3 vols. $1,200 or more

Henty, G.A. — IN THE HEART OF THE ROCKIES. NY, 1894. $50-60

Henty, G.A. — A MARCH ON LONDON. London, 1898. $25-275

Henty, G.A. — THE MARCH TO COOMASSIE. London, 1874. $375-450

Henty, G.A. — THE QUEEN'S CUP. London, 1897, 3 vols. $1,000 or more

Henty, G.A. — BARTHOLOMEW'S EVE. London, 1894. $175-225

Henty, G.A. — SEARCH FOR A SECRET. London, 1867, 3 vols. $1,500 or more

Henty, G.A. — THE TIGER OF MYSORE. London, 1896. $25-275; NY, 1895. $60-75

Henty, G.A. Et Al — BRAINS AND BRAVERY. London, 1903, illustrated by Arthur Rackham. $225-275

Henty, G.A. Et Al — CAMPS AND QUARTERS. NY, 1889, wraps. $1,000 or more

Higginson, Thomas Wentworth — THE BIRTHDAY IN FAIRY-LAND: A STORY FOR CHILDREN. Boston, 1850, wraps. $60-75

Hodgson, William Hope — THE HOUSE ON THE BORDERLAND AND OTHER NOVELS. Sauk City, 1946. $300-350

Hornung, E.W. — MR. JUSTICE RAFFLES. London, 1909. $85-100

Household, Geoffrey — ROGUE MALE. London, 1939. $135-175

Housman, Laurence — A FARM IN FAIRYLAND. London, 1894. $175-225

Howard, Robert E. — ALWAYS COMES EVENING. Sauk City, 1957. $325-375

Howard, Robert E. — THE COMING OF CONAN. NY, (1953). $100-150

Howard, Robert E. — CONAN THE BARBARIAN. NY, (1954). $125-175

Howard, Robert E. — CONAN THE CONQUEROR. NY, (1950). $175-225

Howard, Robert E. — THE DARK MAN AND OTHERS. Sauk City, 1963. $225-275

Howard, Robert E. — KING CONAN. NY, (1953). $110-135

Howard, Robert E. — SKULL-FACE AND OTHERS. SC, 1946. $375-425

Howard, Robert E. — THE SWORD OF CONAN. NY, (1952). $125-175

Hubbard, L. Ron — SLAVES OF SLEEP. Chicago, 1948. $125-175

Hyne, C.J. Cutliffe — THE LOST CONTINENT. London, 1900. $90-125

J

Jackson, Helen Hunt — RAMONA. Boston, 1884. $325-375

Jackson, Shirley — THE ROAD THROUGH THE WALL. NY, (1948). $150-175

Jewett, Sarah Orne — BETTY LEICESTER'S ENGLISH CHRISTMAS. Boston, 1894. $175-225

Jones, James — FROM HERE TO ETERNITY. NY, 1951. $125-150

K

Kesey, Ken — ONE FLEW OVER THE CUCKOO'S NEST. NY, (1962). $275-325

Kingsley, Charles — THE WATER-BABIES. London, 1863. $450-525

Kingsley, Charles — WESTWARD HO! Cambridge (Eng), 1855. $800 or more

Kingsley, Henry — VALENTIN: A FRENCH BOY'S STORY. London, 1872, 2 vols. $85-100

Kipling, Rudyard — "CAPTAINS COURAGEOUS": A STORY OF THE GRAND BANKS. London, 1897. $600 or more

Kipling, Rudyard — THE JUNGLE BOOK & THE SECOND JUNGLE BOOK. London, 1894-95, 2 vols. $650 or more

Kipling, Rudyard — JUST SO STORIES FOR LITTLE CHILDREN. London, 1902. $550 or more

Kipling, Rudyard — KIM. NY, 1902. $450 or more

Kipling, Rudyard — PUCK OF POOK'S HILL. London, 1906. $175-225

Kipling, Rudyard — WEE WILLIE WINKIE AND OTHER CHILD STORIES. Allahabad (India), (1888), wraps. $800 or more

Kosinski, Jerzy — THE PAINTED BIRD. Boston, (1965). $225-275

L

Lardner, Ring W. — GULLIBLE'S TRAVELS. Indianapolis, (1917). $275-325

Lardner, Ring W. — LOSE WITH A SMILE. NY, 1933. $100-125

Lardner, Ring W. — THE LOVE NEST AND OTHER STORIES. NY, 1925. $225-275

Lardner, Ring W. — REGULAR FELLOWS I HAVE MET. Chicago, 1919. $375-450

Lardner, Ring W. — ROUND UP. NY, 1929. $175-225

Lardner, Ring W. — STOP ME IF YOU'VE HEARD THIS ONE. NY, 1929. $125-150

Lardner, Ring W. — THE STORY OF A WONDER MAN. NY, 1927. $225-275

Lardner, Ring W. — TREAT 'EM ROUGH: LETTERS FROM JACK THE KAISER KILLER. Indianapolis, (1918). $225-275

Lardner, Ring W. — WHAT OF IT? NY, 1925. $125-150

Lardner, Ring W. — YOU KNOE ME AL. NY, (1916). $225-275

Larkin, Philip — THE NORTH SHIP. London, (1945). $450-500

Lawrence, D.H. — ENGLAND, MY ENGLAND AND OTHER STORIES. NY, 1922. $175-225

Lawrence, D.H. — LADY CHATTERLEY'S LOVER. (Florence, Italy), 1928, limited & signed. $1,000 or more

Lawrence, D.H. — THE LOST GIRL. London, (1920). $400 or more

Lawrence, D.H. — LOVE AMONG THE HAYSTACKS. London, 1930, limited. $100-125

Lawrence, D.H. — THE LOVELY LADY. London, 1933. $100-125

Lawrence. D.H. — THE MAN WHO DIED. London, 1931. $135-175

Lawrence, D.H. — THE PRUSSIAN OFFICER AND OTHER STORIES. London, (1914). $1,000 or more

Lawrence, D.H. — THE RAINBOW. London, (1915). $2,500 or more

Lawrence, D.H. — RAWDON'S ROOF. London, 1928, limited & signed. $275-325

Lawrence, D.H. — SONS AND LOVERS. London, (1913). $1,000 or more

Lawrence, D.H. — THE WHITE PEACOCK. NY, 1911. $6,500 or more

Lawrence, D.H. — WOMEN IN LOVE. NY, 1920. $175-225

Le Carre, John — CALL FOR THE DEAD. No place, (1962). $225-275

Le Carre, John — THE SPY WHO CAME IN FROM THE COLD. London, 1963. $150-200

Le Fanu, Joseph Sheridan — ALL IN THE DARK. London, 1866, 2 vols. $275-350

Le Fanu, Joseph Sheridan — CHECKMATE. London, 1871, 3 vols. $375-450

Le Fanu, Joseph Sheridan — THE EVIL GUEST. London, (1895). $375-450

Le Fanu, Joseph Sheridan — GHOST STORIES AND TALES OF MYSTERY. Dublin, 1851. $550-650

Le Fanu, Joseph Sheridan — HAUNTED LIVES. London, 1868, 3 vols. $550-650

Le Fanu, Joseph Sheridan — IN A GLASS DARKLY. London, 1872, 3 vols. $450-550

Le Fanu, Joseph Sheridan — MADAME CROWL'S GHOST AND OTHER TALES OF MYSTERY. London, 1923. $275-325

Le Fanu, Joseph Sheridan — THE WYVERN MYSTERY. London, 1869, 3 vols. $450-550

Le Guin, Ursula — THE LEFT HAND OF DARKNESS. NY, (1969). $140-170

Le Guin, Ursula — A WIZARD OF EARTHSEA. Berkeley, (1968). $125-175

Leacock, Stephen — LITERARY LAPSES: A BOOK OF SKETCHES. Montreal, 1910. $125-150

Leacock, Stephen — NONSENSE NOVELS. NY, 1911. $125-150

Lee, Harper — TO KILL A MOCKINGBIRD. Philadelphia, (1960). $125-150

Leiber, Fritz — NIGHT'S BLACK AGENTS. SC, 1947. $100-125

Leinster, Murray (Will F. Jenkins) — SIDEWISE IN TIME. Chicago, 1950. $100-125

Leroux, Gaston — THE PHANTOM OF THE OPERA. Indianapolis, 1911. $125-150

Lessing, Doris — AFRICAN STORIES. London, (1964). $85-100

Lewis, Matthew Gregory — ROMANTIC TALES. London, 1808, 4 vols. $400-500

Lewis, Matthew Gregory — TALES OF WONDER. London, 1801, 2 vols. $450-550

Lewis, Sinclair — BABBITT. NY, (1922). $140-165

Lewis, Sinclair — DODSWORTH. NY, (1929). $110-135

Lewis, Sinclair — FREE AIR. NY, 1919. $140-175

Lewis, Sinclair — THE INNOCENTS. NY, (1917). $550 or more

Lewis, Sinclair — THE JOB. NY, (1917). $350-450

Lewis, Sinclair — MAIN STREET. NY, 1920. $450 or more

Lewis, Sinclair — OUR MR. WRENN. NY, 1914. $425-475

Lewis, Sinclair — THE TRAIL OF THE HAWK. NY, (1915). $425-475

Liebling, A.J. — THE TELEPHONE BOOTH INDIAN. Garden City, 1942. $100-125

London, Jack — THE ABYSMAL BRUTE. NY, 1913. $350-425

London, Jack — THE ACORN PLANTER. NY, 1916. $850 or more

London, Jack — ADVENTURE. NY, 1911. $450-525

London, Jack — BEFORE ADAM. NY, 1907. $275-350

London, Jack — CHILDREN OF THE FROST. NY, 1902. $375-450

London, Jack — THE CRUISE OF THE DAZZLER. NY, 1902. $1,100 or more

London, Jack — A DAUGHTER OF THE SNOWS. Philadelphia, 1902. $375-450

London, Jack — HEARTS OF THREE. NY, 1920. $125-150

London, Jack — THE HOUSE OF PRIDE. NY, 1912. $275-325

London, Jack — THE HUMAN DRIFT. NY, 1917. $650-750

London, Jack — THE IRON HEEL. NY, 1908. $375-450

London, Jack — THE JACKET. London, (1915). $275-350

London, Jack — JOHN BARLEYCORN. NY, 1913. $700 or more

London, Jack — THE SCARLET PLAGUE. NY, 1915. $325-375

London, Jack — SCORN OF WOMEN. NY, 1906. $1,100 or more

London, Jack — THE SEA-WOLF. NY, 1904. $375-425

London, Jack — THE STAR ROVER. NY, 1915. $1,200 or more

London, Jack — TALES OF THE FISH PATROL. NY, 1905. $375-425

Long, Frank Belknap — THE HOUNDS OF TINDALOS. SC, 1946. $100-125

Longfellow, Henry Wadsworth — EVANGELINE: A TALE OF ACADIE. Boston, 1847. $450-500

Longfellow, Henry Wadsworth — TALES OF A WAYSIDE INN. Boston, 1863. $175-225

Loos, Anita — GENTLEMEN PREFER BLONDES. NY, 1925. $100-125

Lovecraft, H.P. — BEYOND THE WALL OF SLEEP. SC, 1943. $600 or more

Lovecraft, H.P. — THE CATS OF ULTHAR. Cassia (FL), 1935. $150-175

Lovecraft, H.P. — THE HAUNTER OF THE DARK. London, 1951. $175-200

Lovecraft, H.P. — MARGINALIA. SC, 1944. $200-250

Lovecraft, H.P. — THE OUTSIDER AND OTHERS. SC, 1939. $800 or more

Lovecraft, H.P. — THE SHADOW OVER INNSMOUTH. Everett (PA), 1936. $1,700 or more

Lovecraft, H.P. — THE SHUNNED HOUSE. Athol (MA), 1928, 59 pp. unbound. $1,500 or more

Lovecraft, H.P. — SOMETHING ABOUT CATS AND OTHER PIECES. SC, 1949. $125-150

Lowry, Malcolm — UNDER THE VOLCANO. NY, (1947). $550 or more

Lucas, Victoria (Sylvia Plath) — THE BELL JAR. London, (1963). $450-525

M

MacDonald, George — DEALINGS WITH THE FAIRIES. London, 1867. $375-450

MacDonald, George — THE PRINCESS AND THE GOBLIN. London, 1897. $375-425

MacFall, Haldane — THE WOOINGS OF JEZEBEL PETTYFER. London, 1898. $175-225

Mailer, Norman — THE NAKED AND THE DEAD. NY, (1948). $275-325

Malamud, Bernard — THE NATURAL. NY, (1952). $150-175

Mann, Thomas — THE MAGIC MOUNTAIN. NY, 1927, 2 vols., limited & signed. $350-425

Mansfield, Katherine — BLISS AND OTHER STORIES. London, (1920). $175-225

Mansfield, Katherine — IN A GERMAN PENSION. London, (1911). $450-525

Marquand, John P. — MING YELLOW. Boston, 1935. $85-125

Marquand, John P. — THE UNSPEAKABLE GENTLEMAN. NY, 1922. $110-135

Marryat, Frederick — MASTERMAN READY. London, 1841-42-43, 3 vols. $450-525

Marryat, Frederick — POOR JACK. London, 1840 $175-225

Marryat, Frederick — THE LITTLE SAVAGE. London, 1848-49, 2 vols. $250-325

Masters, Edgar Lee — SPOON RIVER ANTHOLOGY. NY, 1915. $550-650

Maugham, W. Somerset — A MAN OF HONOUR. London, 1903. $850 or more

Maugham, W. Somerset — AH KING: SIX STORIES. London, (1933). $40-60

Maugham, W. Somerset — ASHENDEN, OR THE BRITISH AGENT. London, 1928. $175-225

Maugham, W. Somerset — LIZA OF LAMBETH. London, 1897. $800 or more

Maugham, W. Somerset — OF HUMAN BONDAGE. NY, (1915). $850-1,000

Maugham, W. Somerset — THE CASUARINA TREE. London, 1926. $175-225

Maugham, W. Somerset — THE MAKING OF A SAINT. Boston, 1898. $225-275

Maugham, W. Somerset — THE MERRY-GO-ROUND. London, 1904. $175-225

McCoy, Horace — NO POCKETS IN A SHROUD. London, (1937). $85-100

McCoy, Horace — THEY SHOOT HORSES, DON'T THEY? NY, 1935. $85-100

McCullers, Carson — REFLECTIONS IN A GOLDEN EYE. (Boston), 1941. $175-225

McCullers, Carson — THE HEART IS A LONELY HUNTER. Boston, 1940. $250-300

McNall, Stanley — SOMETHING BREATHING. LONDON, 1965. $85-110

Melville, Herman — ISRAEL POTTER. NY, 1855. $550-650

Melville, Herman — MARDI: AND A VOYAGE THITHER. NY, 1849, 2 vols. $650-750

Melville, Herman — MOBY-DICK; OR, THE WHALE. NY, 1851. $8,000 or more

Melville, Herman — OMOO: A NARRATIVE OF ADVENTURES IN THE SOUTH SEAS. NY, 1847, wraps. $5,500 or more

Melville, Herman — THE CONFIDENCE-MAN. NY, 1857. $1,100 or more

Melville, Herman — THE PIAZZA TALES. NY, 1856. $1,200 or more

Melville, Herman — TYPEE: A PEEP AT POLYNESIAN LIFE. NY, 1846. $6,000, perhaps much more

Merritt, A. — THE FOX WOMAN AND OTHER STORIES. NY, (1949). $125-175

Metcalfe, John — THE FEASTING DEAD. SC, 1954. $60-75

Millar, Kenneth — BLUE CITY. NY, 1947. $150-200

Millar, Kenneth — THE CHILL, as Ross MacDonald. NY, 1964. $135-175

Millar, Kenneth — THE DARK TUNNEL. NY, 1944. $225-275

Millar, Kenneth — THE DROWNING POOL, as John Ross MacDonald. NY, 1950. $150-200

Millar, Kenneth — THE GALTON CASE, as Ross MacDonald. NY, 1959. $135-150

Miller, Henry — ALLER RETOUR NEW YORK. Paris, (1935), wraps, limited & sgnd. $800 or more

Miller, Henry — BLACK SPRING. Paris, (1936), wraps. $600 or more

Miller, Henry — TROPIC OF CANCER. Paris, (1934), wraps. $5,000 or more

Miller, Henry — TROPIC OF CAPRICORN. Paris, (1939), wraps. $700 or more

Mitchell, Margaret — GONE WITH THE WIND. NY, (MAY) 1936. $650-750

Mitchell, S. Weir — HUGH WYNNE, FREE QUAKER. NY, 1897, 2 vols. $175-225

Moore, Thomas — LALLA ROOKH, AN ORIENTAL ROMANCE. London, 1817. $350-425

Morley, Christopher — THE HAUNTED BOOKSHOP. NY, 1919. $175-225

Morley, Christopher — PARNASSUS ON WHEELS. Garden City, 1917. $450-525

Mundy, Talbot — C.I.D. NY, (1932). $60-75

Mundy, Talbot — THE IVORY TRAIL. Indianapolis, (1919). $125-150

Mundy, Talbot — JIMGRIM. NY, (1931). $100-125

Mundy, Talbot — PURPLE PIRATE. NY, (1959). $30-45

Mundy, Talbot — QUEEN CLEOPATRA. Indianapolis, (1929), limited & signed. $110-135

Mundy, Talbot — TROS OF SAMOTHRACE. NY, 1934. $175-225

N

NABOKOFF, VLADIMIR (Vladimir Nabokov) — LAUGHTER IN THE DARK. Indianapolis, (1938) $250-325

Nabokov, Vladimir — BEND SINISTER. NY, 1947. $150-175

Nabokov, Vladimir — LOLITA. Paris, (1955), 2 vols., wraps. $600-750

Neal, John — THE MOON-HUNTER; OR, LIFE IN THE MAINE WOODS. NY, (1864), wraps. $350-425

Neal, John — RACHEL DYER: A NORTH AMERICAN STORY. Portland (ME), 1828. $350-425

Nin, Anais — THE HOUSE OF INCEST. Paris, (1936), wraps, limited & signed. $425-475

Norden, Charles (Lawrence Durrell) — PANIC SPRING. NY, (1937). $350-425

Normyx (Norman Douglas & Elsa Fitzgibbon) — UNPROFESSIONAL TALES. London, 1901, limited. $325-375

Norris, Frank — YVERNELLE: A LEGEND OF FUEDAL FRANCE. Philadelphia, 1892. $950 or more

Norton, Andre — STAR MAN'S SON, 2250 A.D. NY, (1952). $60-75

O

Oates, Joyce Carol — BY THE NORTH GATE. NY, (1963). $150-175

O'Connor, Flannery — WISE BLOOD. NY, (1952). $275-325

O'Hara, John — BUTTERFIELD 8. NY, (1935). $140-165

Optic, Oliver (William Taylor Adams) — THE BOAT CLUB; OR, THE BUNKERS OF RIPPLETON. Boston, 1855. $225-275

Orwell, George (Eric Arthur Blair) — A CLERGYMAN'S DAUGHTER. London, 1935. $450-525

Orwell, George — ANIMAL FARM: A FAIRY STORY. London, 1945. $450 or more

Orwell, George — NINETEEN EIGHTY-FOUR. London, 1949. $375-450

Orwell, George — KEEP THE ASPIDISTRA FLYING. London, 1936. $350-450

Ouida (Marie Louise De La Ramee) — SYRLIN. London, 1880, 3 vols. $350-425

Ouida — UNDER TWO FLAGS. London, 1867, 3 vols. $350-425

P

Parley, Peter (Samuel G. Goodrich) — THE TALES OF PETER PARLEY ABOUT AMERICA. Boston, 1827. $3,500 or more

Parrish, Randall — PRISONERS OF CHANCE. Chicago, 1908. $50-75

Parry, David M. — THE SCARLET EMPIRE. Indianapolis, 1908. $40-50

Patlock, Robert — THE LIFE AND ADVENTURES OF PETER WILKINS, A CORNISH MAN. London, 1751, 2 vols. $800 or more

Perelman, S.J. — DAWN GINSBERGH'S REVENGE. NY, (1929). $225-275

Poe, Edgar Allan — TALES. NY, 1845, wraps. $15,000 and perhaps much more

Poe, Edgar Allan — TALES OF THE GROTESQUE AND ARABESQUE. Philadelphia, 1840, 2 vols. $12,000, perhaps much more

Poe, Edgar Allan — THE PROSE ROMANCES OF EDGAR A. POE, ETC. UNIFORM SERIAL EDITION..NO.1 CONTAINING THE MURDERS IN THE RUE MORGUE, AND THE MAN THAT WAS USED UP. Philadelphia, 1843, wraps, 40 pages. At least $25,000, perhaps a great deal more.

Porter, Eleanor H. — POLLYANNA. Boston, 1913. $350-425

Porter, Gene Stratton — LADDIE: A TRUE-BLUE STORY. NY, 1913. $125-175

Porter, Jane — THE SCOTTISH CHIEFS: A ROMANCE. London, 1810, 5 vols. $700-850

Post, Melville Davisson — THE CORRECTOR OF DESTINIES. NY, (1908). $550-650

Post, Melville Davisson — UNCLE ABNER. NY, 1918. $450-550

Powell, Anthony — AFTERNOON MEN. London, 1931. $225-275

Powers, J.F. — PRINCE OF DARKNESS AND OTHER STORIES. NY, 1947. $100-125

Pratt, Fletcher — WELL OF THE UNICORN. NY, 1948. $50-75

Pseudoman, Akkad — ZERO TO 80. 1937. $40-50

Puzo, Mario — THE DARK ARENA. NY, (1955). $40-50

Puzo, Mario — THE GODFATHER. NY, (1969). $45-60

Pynchon, Thomas — GRAVITY'S RAINBOW. NY, (1973). $125-150

Pynchon, Thomas — V. Philadelphia, (1963). $325-375

Q

Queen, Ellery (Frederic Dannay & Manfred B. Lee) — THE CHINESE ORANGE MYSTERY. NY, 1934. $110-135

Queen, Ellery — THE DEVIL TO PAY. NY, 1938. $110-135

Queen, Ellery — THE DUTCH SHOE MYSTERY. NY, 1931. $90-110

Queen, Ellery — THE EGYPTIAN CROSS MYSTERY. NY, 1932. $90-110

Queen, Ellery — THE SPANISH CAPE MYSTERY. NY, 1935. $85-100

Queen, Ellery - Editor — THE MISADVENTURES OF SHERLOCK HOLMES. Boston, 1944. $275-325

Quiller-Couch, Sir Arthur — IN POWDER AND CRINOLINE. London, (ca,1913), illustrated by Kay Nielsen. $500 or more

R

Radcliffe, Ann — THE MYSTERIES OF UDOLPHO. London, 1794, 4 vols. $650 or more

Rand, Ayn — ATLAS SHRUGGED. NY, 1957. $125-150

Rand, Ayn — THE FOUNTAINHEAD. Inidanapolis, (1943). $175-225

Rand, Ayn — WE ARE THE LIVING. London, (1936). $600-750

Reade, Charles — THE CLOISTER AND THE HEARTH. London, 1861, 4 vols. $1,200 or more

Reid, Mayne (Thomas M. Reid) — NO QUARTER! London, 1888, 3 vols. $375-425

Reid, Mayne — OSCEOLA THE SEMINOLE. NY, (1858). $325-375

Reid, Mayne — THE QUADROON; OR, A LOVER'S ADVENTURES IN LOUISIANA. London, 1856, 3 vols. $550-650

Reid, Mayne — THE WHITE CHIEF: A LEGEND OF NORTHERN MEXICO. London, 1855, 3 vols. $450-550

Reid, Mayne — THE WILD HUNTRESS. London, 1861, 3 vols. $450-550

Reid, Mayne — THE WOOD-RANGERS. London, 1860, 3 vols. $450-550

Remarque, Erich Maria — ALL QUIET ON THE WESTERN FRONT. London, (1929). $125-175

Richter, Conrad — BROTHERS OF NO KIN AND OTHER STORIES. NY, (ca.1924). $275-325

Riley, James Whitcomb — THE FLYING ISLANDS OF THE NIGHT. Indianapolis, 1892. $175-225

Rinehart, Mary Roberts, With Avery Hopwood — THE BAT: A NOVEL. NY, (1926). $60-75

Rinehart, Mary Roberts — THE MAN IN LOWER TEN. Indianapolis, (1909). $60-75

Rinehart, Mary Roberts — THE RED LAMP. NY, (1935). $125-175

Robbins, Tom — ANOTHER ROADSIDE ATTRACTION. Garden City. $175-225

Rohmer, Sax — SHADOW OF FU MANCHU. GC, 1948. $35-50

Rohmer, Sax — SHE WHO SLEEPS. GC, 1928. $25-35

Roy, Lillian — THE PRINCE OF ATLANTIS. NY, (1929). $40-50

Russell, Eric F. — DEEP SPACE. London, 1956. $50-75

S

Salinger, J.D. — THE CATCHER IN THE RYE. Boston, 1951. $375-450

Salinger, J.D. — NINE STORIES. Boston, (1953). $375-425

Salinger, J.D. — RAISE HIGH THE ROOF BEAM, CARPENTERS, AND SEYMOUR: AN INTRODUCTION. Boston, (1959). $225-275

Sayers, Dorothy L. — GAUDY NIGHT. London, 1935. $110-135

Sayers, Dorothy L., With M. St. Clare Byrne — BUSMAN'S HONEYMOON: A DETECTIVE COMEDY. London, 1937. $225-275

Saroyan, William — THE DARING YOUNG MAN ON THE FLYING TRAPEZE. NY, 1934. $125-175

Serviss, Garrett P. — A COLUMBUS OF SPACE. NY, 1911. $125-175

Shaw, George Bernard — PYGMALION: A ROMANCE IN FIVE ACTS. London, 1913. $700-800

Sherriff, R.C. — THE HOPKINS MANUSCRIPT. London, 1939. $40-50

Shiel, M.P. — CHILDREN OF THE WIND. London, 1923. $175-225

Shiel, M.P. — THE LAST MIRACLE. London, 1906. $125-150

Shiel, M.P. — PRINCE ZALESKI. London, 1895. $350-425

Shiel, M.P. — THE PURPLE CLOUD. London, 1929, limited & signed. $350-425

Shiel, M.P. — SHAPES IN THE FIRE. London, 1896. $275-325

Silverberg, Robert — STARMAN'S QUEST. NY, (1958). $30-45

Simak, Clifford D. — THE CREATOR. (LA, 1946), wraps. $60-75

Siodmak, Curt — F.P.I. DOES NOT REPLY. Boston, 1933. $35-45

Siringo, Charles A. — A COWBOY DETECTIVE. Chicago, 1912. $175-225

Smith, Clark Ashton — THE ABOMINATIONS OF YONDO. SC, 1960. $75-90

Smith, Clark Ashton — THE DARK CHATEAU AND OTHER POEMS. SC, 1951. $275-325

Smith, Clark Ashton — THE DOUBLE SHADOW AND OTHER FANTASIES. (Auburn, CA, 1933), wraps. $175-225

Smith, Clark Ashton — GENIUS LOCI AND OTHER TALES. SC, 1948. $85-100

Smith, Clark Ashton — LOST WORLDS. SC, 1944. $135-160

Smith, Clark Ashton — OUT OF SPACE AND TIME. SC, 1942. $225-275

Smith, Clark Ashton — SPELLS AND PHILTRES. SC, 1958. $325-375

Smith, Clark Ashton — THE STAR-TREADER AND OTHER POEMS. SF, 1912. $150-175

Smith, E.E. — GRAY LENSMAN. NY, n.d. $30-40

Smith, E.E. — SKYLARK THREE. Philadelphia, 1948, limited & signed. $85-110

Smith, E.E. — SPACEHOUNDS OF IPC. Philadelphia, 1947, limited & signed. $100-125

Smith, F. Hopkinson — COLONEL CARTER OF CARTERSVILLE. Boston, 1891. $110-135

Smith, George O. — NOMAD. Philadelphia, (1950). $35-50

Smith, Jessie Wilcox — THE WATER BABIES. NY, (1916). $75-100

Smith, Johnston (Stephen Crane) — MAGGIE: A GIRL OF THE STREETS. (NY, 1893), wraps. $5,500 or more

Smith, Thorne — TURNABOUT. NY, 1931. $35-50

Spenser, Edmund — THE FAERIE QUEENE. London, 1596, 1 or 2 vols. $10,000 or more

Spielberg, Steven — CLOSE ENCOUNTERS OF THE THIRD KIND. NY, (1977). $50-75

Spinrad, Norman — THE MEN IN THE JUNGLE. NY, 1967. $50-75

Spillane, Mickey — I, THE JURY. NY, 1947. $100-125

Stapledon, Olaf — DARKNESS AND THE LIGHT. London, (1942). $175-225

Steinbeck, John — CANNERY ROW. NY, 1945. $125-150

Steinbeck, John — EAST OF EDEN. NY, 1952, trade edition. $125-175

Steinbeck, John — THE GRAPES OF WRATH. NY, (1939). $425-475

Steinbeck, John — IN DUBIOUS BATTLE. NY, (1936), trade edition. $250-325

Steinbeck, John — THE MOON IS DOWN. NY, 1942. $110-135

Steinbeck, John — OF MICE AND MEN. NY, (1937). $175-250

Steinbeck, John — THE PASTURES OF HEAVEN. NY, 1932. $1,000 or more

Steinbeck, John — THEIR BLOOD IS STRONG. San Francisco, 1938, wraps. $375-450

Steinbeck, John — TO A GOD UNKNOWN. NY, (1933). $800 or more

Steinbeck, John — TORTILLA FLAT. NY, (1935). $450 or more

Stephens, James — THE CROCK OF GOLD. London, 1912. $500 or more

Stevenson, Robert Louis — THE BLACK ARROW. NY, 1916, illustrated by N.C. Wyeth. $275-325

Stevenson, Robert Louis — ISLAND NIGHT'S ENTERTAINMENT. NY, 1893. $250-300

Stevenson, Robert Louis — KIDNAPPED. NY, 1913, illustrated by N.C. Wyeth. $275-325

Stevenson, Robert Louis — NEW ARABIAN NIGHTS. London, 1882, 2 vols. $550-650

Stevenson, Robert Louis — THE SILVERADO SQUATTERS. $350-425

Stevenson, Robert Louis — THE STRANGE CASE OF DR. JEKYLL AND MR. HYDE. London, 1886, wraps. $500 or more

Stevenson, Robert Louis — TREASURE ISLAND. Boston, 1884. $800 or more

Stockton, Frank R. — THE FLOATING PRINCE AND OTHER FAIRY TALES. NY, 1881. $175-225

Stockton, Frank R. — THE LADY, OR THE TIGER? AND OTHER STORIES. NY, 1884. $150-175

Stockton, Frank R. — TING-A-LING. NY, 1870. $300-375

Stoker, Bram — DRACULA. (London), 1897. $1,000 or more

Stoker, Bram — THE LADY OF THE SHROUD. London, 1909. $125-150

Stowe, Harriett Beecher — DRED: A TALE OF THE GREAT DISMAL SWAMP. Boston, 1856, 2 vols. $275-350

Stowe, Harriett Beecher — UNCLE TOM'S CABIN. Boston, 1852, 2 vols. $5,000 or more

Stribling, T.S. — THE CRUISE OF THE DRYDOCK. Chicago, (1917). $175-225

Stuart, Jesse — MAN WITH A BULL-TONGUE PLOW. (NY, 1934). $275-350

Sturgeon, Theodore — MORE THAN HUMAN. NY, (1953). $225-275

Sturgeon, Theodore — WITHOUT SORCERY. Philadelphia, (1948). $75-125

Styron, William — LIE DOWN IN DARKNESS. Indianapolis, (1951). $175-225

Styron, William — THIS QUIET DUST. (NY, 1967), wraps. $350-400

Swift, Jonathan — A TALE OF A TUB. London, 1714. $100-125

Swift, Jonathan — TRAVELS INTO SEVERAL REMOTE NATIONS OF THE WORLD, by Lemuel Gulliver. London, 1724, 2 vols. $500 or more

Synge, John M. — IN THE SHADOW OF THE GLEN. NY, 1904, limited to 50 copies. $1,200 or more

T

Taine, John — THE CRYSTAL HORDE. Philadelphia, 1952, limited & signed. $85-110

Taine, John — G.O.G. 606. Philadelphia, (1954), limited & signed. $75-100

Taine, John — SEEDS OF LIFE. Philadelphia, 1951, limited & signed. $65-80

Tarkington, Booth — THE GENTLEMAN FROM INDIANA. NY, 1899. $175-225

Tarkington, Booth — PENROD. Garden City, 1914. $1,100 or more

Tarkington, Booth — PENROD AND SAM. GC, 1916. $275-350

Tarkington, Booth — SEVENTEEN. NY, (1916). $175-225

Tarkington, Booth — THE TWO VANREVELS. NY, 1902. $250-300

Thomas, Jr., Issiah — THE LILLIPUTIAN MASQUERADE. Worcester (MA), 1802 (3rd edition). $459-500

Train, Arthur & Robert Williams Wood — THE MAN WHO ROCKED THE EARTH. NY, 1915. $125-150

Twain, Mark (Samuel L. Clemens) — A CONNECTICUT YANKEE IN KING ARTHUR'S COURT. NY, 1889. $275-350

Twain, Mark — THE CURIOUS REPUBLIC OF GONDOUR. NY, 1919. $175-225

Twain, Mark — THE PRINCE AND THE PAUPER. London, 1881. $300 or more

U

Upfield, Arthur W. — THE HOUSE OF CAIN. London (1928). $325-375

V

Van Dine, S.S. (Willard Huntington Wright) — THE BENSON MURDER CASE. NY, 1926. $225-275

Van Dine, S.S. — THE DRAGON MURDER CASE. NY, 1933. $135-175

Van Dine, S.S. — KENNEL MURDER CASE. NY, 1933. $40-65

Van Vogt, A.E. — SLAN: A STORY OF THE FUTURE. SC, 1946. $175-225

Van Vogt, A.E. — THE WEAPON MAKERS. Providence (RI), (1947). $85-110

Vance, Jack — BIG PLANET. NY, (1957), wraps. $85-100

Verrill, A. Hyatt — THE BRIDGE OF LIGHT. Reading? (PA), 1950, limited & signed. $85-100

W

Wallace, Edgar — THE FOUR JUST MEN. London, 1905. $125-150

Wallace, Edgar — THE MURDER BOOK OF J.G. REEDER. NY, 1929. $125-150

Wallis, Dave — THE ONLY LOVERS LEFT ALIVE. NY, 1964. $30-40

Walter, Elizabeth — IN THE MIST AND OTHER UNCANNY ENCOUNTERS. SC, 1979. $25-35

Wandrei, Donald — DARK ODYSSEY. St. Paul (MN), (1931), limited & signed. $135-160

Wandrei, Donald — THE EYE AND THE FINGER. SC, 1955. $100-125

Wandrei, Donald — POEMS FOR MIDNIGHT. SC, 1964. $85-110

Wandrei, Donals — THE WEB OF EASTER ISLAND. SC, 1948. $60-75

Waterloo, Stanley — ARMAGEDDON. Chicago, (1898). $60-75

Weinbaum, Stanley — THE RED PERIL. Reading?, 1952. $35-50

Wellman, Manley — WORSE THINGS WAITING. (NC), 1973, limited & signed. $85-100

Wells, H.G. — THE ISLAND OF DR. MOREAU. NY, 1896. $150-175

Wells, H.G. — TALES OF SPACE AND TIME. NY, 1899. $125-175

Appendix 6
NORTH AMERICAN BOOK SEARCH SERVICES

When offering books to any of these dealers it is important that you provide as complete a description as possible. All information on the title page, copyright date(s), number of pages and of illustrations, approximate size, color of binding and cover, printing, and *condition*. Mention if there is a dust jacket and its condition. All these things affect the price which will be paid you, as well as the scarcity of the book, and whether the dealer wants the book for stock or has a ready customer for it. If the dealer buys the book it will be subject to inspection and return if it does not meet the description which you furnished. Many of these booksearch services publish regular want's lists — A post card request will usually put you on their mailing list.

ALASKA
The Observatory, POB 1770, Sitka, AK 99835

ARIZONA
Ruby D. Kaufman, 518 East Loma Vista Drive, Tempe, AZ 85282
Bookmans, 18 North Tucson Blvd., Tucson, AZ 85716

ARKANSAS
Jack Bailes - Books, POB 150, Eureka Springs, AR 72632
Yesterday's Books, 258 Whittington Avenue, Box 1728, Hot Springs, AR 71901

CALIFORNIA
Book Baron, 12365 Magnolia Avenue, Anaheim, CA 92804
Black Oak Books, Inc., 1491 Shattuck Avenue, Berkeley, CA 94709
Regent Street Books, 2747 Regent Street, Berkeley, CA 94705
Whaling Research, POB 5034, Berkeley, CA 94715
Peninsula Booksearch, POB 1305, Burlingame, CA 94010
Bookpost, 962 Greenlake Court, Cardiff, CA 92007
Don Discher, 4830 Audrey Drive, Castro Valley, CA 94546
Shuey Book Search, 8886 Sharkey Avenue, Elk Grove, CA 95624
Bookfinder, 2035 Everding Street, Eureka, CA 95501
Terence M. Knaus, 21601 Foster Lane, Fort Bragg, CA 95437
Monroe Books, 809 East Olive, Fresno, CA 93728
American Book Search, POB 4448, Glendale, CA 91202
Hollywood Book Service, 1654 Cherokee Avenue, Hollywood, CA 90028
Buccaneer Books, Inc., POB 518, Laguna Beach, CA 92652
Needham Book Finder, 12021 Wilshire Blvd. - #13, Los Angeles, CA 90025
M.C. Wilson, 1735 Sherbourne, Los Angeles, CA 90035
Donald La Chance, 1032 Bay Oaks Drive, Los Osos, CA 93402
Health Research, 8349 Lafayette Street, Box 70, Mokelumne Hill, CA 95245
This Old House Bookshop, 5399 West Holt, Montclair, CA 91763
M.R. Gildea, POB 13013, Oakland, CA 94614
Wayne Pierce, 4400 Pine Cluster, Oroville, CA 95965
Chimera Books, 405 Kipling, Palo Alto, CA 94301
Book Case Books, 461 North Lake Avenue, Pasadena, CA 91101
Day's Arms & Antiques, 2163 East Main Street, Quincy, CA 95971
The Silver Door, POB 3208, Redondo Beach, CA 90277
Bookie Joint, 7246 Reseda Blvd., Reseda, CA 91335
The Mermaid Books, 433 44th Street, Richmond, CA 94805
'Otento' Books, 3817 Fifth Avenue, San Diego, CA 92103
Academy Library, 2245 Larkin Street, San Francisco, CA 94109
Antiquus Bibliopole, 4147 24th Street, San Francisco, CA 94114
Califia, 2266 Union Street, San Francisco, CA 94123
Louis Collins Books, 1083 Mission Street, San Francisco, CA 94103
Lynn Fuller, Books, 45 Powers Avenue, San Francisco, CA 94110
The Magazine, 839 Larkin Street, San Francisco, CA 94109
Novel Experience, 778 Marsh Street, San Luis Obispo, CA 93401
L.S. Kaiser Books, 1820 Graham Hill, Santa Cruz, CA 95060
A Change of Hobbit, 1853 Lincoln Blvd., Santa Monica, CA 90404
Concord Books, 419 Opal Cove Way, Box 725, Seal Beach, CA 90740
Lois Gereghty Books, 9521 Orion Avenue, Sepulveda, CA 91343
Betsy Hook, Bookfinder, 7345 Healdsburg Avenue, Sebastopol, CA 95472
B. Lynch Book Finder, 8840 Debra Avenue, Sepulveda, CA 91343
Davis & Schorr Art Books, 14755 Ventura Blvd., - #1-747, Sherman Oaks, CA 91403
Arnold Jacobs, 5038 Hazeltine Avenue, Sherman Oaks, CA 91423
Heritage Books, 52 South Washington Street, Sonora, CA 95370
Albatross II Book Shop, 100 Main Street, Tiburon, CA 94920
Lois St. Clair, POB 247, Van Nuys, CA 91408
Kenneth L. Wolf, 6021 Allot Avenue, Van Nuys, CA 91401
Calico Cat Bookshop, 495 East Main Street, Ventura, CA 93001
Blitz Books, POB 1076, Weaverville, CA 96093
221 Books, 760 Carlisle Canyon Road, Westlake Village, CA 91361
Ell Dee Book Finders, POB 1231, Whittier, CA 90609
J. Arthur Robinson Books, 56149 29 Palms Highway, Yucca Valley, CA 92284

COLORADO
Chinook Bookshop, 210 North Tejon, Colorado Springs, CO 80907
Steve Ballinger, 1079 Kearny Street, Denver, CO 80220
Book House, 5870 South Curtice, Littleton, CO 80120
The Cache, 7157 West US 34, Loveland, CO 80537

CONNECTICUT
Bethlehem Book Co., POB 249, Bethlehem, CT 06751
Clipper Ship Book Shop, 12 North Main Street, Essex, CT 06426
Bookcell Books, 90 Robinwood Road, Hamden, CT 06517
David Howland, 99 Marshall Ridge Road, New Canaan, CT 06840
Edgewood Books, 359 Edgewood Avenue, New Haven, CT 06520
Mrs. L. M. Brew, Squash Hollow Road, R.R.2, New Milford, CT 06776
Elliot's Books, POB 6, Northford, CT 06472

Nutmeg Books, 354 New Litchfield Street, Rte. 202, Torrington, CT 06790

Barbara Farnsworth, Route 128, West Cornwall, CT 06796

Bookerie, Simpaug Turnpike, West Redding, CT 06896

DISTRICT OF COLUMBIA

Duff & M.E. Gilfond, 1722 19th Street NW, Washington, DC 20009

Lloyd Books, 1346 Connecticut Avenue NW, Washington, DC 20036

FLORIDA

Tappin Book Mine, 705 Atlantic Blvd., Atlantic Beach, FL 32233

All Books & Prints Store, 4329 SW 8th Street, Miami, FL 33134

Lucile Coleman Books, POB 610813, North Miami, FL 33261

Christopher Ackerman, 180 East Inlet Drive, Palm Beach, FL 33480

Jack Owen, 113 North Country Road, Palm Beach, FL 33480

Brassers, 8701 Seminole Blvd., Seminole, FL 33542

Book Traders, Inc., POB 9403, Winter Haven, FL 33880

GEORGIA

James O. McMeans, POB 429352, Atlanta, GA 30342

Oxford Book Store, 2345 Peachtree Road NE, Atlanta, GA 30305

Book Cottage, 2403 Lawrence Highway, Decatur, GA 30033

Downs Books, 774 Mary Ann Drive NE, Marietta, GA 30067

Margie Sachs — OP Books, Route 2, Box 59, Metter, GA 30439

The Bookman of Arcady, POB 1259, Tybee Island, GA 31328

IDAHO

Boise Book Farm, 5600 Hill Road, Boise, ID 83703

The Book Shop, Inc., 908 Main Street, Boise, ID 83710

Parnassus Books, 218 North 9th Street, Boise, ID 83712

ILLINOIS

Rose Lasley, 5827 Burr Oak, Berkeley, IL 60163

P.J. Henry, 4225 East, Berwyn, IL 60402

KN Enterprises, POB 87397, Chicago, IL 60680

Walter R. Schneemann, 5710 South Dorchester Avenue, Chicago, IL 60637

Thomas W. Burrows, POB 400, Downers Grove, IL 60515

Bookchoice, POB A1497, Evanston, IL 60204

Chicago Book Mart, POB 418, Frankfort, IL 60423

The Book Beautiful, 228 Wentworth, Glencoe, IL 60022

Brainard Book Co., POB 444, La Grange, IL 60525

Bank Lane Books, 782 North Bank Lane, Lake Forest, IL 60045

Prairie Archives, 641 West Monroe, Springfield, IL 62704

Storeybook Antiques/Books, 1325 East Statet Highway 64, Sycamore, IL 60178

Bunter Books, POB 153, Winnetka, IL 60093

INDIANA

Caveat Emptor, 208 South Dunn, Bloomington, IN 47401

Used Book Place, POB 206, Dyer, IN 46311

Larry Schnell Papertique, POB 252, Elberfeld, IN 47613

Books Unlimited, 922 East Washington, Indianapolis, IN 46202

Mason's Books, 264 South Wabash, Wabash, IN 46992

KANSAS

J. Hood Booksellers, 1401 Massachusetts, Lawrence, KS 66044

KENTUCKY

The Sail Loft, 262 Cassidy Avenue, Lexington, KY 40502

Carmichael's Bookstore, 1295 Bardstown Road, Louisville, KY 40204

S-T Associates, 1317 Cherokee Road, Louisville, KY 40204

LOUISIANA

Henry C. Hensel, 657-B Rue Perez, Belle Chasse, LA 70037

Bayou Books, 1005 Monroe Street, Gretna, LA 70053

American Opinion Books, 3804 Canal Street, New Orleans, LA 70119

de Ville Books, 132 Carondelet Street, New Orleans, LA 70130

MAINE

Alfred Search Service, Drawer 1027, Damariscotta, ME 04534

Snowbound Books, RFD Box 620, Madison, ME 04950

The Sail Loft, Newcastle, ME 04553

G.F. Bush, POB 905, Stonington, ME 04681

MARYLAND

Dragoman Books, 680 Americana Drive -#38, Annapolis, MD 21403

Cecil Archer Rush, 1410 Northgate Road, Baltimore, MD 21218

Quill & Brush, 7649 Old Georgetown Road, Bethesda, MD 20814

All Edges Gilt, POB 7625, Silver Spring, MD 20907

Greetings & Readings, 809 Taylor Avenue, Towson, MD 21204

MASSACHUSETTS

Jean S. McKenna Books, POB 397, Beverly, MA 01905

Xanadu Books, POB 91, Braintree, MA 02184

Smith's Book Service, Sunsmith House, Route 6-A, Brewster, MA 02631

Bohdan Zaremba, 3 Livermore Place, Cambridge, MA 02141

Atlantic Book Service, POB 218, Charlestown, MA 02129

Barrow Bookstore, 79 Main Street, Concord, MA 01742

The English Bookshop, 22 Rocky Neck Avenue, Gloucester, MA 01930

Jeffrey H. Weinberg, POB 2122, Lowell, MA 01851

Anthony G. Ziagos Books, POB 28, Lowell, MA 01853

The Book Collector, 375 Elliot Street, Newton, MA 02164

Murray's Bookfinding Service, 115 State, Springfield, MA 01101

Barn Owl Books, POB 323, Wellesley, MA 02181

Book Store, 222 North Main Street, West Bridgewater, MA 02379

Williams Bookstore, 20 Spring Street, Williamstown, MA 01267

MICHIGAN

David's Books, 622 East Liberty, Ann Arbor, MI 48104

Marion the Librarian, 3668 Shimmons Circle South, Auburn Heights, MI 48057

The Necessary Press, POB 313, East Jordan, MI 49727

Curious Book Shop, 307 East Grand River, East Lansing, MI 48823

Great Lake Bookman, POB 162, Houghton, MI 49931

John C. Buckley - Searcher, 27901 Highland Park, Gull Lake, Richland, MI 49083

Barbara J. Rule Books, POB 215, Rochester, MI 48063

Treasures From the Castle, 1720 North Livernois, Rochester, MI 48064

Call Me Ishmael Books, POB 595, Saugatuck, MI 49453

MINNESOTA

Bookmailer, 2730 West Broadway, Minneapolis, MN 55411

Savran's Books, 301 Cedar Avenue, Minneapolis, MN 55454

S & S Books, 80 North Wilder, St. Paul, MN 55104

Northern Lights Bookshop, 103 West Third Street, Winona, MN 55987

Mary Twyce Antiques/Books, 601 East 5th Street, Winina, MN 55987

MISSISSIPPI

James A. Dillon Books, Star Route, Box 23, Carlisle, MS 39049

MISSOURI

Adams Books and Hobbies, 214 North 8th Street, Columbia, MO 65201

Columbia Books, POB 27, Columbia, MO 65205

Red Bridge Books, 2523 Red Bridge Terrace, Kansas City, MO 64131

Shirley's Old Book Shop, 1948 G S Glenstone, Springfield, MO 65804

Elizabeth F. Dunlap, 6063 Westminster Place, St. Louis, MO 63112

Readmore Books, 3607 Meramec, St. Louis, MO 63116

MONTANA

Bird's Nest, POB 8809, Missoula, MT 59807

Book Exchange, Holiday Village, Missoula, MT 59801

NEBRASKA

Niobrara Books, POB 2664, Lincoln, NE 68502

The Book Barn, RR1, Box 304H, South Sioux City, NE 68776

NEW HAMPSHIRE

Dartmouth Bookstore, 33 South Main Street, Hanover, NH 03755

Tainters, POB 36, Temple, NH 03084

NEW JERSEY

Princeton Antiquarian Books, 2917-17 Atlantic, Atlantic City, NJ 08401

Servant's Knowledge, 2915-17 Atlantic Avenue, Atlantic City, NJ 08401

The People's Bookshop, 160 Main Street, Flemington, NJ 08822

Jay's Booktique, 1 Canadian Woods Road, Marlboro, NJ 07746

Wangner's Book Shop, 9 Midland Avenue, Montclair, NJ 07042

Old York Books, 12 French Street, New Brunswick, NJ 08903

Frank Michelli Books, 45 Halsey Street, Newark, NJ 07102

Book Tracers, 869 Chamberlain Avenue, Perth Amboy, NJ 08861

Book House, 218 East Front Street, Plainfield, NJ 07060

Red Bank Book Store, 6 Linden Place, Red Bank, NJ 07701

Kirksco International Bookfinders, 70-212 Cedar Road, Ringwood, NJ 07456

Rena & Merwin L. Orner, 39 North Browning Avenue, Tenafly, NJ 07670

Acres of Books, 35 East State, Trenton, NJ 08608

Books On File, POB 195, Union City, NJ 07087

NEW MEXICO

Book Addict, POB 9134, Albuquerque, NM 87119

Chamisa Bookshop, 1602 Central SE, Albuquerque, NM 87106

Hummingbird Books, 2400 Hannett NE, Albuquerque, NM 87106

Taos Book Shop, POB 827, Taos, NM 87571

NEW YORK

Thomas W. Shaw, 11 Albright Avenue, Albany, NY 12203

Treasures In Books, POB 53, Andes, NY 13731

Baldwin Book Service, POB 157, Baldwin, NY 11510

Books — Past & Present, 428 Pearl Street, Buffalo, NY 14202

Rainbow's End Books, RD3, Country Route 84, Central Square, NY 13036

Seabook Search, Clinton Corners, NY 12514

C.G. Fisher, 62 East Main Street, Cobleskill, NY 12043

Ingeborg Quitzau, POB 5160, Edmeston, NY 13335

Leslie Poste, POB 68, Geneseo, NY 14454

The Book Finder, 471 Exchange Street, Geneva, NY 14456

Alan C. Hunter Books, Harriman Heights Road, Harriman, NY 10926

A Collector's Library, 520 North Greece Road, Hilton, NY 14468

The Bookery, De Witt Mall, Ithica, NY 14850

The Eight-Cent Nickel, 310 South Main Street, Liberty, NY 12754

Hobby Helpers, 7369 East Main Street, Lima, NY 14485

Talbothay's Books, POB 276, Lincolndale, NY 10540

Christian Bookfellowship, POB 763, Millbrook, NY 12545

Cooper Fox Farm — Books, POB 763, Millbrook, NY 12545

Book Finders General, 145 East 27th Street, New York, NY 10016

Book Ranger, 105 Charles Street, New York, NY 10014

Dolphin, Book Shop, 2743 Broadway, New York, NY 10025

Donan Books, 235 East 53rd Street, New York, NY 10022

Peter Thomas Fisher, 41 Union Square West, New York, NY 10003

Timothy Mawson, 134 West 92nd Street, New York, NY 10025

999 Bookshop, 999 Madison Avenue, New York, NY 10021

Paragon Book Gallery, 14 East 38th Street, New York, NY 10016

Russica Book & Art Shop, 799 Broadway, New York, NY 10003

Theatrebooks, Inc., 1576 Broadway - #312, New York, NY 10036

Peter Hennessey Books, POB 393, Peconic, NY 11958

Bengta Woo, 1 Sorgi Court, Plainview, NY 11803

Cabin in the Pines, Route 2, Potsdam, NY 13676

Robert E. Underhill, 85 Underhill Road, Poughkeepsie, NY 12603

Stan Marx, 15 Sinclair Martin Drive, Roslyn, NY 11576

The Book End, 521 Jewett Avenue, Staten Island, NY 10302

Sterling Valley Antiquity, POB 14, Syracuse, NY 13215

Book Look, 51 Maple Avenue, Warwick, NY 10990

Avonlea Books, POB 74, Main Station, White Plains, NY 10602

The Book Gallery, 15 Overlook Road, White Plains, NY 10605

Albert J. Phiebig, Inc., POB 352, White Plains, NY 10602

All Photography Books, POB 429, Yonkers, NY 10702

NORTH CAROLINA

Pacificana, POB 398, Jamestown, NC 27282

OHIO

Susan Heller, 22611 Halburton Road, Beachwood, OH 44122

Barbara Agranoff Books, POB 6501, Cincinnati, OH 45206

Ron-Dor Bookfinders, 4700 Masillon Road, Greensburg, OH 44232

The Amblers, 1123 Hillridge, Reynoldsburg, OH 43068

Burley & Books, Inc., 848 Franklin Park Mall, Toledo, OH 43623

OKLAHOMA

Caravan Books, POB 861, Stillwater, OK 74074

ONTARIO, CANADA

Attic Books, 388 Clarence Street, London, ON, Canada

Glooscap Study, RR1, Pefferlaw, ON L0E 1N0, Canada

Jocelyne Kidston, RR1, Tarzwell, ON P0K 1V0, Canada

Old Favorites Bookshop, 250 Adelaide West, Toronto, ON M5H 1X8, Canada

OREGON

McLaughlin's Books, POB 753, Cottage Grove, OR 97424

Joy A. Wheeler Books, Route 1, Box 49K, Elgin, OR 97827

J. Michaels Books, 376 East 11th Avenue, Eugene, OR 97401

Cameron's Books, 336 SW Third Avenue, Portland, OR 97204

Midvale Books, 155 SW Midvale Road, Portland, OR 97218

The Manuscript, 223 High Street NE, Salem, OR 97301

PENNSYLVANIA

Margaret L. Tyrrell, 117 North 40th Street, Allentown, PA 18104

College Hill Books, 306 Cattell Street, Easton, PA 18042

The Gateway, Ferndale, PA 18921

Helen B. Leech, 7944 Slepian Street, Harrisburg, PA 17112

Hobson's Choice, 511 Runnymede Avenue, Jenkintown, PA 19046

The Tuckers, 2236 Murray Avenue, Pittsburgh, PA 15217

Terry Harper, POB 103, Rouseville, PA 16344

Booksource Ltd., POB 43, Swarthmore, PA 19081

The Hermit's Book House, 34 Mt. Zion Road, Wyoming, PA 18644

RHODE ISLAND

Lincoln Out-of-Print Search, POB 100, Foster, RI 02825

Tyson Books, 334 Westminster Mall, Providence, RI 02903

SOUTH CAROLINA

Norm Burleson - Bookseller, 104 First Avenue, Spartanburg, SC 29302

TENNESSEE

Burke's Book Store, Inc., 634 Poplar Avenue, Memphis, TN 38105

Ollie's Books, 3218 Boxdale Street, Memphis, TN 38118

Crabtree Booksellers, 2905 Taft Highway, Box 282, Signal Mountain, TN 37377

TEXAS

State House Books, 1604 South Congress Avenue, Austin, TX 78704

David Grossblatt, POB 30001, Dallas, TX 75230

The Tracery, POB 30236, Dallas, TX 75230

Colleen's Books, 6880 Telephone Road, Houston, TX 77061

Trackside Books, 8819 Mobud Drive, Houston, TX 77036

All Points of View, POB 321, San Antonio, TX 78292

Maggie Lambeth Books, 136 Princess Pass - #3, San Antonio, TX 78212

Frederick W. Armstrong, 19 North McIlhaney, Stephenville, TX 76401

Book Cellar, 2 South Main, Temple, TX 76501

Von Blon's Books, 1111 Colcord Avenue, Waco, TX 76707

Clark Wright - Book Dealer, 409 Royal Street, Waxahachie, TX 75165

UTAH

Brennan Books, POB 9002, Salt Lake City, UT 84109

Marie Veit, 1852 East 4650 South, Salt Lake City, UT 84117

VERMONT

Bradford Books, West Road, Bennington, VT 05201

Bygone Books, 91 College Street, Burlington, VT 05401

Kneedeep in Books, POB 1314, Manchester Center, VT 05255

Lilac Hedge Bookshop, Main Street, Norwich, VT 05055

The Country Bookshop, RFD2, Plainfield, VT 05667

Bear Book Shop, RFD4, Box 219, West Brattleboro, VT 05301

VIRGINIA

Irene Rouse - Bookseller, 905 Duke Street, Alexandria, VA 22314

B. Tauscher, 102 Norwood Drive, Bristol, VA 24201

Forest Bookshop, POB 5206, Charlottesville, VA 22905

Allbooks, 4341 Majestic Lane, Fairfax, VA 22033

Royal Oak Bookshop, 207 South Royal Avenue, Front Royal, VA 22630

Givens Books, 2345 Lakeside Drive, Lynchburg, VA 24501

Ghent Bookworm, 1407 Colley Avenue, Norfolk, VA 23517

Book Search, 1741 Fairfax Street, Petersburg, VA 23803

Givens Books, 1641 East Main, Salem, VA 24153

The Book House, 209-B North Boundary Street, Williamsburg, VA 23185

WASHINGTON

Peggatty Books, Inc., 609 Maple Street, Clarkston, WA 99403

Comstock's Bindery/Books, 7903 Rainier Avenue, Seattle, WA 98118

WEST VIRGINIA

Appalachia Book Shop, 1316 Pen Mar Avenue, Bluefield, WV 24701

Wolf's Head Books, POB 1048, Morgantown, WV 26507

WISCONSIN

Old Delavan Book Co., 57 East Walworth, Delavan, WI 53115

Webster's Criminal Procedure, 2526 East Webster Place, Milwaukee, WI 53211

The Antiquarian Shop, 1329 Strongs Avenue, Box L, Stevens Point, WI 54481

WYOMING

Backpocket Ranch Bookshop, Star Route 4, Box 27, Sundance, WY 82729

Appendix 7

NORTH AMERICAN SPECIALTY BOOKSELLERS

BOOKSELLERS WHO ISSUE CATALOGS OF COLLECTIBLE BOOKS

All of these booksellers offer catalogs of scarce and rare collectible books and other forms of printed collectibles. Some are specialists in specific genres, i.e., mystery, science fiction, Americana. Many sell by mail only — others also operate shops with regular business hours. Most also buy by mail and a study of their catalogs will give you a good idea of what kind of material is of most interest to them. Some of them also provide a book search service. A post card request will usually put you on the mailing list for their next catalog. It is a courtesy to enclose one or two First Class stamps with your request.

Note: This list is alphabetized by states, and by communities within each state.

ALBERTA, CANADA

Robert C. Scace, POB 7156, Postal Station E, Calgary, AB T3C 3M1, Canada

Tom Williams Books, POB 4126, Stn. C, Calgary T2T 4M9, Canada

ARIZONA

Southwest Books, POB 319, Alpine, AZ 85920

John W. Keuhn, POB 73, Bisbee, AZ 85603

Readex Book Exchange, POB 1125, Carefree, AZ 85377

Russ Todd Books, Star Route 2, Box 872F, Cave Creek, AZ 85331

ARKANSAS

The Kingfisher, Lake Watch Route 1, Box 44, Eureka Springs, AR 72632

Martin House Books, 2212 South T, Fort Smith, AR 72901

Yesterday's Books, Etc., POB 1728, Hot Springs, AR 71901

Appletree Books, Route 1, Box 361, Williford, AR 72482

BRITISH COLUMBIA, CANADA

Okanagan Bookman, 2942 Pandosy Street, Kelowna, BC V1Y 2E6, Canada

Academic Books, POB 86-365, North Vancouver, BC, Canada

Bill Ellis, POB 436, Queen Charlotte City, BC V0T 1S0, Canada

Ainslie Books, 10640 Bridgeport Road, Richmond, BC V6X 1S7, Canada

CALIFORNIA

The Ross Valley Book Co., 1407 Solano Avenue, Albany, CA 94706

House of Books, 1758 Gardenaire Lane, Anaheim, CA 92804

Gail Klemm Books, POB 518, Apple Valley, CA 92307

Rare Oriental Book Co., POB 1599, Aptos, CA 95001

Diane Peterson - Booklady, POB 2544, Atherton, CA 94026

Anacapa Books, 3090 Claremont Avenue, Berkeley, CA 94705

Roy Bleiweiss Fine Books, 92 Northgate Avenue, Berkeley, CA 94708

The Scriptorium, 427 North Canon Drive, Beverly Hills, CA 90210

Books Et Cetera, POB 3507, Chico, CA 95927

John R. Butterworth, 742 West 11th Street, Claremont, CA 91711

Beaver Books, POB 974, Daly City, CA 94017

P.F. Mullins Books, 109 Beachtree Drive, Encinitas, CA 92024

Trophy Room Books, 4858 Dempsey Avenue, Encino, CA 91436

Bookfinder, 2035 Everding Street, Eureka, CA 95501

Symposium Books, 4458 Myrtle Avenue, Long Beach, CA 90807

Art Catalogues, 625 North Almont Drive, Los Angeles, CA 90069

Bennett & Marshall, 8205 Melrose Avenue, Los Angeles, CA 90046

Dawson's Book Shop, 535 North Larchmont Blvd., Los Angeles, CA 90004

Doris Harris Autographs, 5410 Wilshire Blvd., Los Angeles, CA 90036

Heritage Bookshop, 847 North La Cienega Blvd., Los Angeles, CA 90069

George Houle Rare Books, 2277 Westwood Blvd., Los Angeles, CA 90064

Icart Vendor, 7956 Beverly Blvd., Los Angeles, CA 90048

Samuel W. Katz, 10845 Lindbrook Drive-#6, Los Angeles, CA 90024

Joe Martinez, 7057 Lexington Avenue, Los Angeles, CA 90038

Kurt L. Schwarz, 738 South Bristol Avenue, Los Angeles, CA 90049

Sylvester & Orphanos, POB 2567, Los Angeles, CA 90078

Tolliver's Books, 1634 South Stearns Drive, Los Angeles, CA 90035

Vaughns Fine Arts, 214 Medio Drive, Los Angeles, CA 90049

West Los Angeles Book Center, 1650 Sawtelle Blvd., Los Angeles, CA 90025

Zeitlin Periodicals Co., 817 South La Brea Avenue, Los Angeles, CA 90036

Zeitlin & Ver Brugge, 815 North La Cienega Blvd., Los Angeles, CA 90069

Inter-American Books, POB 4154, Malibu, CA 90265

Wessex Books & Records, 1083 El Camino, Menlo Park, CA 94025

Health Research, POB 70, Mokelumne Hill, CA 95245

Sagebrush Press, POB 87, Morengo Valley, CA 92256

Archaeologia, 707 Carlston Street, Oakland, CA 94610

Holmes Book Company, 274 14th Street, Oakland, CA 94612

Robert Perata Books, 3170 Robinson Drive, Oakland, CA 94602

Yosemite Collections, 618 Grand Avenue, Oakland, CA 94610

The Book Sail, 1186 North Tustin, Orange, CA 92667

Fain's First Editions, 693 Amalfi Drive, Pacific Palisades, CA 90272

John P. Slattery, 352 Stanford Avenue, Palo Alto, CA 94306

William P. Wreden, 200 Hamilton Avenue, Palo Alto, CA 94302

William J.B. Burger, POB 832, Pine Grove, CA 95665

Acoma Books, POB 4, Ramona, CA 92065

Joanna Taylor, 2461 El Pavo, Rancho Cordova, CA 95670

Libros Latino, POB 1103, Redlands, CA 92373

The Silver Door, POB 3208, Redondo Beach, CA 90277

Rails Remembered, POB 464, Rosemead, CA 91770

Chloe's Books, POB 255673, Sacramento, CA 95865

Richard L. Press, 1228 "N" Street - No.2, Sacramento, CA 95814

Atticus Books, 728 Broadway, San Diego, CA 92101

Cape Cod Clutter, 3523 Fifth Avenue, San Diego, CA 92103

Golden Hill Antiquarian, 2456 Broadway, San Diego, CA 92101

J. & J. House Booksellers, 5694 Bounty Street, San Diego, CA 92101

Wahrenbrock's Books, 726 Broadway, San Diego, CA 92101

Argonaut Book Shop, 786 Sutter Street, San Francisco, CA 94109

Books America, POB 4006, San Francisco, CA 94101

The Bookstall, 708 Sutter Street, San Francisco, CA 94109

Brick Row Book Shop, 278 Post Street - #303, San Francisco, CA 94108

Drama Books, 511 Geary, San Francisco, CA 94102

Hall, McCormick & Darling, POB 4168, San Francisco, CA 94101

The Holmes Book Company, 22 Third Street, San Francisco, CA 94103

John Howell — Books, 434 Post Street, San Francisco, CA 94102

John Scopazzi Books, 278 Post Street, San Francisco, CA 94108

Sergio Old Prints, 50 Maiden Lane, San Francisco, CA 94108

Alan Wofsy Fine Arts, 4012 China Basin Street, San Francisco, CA 94107

A.S. Fischler Rare Books, 604 South 15th Street, San Jose, CA 95112

R. E. Lewis, Inc., POB 1108, San Rafael, CA 94915

Dave Henson--Books, POB 11402, Santa Ana, CA 92711

Milton Hammer Books, 125 El Paseo, Santa Barbara, CA 93101

Joseph the Provider, 903 State Street, Santa Barbara, CA 93101

Maurice F. Neville Books, 835 Laguna Street, Santa Barbara, CA 93101

Pepper & Stern, POB 2711, Santa Barbara, CA 93120

Second Debut Books, POB 30268, Santa Barbara, CA 93130

L.S. Kaiser Books, 1820 Graham Hill, Santa Cruz, CA 95060

George Robert Kane, 252 Third Avenue, Santa Cruz, CA 95062

Hennessey & Ingalls Inc., 1254 Santa Monica Mall, Santa Monica, CA 90401

Michael S. Hollander, 1433 Santa Monica Boulevard, Santa Monica, CA 90404

Howard Karno--Books, POB 431, Santa Monica, CA 90406

Rancho Books, POB 2040, Santa Monica, CA 90406

Virginia Burgman, 3198 Hidden Valley Drive, Santa Rosa, CA 95404

Eclectic Gallery, POB 1581, Sausalito, CA 94965

Concord Books, Box 275, Seal Beach, CA 90740

Davis & Schorr Art Books, 14755 Ventura Boulevard - #1-747, Sherman Oaks, CA 91403

B.& L. Rootenberg, POB 5049, Sherman Oaks, 91403

Heritage Books, 52 South Washington Street, Sonora, CA 95370

Bay Side Books, POB 57, Soquel, CA 95073

Maxwell's Books, 2103 Pacific Avenue, Stockton, CA 95204

Norman T. Hopper, 1142 Plymouth Drive, Sunnyvale, CA 94087

Len Unger Rare Books, 1575 El Dorado Drive, Thousand Oaks, CA 91362

Air Age Book Company, POB 40, Tollhouse, CA 93667

Book Buddy, 1328 Sartori Avenue, Torrance, CA 90501

Books In Transit, 2830 Case Way, Turlock, CA 95380

Lois St. Clair, POB 247, Van Nuys, CA 91408

Kenneth L. Wolf, 6021 Allott Avenue, Van Nuys, CA 91401

Mari Cyphers Rare Books, 1367 North Broadway, Walnut Creek, CA 94596

Hooked On Books, 1366 North Main Street, Walnut Creek, CA 94596

Blitz Books, POB 1076, Weaverville, CA 96093

221 Books, 760 Carlisle Canyon Road, Westlake Village, CA 91361

J.E. Reynolds, 3801 Ridgewood Road, Willits, CA 95490

Natural History Books, 5239 Tendilla Avenue, Woodland Hills, CA 91364

Robert Ross & Company, 6101 El Escorpion Road, Woodland Hills, CA 91367

Geoscience Books, 13057 California Street, Yucaipa, CA 92399

COLORADO

The King's Market, 1021 Pearl Street-Suite D, Boulder, CO 80302

Rue Morgue Bookshop, 956 Pearl, Boulder, CO 80302

Snatarasa Books, 937 Broadway, Boulder, CO 80302

Book Home Inc., POB 825, Colorado Springs, CO 80901

Hermitage Antiquarian Books, 2817 East Third Avenue, Denver, CO 80206

W J Bookhunter, POB 2795, Denver, CO 80201

William Allen Bookseller, POB 315, Englewood, CO 80151

E. Fithian Books, 1538 Ingalls Street, Lakewood, CO 80214

RGS Books, 14266 Greenway Drive, Sterling, CO 80751

CONNECTICUT

Whitlock Farm Booksellers, 20 Sperry Road, Bethany, CT 06525

Branford Rare Books, 221 Montowese Street, Branford, CT 06405

Chimney Smoke Books, 74 Waller Road, Bridgeport, CT 06606

Bob Cowell Book Seller, 15 Pearsall Way, Bridgeport, CT 06605

Stone of Scone Books, RFD 1, Box 262, Canterbury, CT 06331

Attic Books & Records, POB 53, Colebrook, CT 06021

Colebrook Book Barn, Route 183, Box 108, Colebrook, CT 06021

Rinehart Galleries, Upper Grey, Colebrook, CT 06021

Laurence Golder, POB 144, Collinsville, CT 06022

The Book Block, 8 Loughlin Avenue, Cos Cob, CT 06807

Harrington's, 333 Cognewaug Road, Cos Cob, CT 06807

John Woods, Main Street, Coventry, CT 06238

Extensive Search Service, Squaw Rock Road, Danielson, CT 06239

Clipper Ship Book Shop, 12 North Main Street, Essex, CT 06426

Warren Blake--Bookseller, 131 Sigwin Drive, Fairfield, CT 06430

Museum Gallery Book Shop, 360 Mine Hill Road, Fairfield, CT 06430

R & D Emerson, The Old Church, Main Street, Falls Village, CT 06031

Wolfgang Schiefer, 23 Church Street, Georgetown, CT 06829

Anglers & Shooters Books, Goshen, CT 06576

William & Lois Pinkney, 240 North Granby Road, Granby, CT 06035

American Worlds Books, POB 6162, Hamden, CT 06517

Antique Books, 3651 Whitney Avenue, Hamden, CT 06518

DELAWARE

Oak Knoll Books, 414 Delaware Street, New Castle, DE 19720

Horseshoe Lane Books, 436 New London Road, Newark, DE 19711

Hollyoak Book Shop, 306 West 7th Street, Wilmington, DE 19801

DISTRICT OF COLUMBIA

Bickerstaff & Barclay, POB 28452, Washington, DC 20005

East-West Feature Service, POB 8867, Washington, DC 20003

Folger Shakespeare Books, 201 East Capitol Street SE, Washington, DC 20003

William F. Hale Books, 1222 31st Street NW, Washington, DC 20007

Jean C. Jones Books, 3701 Massachusetts Avenue NW, Washington, DC 20016

Lambda Rising Inc., 2012 "S" Street, Washington, DC 20009

Latin American Books, POB 39090, Washington, DC 20016

Lloyd Books, 1346 Connecticut Avenue NW, Washington, DC 20036

Thomas T. Moebs, 407 "A" Street NE, Washington, DC 20002

Old Print Gallery, 1220 31st Street NW, Washington, DC 20007

Willis Van Devanter, POB 32426, Washington, DC 20007

FLORIDA

Jean Cohen, POB 654, Bonita Springs, FL 33923

Mickler's Floridiana, Box 38, Chuluota, FL 32766

Frank Guarino, POB 89, De Bary, FL 32713

Raintree Books, 432 North Eustis Street, Eustis, FL 32726

Tracy Catledge, POB 583, Fern Park, FL 32730

Wake-Brook House, 990 NW 53rd Street, Fort Lauderdale, FL 33309

McQuerry Orchid Books, 5700 Solerno Road West, Jacksonville, FL 32244

San Marco Bookstore, 1971 San Marci Boulevard, Jacksonville, FL 32207

All Books & Prints Store, 4329 SW 8th Street, Miami, FL 33134

Al Fogel--Books, 2770 NW 32nd Avenue, Miami, FL 33142

The Bookfinders, POB 2021, Miami Beach, FL 33140

The Book Trader, 170 10th Street North, Naples, FL 33940

Mycophile Books, 1166 Royal Palm, Naples, FL 33940

D.E. Whalen--Samadhi, POB 729, Newberry, FL 32669

Dick Hazlett, POB 1935, West Palm Beach, FL 33402

GEORGIA

The Book Studio, POB 13335, Atlanta, GA 30324

Julian Burnett Books, POB 229, Atlanta, GA 30301

James O. McMeans, Box 420352, Atlanta, GA 30342

Old New York Book, 1069 Juniper Street NE, Atlanta, GA 30309

Oxford Book Store, 2345 Peachtree Road NE, Atlanta, GA 30305

Book Search Service, 36 Kensington Road, Avondale Estates, GA 30002

Hound Dog Press Book Shop, 4285 Memorial Drive, Decatur, GA 30032

Robert Murphy--Bookseller, 3113 Bunker Hill Road, Marietta, GA 30062

Margie Sachs--OP Books, Route 2, Box 59, Metter, GA 30439

Coosa Valley Book Shop, 15 East Third Avenue, Rome, GA 30161

Lonnie E. Evans, 414 Bull Street, Savannah, GA 31401

Jacqueline Levine, 107 East Oglethorpe Avenue, Savannah, GA 31401

P.R. Rieber, Box 2202, Thomasville, GA 31792

The Bookstore, Brookwood Plaza, Valdosta, GA 31601

HAWAII

Aldamar World of Books, 409 North King Street, Honolulu, HI 96817

Prints Pacific, R.R.1, Box 276, Wailuku, Maui, HI 96763

ILLINOIS

Rose Lasley, 5827 Burr Oak, Berkeley, IL 60163

P.J. Henry, 4225 East, Berwyn, IL 60402

Abraham Lincoln Book Shop, 18 East Chestnut Street, Chicago, IL 60611

Articles of War Ltd., 7101 North Ashland Avenue, Chicago, IL 60626

Beasley Books, 1533 West Oakdale, Chicago, IL 60657

James M.W. Borg, 8 South Michigan Avenue, Chicago, IL 60603

Richard Cady--Rare Books, 1927 North Hudson Avenue, Chicago, IL 60614

Gerald J. Cielec, 2248 North Kedvale Avenue, Chicago, IL 60639

N. Fagin--Books, 17 North State Street-#1366, Chicago, IL 60602

Joseph J. Gasior, 4814 South Pulaski Road, Chicago, IL 60632

The Globe, POB A3398, Chicago, IL 60690

Elinor Jaksto, 4104 Archer Avenue, Chicago, IL 60632

Thomas J. Joyce & Company, 431 South Dearborn, Chicago, IL 60603

N.L. Laird--Bookseller, 1240 West Jarvis, Chicago, IL 60626

Larry Laws, 831 Cornelia, Chicago, IL 60657

Magic, Inc., 5082 North Lincoln Avenue, Chicago, IL 60625

G.B. Manasek Inc., 5805 South Dorchester, Chicago, IL 60637

Kenneth Nebenzahl Inc., 333 North Michigan Avenue, Chicago, IL 60601

Nelson-Hall Booksellers, 111 North Canal Street, Chicago, IL 60606

Ralph Geoffrey Newman Inc., 175 East Delaware Place, Chicago, IL 60611

A. & A. Prosser--Books, 3118 North Keating Avenue, Chicago, IL 60641

J. Dowd, 38 West 281, Tom's Trail, St. Charles, IL 60174

Seven Oaks Press, 405 South 7th Street, St. Charles, IL 60174

The Gamebag, 973 North Princeton Court, Vernon Hills, IL 60061

Yellowstone Books, POB 69, Villa Park, IL 60181

Richard Owen Roberts, 205 East Kehoe Boulevard, Wheaton, IL 60187

Leekley Book Search, Box 337, Winthrop Harbor, IL 60096

INDIANA

Almagre Books, 3271 Spring Branch Road, Bloomington, IN 47401

Rick Grunder--Books, 915 Maxwell Terrace, Bloomington, IN 47401

Kathleen Rais, 612 North Dunn, Bloomington, IN 47401

G.J. Rausch, POB 2346, Bloomington, IN 47402

Gary Steigerwald, 1500 Maxwell Lane, Bloomington, IN 47401

G.B. Manasek Inc., POB 909, Chesterton, IN 46304

Bookstack, 112 West Lexington Avenue, Elkhart, IN 46516

Campfire Books, 7218 Hogue Road, Evansville, IN 47712

Ft. Wayne Forest Park Books, 1412 Delaware Avenue, Fort Wayne, IN 46805

Back Tracts Inc., POB 30008, Indianapolis, IN 46230

Hoosier Schoolmaster's, 1228 Michigan Avenue, La Porte, IN 46350

Mason's Books, 264 South Wabash, Wabash, IN 46992

Lion Enterprises, R.R.3, Box 127, Walkerton, IN 46574

IOWA

Mike Maddigan, POB 824, Cedar Rapids, IA 52406

Petersen Book Company, POB 966, Davenport, IA 52805

Pauline Millen--Books, 3325 Crescent Drive, Des Moines, IA 50312

Checker Book World, 3520 Hillcrest, Dubuque, IA 52001

William A. Graf--Books, 717 Clark Street, Iowa City, IA 52240

Prairie Lights, 15 South Dubuque Street, Iowa City, IA 52240

Gerald Pettinger Arms Books, Rte.2, Russell, IA 50238

KANSAS

Forsyth Travel Library, Box 2975, Shawnee Mission, KS 66201

S. Jacobs, R.R.6, Box 264, Topeka, KS 66608

Dickey Books, 107 North Clifton, Wichita, KS 67208

KENTUCKY

T & B Books, Box 14077, Covington, KY 41014

Eagle Books, POB 12010, Lexington, KY 40579

Glover's Books, 862 South Broadway, Lexington, KY 40504

Don Grayson, 2600 Meadow Drive, Louisville, KY 40220

Donald S. Mull, 1706 Girard Drive, Louisville, KY 40222

Old Louisville Books, 426 West Oak Street, Louisville, KY 40203

Vernon Owen Books, 1621 Phyliss Avenue, Louisville, KY 40215

Philatelic Bibliopole, POB 36006, Louisville, KY 40233

Don Smith, 3930 Rankin Street, Louisville, KY 40214

S-T Associates, 1317 Cherokee Road, Louisville, KY 40204

The Mt. Sterling Rebel, Box 481, Mount Sterling, KY 40353

LOUISIANA

Taylor Clark, 2623 Government Street, Baton Rouge, LA 70806

Henry C. Hensel, 657-B Rue Perez, Belle Chasse, LA 70037

Bayou Books, 1005 Monroe Street, Gretna, LA 70053

Charles F. Hamsa, 612 Alonda Drive, Lafayette, LA 70503

Books-In-A-Bag, POB 9460, Metairie, LA 70055

American Opinion Books, 3804 Canal Street, New Orleans, LA 70119

Red River Books, POB 3606, Shreveport, LA 71103

MAINE

Robert Canney Rare Books, POB 350, Alfred, ME 04002

Bill Lippincott--Books, 547 Hammond Street, Bangor, ME 04401

Medical Book Service, POB 447, Brewer, ME 04412

Cross Hill Books, POB 798, Brunswick, ME 04011

Leroy Cross, 21 Columbia Avenue, Brunswick, ME 04011

Patricia Ledlie--Books, POB 46, Buckfield, ME 04220

J. Bernard Reynolds, 12 Main Street, Burnham, ME 04922

Varney's Volumes, Quaker Ridge Road, Casco, ME 04015

Alfred Search Service, Drawer 1027, Damariscotta, ME 04534

Skeans & Clifford, POB 85, Deer Isle, ME 04627

Books and Autographs, 287 Goodwin Road, Eliot, ME 03903

George E. Milkey, 50-A Brixham Road, Eliot, ME 03903

MacDonald's Military, Coburn Gore, Eustis, ME 04936

Bunkhouse Books, Route 5A, Box 148, Gardiner, ME 04345

River Oak Books, RFD2, Box 5505, Jay, ME 04239

J.& J. Hanrahan, c/o Post Road Associates, Route 1, Kittery, ME 03909

Deborah Isaacson, Box 932, Lewiston, ME 04240

Maurice E. Owen, RFD2, Bowdoin Center Road, Litchfield, ME 04350

Charles Robinson Books, Pond Road, Box 299, Manchester, ME 04351

Sumner & Stillman, POB 225, Yarmouth, ME 04096

MARYLAND

Dragoman Books, 680 Americana Drive-#38, Annapolis, MD 21403

Artcraft Books, 6701 Cherry Hill Road, Baldwin, MD 21013

The Chirurgical Bookshop, 1211 Cathedral Street, Baltimore, MD 21201

Inscribulus Books, 857 North Howard Street, Baltimore, MD 21201

Key Books, 2 West Montgomery Street, Baltimore, MD 21230

Cecil Archer Rush, 1410 Northgate Road, Baltimore, MD 21218

Sherlock Book Detective, POB 1174, Baltimore, MD 21203

B & K, POB 415, Bowie, MD 20715

Heritage Books, 3602 Maureen, Bowie, MD 20715

Old Hickory Bookshop, 20225 New Hampshire Avenue, Brinklow, MD 20862

Wharf House Books, POB 57, Centreville, MD 21617

Mary Chapman--Bookseller, POB 304, College Park, MD 20740

Jeff Dykes--Western Books, POB 38, College Park, MD 20740

John Gach--Books, 5620 Waterloo Road, Columbia, MD 21045

Firstborn Books, 1007 East Benning Road, Galesville, MD 20765

E. Don Bullian, 7-D Ridge Road, Greenbelt, MD 20770

John C. Rather, POB 273, Kensington, MD 20895

Drusilla's Books, POB 16, Lutherville, MD 21093

Old Quenzel Store, POB 326, Port Tobacco, MD 20677

Harris Books, 12000 Old Georgetown Road-#N805, Rockville, MD 20852

Moers Main Auction, 11910 Lafayette Drive, Wheaton, MD 20902

MASSACHUSETTS

Francis G. Walett, 369 High Street, Abington, MA 02351

Andover Antiquarian Books, 68 Park Street, Andover, MA 01810

Goodspeed's 2, 2 Milk Street, Boston, MA 02108

Daniel F. Kelleher Co., 40 Broad Street, Boston, MA 02109

Ralph Kristiansen, POB 524, Boston, MA 02215

Geoffrey H. Mahfuz, POB 289, Boston, MA 02199

Edward Morrill & Son, 25 Kingston Street, Boston, MA 02111

David L. O'Neal, 308 Commonwealth Avenue, Boston, MA 02115

Ivan Stormgart, POB 1232, Boston, MA 02205

E. Wharton & Co., 36 Hancock Street, Boston, MA 02114

Organ Literature Foundation, 45 Norfolk Street, Braintree, MA 02184

Xanadu Books, POB 91, Braintree, MA 02184

Smith's Book Service, Sunsmith House, Route 6A, Brewster, MA 02631

Thomas G. Boss, 80 Monmouth Street, Brookline, MA 02146

Brookline Village Books, 23 Harvard Street, Brookline, MA 02146

Dan Miranda, POB 145, Brookline, MA 02146

Asian Books, 12 Arrow Street, Cambridge, MA 02138

Blue Rider Books, 1640 Massachusetts Avenue, Cambridge, MA 02138

Grolier Book Shop, 6 Pylmpton Street, Cambridge, MA 02138

In Our Time, POB 386, Cambridge, MA 02139

H.L. Mendelsohn, 1640 Massachusetts Avenue, Cambridge, MA 02138

Pepper & Stern, POB 160, Sharon, MA 02067

Howard S. Mott, South Main Street, Sheffield, MA 01257

Webb Dordick, 15 Ash Avenue, Somerville, MA 02145

Elmcress Books, 161 Bay Road, Route 1A, South Hamilton, MA 01982

J.& J. Lubrano, POB 127, South Lee, MA 01260

T. Small--Books, POB 457, South Yarmouth, MA 02664

Sterling Bookstore, Route 12, Sterling, MA 01564

MICHIGAN

James Babcock, 5055 Point Tremble Road (M29), Algonac, MI 48001

The Bookseller, POB 8163, Ann Arbor, MI 48107

Hartfield Fine & Rare Books, 117 Dixboro Road, Ann Arbor, MI 48105

Keramos, POB 7500, Ann Arbor, MI 48107

Leaves of Grass, 2433 Whitmore Lake Road, Ann Arbor, MI 48103

West Side Book Shop, 113 West Liberty, Ann Arbor, MI 48104

Wine & Food Library, 1207 West Madison Street, Ann Arbor, MI 48103

Gunnerman Books, POB 4292, Auburn Heights, MI 48057

Mayflower Bookshop, 2645 West 12 Mile Road, Berkley, MI 48072

Ceyx, POB 73, Dearborn, MI 48121

Else Fine--Books, POB 43, Dearborn, MI 48121

Cellar Book Shop, 18090 Wyoming, Detroit, MI 48221

Grub Street--A Bookery, 17194 East Warren, Detroit, MI 48224

John K. King--Books, Box 363, Detroit, MI 48232

Curious Book Shop, 307 East Grand River, East Lansing, MI 48823

Joseph L. Lepczyk, POB 751, East Lansing, MI 48823

Albert G. Clegg, 312 West Broad Street, Eaton Rapids, MI 48827

Crabtree's Collection, 2236 Canal Road, Eaton Rapids, MI 48827

Kregel's Bookstore, Box 2607, Grand Rapids, MI 49501

Sportsman's Outdoor Enterprises, POB 192, Grawn, MI 49637

J.E. Sheldon Fine Books, 645 West Green, Hastings, MI 49058

John B. Doukas, 3203 Bronson Boulevard, Kalamazoo, MI 49008

MINNESOTA

J.& J. O'Donoghue-Books, 1926 Second Avenue South, Anoka, MN 55303

ATC Books, 321 East Superior Street, Duluth, MN 55802

Walter Chadde--Books, Star Route 3, Box 629, Grand Marais, MN 55604

Arch Books, 5916 Drew Avenue South, Minneapolis, MN 55410

Bookmailer, 2730 West Broadway, Minneapolis, MN 55411

Thomas Dady, 2223 Sixth Street NE, Minneapolis, MN 55418

Dinkytown Antiquarian Books, 1316 SE 4th Street, Minneapolis, MN 55414

Old Theology Book House, POB 12232, Minneapolis, MN 55412

Rulon-Miller Books, 716 North First Street, Minneapolis, MN 55401

Scientia, POB 14254, Minneapolis, MN 55414

Page One, Highway 53, Orr, MN 55771

Bookdales, 46 West 66th Street, Richfield, MN 55423

Five Quail Books, POB 278, Spring Grove, MN 55974

MISSISSIPPI

James A. Dillon--Books, Star Route, Box 23, Carlisle, MS 39049

Choctaw Books, 406 Manship Street, Jackson, MS 39202

Nouveau Rare Books, 5005 Meadow Oaks Park, Jackson, MS 39211

William M. Hutter, Route 3, Box 123, Ocean Springs, MS 39564

MISSOURI

Leroy Thompson, 3471 Highway A, Festus, MO 63028

Boyce E. McCaslin, POB 1580, Ironton, MO 63650

William J. Cassidy, 109 East 65th Street, Kansas City, MO 64113

Cramer Book Store, POB 7235, Kansas City, MO 64113

Glenn Books, 1227 Baltimore, Kansas City, MO 64105

Klaus Grunewald--Books, 807 West 87th Terrace, Kansas City, MO 64114

Smoky Hill Booksellers, POB 2, Kansas City, MO 64141

Hooked On Books, 2756 South Campbell, Springfield, MO 65807

Reginald P. Dunaway, 6138 Delmar Boulevard, St. Louis, MO 63112

Elizabeth F. Dunlap, 6063 Westminster Place, St. Louis, MO 63112

Swiss Village Books, 711 North First Street, St. Louis, MO 63102

MONTANA

Bay Books & Prints, Grand & Lake Sts., Bigfork, MT 59911

Thomas Minckler, 111 North 30th-Ste.221, Billings, MT 59101

Jane Graham, Box 1624, Bozeman, MT 59715

Blacktail Mountain Books, 42 First Avenue West, Kalispell, MT 59901

Douglas C. Johns, PO Drawer K, Lakeside, MT 59922

Bird's Nest, Box 8809, Missoula, MT 59807

David A. Lawyer--Books, Route 2, Box 95, Plains, MT 59859

NEBRASKA

J.& L. Lee--Booksellers, POB 5575, Lincon, NE 68505

Niobrara Books, POB 2664, Lincoln, NE 68502

D. N. Dupley, 9118 Pauline Street, Omaha, NE 68124

Mostly Books, 1025 South 10th Street, Omaha, NE 68108

1023 Booksellers, POB 3668, Omaha, NE 68103

Wordsmith Stores, POB O, Syracuse, NE 68446

NEVADA

Kalman Appel, 1412 South 16th Street, Las Vegas, NV 89104

Gambler's Book Club, 630 South 11th Street, Las Vegas, NV 89101

NEW BRUNSWICK, CANADA

Artican Books, Box 691, Fredericton, N.B., Canada

P.J. FitzPatrick Books, Spencer Street, Route 4, Fredericton, N.B., Canada

NEWFOUNDLAND, CANADA

Maps & Books, 34 Kingsbridge Road, St. Johns, NF A1C 3R6, Canada

NEW HAMPSHIRE

Kalonbooks, POB 16, Bradford, NH 03221

The Ha'Penny, RFD2, Route 121, Chester, NH 03036

Bert Babcock--Bookseller, Box 1140, Derry, NH 03038

Colophon Book Shop, POB E, Epping, NH 03042

John F. Hendsey, Burley Homestead, Epping, NH 03042

Landscape Books, POB 483, Exeter, NH 03833

Jenny Watson, POB 915, Exeter, NH 03833

The Typographeum Bookshop, The Stone Cottage, Bennington Road, Francestown, NH 03043

Louise Frazier--Books, RFD6, Box 477, Gilford, NH 03246

Sacred and Profane, POB 321, Goffstown, NH 03045

Carry Back Books, Route 10, Dartmouth College Highway, Haverhill, NH 03765

Book Farm, POB 515, Henniker, NH 03242

Old Number Six Book Depot, POB 525, Henniker, NH 03242

Paul Henderson, 50 Berkeley Street, Nashua, NH 03060

Burpee Hill Books, Burpee Hill Road, New London, NH 03257

Sykes & Flanders, POB 86, North Weare Village, NH 03281

NEW JERSEY

Antic Hay Books, POB 2185, Asbury Park, NJ 07712

Bauman Rare Books, 14 South La Clede Place, Atlantic City, NJ 08401

Deskins & Greene Antiques, POB 1092, Atlantic City, NJ 08404

Richard W. Spellman, 610 Monticello Drive, Brick Town, NJ 08723

Edison Hall Books, 5 Ventnor Drive, Edison, NJ 08520

Ruth Woods Oriental Books, 266 Arch Road, Englewood, NJ 07631

Junius Book Distributors, POB 85, Fairview, NJ 07022

The People's Bookshop, 160 Main Street, Flemington, NJ 08822

Ppbk Book Co., 2200 North Central Road, Fort Lee, NJ 07024

Rare Book Co., POB 957, Freehold, NJ 07728

Artifacts, 368 Grove Street, Glen Rock, NJ 07450

J.M. Winters--Books, 680 Summit Avenue, Hackensack, NJ 07601

Old Cookbooks, POB 462, Haddonfield, NJ 08033

Elisabeth Woodburn, Booknoll Farm, Hopewell, NJ 08525

Edenite Society, Imlaystown, NJ 08526

James R. Zimmerman, 32 Terrace Place, Kearny, NJ 07032

DeVictor's Books, 3 Dov Place, Kendall Park, NJ 08824

Oz & Ends Book Shoppe, 14 Dorset Drive, Kenilworth, NJ 07033

The Dictionary, POB 130, Leeds Point, NJ 08220

Stephen Viederman, 108 High Street, Leonia, NJ 07605

Acres of Books, 35 East State, Trenton, NJ 08608

Wilsey Rare Books, 80 Watchung Avenue, Upper Montclair, NJ 07043

Stephen Koschal, POB 201, Verona, NJ 07044

H. Nestler, 13 Pennington Avenue, Waldwick, NJ 07463

Albert Saifer, POB 51, West Orange, NJ 07052

NEW MEXICO

Chamisa Bookshop, 1602 Central SE. Albuquerque, NM 87106

Hummingbird Books, 2400 Hannett NE, Albuquerque, NM 87106

Jack D. Rittenhouse, POB 4422, Albuquerque, NM 87196

Robert R. White, POB 101, Albuquerque, NM 87103

Jane Zwisohn, 524 Solano Drive NE, Albuquerque, NM 87108

Abacus Books, POB 5555, Santa Fe, NM 87502

Ancient Vity Book Shop, POB 1986, Santa Fe, NM 87501

Ancient City Press, POB 5401, Santa Fe, NM 87502

Richard Fitch--Old Maps, 2324 Calle Halcon, Santa Fe, NM 87505

Parker Books of the West, 300 Lomita, Santa Fe, NM 87501

Ean Richards--Books, POB 9141, Santa Fe, NM 87501

Taos Book Shop, 114 Kit Carson Road, Taos, NM 87571

NEW YORK

Joseph Geraci Rare Books, RD1, Box 258, Accord, NY 12404

John Hawley--Books, POB 2061, Albany, NY 12208

Kevin T. Ransom--Books, POB 176, Amherst, NY 14226

Kenneth Lang, 105 Avon Place, Amityville, NY 11701

Oan-Oceanie-Afrique Noire, POB 85, Ancram, NY 12502

Treasures in Books, POB 53, Andes, NY 13731

Autobooks East, POB 1, Babylon, NY 11702

Baldwin Book Service, POB 157, Baldwin, NY 11510

Bayshore Books, 31 West Main Street, Bayshore, NY 11706

Judith Bowman--Books, Pound Ridge Road, Bedford, NY 10506

NORTH CAROLINA

Captain's Bookshelf, 26 1/2 Battery Park Avenue, Asheville, NC 28801

Andrew Cahan, POB 882, Chapel Hill, NC 27514

Keith & Martin--Books, 310 West Franklin Street, Chapel Hill, NC 27514

Carolina Bookshop, 1601 East Independence Boulevard, Charlotte, NC 28205

Little Hundred Gallery, 6028 Bentway Drive, Charlotte, NC 28226

B.L. Means, 5935 Creola Road, Charlotte, NC 28226

Book House, Brightleaf Square, Durham, NC 27707

Book Trader, POB 603, Fairmont, NC 28304

Albemarle Books, POB 587, Gatesville, NC 27938

Pacificana, POB 398, Jamestown, NC 27282

NOVA SCOTIA, CANADA

Nautica Booksellers, 1579 Dresden Row, Halifax, NS B3J 2K4, Canada

Schooner Books, 5378 Inglis Street, Halifax, NS B3H 1J5, Canada

D.A. Butcher, 87 McLean Street, Trurd, NS B2N 4W2, Canada

The Odd Book, 8 Front Street, Wolfville, NS, Canada

OHIO

The Bookseller Inc., 521 West Exchange Street, Akron, OH 44302

The Odyssey, 1743 South Union, Alliance, OH 44601

Croissant & Company, POB 282, Athens, OH 45701

D. Gratz, Route 2, Box 89, Bluffton, OH 45817

De Anima, 122 East Evers, Bowling Green, OH 43402

Barbara Agranoff--Books, POB 6501, Cincinnati, OH 45106

Old Erie Street Bookstore, 2128 East 9th Street, Cleveland, OH 44115

OKLAHOMA

Ron Bever, Rte.3, Box 243-B, Edmond, OK 73034

The Book Sheet, POB 1461, Lawton, OK 73502

Arcane Books, 3120 Harvey Parkway, Oklahoma City, OK 73118

Melvin Marcher, 6204 North Vermont, Oklahoma City, OK 73112

Caravan Books, Box 861, Stillwater, OK 74074

Oklahoma Bookman, 1107 Foreman Road NE, Yukon, OK 73099

ONTARIO, CANADA

Huronia-Canadiana, POB 685, Alliston, ON, Canada

Madonna House Bookshop, Combermer, ON, Canada

The House of Antique Books, 130 Shaftersbury Street, Downsview, ON, Canada M3H 5M1

D.W. Goudy, 10 Douglas Street, Guelph, ON, Canada N1H 2S9

Rising Trout Sporting Books, POB 1719, Guelph, ON, Canada N1H 6Z9

OREGON

McLaughlin's Books. POB 753, Cottage Grove, OR 97424

Authors of the West, 191 Dogwood Drive, Dundee, OR 97115

Backstage Books, POB 3676, Eugene, OR 97403

B.L. Bibby Books, 1225 Sardine Creek Road, Gold Hill, OR 97525

Ernest L. Sackett, 100 Waverly Drive, Grants Pass, OR 97526

PENNSYLVANIA
Philip G. LeVan, 2443 Liberty Street, Allentown, PA 18104
Margaret L. Tyrrell, 117 North 40th Street, Allentown, PA 18104
Hive of Industry, POB 602, Easton, PA 18042
James S. Jaffe, POB 496, Haverford, PA 19041
Medical Manor Books, Benjamin Fox Pavilion, Box 647, Jenkintown, PA 19046

PUERTO RICO
Poe Book Shop, Bzn.119, Barrio Mani, Mayaguez, P.R. 00708

QUEBEC, CANADA
J.A. Benoit, 3465 Sherbrooke East, #1, Montreal, Quebec, Canada H1W 1C9
Bibliography of the Dog, 4170 Decarie Boulevard, Montreal, Quebec, Canada 4H4 3K2
Mme. Lucie Javitch, 1589 Dr. Penfield Avenue, Montreal, Quebec, Canada H3G 1C6
Helen R. Kahn, POB 323, Victoria Station, Montreal, Quebec, Canada H3Z 2V8
Jean Gagnon, 402-764 St. Joseph Street, Bp.653 H-V, Quebec, Quebec, Canada G1R 4S2

RHODE ISLAND
Jack Clinton, POB 1098, Hope Vallet, RI 02832
Anchor & Dolphin Books, POB 823, Newport, RI 02840
Armchair Sailor Bookstore, Lee's Wharf, Newport, RI 02840
Sign of the Unicorn, POB 297, Peacedale, RI 02883
Cornerstone Books, 163 Brook Street, Providence, RI 02906

SASKETCHEWAN, CANADA
Northland Books, 813 Broadway Avenue, Saskatoon, SK, Canada S7N 1B5

SOUTH CAROLINA
Harpagon Associates, 369 King Street, Charleston, SC 29401
Noah's Ark Book Attic, Stony Point, Rte.2, Greenwood, SC 29646
The Attic, Inc., POB 123, Hodges, SC 29653
The Book Shoppe, 9900 Kings Highway North, Myrtle Beach, SC 29577
Hampton Books, Route 1, Box 202, Newberry, SC 29108

UTAH
Bekker Antiquarian Books, 903 South 10th Street, East, Salt Lake City, UT 84105
Cosmic Aeroplane Books, 258 East First Street, South, Salt Lake City, UT 84111

Scallawagiana Books, POB 2441, Salt Lake City, UT 84110
Ute-or-Ida Books, POB 279, West Jordan, UT 84084

VERMONT
Aislinn books, POB 589, Bennington, VT 05201
New Englandia, POB 589, Bennington, VT 05201
Kenneth Leach, POB 78, Brattleboro, VT 05301
Tuttle Antiquarian Books, 28 South Main Street, Rutland, VT 05701
Weston Books, RD1, Box 90, Landgrove Road, Weston, VT 05161

VIRGINIA
Irene Rouse, Bookseller, 905 Duke Street, Alexandria, VA 22314
Virginia Book Company, POB 431, Berryville, VA 22611
B. Tauscher, 102 Norwood Drive, Bristol, VA 24210
Heartwood Books, 9 Elliewood, Charlottesville, VA 22903
Louis Ginsberg, POB 1502, Petersburg, VA 23805

VIRGIN ISLANDS
Rulon-Miller Books, Red Hook, Box 41, St. Thomas, VI 00802

WASHINGTON
Tolstoi's Ink, Third & State Sts., Marysville, WA 98270
Aero Literature, POB 1441, Olympia, WA 98507
Bainbridge Books, 322 Boylston Street, Seattle, WA 98102
Bibelots & Books, 112 East Lynn, Seattle, WA 98102
Catweasel Books, POB 20695, Seattle, WA 98102

WEST VIRGINIA
Book Store, 104 South Jefferson Street, Lewisburg, WV 24901
Wooden Porch Books, Route 1, Box 262, Middlebourne, WV 26149
Wolf's Head Books, POB 1048, Morgantown, WV 26507
Sebert's Books, Route 3, Box 325, Mount Nebo, WV 26679
The Bishop of Books, 117 15th Street, Wheeling, WV 26003

WISCONSIN
Old Delavan Book Company, 57 East Walworth, Delavan, WI 53115
W. Bruce Fye, 1607 North Wood Avenue, Marshfield, WI 54449
Constant Reader Bookshop, 1901 North Prospect Avenue, Milwaukee, WI 53202
Littlwoods Book House, 200 East Park Avenue, Waukesha, WI 53186

WYOMING
Backpocket Ranch Bookshop, Star Route 4, Box 27, Sundance, WY 82729

Appendix 8
RECOMMENDED READING

Your local library may have a copy of these books. If not, your local NEW book store should be able to tell you if any particular title is still in-print, the cost, and order it for you if you wish. If the book is out-of-print, check with your nearest used-book or antiquarian book store. They may be able to locate a copy for you if they operate a search service. Or you can advertise for yourself in *The Antique Trader Weekly, Collector's News, or AB The Antiqaurian Bookman,* for a copy.

A

AB BOOKMAN'S YEARBOOK. Annual.

Adams, Ramon F. — MORE BURS UNDER THE SADDLE: BOOKS AND HISTORIES OF THE WEST. 1979.

Aldiss, Brian — BILLION YEAR SPREE: A HISTORY OF SCIENCE FICTION. 1973.

Aldiss, Brian & Harry Harrison — HELL'S CARTOGRAPHERS: SOME PERSONAL HISTORIES OF SCIENCE FICTION WRITERS. 1975.

AMERICAN BOOK PRICES CURRENT. Annual.

Amis, Kingsley — THE JAMES BOND DOSSIER. 1965.

Ash, Brian — WHO'S WHO IN SCIENCE FICTION. 1976.

Atteberry, Brian — THE FANTASY TRADITION IN AMERICAN LITERATURE. 1980.

B

Bain, Robert — Editor — SOUTHERN WRITERS: A BIOGRAPHICAL DICTIONARY. 1979.

Baron, Herman — AUTHOR INDEX TO ESQUIRE, 1933-1973. 1976.

Barron, Neil — ANATOMY OF WONDER: A CRITICAL GUIDE TO SCIENCE FICTION. 1981.

Baym, Nina — WOMAN'S FICTION: A GUIDE TO NOVELS BY AND ABOUT WOMEN IN AMERICA, 1820-1870. 1978.

Baynton-Williams, Roger — INVESTING IN MAPS. 1969.

Bleiler, Everett F. — THE CHECKLIST OF SCIENCE FICTION AND SUPERNATURAL FICTION. 1979.

Bleiler, Everett F. — THE GUIDE TO SUPERNATURAL FICTION. 1982.

Blum, Eleanor — BASIC BOOKS IN THE MASS MEDIA: AN ANNOTATED SELECTED BOOKLIST. 1980.

Bradley, Van Allen — THE BOOK COLLECTOR'S HANDBOOK OF VALUES. Latest edition.

Brandes, George Morris Cohen — MAIN CURRENTS IN NINETEENTH-CENTURY LITERATURE. 6 vols. 1972.

Breen, Jon L. — WHAT ABOUT MURDER? A GUIDE TO BOOKS ABOUT MYSTERY AND DETECTIVE FICTION. 1981.

Bruccoli, Matthew, Et Al — DICTIONARY OF LITERARY BIOGRAPHY. 19 vols. 1978-82.

Bruccoli, Matthew, Et Al — FIRST PRINTINGS OF AMERICAN AUTHORS. 4 vols. 1977-78.

Bruccoli, Matthew & C.E. Frazer Clark, Jr. — PAGES: INSIDE THE WORLD OF BOOKS, WRITERS, AND WRITING. 1976.

Bruns, Hank F. — ANGLING BOOKS OF THE AMERICAS. 1983.

Burke, W.J. & W.D. Howe — AMERICAN AUTHORS AND BOOKS. 1972. Latest edition.

C

Clareson, Thomas D. — SCIENCE FICTION CRITICISM: AN ANNOTATED CHECKLIST. 1972.

Clarie, Thomas C. — OCCULT BIBLIOGRAPHY: AN ANNOTATED LIST OF BOOKS PUBLISHED IN ENGLISH, 1971-75. 1978.

Clark, Joseph D. — BEASTLY FOLKLORE. 1968.

Cohen, Norman — LONG STEEL RAIL: THE RAILROAD IN AMERICAN FOLKLORE. 1981.

Cohen, Sarah Blacher — Editor — COMIC RELIEF: HUMOR IN CONTEMPORARY AMERICAN LITERATURE. 1978.

Commire, Anne — YESTERDAY'S AUTHORS OF BOOKS FOR CHILDREN. 1976.

Conningham, Frederic A. — CURRIER & IVES PRINTS: AN ILLUSTRATED CHECK LIST. 1970.

CONTEMPORARY DRAMATISTS. 1982.

Cook, Michael L. — DIME NOVEL ROUND-UP: AN ANNOTATED INDEX, 1931-1981. 1982.

Cook, Michael L. — MYSTERY FANFARE: A COMPOSITE ANNOTATED INDEX TO MYSTERY AND RELATED FANZINES, 1963-1981. 1982.

Cook, Michael L. — MURDER BY MAIL: INSIDE THE MYSTERY BOOK CLUBS, WITH COMPLETE CHECKLISTS. 1979.

Coven, Brenda — AMERICAN WOMEN DRAMATISTS OF THE TWENTIETH CENTURY: A BIBLIOGRAPHY. 1982.

Cowart, David & Thomas L. Wymer — TWENTIETH-CENTURY AMERICAN SCIENCE FICTION WRITERS. 2 vols. 1981.

Cunningham, Eugene. — TRIGGERNOMETRY. Latest printing.

Currey, L.W. — SCIENCE FICTION AND FANTASY AUTHORS: A BIBLIOGRAPHY OF FIRST PRINTINGS. 1979.

D

Dahl, Svend — HISTORY OF THE BOOK. 1968.

Davis, David Brion — HOMICIDE IN AMERICAN FICTION, 1798-1860: A STUDY IN SOCIAL VALUES. 1968.

Day, A. Grove — BOOKS ABOUT HAWAII: FIFTY BASIC AUTHORS. 1977.

Day, A. Grove — PACIFIC ISLANDS LITERATURE: ONE HUNDRED BASIC BOOKS. 1971.

Debo, Angie — A HISTORY OF THE INDIANS OF THE UNITED STATES. 1979.

Derleth, August — A PRAED STREET DOSSIER. 1968.

De Vinne, Theodor L. — THE PRACTICE OF TYPOGRAPHY: A TREATISE ON TITLE PAGES. 1968.

De Waal, Ronald B. — THE WORLD BIBLIOGRAPHY OF SHERLOCK HOLMES AND DR. WATSON. 1975.

Dinan, John A. — THE PULP WESTERN: A POPULAR HISTORY OF THE WESTERN FICTION MAGAZINE IN AMERICA. 1981.

Dobyns, Henry F. & Robert C. Euler — INDIANS OF THE SOUTHWEST: A CRITICAL BIBLIOGRAPHY. 1981.

Dow, George Francis — SLAVE SHIPS AND SLAVING. 1968.

Drazan, Joseph G. — THE PACIFIC NORTHWEST: AN INDEX TO PEOPLE AND PLACES IN BOOKS. 1979.

Duff, E. Gordon — EARLY PRINTED BOOKS. 1968.

Duffy, John — THE HEALERS: A HISTORY OF AMERICAN MEDICINE. 1979.

E

Earle, Alice M. — STAGE-COACH AND TAVERN DAYS. 1968.

Eastman, Mary H. — INDEX TO FAIRY TALES, MYTHS AND LEGENDS. 3 vols. 1926,-37,-52.

Eisenstein, Elizabeth — THE PRINTING PRESS AS AN AGENT OF CHANGE. 2 vols. 1979.

ELLERY QUEEN'S BOOK OF FIRST APPEARANCES. 1982.

Eppink, Norman R. — 101 PRINTS: THE HISTORY AND TECHNIQUES OF PRINTMAKING. 1971.

E

Fairbanks, Carol & Eugene A. Engeldinger — BLACK AMERICAN FICTION: A BIBLIOGRAPHY. 1978.

Faunce, Patricia S. — WOMEN AND AMBITION: A BIBLIOGRAPHY. 1980.

Faye, Christopher U. — FIFTEENTH-CENTURY PRINTED BOOKS AT THE UNIVERSITY OF ILLINOIS. 1949.

Feiffer, Jules — THE GREAT COMIC BOOK HEROES. 1965.

Fisher, Vardis & Opal Laurel Holmes — GOLD RUSHES AND MINING CAMPS OF THE EARLY AMERICAN WEST.

Flanagan, Cathleen C. & John T. — AMERICAN FOLKLORE: A BIBLIOGRAPHY, 1950-74. 1977.

Foster, Thomas Henry — BEADLES, BIBLES AND BIBLIOPHILES. 1948.

Franklin V, Benjamin — BOSTON PRINTERS, PUBLISHERS AND BOOKSELLERS, 1640-1800. 1980.

Franklin, Linda C. — ANTIQUES AND COLLECTIBLES: A BIBLIOGRAPHY OF WORKS IN ENGLISH, 16TH CENTURY TO 1976. 1978.

G

Gee, Ernest Richard — EARLY AMERICAN SPORTING BOOKS, 1734-1844. 1975.

Georges, Robert A. & Stephen Stern — AMERICAN IMMIGRANT AND ETHNIC FOLKLORE: AN ANNOTATED BIBLIOGRAPHY. 1982.

Glover, Dorothy & Graham Greene — VICTORIAN DETECTIVE FICTION: A CATALOGUE. 1966.

Goodwater, Leanne — WOMEN IN ANTIQUITY: AN ANNOTATED BIBLIOGRAPHY. 1975.

Goulart, Ron — CHEAP THRILLS: AN INFORMAL HISTORY OF THE PULP MAGAZINES. 1972.

Goulart, Ron — THE HARDBOILED DICKS: AN ANTHOLOGY AND STUDY OF PULP DETECTIVE FICTION. 1965.

Greiner, Donals — Editor — AMERICAN POETS SINCE WORLD WAR II. 2 vols. 1980.

Gribbin, Lenore S. — WHO'S WHODUNIT: A LIST OF 3,218 DETECTIVE STORY WRITERS AND THEIR 1,100 PSEUDONYMS. 1968.

Grimes, Janet & Diva Daims — NOVELS IN ENGLISH BY WOMEN, 1891-1920: A PRELIMINARY CHECKLIST. 1979.

Grobani, Anton — GUIDE TO BASEBALL LITERATURE. 1975.

Grobani, Anton — GUIDE TO FOOTBALL LITERATURE. 1975.

Gruber, Frank — THE PULP JUNGLE. 1967.

Grumet, Robert Steven — NATIVE AMERICANS OF THE NORTHWEST COAST: A CRITICAL BIBLIOGRAPHY. 1980.

Gunn, Drewey W. — MEXICO IN AMERICAN AND BRITISH LETTERS: A BIBLIOGRAPHY OF FICTION AND TRAVEL BOOKS. 1974.

H

Hancer, K. — THE PAPERBACK PRICE GUIDE. Annual.

Heard, J. Norman — BOOKMAN'S GUIDE TO AMERICANA. The most recent editions.

Hubin, Allen J. — THE BIBLIOGRAPHY OF CRIME FICTION, 1749-1975. 1979.

Hudgeons, Thomas E. — OFFICIAL PRICE GUIDE TO OLD BOOKS & AUTOGRAPHS. Latest edition.

K

Kirkpatrick, Daniel - Editor — TWENTIETH-CENTURY CHILDREN'S WRITERS. 1978.

L

Le Fontaine, Joseph Raymond — THE BOOK OF AUTHORS.

Le Fontaine, Joseph Raymond — A HANDBOOK FOR BOOKLOVERS. 1988.

Le Fontaine, Joseph Raymond — INTERNATIONAL BOOK COLLECTORS DIRECTORY, 1983.

Lowery, Lawrence F. — THE COLLECTOR'S GUIDE TO BIG LITTLE BOOKS AND SIMILAR BOOKS. Latest edition.

M

Matthews, Jack — COLLECTING RARE BOOKS FOR FUN AND PROFIT. 1981. (In my opinion the best book on the subject ever written for the neophyte).

Mcgrath, Daniel F. - Editor — BOOKMAN'S PRICE INDEX. Latest editions.

Molnor, John E. — AUTHOR-TITLE INDEX TO JOSEPH SABIN'S DICTIONARY OF BOOKS RELATING TO AMERICA. 3 volumes. 1974.

Mossman, Jennifer - Editor — PSEUDONYMS AND NICKNAMES DICTIONARY. 3 volumes. 1982.

P

Pelton, Robert W. — COLLECTING AUTOGRAPHS FOR FUN AND PROFIT. 1987.

Peters, Jean-Editor — BOOK COLLECTING: A MODERN GUIDE. 1977.

R

Raymond, Joseph — INTERNATIONAL BOOK COLLECTORS DIRECTORY. Latest edition.

Reilly, John M. - Editor — TWENTIETH-CENTURY CRIME AND MYSTERY WRITERS. 1980.

S

Sabin, Joseph — A DICTIONARY OF BOOKS RELATING TO AMERICA. 2 volumes. Latest edition.

Sampson, George - Editor — THE CONCISE CAMBRIDGE HISTORY OF ENGLISH LITERATURE. Latest edition.

Sharp, Harold S. — HANDBOOK OF PSEUDONYMS AND PERSONAL NICKNAMES. 5 volumes. 1972-82.

Smith, Curtis - Editor — TWENTIETH-CENTURY SCIENCE FICTION WRITERS. 1981.

T

Tebbell, J.A. — HISTORY OF BOOK PUBLISHING IN THE UNITED STATES, 1630-1980. 4 vols., 1972-1981.

V

Vinson, James, Et Al — TWENTIETH-CENTURY ROMANCE AND GOTHIC WRITERS. 1982.

Vinson, James — TWENTIETH-CENTURY WESTERN WRITERS. 1982.

Vinson, James And D.L. Kirkpatrick - Editors — CONTEMPORARY NOVELISTS. Latest edition.

W

Wolff, R.L. — NINETEENTH-CENTURY FICTION: A BIBLIOGRAPHIC CATALOGUE. 2 vols., 1980.

Appendix 9

ORGANIZATIONS FOR BOOK PEOPLE

Most of these organizations focus on specific genres or authors as you can tell by the names. However, they can be a fascinating source of obscure factual information as well as trivia. Many of them publish periodic newsletters or bulletins which you can receive as a member, or simply subscribe to.

In addition, their membership also is a potential customer source for you since most members will also have additional collecting interests.

In any event, it will be well worth your while to write and request membership information and cost for their publication if they have one. Be patient, however, since addresses change frequently and your letter may have to be forwarded several times before reaching the right person.

The Horatio Alger Society, 4907 Allison Drive, Lansing, MI 48910

The Sherwood Anderson Society, University of Richmond, Richmond, VA 23173

Antiquarian Society of America, 185 Salisbury Street, Worcester, MA 01609

Society of American Archivists, 330 South Wells Street, Chicago, IL 60606

Universal Autograph Collector's Club, c/o Herman Darvick, 562 Lakeview Avenue, Rockville Centre, NY 11570

Automobile License Plate Collector's Association, POB 712, Weston, WV 26452

Aviation Historical Society, American, POB 99, Garden Grove, CA 92642

American Battleship Association, POB 11247, San Diego, CA 92111

International Society of Bible Collectors, POB 2485, El Cajon, CA 92021

American Bible Society, 1865 Broadway, New York, NY 10023

Society of Biblical Literature, 2201 South University Boulevard, Denver, CO 80210

Book Club of California, 545 Sutter Street, San Francisco, CA 94102

American Society of Bookplate Collectors and Designers, 1206 North Stoneman Avenue -- #15, Alhambra, CA 91801

Organization for Collectors of Covered Bridge Postcards, 605 East 105th Street, Kansas City, MO 64131

British Fantasy Society, 447a Porter Avenue, Dagenham, Essex, England RM9 4ND

Aaron Burr Association, RD1, Route 33, Box 429, Hightstown-Freehold, Hightstown, NJ 08520

The Burroughs Bibliophiles, 454 Elaine Drive, Pittsburgh, PA 15236

Samuel Butler Society, Chaplain Library, Williams College, POB 426, Williamstown, MA 01267

The Byron Society, 259 New Jersey Avenue, Collingswood, NJ 08108

James Branch Cabell Society, 665 Locust Avenue, Oradell, NJ 07649

California Pioneers, The Society of, 456 MacAllister Street, San Francisco, CA 94102

Calligraphy and Handwriting, The Society of, c/o Factory of Visual Arts, 4649 Sunnyside North, Seattle, WA 98103

Calligraphy, Society for, 1161 Embury Street, Pacific Palisades, CA 90272

Canal Society, The American, 809 Rathton Road, York, PA 17403

Cannon Hunter's Association of Seattle, 1520 Northeast 62 Street, Seattle, WA 98115

Carroll Society of North America, The Lewis, 617 Rockford Road, Silver Spring, MD 20902

Cather Pioneer Memorial and Educational Foundation, The Willa, Red Cloud, NE 68970

Chesapeake & Ohio Historical Society, The, POB 417, Alderson, WV 24910

Check Collectors Roundtable, POB 125, Milford, NH 03055

Chinese Historical Society of America, 17 Adler Place, San Francisco, CA 94133

Circus Fans Association of America, 4 Center Drive, Camp Hill, PA 17011

Civil War Round Table Association, POB 7388, Little Rock, AR 72217

Clowns of America, POB 3906, Baltimore, MD 21222

American Collectors Association, 4040 West 70 Street, Minneapolis, MN 55435

Society of Colonial Wars, 840 Woodbine Avenue, Glendale, OH 45246

Crawford Memorial Society, F. Marion, Saracinesea House, 3610 Meadowbrook Avenue, Nashville, TN 37205

Deltiologists of America (Antique picture postcards), 3709 Gradyville Road, Newton Square, PA 19073

Derleth Society, August, 418 East Main Street, Sparta, WI 54656

Dickens Society, The (Charles), Office of Academic Publications, University of Louisville, Louisville, KY 40201

National Ding-A-Ling Club, POB 2188, Glen Ellyn, IL 60137 (With a name like that who wouldn't want to be member -- aren't most of us qualified?)

Dracula Fan Club, The Count, Penthouse North, 29 Washington Square West, New York, NY 10011

Dracula Society, Count, 334 West 54 Street, Los Angeles, CA 90037

Dracula Society, The, c/o Bruce Wightman, 36 High Street, Upper Upnor, Rochester, Kent, England

Flat Earth Society, International, POB 2533, Lancaster, CA 93534

Epigraphic Society, The (Inscriptions), POB 335, Cambridge, MA 02138

Fantasy Association, The, POB 24560, Los Angeles, CA 90024

Fantasy Fan Federation, National, c/o Janie Lamb, Rt.1, Box 364, Heiskell, TN 37754

Fantasy Society, British, c/o Rob Butterworth, 79 Rochdale Road, Milnrow, Rochdale, Lancs., England OL16 4DT

Folklife Center, American, Library of Congress, First & Independence Avenue SE, Washington, DC 20540

Folklore, Center for Southern, POB 4081, Memphis, TN 38104

Folklore Society, Northeast, South Stevens Hall--Room B, University of Maine, Orono, ME 04473

Foreign Relations, The Society for Historians of American, National Office, Department of History, University of Akron, Akron, OH 44325

Genealogical Society, National, 1921 Sunderland Place NW, Washington, DC 20036

Ghosts, International Society for the Investigation of, 369J Western Drive, Santa Cruz, CA 95060

Great Lakes Historical Society, 480 Main Street, Vermilion, OH 44089

Greystoke, House of (Edgar Rice Burroughs), 6657 Locust, Kansas City, MO 64131

Hawthorne Society, Nathaniel, Department of English, North Texas State University, Denton, TX 76203

Herpetological Society, Chicago (Reptiles and amphibians), 2001 North Clark Street, Chicago, IL 60614

Historical Association, American, 400 "A" Street SE, Washington, DC 20003

History, American Association for State and Local, 1400 8th Avenue South, Nashville, TN 37203

History and Culture, The Institute of Early American, College of William & Mary/Colonial Williamsburg Foundation, POB 220, Williamsburg, VA 23185

Hyborean Legion, POB 8243, Philadelphia, PA 19101

Historical Association, American Italian, 209 Flagg Place, Staten Island, NY 10304

Jamestown Society, POB 7389, Richmond, VA 23221

Jazz Museum, New York, 236 West 54 Street, New York, NY 10019

Jewish Historical Society, American, Two Thornton Road, Waltham, MA 02154

Lepidopterist's Society (Butterflies and moths), 257 Common Street, Dedham, MA 02026

Lewis Society, New York C.S., 332 Park Drive, Ossining, NY 10562

Lovecraft Society, The H.P., c/o Scott Connors, 6004 Kingston Drive, Aliquippa, PA 15001

Museum of Magic, American (Conjuring), POB 5, Marshall, MI 49068

Manuscript Society, 1206 N. Stoneman Avenue-#15, Alhambra, CA 91801

Melville Society, The (Herman), c/o Donald Yanella, Department of English, Glassboro State College, Glassboro, NJ 08028

Memorabilia Americana, 1211 Avenue "I", Brooklyn, NY 11230

Mythopoeic Society (Myths), POB 4671, Whittier, CA 90607

Newspaper Collectors Club, International, POB 7271, Phoenix, AZ 85011

Outlaw and Lawman History, National Association and Center for, Utah State University, Merrill Library, Logan, UT 84321

Peake Society, Mervyn, Central Library, Northgate Street, Ipswich, Suffolk, England 1P1 3DE

Penn Association, William, 429 Forbes Avenue, Pittsburgh, PA 15219

Pilgrim Society, 75 Court Street, Plymouth, MA 02360

Political Items Collectors, American, 1054 Sharpsburg Drive, Huntsville, AL 35803

Printing History Association, The American, c/o Professor Catherine T. Brody, New York City Community College Library, 300 Jay Street, Brooklyn, NY 11201

Puppeteers of America, 5 Cricklewood Path, Pasadena, CA 91107

Railway Historical Society, National, POB 2051, Philadelphia, PA 19103

Russell Society, Bertrand, RD1, Box 409, Coopersburg, PA 18036

Science Fiction, Fantasy & Horror Films, Academy of, 334 West 54 Street, Los Angeles, CA 90037

Shakespeare Society of America, POB 6328, Vanderbilt Station, Nashville, TN 37235

READY RECKONER VALUE GUIDE
Book Value versus Condition

How to use the Ready Reckoner: You must have a value to start with, for a book in a specific condition. From that, you can determine the value for a book in any other condition. Example's:

You have a book in Fine condition and have determined that this same book in good condition is worth $38. Find $38 in the GOOD column. Read across to the FINE column — the value is $85.

You have a book in FAIR condition and know that in FINE condition it should sell for $100. Find $100 in the FINE column. Read across to the FAIR column — the value is $10.

You have two copies of the same book. One is MINT, the other is GOOD. You have determined the price for the one in GOOD condition should be $15. Read across to the MINT column — the price should be $42.

For values not listed find the nearest lower and higher value add them together, then average the values.

Caution: All values listed are for books with dust jackets in the same condition as the book, (if originally issued with a dust jacket) AND generally for first editions. If, however, you find a recorded price for a later edition which can matched in any of the columns, you could use the other columns with some downgrading of the prices since the value spread will be much smaller.

MINT $	FINE $	VERY GOOD $	GOOD $	FAIR* $	POOR** $
12.00	10.00	8.00	4.00	1.00	--
18.00	15.00	12.00	7.00	1.50	--
24.00	20.00	16.00	9.00	2.00	--
30.00	25.00	21.00	11.00	2.50	--
42.00	35.00	29.00	15.00	3.50	2.00
54.00	45.00	37.00	20.00	4.50	2.50
66.00	55.00	49.00	24.00	5.50	3.00
78.00	65.00	54.00	29.00	6.50	3.50
90.00	75.00	62.00	33.00	7.50	4.00
102.00	85.00	71.00	38.00	8.50	4.50
120.00	100.00	83.00	44.00	10.00	5.50
150.00	125.00	105.00	55.00	12.50	7.00
180.00	150.00	125.00	65.00	15.00	8.00
210.00	175.00	145.00	80.00	20.00	9.00
240.00	200.00	165.00	90.00	20.00	11.00
300.00	250.00	210.00	110.00	25.00	14.00
360.00	300.00	250.00	135.00	30.00	16.00
420.00	350.00	290.00	155.00	35.00	19.00
480.00	400.00	335.00	180.00	40.00	22.00
540.00	450.00	375.00	200.00	45.00	25.00
600.00	500.00	415.00	220.00	50.00	27.00
720.00	600.00	500.00	265.00	60.00	33.00
840.00	700.00	585.00	310.00	70.00	38.00
960.00	800.00	665.00	355.00	80.00	44.00
1080.00	900.00	750.00	400.00	90.00	50.00
1200.00	1000.00	835.00	445.00	100.00	55.00
1440.00	1200.00	1000.00	535.00	120.00	65.00
1800.00	1500.00	1250.00	665.00	150.00	85.00
2400.00	2000.00	1665.00	890.00	200.00	110.00

* Collectors will buy books in FAIR condition as "reading copies" only and only if it is a scarce title.

**Copies of titles in "POOR" condition must be rare to justify purchase even at these prices. The only useful purpose they serve is to supply missing illustrations, or inside and title pages, for better, but defective, copies. This applies primarily to non-fiction titles — there is virtually no market for novels in this condition.

INDEX